All the programs from Turbo Pascal Solutions are also available on diskette for the IBM PC. This diskette has been given to many major national IBM PC user groups and to TUG, the Turbo Users Group. These groups will provide this diskette as part of their own ongoing software library programs. Contact your local user group or TUG for current prices and ordering information.

Or, you can order this diskette directly from the author for $10.00, using the order form below.

Order Form

Shipping information—please print

Name ____

Street ____

City ___________________________ State _________ Zip _________

Date ____

Please send me

____________ diskettes to accompany **Turbo Pascal Solutions,** at $10.00 each; $15.00 each outside U.S. and Canada.

Check method of payment:

☐ check   ☐ money order   ☐ cash

(Credit cards and C.O.D. payments are not accepted.)

Amount enclosed $ ___________________________________

Mail to: Jeff Duntemann
103 Hidden Drive
Scotts Valley, CA 95066

Price includes postage and handling and applicable sales tax. Price and availability subject to change without notice.

TURBO PASCAL SOLUTIONS

JEFF DUNTEMANN

Scott, Foresman and Company

Glenview, Illinois   London

ISBN 0-673-18584-2

Library of Congress Cataloging-in-Publication Data

Duntemann, Jeff.
   Turbo Pascal solutions.

   Includes indexes.
   1. PASCAL (Computer program language)   2. Turbo
Pascal (Computer program)   I. Title.
QA76.73.P2D87   1988   005.13′3   87-12759
ISBN 0-673-18584-2

1 2 3 4 5 6 RRC 92 91 90 89 88 87

Turbo Pascal is a trademark of Borland International. IBM PC, IBM PC/XT, and IBM PC/AT are trademarks of International Business Machines Corporation.

Notice of Liability

Scott, Foresman Professional Publishing Group books are available for bulk sales at quantity discounts. For information, please contact the Marketing Manager, Professional Books, Professional Publishing Group, Scott, Foresman and Company, 1900 East Lake Avenue, Glenview, IL 60025.

To the eternal memory of

Frank W. Duntemann, Engineer
1922-1978

Who said, When you build 'em right, they fly.

You did. And I do.

Preface

The Secret to the Universe

As far as I'm concerned, the secret to the universe is only this: Know how something works, and you've got it in your hip pocket. There is no such thing as magic; there are only varying degrees of ignorance. Etch away that coating of ignorance and watch the wheels turn.

This is the single greatest truth I learned from the man to whom this book is dedicated, and in 35 years it has never failed me. My early efforts in amateur radio were an excellent object lesson: I pulled grimy electronic components out of discarded radios and TV sets and soldered them together into Chinese copies of radio projects appearing in the ham radio magazines. Two out of three of these projects didn't work. They didn't work because I didn't know *how* they worked. I was flying blind and missing things, things that a knowledgeable radio technician would have unconsciously included in the construction process. These days, my radio project success rate has climbed to two out of three, with that third failure generally due to the faulty components I pulled out of discarded TV sets in my younger years. But that's a different issue altogether.

In writing *Complete Turbo Pascal*, I explained in detail how the Turbo Pascal implementation of the Pascal language worked. At this writing (January 1987), the book has sold more than 50,000 copies in two editions. Placing my address on the flyleaf has garnered a lot of mail for me. Much of that mail consisted of questions—not about Turbo Pascal (most readers said I covered that well), but about using Turbo Pascal to "get at" certain parts of one machine or another. "Could you send me a procedure that reads the PC joystick?" was one of the most common requests. Sure, no problem—but why couldn't they write one themselves?

It occurred to me at that time that there are generally two kinds of people in this world: those who follow recipes and those who write them. I've stood on both sides of that fence, and, once again, the difference is how much you know about the subject of the recipe. I can write you a recipe for chicken soup right now; gazpacho I'd have to read up on. Furthermore, once I understood what gazpacho is supposed to be, I might have to make it once or twice to get it right.

So it works with computer programming. I don't care for joysticks, but I read the literature on their theory of operation and worked out a procedure to send to people who needed it. About that time, I noticed other books appearing on the market for Turbo Pascal, designed as "libraries" or "cookbooks," full of functions and procedures to do anything under the sun. I imagined making a quick buck by turning the \TURBO\HACKS subdirectory of my hard disk upside down and pouring 400 pages or so of code onto paper and calling it a book.

I decided not to.

In creating *Turbo Pascal Solutions*, I have a higher aim in mind: I want to demonstrate how you, too, can write recipes rather than follow them. The thrust of this book is not the code examples, but the theory behind them. That's why it is less a book about Turbo Pascal than about the IBM PC/XT/AT hardware and how that hardware works.

If I drag you through enough thickets, you'll pick up the method of hacking your own way through in time, when you need to—and you will need to. The PC industry changes constantly. New products are appearing all the time. You might buy a great new printer that doesn't *quite* follow the venerable Epson standard. It might have seventeen new modes allowing you to print reverse-reading graphics images on your T-shirts—but that won't help you if you can't control the new modes from within your programs. If you are, in fact, the first kid on your block with that particular printer, you'd better crack the manual and understand how it works, or your T-shirts will be none the livelier.

We do have to settle a few other things. I have been excoriated more than once for writing deliberately nonportable code in Pascal. Guilty. And unrepentant. Portability in Pascal is generally achieved by ignoring about 60 percent of the machine its programs run on. However, since I paid for 100 percent of the machine, I say portability be damned. I want to write a PacMan game. I need the joystick.

The problem here is that portability is an ideal to be approached, not an ikon to be worshipped. You can structure your Pascal programs such that highly machine-dependent code is set off in clearly marked functions and procedures. Moving the code to a new machine (or even to a new type of peripheral running on the old machine) will only require changing the machine-dependent subprograms, and not an endless search-and-destroy mission through 3000 lines of main program code.

All of the subprograms in this book are machine dependent—some more than others. Keep that in mind as you design them into your programs, and especially as you use the principles I explain to design your own machine-dependent code. Work smart now and work less later on.

There is a great deal that I wanted to cover in this book and could not, for space reasons. Interrupt-service routines for Turbo Pascal could fill an entire book by themselves. That goes double for graphics. As time permits, I hope to present further books on getting machine-dependent things done with Turbo Pascal. Watch for them.

I would also like to acknowledge certain people who offered me help along the way: Ted Mirecki, on assembly language specifics; Michael Abrash and John Cockerham on the EGA; Marshall Brain for showing me just how arcane the subject of interrupts really is; and my fabulous wife Carol for tossing my rear end into bed when the smoke started to pour out of my ears.

Feel free to write. I may not always be able to answer personally (not if I ever intend to get another book out the door), but I always enjoy hearing from you. If you've got a good recipe, pass it along.

As for mine—well, the chicken soup's in the can. The gazpacho's cooking.

—Jeff Duntemann
103 Hidden Drive
Scotts Valley, CA 95066

Contents

A Note on Software Releases

The bulk of the software included in this book was developed using Turbo Pascal Release 3.01A under PC DOS 3.0 and (later) PC DOS 3.1. Virtually all of the routines will operate identically under DOS 2.0 and 2.1 as well, but I haven't tested it and can't guarantee it. Much of the material on PC DOS and *all* of the material on organizing your disk system into subdirectories is *not* valid for DOS 1.0 and 1.1, and I strongly encourage anyone still using those releases to abandon them for newer releases. (Note that Turbo Pascal V3.0 will *not* work *at all* under DOS 1.X.)

Indications from Borland International are that Turbo Pascal Release 3.0 will be current for some time to come. It is unlikely that a future change in Turbo Pascal will invalidate any of the material in this book. However, future additions to Turbo could make certain things I offer obsolete. There's no helping that; it's the way this crazy computer business operates.

If there continues to be a market for my books in future years, I intend to update them periodically to reflect current releases of both PC DOS and Turbo Pascal. And, of course, there's always the possibility that unforeseen developments will push both PC DOS and Turbo Pascal into obscurity . . .

. . . but I wouldn't wait up for it.

Working Smart

1.1 Organizing Your Working Disks

Clutter kills.

I'm not talking about rakes lying prongs-up in the garage, or piles of round metal stock rolling around the basement floor. I mean *software* clutter—a root directory brimming with experimental programs, incomplete functions and procedures, and data structure definition-include files—not to mention old versions of all of the above, mixed freely with the Turbo Pascal compiler and purchased source-code libraries like the Turbo Access Toolbox.

Turbo Pascal program development naturally tends toward such a condition. The seductive power that Turbo gives you to throw something together in ten minutes—"just to see what blows up"—leads to huge numbers of small Pascal source-code files, mostly uncommented, often given names in sequences similar to this:

```
TEST.PAS
TESTER.PAS
TESTER00.PAS
TST01.PAS
TST02.PAS
TST02-1.PAS
```

and so on. When you're unsure of a certain technique, you tend to move forward in small steps, saving the prior version of your program under a slightly different name, in case the whole thing backfires and you need to back up a step and try something else.

If you have four or five projects underway at once, this method leads to huge numbers of source files, some of which have been left behind by development, sitting around for months doing nothing. You may already have forgotten what most of them were for.

Even if your habits don't include such messiness, the problem of "interfering-include files" may have arisen. It doesn't take long before a large program needs to be cut into include files to be compilable. If your programs develop along similar lines, the tendency will be to cut out similar portions of the program—for example, a variable initialization procedure. Perhaps, in cutting up your newest program, you extract the initialization procedure into a file called **INIT.SRC.** You already have another program with an include file called **INIT.SRC,** written four months ago, but, in the red heat of creation, you ignore Turbo's warning and overwrite the older file. All is well for weeks until you go back to the earlier program and find that it won't compile. The initialization procedure is initializing a group of undeclared variables. And no wonder—it's the initialization procedure from an entirely different program.

Your programs are structured to keep them comprehensible. Your development environment should be structured for the very same reason. Organizing your Turbo Pascal development environment is no particular problem, even if you only have floppy disks. If you have a hard disk, it's a snap.

Using DOS Subdirectories

It's all done with subdirectories. Subdirectories first appeared with Release 2.0 of PC DOS. If you are still using DOS 1.1 or (God save us) DOS 1.0, you are out of luck, and almost certainly out of your mind. Much of this book deals with PC DOS features existing only in Release 2.0 of DOS or later. Don't work any harder than you have to. Upgrade to DOS 2.0 (or better still, DOS 3.3) right away.

The next few pages will give you a brief review of DOS subdirectories and how to use them. If you are new to DOS, it might pay to pick up a separate text on using PC DOS and go through it from cover to cover. The best book by anyone on this subject (for the beginner, at least) is Peter Norton's *MS DOS and PC DOS User's Guide* (Brady Books, 1984. ISBN 0-89303-645-5).

If, on the other hand, you're a DOS wizard, you might skip past this section entirely. I wouldn't want to bore you.

Subdirectories came along when hard disks appeared, offering the capacity to store hundreds or thousands of files. As you might expect, entering a **DIR** command and watching several hundred filenames scroll by your screen is the fast track to madness.

Files on a hard disk are often related to one another by function. A group of files may pertain to a word processing program or (in our case especially) to a programming language like Turbo Pascal. DOS allows you to create separate directories on a single disk drive to contain groups of related files.

Each disk drive always has one main directory, called the "root" directory. This is the directory you enter when first specifying a drive unit on the command line. In other words, if you want to look at what's in drive C, at the DOS prompt type:

```
A>C:
```

and enter the root directory for drive C. The prompt reflects the change:

```
C>
```

Typing the **DIR** command here will display the list of files on drive C's root directory. Locate the root directory in Figure 1.1, and follow this figure along with the rest of the discussion on subdirectories.

DOS allows you to create subdirectories that "branch off" the root directory. From a functional standpoint, such subdirectories are identical to the root directory. You create subdirectories with the MD (Make Directory) DOS command:

```
C>MD TOOLKIT
```

This command will create a subdirectory on drive C called **TOOLKIT**. It only creates **TOOLKIT**; it puts nothing in **TOOLKIT** nor does it change the current

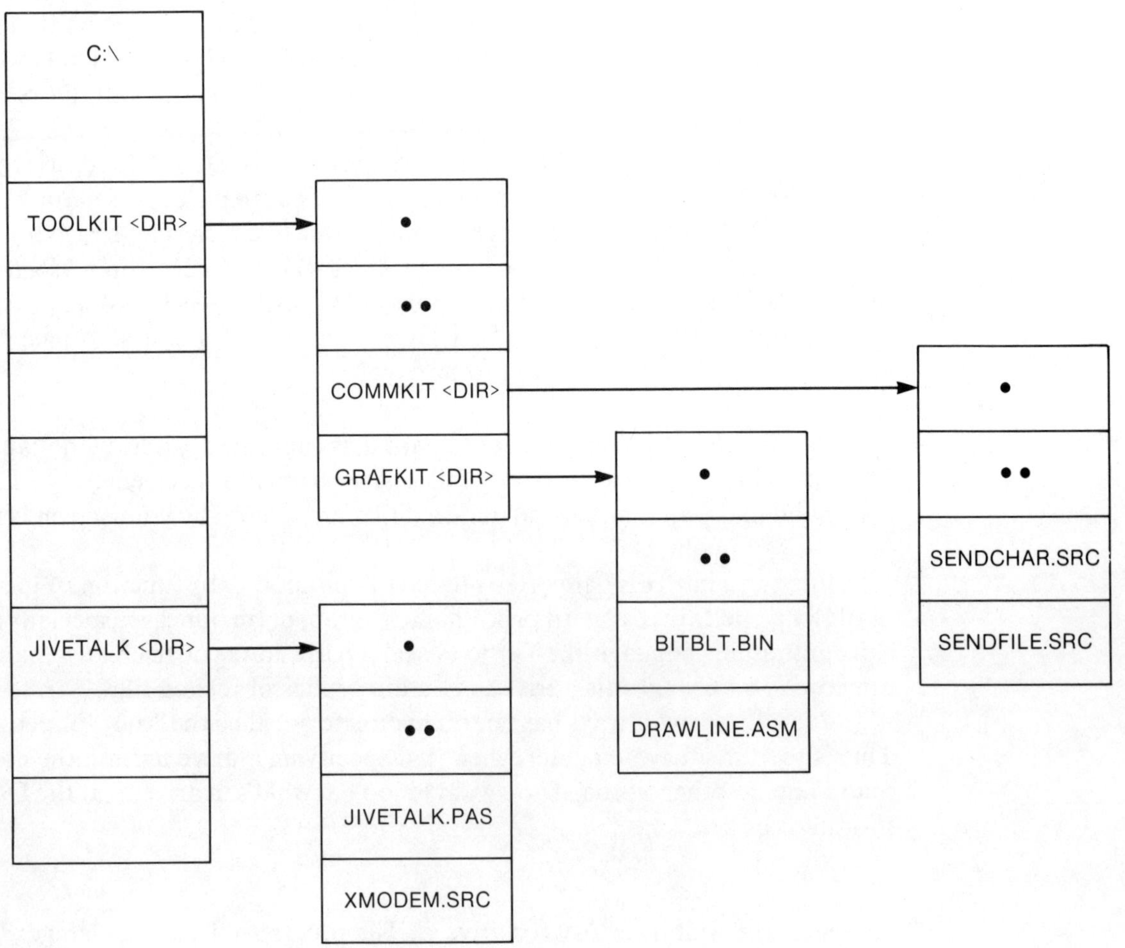

Figure 1.1   **A structured directory**

directory to **TOOLKIT**. To change the current directory to **TOOLKIT**, you use the CD (Change Directory) command:

```
C>CD TOOLKIT
```

Now the current directory is **TOOLKIT**. (Or, when the fellow asks you, "Where are you?" answer back, "I'm in **TOOLKIT**.") When you use the **DIR** command, you will see listed *only* the files in subdirectory **TOOLKIT**. When you issue an **ERASE *.*** command, you will erase *only* the files in subdirectory **TOOLKIT**.

One bit of jargon I'll be using in this book is the concept of "parent" and "child" directories. The current directory when we created **TOOLKIT** was the root directory. The root directory is said to be the "parent directory" to **TOOLKIT**. Conversely, **TOOLKIT** is said to be a "child directory" of the root directory. Every directory except the root directory has one parent directory. Every directory can have one or more child directories. From within **TOOL-KIT**, for example, we could define a child subdirectory named **COMMKIT** to contain data communications toolkit routines, and another named **GRAFKIT** to contain graphics routines.

DOS recognizes a shorthand notation associated with this jargon. The root directory is represented by "\" (backslash; the notation does *not* include the quote marks). The current directory is represented by a single period: "." Any subdirectory's parent directory is represented by two periods: ".." There is *no* shorthand form for a child directory, since there can be many child directories branching off from any given directory. To access a child directory, you must give its name.

Now, an important question: When you start wandering around a complicated system of directories and subdirectories, how do you tell which directory is the current directory? In other words, which directory you are currently "in"? The **CD** command, issued without a directory name, will display the name of the current directory:

```
C>CD
C:\TOOLKIT\COMMKIT
```

The second line is displayed by DOS, and it is called a "pathname." A "path" is the route you must take through the disk directory system to reach a certain directory or a file within that directory. The pathname returned by the **CD** command as shown above describes the path from the root directory to the current directory. The path to a file named **SENDCHAR.SRC** within the subdirectory **COMMKIT**, for example, would be specified by this pathname:

```
C:\TOOLKIT\COMMKIT\SENDCHAR.SRC
```

This sample pathname indicates that file **SENDCHAR.SRC** exists in the current directory **COMMKIT**, which is a child directory of another directory named **TOOLKIT**, which, in turn, is a child directory of the root directory (indicated by the initial backslash) on drive C. The pathname need not include the drive unit if you wish the path to begin on the current drive unit. If the current drive were drive C and you wished to describe a path on drive B, the pathname would have to begin with **B:**.

Backslashes are used to separate the names of parent and child subdirectories. A backslash *by itself* always indicates the root directory; a backslash which *begins* a pathname indicates that the path described by the pathname begins at the root directory.

You can also specify a path which begins at the current directory. Any pathname which does *not* begin with a backslash starts at the current directory. If the current directory were **TOOLKIT**, for example, we could specify a path to **SENDCHAR.SRC** this way:

```
COMMKIT\SENDCHAR.SRC
```

Note that there is no backslash at the beginning of this pathname. This indicates that the path starts at the current directory (which is **TOOLKIT**) through **TOOLKIT**'s child directory **COMMKIT** to the file **SENDCHAR.SRC**.

There is a good trick we can use to make DOS indicate the current directory at all times. The DOS command **PROMPT** allows us to set up the DOS prompt in various ways. I won't describe **PROMPT** in detail, but I recommend that you always execute the following **PROMPT** command before starting work on your machine:

```
PROMPT $P$G
```

You can enter this command from the DOS prompt or, better still, add it to your **AUTOEXEC.BAT** batch file, from which it will be executed every time you reboot your computer.

PROMPT PG instructs DOS to display the pathname of the current directory within the DOS prompt. If we use the **CD** command to move from the root into subdirectory **TOOLKIT**, the DOS prompt changes to this:

```
C:\TOOLKIT>
```

If we used the **CD** command to move one level further into the child subdirectory **COMMKIT**, the prompt would automatically change to:

```
B:\TOOLKIT\COMMKIT>
```

Once you execute **PROMPT PG**, this changing of the DOS prompt is done by DOS automatically without any further commands from you.

Throughout this book, when I give examples of the DOS command line, I will assume that the **PROMPT PG** command has been given, and the prompt will indicate the current directory.

Specifying a path from the root to **SENDCHAR.SRC** (as we just did a few paragraphs back) is a straightforward descent from the root through two subdirectories. A path need not start at the root, nor must it always travel "downward" on the directory structure. Suppose we have defined another child directory from the root called **JIVETALK**. In that subdirectory are Pascal files for a program called **Jivetalk**. Since **Jivetalk** is a communications program, it will need to include some of the source files in the **COMMKIT** subdirectory. How is this done?

The path from **JIVETALK.PAS** to **SENDCHAR.SRC** goes up into the root directory, over to subdirectory **TOOLKIT**, and down again through subdirectory **COMMKIT** to **SENDCHAR.SRC**. Going "up" from a subdirectory to its parent is done with the double-dot notation previously mentioned:

```
{$I..\TOOLKIT\COMMKIT\SENDCHAR.SRC}
```

You need to have this include statement inside **JIVETALK.PAS** to include **SENDCHAR.SRC** into the compilation of **JIVETALK.PAS**. The two dots indicate a path up from the current directory (which, for **JIVETALK.PAS**, is subdirectory **JIVETALK**; see Figure 1.1) into the root directory, and down from the root into **TOOLKIT**.

Now, since we can always specify a path from the root by starting the pathname with a "\", wouldn't it be just as easy to do without the two dots and write the include statement this way:

```
{$I \TOOLKIT\COMMKIT\SENDCHAR.SRC}
```

No! In this particular case, the parent directory of **JIVETALK** happens to be the root. *This is not necessarily always the case*. In fact, for the specific hard disk directory structure I'll be discussing shortly, the topmost directory of the structure will not be the root but a subdirectory named **TURBO**. The **TOOLKIT** subdirectory and your various project subdirectories (like my example of **JIVETALK**) will be child subdirectories of subdirectory **TURBO**. The two dots are essential to point the path up to the immediate parent directory. The two dots make no assumptions about the root; they simply backtrack one level "up" the directory structure. This is a subtle and important point that can get you into trouble if forgotten.

Organizing Floppy Disks

Turbo Pascal is the only important Pascal that can be used conveniently on floppy disks, because it is small. Once you have installed Turbo Pascal for your particular machine, you can delete the **TINST** (install utility) files from your disk. The sample programs don't need to be on the compiler disk at all; if you are using floppy disks and want to play with the sample code, move all of Borland's supplied .PAS files to a separate floppy disk for use in drive B. In fact, all you need for complete use of the Turbo Pascal compiler for the IBM PC are these files:

```
TURBO.COM
TURBO.MSG
GRAPH.BIN
GRAPH.P
```

If you do not have a graphics card in your system, the **GRAPH** files can be deleted as well. Even with the **GRAPH** files, you have used only 50K out of a 360K floppy disk. The rest of the disk should be used for holding "toolkit" collections of functions and procedures.

One toolkit is, of course, your own: the routines you write and perfect for your own purposes. These should go into a subdirectory called **TOOLKIT**. There are other toolkit products which you can buy from various software companies. Some of the best-known come, like Turbo Pascal itself, from Borland International. The Turbo Access Toolkit, for example, might be placed in a subdirectory named **ACCESS**. The Turbo Editor Toolkit (TET) could be stored in a subdirectory named **TET**. See Figure 1.2.

The structure in Figure 1.2 will probably be all you can expect to fit on one 360K floppy disk. You may not need Turbo Access or TET, and without them you will have all the more space for your own toolkit. The important thing is to group related pieces of Turbo Pascal source code in separate subdirectories.

Aside from imposing some order on disk-drive chaos, file backup is another good reason to arrange your Pascal work disk this way. If you make **TOOLKIT** the current directory and put a blank disk in drive B, you can back up all of your toolkit routines to drive B with one simple command:

```
A:\TOOLKIT>COPY *.* B:
```

This will copy *only* your toolkit routines to drive B, without making an unnecessary backup copy of Turbo Pascal or other files in other directories.

All of your actual program code (like the **Jivetalk** program mentioned above) should be stored on a separate floppy disk and used in drive B. Your work disk in drive A will change infrequently. To work on a different project, simply change the floppy disk in drive B. Don't try to cram more than one major programming project onto a single floppy disk. With mail-order diskettes hovering at about 45 cents each, it's foolish economy to save on diskettes by mixing multiple projects together. Torn hair is worth more than that.

Organizing a Hard Disk

The cost of Winchester hard-disk systems has come down dramatically since IBM PCs first appeared in quantity in 1982. In early 1984, a 10-megabyte hard disk cost $2000 and worked badly. I paid $765 for my first 20-megabyte disk system in March 1985; currently (January 1987), you can buy a 20-megabyte hard-disk system for $385. I recently bought a fast AT-style 43-megabyte disk

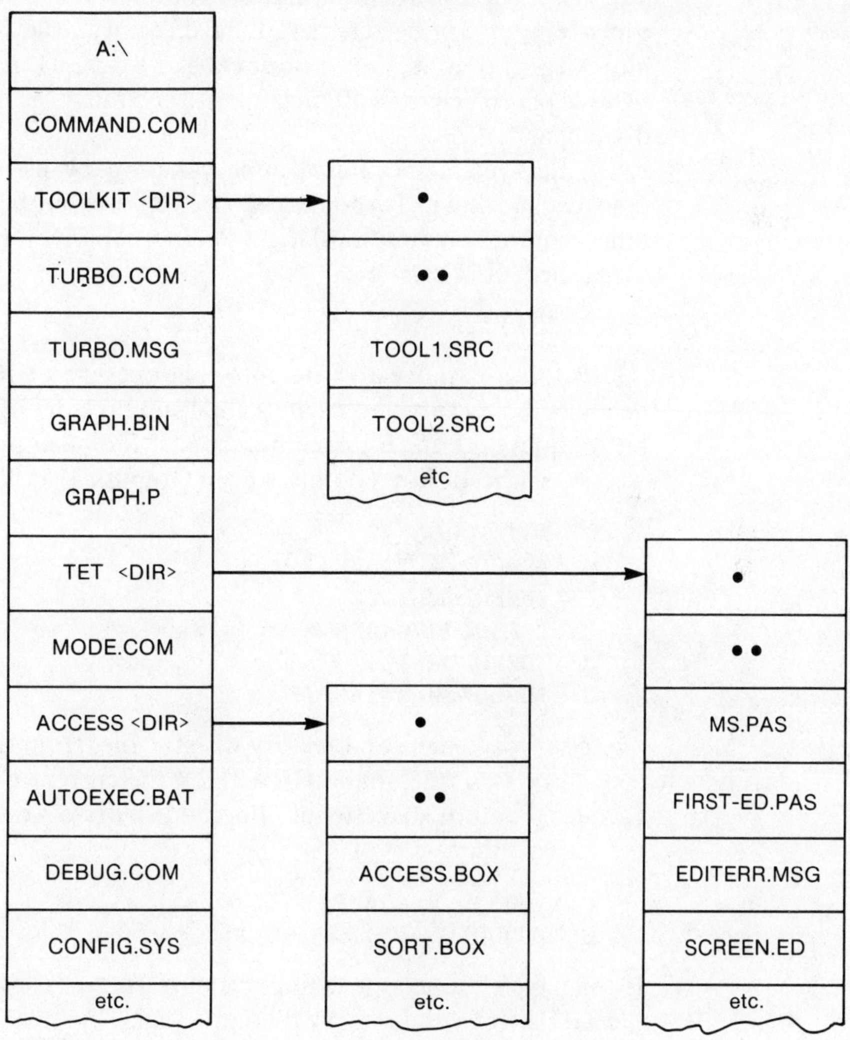

Figure 1.2   **Compiler diskette structure**

drive for $595. In 1982, I paid $325 for one double-sided, 360K floppy-disk drive and thought I had done well. (The going price was more like $400.) Today they cost $89. PC DOS didn't even support hard disks until early 1983, and then add-in 10-megabyte systems cost about $2500. We have indeed come a long way.

I say all this to encourage you to set money aside for a hard disk if you don't already own one. It will make life enormously easier for you in a great many ways.

A hard disk can also get cluttered in a hurry, and 10 megabytes is room for a lot of clutter. The need for a rational directory structure on a hard disk is even more urgent than it is for a floppy-disk system, because with 10 or 20 megabytes to play in, chaos will catch up with you much faster than the limits of your disk capacity.

Unless you are beyond all hope, you probably use your computer for more than just hacking in Turbo Pascal. To keep your Turbo material separate from other material on your hard disk, set up a subdirectory from your root directory called **TURBO**:

```
C:\>MD TURBO
```

Before you move any files into subdirectory **TURBO**, make **TURBO** the default subdirectory and create a child subdirectory of **TURBO** for your toolkit routines and one for each purchased "toolbox" product you own (Turbo Access, Turbo Editor Toolkit, Turbo Graphix Toolbox, MetaWindow, etc.):

```
C:\>CD TURBO
C:\TURBO>MD TOOLKIT
C:\TURBO>MD ACCESS
C:\TURBO>MD GRAPHIX
C:\TURBO>MD TET
C:\TURBO>MD METAGRAF
```

Now load each subdirectory with the files from the vendors' distribution disks. For example, make **GRAPHIX** the current directory, put the Turbo Graphix Toolbox diskette into floppy-disk drive **A:**, and copy all its files into the subdirectory:

```
C:\TURBO>CD GRAPHIX
C:\TURBO\GRAPHIX>COPY A:*.*
```

If you have obtained the listings disk for *Turbo Pascal Solutions*, copy it into the **TOOLKIT** subdirectory the same way.

At this point, go back "up" into the **TURBO** subdirectory, place the Turbo Pascal distribution disk into **A:**, and copy all files into the **TURBO** subdirectory:

```
C:\TURBO\GRAPHIX>CD..
C:\TURBO>COPY A:*.*
```

You might want to cull the various sample Pascal source-code files from the **TURBO** subdirectory at this point if you don't wish to use them. The idea is to have as little unnecessary material in your Turbo Pascal work area as possible.

Most people keep program files in development in the the same subdirectory with the Turbo Pascal compiler. This is unwise if you intend to have more than one project going at the same time. Similar include files from different projects have a way of getting confused, as I mentioned before. The safe philosophy puts every project in its own subdirectory. Create a child subdirectory of **TURBO** for each major project you have underway:

```
C:\TURBO>MD JIVETALK
C:\TURBO>MD IKONYX
C:\TURBO>MD STELLA
```

To keep things neat and clean, one more subdirectory is needed for those 10-minute hacks that don't qualify as separate projects. I call that subdirectory **HACKS**. Create **HACKS** and do your best to resist creating program files up in the parent subdirectory **TURBO**.

The essential structure should be this: A parent directory called **TURBO** contains separate subdirectories for your own personal toolkit (including the routines in this book) and each commercial toolkit product that you own. **TURBO** also contains child directories for each of your major projects, plus a catchall subdirectory called **HACKS** for little items which don't qualify as projects.

1.2 Working with the System

If you're used to having everything—compiler, programs, toolkit routines, and so on—in the same directory, using this structure takes practice and a measure of discipline. Here are some tips to follow:

Always work from a project subdirectory. This is easy enough to do, if you have installed Turbo Pascal with the correct pathname to its **TURBO.MSG** message file. When Turbo Pascal begins running, it attempts to load this error message file. *Unless you tell it otherwise, it looks in the current directory.* In other words, if you are in a child directory of subdirectory **TURBO** instead of in **TURBO** (where **TURBO.MSG** resides), you will get that maddening "File not found. Press <esc>" message following "Loading TURBO. MSG."

Some people have solved this problem in brute-force fashion by copying **TURBO.MSG** into every subdirectory they have! Not necessary. The "well-behaved" way to solve this problem is to run **TINST**, the Turbo Pascal install program. If you are using an IBM PC, you can get along quite well without ever installing Turbo; it comes preinstalled *except* for the message file pathname.

TINST, when it runs, shows you a menu that looks like this:

```
              TURBO Pascal installation menu.
          Choose installation item from the following:
  [S]creen type¦ [C]ommand installation¦ [M]sg file path¦ [Q]uit
                    Enter S,C,M, or Q:
```

The option marked **[M]sg file path** is the one you want. Type **M**. The prompt that appears will look like this:

```
MSG file path and name (eg. A:\TURBO.MSG)
TURBO.MSG ->
```

The **TURBO.MSG** in the second line is the current path to the file; in other words, no path at all. The name of the file itself without any disk-drive unit or subdirectory names will only allow the computer to find it in the current directory on the logged disk drive. You should always type in the pathname where Turbo Pascal can expect to find its message file.

If you are using my suggested floppy-disk setup, type this:

```
A:\TURBO.MSG
```

If you're using my suggested hard-disk setup, you should probably type this:

```
C:\TURBO\TURBO.MSG
```

I say "probably" because you may have your disk system set up a little differently. Most hard disks become drive C, but if you have two, the second is often drive D. I've seen cases where disk drives extend to G; some people just don't know when to quit. Also, you are under no obligation to put the **TURBO** subdirectory right off the root. Some people have a subdirectory off the root for programming languages in general, perhaps called **LANGUAGE**. The **TURBO** subdirectory is a child subdirectory of **LANGUAGE**, and the full pathname (assuming drive C) would be:

```
C:\LANGUAGE\TURBO\TURBO.MSG
```

The idea is to type the full pathname of file **TURBO.MSG**, so that **TINST** can store the pathname into your copy of Turbo Pascal. Once your copy of Turbo has the pathname embedded within it, it will always look for the **TURBO .MSG** file at that pathname, and you won't have to worry about it anymore.

You must also set a DOS path to **C:\TURBO** in your **AUTOEXEC.BAT** file, so that, no matter what directory you are in, you can run the Turbo Pascal compiler simply by typing **TURBO** at the command line. If you already have a **PATH** command in your **AUTOEXEC.BAT** file, you can add a path to your **TURBO** subdirectory by adding **C:\TURBO** to the path specifier. The following is a typical path command including the **TURBO** path specifier:

```
PATH C:\DOS;C:\SIDEKICK;C:\UTILS;C:\TURBO
```

This **PATH** command specifies four different directories in which DOS is to look for program files if the requested file is not in the current directory. Given the above path specifier, if you type "TURBO" at the command line from a project subdirectory, DOS will first look for **TURBO.COM** in the project subdirectory. Not finding it there, DOS will check **DOS**, **SIDEKICK**, **UTILS**, and finally **TURBO**, from which it will load and run **TURBO .COM**.

There is some small chance that in one of the first three subdirectories DOS checks, you may have another program file named **TURBO.COM** or **TURBO.EXE**. If so, Turbo Pascal will never be found and the other program will be run. "Turbo" is entirely too popular a word in the software world these days. [Moral: *Be careful what you load by the bushel into your hard disk*.]

The benefits of working within a project subdirectory are mostly a matter of keeping a multitude of files straight. Each project you do may have an include file called **INIT.SRC**. This is fine, as long as each **INIT.SRC** is in its own separate project subdirectory.

Use the "..." notation in include file specifiers. When you wish to include a toolkit routine from a program file residing in a project subdirectory, use the "..." notation to "reach up" into the parent subdirectory before "reaching down" into the proper toolkit subdirectory. For example, when you wish to access the **MARKTIME.SRC** routine in subdirectory **TOOLKIT** from within your program source file in subdirectory **JIVETALK**, use this include command:

```
{$I ..\TOOLKIT\MARKTIME.SRC}
```

You could specify the same include file starting from the root directory, like this:

```
{$I \TURBO\TOOLKIT\MARKTIME.SRC}
```

but *don't*. This include command assumes that the **TURBO** subdirectory is a child of the root directory. In our case it is, but it doesn't have to be. As mentioned above, you might wish to arrange your hard disk differently. Perhaps you are using a subdirectory off the root called **LANGUAGE**, and within **LANGUAGE** create subdirectories **TURBO**, **ZBASIC**, and **LETSC**. The first include command would still work fine. The second one, obviously, would generate a "file not found" error, since there is no **TURBO** subdirectory under the root. *Any pathname beginning with a backslash starts at the root.*

1.3 Backing Up Turbo Files

Somewhere the goblins have written that *anything you do not back up you will eventually lose.* The little devils are correct. For this reason, I powerfully suggest that you back up your *entire* hard-disk system regularly, preferably once a week. If you have a tape backup system, you are among the few, the proud, the safe. If you have a Bernoulli Box, you are all of the above, and rich as well.

There are alternatives to cartridge disks and tape backup that are, in fact, better. By a wide margin, the best disk backup utility is Fifth Generation Systems' **Fastback**. It is incredibly fast—faster, in fact, than most streaming tape systems for small computers. You can back up five megabytes in 10 minutes or less if you're quick with a disk drive door. I use **Fastback** once a week, or anytime I've been working at the console for more than four hours.

If you can't do that, keep a set of backup disks for each child subdirectory under **TURBO**. You needn't back up the **TURBO** subdirectory itself because all its files are presumably safe and sound on your Turbo Pascal distribution disks.

1.4 Documentation

Even if you adhere to the system outlined above, clutter will accumulate. The magical thing about Turbo Pascal is that it allows you to try a technique quickly without investing a lot of time in the test. Over a period of months, little files like **TEST.PAS** will collect in all your project subdirectories. **HACKS**, in particular, will be full of such debris.

It's too simplistic to advise erasing them regularly. You wouldn't have created each of those files without something in mind. In trying a technique, you probably learned something—either a new way to accomplish a task or a dead end to be avoided.

Unless you keep a programmer's log, much of this experience will be forgotten and lost over time. Keeping the little test files on disk as memory-joggers will clog your disk or (if you're using a lot of include files) possibly confuse programs incorporating several source files.

I advise keeping a loose-leaf or spiral-bound notebook beside your monitor, ready to grab at a moment's notice. Every time you try something in a little 15-liner, take 30 seconds to jot down why you needed to try it and what the results were. Then you can erase the 15-liner without risk of losing the experience.

Yes, I know, programmers should keep logs in disk files. I've tried it, and it doesn't work. When I'm staring at the screen, puzzling out a source file that I don't understand, I want my log lying flat on the desk next to the keyboard. Someday, when we have monitors capable of holding two full pages side-by-side (I've worked with the Xerox Star and I'm spoiled), perhaps I'll try it again.

"Self-documenting" Code

There is no such thing as self-documenting code, nor will there ever be. Program code can only say *how*; it cannot say *why*. "Why" is the far more important question in any process, since a knowledgeable professional can often work backwards from the "why" to the "how." (This is how programs get designed in the first place. A set of requirements is actually a "why" for a "how" that hasn't been written yet.)

Your code should at very least tell a person conversant in Pascal what it's doing. You will have to add some comments as indication of why it's doing what it's doing.

Comments are important. Every routine in your toolkit should begin with a comment header block. This block should contain the name of the file under which the routine is saved, required inputs, and defined outputs. If any of the input or output values are peculiar or nonobvious for some reason, the header should shed some light on them.

Most important, if the routine requires that something be defined before it (a type, a variable, or another procedure or function) the header *must* explain exactly what must precede it. This includes programmer-defined types. A person (and it shouldn't have to be you) should be able to take any routine in your toolkit and use it by itself, unless it calls another routine in the toolkit. And if it does, that routine should be clearly named.

The comment header should contain the date the routine was last modified. *Update this date religiously.* You can tell from a directory listing which of two files was modified more recently, but if you keep hardcopy listings of your toolkit in a three-ring binder, the date becomes essential.

A simple toolkit routine follows. "Deedle" is for people who have gotten tired of ordinary beeps. There is a class of telephones (usually found in the offices of expensive lawyers) that makes a kind of refined warbling birdcall. Deedle approximates that sound. The parameter indicates how many two-tone "deedles" will be generated by the call. Note the comment header.

```
1        {->>>>Deedle<<<<------------------------------------------------}
2        {                                                               }
3        { Filename: DEEDLE.SRC -- Last Modified 10/20/85                 }
4        {                                                               }
5        { This routine makes a sound not unlike certain electronic      }
6        { telephone ringers you hear in lawyers' offices.  The number   }
7        { of "deedles" is given by the value passed in Deedles.         }
8        {                                                               }
9        {                                                               }
10       {                                                               }
11       {---------------------------------------------------------------}
12
13       PROCEDURE Deedle(Deedles : Integer);
14
15       VAR I : Integer;
16
17       BEGIN
18         FOR I := 1 TO Deedles DO
19           BEGIN
20             Sound(800); Delay(50); Sound(500); Delay(50)
21           END;
22         NoSound
23       END;
```

Copyright and the Public Domain

Comment header blocks are a good place for your copyright notice. I usually don't bother with copyright notices on individual toolkit routines, since I pass those out freely. If your routines represent a commercial endeavor, however, the notice is *essential* if you ever intend to win an infringement suit.

It is possible to distribute source code freely and yet retain copyright. Things do not go into the public domain unless you explicitly place them there. It is perfectly legal to copyright a program and then distribute it for noncommercial uses only. You created it and all rights to it are yours—to assign or retain as you desire. There is no contradiction in saying:

```
(c) 1987 by Jeff Duntemann
Feel free to copy and distribute for noncommercial purposes.
```

What this means is that you are granting free rights to copy and use your code. Nonetheless, you still *own* the code, and can specify conditions under which it may be used (e.g., for noncommercial applications by hackers). To be honest, I don't care what people do with my toolkit routines, but you should be aware of the options available to you.

One thing to remember about the public domain is that it is irrevocable. If you place code in the public domain it stays there. Furthermore, you lose all control over the material, and if Lotus Development decides to use it in their upcoming 4-5-6 five-dimensional spreadsheet, it's money in Uncle Mitch's pocket and not yours.

I find it convenient to keep an empty comment header block as a text file in my toolkit subdirectory. Whenever I build a new toolkit routine, it's an easy matter to copy the boilerplate comment header into the current workfile and fill in the details. File **HEADER.SRC** in the Turbo Pascal Solutions toolkit is such a boilerplate comment header.

```
1    {->>>>SubprogramName<<<<------------------------------------------}
2    {                                                                 }
3    { Filename : MYSUB.SRC -- Last Modified 1/6/87                     }
4    {                                                                 }
5    { <First describe your routine>                                   }
6    { <Then tell what must be predefined for it to compile>           }
7    {                                                                 }
8    {                                                                 }
9    {-----------------------------------------------------------------}
```

Patches and Fixes

Any product widely used by programmers is going to be patched. If a bug is found, the wild-eyed among us will immediately dive in with **DEBUG** or Brett Salter's remarkable Periscope system and start looking for patches. If the product doesn't quite do what some of us would like, the hackers are going to devise a patch to change things for the better.

It is a credit to the maturity of Borland International that they have not only condoned investigation and patching of Turbo Pascal's code but have encouraged it, particularly through the Borland CompuServe SIG. Most of the patches in this section originated on CompuServe.

2.1   Using DEBUG to Patch Files

Among the standard DOS utilities is a creature called **DEBUG**, a useful creature indeed, considering its small size and the fact that it's "free." Using **DEBUG** to trace program execution is a subtle business that takes some practice and late evenings in a soundproof room; however, patching Turbo Pascal or your own code files with **DEBUG** isn't the least bit difficult. This section is intended for people who have shied away from using **DEBUG** because of its mystique or because of an aversion to cryptic commands (DOS jockeys be aware that I probably won't be telling you anything you don't already know).

DEBUG is itself a program (albeit a special one in many ways) that loads and remains resident above DOS. It "becomes" the command processor, and changes the prompt to make this preemption of **COMMAND.COM** apparent. The prompt becomes a dash symbol (−). **DEBUG** displays the dash prompt and waits for keyboard input, just as DOS does.

The valid commands, however, are completely different, and are all single characters. (This restriction is part of the reason **DEBUG** is as small as it is. It doesn't have to parse English-like commands, or even figure out how large they are.)

Loading a File into DEBUG

Patching a file with **DEBUG** requires that the file be loaded into memory above **DEBUG**. There are two ways to do this: from the command line when you invoke **DEBUG**, or from within **DEBUG** after **DEBUG** has been loaded.

Do it the easy way: Include the name of the file to be patched as a command-line parameter when you load **DEBUG**:

```
C:\>DEBUG TURBO.COM
```

This command loads **DEBUG** into memory, and causes **DEBUG** to load the Turbo Pascal program file. It will then display its taciturn little dash prompt and wait for your input. If, for some reason, you forget to load your file this way, you must execute two **DEBUG** commands to load a file into memory. The first is the N(ame) command, which gives **DEBUG** the name of the file you wish to load:

```
-N TURBO.COM
```

Again, **DEBUG** will respond with the dash prompt, nothing more. You then must type the L(oad) command to actually load your file:

```
-L
```

and the file will load. Your only verification is that the dash prompt will reappear. Anything else indicates an error.

Getting out of **DEBUG** from the dash prompt is only a matter of typing a Q for Q(uit).

Examining the Loaded File

If you wish to look at what the file you loaded contains, the D(ump) command is used. Dumping the first 128 bytes of Turbo Pascal can be done this way:

```
-D
```

and you will see:

```
4CD4:0100   E9 79 2C 90 90 CD AB 43-6F 70 79 72 69 67 68 74   .y,....Copyright
4CD4:0110   20 28 43 29 20 31 39 38-35 20 42 4F 52 4C 41 4E    (C) 1985 BORLAN
4CD4:0120   44 20 49 6E 63 02 04 00-B1 57 00 3C 33 00 00 00   D Inc....W.<3...
4CD4:0130   00 00 00 00 00 00 00 00-00 00 00 00 00 00 00 00   ................
4CD4:0140   00 00 00 00 00 00 00 00-00 00 00 00 00 00 00 00   ................
4CD4:0150   00 00 00 00 00 14 44 65-66 61 75 6C 74 20 64 69   ......Default di
4CD4:0160   73 70 6C 61 79 20 6D 6F-64 65 50 42 01 FF FF 0F   splay modePB....
4CD4:0170   07 07 70 0F 07 07 70 0E-07 07 4F 2E 8A 27 0A E4   ..p...p...O..'..
```

Some of this is readable in the ASCII column on the right (notably Borland's copyright notice), but most of it is binary data and executable code that either displays in ASCII as gobbledygook or else as period characters (.), indicating a binary code that corresponds to no ASCII character.

You can "step through" the file, 128 bytes at a time, by repeatedly pressing D. Note the numbers at the left margin. They indicate the actual memory location, given as segment : offset addresses, at which the dumped line begins. The segment column is the left of the two columns separated by a colon. In the example given above, all the numbers in the segment column are the same, $4CD4. (Remember that this is all in hex, even though **DEBUG** does not use the familiar dollar sign prefix used by Turbo Pascal to indicate the presence of hexadecimal numbers.) This number will be different for your system, and may be different from one invocation of **DEBUG** to another, depending on what resident programs you may happen to have loaded at the time. Since all of Turbo Pascal, as well as any program file created by Turbo Pascal, fall within a single 64K segment, this number can be ignored, as it will be the same no matter where you are within the program being examined.

The number to the right of the colon is the offset address of the first byte in the line. The offset addresses begin at $0100, since **.COM** files are always loaded by DOS at offset $0100 into the code segment. (The region from $0000 to $0100 is known as the Program Segment Prefix, and it may be examined, but it is *not* stored on disk with the program itself. DOS creates it and fills it while the program is being loaded from disk.)

When you want to examine a specific byte in a file, the offset is the number you need to look for. For example, if someone tells you to "look at the byte at $016B in **TURBO.COM**," he means the byte at offset $016B into the code segment. The way to find this byte in a hexdump like the one displayed by the **DEBUG** D(ump) command is to follow the offset address column down until you find the first number *larger* than the offset you're seeking. Then back up one line; the byte you want is within that line.

Notice that the offset addresses are 16 bytes apart. Move across on the selected line, counting from the closest multiple of sixteen. For example, to find $016B on the hexdump, move down the offset address column until you find the first number larger than $016B. The number is $0170. Move to the *previous* line, the one that begins with $0160. Count across by 11 ($0B) bytes, and that byte will be $016B.

With this method, however, you do run the risk of counting incorrectly, especially if you're unaccustomed to using hexadecimal and start counting in base ten instead. There is an easier way to look at a particular byte in a file. **DEBUG** has a command called E(nter) that serves two purposes: One is to look at specific bytes in a file without having to poke through a dump of 128 bytes; the other use, as you'll see below, is to change those bytes after they're displayed. To examine the byte at $016B with no mistake, type this:

```
-E 016B
```

(Note that you *don't* use Turbo's dollar sign prefix here.) **DEBUG** will respond with this display:

```
4CD4:016B  19.
```

The cursor will be flashing immediately to the right of the period character (we'll explain why in a moment). You can look at the next byte after $016B (offset $016C) by pressing the space bar. Ultimately, return to the dash prompt by pressing Enter.

Patching Locations in the File

The real purpose of the E(nter) command is to *change* the byte at the address it displays. This is the reason the cursor is shown immediately to the right of the period after the display of the byte itself. **DEBUG** will allow you to type in a hexadecimal number after the period that will replace the number originally displayed. This, in a nutshell, is how code patching is done in **DEBUG**: Find the right location, and use E(nter) to display and then type in a new value for the desired location.

Recall, for a moment, the process used to display a byte in a file using the E(nter) command. **DEBUG** displays the address of the byte, the value of the byte in hex, and then a period. The cursor is positioned after the period. You can enter a new value here to take the place of the old value.

For example, to change the value of the byte at $016B, you would first display the value of the byte using E(nter):

```
-E 016B
4CD4:016B  19.
```

Then type the new value immediately after the period. Then press Enter:

```
4CD4:016B  19.42
```

The dash prompt will again appear. You can recheck your work by requesting a redisplay of the same location:

```
-E 016B
4CD4:016B  42.
```

Press Enter and the dash prompt will reappear.

Saving the Patched File to Disk

At this point, the file is patched—that one byte is, at least. You may need to patch several bytes, and they can all be done the same way, using **DEBUG**'s

E(nter) command. In any event, you will need to save the patched file back out to disk. The **DEBUG** command W(rite) will accomplish this:

```
-W
Writing 9A39 bytes
```

Your changes have been saved, and you can use **DEBUG**'s Q(uit) command to return to DOS. Need I add that you should experiment with duplicate copies of files, and not your *only* copy?

2.2   Altering the Screen Size

The IBM PC version of Turbo Pascal does not go through the ROM BIOS (Basic Input/Output System) for screen display. It writes directly to display adapter memory. This accounts for the rapid screen refresh you see when scrolling a screen in the Turbo Editor.

Currently, almost all PC-compatible video displays are 25 lines high and 80 columns wide. The machinery that Turbo Pascal uses to directly address the display adapter memory is easily patched to work with a display format larger or smaller than 25×80, *if* the memory mapping is identical to the PC's—a 4K or larger region of RAM beginning at either $B0000 or $B8000.

The tyranny of 25×80 displays is only beginning to be questioned and broken. I myself own two displays which go beyond 25×80. The main console of my IBM PC is a marvelous thing indeed: A 66×80 monochrome display in eggshell white with a 9×14 pixel character cell. It's a "portrait" screen, meaning that the long side of the CRT tube is vertical. (A traditional 25×80 display is referred to as a "landscape" screen. Paintings of landscapes tend to be long in the horizontal, while portraits of people tend to be higher than they are wide.)

The Micro Display Systems Genius VHR Display is the closest thing to electronic paper I have ever seen, as it will show you *more* than a full 54-line page at one time. If your cranial bandwidth is greater than 25 lines, you should consider it. At about $1500, it is not by any means cheap, but if you must spend any significant part of your day staring at a screen (as most writers do), it will quickly prove worth that and more. No writer friend I have ever shown it to has gone away without a little lust in his or her heart.

In my 386 machine, I have an EGA clone. The "EGA" refers to IBM's Enhanced Graphics Adapter, a 1984-era board that combines the monochrome and most of the color graphics modes supported by the PC onto one card, along with some great new modes. Most of the EGA's press has emphasized the 640×350 color mode, which is lovely, if confusing to program for. Less well-known is the fact that the EGA has a 43×80 mode using an 8×8

pixel character cell. While not as crisp and well-formed as the EGA's color 25×80, 8×14 pixel character cell, it is nonetheless quite readable on a good-quality monitor.

The downside of the EGA is that the best graphics modes require a special type of monitor which is still considerably more expensive than your standard RGB color monitor. Prices are falling, but slowly. Keep your eye on what are being called "multisync" monitors, which can adapt broadly to the video frequencies presented to their inputs. You can plug a monochrome adapter, a color graphics adapter, or an EGA into such a monitor, and its circuits will "lock" onto the horizontal and vertical sweep frequencies and present you with a clean, steady image without having to adjust the monitor or fiddle with jumpers or software parameters on the video board. Both NEC and Sony have a multisync monitor on the market, and both are excellent. My 386 machine uses the Sony Multiscan monitor, and if there is a better color screen for less than $1000, I have yet to see it.

In the other direction, certain lapheld machines have a display format smaller than 25×80—typically, 16×80. Turbo Pascal can be patched to operate at 16×80 as well as 66×80 or 43×80.

The patch is simple: Two bytes at offset $016A into **TURBO.COM** describe the current screen column and row size. Use **DEBUG** (or any other binary editor) to alter these two bytes to reflect your desired screen size figures.

The default value of the byte at offset $016A is $50, which is 80 decimal. This is the default column size. The following byte (offset $016B) is shipped as $19, or decimal 25. Change either or both to suit your needs and save the modified copy of **TURBO.COM** back out to disk. Needless to say, do *not* perform this kind of surgery on your distribution disk! In fact, make a separate copy for experimentation until you're sure the operation has been a success.

I have successfully tested this patch with both Turbo 2.0 and Turbo 3.0. Turbo 1.0 uses ROM BIOS calls for screen control and is thus not amenable to this kind of modification. Current releases of Turbo 87 and Turbo BCD are patched exactly the same way to the same location.

An interesting bonus to all of this is that **.COM** files compiled with a patched copy of Turbo Pascal carry the screen size patch along. At offset $016A into a Turbo-compiled **.COM** file, you will find the same column and row size bytes, typically set to $50 $19. Patching a compiled program to a larger screen size will enable that program to use the larger screen *if and only if* the program's logic allows use of the larger screen area. In other words, if you are patching a text editor which has tests written in Pascal to prevent the cursor row value from exceeding 25, your cursor will not budge past line 25.

I have not yet found a single full-screen application on the market or on the various Turbo Pascal bulletin board treasure troves that will readily expand its turf into a larger screen. In general, to work with an unusual screen size, you'll have to roll your own. A *very* bright program would examine the two bytes at offset $016A into its code segment to see how big a screen it had to work with. This simple procedure (which is essentially two memory peeks) will do the job:

```
1          {->>>>ScreenSize<<<<---------------------------------------------}
2          {                                                                }
3          { Filename: SCRNSIZE.SRC -- Last modified 12/14/85               }
4          {                                                                }
5          { This routine uses MEM to peek at the screen size bytes at      }
6          { offset $16A into the program's code segment, and returns       }
7          { row and column size figures as integer parameters.  For most  }
8          { (or nearly all!) programs this will be 80 & 25, but both       }
9          { Turbo Pascal and .COM files produced by Turbo Pascal can be    }
10         { patched for different size screens by altering the two bytes   }
11         { at CS : $16A.  As 43 and 66 line screens become commoner, it   }
12         { will be smart to see what size screen is available in order    }
13         { to make the most of it.                                        }
14         {                                                                }
15         {                                                                }
16         {                                                                }
17         {----------------------------------------------------------------}
18
19         PROCEDURE ScreenSize(VAR Columns,Rows : Integer);
20
21         BEGIN
22           Columns := MEM[CSeg : $16A];
23           Rows    := MEM[CSeg : $16B];
24         END;
```

If you were to write a text editor, it could first call **ScreenSize** and use the row and column values returned to enable full-screen refresh and full-screen cursor positioning, no matter what the size of the screen. (Refer to Chapter 5 for a more detailed discussion of screen sizes.)

2.3   Changing the Video Attributes

Turbo Pascal's use of video attributes is idiosyncratic, to say the least. Text in the editor and text output to the display via **Write** and **Writeln** are normally displayed with the intensity bit set, making such text bright compared to the text displayed by DOS output. When Turbo is installed for use with a color screen, the default output text is yellow (in the PC's peculiar color scheme, "bright brown"), while text displayed after executing the **LowVideo** procedure is ordinary white (i.e., not bright). Marking a block of text in the editor makes the block of text revert to normal (not bright) intensity. This seems backwards to me—but it can be changed with a simple one-byte patch.

Turbo Pascal maintains a 12-byte table of video attributes in the first 128 bytes of its code segment. This table actually consists of three independent tables of four bytes each for the three installable "color" possibilities understood by **TINST.COM**, the Turbo Pascal install utility. The first table contains the attributes for use with the IBM Monochrome Display Adapter (MDA). The second and third are for use with either the Color Graphics Adapter (CGA) or Enhanced Graphics Adapter (EGA). The second table applies to situations where a composite monochrome display is connected to the CGA (The IBM EGA does not support such a display, although some EGA clone boards do), and the third table for situations when a full-color screen is desired.

These tables contain default values for the video attributes to be used for four different text display situations:

1. *Normal text.* This is text as displayed in the editor, and text displayed by **Write** and **Writeln** during program execution.
2. *"Low" text.* This is text as displayed after the **LowVideo** procedure is executed. This is also the attribute used for the status-line information at the top of the editor screen.
3. *Block text.* This is text that has been set off as a block by the ˆ**KB**/ˆ**KK** editor command keystrokes. The attribute for block text is also used when Turbo Pascal displays the message "New File" when it creates a new disk file for the editor.
4. *Error messages.* When the compiler displays an error message, it will use an attribute different from the others. On color displays, this is white text on a red background for greatest visibility.

Only one of the three tables is used at any one time, depending on what display you selected when installing Turbo Pascal via **TINST.COM**.

The tables begin at offset $016F into the code segment. A summary of the patch points and the default values ordinarily stored there is given in Figure 2.1. (You can decode the attributes themselves by looking ahead in Chapter 5 to Figures 5.5 and 5.6.)

The best example of the use of these tables concerns the block-text attribute. I have always found Turbo Pascal's way of marking blocks in "half-bright" video (half-bright compared with the intense video used for normal editor text displays) to be very annoying. The reverse-video attribute used by Word Perfect and P-Edit is considerably better, not only because it is more visible, but also because it highlights spaces within a block as well as visible char-

		Normal	Low	Block	Error
Monochrome Display	Offset	$016F	$0170	$0171	$0172
	Default value	$0F	$07	$07	$70

		Normal	Low	Block	Error
CGA/EGA in B&W mode	Offset	$0173	$0174	$0175	$0176
	Default value	$0F	$07	$07	$70

		Normal	Low	Block	Error
CGA/EGA in color mode	Offset	$0177	$0178	$0179	$017A
	Default value	$0E	$07	$07	$4F

Figure 2.1 **Video attribute patch points**

acters. Highlighting spaces can be important when a block of text begins or ends within a series of space characters. Under the default block-highlighting attribute, you can't tell at which space the block begins or ends.

The default block-text attribute is $07 in all cases. $07 produces normal text on the monochrome screen and "light grey," or "dark white" (the ordinary color DOS uses to display its text) on color screens. To change this to black-on-white reverse video, use a $70 attribute. If you have a color screen, you can get a little more creative simply by placing a dark foreground color on a light background color. For example, to display text in blue on a brown background (which looks better than you might think), use an attribute of $61.

The tables can be patched from **DEBUG** exactly as described in Section 2.1. (Many thanks to Corey Vavrik for pointing out that it is, in fact, three tables and not a single table, as I had originally assumed.)

2.4 Eliminating the "Include error messages (Y/N)?" Prompt

Perhaps the most popular and useful Turbo Pascal patch of all is the one that eliminates that annoying (especially when you're working in a caffeine fever hurry) prompt to "Include error messages (Y/N)?" It's certainly easy enough to do. It has a further distinction in that there is a reliable method of locating the patch for any given version of Turbo Pascal up through version 3.01B. As Turbo Pascal V4.0 is being completely redesigned as an **.EXE** file with an interface similar to that of Turbo Prolog and Turbo BASIC, this patch won't be necessary for the next major release of Turbo Pascal.

The theory behind the patch is this: When Turbo displays the prompt, it waits for user input, accepts a character from the user, and places that character in a particular storage location in low memory—somewhere between offsets $0300 and $0400 into the code segment. It then calls another routine that examines the character in low memory, and, based on that character, either loads the message file or doesn't.

What we need to do is "short-circuit" the request for user input, and yet still satisfy the routine that tests the temporary variable in low memory. Short-circuiting the user input request is easy—we can "NOP it out" with NOP (No Operation) instructions. But we also have to move the correct character value into the location in low memory. This means it will *not* be a one-byte patch, as were the patches I've described so far. The patch entails entering four 8086 mnemonics through **DEBUG**.

Finding the patch point is the first step. The point is different for the different versions of Turbo Pascal: Turbo, Turbo-87, and Turbo BCD. It is also different for V2.0 and V3.0, and although it doesn't always vary between minor releases like 3.01A and 3.01B, it might. There's nothing to guarantee against it. Therefore, *always* check before you patch to make sure you're hitting the correct point. (And *always* do your patch on a duplicate copy of Turbo Pascal.)

Finding this patch point is easier than many because it always seems to occur two bytes past the end of the prompt string itself. Thus, if you can find the string "Include error messages" within **TURBO.COM** (the "(Y/N)?" is stored elsewhere), you can identify the patch point as well.

DEBUG has a S(earch) command which makes this child's play. Load the desired version of Turbo into memory from **DEBUG** and execute this command:

```
-S CS:100 4000 "error messages"
```

Use lowercase when entering the actual quoted string as I did here, since **DEBUG** does not automatically capslock quoted strings as it does command characters. The **CS:100 4000** command is the range of memory locations to be searched. $4000 is high enough, since the point is always somewhere between $2000 and $3000.

DEBUG will search, and, if you've entered the command correctly, will respond with the location of the string as a segment : offset address. Again, ignore the segment value. The offset is the one you want.

To find the address of the patch point, you must dump memory starting at the location returned by **DEBUG**:

```
-D XXXX
```

where you enter the offset in place of "XXXX." You will see something like this:

```
4CB8:2E80                                              65                    e
4CB8:2E90  72 72 6F 72 20 6D 65 73-73 61 67 65 73 00 E8 21    rror messages..!
4CB8:2EA0  03 A2 7C 03 74 03 E8 FA-0D E8 8B 0D E8 60 00 8B    ..|.t........`..
4CB8:2EB0  26 98 02 BB AF 2E 53 80-3E FE 01 00 74 03 E9 62    &.....S.>...t..b
4CB8:2EC0  09 E8 E8 0F 8D 8A BE 00-E8 0D 10 E8 A7 DB E8 CF    ................
4CB8:2ED0  DB 50 E8 C4 DB 58 BE 18-32 E8 2C 03 72 31 2E FF    .P...X..2.,.r1..
4CB8:2EE0  64 01 FC BF 36 00 1E 07-AC AA 0A C0 75 FA E8 90    d...6.......u...
4CB8:2EF0  DB 3A 20 00 E8 C3 F5 BB-36 00 E8 9C DB 8A 07 3C    .: .....6......<
4CB8:2F00  1A 74 07 3C 20 75 03 43-EB F3 C3 80 3F 1A C3       .t.< u.C....?..
```

Notice on the hexdump that there is a $00 byte immediately after the string "error messages." This is the terminator byte for the string, which (as DOS requires) is formatted in the ASCIIZ manner. Immediately after the $00 byte is an $E8 byte. This is the start of the patch point (see Figure 2.2). To get the actual address of the patch point, count across the dump to get the address of the $E8 byte. (It might not always be an $E8 byte as it is in this example. What you want is the address of the first byte *after* the $00 byte.) In the dump shown above, the address would be $2E9E.

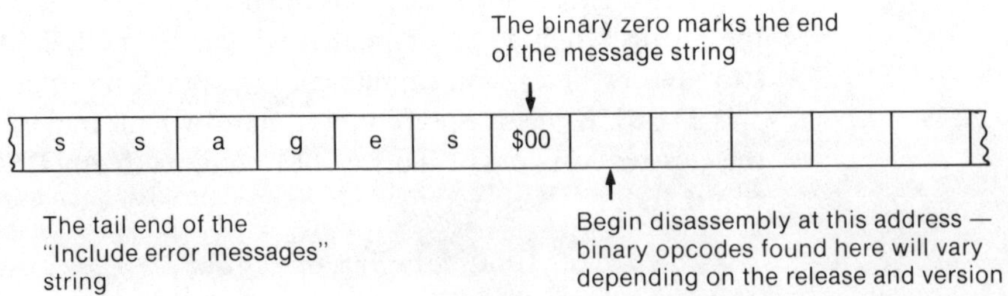

Figure 2.2   **Finding the patch point**

To be doubly sure, disassemble the code starting at the patch point. **DEBUG** has an U(nassemble) command [they might have called it D(isassemble), but D was already taken for D(ump)] that will work backwards from the binary machine code in the file and produce its best guess as to the 8086 mnemonics corresponding to those codes. I call it a guess because this command cannot tell the difference between code and data; where they are freely mixed within the code segment (as they are within Turbo Pascal), trying to disassemble data can become confusing indeed, as can beginning a disassembly within a multibyte opcode. Use the A command with some care, and think hard about what it tells you.

Enter the U(nassemble) command with the offset you derived from the hexdump:

```
-U XXXX
```

where you enter your offset in place of "XXXX." You should see something similar to this:

```
4CB8:2E9E E82103       CALL    31C2
4CB8:2EA1 A27C03       MOV     [037C],AL
4CB8:2EA4 7403         JZ      2EA9
4CB8:2EA6 E8FA0D       CALL    3CA3
4CB8:2EA9 E88B0D       CALL    3C37
4CB8:2EAC E86000       CALL    2F0F
4CB8:2EAF 8B269802     MOV     SP,[0298]
4CB8:2EB3 BBAF2E       MOV     BX,2EAF
4CB8:2EB6 53           PUSH    BX
4CB8:2EB7 803EFE0100   CMP     BYTE PTR [01FE],00
4CB8:2EBC 7403         JZ      2EC1
```

Some of the numbers may be different, but for the mnemonics you should see this pattern: CALL MOV JZ CALL CALL CALL. If you see that pattern, and the *first* mnemonic is the CALL, you have the right point. Make absolutely sure, however, that the first instruction displayed is a CALL instruction, and not something peculiar like DB, JNB, or AND. (Disassembling the $00 byte at the end of the message string will display an AND mnemonic.) If it is, you've probably counted wrong in reading the hexdump to determine the patch point. Go back and recheck, or you will patch the wrong spot and create a suicidal copy of the compiler.

Now to perform the patch itself. Notice in the MOV mnemonic a hexadecimal operand within square brackets ($037C in the example above). This number will vary between versions; it is the offset into the data segment of the variable that holds the responds from the user input that we are trying to fake. Copy it down—you'll need it to make the patch.

Here we need to replace some of the 8086 instructions at the patch point with a few of our own. For this we use the A(ssemble) command in **DEBUG**. It accepts 8086 assembly-language mnemonics and translates them to binary opcodes at the location we specify. We invoke the A command with our patch point as the location. **DEBUG** will display the current location, and wait for you to enter mnemonics. The session should look like the following genuine captured (via DOS redirection) **DEBUG** session:

```
-A 2E9E
4CB8:2E9E MOV BYTE PTR [037C],0B
4CB8:2EA3 NOP
4CB8:2EA4 NOP
4CB8:2EA5 NOP
4CB8:2EA6
-W
Writing 9A39 bytes
-Q
```

Your input consists of the A command, the MOV mnemonic and its parameters, the three NOP mnemonics, the W command, and finally the Q command. The dash prompts and the segment : offset address indicators are provided by **DEBUG**.

Remember that the bracketed number in the MOV mnemonic is not always $037C. That number must be the number you discovered in disassembling the code at the patch point. It is the offset into the data segment of the variable into which the "yes" value is stored by the MOV instruction. If you use another number arbitrarily, you could lock up your machine in running the patched version of the compiler.

As explained earlier, the W(rite) **DEBUG** command writes the patched compiler file back out to disk under its original name, and tells you how many bytes were actually written.

When you run the patched version of the compiler, the prompt will appear momentarily, then vanish as the compiler answers its own question and proceeds to load the message file.

For Turbo Pascal V3.01A, the patch points for the three versions are as follows: Turbo Pascal : $2F7D; Turbo-87 Pascal : $2A46; and Turbo BCD Pascal : $2E9E. But don't take my word for it; these things can change. Double check before you patch. As I do not have V2.0 of Turbo-87 or Turbo BCD, I leave all of Turbo Pascal V2.0 as an exercise for the reader.

One final note: Once you find the patch point for your particular copy of Turbo Pascal, make a note of it in your user guide somewhere, or in the margin of this book. You may decide someday to unpatch the compiler, or repatch another copy, and you can save yourself the trouble of searching for the patch all over again. This goes for any changes you make to Turbo Pascal, and I feel that it pays to keep a "virgin" copy handy, in case things ever start acting peculiar. Before you ring up Borland International, load an unpatched version of the compiler and give it a try. The patches I've described here have a long pedigree, and I have used all of them for a long time (which is why there are not half a dozen more patches here—I have others that run the gamut from risqué to totally bonkers), but I've been surprised before, and may be again.

So will you.

Turbo Pascal and the 8088

This is fundamentally a book about low-level interface to the IBM PC, and that implies low-level interface to the 8088 CPU. As the 8088 is an electrical variant of the 8086, this applies to 8086 machines as well, *if* they are very compatible with the PC in other ways. In most cases, the PC/AT with its 80286 processor will also run identically to the 8086 and 8088, and I will call out any important differences where they occur.

3.1   8088 Software Interrupts

Most people think that IBM PC DOS is the controlling hand within the IBM PC, and while largely true, it doesn't credit the assistance of the IBM ROM BIOS (Basic Input/Output System), which does much of the work for PC DOS. The great majority of the toolkit routines in the Turbo Pascal Solutions Toolkit rely on either PC DOS or ROM BIOS calls. In both instances, those calls are accomplished with software interrupts. In this short section, I'll review the concept of a software interrupt and how the concept is made real in the 8088.

An interrupt is a tap on the CPU's shoulder, indicating that it must pay attention to something else *now*. Interrupt mechanisms have always been part of microprocessor systems. Until the development of the 8086 and 8088, all interrupts were *hardware* interrupts.

Hardware interrupts work this way: An electrical signal on one pin of the CPU chip causes the CPU logic to save the program counter, stack pointer, and general-purpose registers. The CPU is then free to service the request from outside the chip to execute some bit of code unrelated to its ongoing task. Once the request for service is satisfied, the CPU restores the registers it had saved and picks up its ongoing task as though nothing had happened.

With the 8086 family architecture, Intel presented the concept of the *software* interrupt. Software interrupts work exactly the same way as hardware interrupts do, except that the triggering request is a machine instruction (software) rather than an electrical signal on a CPU pin (hardware).

There were a number of reasons for doing this. Since the only difference between hardware and software interrupts is the means by which the interrupt request is triggered, it is possible to test hardware interrupt service routines before the interrupting hardware is perfected, by using software interrupts to simulate the incomplete external hardware device.

A far more important use of software interrupts is in the devising of a system of standard entry points to system software. When any kind of interrupt occurs, the CPU first saves essential registers, and then performs a "long jump" to the location of the interrupt service routine somewhere in memory.

The way the CPU locates this interrupt service routine is critical. The 256 8088 interrupts are numbered from 0 to 255. When an interrupt happens, the CPU must receive the number of the requested interrupt. For hardware interrupts, this number comes from the interrupt priority controller chip outside the CPU. For software interrupts, the interrupt number is built into the interrupt instruction. For example, the 8088 instruction

```
INT 21
```

will trigger software interrupt hex 21.

The first 1024 bytes of the 8088 memory map are reserved for interrupt vectors. "Vector" is taken to mean "pointer" here, since pointers are exactly what occupy those 1024 bytes of memory. Each of the 256 different interrupts has its own 4-byte region within this 1024-byte memory block ($256 \times 4 = 1024$). This 4-byte region contains a 32-bit pointer to the first instruction of the interrupt's service routine.

The first four bytes of 8088 memory contain the interrupt vector for interrupt 0. The next four bytes of memory contain the vector for interrupt 1, and so on up to 255 (see Figure 3.1). Obviously, if the CPU knows the interrupt number, it can multiply that number by four and go immediately to the interrupt vector for any given interrupt. The first two bytes of the interrupt vector represent the program counter value for the start of the service routine, and the second two bytes are the code segment value where that service routine exists. The CPU need only load the code segment value into the CS register and the program counter value into the program counter register, and it is off and running the interrupt service routine.

Interrupt 0				Interrupt 1				Interrupt 2		
Offset		Segment		Offset		Segment		Offset		
LSB	MSB	LSB	MSB	LSB	MSB	LSB	MSB	LSB	MSB	
0	1	2	3	4	5	6	7	8	9	

Memory addresses ➡

$0000 : $0000

Figure 3.1   **The 8086 interrupt vector table**

The important fact here is that the code which seeks to use a software interrupt service routine need not know where that routine is in memory. It only needs to know the interrupt number. Indeed, the actual location of the service routine can change over time, as the routine is altered or expanded. As long as the computer's boot or startup code stores the correct interrupt vectors into the lowermost 1024 bytes of memory, software interrupt service routines may be located anywhere and still be accessed easily by application programs.

This is the spirit of the IBM PC's ROM BIOS. The BIOS is a collection of software interrupt service routines stored in a ROM (Read-Only Memory) at the top of the 8088's memory address space. The interrupt numbers are assigned according to the general function performed by the interrupt service routine. For example, interrupt 16 ($10) controls video services for the PC. Interrupt 22 ($16) controls access to the keyboard.

Not all software interrupts are reserved for the use of the ROM BIOS. PC DOS uses a few; most of them are not used at all. The Microsoft mouse driver makes use of a software interrupt. Many peripheral driver programs, in fact, make use of software interrupts. The IBM PC as we know it would have been impossible without them.

Exploring the interrupt vector jump table (the first 1024 bytes of 8086 memory where all the vectors are stored) can be done with **DEBUG**, but a simple program can make the vectors easier to read and change. **VECTORS .PAS** contains a utility called **Vectors** that can display and change interrupt vectors, and also display a hexdump of the first 256 bytes of memory pointed to by a vector. Changing an interrupt vector can be strong medicine, and shouldn't be attempted unless you know what you're doing. Altering the timer-tick interrupt carelessly will freeze your machine solid in 55 milliseconds flat. However, if you intend to write programs that intercept interrupt vectors, **Vectors** can save a lot of aggravation during development.

The **Vectors** program is a good example of the use of MEM and MEMW, and untyped VAR parameters. (See Section 3.4 for further discussion.)

3.2   Registers and Register Structures

In broad strokes, the previous section described the nature and use of software interrupts. Your Turbo Pascal programs can make efficient use of software interrupts. Understanding how requires some discussion of 8088 machine registers.

A *register* is nothing more than a storage location inside the CPU chip itself. The 8088 has numerous registers, nearly all of which are 16 bits, or two bytes, wide. Some of the registers have specific duties to perform in the 8088's execution of its programs; many are simply convenient places to tuck things away for a moment. (How the registers contribute to the 8088 instruction set is too large a topic to cover here in detail. What's important now is to understand how machine registers are used in connection with calling software interrupt service routines from Turbo Pascal.)

Most software interrupt service routines—like those in the PC's ROM BIOS—require input values, and return output values when processing is finished. These values are passed back and forth between a Turbo Pascal program and the interrupt service routine in machine registers.

Turbo Pascal's **Intr** procedure invokes software interrupts. **Intr** requires an interrupt number and a special data structure containing integer fields corresponding to most of the 8088's registers:

```
Intr(<interrupt #>,<register structure>);
```

The Turbo Pascal Reference Manual refers to the register structure as **"Result"**, but the structure also passes values *to* the interrupt service routine as well as returning results. The manual defines the type of the register structure this way:

```
RegPack = RECORD
                AX,BX,CX,DX,BP,SI,DI,DS,ES,Flags : Integer
          END;
```

"RegPack" is an arbitrary name that is not built into the compiler; you may call it whatever you like. Also, remember that it is *not* predefined. Whenever you intend to use it, it must be declared in the type declaration part of the program, procedure, or function in which it is used. To lessen the possibility of confusion, I will keep the name **RegPack** in the Turbo Pascal Solutions Toolkit routines.

Each of the 10 fields of type **RegPack** is named after an 8088 machine register. When **Intr** is called by your program, it copies the 10 values from **RegPack**'s 10 fields into each field's corresponding 8088 register, then invokes the software interrupt you requested. When the interrupt service routine returns control to **Intr**, **Intr** copies each of the ten 8088 registers into its corresponding field in **RegPack**. The interrupt service routine may or may not have changed any of the 10 machine registers, but if any *were* changed, the altered values will be available in **RegPack** for your program to use.

At first glance, this seems straightforward enough. One persistent problem is that many of the 8088's registers are treated by interrupt service routines not as single 16-bit quantities, but as independent 8-bit quantities. In particular, registers AX, BX, CX, and DX are often treated as pairs of 8-bit registers.

Within AX are AH and AL (Think, "A High" and "A Low"); within BX are BH and BL, and so on for CX and DX. It is often necessary to place separate values in the two halves of a given register.

For example, consider the BIOS VIDEO routine which positions the cursor to a particular location on the CRT screen. Before you call software interrupt 16 (VIDEO) you have to place the desired row/column position in register DX. The row number goes in DH, and the column number in DL. **RegPack** considers DX an integer. How do you put two different values into the two halves of an integer?

The crude way is to shift the value intended for DH eight bits to the left, and then add the shifted quantity to the value intended for DL. This can best be understood by looking at an integer as two bytes. Turbo Pascal's **SHL** operator shifts the bits in an integer a given number of bit-places to the left—that is, from bit 0 toward bit 15. If some number exists in the low byte of an integer, shifting it eight bit-positions to the left shifts that number into the high byte. The low byte has been filled with zero bits; adding another number to the shifted integer simply puts that number into the integer's low byte. Voila! You have placed two separate values into a single integer.

In symbolical terms, storing byte quantity B1 into the high byte of integer I and byte quantity B2 into the low byte of integer I is done this way:

```
I := (B1 SHL 8) + B2;
```

Doing the reverse (in Turbo Pascal, at least) is much easier. Turbo Pascal provides a pair of functions, **HI(I)** and **LO(I)**, which return the high and low bytes of integer argument I. Getting B1 and B2 back out of integer I is as simple as typing:

```
B1 := HI(I);
B2 := LO(I);
```

While they may appear neater on the surface, this pair of functions is just as crude as the previous method we discussed; the crudeness has simply gone underground. Both loading and unloading byte halves of integers in the ways shown above are inefficient, in that shift operations and add operations take time. There is a much faster method that involves no arithmetic calculation at all. The key to the whole process is the notion of a "free-union variant record."

I covered free-union variants in *Complete Turbo Pascal*, Section 9.4. It's a tricky concept, best approached by starting with an ordinary Pascal variant record:

```
TYPE
  Register = RECORD
               CASE AsBytes : Boolean OF
```

```
            False : (Word : Integer);
            True : (LoByte,HiByte : Byte)
      END;
```

Type **Register** is a variant record. The tag field **AsBytes** is a Boolean variable. The value contained in **AsBytes** determines how the rest of the record will be looked upon by Pascal. If **AsBytes** contains a value of **True**, the remainder of the record contains two 8-bit byte values. If **AsBytes** contains a value of **False**, the remainder of the record contains a single 16-bit integer value.

By changing the value of **AsBytes**, we can change the sense of the record from one of storing two bytes to one of storing a single integer. Is this what we want? Close . . . but not quite.

Here's the snag: When the value of **AsBytes** changes, the value of the rest of the record becomes undefined. If we loaded two bytes into **LoByte** and **HiByte** when **AsBytes** was **True**, changing **AsBytes** to **False** wipes out the two values.

The Pascal definition, in one of its more bizarre turns, allows us to eliminate the *name* of the tag field but not its *type*:

```
TYPE
  Register = RECORD
             CASE Boolean OF
                 False : (Word : Integer);
                 True : (LoByte,HiByte : Byte)
             END;
```

Type **Register** is now a free-union variant record. (The earlier example which had a tag field name is sometimes called a "discriminated-union" variant record, though the name is not widely used.)

What sort of creature is this? Quite tersely, both possible interpretations of the data in a **Register** record are valid *at the same time*. We can load an integer into a **Register** record, and then immediately turn around and read that value as two distinct byte values. In other words:

```
VAR
  AX : Register;         { AX is type Register, see above }

AX.Word := 26436;        { Assign a value to AX as an integer }
Writeln(AX.HiByte);      { Display low half: 68 }
Writeln(AX.LoByte);      { Display high half: 103 }
```

What happened here is that we loaded a 16-bit quantity into AX by accessing the **Word** field of AX. Then we turned around and fished out the two halves of the integer we just stored by accessing the **LoByte** and **HiByte** fields. No conversion was necessary.

The secret is that **Word,** and the two fields **LoByte** and **HiByte,** actually occupy the *same* two physical bytes in memory. The free-union variant record structure is really doing nothing more than providing two different ways of naming the same two bytes of memory. Chucking the tag field saves us a byte of memory to boot!

A Better Version of RegPack

By using the free-union variant record concept, we can provide a much more useful register structure to **Intr.** By making each register field in **RegPack** itself a free-union variant record, we can at our whim access the entire 16 bits of a register, or access either 8-bit half of a register. The following two record type definitions are an essential part of the Turbo Pascal Solutions Toolkit:

```
TYPE
  Reg = RECORD
          CASE Boolean OF
            False : (Word : Integer);
            True  : (LoByte,HiByte : Byte)
        END;

RegPack = RECORD
            AX,BX,CX,DX,BP,SI,DI,DS,ES,Flags : Reg
          END;
```

Notice that while the fields of **RegPack** are no longer integers, each is still only two bytes long, which is what the machinery of **Intr** expects.

The best way to show you how to use the new **RegPack** definition is with a simple toolkit routine that depends on it. Read the definition of **FlushKey** carefully:

```
1        {->>>>FlushKey<<<<------------------------------------------------}
2        {                                                                 }
3        { Filename: FLUSHKEY.SRC -- Last modified 11/29/85                 }
4        {                                                                 }
5        { This routine uses ROM BIOS services to flush waiting            }
6        { characters from the keyboard buffer.  This should be done       }
7        { immediately before user prompts which must NOT be answerable    }
8        { via type-ahead:  Go-aheads for file erasures, things like       }
9        { that.                                                           }
10       {                                                                 }
11       {                                                                 }
12       {                                                                 }
13       {-----------------------------------------------------------------}
14
```

(continued)

```
15          PROCEDURE FlushKey;
16
17          TYPE
18            Reg      = RECORD
19                          CASE Boolean OF
20                             False : (Word : Integer);
21                             True  : (LoByte,HiByte : Byte)
22                        END;
23
24            Regpack = RECORD
25                          AX,BX,CX,DX,BP,SI,DI,DS,ES,Flags : Reg
26                        END;
27
28          VAR Registers : Regpack;
29
30          BEGIN
31            Registers.AX.HiByte := $01;      { AH=1: Check for keystroke }
32            INTR($16,Registers);                 { Interrupt $16: Keyboard services}
33            IF (Registers.Flags.Word AND $0040) = O THEN   { If chars in buffer }
34              REPEAT
35                Registers.AX.HiByte := O;    { Char is ready; go read it... }
36                INTR($16,Registers);             { ...using AH = 0: Read Char }
37                Registers.AX.HiByte := $01; { Check for another keystroke... }
38                INTR($16,Registers);             { ...using AH = 1 }
39              UNTIL (Registers.Flags.Word AND $0040) <> 0;
40          END;
```

FlushKey flushes the keyboard typeahead buffer. In other words, if any characters are waiting to be read in the typeahead buffer, **FlushKey** reads them and throws them away. Why is this useful? There are times when you do *not* want to allow a user to answer a question by typing ahead, presumably before the question's prompt appears on the screen. If you are asking a user whether or not he wants to delete the old version of his master data file, you would prefer that he read the question and think about it for a moment, rather than insert an answer in the typeahead queue and wait for the machine to catch up with his responses. He might slip and type the wrong character, or forget that the question comes up. Therefore, immediately before prompting the user for responses which may have drastic consequences, call **FlushKey** to empty the typeahead buffer.

FlushKey uses the keyboard services interrupt of ROM BIOS, interrupt 22 (16 hex, or $16 in the listing). The very first line of the body of **FlushKey** loads a value of 1 into the high byte of register AX:

```
Registers.AX.HiByte := $01;
```

This notation selects two nested record fields: Field **AX** of record **Registers**, and field **HiByte** of record **AX**.

Now, consider line 33:

```
IF (Registers.Flags.Word AND $0040) = 0 THEN
```

This time, we're testing for one bit (the zero bit) out of the **Flags** register. **Flags** is treated here as a 16-bit integer quantity. **Flags** is not traditionally broken into halves as AX, BX, CX, and DX so often are. While we could separately access **HiByte** and **LoByte** for **Flags**, I recommend against it for clarity's sake. There is no speed advantage to testing a single bit within an 8-bit byte over testing for that same bit within a 16-bit integer.

3.3 BIOS and BIOS Services

FlushKey provides a good introduction to the concept of ROM BIOS services. As I explained earlier, each broad function of BIOS (video, keyboard, printer, serial port) has its own software interrupt. However, within most BIOS functions are two or more separately invocable services that are called using the same software interrupt. Within the video function (software interrupt 16), for example, are services to position the cursor, write a character to the screen, scroll a rectangular window up or down, change text and graphics modes, write pixels to a graphics screen, read characters from a text screen, and many more.

The BIOS video function is selected by invoking software interrupt 16. Invoking an individual video service is done by placing a service code in the high half of the AX register, AH. This is a custom in the use of the IBM PC's ROM BIOS services: To select a service within a function, place the service code in AH.

FlushKey does this several times, initially at line 31. Service 1 for the BIOS keyboard function checks for the availability of a character in the typeahead buffer. **FlushKey** first checks to see if there is at least one character in the buffer by examining the Zero bit in the **Flags** register. Service 1 communicates its result to the calling logic by setting or clearing the Zero bit. If the Zero bit comes back cleared (i.e., set to 0), a character is in the buffer. If the Zero bit comes back set (i.e., set to 1), no character is waiting in the typeahead buffer.

Notice that if the first check for waiting characters comes back positive, **FlushKey** enters a **REPEAT/UNTIL** loop. The loop is entered only if a character is known to be in the buffer, so keyboard service 0 is called immediately. Service 0 returns the first waiting character in the typeahead buffer. If no character is waiting to be read, service 0 will wait for a character to be typed. This is the reason we must check for the presence of a character before attempting to read one with service 0. Trying to read a character when none has been typed will give the appearance of a hung system until some key is pressed.

The loop reads a character and then checks for the presence of yet another character. If no further characters are detected via keyboard service 1, the buffer is empty and **FlushKey** has done its job. If more characters are detected, the read-and-check-for-more loop is repeated until the buffer comes up empty. This state is indicated by a set Zero flag. Note that nothing is done with the characters read; **FlushKey** simply reads them and throws them away to clear the buffer. You could expand **FlushKey** to return a string variable containing any characters found in the typeahead buffer if it was important not to ignore an important keypress, such as an "escape" code or other "hot key."

Polling the Keyboard with GetKey

With a little more complication, we can draw from the BIOS virtually all it has to offer in terms of keyboard support. There are only three services available under the BIOS keyboard function, interrupt 22. **FlushKey** uses 0 and 1. Service 2 returns the current state of the IBM PC's various shift-type keys.

There are four shift-type keys on the PC keyboard, and four lock-type keys. Shift-type keys create a condition only when pressed; when released, that condition goes away. The four shift-type keys are Control (Ctrl), Alt, Left Shift and Right Shift. In terms of uppercase and lowercase characters, Left Shift and Right Shift are identical, but at the BIOS level they are two separate keys which may be tested for independently.

The lock-type keys are Insert (Ins), Caps Lock, Num Lock, and Scroll Lock. These keys control keyboard "toggles"—flags which can be switched between two states but which remain in a given state until switched to the opposite state, much like a toggle switch controlling a light fixture. Flip it once, and the light goes on and stays on, until you flip it again to turn it off. (This analogy is especially appropriate for some non-IBM keyboards, which have LED lamps built into the lock-type keys so that you can always tell which state the key is in at a glance. With the IBM keyboard, you have to remember your present state, or take a chance by pressing a key and seeing what happens.)

Keyboard interrupt service 2 returns an 8-bit byte in AL containing eight flag bits. The meaning behind each bit is shown below:

Bit #	Meaning	Type
0	1 = Left Shift depressed	Shift
1	1 = Right Shift depressed	Shift
2	1 = Ctrl depressed	Shift

Bit #	Meaning	Type
3	1 = Alt depressed	Shift
4	1 = Scroll Lock active	Lock
5	1 = Num Lock active	Lock
6	1 = Caps Lock active	Lock
7	1 = Insert active	Lock

The states of the shift-type keys (bits 0-4) are returned for the moment the interrupt call is made. There is *no* buffering of shift keys.

Below is **GetKey**, a keyboard-sampling routine which will tell you everything the BIOS is capable of telling you about the IBM PC keyboard. **GetKey** is a "polling" routine. It doesn't wait for a character or a string to be typed at the keyboard. At the moment you call **GetKey**, it jumps out and takes a look at the keyboard and the typeahead buffer. If a character is waiting in the typeahead buffer, **GetKey** will grab it and bring it back, setting its function return value to **True**. If no character is ready, **GetKey**'s function-return value will come back as **False**. In either case, **GetKey** returns the current state of the shift-type keys and the lock-type keys in a byte named **Shifts**.

```
1      {->>>>GetKey<<<<---------------------------------------------------}
2      {                                                                  }
3      { Filename: GETKEY.SRC -- Last modified 11/28/85                   }
4      {                                                                  }
5      { This routine uses ROM BIOS services to test for the presence }
6      { of a character waiting in the keyboard buffer and, if one is }
7      { waiting, return it.  The function itself returns a TRUE       }
8      { if a character has been read.  The character is returned in   }
9      { Ch.  If the key pressed was a "special" (non-ASCII) key, the }
10     { Boolean variable Extended will be set to TRUE and the scan    }
11     { code of the special key will be returned in Scan.  In         }
12     { addition, GETKEY returns shift status each time it is called }
13     { regardless of whether or not a character was read.  Shift     }
14     { status is returned as eight flag bits in byte Shifts,         }
15     { according to the bitmap below:                                }
16     {                                                               }
17     {           BITS                                                }
18     {     7 6 5 4 3 2 1 0                                           }
19     {     1 . . . . . . .   INSERT       (1=Active)                }
20     {     . 1 . . . . . .   CAPS LOCK    (1=Active)                }
21     {     . . 1 . . . . .   NUM LOCK     (1=Active)                }
22     {     . . . 1 . . .  .  SCROLL LOCK  (1=Active)                }
23     {     . . . . 1 . . .   ALT          (1=Depressed)            }
```

(continued)

```pascal
24        {           .  .  .  .  .  1  .  .   CTRL          (1=Depressed)      }
25        {           .  .  .  .  .  .  1  .   LEFT SHIFT    (1=Depressed)      }
26        {           .  .  .  .  .  .  .  1   RIGHT SHIFT   (1=Depressed)      }
27        {                                                                    }
28        { Test for individual bits using masks and the AND operator:     }
29        {                                                                    }
30        {    IF (Shifts AND $0A) = $0A THEN CtrlAndAltArePressed;        }
31        {                                                                    }
32        {                                                                    }
33        {                                                                    }
34        {-------------------------------------------------------------------}
35
36        FUNCTION GetKey(VAR Ch        : Char;
37                        VAR Extended : Boolean;
38                        VAR Scan     : Byte;
39                        Var Shifts   : Byte) : Boolean;
40        TYPE
41          Reg      = RECORD
42                       CASE Boolean OF
43                         False : (Word : Integer);
44                         True  : (LoByte,HiByte : Byte)
45                     END;
46
47          Regpack = RECORD
48                      AX,BX,CX,DX,BP,SI,DI,DS,ES,Flags : Reg
49                    END;
50
51        VAR Registers : Regpack;
52            Ready     : Boolean;
53
54        BEGIN
55          Extended := False; Scan := 0;
56          Registers.AX.HiByte := $01;       { AH=1: Check for keystroke }
57          INTR($16,Registers);              { Interrupt $16: Keyboard services}
58          Ready := (Registers.Flags.LoByte AND $40) = 0;
59          IF Ready THEN
60            BEGIN
61              Registers.AX.HiByte := 0;         { Char is ready; go read it... }
62              INTR($16,Registers);              { ...using AH = 0: Read Char }
63              Ch := CHR(Registers.AX.LoByte);   { The char is returned in AL }
64              Scan := Registers.AX.HiByte;      { ...and scan code in AH.    }
65              IF CH = CHR(0) THEN Extended := True ELSE Extended := False;
66            END;
67          Registers.AX.HiByte := $02;    { AH=2: Get shift/alt/ctrl status }
68          INTR($16,Registers);
69          Shifts := Registers.AX.LoByte;
70          GetKey := Ready
71        END;
```

There is an additional complication to the notion of "returning a character" from the PC keyboard. There are keys which do not represent characters—the function keys and arrow keys being prime examples. Your programs may need to use those keys. How do you get them?

The BIOS divides keystrokes into "ASCII" and "extended" keys. ASCII keys are those which stand for an ASCII letter, numeral, or symbol having a numeric code from 0 to 127. If an ASCII key is pressed, **GetKey** returns the ASCII character in its character parameter **Ch**. The extended keys are the function keys, arrow keys, PgUp, PgDn, Home, End, and various combinations of those keys with Ctrl, Alt, and Shift. Each extended key has a code from 0 to 255. This code is returned for extended keys in **GetKey**'s **Scan** parameter. If an extended code is being returned, **GetKey** will also return a Boolean value of **True** in its **Extended** parameter.

Using the PC's Cassette-Control Relay

One of the stranger and today nearly-forgotten aspects of the original IBM PC was that it contained a complete digital cassette interface for program and data storage. IBM was covering all the bases with its PC; in addition to a fully disk-based machine, it intended to deliver an inexpensive ("only" $2000 or so) version of the PC for use in the home, without any disk drives at all. In place of DOS and disk drives, it had a version of BASICA in ROM that could store and retrieve programs and data from ordinary audio cassettes.

Nobody had told IBM that there was no home computer market for $2000 computers, and the cassette port went generally unused. The cassette port remains on all PC motherboards, however, and while the data transfer logic is of little use, the small relay that turned the cassette drive motor on and off can be used for other purposes. Keep in mind that I mean "PC" here in the specific; the cassette port is *not* part of the PC/XT or PC/AT machines.

The relay is an SPST type, with contacts rated at one amp current. Having taken a long look at the relay, however, I would play it safe and limit the current through the relay to half an amp or slightly more. The relay contacts are brought out through the other five-pin DIN connector on the back panel of the PC (into which you are always connecting the PC keyboard by mistake). The DIN connector pinouts are shown in Figure 3.2.

Support for the cassette interface is part of ROM BIOS, and is accessed through software interrupt $15. Service 0 turns the motor on, and service 1 turns the motor off. No other parameters need to be passed, and none are returned.

The two procedures for turning the relay on and off are essentially trivial invocations of software interrupt $15.

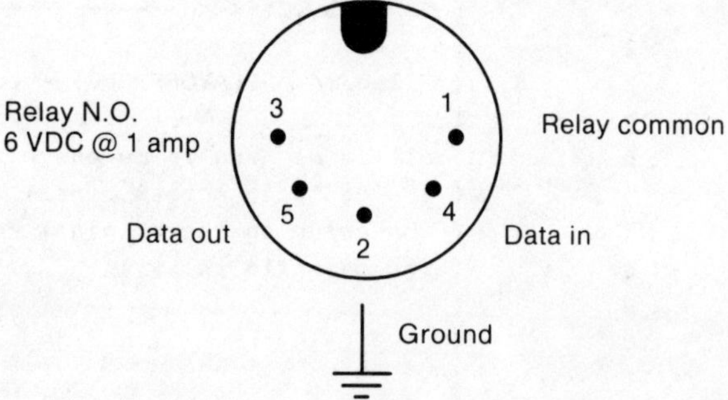

Figure 3.2   **The PC's cassette port interface**

```
1        {->>>>RelayOn<<<<----------------------------------------------------}
2        {                                                                     }
3        { Filename: RELAYON.SRC -- Last modified 12/29/85                     }
4        {                                                                     }
5        { This one quite simply energizes the cassette relay, which          }
6        { closes the contacts across pins 1 and 3 of the cassette DIN         }
7        { connector on the original PC.  (XT's and AT's do not have           }
8        { the cassette relay.)  The specs allow for 1 amp through the         }
9        { relay, but having inspected the relay I would play it safe          }
10       { and attempt no more than half an amp.                              }
11       {                                                                     }
12       {                                                                     }
13       {                                                                     }
14       {---------------------------------------------------------------------}
15
16       PROCEDURE RelayOn;
17
18       TYPE
19         Reg       = RECORD
20                       CASE Boolean OF
21                         False : (Word : Integer);
22                         True  : (LoByte,HiByte : Byte)
23                     END;
24
25         Regpack = RECORD
26                       AX,BX,CX,DX,BP,SI,DI,DS,ES,Flags : Reg
27                     END;
28
29       VAR
30         Registers : Regpack;
31
32       BEGIN
33         Registers.AX.HiByte := 0;    { Service that turns motor on }
34         INTR($15,Registers)
35       END;
```

```
 1          {->>>>RelayOff<<<<---------------------------------------------------}
 2          {                                                                     }
 3          { Filename: RELAYOFF.SRC -- Last modified 12/29/85                     }
 4          {                                                                     }
 5          { All we do here is de-energize the cassette relay, opening           }
 6          { the contacts across pins 1 and 3 of the cassette DIN                }
 7          { connector on the original PC.  (XT's and AT's do not have           }
 8          { the cassette relay.)                                                }
 9          {                                                                     }
10          {                                                                     }
11          {                                                                     }
12          {---------------------------------------------------------------------}
13
14          PROCEDURE RelayOff;
15
16          TYPE
17            Reg      = RECORD
18                          CASE Boolean OF
19                             False : (Word : Integer);
20                             True  : (LoByte,HiByte : Byte)
21                       END;
22
23            Regpack = RECORD
24                          AX,BX,CX,DX,BP,SI,DI,DS,ES,Flags : Reg
25                       END;
26
27          VAR
28            Registers : Regpack;
29
30          BEGIN
31            Registers.AX.HiByte := 1;   { Service that turns motor off }
32            INTR($15,Registers)
33          END;
```

The only time I have used the cassette relay was in keying a small FM amateur radio transceiver; in the process, I learned that the PC is also a radio transmitter of considerable power. The square waves coursing about inside the PC are rich in harmonics, and unless you bypass the relay control lines at the DIN connector, you will hear the buzzsaw rasp of the timer interrupts in your receiver to the exclusion of just about everything else.

In addition, although I had no trouble working at three watts RF, more powerful transmitters could send enough loose RF energy into the PC to disrupt system memory. If things act strangely when you connect a transmitter to the cassette port, bypass. Then bypass some more. Of course, keep in mind that the PC radiates RF through the air as well as through connecting cables. If your antenna is in the same room as the PC, you will almost certainly hear nothing but the PC, regardless of how well the cassette port is bypassed. Rubber duckies won't cut it!

A Morse Code Generator

This seems the best place in the book to include a short routine that converts plain text to Morse code for amateur radio purposes. Procedure **SendMorse** accepts strings containing plain ASCII text, and will use the computer speaker to transmit the code audibly. Two additional parameters specify the code speed in words per minute (WPM) and the frequency (in hertz) of the speaker tone used.

The amateur practice of blending two separate Morse characters together for certain purposes (such as SK, meaning "end of contact") is handled by prefixing the pair to be "blended" with an asterisk (*), a character for which there is no common Morse equivalent. The blended SK would then be passed to **SendMorse** as *SK.

Local procedure **Morse** accepts strings containing information already encoded as "dits" and "dahs," where the ASCII period character (.) represents a dit and the ASCII dash (-) represents a dah. **Morse** was set out apart from the body of **SendMorse** so that it could be rewritten to output the code through some port other than the audible speaker. One obvious place is through the PC's cassette relay, as described above.

SendMorse uses the ARRL's published definition for WPM as:

```
WPM = 1.2 * B
```

where B is the baud rate of the transmission—essentially, the rate at which the smallest units of information are passed. This unit is the length of the audible portion of a dit, though it must be remembered that the dit properly includes the dit-length silence following it. The baud rate is thus *twice* the rate of an uninterrupted series of dits. The length of each dit can be derived from the above formula as:

$$\text{DitLength} = \frac{1.2}{\text{WPM}}$$

which, when multiplied by 1000, becomes an integer that can be passed to Turbo Pascal's **Delay** procedure as the integer number of milliseconds by which to delay.

The **Delay** procedure is tolerably clock-speed independent, and **Send-Morse** will transmit code within a few percent of the passed code speed figure regardless of the speed of the host computer. I have tested this on a 4.77-Mhz PC and a 16-Mhz 80386 AT compatible, and the speeds are close enough to count on for code practice leading to the FCC amateur exams.

```
1        {->>>>SendMorse<<<<-------------------------------------------}
2        {                                                             }
3        { Filename : SENDMORS.SRC -- Last Modified 1/29/87            }
4        {                                                             }
5        { This procedure converts plain text to audible Morse Code at }
6        { a specified code speed and tone frequency.  The times are   }
7        { fairly accurate and have been tested on a 4.77 Mhz PC and a }
8        { 16 Mhz 80386 machine without significant difference in      }
9        { code speed.  (Turbo's V3.0 DELAY procedure is finally clock }
10       { speed independent.)  The useful range of the procedure is   }
11       { from 10-35 WPM, with best "feel" at 15-25 WPM.              }
12       {                                                             }
13       { Text is passed to SendMorse as quoted strings of plain      }
14       { text.  If two characters are to be sent as one without an   }
15       { intermediate delay, an asterisk ('*') must precede the two  }
16       { characters.  This replaces the overbar used in most amateur }
17       { literature.                                                 }
18       {                                                             }
19       { Types String255 and String80 must be predefined.           }
20       {                                                             }
21       {                                                             }
22       {                                                             }
23       {-------------------------------------------------------------}
24
25
26       PROCEDURE SendMorse(PlainText : String255;
27                           ToneFrequency : Integer;
28                           CodeSpeed     : Integer);
29
30
31       VAR
32          I             : Integer;
33          ToneLength    : Integer;
34          DitLength     : Integer;
35          CodeChar      : String80;
36          BlendNextTwo  : Boolean;
37
38
39       { Code is passed to local procedure Morse as literal dots and }
40       { dashes:  '-.-.' = 'C', and so on.  SendMorse converts from  }
41       { text to the dot/dash code representation. }
42
```

(continued)

```
43        PROCEDURE Morse(CodeChar : String80);
44
45        VAR
46          I : Integer;
47
48        BEGIN
49          FOR I := 1 TO Length(CodeChar) DO
50            BEGIN
51              IF CodeChar[1] IN ['.','-'] THEN
52                BEGIN
53                  IF CodeChar[I] = '.' THEN ToneLength := DitLength
54                    ELSE ToneLength := DitLength * 3;
55                  Sound(ToneFrequency);
56                  Delay(ToneLength);
57                  NoSound;
58                  Delay(DitLength)
59                END
60            END
61        END;
62
63        BEGIN
64          BlendNextTwo := False;
65          { Code speed calculation is derived from formulae published in }
66          { the 1986 ARRL Handbook, Section 9-8.   I recommend running   }
67          { this procedure at 10 WPM or greater; 15-20 WPM is its most   }
68          { effective range.   Timer resolution interferes above 35 WPM. }
69          DitLength := Round((1.2 / CodeSpeed) * 1000.0);
70          FOR I := 1 TO Length(PlainText) DO IF PlainText[I] = '*' THEN
71            BlendNextTwo := TRUE ELSE
72            BEGIN
73              PlainText[I] := UpCase(PlainText[I]);
74              CASE PlainText[I] OF
75                'A' : CodeChar := '.-';
76                'B' : CodeChar := '-...';
77                'C' : CodeChar := '-.-.';
78                'D' : CodeChar := '-..';
79                'E' : CodeChar := '.';
80                'F' : CodeChar := '..-.';
81                'G' : CodeChar := '--.';
82                'H' : CodeChar := '....';
83                'I' : CodeChar := '..';
84                'J' : CodeChar := '.---';
85                'K' : CodeChar := '-.-';
86                'L' : CodeChar := '.-..';
87                'M' : CodeChar := '--';
88                'N' : CodeChar := '-.';
89                'O' : CodeChar := '---';
90                'P' : CodeChar := '.--.';
91                'Q' : CodeChar := '--.-';
```

(continued)

```
 92                      'R' : CodeChar := '.-.';
 93                      'S' : CodeChar := '...';
 94                      'T' : CodeChar := '-';
 95                      'U' : CodeChar := '..-';
 96                      'V' : CodeChar := '...-';
 97                      'W' : CodeChar := '.--';
 98                      'X' : CodeChar := '-..-';
 99                      'Y' : CodeChar := '-.--';
100                      'Z' : CodeChar := '--..';
101                      '1' : CodeChar := '.----';
102                      '2' : CodeChar := '..---';
103                      '3' : CodeChar := '...--';
104                      '4' : CodeChar := '....-';
105                      '5' : CodeChar := '.....';
106                      '6' : CodeChar := '-....';
107                      '7' : CodeChar := '--...';
108                      '8' : CodeChar := '---..';
109                      '9' : CodeChar := '----.';
110                      '0' : CodeChar := '-----';
111                      '?' : CodeChar := '..--..';
112                      '.' : CodeChar := '.-.-.-';
113                      ',' : CodeChar := '--..--';
114                      '/' : CodeChar := '-..-.';
115                      '$' : CodeChar := '...-..-';
116                      '-' : CodeChar := '-....-';
117                      ELSE CodeChar := ''
118                    END; {CASE}
119                    Morse(CodeChar);
120                    IF NOT BlendNextTwo THEN Delay(DitLength * 2);
121                    BlendNextTwo := FALSE
122                  END;
123              END;
```

SendMorse works best at code speeds between 15 and 25 WPM, and gets
dicey below 10 or above 35. For practice at lower speeds, it would make sense
to modify the code to insert additional "dead time" between characters and
keep the character elements themselves at 10 WPM or faster.

The short program **MorseTest** demonstrates the use of **SendMorse**.

```
1              PROGRAM MorseTest;
2
3
4              TYPE
5                String255 = String[255];
6                String80  = String[80];
7
```

(continued)

```
 8          {$I SENDMORS.SRC}
 9
10
11          BEGIN
12            ClrScr;
13            SendMorse('CQCQCQ DE KB2JN *SK',850,15);
14          END.
15
16
17
18
```

3.4   Seeing What You're Doing

The Problem with Symbolic Debuggers

Most computer programs can be debugged simply by checking to see what the variables contain from time to time. This is the reason for a whole class of utilities called "symbolic debuggers." In a symbolic debugger, the programmer can interrupt a program, ask for the value of a variable *by name*, and get a hexdump of the data currently stored within that variable. Symbolic debuggers make it less necessary to know the binary address of every single variable you'd like to watch.

One of the more aggravating things about symbolic debuggers is that they don't work with Turbo Pascal programs. A friend of mine, Brett Salter, sells a superb symbolic debugger named Periscope. He gets a lot of calls from people who want to use Periscope with Turbo Pascal, and the answer is as agonizing as it is inescapable: you can't.

Symbolic debuggers cannot display variables in Turbo Pascal programs by name because Turbo Pascal throws away the symbolic names for variables during the compilation process. Assemblers and language compilers which create linkable (.OBJ) output files can build variable names into a special .OBJ record type, which is then used by the symbolic debugger. Turbo Pascal does not generate .OBJ files and therefore has no way to associate symbolic names from the program variables in the executable (.COM) machine code file.

Supposedly, Release 4.0 of Turbo Pascal will solve this problem. In the meantime, there are certain things you can do to make variable inspection easier.

The most basic of all Pascal debugging techniques is including **Writeln** statements throughout your program to write the current value of a variable to the screen or (if writing to the screen would disrupt the workings of the program) to the system printer. This certainly slows the program down, but there's no better way to prove that a variable is getting out of hand within a program loop than to print out the value of that variable at each pass through the loop.

The boulder-sized hole in this technique is that **Writeln** will only print simple variable types like **String**, **Char**, **Byte**, **Integer**, **Real**, and **Boolean**. Enumerated types, records, sets, and, in general, any data which has no printable interpretation cannot be displayed via **Writeln**.

What is needed here is a general-purpose procedure which will accept any variable, printable or not, and display it to the screen or printer in hexadecimal format. These mini-hexdumps would be harder to read than clear character displays of printable data, but nevertheless would provide an unambiguous look at any conceivable program variable.

In traditional Pascal, such a routine is impossible. The problem is that procedure parameters are typed, and you cannot pass a record variable in a parameter having a string type—or vice versa—or have a type different from the type declared in the procedure parameter line. **Write** and **Writeln** are special cases built into the compiler.

Once again, Turbo Pascal provides a trapdoor out of this predicament. In another bizarre enhancement to the standard Pascal definition, Turbo Pascal allows untyped **VAR** parameters. In other words, it is perfectly legal to declare a procedure this way:

```
PROCEDURE VarDump(VAR Target);
```

Turbo Pascal will compile this without a whimper. What, however, does an untyped **VAR** parameter mean within a procedure body? What can be done with it?

Very little, in fact. The type of a variable tells program code two important things: 1) How large a variable is, and 2) what may be legally done with it. Without a type, the code in the body of a procedure has very little to go on when dealing with the untyped parameter. Untyped **VAR** parameters cannot be assigned to any other type, including other untyped **VAR** parameters, nor can they be passed to any standard procedure or function.

What *can* be done is, in one respect, a base trick, but it works: An untyped **VAR** parameter, like any **VAR** parameter, is not itself a variable but actually a 4-byte pointer to the actual parameter in the program's code segment. Since it is, in effect, a machine address, an untyped **VAR** parameter can provide an absolute variable declaration with an address. In other words, within a procedure, you can declare an absolute variable at the address represented by the untyped **VAR** parameter:

```
PROCEDURE VarDump(VAR Target);
VAR
  DumpArray : ARRAY[0..Maxint] OF Byte ABSOLUTE Target;
```

This works only because the address of an absolute variable in Turbo Pascal does *not* have to be set at compile time. Whenever **VarDump** begins executing, it will take the address represented by **Target** and map the variable **DumpArray** at that address. This lays **DumpArray** over whatever actual parameter was passed to **VarDump** in **Target**. Element 0 of **DumpArray** is in the same physical place as the first byte of the actual parameter passed in **Target**—whatever type it happens to be. This allows us to treat the actual parameter passed in **Target** as an array of bytes, to do with as we please.

There is one snag: We don't know how large **Target**'s actual parameter is. We may pass a gigantic record structure in **Target** the first time we call **Var-Dump**, and a one-byte enumerated type in it the next time. Obtaining the size requires a second parameter:

```
PROCEDURE VarDump(VAR Target; ItSize : Integer);
```

Now we have everything we need to examine or change every byte within any variable that happens to get passed in **Target**, irrespective of its type.

For our immediate purposes in trying to display a hexdump of an arbitrary variable, we can take the actual parameter passed in **Target** and display a hexdump of it byte by byte. This requires a hexadecimal output routine:

```
1          {->>>>WriteHex<<<<------------------------------------------------}
2          {                                                                 }
3          { Filename: WRITEHEX.SRC -- Last modified 12/15/85                 }
4          {                                                                 }
5          { This routine cerates a 2-character hexadecimal                   }
6          { representation of any arbitrary byte value and passes the        }
7          { representation to Device.  Device is any variable of type        }
8          { Text.  This is typically a device file like CON or PRN but       }
9          { could be any open text file as well.  This works by             }
10         { isolating the high and low nybbles of the target byte and        }
11         { using the isolated nybbles (after bringing the high-order        }
12         { nibble down to the low four bits) to index into an array         }
13         { of hexadecimal digits.                                          }
14         {                                                                 }
15         {                                                                 }
16         {                                                                 }
17         {-----------------------------------------------------------------}
18
19
20         PROCEDURE WriteHex(VAR Device : Text; BT : Byte);
21
22         CONST
23           HexDigits : ARRAY[0..15] OF Char = '0123456789ABCDEF';
24
25         VAR
```

(continued)

```
26            BZ : Byte;
27
28        BEGIN
29          BZ := BT AND $0F;
30          BT := BT SHR 4;
31          Write(Device,HexDigits[BT],HexDigits[BZ])
32        END;
```

WriteHex breaks byte parameter **BT** apart into two 4-bit nybbles. The lower nybble is used directly as an index into an array of hex digit characters from 0 to F. If the value in the lower nybble is 12, **WriteHex** displays the twelfth character in **HexDigits**, which is C. The higher nybble must first be shifted four bits to the right, dividing its value by 16, before it, too, is used to index into **HexDigits** in search of a character equivalent to its value. The two characters taken together provide a hexadecimal equivalent for any 8-bit byte.

WriteHex has a parameter called **Device**, which is an open text file. Device files are text files, and, in most cases, the open text file passed in **Device** will be either **CON** or **LST**. Of course, **CON** will route the hex display to the screen, and **LST** to the printer. As an alternative, you could open an ordinary disk-resident text file and send the hex output of **WriteHex** into that file, allowing you to "capture" variables dumped during a test session.

Given **WriteHex**, creating the generalized variable dump routine is straightforward:

```
1          {->>>>VarDump<<<<----------------------------------------------}
2          {                                                              }
3          { Filename: VARDUMP.SRC -- Last modified 10/26/85              }
4          {                                                              }
5          { This routine displays a hexdump of ANY arbitrary variable,   }
6          { regardless of type.  The variable to be dumped is passed in  }
7          { Target, and the size of Target (calculated using SizeOf to   }
8          { be safe) is passed in ItSize.  Target is untyped and can     }
9          { accept as its actual parameter ANY valid type except a file  }
10         { type.  The hex dump is sent to Device, which can be any open }
11         { text file including CON (for output to the console) and PRN  }
12         { (for output to the system printer.)                          }
13         {                                                              }
14         { CALLS:                                                       }
15         {   WRITEHEX.SRC, which must be included before it in the      }
16         {   compilable source file.                                    }
17         {                                                              }
18         {                                                              }
19         {                                                              }
20         {--------------------------------------------------------------}
21
```

(continued)

```
22        PROCEDURE VarDump(VAR Device : Text; VAR Target; ItSize : Integer);
23
24        CONST
25          Printables : SET OF Char = [' '..'}'];
26
27        VAR
28          I,J        : Integer;
29          Full,Left : Integer;
30          Dumpit     : ARRAY[0..MaxInt] OF Byte ABSOLUTE Target;
31
32
33        PROCEDURE DumpLine(Offset,ByteCount : Integer);
34
35        VAR
36          I : Integer;
37
38        BEGIN
39          FOR I := 0 TO ByteCount-1 DO                  { Hex dump the data }
40            BEGIN
41              WriteHex(Device,Dumpit[(Offset*16)+I]);
42              Write(Device,' ')
43            END;
44          FOR I := 0 TO 56 - (ByteCount*3) DO Write(Device,' ');  { Space interval }
45            Write(Device,'|');                          { Show first boundary bar }
46          FOR I := 0 TO ByteCount-1 DO                 { Show printable equivalents }
47            IF Chr(Dumpit[(Offset*16)+I]) IN Printables THEN
48              Write(Device,Chr(Dumpit[(Offset*16)+I]))
49            ELSE Write(Device,'.');
50          Writeln(Device,'|')                          { Final boundary bar }
51        END;
52
53
54        BEGIN
55          Full := ItSize DIV 16;    { Number of 16-byte chunks in TARGET }
56          Left := ItSize MOD 16;    { 'Leftover' bytes after last 16-byte chunk }
57          FOR I := 0 TO Full-1 DO   { Not executed if less than 16 bytes in TARGET }
58            DumpLine(I,16);
59          IF LEFT > 0 THEN          { Not executed if size of TARGET divides by 16 }
60            DumpLine(Full,Left);
61          Writeln(Device)           { Space down one line after dump }
62        END;   { VarDump }
```

VarDump does its work line by line, where each line contains 16 or fewer
bytes of the parameter **Target**. The local procedure **DumpLine** does the actual
dump of each line. **DumpLine** first displays its line as hexadecimal equivalents.
Then it spaces over to the right and displays the character equivalents for each
printable character in its line, or a period character (.) for each nonprintable

character. Two vertical bar characters (¦) delineate the character equivalent part of the dump.

All that the main body of the **VarDump** procedure does is decide how many full lines of 16 characters are contained in **Target**, and how large a partial line (if any) will remain to be dumped after all the full lines have been dumped. With those figures in hand, it calls **DumpLine** to do the actual line dumps.

You can call **VarDump** from anywhere in a program and plug any variable into **Target**, so long as the variable is less than **MaxInt** (32,767) bytes long. (That shouldn't be a serious limitation, as watching 32,767 characters of hexdump scroll by is enough to drive anyone to watch *Love Boat*.)

Use untyped **VAR** parameters with some care. In cases when the actual parameter passed to a procedure in an untyped **VAR** parameter is smaller than the size of the absolute array variable, it is easy to index past the end of the variable into other variables or system resources. Needless to say, this can be a superb education in the value of letting sleeping variables lie.

Exploring the Interrupt Vector Jump Table with WriteHex

It is possible to inspect and change the vector jump table with **DEBUG**, but that's the hard way. The vectors' components are stored backwards in memory from the way we generally write them (see Figure 3.1). The offsets are stored *before* the segments, and the least significant bytes of both segments and offsets are stored *before* the most significant bytes.

The small utility program **Vectors** reformats the table for our eyes, and allows us to perform certain operations on the table. **Vectors**, for example, allows us to zero-out all 32 bits of a vector. It also allows us to change the offset or segment portion of any vector to the value of our choice.

Most interestingly, **Vectors** can provide a look at what any vector is actually pointing to. Any initialized interrupt vector points to an interrupt service routine of some sort. **Vectors** will, on command, hexdump the first 256 bytes of memory pointed to by any given interrupt vector. People who can read 8086 binary machine code in their heads can track the logic of simple service routines. The rest of us can look for service routine "signatures," typically in the form of copyright notices embedded in the binary machine code. If you have the Logitech mouse driver loaded, **Vectors** will show you the Logitech signature at an offset of 16 bytes into the driver, pointed to by interrupt 51 ($33).

Vectors tests every vector it displays and indicates whether the vector points to a binary $CF value. This is the machine-code equivalent of the IRET (Interrupt Return) mnemonic. Pointing an interrupt to an IRET instruction is a safety measure that prevents havoc in case an interrupt occurs for which the vector is uninitialized. If an unused vector is made to point to an IRET, the worst that can happen if that interrupt is triggered is nothing at all—the IRET sends execution back to the caller without taking any action.

In the best of all worlds, all unused interrupt vectors are initialized to point to an IRET. But as you'll see once you run **Vectors**, only a few vectors are so disarmed. Most point to segment zero, or offset zero, which is in fact an interrupt vector itself (for interrupt 0, the first entry in the jump table). If such an interrupt occurs, the CPU will attempt to execute the interrupt jump table as though it were code—which will almost certainly crash the machine hard.

Vectors is simple in operation. It cycles through the 256 interrupt vectors one at a time, displaying the current value of the current interrupt vector, and then pausing for a command. "Jumping" to another interrupt vector is done by entering its value as either a decimal number or a hexadecimal value preceded by a "$".

Changing a vector value is done with the E command. E prompts individually for the segment and offset portion of the vector. If you don't wish to change one or both, simply press Enter and nothing will be altered. As with jumping to a new value, vector values can be entered in either decimal or hex.

D dumps the 256 bytes pointed to by the current vector. If the first byte of the block is an IRET instruction, **Vectors** will say so.

Z changes both the offset and segment portion of a vector to zero. This can be useful in cases where you are testing software that modifies interrupt vectors—and may be modifying the wrong ones. Zeroing a vector allows you to come back after your test software has run, and tell at a glance if the zeroed vector or vectors have stayed zeroed.

Either Q or X will exit **Vectors**.

WriteHex figures prominently in **Vectors** as the mechanism by which the interrupt vectors are displayed, and also as the core of a hexdump routine, **DumpBlock**, that dumps 256 bytes of memory at the location pointed to by the current vector.

Vectors also makes considerable use of **MEM** and **MEMW**. The final statement of **DisplayVector**, in fact, nests two **MEMW**'s within a **MEM** by way of testing for an IRET at the vector address. Unlike Turbo Pascal's **PortW**, which should only be used on 8086 or 80286 machines with true 16-bit port I/O, **MEMW** is fully defined on 8-bit 8088 machines. It simply picks up two bytes starting at the given address, rather than one, as does **MEM**.

It is largely the presence of powerful primitives such as **MEM** and **MEMW** that led me to write system utility programs like **Vectors** in Pascal rather than C. C is hard to read and hard to use, and no one has yet proven to me that it is more powerful than a well-implemented Pascal or Modula 2.

```
1        {-------------------------------------------------------------------}
2        {                          VECTORS                                  }
3        {                                                                   }
4        {                   Interrupt vector utility                        }
5        {                                                                   }
6        {                              by Jeff Duntemann                    }
7        {                              Turbo Pascal V3.01A                  }
8        {                              Last update 2/9/87                   }
9        {                                                                   }
10       { This program allows you to inspect and change 8086 interrupt }
11       { vectors, and look at the first 256 bytes pointed to by any    }
12       { vector.  This allows the spotting of interrupt service        }
13       { routine "signatures" (typically the vendor's copyright        }
14       { notice) and also indicates when a vector points to an IRET.   }
15       {                                                                   }
16       {                                                                   }
17       {                                                                   }
18       {-------------------------------------------------------------------}
19
20
21       PROGRAM Vectors;
22
23       {$V-}     { Relaxes type checking on string lengths }
24
25       CONST
26         Up = True;
27
28       TYPE
29         String80    = String[80];
30         String255   = String[255];
31         Block       = ARRAY[0..255] OF Byte;
32
33       VAR
34         I             : Integer;
35         VectorNumber  : Integer;
36         VSeg,VOfs     : Integer;
37         NewVector     : Integer;
38         MemBlock      : Block;
39         ErrorPosition : Integer;
40         Quit          : Boolean;
41         Command       : String80;
42         CommandChar   : Char;
43         Device        : Text;
44
45
46       {$I WRITEHEX.SRC}
47
48
49       PROCEDURE StripWhite(VAR Target : String255);
```

(continued)

```
50
51     CONST
52       Whitespace  : SET OF Char = [#8,#10,#12,#13,' '];
53
54     BEGIN
55       WHILE (Length(Target) > 0) AND (Target[1] IN Whitespace) DO
56          Delete(Target,1,1)
57     END;
58
59
60     {<<<< ForceCase >>>>}
61     { From: COMPLETE TURBO PASCAL by Jeff Duntemann   }
62     { Scott, Foresman & Co. 1986   ISBN 0-673-18600-8 }
63     { Described in section 15.3 -- Last mod 2/1/86    }
64
65     FUNCTION ForceCase(Up : BOOLEAN; Target : String255) : String255;
66
67     CONST
68       Uppercase : SET OF Char = ['A'..'Z'];
69       Lowercase : SET OF Char = ['a'..'z'];
70
71     VAR
72       I : INTEGER;
73
74     BEGIN
75       IF Up THEN FOR I := 1 TO Length(Target) DO
76         IF Target[I] IN Lowercase THEN
77           Target[I] := UpCase(Target[I])
78         ELSE { NULL }
79       ELSE FOR I := 1 TO Length(Target) DO
80         IF Target[I] IN Uppercase THEN
81           Target[I] := Chr(Ord(Target[I])+32);
82       ForceCase := Target
83     END;
84
85
86
87     PROCEDURE DumpBlock(XBlock : Block; VAR Device : Text);
88
89     VAR
90       I,J,K : Integer;
91       Ch    : Char;
92
93     BEGIN
94       FOR I:=0 TO 15 DO          { Do a hexdump of 16 lines of 16 chars }
95         BEGIN
96           FOR J:=0 TO 15 DO    { Show hex values }
97             BEGIN
98                WriteHex(Device,Ord(XBlock[(I*16)+J]));
```

(continued)

```
 99                       Write(Device,' ')
100                     END;
101                   Write(Device,'   |');       { Bar to separate hex & ASCII }
102                   FOR J:=0 TO 15 DO          { Show printable chars or '.' }
103                     BEGIN
104                       Ch:=Chr(XBlock[(I*16)+J]);
105                       IF ((Ord(Ch)<127) AND (Ord(Ch)>31))
106                       THEN Write(Device,Ch) ELSE Write(Device,'.')
107                     END;
108                   Writeln(Device,'|')
109                 END;
110             FOR I:=0 TO 1 DO Writeln(Device,'')
111           END;  { DumpBlock }
112
113
114           PROCEDURE ShowHelp;
115
116           BEGIN
117             Writeln;
118             Writeln('Press RETURN to advance to the next vector.');
119             Writeln;
120             Writeln('To display a specific vector, enter the vector number (0-255)');
121             Writeln('in decimal or preceded by a "$" for hex, followed by RETURN.');
122             Writeln;
123             Writeln('Valid commands are:');
124             Writeln;
125             Writeln('D : Dump the first 256 bytes pointed to by the current vector');
126             Writeln('E : Enter a new value (decimal or hex) for the current vector');
127             Writeln('H : Display this help message');
128             Writeln('Q : Exit VECTORS ');
129             Writeln('X : Exit VECTORS ');
130             Writeln('Z : Zero segment and offset of the current vector');
131             Writeln('? : Display this help message');
132             Writeln;
133             Writeln
134             ('The indicator ">>IRET" means the vector points to an IRET instruction');
135             Writeln;
136           END;
137
138
139
140           PROCEDURE DisplayVector(VAR Device : Text; VectorNumber : Integer);
141
142           VAR
143             Bump : Integer;
144
145           BEGIN
```

(continued)

```
146                Bump := VectorNumber * 4;
147                Write(Device,VectorNumber : 3,'  $');
148                WriteHex(Device,VectorNumber);
149                Write(Device,'  [');
150                WriteHex(Device,MEM[O : Bump + 3]);
151                WriteHex(Device,MEM[O : Bump + 2]);
152                Write(Device,':');
153                WriteHex(Device,MEM[O : Bump + 1]);
154                WriteHex(Device,MEM[O : Bump]);
155                Write(Device,']');
156                IF MEM[MEMW[O:(VectorNumber*4)+2] : MEMW[O:VectorNumber *4]] = $CF
157                  THEN Write(Device,' >>IRET ')
158                  ELSE Write(Device,'        ');
159            END;
160
161
162            BEGIN
163              Quit := False;
164              VectorNumber := O;
165              Assign(Device,'CON:');
166              Reset(Device);
167              Writeln('>>VECTORS<<');
168              Writeln('By Jeff Duntemann');
169              Writeln('From the book: TURBO PASCAL SOLUTIONS');
170              Writeln('ISBN ');
171              ShowHelp;
172
173              REPEAT
174                DisplayVector(Device,VectorNumber);      { Show the vector # & address }
175                Readln(Command);                         { Get a command from the user }
176                IF Length(Command) > O THEN              { If something was typed:      }
177                  BEGIN
178                    { See if a number was typed; if one was, it becomes the current }
179                    { vector number.  If an error in converting the string to a      }
180                    { number occurs, Vectors then parses the string as a command.    }
181                    Val(Command,NewVector,ErrorPosition);
182                    IF ErrorPosition = O THEN VectorNumber := NewVector
183                      ELSE
184                        BEGIN
185                          StripWhite(Command);           { Remove leading whitespace   }
186                          Command := ForceCase(Up,Command); { Force to upper case     }
187                          CommandChar := Copy(Command,1,1); { Isolate first char.     }
188                          CASE CommandChar OF
189                            'Q','X' : Quit := True;    { Exit VECTORS }
190                            'D'     : BEGIN            { Dump 256 bytes at vector }
191                                        VOfs := MEMW[O : VectorNumber*4];
192                                        VSeg := MEMW[O : (VectorNumber*4) + 2];
```

(continued)

```
193                                      FOR I := 0 TO 255 DO
194                                        MemBlock[I] := MEM[VSeg : VOfs+I];
195                                      IF MemBlock[0] = $CF THEN
196                                        Writeln('Vector points to an IRET.');
197                                      DumpBlock(MemBlock,Device)
198                                    END;
199                  'E'       : BEGIN              { Enter new vector value }
200                                    Write('Enter segment ');
201                                    Write('(RETURN retains current value): ');
202                                    Readln(Command);
203                                    StripWhite(Command);
204                                    IF Length(Command) > 0 THEN
205                                      BEGIN
206                                        Val(Command,VSeg,ErrorPosition);
207                                        IF ErrorPosition = 0 THEN
208                                          MEMW[0:(VectorNumber*4)+2] := VSeg
209                                      END;
210                                    DisplayVector(Device,VectorNumber);
211                                    Writeln;
212                                    Write('Enter offset  ');
213                                    Write('(RETURN retains current value): ');
214                                    Readln(Command);
215                                    StripWhite(Command);
216                                    IF Length(Command) > 0 THEN
217                                      BEGIN
218                                        Val(Command,VOfs,ErrorPosition);
219                                        IF ErrorPosition = 0 THEN
220                                          MEMW[0:VectorNumber*4] := VOfs
221                                      END
222                                    END;
223                  'H'       : ShowHelp;
224                  'Z'       : BEGIN              { Zero the vector }
225                                    FOR I := 0 TO 3 DO
226                                      MEM[0:(VectorNumber*4)+I] := 0;
227                                    DisplayVector(Device,VectorNumber);
228                                    Writeln('zeroed.');
229                                    VectorNumber := (VectorNumber + 1) MOD 256
230                                    END;
231                  '?'       : ShowHelp;
232                END {CASE}
233              END
234            END
235        { The following line increments the vector number, rolling over to 0 }
236        { if the number would have exceeded 255: }
237        ELSE VectorNumber := (VectorNumber + 1) MOD 256
238      UNTIL Quit;
239    END.
```

3.5   Coping with the 8087/80287

Turbo Pascal is not especially accommodating with regards to Intel's math coprocessors, the 8087 (for use with 8086 and 8088 CPU's) and the 80287 (for use with the 80286). The stock version of Turbo Pascal makes no use of the coprocessor whatsoever. The version of Turbo Pascal designed to make use of the coprocessor (Turbo-87 Pascal) *must* have one installed in the machine, or the environment will lock your system up tight.

Certain other Pascal compilers contain code to detect whether a math coprocessor is installed in a machine. These clever compilers will use it if one is there, or "emulate" it if one is not. Emulating an 8087 or 80287 is accomplished by writing machine-code subroutines that perform precisely the same numeric operations as the opcodes embedded in silicon inside the math coprocessor. These emulation subroutines will be slower than a real '87, and take up considerable memory. Programs developed by these smart compilers will perform real number math at normal speed in a machine without an '87, and much faster in a machine with an '87—using the same physical .EXE file, without any recompilation or relinking. (Of all common Pascal compilers, only Turbo Pascal produces .COM files.) Before the program begins running, it checks for the presence of the math coprocessor, and sets itself up accordingly.

This is possible in programs produced by smarter compilers because the *same* real number variables may be acted upon by *either* the '87 or the emulation code. This is not the case with Turbo Pascal. The reason is simple: Turbo Pascal real numbers and Turbo-87 Pascal real numbers are of different sizes.

A Turbo Pascal real number is expressed as six bytes. This format (described in detail in *Complete Turbo Pascal*) was developed by Borland International for use with Turbo Pascal and is not used anywhere else, to my knowledge. Turbo-87 Pascal, by contrast, must express its real numbers in a format that the 8087 and 80287 can understand. The '87 coprocessors understand several real-number formats, but the format most widely used expresses real numbers as eight bytes. This is the format used by Turbo-87 Pascal; it is not in any way compatible with the 6-byte format used by the original Turbo Pascal.

What does this mean to you as a Turbo Pascal software developer? If you intend to support both machines with '87's and machines without '87's, you have to provide two versions of your product: one compiled with Turbo Pascal and the other compiled with Turbo-87 Pascal. Furthermore, you have to be sure your customers do not try to run the version of your product compiled with Turbo-87 Pascal on a machine without an 8087 or an 80287. If they do, their systems will lock up. They will have to reboot and could lose data. They will not be pleased.

You could put warnings in the manual, but most users don't even open the manual unless they get hopelessly stuck trying to run the software by the seat of their pants. Your computer is smart enough to determine whether it has an '87 or not. Let's see how, and then put that knowledge to work.

Detecting the Math Coprocessor

The 8088 and the 8087 are almost in parallel on the system board. They share the exact same address and data bus. Both processors "watch" the stream of instructions being executed, but the '87 remains dormant until it detects one of its own instructions on the bus. When the parallel-connected 8088 and 8087 see an 8087-specific instruction on the bus, the 8088 "allows" the 8087 to pick up the instruction and process it.

In case I've startled you with all this technical detail, be assured that you don't have to worry about how the 8087 works in most cases. In the Turbo Pascal world, you can't make use of the '87 except through Turbo-87 Pascal, and in that case the compiler does it all and you need only enjoy.

You only have to understand what happens when two 8087-specific instructions are executed: FNINIT and FNSTCW.

At the highest level, detecting an '87 is simple: You try to initialize the '87 chip, and if it acknowledges the initialization, it's present and usable. On the other hand, if no acknowledgement comes back, the '87 is not there.

Now, if you try to run Turbo-87 Pascal (or a program compiled under Turbo-87 Pascal) on a machine without an '87, the system will hang, requiring a soft boot (Ctrl/Alt/Del) to get free. Why? Because, in most cases, the 8088 and 8087 (or 80286 and 80287) operate asynchronously. In other words, when the 8088 hands the 8087 something to do, it waits until the 8087 signals that the operation is complete. The danger here is that if the 8088 *assumes* that the 8087 is present, it will put an 8087 instruction out on the bus and then wait forever if no 8087 is installed. That's the nature of the system-hang. Technically speaking, the 8088 executes a WAIT instruction and sits there, waiting for the 8087 to place a signal on a hardware bus line called TEST, indicating that the 8087 has finished its work. The 8088 samples TEST once every few cycles, and when TEST becomes true, it breaks out of WAIT and continues executing instructions.

There are two instructions that initialize the '87 chip. One, FINIT, plays the game we just described. It tells the '87 to initialize itself and then waits for a response. The other instruction, FNINIT, does the very same thing except it does *not* wait for a reply from the '87.

So far so good. But to be sure that an '87 is installed on the bus, a response must be able to get from the '87 to the '88. This is done, again, by two related instructions. FSTCW tells the '87 to take its "status control word" (rather like the 8088's flags word) and store it somewhere in memory, then waits for a response. As with FINIT, there is a "no wait" version of FSTCW, FNSTCW, that does the same thing, except it doesn't wait. If the '87 is there, fine; the control word gets stored and can be examined. If the '87 is *not* there, nothing gets stored. Either way, the 8088 gets control back as soon as it passes the instruction onto the bus. The 8088 then examines the location where the '87 was to store its status control word. If an "A-OK" bit pattern is there, the 8088 knows that an '87 is safely on the bus. If the location has not changed, the 8088 knows that no '87 lives on the bus.

Doing this in Turbo Pascal involves the **INLINE** statement, so that we can set up a FNINIT instruction and an FNSTCW instruction. The whole procedure for detecting the 8087/80287 is quite brief:

```
 1          {->>>>Is87There<<<<------------------------------------------------}
 2          {                                                                  }
 3          { Filename: 87THERE.SRC -- Last modified 6/21/86                    }
 4          {                                                                  }
 5          { This routine detects the presence of an 8087 or 80287 by         }
 6          { attempting to initialize the chip and seeing if a control        }
 7          { word value is returned.  If no control word value comes back     }
 8          { (it will typically be 3 though I have seen 118 as well) then      }
 9          { no coprocessor is installed in the host system.                  }
10          {                                                                  }
11          {                                                                  }
12          {                                                                  }
13          {------------------------------------------------------------------}
14
15          FUNCTION Is87There : Boolean;
16
17          TYPE
18            Reg      = RECORD
19                          CASE Boolean OF
20                             False : (Word : Integer);
21                             True  : (LoByte,HiByte : Byte)
22                        END;
23
24          VAR
25            ControlWord : Reg;
26
27          BEGIN
28            ControlWord.Word := 0;  { Clear control word storage to 0 }
29            INLINE
30              ($90/$DB/$E3/                      { FNINIT }
31               $90/$D9/$7E/<ControlWord);        { FNSTCW ControlWord }
32            IF ControlWord.HiByte = 0 THEN Is87There := False
33              ELSE Is87There := True
34          END;
```

Both FNINIT and FNSTCW are three bytes long. Note the <Control-Word after the FNSTCW instruction. The "<" forces the address of **ControlWord** to a single byte, which is what FNSTCW expects. **ControlWord** is a local variable, allocated on the stack when function **Is8087There** is invoked. When the compiler encounters the identifier **ControlWord** in the **INLINE** statement, it replaces the identifier **ControlWord** with its offset from 8088 base pointer register BP. BP is the "anchor point," indicating the top of the stack just before **Is8087There** was invoked. Within a procedure or function, all parameters and local variables are referenced as offsets from the BP register.

FNSTCW thus knows where to find local variable **ControlWord**, and if the '87 is there, the FNSTCW instruction will place the value of the '87's status control word in **ControlWord**. **ControlWord** was cleared to zero before anything was sent to the '87, so, theoretically, any non-zero value in **ControlWord** after the FNSTCW is put out on the bus should indicate that an '87 is present.

What should come back is the value 3. Oddly, I have seen a fully functional PC/AT whose 80287 returns a value of 118. It is unclear why this happens. I suspect that any non-zero value indicates a working 8087 or 80287.

Detecting Turbo-87 Pascal

Function **Is8087There** will tell you whether or not an 8087 or 80287 lives on the bus. Unfortunately, that's only half the story. Just as important, a program must know whether or not it was compiled with Turbo-87 Pascal.

Determining which compiler compiled a program from inside the program is easy. All you have to do is see how large a real-number variable is. Turbo Pascal allocates six bytes to each real-number variable; Turbo-87 Pascal allocates eight bytes to each real-number variable. Create a function that measures the size of a real number:

```
 1       {->>>>CompiledFor8087<<<<-------------------------------------------}
 2       {                                                                   }
 3       { Filename : COMP87.SRC -- Last Modified 2/9/87                      }
 4       {                                                                   }
 5       { This routine returns TRUE if the program in which it resides }
 6       { was compiled with Turbo-87 Pascal.  It does this by testing  }
 7       { the length of the real number type; standard Turbo uses a     }
 8       { six-byte real while Turbo-87 uses the IEEE eight-byte real.   }
 9       {                                                                   }
10       {                                                                   }
11       {                                                                   }
12       {-------------------------------------------------------------------}
13
```

(continued)

```
14            FUNCTION CompiledFor8087 : Boolean;
15
16            VAR
17              R : Real;
18
19            BEGIN
20              R := 42.0;
21              IF SizeOf(R) = 8 THEN CompiledFor8087 := True
22                ELSE CompiledFor8087 := False
23            END;
```

Given these two functions, your first impulse would be to create message logic similar to this:

```
IF Is87There AND NOT(CompiledFor87) THEN
  BEGIN
    Writeln('You have an 8087 or 80287 in your system,');
    Writeln(' but this version of IKONYX does not use it.');
    Writeln(' For faster performance on this machine,');
    Writeln(' run IKONYX87.COM instead.');
    Writeln;
    Write('>>Continue this version of IKONYX? (Y/N): ');
    Read(InChar);
    IF NOT (InChar IN ['Y', 'y']) THEN Halt
  END
ELSE
  IF NOT(Is87There) AND CompiledFor87 THEN
    BEGIN
      Writeln('WARNING!  This program was compiled for use');
      Writeln('          with an 8087 or 80287, and none is');
      Writeln('          installed in this computer. Returning');
      Writeln('          to DOS . . .');
      Halt
    END;
```

Alas, although this method makes good logical sense, it doesn't work in the second case. For reasons that I have never been able to crisply define, a program compiled under Turbo-87 Pascal will lock up an 8087-less computer *immediately*. In other words, it crashes before the program has a chance to notice the problem and display the error message. The Turbo Pascal runtime code apparently uses some of the special 8087 opcodes during its initialization, perhaps in allocating memory for real-number variables. As soon as the program attempts to use an 8087 opcode on an 8087-less machine, it goes into an endless wait condition, from which reboot is the only exit.

The other option—using the **Execute** procedure to execute one of two versions of a program, one compiled with Turbo Pascal and the other compiled with Turbo-87 Pascal—doesn't work either (again, for reasons I do not fully understand). In other words, given two compiled versions of the program SPIRO.PAS, SPIRO88.COM compiled with Turbo Pascal and SPIRO87 .COM compiled with Turbo-87 Pascal, you might like to (but cannot) do the following:

```
PROGRAM SpiroExecute;     {Sorry, this program doesn't work!}
{$I 87THERE.SRC}

BEGIN
  IF Is87There THEN Execute('SPIRO87.COM')
       ELSE Execute('SPIRO88.COM');
END.
```

This is a shame, as it would be an elegant way to solve the 87/no 87 program at runtime without any intervention by the user (who may not know an 8087 from the Starship Enterprise). As best I can tell, the Turbo Pascal runtime makes assumptions about the .COM file it is loading and executing that preclude its working across the Turbo Pascal versions.

The Way Out

The bottom line is that you can't currently "autodetect" the 8087/80287 and run an appropriate version without going to the DOS batch facility. Batch has a slightly "clunky" air to it, but it often comes through in a pinch. The way to autodetect through batch is to create a short utility that calls **Is87There** and sets the DOS ERRORLEVEL flag to one of two values depending on the return value of the function. Setting ERRORLEVEL is done through the use of Turbo Pascal's built-in **Halt** procedure, which terminates program execution and optionally returns a value to DOS for reporting in ERRORLEVEL. Such a utility is essentially one IF statement:

```
 1       {------------------------------------------------------------}
 2       {                         CHECK87                            }
 3       {                                                            }
 4       {            Batch file '87 detection utility                }
 5       {                                                            }
 6       {                              by Jeff Duntemann             }
 7       {                              Turbo Pascal V3.01A           }
 8       {                              Last update 2/9/87            }
 9       {                                                            }
10       { This short utility is intended to be run from a batch file }
11       { to allow the selective running of programs compiled by     }
```

(continued)

```
12        { standard Turbo Pascal (on machines without an 8087 or 80287  }
13        { installed) or by Turbo-87 Pascal (for machines with an '87.) }
14        { Check87 sets the ERRORLEVEL value through the Halt procedure }
15        { and then exits.  A batch routine might test ERRORLEVEL and   }
16        { then run a program compiled by Turbo-87 if an 8087 is        }
17        { detected, or a program compiled with standard Turbo if no    }
18        { '87 is found.                                                }
19        {                                                              }
20        {                                                              }
21        {                                                              }
22        {--------------------------------------------------------------}
23
24        PROGRAM Check87;
25
26        {$I 87THERE.SRC}
27
28        BEGIN
29          IF Is87There THEN Halt(5) ELSE Halt(0)
30        END.
```

If **Is87There** finds an '87 in the machine, it returns a 5 through ERROR-LEVEL; if no '87 is found, it returns a 0 instead. That's all it does, because that's all it needs to do.

I described a strictly-for-fun graphics program in *Complete Turbo Pascal, Second Edition.* It's a software SpiroGraph, and it generates complex cyclic patterns on the graphics screen using only straight line draws. I won't list or describe the program again here (it's several hundred lines long) but I will include it on the listings diskette for *Turbo Pascal Solutions.* The identical program source can be compiled with either standard Turbo Pascal or Turbo-87 Pascal. Assume for this example that the program compiled with standard Turbo Pascal is called SPIRO88.COM and the program compiled with Turbo-87 Pascal is called SPIRO87.COM.

If we wanted to use CHECK87.PAS to automatically run the appropriate compiled version of **SpiroGraph**, we would need the following batch file:

```
1        CHECK87
2        IF ERRORLEVEL 5 GOTO YES87
3        SPIRO88
4        GOTO Exit
5        :YES87
6        SPIRO87
7        :EXIT
```

DOS batch has primitive conditional branching facilities, though they are completely unstructured and hearken back to the days of mainframes. Labels are named and begin with colons. The batch file runs **Check87**, and then tests

ERRORLEVEL against a constant of 5. If ERRORLEVEL has a value of 5 or larger, a GOTO is executed to the target label YES87. Batch execution resumes at YES87 and SPIRO87.COM is executed. If no '87 is detected, the ERROR-LEVEL test falls through, and SPIRO88.COM is executed, after which an unconditional branch to the end of the batch file is taken.

What the user must do is type SPIRO at the command prompt; he's running a batch file rather than a Turbo Pascal program, but the bottom line is that the combination of **Check87** and DOS batch can (awkwardly) autodetect and run '87 and non-87 versions of the same program. Rumor has it that Turbo Pascal V4.0 will incorporate true coprocessor autodetection similar to that of Microsoft C and Pascal. In the meantime, batch it!

CHAPTER 4

The Agony of Assembly-Language Interface

Given that the whole reason for inventing high-level languages like Pascal was to *avoid* having to code in assembler, the current obsession with assembly-language interface to Turbo Pascal makes me smile. It is by far the question I am asked most about Turbo Pascal, aside from fantasies such as, "How can I make Turbo generate .OBJ files?" (Some people refuse to believe that certain things can't be done with a one-byte patch.) It's a head scratcher. Assembly language smells too much like work to me; I see it as programming with all the fun squeezed out. But there are people who build ships in bottles, or who model entire railroads in Z scale. There are people who sail the Pacific in hollow trees. This section is dedicated to them.

There are two good reasons for writing Turbo Pascal subprograms in assembly code. The first reason is to do something that Turbo Pascal can't do on its own. Many people think this is a long list (after all, Pascal is *Pascal*). In fact, the list is short indeed.

Turbo Pascal's suite of extensions for systems programming is nothing short of brutal. You have complete read/write access to every byte in the 8086's megabyte of address space, even though Turbo Pascal executable code is limited to a single 64K segment. You have access to every I/O port in the 8086's 64K I/O address range. You can map a variable at any memory address, or make 8086 software interrupts. You can read the current contents of the CS, DS, or SS registers, or extract the current segment and offset address of any data item. A high-speed fill and a high-speed block move procedure are available, as well as a host of sneaky tricks for defeating Pascal's strong typing. The point is this: Before you *assume* that something needs to be done in assembly language, think it over, keeping the above weaponry in mind.

The following is a list of things that require at least *some* machine-code intervention to be performed:

1. Interrupt service routines. Not for the faint-hearted.
2. Resident utilities. Ditto.
3. Multitasking. *Double* ditto.
4. DOS program execution from within a Turbo program.
5. Register peeks and pokes. Easy.

That's a short list. With the exception of item 5, it's also a mean one. I'm not going to take on goblins 1-4 in this book, since doing so would blow it up to the size of a Sears catalog. A separate book on using interrupts would cover them, and it would *not* be a thin book.

The second reason for writing Turbo Pascal subprograms in assembly code is more subjective: to do things that can't be done quickly enough in Pascal itself. Purists and other madmen would say *everything*, but let's be reasonable. My list follows:

1. Joystick interface.
2. Text buffer clearing.
3. Text region (window) moving and scrolling.
4. Fast polled serial communications.
5. Nearly *anything* involving graphics.
6. Matrix math (including spreadsheet recalculation).

Surprise! Another short list. Actually, item 5 contains a universe of complication that could fill one book or several. The bottom line is that the 8088 processor running at PC speeds just doesn't have the horsepower to do acceptable graphics, even in assembler—so Pascal graphics have to be even worse. And they are. Human nature being what it is, no machine will ever do graphics quickly enough to suit an unappreciative user, so the best you can do is hand-code the critical routines in assembler and apologize frequently.

If you're working in assembler outside these areas, you may be fooling yourself into working too hard. Think again. (And if you know you're right, share your discovery with me, and I'll add it to my list.)

Use an Assembler!

There are two ways to use machine code from within a Turbo Pascal program. One is the **INLINE** statement, which accepts numeric literals as arguments and inserts them verbatim into the generated program code at that point. There's no protection in it; if the codes tell the CPU to walk off the edge of the world, it will, smiling. **INLINE** does not understand assembler mnemonics like **MOV AX,$F6**. You must hand-assemble your mnemonics into binary numbers, such as **$B8/$F6**, before **INLINE** will accept them. Doing this to more than a handful of mnemonics is ugly, grueling work, prone to many errors and nasty ones. Moreover, it's all unnecessary, because the best assembler you can buy (as far as I'm concerned) will do all that and more, and costs only $100. If you intend to do a sizeable amount of assembly-language interface, and if you value your time at more than 25 cents an hour, Microsoft's MASM 4.0 will pay for itself in two weeks flat.

Actually, if all you want to do is translate short and simple sequences of mnemonics into binary opcodes, DOS **DEBUG** can do that well enough. But if you're serious enough to work in assembler at all, you should be serious enough to buy the proper tools. The remaining discussion of non-**INLINE** assembly-language techniques in this book will assume the use of Microsoft's dazzling Macro Assembler (MASM) version 4.0, the current version as of mid-1986.

The other method, external machine-code routines, *requires* an assembler, giving you no choice in the matter.

I won't be exhaustively explaining either the 8086 architecture or 8086 machine instructions in any great detail here. Good books on the subject are rare; bad books are everywhere. [My favorite is *Assembly Language Primer for the IBM PC and XT*, by Robert Lafore (ISBN 0-452-25497-3).] New, possibly better books could appear at any time. Keep your ears open at your user group meetings. Ask the man who already does assembler how *he* learned.

4.1   The Runtime Memory Map

One of the luxuries of programming in a high-level language like Pascal is not having to worry about where everything is located in memory. By and large, that's the compiler's job. The programmer defines a variable by naming an identifier and giving it a type. The compiler allocates room for it in the data segment, and keeps track of what operations are performed on any data you might load into that variable. You can find the 8086 machine address of that variable with the **Seg** and **Ofs** built-in functions, but you don't *need* to know the address to use the variable. Knowing the variable's identifier is enough.

Similarly, when a procedure or function is invoked, you don't have to be aware of the fact that the compiler pushes the addresses of VAR parameters onto the stack, rather than actual copies of the ordinary value parameters. You needn't know that the stack is involved at all. You might program for years and not realize that such a thing as a stack exists; that's the power of a high-level language.

This all changes when you dip into assembly language. Abruptly, memory breaks into several critical segments. Variables lose their names, pointers and VAR parameters turn into pure machine addresses, and the stack moves to a position somewhere close to the center of creation. Lose track of any part of it, and you can lose it all in 16 machine cycles or less.

Thus warned, carefully study the runtime memory map in Figure 4.1. This is the map of a standalone Turbo Pascal program—one compiled to disk rather than to memory—within the Turbo Pascal Environment. Adding the Environment to the memory map complicates things to some extent, but it doesn't *change* much. All it does is move the beginning of the program's code segment about 44K up-memory to make room for the compiler and editor beneath it.

The first 256 bytes of the code segment comprise the program segment prefix (PSP). Interesting information about the program lives here, as does the command line tail. Immediately following the PSP is the program code itself.

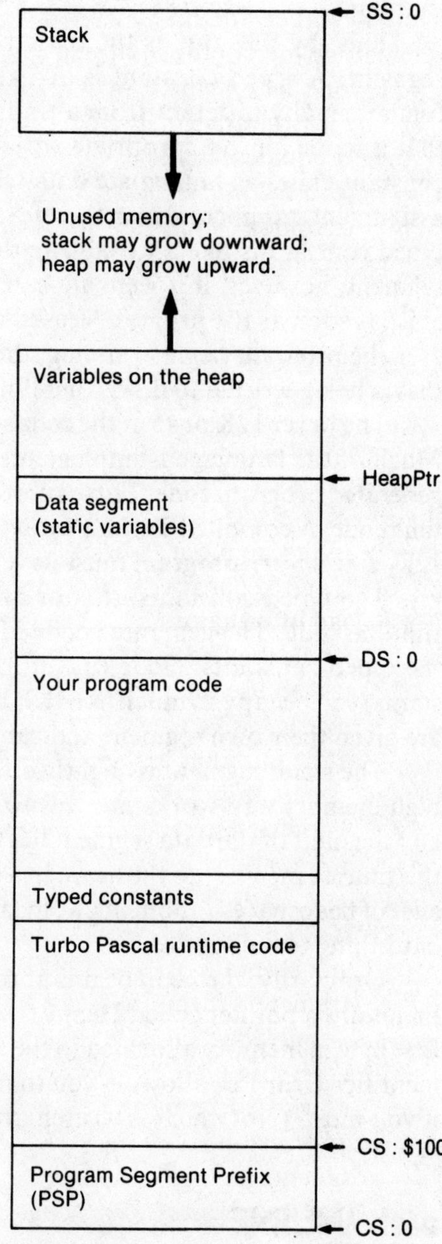

Figure 4.1 **The runtime memory map**

The PSP and the program code are saved to disk as the program file, and that's all. The data segment, heap, and stack are allocated when the program begins running.

This, by the way, is the reason that typed constants reside in the code segment. A typed constant is actually a variable with an initial value. It is fundamentally different from a traditional Pascal constant, which is a *value* that is loaded into appropriate variables as immediate data. A "copy" of the constant exists as immediate data whenever it is used in an expression or an assignment statement. It can therefore have no single, unambiguous address. A typed constant is like a variable in that it exists in only one place in the code segment; however, if it were allocated in the data segment, it would cease to exist as soon as the program ceased running. To store its value for use whenever the program begins running, the compiler has to write it to the code file that is being written to disk. Therefore, it must be placed in the code segment.

The lower 12K or so of the code segment is the Turbo Pascal runtime code. Much of the language is implemented as a suite of subroutines called by the generated program code. These subroutines, taken together, are called the runtime code. A compiled Turbo Pascal program file cannot be smaller than about 12K, since *every* program must have a copy of the runtime code.

The typed constants, if your program has any, are allocated above the runtime code. The generated code of your own Pascal program begins above the typed constants. Code (including the runtime code and any typed constants) can occupy as much as 64KB by itself. Data, generally global variables, are given their own segment and can occupy an additional 64KB.

The stack segment is slightly different from the others in that it begins in high memory and works *downward*. Between the limit of the stack segment and the limit of the data segment lies the rest of your memory. Turbo allocates this unused memory to the heap. In a 640K PC, as you can imagine, this creates a *lot* of heapspace—about 400K, in fact. Use the heap whenever you can—it's a hard thing to run out of.

Ordinarily, the heap begins at the end of the data segment. Turbo Pascal maintains a pointer called **HeapPtr** within the runtime code that points to the first byte in memory allocated to the heap. The pointer is available through the identifier **HeapPtr**, allowing you to move the start of the heap somewhere else if you must. (Not much is written about this, and I don't recommend it.)

4.2   Working with INLINE

The portion of the Turbo Pascal compiler that actually writes out the opcodes that comprise your machine-readable program is called the *code generator*. Code generation is an art approaching black magic, and I don't pretend to know a great deal about it. Ordinarily, the code generator takes its cues from the portion of the compiler that parses and analyzes your ASCII source-code file, and, based on those cues, it creates your program-code file.

However, there are two instances in which the code generator takes a break and stops generating code. One is at the reserved word **EXTERNAL**, which indicates that code is going to be read from a disk file for awhile. The other instance is when it encounters the **INLINE** reserved word. An **INLINE** statement is in some ways like an internally stored version of an external machine-code file. The code generator stops generating code and simply pulls it verbatim from the list of binary numbers you have written as arguments to the **INLINE** statement.

An **INLINE** statement can be dropped in anywhere. It is *not* a procedure call. The statement

```
INLINE($CD/$05);
```

causes the code generator to pause and insert the two binary numbers **$CD** and **$05** into the code file it's generating for you. Those two numbers are the op-codes for the instruction

```
INT 05
```

which you should recognize as the Print Screen interrupt from the IBM PC ROM BIOS.

The general form of an **INLINE** statement is the following:

```
INLINE(<arg>/<arg>/<arg>/<arg> . . . <arg>);
```

Each **<arg>** is an argument for the **INLINE** statement. Most arguments are numbers. A number may be expressed as an integer literal in decimal or hexa-decimal form, or it may be a named integer constant. Any other type of literal or constant (real, string, or Boolean, for example) will generate compiler error **22: Integer constant expected**.

Numeric constants and literals passed as arguments to **INLINE** will be evaluated down to either one or two binary bytes by the code generator. If they fall into the range of 0 to 255, they will generate a single binary byte. Any value greater than or equal to 256 will generate two bytes.

For example, consider some integer constants:

```
CONST
  BAR = 291;
  FOO = 11;
```

The constant **FOO**, when passed to **INLINE**, will generate the single binary byte $OB. **BAR**, on the other hand, will generate the two bytes $23 $01. If that seems suspiciously high for the hex equivalent of 291, remember that integers are stored in memory by the 8086 with the *least* significant byte *first* in memory.

What we see for **BAR** is not the hexadecimal number $2301 but the number $0123, which is the hex equivalent of decimal 291. This inversion of common sense is logical from the CPU's perspective, but we humans will simply have to get used to it.

Identifiers other than integer constants may also be passed as arguments to **INLINE**. Care must be taken here, as the sense of what **INLINE** does with these identifiers is not always the same as what the identifiers do in a normal Pascal program. Variables, for example, do not evaluate out to their values. If you pass a global variable's identifier to **INLINE**, it will be replaced with that variable's offset into the data segment. (Local variables and procedure parameters are a much more involved affair and will be discussed in detail in Section 4.4.) A typed constant's identifier will evaluate down to the typed constant's offset into the code segment, which is where typed constants are stored. Remember that whenever you are passing an *offset* to **INLINE**, it will be expressed as two bytes, even if the value of the offset is less than 256. If, for example, a global variable **BAS** is passed to **INLINE**, and the offset of **BAS** is $22, **INLINE** will express that offset as $22/$00.

The symbol "*" may be an argument to **INLINE**, either alone or as part of a legal numeric expression that evaluates to an integer. It is replaced with the current instruction pointer (IP), often referred to generically as the *program counter*. This is a 2-byte value containing the offset into the code segment from which the next machine instruction will be summoned. One common mistake made by beginners is to follow a **JMP** opcode ($E9 or $EB) with the "*" and an offset: $EB/*+8. The intent is to perform a relative jump (in this example, 8 bytes forward) from the current position of the program counter. *It doesn't work that way*, and trying to do so will lock up your system. (The circumstances under which the program counter reference "*" would be useful are unclear to me, but I am not primarily an assembly-language programmer. If you find a compelling use for it, drop me a line and help me learn something.)

Two additional symbols may be used within **INLINE**: "<" and ">". These are **INLINE**'s override operators. Ordinarily, a numeric literal argument to **INLINE** is encoded as one byte if it falls in the range of 0 to 255, or two bytes if it has a value higher than 255. Variable and constant identifiers and program counter references generate two bytes.

The override operators allow you to force a single-byte value to be encoded as two bytes, or a 2-byte value to be coded as a single byte. The "<" operator instructs the code generator to encode only the least significant byte of a 2-byte argument. The ">" operator instructs the code generator to encode a single-byte argument as two bytes by adding a zero byte after the single-byte value. Examples of the functions of override operators are as follows:

```
INLINE($1122/<$3344);    {Generates $11 $22 $44}
INLINE($5566/>$77);      {Generates $55 $66 $77 $00}
```

Again, this feature of **INLINE** is not likely to be useful in many situations, but do be aware of it. (An example of the override operator "$<$" in use can be seen in the **Is87There** function at the end of Chapter 3.)

Register Peeks and Pokes

Turbo Pascal allows little direct access to the 8086 registers; there are only functions to return the current values of segment registers DS, CS, and SS (**DSeg**, **CSeg**, and **SSeg**). Going directly to the registers is not something you need to do frequently, but there are some arcane occasions that call for it. The **MSDOS** and **Intr** built-in routines return most of the 8086 registers, but you may wish to inspect or change the registers without doing either a DOS call or a software interrupt. (Doing a dump of the stack from within a function or procedure is one good example that we'll examine in detail a little later.)

INLINE is tailor-made for this sort of thing. Four or five binary bytes in an **INLINE** statement will allow you to peek or poke just about any programmer-accessible 8086 register.

The *modus operandi* is simple: Define a global variable which is to contain the returned register value. There's nothing predefined or sacred about the names of the 8086 register in Turbo Pascal. You can define identifiers AX, BX, CX, DX, and all the others, just as given in the 8086 documentation. As most 8086 registers are 16 bits wide, type **Integer** will easily hold them. If you need to access register halves in addition to the register as a whole, you might define a register variable as the free-union variant record type **Reg** (as described in Section 3.2).

Make sure that they are *global* variables, defined in the main program variable definition part, and not within one of the procedures or functions. The methods described in this section work *only* with global variables. It is certainly possible to return register values to local variables within a Pascal subprogram, but the methods are not as simple as with global variables. They require considerable understanding of the various addressing modes that the 8088 offers, particularly those involving indirect references offset from register BP.

For simplicity's sake, assume throughout this section that you have defined a suite of global integer variables as

```
VAR
   AX,BX,CX,DX,BP,SI,DI,ES,SP,FLAGS : Integer;
```

The simplest case is the return of 8086 register AX. The following **INLINE** statement will do it:

```
INLINE($A3/AX);      {MOV DS:<var>,AX}
```

One of the arguments to **INLINE** is a binary number; the other is the name of variable **AX**. When Turbo Pascal compiles this statement, it replaces the identifier **AX** with variable **AX**'s offset relative to the data-segment register **DS**. **$A3** is a special form of the 8086 **MOV** instruction that assumes **DS** is acting as a segment register and that an immediate offset is given as part of the instruction. In other words, once Turbo Pascal compiles this statement, it might be expanded to:

```
$A3/$14/$00
```

The **$14/$00** is actually an immediate offset supplied by the compiler, representing variable **AX**'s position in the data segment. The **$00** was added since **$A3** requires a 16-bit offset; rather than simply giving an offset of **$14**, Turbo dutifully supplies an offset of **$0014**. The **$00** comes *after* the **$14** because the 8086 stores 16-bit quantities low-byte first, followed by high-byte. (Yes, it's screwy, but as Intel will tell you again and again, the 8086 architecture was *not* designed to make it easy on assembly-language programmers.)

The $A3 opcode is a special case in that it operates only on register AX. We can't use it directly to return any of the other registers. However, moving one register into another takes only four clock cycles; so, for the rest of the 8086's registers, all we need to do is move the other register values into AX, then move the contents of AX into the variables defined for the other registers. The additional time required is minute, and it makes coding up the rest of our register peeks easy.

The general-purpose register-register move opcode is $89, but it requires a second opcode byte to tell the CPU which register is being moved to which register. The complete two-byte opcode to move register BX to register AX is $89/$D8. Adding this before our previous code for returning the value of register AX gives us a complete register peek statement for register BX:

```
INLINE($89/$D8/$A3/BX);     {MOV AX,BX; MOV DS:<var>,AX}
```

$89/$D8 moves the contents of register **BX** into register **AX**; **$A3/BX** then moves the contents of register **AX** into the global variable **BX**.

Pushing and Popping the Stack

The above **INLINE** statement will, of course, destroy whatever might previously have been in register AX. If protecting the current value of AX is important, you can temporarily push AX's current value onto the system stack, perform the peek, and then pop AX's contents back off the stack into the AX register. This adds considerably to the number of machine cycles used, but we're still talking about a handful of milliseconds at the most. Adding the opcodes for push and pop expands our **INLINE** statement like this:

```
INLINE($50/$89/$D8/$A3/BX/$58)
```

Here, **$50** is the PUSH AX opcode, and **$58** is the POP AX opcode.

Push and pop operations are also helpful when you want to peek the 8086 flags. The flags reside in a 16-bit word, of which only nine bits are significant. Each bit is a flag, and each flag is set or cleared under specific machine conditions, often as the result of executing some 8086 opcode. (Again, a good book on 8086 assembly language will tell you what each individual flag stands for.)

There is no instruction for moving the flag word into a register. There is, however, an instruction (PUSHF) that pushes the flag word onto the stack. We've already examined the POP AX instruction, which pops a word off the top of the stack into AX. Executing PUSHF followed by POP AX pushes the flags onto the stack and then pops them off into AX, effectively moving the flag word into AX. Because pushing or popping the stack involves access to system memory, it takes a lot more time than moving a value from one internal 8086 register into another, but we're still speaking of scant milliseconds.

This can still be done without losing the current contents of AX by pushing AX onto the stack first, then pushing the flags, popping the flags into AX, moving AX into a global variable, and, finally, popping the original contents of AX back off the stack into AX:

```
INLINE($50/          {PUSH AX}
       $9C/          {PUSHF}
       $58/          {POP AX}
       $A3/FLAGS/     {MOV <var>,AX}
       $58);         {POP AX}
```

Notice that this **INLINE** statement has been stacked vertically rather than run out on a single line, as the earlier examples were. This was done to allow comments to the left of each group of binary bytes that represents a machine instruction. The comments can, of course, be anything at all, but good practice for **INLINE** is to use the assembly-language mnemonic within a comment beside each binary machine instruction. For **INLINE** statements of more than four or five bytes, this is essential. You may remember what all those binary numbers do *now*, but come back in six weeks and have another look. . . . Make it easy on yourself. Comment heavily and consistently.

Accessing Typed Constants

As explained earlier, typed constants are stored, not in the data segment, but in the code segment. Moreover, typed constants can be changed, like variables. They are essentially global variables that are stored in the code segment with an initial value at compile time.

Although I have never heard of anyone burning Turbo Pascal code into

ROM or EPROM, it's not outside the bounds of possibility. If you ever try it, remember not to attempt altering a typed constant, since that is tantamount to writing into ROM.

As with global variables, **INLINE** replaces the name of a typed constant with a 2-byte offset. This offset is into the code segment rather than the data segment. However, **INLINE** does *nothing* to indicate the fact that the offset is relative to register CS rather than DS. You have to do that yourself; but it's not a difficult procedure.

The 8086 instruction set contains four special opcodes called *segment prefixes*. There is one such prefix for each of the four segment registers: DS (data segment), CS (code segment), SS (stack segment), and ES (extra segment). The prefixes perform no active functions; they do not move or test data or transfer control to a different location in memory. However, they do alter the sense of certain opcodes when they are placed in front of those opcodes.

The best example involves moving a register value into a global variable (discussed previously in this section). The **INLINE** code to move register AX into a global integer variable named **GoshWow** looks like this:

```
INLINE($A3/GoshWow);     {MOV DS:GoshWow,AX}
```

Note the use of **DS:** in the comment. It indicates that the location of <var> is specified as an offset relative to the **DS** segment register. This is the default sense of opcode **$A3**.

Placing the code segment prefix in front of the $A3 opcode alters the sense of the action significantly:

```
INLINE($2E/$A3/OhBoy);     {MOV CS:OhBoy,AX}
```

Here, **OhBoy** is an integer typed constant, which, like all other typed constants, is stored in the code segment. Putting prefix **$2E** in front of opcode **$A3** tells the 8086 that the offset that follows **$A3** is into the code segment, represented by the segment address in register **CS**. The 8086 thus copies the contents of register **AX** into the memory location at **CS:** <var> rather than **DS:** <var>. The effect is to copy the contents of **AX** into typed constant **OhBoy**.

As you might expect, it works just as well in the opposite direction. This **INLINE** statement copies the value stored in typed constant **OhBoy** into register AX:

```
INLINE($2E/$A1/OhBoy);     {MOV AX,CS:OhBoy}
```

Segment Prefixes

Register	Prefix	Example in use	Mnemonic
DS	$3E	INLINE($3E/$A3/<gl. var>);	{MOV DS:<var>,AX}
CS	$2E	INLINE($2E/$A3/<str. con.>);	{MOV CS:<var>,AX}

| SS | $36 | INLINE($36/$A3/<offset>); | {MOV SS:<var>,AX} |
| ES | $26 | INLINE($26/$A3/<offset>); | {MOV ES:<var>,AX} |

The above table summarizes the four segment-register prefixes and gives examples of their use. Note that the first case, for **DS**, is redundant. **DS** is the default register in this case and no prefix is needed; however, using one does no harm, aside from using more space and a few more machine cycles.

Some cautions about the use of the examples in the table: Only the first two cases are generally useful. The existence of the **SS** prefix suggests that it can be used to access subprogram local variables that exist on the stack. *Not so.* **INLINE** replaces the identifier of a local variable with its offset from base pointer BP, and automatically selects **SS** as the segment register. (This requires a different strategy, which will be discussed in Section 4.3, after describing exactly what happens to the stack when a subprogram is executed.)

For now, consider the use of prefixes limited to accessing typed constants in the code segment. You may find a more exotic use for the other prefixes, but in that case you are far better off working with MASM in creating external machine-code files (described in Section 4.5).

Jumps within INLINE

Turbo Pascal's **INLINE** feature does little or nothing to make jumps easy to write. You have nothing similar to the labels available in a real assembler. All jumps have to be followed by a *displacement value* that you must calculate manually. This is the number of bytes away from the current position of the program counter to which execution will pass. If you miss it by even a single byte, you could be reaching for the power switch.

Jumps should therefore be handled with some care. Particularly, dropping new code into an **INLINE** statement that contains jumps can throw all your displacements off, forcing you to recalculate them every time you change the number of bytes between a jump instruction and its destination. Having been through this a few times, my recommendation is that once your **INLINE** statement gets complicated enough to start handing you that kind of grief, convert it to an external routine and begin using an assembler.

There are several different flavors of jump instruction in the 8088 instruction set. The two main groups are *long* and *short* jumps. Long jumps require both a segment and an offset address, and will therefore not only take you out of the **INLINE** statement, but outside of Turbo Pascal entirely, since Turbo Pascal programs have only one single code segment.

In most cases, short jumps will do. Short jumps remains within the current code segment and come in two flavors of their own: conditional and unconditional. An unconditional jump is like Pascal's **GOTO**; execution moves to the destination and that's that. Conditional jumps perform the jump only if some condition is met.

All short jumps specify their destinations by way of a displacement value, which can be either negative (for backward jumps) or positive. *This is not an offset into the code segment.*

To further complicate matters, all conditional jumps are limited to 128 bytes forward or 128 bytes backward, since they can only accept a single-byte displacement. Only the unconditional short jump can use a 16-bit displacement and move 32K bytes forward or backward.

Expressing negative numbers (which includes negative displacements) in binary notation uses an interesting notation called *two's complement*. A binary number added to its two's complement yields zero. The best way to explain it is in a table, as shown below. Study the table for a moment until the scheme seems natural to you.

Two's Complements

− 1 = $FF	−17 = $EF	−33 = $DF	−49 = $CF
− 2 = $FE	−18 = $EE	−34 = $DE	−50 = $CE
− 3 = $FD	−19 = $ED	−35 = $DD	−51 = $CD
− 4 = $FC	−20 = $EC	−36 = $DC	−52 = $CC
− 5 = $FB	−21 = $EB	−37 = $DB	−53 = $CB
− 6 = $FA	−22 = $EA	−38 = $DA	−54 = $CA
− 7 = $F9	−23 = $E9	−39 = $D9	−55 = $C9
− 8 = $F8	−24 = $E8	−40 = $D8	−56 = $C8
− 9 = $F7	−25 = $E7	−41 = $D7	−57 = $C7
−10 = $F6	−26 = $E6	−42 = $D6	−58 = $C6
−11 = $F5	−27 = $E5	−43 = $D5	−59 = $C5
−12 = $F4	−28 = $E4	−44 = $D4	−60 = $C4
−13 = $F3	−29 = $E3	−45 = $D3	−61 = $C3
−14 = $F2	−30 = $E2	−46 = $D2	−62 = $C2
−15 = $F1	−31 = $E1	−47 = $D1	−63 = $C1
−16 = $F0	−32 = $E0	−48 = $D0	−64 = $C0

This table should eliminate any need to calculate two's complements on your own; if your **INLINE** statements ever require a backward jump longer than 64 bytes, you are a brave soul indeed.

Here is an example of a backward jump coded in **INLINE**:

```
INLINE($31/$C0/           {XOR AX,AX}
       $B9/$64/$00/        {MOV CX,100}
       $81/$C0/$03/$00/    {ADD AX,3}
       $49/                {DEC CX}
       $75/$F9);           {JNZ -7}
```

The code itself doesn't do anything useful; I chose it because it was easy to understand and follow. The first line **XOR**s the **AX** register against itself. This is probably the first performance "tweak" assembly-language programmers ever learn. It clears **AX** to zero in three machine cycles, while the equivalent MOV AX,0 takes four machine cycles. (In some circles every cycle counts.)

The next line loads **100** into **CX** as immediate data. This will become the counter for a loop we're going to assemble. The third opcode does some "work": It adds three to the **AX** register. The next line *decrements* **CX** (decreases it by one byte), which, in this case, is acting as a count register. It was loaded originally with the number of times we wish to execute this particular loop, and with each pass through the loop, it is decremented by one.

The last line is the jump instruction, "Jump Not Zero," or JNZ. It checks an 8086 flag (called the *zero flag*) and makes its decision whether to jump or not based on the state of that flag. The decrement instruction that comes just before the jump affects the zero flag; if, in decrementing CX, CX goes to zero, the zero flag becomes true.

JNZ will jump as long as the zero flag is not true. The zero flag is set to false each time CX is decremented, but does not go to zero. As long as there remains a non-zero value in CX, JNZ will make its backward jump by seven bytes. However, as soon as CX goes to zero, the zero flag becomes true, and JNZ will not jump but simply let control "fall through" to the next instruction. In this case, there are no more instructions in the **INLINE** statement, so the next instruction in the Pascal program takes over.

The only tricky part of setting this up is deciding exactly what displacement value to use for JNZ; you have to count backward from the location immediately after the displacement value. Count seven bytes backward from just past the $F9 displacement byte, and you'll find yourself at the beginning of the ADD instruction, which is where you want to be.

The easiest mistake to make in coding jumps like this is to count from the position following the jump opcode rather than the position after the displacement value. This is especially true if you haven't calculated the displacement and written down a value for it in its proper place. (Don't ever forget: The displacement byte is part of the jump instruction!) By the time the displacement is added to the instruction pointer, the instruction pointer is already pointing to the first byte past the end of the instruction. So even if you don't yet know what value the displacement is going to be, fill the byte position with a $00 so that you can be sure you're counting it as you figure the displacement.

The second easiest mistake to make is inserting an instruction in the middle of a sequence of **INLINE** instructions without adjusting any affected jump displacements. Jumping into the middle of a multibyte instruction is fatal more often than not. Every time you add instructions to, or remove instructions from, an **INLINE** statement with jumps, check those displacements.

There's little else to do in coding jumps, but that nasty business of calculating correct displacements makes it thoroughly unpleasant work. Minimize jumps in **INLINE** code—or start using that assembler!

4.3 Functions, Procedures, and Local Variables

The trickiest part to using variables from machine code is knowing where they are. As we've seen, global variables and typed constants are easy to pin down: Global variables exist at one unchanging offset from the DS register, while typed constants exist at one unchanging offset from the CS register.

When we begin talking about subprograms (procedures and functions) the whole game changes shape drastically. This has to do with the nature of subprograms in Pascal. Although a subprogram's code is created at compile time and always exists somewhere in the code segment, a subprogram's parameters and data literally *do not exist* until the subprogram is invoked. No space is reserved in the data segment for a subprogram's parameters, nor for its local variables. These critters come into being when a subprogram is called, and they are created on the stack.

It is helpful to remember at this point that the 8088 CPU decrements the stack pointer *first* and then stores the pushed value at the stack location. This means that the stack pointer always points to real data, *not* to unused, empty space. Not all CPU's work this way; some store information at the stack location first and then decrement, leaving the stack pointer pointing at free space. Think: First decrement, *then* store . . . and you won't get confused.

When a subprogram is invoked, Turbo Pascal's runtime code *instantiates* the subprogram on the stack. It can best be explained by using an example. Consider these declarations:

```
TYPE
  String30 = String[30];
  IntArray = ARRAY[0..99] OF Integer;

FUNCTION Dummy(VAR Values  :  IntArray;
               Fudge    :   Integer;
               Level,Clearance  :  Char;
               Message :  String30)  :  Boolean;

VAR
  Grade  :  Char;
  Cutoff :  Char;
```

```
BEGIN
  Grade  := 'A';
  Cutoff := 'Q';
END;
```

This is not intended to be a useful function declaration. It was defined with the parameters and data items shown to make it interesting on the dissection table. Let's follow what happens when **Dummy** is invoked, step by step. As virtually all these steps involve the stack, a diagram of the condition of the stack *after* instantiation is given in Figure 4.2. If you get confused while reading, follow along on the diagram as well.

1. *Space for the function result is pushed onto the stack.* In **Dummy**'s case, this is a single byte for a Boolean value. For an integer, it would be two bytes; for a non-8087 real, six bytes, and so on. (Representation of various data types is discussed more fully in Section 4.7.) In Standard Pascal, only simple types may be returned from functions, whereas Turbo Pascal also allows functions to return strings.

Oddly enough, this space is *not* used to return the value to the Turbo Pascal runtime when the function returns control to the calling logic, except in certain cases. (More on the sticky matter of function results can be found in Section 4.6.)

If **Dummy** had been a procedure, no space would have been pushed onto the stack for function results.

2. *The parameters are pushed onto the stack.* In our example, **Values** is pushed first. **Values** is a VAR parameter, meaning that what the subprogram gets is not a copy of **Values**, but the *address* of **Values**. What is pushed onto the stack is, essentially, a pointer to the actual parameter passed to **Dummy** as **Values**. The 16-bit segment part of the address is pushed first, followed by the 16-bit offset part of the address.

Remember that we're starting from high memory and moving toward low memory with each item pushed onto the stack.

Parameter **Fudge** is pushed onto the stack next. **Fudge** is a value parameter, so a copy of the actual parameter is pushed onto the stack. This copy is, like all integers, represented as two bytes. The most significant byte of the integer value is higher in memory. In other words, if, at invocation time, **Fudge** is passed a value of 17,642 (hex $44EA) the hex byte $44 will be located one byte higher on the stack than the byte $EA.

The next two parameters, **Level** and **Clearance**, are both characters. Now, while characters are represented as a single byte in Pascal, they are pushed onto the stack as words (two bytes), *except* when used as function results. (Confusing? You bet. More on this in Section 4.6.) Here, **Level** and **Clearance** are being passed as parameters, so they are passed as two bytes. Of the two bytes pushed onto the stack for each character, the byte higher in memory is a zero byte ($00), followed by the byte containing the actual character value.

Finally, parameter **Message** is pushed onto the stack. **Message** is a **String30**, meaning that it consists of one length byte plus 30 character data bytes. String values are pushed onto the stack backward in a sense: The *last* character in the string is pushed first, followed by the second-to-last, and so on, until, finally, the first character is pushed onto the stack. The very last byte of

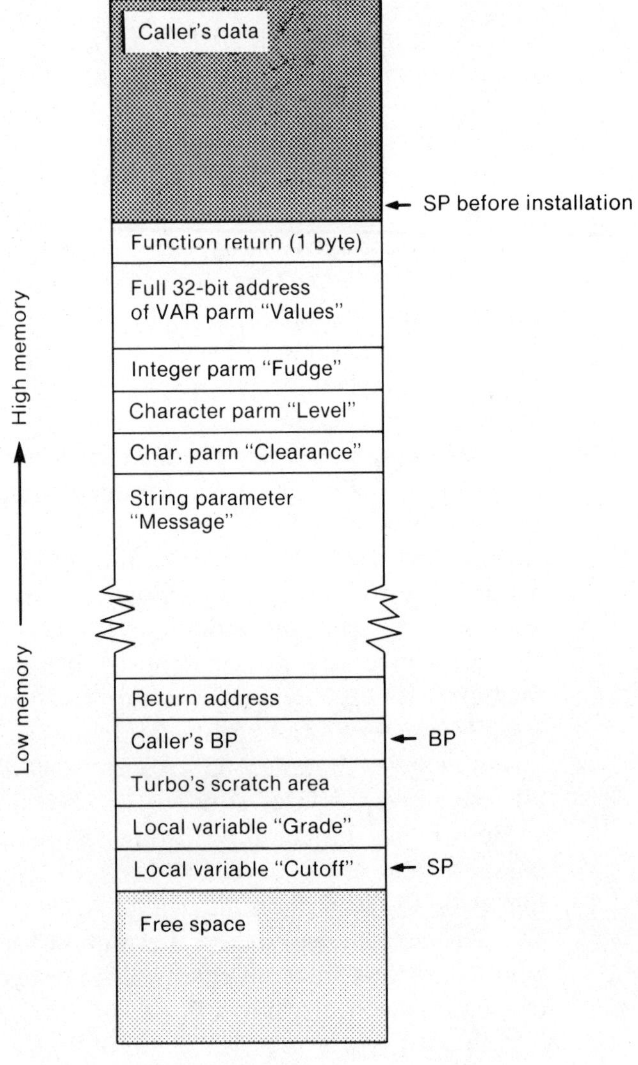

Figure 4.2 **Instantiation of a subprogram**

the string pushed onto the stack is the length byte, element 0 of the string variable. Note that although individual character variables are pushed onto the stack as words, the characters comprising a string are pushed onto the stack as bytes. This is a slower process, but it saves valuable stack space.

3. *All the parameters are now on the stack*. The return address is now pushed onto the stack. Unlike the full 32-bit address pushed onto the stack for VAR parameters like **Values**, this address is a 16-bit offset into the code segment. There's no need to specify a code segment address because Turbo Pascal programs only have one code segment, which is known throughout the program and never changes. (You can examine the code segment value by way of the built-in function **CSeg**, which returns the current code-segment address.)

There is a conceptual break at this point. Everything so far is done by the Turbo Pascal runtime code, whether the subprogram being instantiated is written in Pascal or declared as an external machine-code file. From here on, however, external machine-code subprograms are on their own.

4. *The stack pointer SP now points to the least significant byte of the return address*. To allow easy access to the parameters currently on the stack, the stack pointer must be copied into the base pointer BP. This will free the stack pointer to run up and down as the code requires during subprogram execution while still providing a fixed base from which to access parameters.

The Turbo Pascal runtime code, however, requires that subprograms leave certain registers (BP, CS, DS, and SS) alone when they execute, since these registers are literally the only way the program code keeps track of where its code, data, and stack are. The runtime has its own uses for the BP (base pointer) register, even when the main program is executing and variables are allocated in the data segment rather than on the stack. Additionally, subprograms can have their own local subprograms, and if a subprogram is executed *within* another subprogram, the outer subprogram depends on BP to keep track of its local variables and parameters. If the inner subprogram loaded its own value into BP without saving the outer program's copy of BP, the outer subprogram would no longer know where its parameters and local variables were when it resumed control.

Therefore, before loading the stack pointer into BP, the previous value of BP must be saved on the stack. Once BP has been pushed onto the stack, the SP (stack pointer) register can be loaded into BP, providing an anchor point for access to items stored previously on the stack, and allowing the stack to proceed and serve the executing code as needed.

In subprograms written in Pascal, the code generator does all of this. In your external machine-code subprograms, you will have to explicitly push BP and move the stack pointer into BP. It's simple enough:

```
PUSH  BP
MOV   BP,SP
```

At this point, both **BP** and **SP** point to the old value of **BP**, now safely ensconced on the stack.

5. *Local variables must now be allocated on the stack*. In subprograms written in Pascal, of course, this happens invisibly. Interesting things happen here. In tracing code generated by Turbo Pascal, I have found that the runtime code allocates single bytes on the stack for variables such as characters, bytes, and Booleans that only require single bytes. Ordinarily, space on the stack is only allocated in chunks of two bytes (one word) at a time. The **PUSH** and **POP** 8088 instructions only manipulate words, not bytes. The Turbo Pascal runtime, however, fakes single-byte pushes by performing a **DEC SP** instruction, which moves the stack pointer down by one byte. As there is no initial value to push into a local variable, this is all that is required.

I said only a little about it in previous paragraphs to avoid confusion, but this same method is used when allocating string parameters on the stack. The length byte and the individual data characters in a string are all single bytes; they are pushed individually onto the stack by a process of decrementing SP by one and then storing the bytes on the stack with a **MOV** instruction rather than a **PUSH** instruction.

Function results are also allocated on the stack this way, so that types represented as single bytes are allocated on the stack as single bytes when they are function results, even though they are allocated as two bytes if they are value parameters.

The Turbo Pascal runtime code also has the option of allocating storage on the stack for temporary values generated during the execution of a subprogram written in Pascal. These are allocated before local variables.

If your external machine-code subprograms require local workspace, you must allocate it yourself by pushing an appropriate number of words onto the stack, or by subtracting the number of bytes needed from the value in the stack pointer:

```
SUB SP,WORKSPACE_SIZE
```

If **WORKSPACE_SIZE** had earlier been equated to 12, a total of 12 bytes of memory would have been allocated on the stack.

At this point, all initial work connected with the stack is finished, and the subprogram gets on with its real work. When that work is completed, however, what was done to the stack must be undone for control to return to the calling logic in an orderly fashion.

Cleaning up the stack is not difficult. The first step is to move the subprogram's current value of BP into the stack pointer SP:

```
MOV SP,BP
```

If you recall, **BP** had been left pointing to the calling logic's older copy of **BP** on the stack. The above instruction brings **SP** up to that point, which, in effect, destroys any local variables and temporary workspace that had been allocated on the stack. Next, the calling logic's copy of **BP** is restored by popping it off the stack:

```
POP BP
```

This instruction takes whatever lies at **SS:SP** and moves it into the **BP** register. Since **SP** points to the old copy of **BP**, that copy of **BP** is restored into the **BP** register. Now **BP** is no longer in the service of the subprogram, but has gone back to the control of the calling logic. The stack pointer, however, now points to the least significant byte of the return address. All remaining cleanup is combined with the process of returning control to the calling logic with one single instruction:

```
RET <bytes>
```

The <**bytes**> parameter is the exact number of bytes of the subprogram's data remaining on the stack, including any function results but *not* including the two bytes of return address. For our sample function **Dummy**, this would be 41 bytes for parameters plus one byte for the function result, for a total of 42.

Peeking the Stack

You don't have to be content with inferences in working out the contents of the stack during a function or procedure call. You can go right in and *look* at it if you like.

Recall from the previous section that, during subprogram instantiation, the Turbo Pascal runtime code pushes parameters onto the stack, and then copies the stack-pointer register SP into the base-pointer register BP. This allows the runtime to use the stack pointer for other things during subprogram execution while "keeping its finger" at the point in the stack where parameters are stored. BP does not change at any point later in the subprogram (unless you explicitly change it—not a good idea!), so it can be used as a base from which to reference parameters on the stack.

The value of the stack-segment register SS is always accessible through the Turbo Pascal built-in function **SSeg**. Thus, looking at parameters on the stack is as simple as obtaining the value in BP, combining the return value from **SSeg** with the value of BP into a pointer, and passing that pointer to the **VarDump** procedure described in Section 3.4. Obtaining the value of BP is done with a short **INLINE** statement, as described earlier. Creating this pointer can be done with Turbo Pascal's **Ptr** function, which returns a pointer given two integer values, one specifying the segment part of the pointer and the other the offset part of the pointer.

VarDump also requires a size parameter to tell it how many bytes to dump. For simplicity's sake, just add up the sizes of all parameters you're passing, and hard-code that figure into **VarDump**'s **ItSize** parameter.

You can also let the machine calculate how many bytes of parameter are on the stack, and dump only that number of bytes. (It involves a little more coding, but I think it's more satisfying to let computers do what they do best.) Consider that *just before* a subprogram is called, the SP register is pointing to the *last* byte allocated on the stack by the Turbo Pascal runtime code for whatever block that had control when the subprogram was called. When the subprogram is called, parameters are allocated on the stack from that point downward. When the subprogram begins executing, the BP register points to the last byte of parameter data allocated for the subprogram.

Figure 4.3 shows a before-and-after view of the stack when a subprogram is called. The calling logic has been labeled "Block A," and the subprogram "Block B." Before Block B is called, the stack pointer points to the last byte of data local to Block A. Beneath SP is free space, available for stack growth. SP can be captured at this point as a "before" pointer for the stack-peeking trick. You have two choices for the "after" value, as described below.

By saving the value of the stack pointer just before the subprogram is called (a "before" value), and then saving BP after the subprogram begins running (an "after" value), the number of bytes of parameter data pushed onto the stack for the subprogram will be equal to the difference between the "before" and "after" values. This value can then be given to **VarDump**'s **ItSize** parameter, and **VarDump** will always dump exactly the right number of bytes of parameter data from the stack—no more, no less.

The short program **Look1** dumps the parameter data from function **Dummy** that we described previously. Figure 4.4 annotates the first of the two dumps of the stack which **Look1** creates and relates it to the parameter list for **Dummy**. The dump shows the status of the parameter stack immediately upon execution of **Dummy**.

Program **Look1** dumps the stack from the stack pointer just before **Dummy**'s invocation, down to BP after instantiation. Between these two points are **Dummy**'s parameters. **Dummy** has local variables in addition to parameters, however. To view them, you need to follow the stack further down, beyond BP to the new position of the stack pointer SP. After **Dummy** has begun executing, SP points to the last word of data in whatever local variables **Dummy** may contain.

With some minor modifications, **Look1** shows us the stack from the "before" position of the stack pointer to the "after" position of the stack pointer,

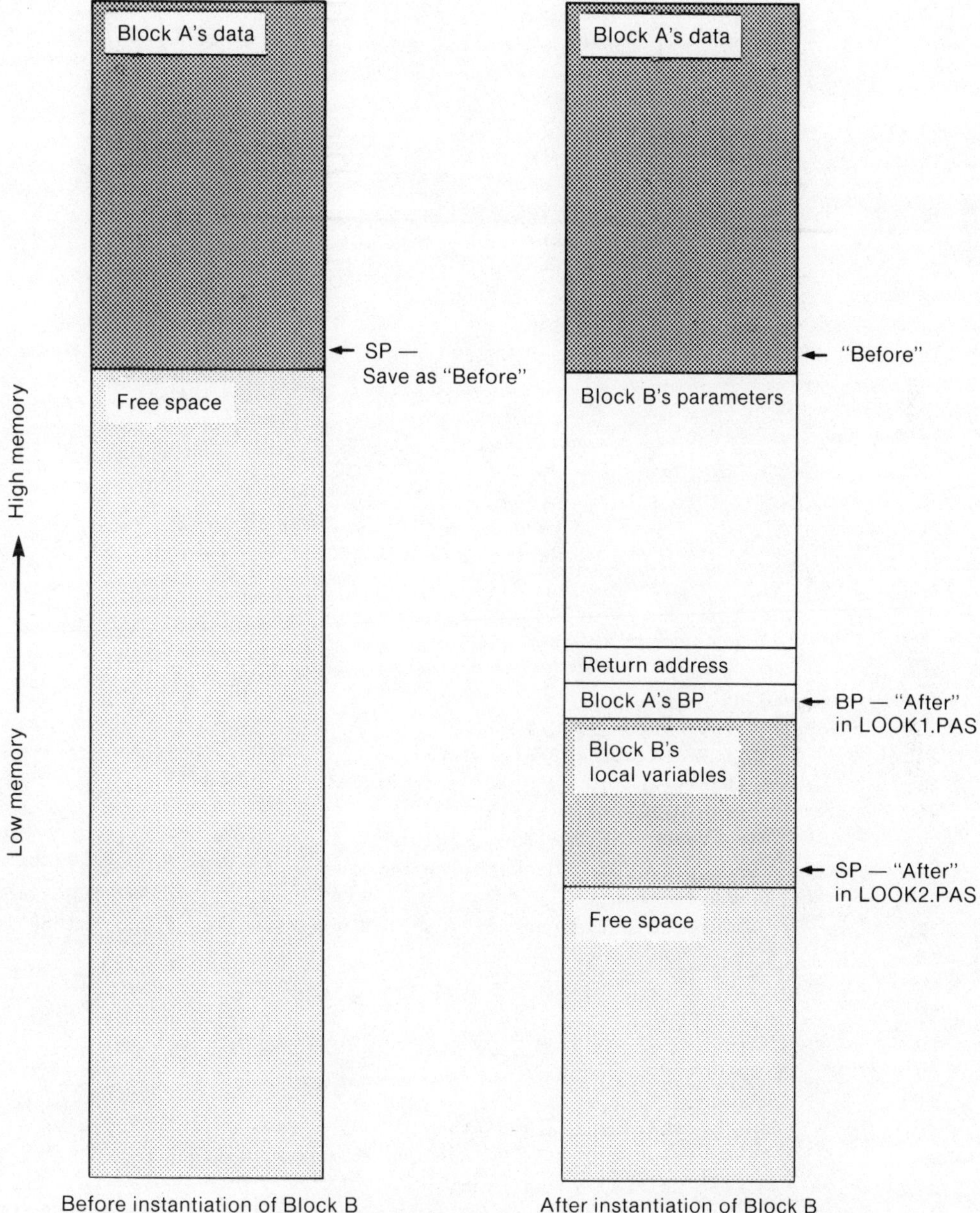

Figure 4.3 **Peeking the stack**

```
 1            PROGRAM Look1;
 2
 3            TYPE
 4              String30 = String[30];
 5              IntArray = ARRAY[0..99] OF Integer;
 6
 7            VAR
 8              OK          : Boolean;
 9              Register    : Integer;
10              StackMarker : ^Byte;
11              Before,After : Real;
12              MyArray     : IntArray;
13
14            {$I ..\TOOLKIT\WRITEHEX.SRC}
15            {$I ..\TOOLKIT\VARDUMP.SRC}
16
17
18
19            FUNCTION Dummy(VAR Values    : IntArray;
20                              Fudge     : Integer;
21                              Level,Clearance : Char;
22                              Message   : String30) : Boolean;
23
24            VAR
25              Grade,Cutoff : Char;
26
27            BEGIN
28              INLINE($90/$90/$90/$90);
29              INLINE($8B/$C5/$A3/Register);              { Save BP into Register }
30              IF Register < 0 THEN After := Register + 65536.0
31                ELSE After := Register;
32              StackMarker := Ptr(SSeg,Register);      { Make a pointer SS : BP    }
33              VarDump(Con,StackMarker^,Trunc(Before-After));  { Dump stack }
34              Dummy := True;                                  { Set function value }
35              VarDump(Con,StackMarker^,Trunc(Before-After));  { Dump stack again }
36            END;
37
38
39
40            BEGIN
41              ClrScr;
42              INLINE($8B/$C4/$A3/Register);           { Save BP into Register }
43              IF Register < 0 THEN Before := Register + 65536.0
44                ELSE Before := Register;
45              OK := Dummy(MyArray,42,'Q','Z','I was born on a pirate ship.  ');
46            END.
```

```
FUNCTION Dummy (VAR Values      : IntArray;
                    Fudge       : Integer;
                    Level,Clearance  : Char;
                    Message     : String30) :  Boolean;
```

When function "Dummy" is instantiated, its stack looks like this:

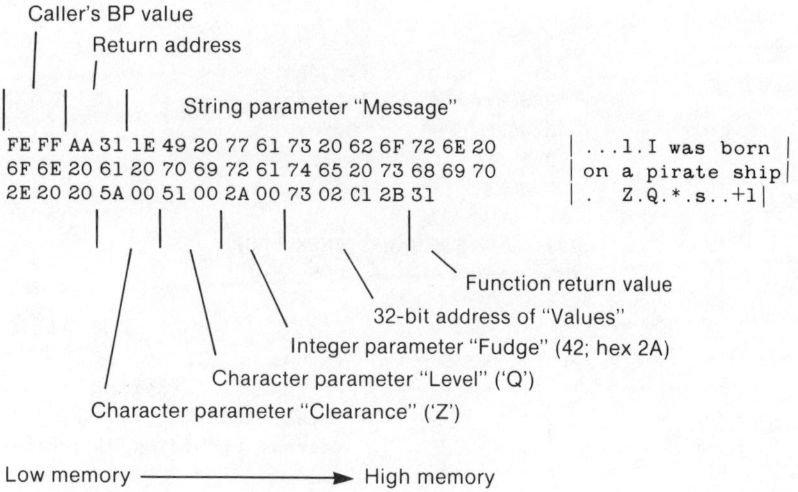

```
Caller's BP value
      |        Return address
      |          /
      |          /        String parameter "Message"
|     |    |
FE FF AA 31 1E 49 20 77 61 73 20 62 6F 72 6E 20     | ...1.I was born |
6F 6E 20 61 20 70 69 72 61 74 65 20 73 68 69 70     | on a pirate ship|
2E 20 20 5A 00 51 00 2A 00 73 02 C1 2B 31           | .   Z.Q.*.s..+1|
         |    |    |      |           |
          \    \    \      \           \
           \    \    \      \           \  Function return value
            \    \    \      \        32-bit address of "Values"
             \    \    \   Integer parameter "Fudge" (42; hex 2A)
              \    \  Character parameter "Level" ('Q')
               \  Character parameter "Clearance" ('Z')

Low memory ───────────────▶ High memory
```

Figure 4.4   **Look1's stack**

including not only all parameters and the return address, but the local variables as well. This modified program becomes **Look2**. The only difference is that SP is taken as the "after" stack marker, rather than BP.

Figure 4.5 shows the second of the two dumps of the stack created by **Look2**. The function **Dummy** is the same as that shown in **Look1**. The dump is very similar to the dump produced by **Look1**, except that it goes further into low memory, past the caller's BP value and the return address. The dump was made *after* the two local variables were assigned values so that the values would appear in the dump. This particular procedure is allocated two bytes of "scratch" area by the Turbo Pascal runtime code; this number varies according to rules that are not documented. In your own explorations, you may need to use this same trick to figure out how much scratch has been allocated. Declare a local variable if one does not already exist and assign it a recognizable value. Then peek the stack. The scratch area will consist of all memory between the recognizable local variable value and four bytes below the end of the last parameter. (The four bytes contain the return address and caller's BP value.)

```
 1          PROGRAM Look2;
 2
 3          TYPE
 4            String30 = String[30];
 5            IntArray = ARRAY[0..99] OF Integer;
 6
 7          VAR
 8            OK          : Boolean;
 9            Register    : Integer;
10            StackMarker : ^Byte;
11            Before,After : Real;
12            MyArray     : IntArray;
13
14          {$I ..\TOOLKIT\WRITEHEX.SRC}
15          {$I ..\TOOLKIT\VARDUMP.SRC}
16
17
18          FUNCTION Dummy(VAR Values   : IntArray;
19                             Fudge    : Integer;
20                             Level,Clearance : Char;
21                             Message  : String30) : Boolean;
22
23          VAR
24            Grade,Cutoff : Char;
25
26          BEGIN
27            INLINE($8B/$C4/$A3/Register);          { Save BP into Register }
28            IF Register < 0 THEN After := Register + 65536.0
29              ELSE After := Register;
30            StackMarker := Ptr(SSeg,Register);     { Make a pointer SS : SP   }
31            VarDump(Con,StackMarker^,Trunc(Before-After));  { Dump stack }
32            Dummy := True;                                  { Set function value }
33            Grade := 'A';
34            Cutoff := 'C';
35            VarDump(Con,StackMarker^,Trunc(Before-After));  { Dump stack again }
36          END;
37
38
39
40          BEGIN
41            ClrScr;
42            INLINE($8B/$C4/$A3/Register);          { Save SP into Register  }
43            IF Register < 0 THEN Before := Register + 65536.0
44              ELSE Before := Register;
45            OK := Dummy(MyArray,42,'Q','Z','I was born on a pirate ship.  ');
46          END.
```

```
FUNCTION Dummy (VAR Values    : IntArray;
                    Fudge     : Integer;
                    Level,Clearance : Char;
                    Message   : String30) : Boolean;

VAR
  Grade,Cutoff : Char;
```

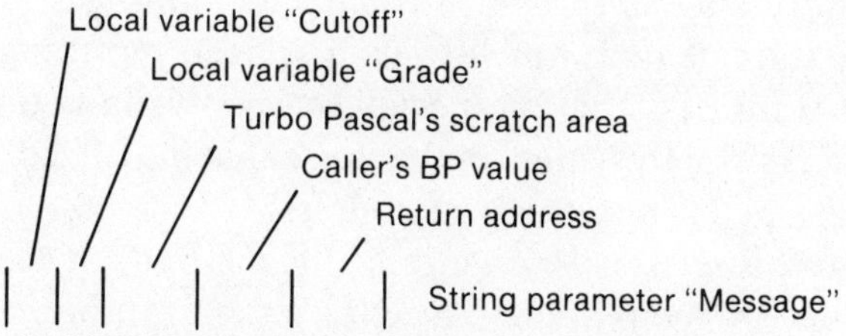

```
             Local variable "Cutoff"
               Local variable "Grade"
                 Turbo Pascal's scratch area
                 Caller's BP value
                   Return address

| | |   |   |    String parameter "Message"
43 41 D0 FF FE FF B6 31 1E 49 20 77 61 73 20 62    | CA.....l. I was b |
6F 72 6E 20 6F 6E 20 61 20 70 69 72 61 74 65 20    | orn on a pirate   |
73 68 69 70 2E 20 20 5A 00 51 00 2A 00 73 02 C2    | ship .   Z.Q.*.s.. |
2B 01                                              | +. |
```

This dump was taken AFTER local variables "Grade" and "Cutoff"
were assigned values.

Figure 4.5   **Look2's stack**

Relate the stack dump from **Look2** to the stack diagram in Figure 4.5 for additional clarification of how the stack peek works.

This method of looking at the parameter stack can be a useful first step in designing an external machine-language subprogram. Once you decide what parameters will be passed to the subprogram, create a dummy subprogram in Pascal (like **Dummy** in the above example), using those parameters exactly as they will exist in the external subprogram. Pass some easily recognizable values to the subprogram as actual parameters, and then dump the stack from inside the subprogram. Use the hexdump to establish offsets from BP, or to create an assembly-language structure for the parameters (discussed in detail in Section 4.5).

Never be too embarrassed to actually *draw* the stack on graph paper to get all the offsets and parameter sizes straight. The biggest problems with simple external subprograms are caused by simply not getting the parameters passed correctly. Paper is cheap. Time is not. Do whatever you must to get it all straight in your mind, and you will save a great deal of time.

Accessing Local Variables and Parameters from INLINE

Accessing global data items from **INLINE** is best done through register AX, as described earlier. Turbo Pascal conveniently replaces global variable identifiers with their offset relative to DS, and a special form of the MOV instruction works handily with AX and offsets from DS.

Accessing subprogram parameters and local variables from within **INLINE** statements is much trickier, since everything has to be specified as an offset from BP. This is especially tricky when you want to get at a VAR parameter, since the value on the stack at some offset from BP is not the value of the parameter, but its 32-bit address.

In this section we'll examine the methods of accessing these variables and parameters. As in previous sections, the examples will focus on working with type **Integer**, since the bulk of data passed between machine-code routines and Pascal code is either two bytes in size or some multiple of two. The important thing to learn is the general method, so that, for each specific case, you can puzzle out the details without a great deal of trouble.

Accessing local variables from within **INLINE** is fairly straightforward. Turbo Pascal replaces the names of local variables with their offset from BP, relative to the stack-segment register SS. For example, to move the value of AX into a subprogram's local variable, code up this:

```
MOV SS:BP+<var>,AX
```

Turbo will obligingly provide the offset from **BP** represented by **<var>**. But what is the opcode? This is an especially messy instance of the 8086 instruction set coming to the fore. It represents one specific case of the general mnemonic

```
MOV mm,rr
```

which means, move a 16-bit register into a 16-bit memory location. This mnemonic evaluates to a 2-byte opcode. The first byte, $89, is common to all instances of the generic mnemonic shown above. The second byte is different depending on two things: 1) How we specify mm; in other words, from some register. Is the offset given as BP? BP plus a displacement? Or one of the many other possible combinations of registers and displacements? 2) Which 8086 register is being moved to mm.

For the example above, the 2-byte opcode is $89/$86. But remember, that's *only* for register AX. The coding for all the other registers is best shown as a table:

```
MOV mm,rr
First byte                    Second byte
  [BP+dd]      AX    BX    CX    DX    BP    SI    DI    SP
    $89       $86   $9E   $8E   $96   $AE   $B6   $BE   $A6
```

Here **[BP+dd]** means "the word at the address given by register BP plus a 16-bit offset dd." This offset is what Turbo Pascal uses to replace a local variable identifier.

The following program is a simpleminded example of moving data between machine registers and subprogram local variables:

```
PROGRAM MOVLocal;

PROCEDURE Foo;

VAR
  Fee,Fie : Integer;

BEGIN
  Fee := 0; Fie := 0;
  INLINE($B8/$11/$00);        {MOV AX,17}
  INLINE($89/$86/Fee);        {MOV Fee,AX}
  Writeln( 'Fee=',Fee);
  Readln;
  INLINE($8B/$9E/Fee);        {MOV BX,Fee}
  INLINE($89/$9E/Fie);        {MOV Fie,BX}
  Writeln( 'Fie=',Fie);
  Readln;
END;

BEGIN
  ClrScr;
  Foo;
END.
```

Procedure **Foo** has two local variables, **Fee** and **Fie**. Both these local variables are initialized to zero. An immediate value of 17 is loaded into register AX. Then, the contents of AX are moved into **Fee** by the statement **INLINE ($89/$86/Fee);**. This can be verified by displaying **Fee** to the screen. Next, the contents of **Fee** are moved into register BX; from BX they are moved into local variable **Fie**, which is then displayed to verify that the value of 17 was moved from AX into **Fee**, from **Fee** into BX, and from BX into **Fie**.

Make sure you understand how the second bytes of the move opcodes were selected from the table.

Accessing subprogram parameters is done in much the same way. As with local variable references, when Turbo encounters a value parameter reference within a subprogram, it replaces the reference with the value parameter's offset from BP on the stack. Moving data between registers and value parameters thus requires the identical 8086 opcodes that moving local variables did. Study this program carefully:

```
PROGRAM MOVParameter;

PROCEDURE Foo(Foe,Fum : Integer);

VAR
  Fee,Fie : Integer;

BEGIN
  Fee := 0; Fie := 0;
  Writeln('Fum=',Fum);
  INLINE($8B/$8E/FOE);        {MOV CX,Foe}
  INLINE($89/$8E/Fee);        {MOV Fee,CX}
  Writeln('Fee=',Fee);
  Readln;
  INLINE($8B/$96/Fee);        {MOV DX,Fee}
  INLINE($89/$96/Fum);        {MOV Fum,DX}
  Writeln('Fum=',Fum);
  Readln;
END;

BEGIN
  ClrScr;
  Foo(42,17);
END.
```

One difference here is that we're using registers CX and DX rather than AX and BX. Notice how that changes the second byte of the opcode, and relate it to the table on page 102.

Program **MOVParameter** takes an integer value from parameter **Foe** and moves it into local variable **Fee** by way of register CX. Then, the same value is moved from **Fee** into DX, and from DX into value parameter **Fum**. The important thing to remember in comparing **MOVLocal** and **MOVParameter** is that, from **INLINE**'s perspective, subprogram local variables and subprogram value parameters are exactly the same thing, accessed in exactly the same way, with the same 8086 instruction.

Now, while it doesn't alter the sense of the opcode, you should keep in mind (in case you have to go troubleshooting your **INLINE** code) that these offsets from BP can be either positive or negative values. For example, in the little program **MOVLocal** given above, if you add code to examine the value of the offset that Turbo replaces the local variable references with, you'll see that the offsets of both **Fee** and **Fie** are negative numbers.

The offsets for value parameters **Foe** and **Fum** in program **MOVParameter**, however, are positive numbers. (For an excellent exercise, code up the **INLINE** statements it would take to examine and display the offset values for **Fee**, **Fie**, **Foe**, and **Fum** in **MOVParameter**.) What goes on here?

Recall the process of instantiating a subprogram on the stack, and think of the position of BP relative to value parameters and local variables on the stack. The stack pointer is copied into BP *after* value parameters are allocated on the stack, but *before* local variables are allocated on the stack (see Figure 4.3). Thus, the value parameters must be accessed by adding an offset to BP, while the local variables are accessed by subtracting an offset from BP. Adding a negative offset gives the same result as subtracting an offset. This is why the offsets for **Fee** and **Fie** are negative.

A reminder to beginners: Negative numbers in the 8086 world are encoded in two's complement form, such that $-1 = \$FF$; $-2 = \$FE$; $-3 = \$FD$.

Figure 4.6 highlights program **MOVParameter**'s stack as a group of *words* rather than bytes. The dashed lines represent byte boundaries within words. Offsets from BP, however, are always given in bytes. The word at offset -2 from BP (shown as "???") is allocated by the Turbo Pascal runtime code for its own purposes, perhaps as a scratch word for temporary storage of registers.

Using VAR Parameters from within INLINE

Compared to using VAR parameters, dealing with local variables and value parameters is a snap. Recall that for VAR parameters, the value that is pushed onto the stack is not the value contained in the actual parameter, but the address of the variable that is the actual parameter. This introduces another level of indirection in accessing VAR parameters: Before we can access the parameter, we have to access its address. Once its address has been moved off the stack and into the right registers, we can work with the parameter itself.

Yes, it's a lot more fooling around than working with value parameters, but the bad news ends there. The good news is that the 8086 contains the instruction LES (Load Pointer Using ES), designed precisely for taking an address off the stack and putting it in the appropriate register for this kind of indirect addressing. This instruction pulls a 32-bit address from somewhere in memory and puts the segment portion of that address into register ES, and the offset portion of the address into the register of your choice. The location "somewhere in memory" can be set up to exist at an offset from BP given as a VAR parameter identifier within **INLINE**.

Register ES represents what is called the *extra segment*, and it is precisely that—a spare segment that can be changed and used for various purposes without disrupting the data segment (DS), code segment (CS), or stack segment (SS). We're going to use the extra segment as a spare-data segment, and load the offset from ES into the DI register.

LES is a two-byte opcode. The first byte is always $C4, and the second byte varies depending on where the address is to be found, and into which register the offset portion of the address is to be loaded. For our purposes in

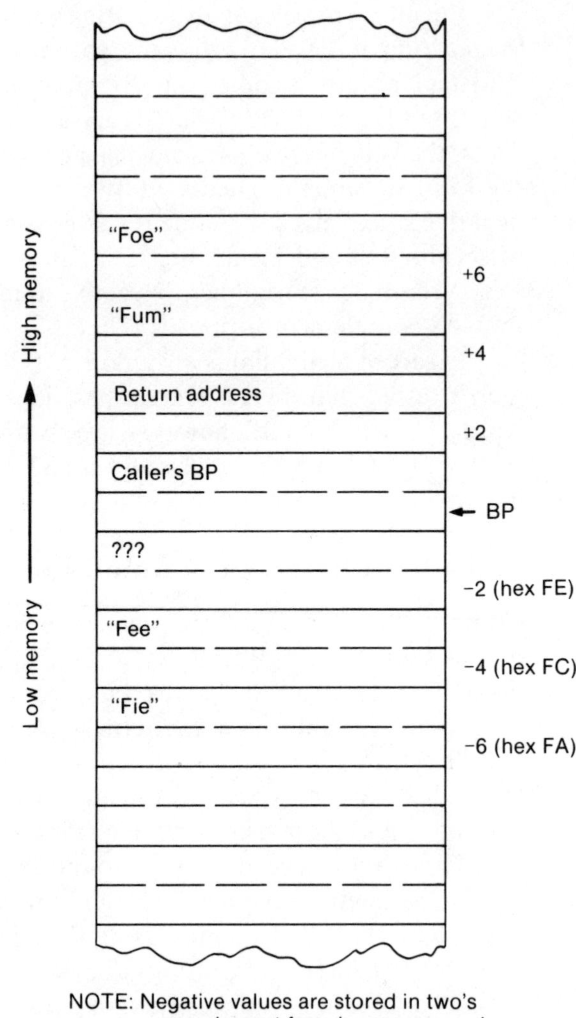

Figure 4.6 **Offsets from BP**

using LES to access VAR parameters, the address is found at an offset from BP. Given that, the second byte can be chosen from a simple row of values related to the offset register:

LES coding for accessing VAR parameters:

First byte				Second byte				
	AX	BX	CX	DX	BP	SI	DI	SP
$C4	$86	$9E	$8E	$96	$AE	$B6	$BE	$A6

For our use of **DI**, the second byte becomes **$BE**. This table ought to look familiar . . . it's the same set of second-byte values used in the table of register/memory MOV opcodes on page 102.

This simple example should give you a feel for how LES is used from **INLINE** to access a VAR parameter:

```
PROGRAM VARParmINLINE;

VAR
  Flarf : Integer;

PROCEDURE Foo(VAR Fum : Integer);

BEGIN
  INLINE($C4/$BE/Fum);       {LES DI,[BP+<offset>]}
  INLINE($BA/$71/$00);       {MOV DX,$71}
  INLINE($26/$89/$15);       {MOV ES:[DI],DX}
END;

BEGIN
  ClrScr;
  Flarf := 0;
  Foo(Flarf);
  Writeln( 'Flarf=' ,Flarf);
  Readln
END.
```

This small program contains a procedure, **Foo**, that has one **VAR** parameter. Procedure **Foo** does only one thing: It places a value of 113 (hex **$71**) into the **VAR** parameter. If you recall, in Pascal, only **VAR** parameters can be changed by subprogram logic, and that is all we're doing in this example.

Inside procedure **Foo**, the first **INLINE** statement takes the address of **VAR** parameter **Fum** off the stack and loads it into registers **ES** and **DI**. The second **INLINE** statement loads the immediate value **$71** into register **DX**. The last **INLINE** statement moves the contents of **DX** into **VAR** parameter **Fum**.

This last **INLINE** statement merits a closer look: It's our old friend **MOV**, but coded up in a different way. First of all, notice the **$26** byte. This is the extra-segment prefix. When a segment is not implied (as the stack segment SS is by specifying an offset from BP), the default segment for using **MOV** is DS. The extra-segment prefix tells the 8086 that the segment register for the following instruction is to be **ES**. Without the prefix, the **MOV** instruction would have moved data out to the word at DS:DI, whatever that might be.

Try to associate in your mind the use of the **ES** segment override prefix with access to **VAR** parameters from **INLINE**. It's possible to push the caller's value of DS onto the stack and use the LDS (Load Pointer Using DS) instruction rather than LES. This would make DS the default-segment register, eliminating the need for override prefixes; however, you must remember to pop the caller's DS value off the stack before the **INLINE** code finishes up. (Using **ES** seems tidier to me, and the memory fetch overhead incurred for using the prefix is minimal, when balanced against the time required to push and pop DS.)

The **$89** opcode for **MOV** is familiar enough; it stands for the MOV mm,rr variant of the **MOV** instruction. Its second byte is not familiar, however; it depends both on the register operand (in this case, **DX**) and on the method of addressing the destination memory location. The shorthand for that location is **ES:[DI]**, meaning "the location pointed to by offset **DI** from segment register **ES**." (The square brackets indicate that we're referring to the memory location itself rather than its address.) Given these two criteria, a second byte can be chosen from the list of possible values:

```
MOV mm,rr coding for accessing VAR parameters at ES:[DI]:

First byte                  Second byte
                AX    BX    CX    DX    BP    SI    DI    SP
    $89        $05   $1D   $0D   $15   $2D   $35   $3D   $25
```

Since we're using **DX** in the **MOV** operation, the second byte (per the table) is **$15**. Had the operation been **MOV mm,BX** instead, the second byte would have been **$1D**.

To recap: Working with a VAR parameter first requires that the actual parameter's address be copied from the stack into a segment register and an appropriate offset register. For simple work within **INLINE**, let's standardize ES as the segment register and DI as the offset register. The instruction LES, when coded correctly for DI and given the offset from BP of the VAR parameter's identifier, will take the address from the stack and load it appropriately into ES and DI.

Once the address is in ES:DI, the register/memory instructions can be coded to use that address to access the VAR parameter.

Note here that we can do more than MOV values between registers and VAR parameters. Any of the following instructions can be used anywhere that MOV is used:

```
ADC    Add with carry            ADD    Add without carry
AND    Logical AND               CMP    Compare
MOV    Move                      OR     Logical OR
SBB    Subtract with borrow      SUB    Subtract without borrow
TEST   Test bit or bits          XCHG   Exchange memory and register
XOR    Logical XOR
```

In Appendix A, you will find a table that lists the proper opcodes for all instructions between the 8086 registers and memory, where "memory" means global variables, local variables, value parameters, and VAR parameters.

The program shown below provides a slightly more complicated—but considerably more useful—example of working with VAR parameters from within **INLINE**:

```
1        PROGRAM FastIncrement;
2
3        TYPE
4          IntArray = ARRAY[0..16000] OF Integer;
5
6        VAR
7          I      : Integer;
8          Scores : IntArray;
9
10
11       PROCEDURE Increment(VAR Scores : IntArray;
12                           ByHowMuch  : Integer);
13
14       BEGIN
15         INLINE($C4/$BE/Scores/       {LES DI,[BP+<offset>]}
16               $B9/$80/$3E/           {MOV CX,16000}
17               $8B/$9E/ByHowMuch/     {MOV BX,ByHowMuch}
18               $26/$01/$1D/           {ADD ES:[DI],BX}
19               $47/                   {INC DI}
20               $47/                   {INC DI}
21               $E2/$FA);             {LOOP -6}
22
23       END;
24
25
26       BEGIN
27         ClrScr;
28         { First, zero out the array: }
29         FillChar(Scores,SizeOf(Scores),Chr(0));
30         FOR I := 0 TO 10 DO
31           Writeln(Scores[I]);   { Show first ten values }
32         Readln;
33         Increment(Scores,72);   { Increment the array }
34         FOR I := 0 TO 10 DO
35           Writeln(Scores[I]);   { Show first ten values again }
36         Readln
37       END.
```

Procedure **Increment** is the star of this show. It adds a specific number (given in **ByHowMuch**) to every element of a 16,000-element integer array. For large arrays, this can be time-consuming; therefore, writing a process like this in machine code can be worthwhile in terms of time saved.

Scores, the array to be incremented, is passed to procedure **Increment** as a VAR parameter. Its address is therefore passed on the stack, and the sequence **$C4/$BE/Scores** copies the address from the stack, placing the segment portion in ES and the offset portion in DI. The number of elements in the array (16,000) is loaded as immediate data into register CX. The value parameter **ByHowMuch** is copied from the stack into register BX.

So much for setup. What happens next is an 8086 loop. **Increment**'s real work is done by the ADD instruction coded as the sequence **$26/$01/$1D**. (Notice the ES prefix.) The value in register BX is added to the word pointed to by ES:DI. At the outset, this is the first element of the array **Scores**. Now, after the first element of the array has been processed, the DI register is incremented twice. Why? Each element of **Scores** is an integer, and integers are two bytes long. The idea is to point ES:DI to the *next* integer in **Scores**. DI has to be incremented by two to move past both bytes of the integer it is currently pointing to, so it can point to the next integer in line.

The LOOP instruction is a goodie. It decrements the value in CX (which is the number of elements in **Scores**) and then branches *back* by six bytes. If you count six bytes back from the LOOP opcode, you'll find yourself back at the beginning of the ADD opcode, ready to process the next element of **Scores**.

This loop executes again and again, each time decrementing the count in CX. When CX eventually gets to zero, LOOP ceases to branch back, and simply passes control on to the next instruction. In this case, there are no more instructions in the **INLINE** statement, so procedure **Increment** finishes up and returns to the main program.

Notice that −6 is represented in binary fashion as $FA. $FA is the two's complement of 6, and, in the 8086 world, the negative of a number is given by its two's complement. You can calculate two's complements easily by using a programmer's calculator, or the calculator in Borland International's Sidekick desk organizer program.

I coded the machine-code portion of **Increment** as a single **INLINE** statement here, as this is standard practice, rather than placing each separate machine instruction in its own **INLINE** statement as I have been doing so far for clarity's sake.

Once you have a pointer to your VAR parameter loaded into ES:DI, accessing VAR parameters is no more difficult than accessing data in value parameters or subprogram local variables.

There is a truly obnoxious misstatement in the Turbo Pascal V3.0 Reference Manual concerning parameter passing. On page 224, while describing the details of parameter passing, the manual says:

"Even when used as value parameters, **Array** *and* **Record** *parameters are not actually passed on the stack. Instead, two words containing the base address and offset of the first byte of the parameter are transferred. It is then the responsibility of the subroutine to use this information to make a local copy of the variable."*

This simply isn't true. *All* value parameters are passed on the stack, no matter how big they are. I'm not sure where a subprogram would put a local copy of a large value parameter *except* on the stack.

Pointer References from INLINE

One other use of the ES:DI addressing mode from **INLINE** involves accessing dynamic variables from within an **INLINE** statement, through pointers. Like a VAR parameter, a pointer is a 32-bit address that specifies some location within the 8086's 1-megabyte address space. Also like a VAR parameter, a pointer can be loaded into the ES and DI registers, and the pointer's referent (the variable it points to) can be accessed using the same opcodes one would use to access a VAR parameter. The only difference between working with VAR parameters and working with pointers is the way ES and DI are loaded via the LES instruction.

First of all, keep this (rather confusing) fact in mind: A VAR parameter and a pointer passed to a subprogram as a value parameter are identical on a binary basis. After all, a VAR parameter *is* a pointer to the actual parameter, even though it is not called a "pointer" in the parameter declaration. Therefore, the *same* LES opcodes can be used for both VAR parameters and pointers passed as value parameters:

```
INLINE($C4/$BE/Scores      {LES DI,[BP+<offset>]}
       $26/$01/$1D)        {ADD ES:[DI],BX}
```

This example demonstrates this feature. Here, the identifier **Scores** could be *either* a VAR parameter (as it was in the previous example program **FastIncrement** *or* a pointer passed to the subprogram containing the **INLINE** statement as a value parameter. In either case, an address has been passed to the subprogram on the stack, under the identifier **Scores**. **LES** takes this address from the stack and loads the segment portion into **ES** and the offset portion into **DI**. The second opcode adds the contents of register **BX** to whatever is pointed to by the address passed on the stack—whether that address was a VAR parameter or a pointer passed as a value parameter.

Pointers, of course, do not have to be passed as parameters. Using a pointer declared as a global variable requires a different LES opcode than the one shown above. A pointer declared as a global variable is simply an address stored in Turbo Pascal's data segment, and it has an offset from data-segment base address in the DS register. The addressing method is the same used with any global variable; that is, as a 16-bit offset from DS. Assuming a pointer **MyPtr** is declared as a global variable, the LES opcode would look like this:

```
INLINE($C4/$3E/MyPtr/          {LES DI,DS:[<offset>]}
       $26/$80/$05/$03);       {ADD WORD PTR ES:[DI],03H}
```

Again, only the second opcode byte is different; **LES** always has an initial opcode byte of **$C4**. Turbo Pascal replaces the global identifier **MyPtr** with **MyPtr**'s offset from the DS register, which is what the **$C4/$3E** opcode requires.

A short program demonstrating pointer access from **INLINE** is given below. A pointer (**MyPtr**) is declared as a variable, and an integer variable is allocated on the heap and given to **MyPtr** as its referent. This dynamic integer variable is given a value of 42 through a normal assignment statement. Then, the **INLINE** statement accesses the dynamic variable pointed to by **MyPtr** and adds 3 to it. The value of **MyPtr**^ is displayed before and after to prove that these shenanigans actually work.

For dynamic variables larger than integers, the offset value in DI may be increased or decreased so that ES:DI points to different parts of the dynamic variable. Keep in mind that on an assembler level within **INLINE**, you can only access one byte or one word (two bytes) at a time. To access larger data items, you must loop through them, incrementing or decrementing DI after each access.

```
PROGRAM PointerINLINE;

TYPE
  IntPtr = ^Integer;

VAR
  MyPtr : IntPtr;

BEGIN
  ClrScr;
  New(MyPtr);
  MyPtr^ := 42;
  Writeln('Before: ',MyPtr^);
```

```
INLINE($C4/$3E/MyPtr/          {LES DI,MyPtr}
       $26/$80/$05/$03);       {ADD WORD PTR ES:[DI],03H}
Writeln( 'After: ',MyPtr^);    {'45' should be new value.}
Readln
END.
```

4.4   A Summary of Register/Memory Operations from INLINE

By now, you should be getting the hang of coding up short assembly-language sequences via **INLINE**. The real trick—aside from knowing where things are—lies in getting the assembly-language mnemonic translated correctly into one or more binary opcodes. Most of the examples in the previous section involved the MOV opcode, since that is one of the simplest and commonest of assembly-language operations.

There are a number of other 8086 instructions that can be made to operate on variables and value parameters in a similar fashion. These operations include addition, subtraction, AND, OR, XOR, exchange, compare, and test. In all of these cases, the opcode you must place in the **INLINE** statement consists of two bytes. The first byte specifies the operation (unless the first byte is a segment-override prefix), and the second byte specifies which register is acting or acted upon. In all cases, a Pascal identifier must be supplied to **INLINE** that specifies which parameter or local variable is acting or being acted upon.

All of these operations can be performed on either 8-bit or 16-bit operands. The opcode bytes are *not* the same in both cases. In all operations, the results of the operation (for example, the sum when you add memory to a register) are placed in the first operand. In other words, for ADD rr,mm, the sum is placed in the register.

To assemble an opcode from the tables on pages 114-115, first decide which operation you want to perform—say, subtract with borrow (SBB). The opcodes exist in two types of pairs, depending on whether the results of the operation are to be placed in the variable or in the register. Choose the destination for the results and pick one of the two alternative rows:

```
SBB mm,rr    Difference is placed in the variable (mm)

SBB rr,mm    Difference is placed in the register (rr)
```

Then, decide whether the operation is performed on 8-bit or 16-bit operands. Move across to either the 8-bit column or the 16-bit column, as appropriate. There's your first opcode byte!

Choose the second opcode byte from the Second-byte Tables on pages 115-116. First, zero in on one of the four tables by deciding the addressing method your operation is to use. In Turbo Pascal **INLINE** terms, this comes down to deciding whether you're working with subprogram value parameters or local variables (which are addressed as offsets from BP); global variables (addressed as offsets from DS); or subprogram VAR parameters (addressed through the 32-bit address you must construct in ES:DI); There is one table for global variables and another for subprogram VAR parameters. But . . . there are *two* tables for subprogram local variables and value parameters.

Subprogram local variables and value parameters are addressed as offsets from BP. In 99.9999999 percent of the cases, that offset will be an 8-bit quantity. (In other words, the offset will be 255 bytes or less.) There is a table for local variables and value parameters where the offset is an 8-bit quantity. I'm also including the table to use when you are ranging more than 255 bytes from BP. This is obviously a *lot* of stack space to be traversing, and it won't happen often—but when it does, choose the 16-bit offset table.

Now that you have decided which second-byte table to use, the only remaining decision is which register to apply. Find the register that will be involved in your operation, and move down to find your second byte. Finally, if you're using ES as the segment register in accessing a VAR parameter, insert the $26 ES segment-override prefix *in front of* the opcodes you have just assembled. And that's all there is to it!

Follow this process using the examples listed below until you're sure you know what you're doing:

```
SUB  Parm8,AH        INLINE($28/$66/Parm8);
XOR  SI,Global16     INLINE($33/$36/Global16);
ADC  BL,Local8       INLINE($12/$5E/Local8);
OR   DX,Parm16       INLINE($0B/$96/Parm16);
SBB  Local16,DI      INLINE($19/$BE/Local16);
CMP  Global8,CH      INLINE($38/$2E/Global8);
```

("Parm" = parameter)

First Opcode Bytes for Register/Memory Operations

	First opcode byte	
	16-bit mm/rr	8-bit m/r
ADC mm,rr Add with carry	$11	$10
ADC rr,mm	$13	$12
ADD mm,rr Add	$01	$00
ADD rr,mm	$03	$02

AND	mm,rr	Logical AND	$21	$20
AND	rr,mm		$23	$22
CMP	mm,rr	Compare	$39	$38
CMP	rr,mm		$3B	$3A
MOV	mm,rr	Move	$89	$88
MOV	rr,mm		$8B	$8A
OR	mm,rr	Logical OR	$09	$08
OR	rr,mm		$0B	$0A
SBB	mm,rr	Sub. w. borrow	$19	$18
SBB	rr,mm		$1B	$1A
SUB	mm,rr	Subtract	$29	$28
SUB	rr,mm		$2B	$2A
TEST	rr,mm	Test bit(s)	$85	$84
XCHG	rr,mm	Exchange	$87	$86
XOR	mm,rr	Logical XOR	$31	$30
XOR	rr,mm		$33	$32

All operations must be coded as:
INLINE(<Byte1>/<Byte2>/<identifier>);

For example:
ADD DX,Fum   codes as   **INLINE($03/$96/Fum);**

Second-byte Tables

For use with VAR parameters:
i.e., where mm is ES: [DI]
(Don't forget the $26 segment override prefix!)

register =	AX	BX	CX	DX	BP	SI	DI	SP
	AL	BL	CL	DL	CH	DH	BH	AH
	$05	$1D	$0D	$15	$2D	$35	$3D	$25

For use with global variables:
i.e., where mm is [DS+<offset>]

register =	AX	BX	CX	DX	BP	SI	DI	SP
	AL	BL	CL	DL	CH	DH	BH	AH
	$06	$1E	$0E	$16	$2E	$36	$3E	$26

For use with local variables and value parameters:
i.e., where mm is [BP+<offset>]

For use with an 8-bit <offset>:

register =	AX	BX	CX	DX	BP	SI	DI	SP
	AL	BL	CL	DL	CH	DH	BH	AH
	$46	$5E	$4E	$56	$6E	$76	$7E	$66

For use with a 16-bit <offset>:

register =	AX	BX	CX	DX	BP	SI	DI	SP
	AL	BL	CL	DL	CH	DH	BH	AH
	$86	$9E	$8E	$96	$AE	$B6	$BE	$A6

Selecting opcodes for operations that take place between registers or between registers and immediate data is much less complex; it is straightforward enough, in fact, to allow the generation of a (large) table containing all the various combinations. This table (called the Eyeball INLINE Assembler) can be found in Appendix A.

4.5 Writing External Machine-code Subprograms

Popular as it is, there are two good reasons not to do any considerable amount of machine-code work in **INLINE**:

1. *It's too much work.* Cobbling up a complicated MOV opcode by hand can take up to a minute or longer. An assembler can generate hundreds of them per second. Also, each time you insert an instruction into the middle of an **INLINE** statement, you must recalculate (manually) every offset and jump destination. (At the risk of sounding too flip, I have to say, hey, man, that's what *computers* are for.)

2. *There are many more ways to go wrong.* (This is both a corollary and a consequence of reason #1.) Calculate an opcode or an offset wrong by a single bit, and your program runs off into the bushes. Assemblers do such things perfectly every time. Assembly language is hard enough to do well without having one eye closed and one arm in a sling.

To do machine-code work properly, buy Microsoft's Macro Assembler and write your machine-code subprograms as Turbo Pascal external routines. Once you do this, you'll wonder why you ever bothered with **INLINE**. Throughout this section (throughout this entire book, in fact), when I refer to "the assembler" or "MASM," I am referring to Microsoft's Macro Assembler

V4.0, which is current as of this writing. It is possible to use other assemblers, but I make no promises that the pseudo-opcodes or even the assembly-language mnemonics will be the same. In particular, the popular "shareware" assembler CHASM (CHeap ASseMbler) does not follow Microsoft's conventions, and the source files given here will not work under it.

I recommend creating a separate subdirectory on your hard disk (if you are using one) for MASM. MASM comes with a number of utilities that are best not mixed with all your Turbo Pascal work. Gaining easy access to MASM's subdirectory is done by adding the name of the subdirectory to your PATH statement:

```
PATH C:\DOS;C:\TURBO;C:\UTILS;C:\MASM
```

This path statement includes the names of four subdirectories: **DOS**, **TURBO**, **UTILS**, and **MASM**. Yours may be different, and they may be in any order—just as long as both **TURBO** and **MASM** are in the list somewhere.

Turbo Pascal's facility for handling externally assembled machine-code subprograms is simple and works well. A typical external machine-code subprogram declaration looks like this:

```
PROCEDURE Foo(Bar,Bas : Integer); EXTERNAL 'FOO.BIN';
```

Basically, when the Turbo Pascal code generator encounters the reserved word **EXTERNAL**, it stops creating object code from source and opens the filename immediately following **EXTERNAL**. It then draws its code from the external code file until the code file ends. Then, normal Pascal code generation resumes with the statement following the **EXTERNAL** subprogram definition statement.

In building external machine-code subprograms, it is critical to understand exactly what has already been done by the code generator before the first opcode in the external file is executed. As described in Section 4.3, all parameters are pushed onto the stack (preceded by a function result in some cases), followed by the 16-bit return address offset into the code segment.

The Absolute Minimum External Assembly-language File

A good way to begin explaining how to set up an external assembly-language program is to show you the least involved file you can successfully pass through MASM:

```
MYCODE   SEGMENT  PUBLIC
         ASSUME   CS:MYCODE
         PUBLIC   GRONK
```

```
GRONK      PROC       NEAR
GRONK      ENDP
MYCODE     ENDS
           END
```

This little snippet will successfully assemble, but no code will be generated, as there are no actual assembly-language mnemonics in it. (I wrote this example in uppercase strictly as a typographical convention. It may date me, but I am more comfortable reading assembly language in uppercase. You can use any combination of uppercase and lowercase that pleases you, since the assembler, like Turbo Pascal, forces all lowercase characters to uppercase internally before using them.)

The symbol **MYCODE** names a code segment that we are creating. The **PUBLIC** declaration is vestigial in a sense, since we are not going to link the code to an .OBJ file. The **ASSUME** directive is important, since it tells the assembler that the segment value for certain operations that work on the code segment is to be found in CS. Certain peculiar tricks can be accomplished by making this some *other* register at some point within the program—say, by assuming that the code-segment value is in SS. (Microsoft's BASICA obtains some of its graphics speed by executing code on the stack, but the thought of doing that makes my hair curl.)

Within the segment **MYCODE** is an assembly-language procedure called **GRONK**. To the assembler, **GRONK** is a **PROC**, whether it was declared as a function or as a procedure in the Pascal program. In assembly language, there is no syntactic difference between a Pascal function and a Pascal procedure; the difference is in the way the Pascal program treats register values left behind by the external subprogram.

GRONK is a "near" procedure, or *near proc*, meaning that it exists within some larger code segment and is located by a 16-bit offset within that code segment. Remember that in a Turbo Pascal program, there is only one code segment, and that code segment encompasses external subprograms as well as Pascal code. One consequence of declaring **GRONK** as a near proc is that it will expect a 16-bit return address offset on that stack at return time rather than a full 32-bit 8086 machine address.

Although **GRONK** is the only proc named in this particular file, there can be any number of procs within segment **MYCODE**, assuming that together they contain less than 64K of code. The **GRONK ENDP** directive tells the assembler that the proc is finished, and the **MYCODE ENDS** directive tells the assembler that segment **MYCODE** is finished. Finally, the **END** directive tells the assembler that the source file is finished.

A word about names used in external assembly-language files: There is *no* necessary correspondence between identifiers used in your Pascal program and symbols used in your assembly-language source file. In other words, the symbol **GRONK** does *not* have to appear in your Pascal source file. Pascal can call the external procedure or function anything it likes. The **MYCODE** symbol is there only to keep the assembler happy, since the assembly-language files we'll be discussing do not define more than one segment within a file. Assembly-language files are cooked down into .COM files (more on this shortly), which are pure memory images and contain *no* assembler symbols at all—only opcodes and offsets.

A Boilerplate External Assembly-language Source File

In Section 4.4, we described what happens when Turbo Pascal instantiates a subprogram. For externals, the compiler will push function results, parameters, and the return address onto the stack, but everything from that point on must be done by the external routine.

The most important task here is the saving of the old BP on the stack, and the saving of the stack-pointer value as the new value of BP. Any external subprogram *with* parameters must perform these steps; a subprogram *without* parameters won't be especially useful.

I have set up a "boilerplate" external assembly-language source file that builds this necessary BP management into our minimal source-code file, and adds a comment header. I cannot overemphasize the importance of commenting in assembly-language files. *One comment per line* is often called "the IBM standard for commenting code." One comment per line (as far as I'm concerned) is the *minimum* safe level of commenting. Comment until your friends can read it and understand it—then you're probably safe.

```
1    ;=============================================================================
2    ;
3    ;     B O I L E R  -  Boilerplate external assembly language source file
4    ;
5    ;=============================================================================
6    ;
7    ;
8    ;
9    ;
10   ;
11   ;
12   ; BOILER is written to be called from Turbo Pascal V3.0 using the
13   ; EXTERNAL procedure convention.
14   ;
15   ; Declare the procedure itself as external using this declaration:
```

(continued)

```
16              ;
17              ; PROCEDURE Boiler; EXTERNAL 'BOILER.BIN';
18              ;
19              ; To reassemble/relink BOILER:
20              ;------------------------------------
21              ; 1. Assemble this file with MASM.   "C>MASM BOILER;"
22              ; 2. Link it into a .EXE file.       "C>LINK BOILER;"
23              ; 3. Use EXE2BIN to make a .COM file. "A> EXE2BIN BOILER.EXE BOILER.COM"
24              ; 4. Declare as shown above in your Turbo Pascal program.
25              ; 5. Ignore any minor diagnostic messages that may be generated when
26              ;    this file is assembled and linked.  EXE2BIN is supplied with the
27              ;    supplemental programs for PC-DOS; see the DOS manual.
28              ;
29
30      CODE    SEGMENT PUBLIC
31              ASSUME  CS:CODE
32              PUBLIC  BOILER
33
34      BOILER  PROC    NEAR
35              PUSH    BP                      ;SAVE PREVIOUS VALUE OF BP ON STACK
36              MOV     BP,SP                   ;SP BECOMES NEW VALUE OF BP
37
38
39              ; THE BODY OF YOUR EVENTUAL PROC GOES HERE...
40
41
42              MOV     SP,BP                   ; RESTORE PRIOR STACK POINTER & BP
43              POP     BP                      ;   IN CONVENTIONAL RETURN
44              RET
45
46      BOILER  ENDP
47      CODE    ENDS
48              END
```

Turning Source Code into External Machine-code Files

There are three steps required to turn a syntactically correct assembly-language source file into an external machine-code file suitable for loading into a Turbo Pascal program. They are as follows:

   1. *Assembly*. This is done by invoking MASM. MASM reads the source-code file, performs its magic, and writes out a relocatable object module to disk. This module is actually a DOS file. The filename is the same as the name of your source file, but with an added extension of .OBJ.

   From the DOS prompt, a successful MASM session looks like this:

```
C:>MASM BOILER;

Microsoft (R) Macro Assembler Version 4.00
Copyright (C) Microsoft Corp 1981, 1983, 1984, 1985. All
rights reserved

51062 Bytes symbol space free

    0 Warning Errors
    0 Severe Errors

C:>
```

Note the semicolon after **BOILER**. It tells **MASM** that you want all the standard defaults for code and listing files. If you omit the semicolon, **MASM** will ask you a series of questions about the names you wish to give the various output files. While this is not harmful to the operation, it will prevent you from automatically generating finished machine-code files from a batch-command file (described in detail shortly).

2. *Linking.* All the really hard work is done by the assembler. It fathoms out the logic of the source-code file and selects the correct 8088 opcodes to correspond to specific assembler mnemonics. The linker's job is simpler in our case, since it really doesn't have to link anything together. Our machine-code file is a lonely creature, self-sufficient and without any need to call upon routines contained in other code files on disk.

But the linker must go through the motions anyway. In the process, it converts the output of the assembler (an .OBJ file) to a DOS executable file, which has the same filename as your source file, but with the extension .EXE.

Here is a typical linker session:

```
C:>LINK BOILER;

IBM Personal Computer Linker
Version 2.30 (C) Copyright IBM Corp. 1981, 1985

Warning: no stack segment

C:>
```

As with MASM, the semicolon after **LINK** in the command line instructs **LINK** to use all the default names in processing your file. It will look for **BOILER.OBJ** in our example, and output **BOILER.EXE**.

The warning message can be safely ignored. There is indeed no stack segment in any Turbo Pascal external machine-code file (which is, in fact, a good thing).

3. *Converting .EXE to pure binary.* An .EXE file is actually an executable file, but not one that can be executed from inside a Turbo Pascal program. It

contains a header full of information useful to DOS but irrelevant to Turbo Pascal. To make use of the file, it must be converted to pure binary by lopping off the header and cleaning up a few other things as well.

There is a DOS utility called EXE2BIN that performs this function. It accepts an .EXE file and outputs a pure binary memory image of the assembled machine code. A *memory image* is simply a disk file that is equivalent byte for byte to the machine code as it will exist and execute in memory. No other processing of the file will be done in moving it between disk and memory.

The third step is the simplest of all:

```
C:>EXE2BIN BOILER.EXE BOILER.BIN

C:>
```

After **EXE2BIN** runs, you will have the file **BOILER.BIN** on disk. **BOILER .BIN** is the actual disk file that will be read into memory by Turbo Pascal when it compiles a Pascal program with a subprogram declared as **EXTERNAL**. (Many people give the binary file an extension of .COM, but I avoid that, since a .COM file can be executed from the command prompt, and executing an external machine-code procedure will almost certainly crash your machine hard. I believe in making accidents as unlikely as possible.)

All three steps can be executed automatically with minimal keystroking on your part by creating a batch file that can be run from DOS. *Batch* is a sort of pseudo-language understood by the DOS command processor. It executes DOS commands and programs in sequence, and has some capability to test the results of programs—typically through a DOS flag called ERRORLEVEL— and branch. (Batch has been discussed in many other books; therefore, I won't explain it in detail here.) The following batch file should serve all your simple Turbo Pascal external machine-code file generation work. The logic in it should be obvious, even if you aren't familiar with batch files:

```
MASM %1;
IF ERRORLEVEL 1 GOTO EXIT
LINK %1;
IF ERRORLEVEL 1 GOTO EXIT
EXE2BIN %1.EXE %1.BIN
IF ERRORLEVEL 1 GOTO EXIT
REM External file %1.BIN created successfully
:EXIT
```

The **%1** allows substitution of a name from the command line. You can name this batch file anything you like; I call mine CREATE.BAT. When you invoke this batch file:

```
C:>CREATE BOILER
```

the word **BOILER** is substituted anywhere the batch file finds **%1**. Note that the file extension for the batch file *must* be .BAT, or DOS will not recognize it as a batch file.

Each of the three steps is tested for successful completion by testing the state of the **ERRORLEVEL** flag. Normal completion of **MASM**, **LINK**, or **EXE2BIN** sets **ERRORLEVEL** to 0. Any error will set it to 1 or higher. The batch **IF** tests for the specified value *or any higher value*. In other words, if **MASM** returned an error code of 7 (and there are lots of MASM error codes), the batch file would still recognize it as an error and terminate immediately, even though the specified value in the batch file is 1.

With the batch file underway, you can go back to the fridge for another Mountain Dew and let the machine crunch without being afraid of missing an error. Unless you see the message

```
REM External file BOILER.BAT created successfully
```

when you get back, you'll know something didn't work correctly.

A Simple External Machine-code Routine

Now that the mechanics are in place, it's time to look at a useful real-world example of a Turbo Pascal external machine-code procedure. This first example is conceptually simple, so even if you haven't yet studied 8088 assembly language in great detail, you should be able to follow it. (In Chapter 5 I'll describe a whole suite of Pascal routines for performing text video I/O on "virtual" screens allocated and stored on the heap. These screens are accessed by way of pointers, and can be "flashed" into the visible screen buffer by using Turbo Pascal's built-in **Move** procedure.)

One benefit of using my routines over Turbo Pascal's built-in video routines is that mine peek at the screen-size bytes stored in the first 128 bytes of every Turbo Pascal program (see Section 2.2) and configure themselves to the appropriate screen size. Without recompiling, a single program can work with ordinary 80×25 screens, the 80×16 screens found on many lapheld portables, or the enormous MDS Genius VHR 80×66 screen (which I use for most of my work these days).

Whenever you have screens, you will have a need to clear them occasionally. Turbo's **ClrScr** routine clears only the visible buffer. Furthermore, it only clears screens to blank (i.e., fills the screen with space characters—ASCII character 32). There are several "halftone" characters in the high half of the IBM PC's character set (characters 176–178). Clearing a text screen to one of those halftone characters can impart a certain classy look to your screens, reminiscent of Ashton-Tate's elegant Framework product.

The assembly-language external routine **ClearScreen** addresses all of these issues. The actual machine-code file is stored on disk under the name **CLEARS.BIN**. It is defined this way:

```
PROCEDURE ClearScreen(Target : ScreenPtr; ScreenSize : Integer;
                      Attribute : Integer; CharFill : Byte);
                      EXTERNAL 'CLEARS.BIN';
```

You pass it **TARGET**, a pointer to the screen you wish cleared. A pointer to the visible screen is generated easily enough by using Turbo Pascal's **Ptr** function; screens on the heap already have pointers linking them to reality. Since a screen, as understood by the Pascal program, may be a different size at different times, a size parameter, **ScreenSize**, must also be passed to **ClearScreen**. **ScreenSize** specifies the total size in bytes of the buffer being cleared. Making sure the pointer **Target** points to a buffer that is actually **ScreenSize** bytes long is up to the programmer; clear a larger buffer than the one **Target** points to and you could destroy essential things contained in memory, leading to corrupted data or program crashes.

ClearScreen can specify both the attribute of the characters filling the buffer and the characters themselves. In other words, you can fill a buffer with underlined space characters, or high-intensity halftone characters if you like. Note that parameter **Attribute** is declared as an integer, and that the actual attribute information must be placed in the *high* eight bits of the integer value. In other words, if you want to use an attribute byte of $07 (for normal text), you must pass a value of $0700 in **Attribute**. (This was done to make attribute handling a little easier for several other routines that will be discussed in Chapter 5, along with additional information on **ClearScreen**.)

```
 1  ;==========================================================================
 2  ;
 3  ;      C L E A R S C R E E N   -   Screen clear primitive for Turbo Pascal
 4  ;
 5  ;==========================================================================
 6  ;
 7  ;
 8  ;
 9  ;
10  ;
11  ;
12  ; CLEARSCREEN is written to be called from Turbo Pascal V3.0 using the
13  ; EXTERNAL procedure convention.  It has the advantage over ClrScr in that
14  ; it can clear a screen stored on the heap, and also that a screen can be
15  ; cleared with a character other than space, like the IBM PC's halftone
16  ; characters, for the Framework effect.  An attribute can be written to the
17  ; cleared buffer as well as a clear character.
```

(continued)

```
18      ;
19      ; To use CLEARSCREEN, you must have predeclared a screen array and a
20      ; pointer type to that screen array.  For a typical 25 X 80 screen, these
21      ; declarations would like like this:
22      ;
23      ; TYPE
24      ;   Screen    = ARRAY[0..1999] OF Integer;
25      ;   ScreenPtr = ^Screen;
26      ;
27      ; To use CLEARSCREEN on the visible screen, you must "doctor" a declared
28      ; pointer to point to either the monochrome or graphics text buffer:
29      ;
30      ; VAR
31      ;   VisibleScreen : ScreenPtr;
32      ;
33      ; VisibleScreen := Ptr($B000,0);  { For the monochrome adapter }
34      ; VisibleScreen := Ptr($B800,0);  { For the color graphics adapter }
35      ;
36      ; Declare the procedure itself as external using this declaration:
37      ;
38      ; PROCEDURE CLEARSCREEN(Target : ScreenPtr; ScreenSize : Integer;
39      ;                       Attribute : Integer; CharFill : Byte);
40      ;                       EXTERNAL 'CLEARS.BIN'
41      ;
42      ;
43      ; Pass CLEARSCREEN the attribute code you wish to use in Attribute
44      ; (typically $0700 for "normal" text display) and the character to "clear"
45      ; with in CharFill.  Use 32 or Ord(' ') to fill with blanks, or you may use
46      ; the "halftone" characters (176-178) for Framework style screens.  Keep
47      ; in mind that the attribute code must be in the HIGH byte of the actual
48      ; parameter passed to Attribute.
49      ;
50      ; EXAMPLES:
51      ;
52      ; To clear the visible screen to normal blanks:
53      ;     CLEARSCREEN(VisibleScreen,4096,$0700,' ');
54      ;
55      ; To clear a screen on the heap to a halftone screen:
56      ;     CLEARSCREEN(NewScreen,4096,$0700,176);
57      ;
58      ; Obviously, you must have declared VisibleScreen and NewScreen and set
59      ; them up so that they both point to either a screen on the heap or the
60      ; visible screen buffer.  If the pointer Target has a value of NIL,
61      ; CLEARSCREEN will return to the calling logic without taking any action.
62      ; Good thing, too--if it did, it would blank your interrupt vector table!
63      ;
64      ;
65      ; To reassemble/relink CLEARSCREEN:
66      ;---------------------------------------
```

(continued)

```
67        ; 1. Assemble this file with MASM.   "A> MASM CLEARS;"
68        ; 2. Link it into a .EXE file.       "A> LINK CLEARS;"
69        ; 3. Use EXE2BIN to make a .COM file. "A> EXE2BIN CLEARS.EXE CLEARS.COM"
70        ; 4. Declare as shown above in your Turbo Pascal program.
71        ; 5. Ignore any minor diagnostic messages that may be generated when
72        ;      this file is assembled and linked.  EXE2BIN is supplied with the
73        ;      supplemental programs for PC-DOS; see the DOS manual.
74        ;
75
76        CODE    SEGMENT PUBLIC
77                ASSUME  CS:CODE
78                PUBLIC  CLEARS
79        ;
80        ; This structure maps the stack at entry to CLEARSCREEN:
81        ;
82        ONSTACK STRUC
83        OLDBP   DW ?     ;CALLER'S BP VALUE SAVED ON STACK
84        RETADDR DW ?     ;RETURN ADDRESS OFFSET
85        FILLER  DW ?     ;CHARACTER THAT FILLS THE CLEARED BUFFER
86        ATTRIB  DW ?     ;ATTRIBUTE FOR THE CLEARED BUFFER
87        BUFSIZE DW ?     ;SIZE OF THE BUFFER TO BE CLEARED, IN BYTES
88        BUFOFS  DW ?     ;OFFSET OF BUFFER ORIGIN
89        BUFSEG  DW ?     ;SEGMENT OF BUFFER ORIGIN
90        ENDMRK  DB ?     ;DUMMY LABEL TO MARK END OF DATA ON STACK
91        ONSTACK ENDS
92        ;
93
94
95        CLEARS  PROC    NEAR
96                PUSH    BP
97                MOV     BP,SP                       ; CALLING CONVENTION
98        ;
99        ;----------------------------------------------------
100       ; FIRST WE TEST FOR BUFFER = NIL...QUIT IF SO
101       ;----------------------------------------------------
102       ;
103               CMP     WORD PTR [BP].BUFSEG,0  ; A NIL POINTER IS A SEGMENT AND
104               JNE     START                   ; OFFSET BOTH SET TO 0
105               CMP     WORD PTR [BP].BUFOFS,0
106               JE      BYE
107
108       ;
109       ;----------------------------------------------------
110       ; PREPARE THE REGISTERS FOR THE STORE WORD OPERATION
111       ;----------------------------------------------------
112       ;
113       START:  CLD                                 ; CLEAR DIRECTION FLAG
114               MOV     AX,[BP].ATTRIB              ; LOAD ATTRIBUTE CODE INTO AX
115               AND     AX,0FF00H                  ; MASK OUT LOW BYTE OF ATTRIBUTE CODE
```

(continued)

```
116                   MOV      BX,[BP].FILLER          ; LOAD FILLER CODE INTO BX
117                   AND      BX,0FFH                 ; MASK OUT HIGH BYTE OF FILLER CODE
118                   OR       AX,BX                   ; AND COMBINE ATTRIB & FILLER INTO AX
119                   MOV      BX,[BP].BUFOFS          ; SET DI TO TARGET BUFFER OFFSET
120                   MOV      DI,BX                   ;   BY WAY OF BX
121                   MOV      BX,[BP].BUFSEG          ; SET ES TO TARGET BUFFER SEGMENT
122                   MOV      ES,BX                   ;   BY WAY OF BX
123          ;
124          ;-----------------------------------------------------------------
125          ; LOOP TO STORE CHARACTER AND ATTRIBUTE INTO BUFFER BY WORD MOVE
126          ;-----------------------------------------------------------------
127          ;
128                   MOV      CX,[BP].BUFSIZE         ; SET UP COUNTER WITH BUFFER SIZE
129                   REP      STOSW                   ; DO THE STRING STORE
130          ;
131          ;------------------------------------------
132          ; DONE.. CLEAN UP THE STACK AND LEAVE
133          ;------------------------------------------
134          ;
135          BYE:     MOV      SP,BP                   ; RESTORE PRIOR STACK POINTER & BP
136                   POP      BP                      ;   IN CONVENTIONAL RETURN
137                   RET      ENDMRK-RETADDR-2        ; TRASH 10 BYTES FOR PARMS
138
139          CLEARS   ENDP
140          CODE     ENDS
141                   END
```

As I've said before, the worst part about writing external machine-code routines is passing parameters between Pascal and the external routine. The parameters are on the stack when the external routine takes over; that much, at least, is done for you.

But getting material off the stack takes a little care. As explained earlier, the stack pointer is copied into BP when the external routine begins executing, so that an unmoving base exists from which to reference parameters on the stack. All parameters have to be named by way of an offset from BP. You can do that manually for each parameter, by using an **EQU** (equate) directive:

```
FILLER    EQU    4[BP]
ATTRIB    EQU    6[BP]
BUFSIZE   EQU    8[BP]
BUFOFS    EQU    10[BP]
BUFSEG    EQU    12[BP]
```

This commonly used notation takes the location pointed to by the BP register (indicated by the square brackets around BP) and adds an offset to them. **4[BP]** means "4 higher than the address pointed to by BP."

This system works fine. However, suppose you decide to add another parameter to the list, and insert it between **ATTRIB** and **BUFSIZE**? You would have to manually recalculate all the offsets past **ATTRIB**.

The assembler can do that more reliably than you can. The way to make the assembler do the hard work is to define a *structure* that can be mapped onto the stack. The five equate directives shown above have been replaced (in **ClearScreen**) with the following assembly-language structure:

```
ONSTACK   STRUC
OLDBP     DW      ?   ;CALLER'S BP VALUE SAVED ON STACK
RETADDR   DW      ?   ;RETURN ADDRESS OFFSET
FILLER    DW      ?   ;CHARACTER THAT FILLS THE CLEARED BUFFER
ATTRIB    DW      ?   ;ATTRIBUTE FOR THE CLEARED BUFFER
BUFSIZE   DW      ?   ;SIZE OF BUFFER TO BE CLEARED, IN BYTES
BUFOFS    DW      ?   ;OFFSET OF BUFFER ORIGIN
BUFSEG    DW      ?   ;SEGMENT OF BUFFER ORIGIN
ENDMRK    DB      ?   ;DUMMY LABEL TO MARK END OF DATA ON STACK
ONSTACK   ENDS
```

An assembly-language structure is very much like a record in Pascal. The structure is named **ONSTACK**, and it includes everything between the directive **ONSTACK STRUC** and **ONSTACK ENDS**, just as a Pascal record includes everything between the reserved words **RECORD** and **END**.

Both records and structures have component parts called fields. All of **ONSTACK**'s fields, except **ENDMRK**, are 16-bit words (the directive **DW** means "Define Word"), but they don't have to be; if you had a Boolean function result in the structure, it would be a byte, and you would use the **DB** ("Define Byte") directive instead.

You have probably noticed that there are more fields in **ONSTACK** than there were equate directives in the parameter list given earlier. The fields **OLDBP** and **RETADDR** have been added to the structure, even though (as the sharper among you may have already checked) neither is referenced anywhere within **ClearScreen**. These two new fields are, in fact, placeholders. As you'll remember, when the real work of **ClearScreen** begins, register BP is pointing to the old value of BP, above which is the return address, and above which are the parameters. (Refer back to Figure 4.2.) We don't care what we name **OLDBP** and **RETADDR**; we only need them to hold their places because of the way we reference the individual fields within structure **ON-STACK**.

Like Pascal, assembly-language structures specify individual fields by *dotting*. In other words, to specify the field **PatientAge** in Pascal record **MedHistory**, you would use the notation **MedHistory.PatientAge**. Assembly language isn't quite so easy, unfortunately. In **ClearScreen**, we defined a structure called **ONSTACK** but we didn't say *where* it was; it is at the address pointed to by register BP. In assembly language, we can specify the structure itself by its address rather than its name. In this case, that address is the one contained in BP. Therefore, specifying a field within **ONSTACK** is done with this notation:

```
MOV CX,[BP].BUFSIZE
```

When the assembler encounters notation like this, it is smart enough to figure out that the symbol **BUFSIZE** is a field within a structure called **ON-STACK**, and it counts the appropriate number of bytes up-memory from **[BP]** and grabs the parameter from the structure that we have mapped over the stack. Now, if we are to start the structure at **[BP]**, we have to include the two fields **OLDBP** and **RETADDR** to hold the space between the address contained in **BP** and the location where the parameters actually begin.

Oddly enough, we don't use the structure's name **ONSTACK** at all. The name only exists to keep the assembler happy; it likes every entity in a program to have a name—even if that name is never put to any use within the program.

Once you understand the way parameters on the stack are referenced, understanding the rest of **ClearScreen** is easy. The first block of code is a safety feature. A Pascal pointer is an address, and the address passed to **ClearScreen** as **BUFOFS** and **BUFSEG** becomes the starting point for a buffer that is going to be cleared to some value, wiping out whatever was previously in that buffer.

In Turbo Pascal, a pointer with the value **NIL** is two words of zeroes. If we treated it as an address, it would be 0000:0000, which is the start of the 8088 interrupt vector table—and we really *really* don't want to fill any part of that with anything. Plainly, we have to test for **NIL** pointers and return control to the calling logic without taking any action when a **NIL** pointer is detected. If the two compares both come up with zero (indicating a **NIL** pointer), the routine branches to stack cleanup and returns without doing anything else.

The rest of **ClearScreen** is essentially one operation: a block move of some 16-bit word into the buffer, using the 8088 block-move instruction **STOSW** (STOre String Word). This operation consists mainly of filling registers with the proper values before actually executing the block move itself. The filler character and the attribute byte are combined into one word stored in AX. The segment and offset portions of the pointer indicating the start of the buffer to be cleared are loaded into ES and DI by way of BX. (You can't directly load either ES or DI from memory—in this case, from the stack. You must load from memory into a general purpose register like BX, and from that register into ES or DI.)

Finally, the number of bytes to be moved is stored into the count register CX, and we let 'er rip with **STOSW**. *Zap!* The buffer is filled with whatever was in register AX. After that, we just clean up the stack and go home.

Simple as it is, **ClearScreen** is versatile and very effective. When you use it to clear a screen (even a screen 66 lines high, as mine is), the screen clears *instantaneously*. You simply cannot see the progression of the fill from the top to the bottom of the screen.

Such is the power of assembly language.

Reading the Joystick via Assembly Language

One of the more peculiar omissions from Turbo Pascal V3.0 (considering the kitchen-sink quality of the product otherwise) is joystick interface. This is all the more puzzling because joystick interface is one of those few areas that requires assembly language to work well, even though a crude interface can be cobbled up in Pascal.

A joystick-reading routine is a good second example of external assembly-language subroutines, since it incorporates two VAR parameters that return information to the calling program. Getting information into and out of VAR parameters is much subtler than simply picking value parameters off the stack.

Before we get into the actual assembly language, let's take a look at the IBM PC joystick interface and how it works.

In reading the PC's joystick, we're actually working through a peripheral that IBM refers to as the *game control adapter*. This is either a short-slot expansion board or a feature built into a multifunction board. The joystick itself is a pair of potentiometers (variable resistors) mechanically coupled to the stick itself, in such a way that moving the stick in two dimensions runs the two potentiometers up and down their ranges. One potentiometer records the motion in the X axis, and the other records motion in the Y axis.

The game control adapter board itself is actually a generalized means of reading resistance values attached to its inputs. You can actually use the board as a rather crude ohmmeter of limited range and accuracy, and there is nothing special about the joystick mechanism. Any variable resistance of a suitable range can be read through the adapter.

At the core of the game control adapter is a logic element called a *one-shot*. This is a circuit that maintains an output line at a logic one (high) until a brief input pulse is applied to its input line. Then the output line goes low and stays low until a resistance-capacitance network "times out;" that is, until the resistance bleeds off the charge stored in the capacitor. The lower the resistance, the more quickly the charge will flow out of the capacitor, and the sooner the output line will return high. If graphed against time, this produces long pulses for high resistance values, and short pulses for low resistance values (see Figure 4.7).

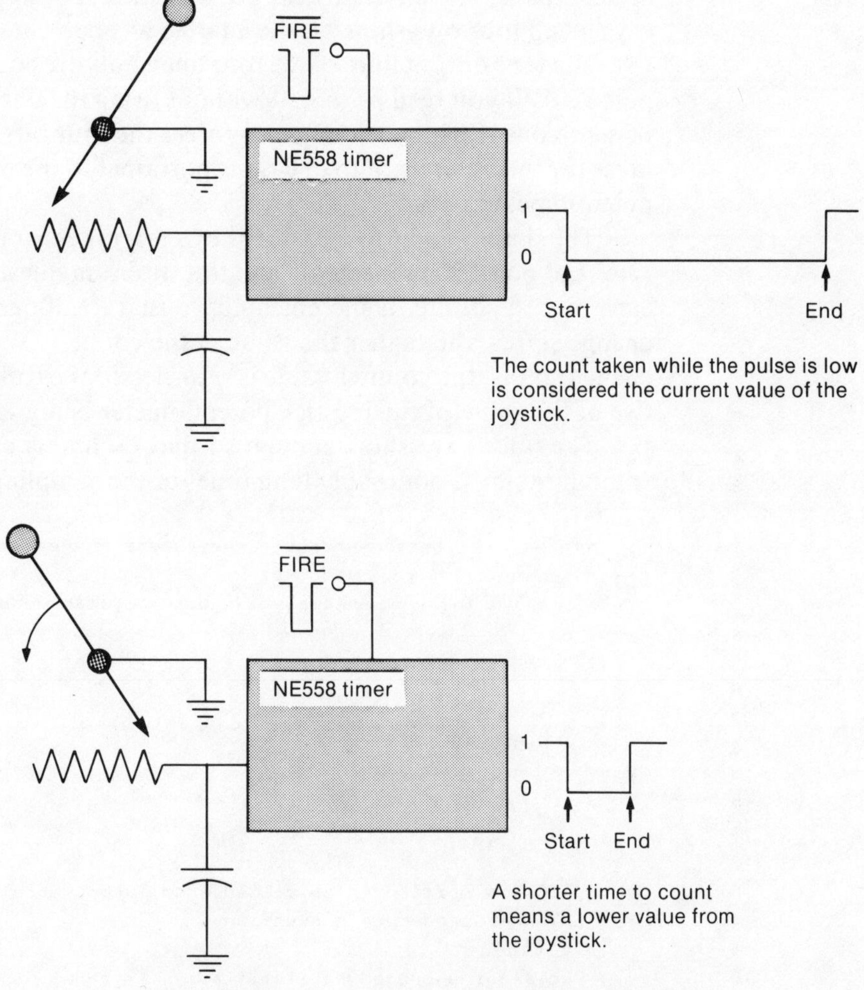

Figure 4.7   **The game controller one-shots**

Each joystick requires two one-shot circuits—one for each axis of the joystick. The resistance is supplied by the two potentiometers in the joystick. On the output side, the output lines of the one-shots are coupled to an I/O port with an address of $201.

Software interface is complicated by the fact that each game control adapter supports up to two joysticks, and both joysticks are sampled at once, whether or not any physical joysticks are connected to the adapter.

Sampling works like this: A value is written to I/O port $201. The value doesn't matter; it can be anything at all. The act of writing to the port is what triggers all four one-shots on the adapter at once.

The four output lines of the four one-shots are coupled to bits 0–3 of I/O port $201. If you read port $201 without firing the one-shots, all four bits will be set to one. Firing the one-shots forces the four bits to zero, and the time it takes for them to return to one is proportional to the resistance of the joystick potentiometers.

The simplest way to measure the time it takes for the bits to change status is to read port $201 repeatedly and test the bit in question until it changes. At each read, a counter is incremented, so that the longer it takes for the bit to change status, the higher the value in the counter. When the bit finally does change status, the counter value is returned to the calling logic as representative of the value of the joystick potentiometer being tested.

The pulses are short enough so that each axis can be tested separately without taking a noticeably long time for the sampling operation.

```
 1          ;==========================================================================
 2          ;
 3          ;    S T I C K  -  Assembly language joystick input for Turbo Pascal
 4          ;
 5          ;==========================================================================
 6          ;
 7          ;
 8          ;
 9          ;
10          ;
11          ;
12          ;
13          ; STICK is written to be called from Turbo Pascal V3.0 using the
14          ; EXTERNAL procedure convention.
15          ;
16          ; Declare the procedure itself as an external using this declaration:
17          ;
18          ;     PROCEDURE STICK(StickNumber : Integer VAR X,Y : Integer);
19          ;                                     EXTERNAL('STICK.BIN');
20          ;
21          ; StickNumber specifies which joystick to read from, and the X and Y
22          ; parameters return integers proportional to the joystick's position
23          ; at the moment the stick is sampled.  These integers will vary from
24          ; stick to stick depending on the resistance of the potentiometers
25          ; used within the stick, but will typically from from 3 to 150.
26          ;
27          ; The IBM standard game controller board consists of two pairs of
28          ; one-shots, which output a pulse when triggered by an I/O write to
29          ; I/O port $201.  The length of this pulse is determined by an RC
30          ; time constant circuit the resistance portion of which is the
```

(continued)

```
31        ; potentiometer in the joystick.  As the handle is moved around, the
32        ; two potentiometers (one for X, one for Y) run up and back, changing
33        ; resistance as they go.
34        ;
35        ; To read one of the two joysticks, a dummy value (which may be anything
36        ; at all) is written to I/O port $201.  Port $201 must then be polled
37        ; continuously, incrementing a register at each polling event.  When
38        ; the bit corresponding to that stick's X or Y coordinate changes state,
39        ; the count in the register is returned as that coordinate value at the
40        ; time the stick was sampled.
41        ;
42        ; Here is a map of the joystick bits as returned by port $201:
43        ;
44        ;      |7 6 5 4 3 2 1 0|
45        ;            | | | |
46        ;            | | | - - - - - - -> X coordinate, joystick #1
47        ;            | | - - - - - - - -> Y coordinate, joystick #1
48        ;            | - - - - - - - - -> X coordinate, joystick #2
49        ;            - - - - - - - - - -> Y coordinate, joystick #2
50        ;
51        ; One thing to keep in mind is that a bit goes LOW when sampled, and
52        ; you must test for a HIGH on that bit to indicate that the one-shot has
53        ; timed out.
54        ;
55        ;
56        ; To reassemble/relink STICK:
57        ;-----------------------------------
58        ; 1. Assemble this file with MASM.  "C>MASM STICK;"
59        ; 2. Link it into a .EXE file.      "C>LINK STICK;"
60        ; 3. Use EXE2BIN to make a .COM file. "A> EXE2BIN STICK.EXE STICK.BIN"
61        ; 4. Declare as shown above in your Turbo Pascal program.
62        ; 5. Ignore any minor diagnostic messages that may be generated when
63        ;    this file is assembled and linked.  EXE2BIN is supplied with the
64        ;    supplemental programs for PC-DOS; see the DOS manual.
65        ;
66        ;
67        ; This structure defines the layout of parameters on the stack.
68        ;
69        ONSTACK    STRUC
70        OLDBP      DW   ?                    ;TOP OF STACK
71        RETADDR    DW   ?                    ;NEAR RETURN ADDRESS
72        YADDR      DD   ?                    ;FAR ADDRESS OF X VALUE
73        XADDR      DD   ?                    ;FAR ADDRESS OF Y VALUE
74        STIK_NO    DW   ?                    ;STICK NUMBER
75        ONSTACK    ENDS
76
77        CODE       SEGMENT PUBLIC
78                   ASSUME  CS:CODE
79                   PUBLIC  STICK
```

(continued)

```
80
81              ;   EQUATES FOR ONE-SHOT BITS FOR STICKS 1 & 2
82
83      STICK_X     EQU         1
84      STICK_Y     EQU         2
85
86
87      STICK       PROC        NEAR
88                  PUSH        BP              ;SAVE CALLER'S BP
89                  MOV         BP,SP           ;STACK POINTER BECOMES NEW BP
90                  PUSH        DS
91
92          ;   GET THE X AXIS VALUE FIRST
93
94                  MOV         AH,STICK_X          ; MOVE IN THE X TEST BIT
95                  CMP         [BP].STIK_NO,2    ; SEE IF WE'RE TESTING STICK #1 OR #2
96                  JNE         TEST_X
97                  SHL         AH,1            ; SHIFT BIT NUMBERS 2 LEFT FOR STICK #2
98                  SHL         AH,1
99      TEST_X:     MOV         AL,1            ; INITIALIZE OUTPUT VALUE
100                 MOV         DX,201H         ; SET PORT ADDRESS
101                 MOV         BX,0            ; AND KEEPING THE RUNUP COUNT IN BX
102                 MOV         CX,BX           ; LOOP 64K TIMES MAX
103                 OUT         DX,AL           ; TRIGGER THE ONE-SHOTS
104     AGAIN_X:    IN          AL,DX           ; READ THE ONE-SHOT BITS
105                 TEST        AL,AH           ; TEST FOR A HIGH BIT 0
106                 JE          DELAY           ; WE'RE DONE IF BIT 0 IS HIGH
107                 INC         BX              ; OTHERWISE INCREMENT BX AND LOOP AGAIN
108                 LOOP        AGAIN_X
109                 MOV         BX,-1           ; SET X=-1 IF NO RESPONSE
110
111         ;   DELAY HERE TO LET THE OTHER THREE PULSES MAX OUT
112
113     DELAY:      MOV         CX,512
114     WAIT:       LOOP        WAIT
115
116         ;   NOW WE GET THE Y AXIS VALUE
117
118                 MOV         AH,STICK_Y          ; MOVE IN THE Y TEST BIT
119                 CMP         [BP].STIK_NO,2    ; SEE IF WE'RE TESTING STICK #1 OR #2
120                 JNE         TEST_Y
121                 SHL         AH,1            ; SHIFT BIT NUMBERS 2 LEFT FOR STICK #2
122                 SHL         AH,1
123
124     TEST_Y:     MOV         SI,0            ; KEEP THE RUNUP COUNT FOR Y IN SI
125                 MOV         CX,SI           ; SET LOOP LIMIT TO 64K
126                 OUT         DX,AL           ; FIRE THE ONE-SHOTS AGAIN
127     AGAIN_Y:    IN          AL,DX           ; READ THE ONE-SHOT BITS
128                 TEST        AL,AH           ; TEST FOR A HIGH BIT 1
```

(continued)

```
129                    JE      DONE          ; WE'RE DONE IF BIT 1 IS HIGH
130                    INC     SI            ; OTHERWISE INCREMENT SI AND LOOP AGAIN
131                    LOOP    AGAIN_Y
132                    MOV     SI,-1         ; SET Y=-1 IF NO RESPONSE
133
134           ;   MOVE RETURN VALUES FROM REGISTERS INTO VAR PARAMETERS X & Y
135
136           DONE:    LDS     DI,[BP].XADDR           ;ADDR OF X INTO DS:DI
137                    MOV     [DI],BX                 ;X VALUE FROM BX TO DS:DI
138                    LDS     DI,[BP].YADDR           ;DITTO FOR Y VALUE FROM SI
139                    MOV     [DI],SI
140
141           ;   IT'S OVER...NOW CLEAN UP THE STACK AND LEAVE
142
143                    POP     DS
144                    MOV     SP,BP                   ; CLEAN UP STACK AND LEAVE
145                    POP     BP                      ; RESTORE CALLER'S BP
146
147                    RET     10
148
149           STICK    ENDP
150           CODE     ENDS
151                    END
```

Take a look at the assembly language routine **Stick**, which can read either joystick 1 or joystick 2, depending on the value passed in parameter **Stick-Number**. VAR parameters **X** and **Y** return values proportional to the joystick position in both X and Y axes.

Our friend **ONSTACK** is here again, with something new: The **DD** directives after fields **XADDR** and **YADDR** mean "Define Double;" they allocate four bytes on the stack for the full 32-bit addresses of the actual parameters plugged into **X** and **Y**.

Before we test anything, we have to determine whether to read joystick 1 or joystick 2. The only difference between testing joysticks 1 and 2 lies in which bits must be watched when reading port $201. Joystick 1 is read on bits 0 and 1, and joystick 2 is read on bits 2 and 3. The equate directives **STICK_X EQU 1** and **STICK_Y EQU 2** are for joystick 1, and represent bit *values*, not bit *numbers*. In order to be used in reading joystick 2, both these values must be shifted two bits to the left.

At label **TEST_X**, a dummy value is loaded into register AL, and output to port $201. As mentioned above, this value is not significant; it could be absolutely anything. The important work is done by the address circuitry on the game control board; whenever *anything* is sent to port $201, the one-shot time-out process begins.

The runup count is kept in BX, which is initialized to zero. A maximum runup of 65,536 will be used to prevent the system from hanging up in case the game control board has failed electrically and the one-shots never time out. This is done by loading another zero into CX; the LOOP opcode decrements CX each time it executes, and will "fall through" if CX becomes zero *after* a LOOP opcode. (This is why the loop doesn't end immediately, even though we have set CX to zero; LOOP has already decremented CX by one by the time it tests CX for zero, and decrementing a zero value in a 16-bit register yields 65,535.)

If LOOP ever terminates after 65,536 iterations, it loads a value of -1 into the return register to indicate to the calling logic that the joystick read has failed.

After outputting the dummy value to port $201 at line 103, a loop is entered that continually reads the one-shots and tests for a high bit. If no high bit is detected, BX is incremented and the loop repeats. Eventually a high bit will be detected, and the count in BX will be proportional to the time it took for the bit to go high.

The X value is returned in BX. The Y value is tested in precisely the same way, except that the runup count is kept in SI rather than in BX.

Perhaps the most important and nonobvious technique demonstrated by **STICK** is the way values are returned from the assembly-language subprogram to the pair of Pascal VAR parameters X and Y. From the perspective of the assembly code, X and Y are not values, but addresses of two variables somewhere in the Pascal universe. Returning a value in X and Y means using those addresses to store values into the variables to which they point.

The means to this end is the LDS opcode. LDS was designed to take a 32-bit address from some location in memory (in this case, on the stack) and break it into two halves. One half (the segment portion) is put into DS (the "DS" in the mnemonic "LDS"), and the other half (the offset portion) is loaded into the register specified after the LDS mnemonic. In the case of **STICK**, this is the DI register. The pointer thus constructed in those two registers DS:DI is then used to MOV a value from a register into one of the variables whose address was passed to **STICK** on the stack.

There are other ways of getting data into a VAR parameter, but using LDS (or its brother LES, identical except in using ES where LDS uses DS) is by far the simplest and most efficient.

4.6   Returning Values from External Functions

A function in Pascal is a subprogram that returns a value to an expression. A procedure, by contrast, is a statement, and stands alone without returning a value. In Standard Pascal, functions can return only simple types: Integers, reals, Booleans, characters, ordinal types, pointers, and subranges. Turbo Pascal functions, additionally, can return string values as function results.

Pascal functions *cannot* return arrays, records, files, or (sadly) sets. Note that a typographical error on page 224 of the *Turbo Pascal Reference Manual* implies that sets can be returned as function results, but careful reading shows that the word "sets" in boldface should have been "strings."

As mentioned earlier, there is no difference between functions and procedures at an assembly-language level. To return a value, an external machine-code subprogram leaves behind a value in an appropriate place; after it returns control to the calling logic, the Turbo Pascal runtime code pulls the value from that appropriate place and plugs it into the expression containing the external function invocation.

The *type declaration* of the function tells the runtime code where to look for the value. (Every function must be declared with a type, or a Pascal error is generated.) For example, integer values are left behind in the AX register. If you define an external function of type **Integer**, the Turbo Pascal runtime will take whatever value is left behind in AX and replace the function's identifier with that value in the expression being evaluated. A function defined as a pointer type, by contrast, will be expected to leave behind the pointer's segment part in DX and its offset part in AX.

A potential source of confusion lies in the fact that a variable is always allocated on the stack for the function-return value, even for data types which are returned to the calling logic in registers or the zero flag. At instantiation time, this variable is allocated on the stack first, before any parameters are allocated. It exists so that Turbo Pascal has someplace to put the return value during the execution of the function. For example, consider this function definition:

```
FUNCTION Negative(Foo : Integer) : Boolean;

BEGIN
  IF Foo < 0 THEN
    BEGIN
      Negative := True;
      Writeln('Warning: Value is negative!')
    END
  ELSE
    Negative := False
END;
```

Notice that the function-return value here is set early in the function, after which a message must be displayed. If the generated code simply set the zero flag at the point in the function corresponding to the assignment statement that sets the return value, the zero flag could easily be changed by instructions required to display the message. To avoid such conflicts, the runtime code keeps return values on the stack temporarily, and then sets the zero flag appropriately immediately before returning to the calling logic.

Why all function return values are not returned on the stack (as are strings and real-number values) is a mystery. It was probably a shortcut to keep the compiler small. Almost everything about Turbo Pascal that is difficult to understand can be traced to a desire to keep the compiler as small as possible.

The following summaries explain in detail how to return the permissible Pascal types as function results from external functions.

Integers and Integer Subranges

Integer values must be returned in the AX register. The high-order byte of the integer must be in AH, and the low-order byte must be in AL.

Characters, Bytes, Enumerated Types, and Subranges

These data types are all 8-bit types, and are returned in the AL register. In addition, AH must be set to zero. Another thing to remember is that the Turbo Pascal runtime code pushes only a single-byte function-return value onto the stack for single-byte types. (It's not done by using the PUSH opcodes, which only work on words, but by decrementing the stack pointer by one byte.)

Pointers

The segment portion of a pointer is returned in DX, and the offset portion is returned in AX. The high-order byte of the segment is returned in DH, the low-order byte in DL, and the offset is returned similarly in AH and AL. Again, remember to allocate four bytes on the stack for the return-value copy of the pointer, even though the pointer itself is returned in DX:AX.

Booleans

A Boolean value is returned by way of the Z (Zero) flag in the Flags register. If the Z flag is set, the value returned is **False**. If the Z flag is cleared, the value returned is **True**.

From a coding standpoint, this is a little subtler than simply moving a value into the proper register and going home. Many 8086 instructions affect the flags register, and a fair number affect the Z flag itself. Presumably, an assembly-language operation sets the Z flag, and then the function has done its work. Be careful not to execute some other instruction that affects the Z flag *after* the point where your significant operation occurs. As a rule of thumb, execute the instruction that affects the Z flag in the way you want returned to the calling logic *last*. Don't do anything after that except return or jump to a return.

For an example of an external function that returns a Boolean value, consider the problem of returning the state of the switches on a PC joystick (see Figure 4.8). There are two switches on each joystick, and the PC hardware supports two joysticks. The status of all four switches can be read at one time from I/O port $201. If you'll remember from the previous section, the four one-shots that track the X/Y position of the two joysticks are also returned as bit fields in the byte returned from port $201. Bits 0–3 are used in determining the joystick positions, and bits 4–7 return the current state of the four joystick switches. The four switch bits are normally high—that is, set to a value of one. When a button is pressed, its bit goes from one to zero. The bit remains zero until the button is released, at which time the bit immediately returns to a value of one.

I have to be up-front at this point and admit that there is nothing in reading the joystick buttons that can't be done perfectly well from Turbo Pascal. There really isn't any need to read the joystick buttons from an external func-

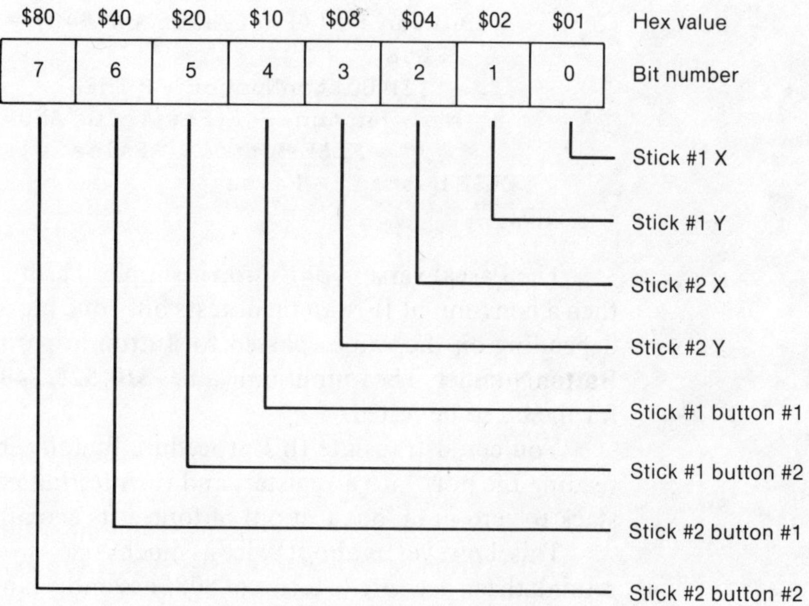

***Figure 4.8*   Game controller bits at port $201**

tion; I only provide the external routine because it shows how to return a Boolean value and is both useful and easy to comprehend.

In fact, showing you how to read the buttons in Pascal illustrates an important point often forgotten in designing external machine-code routines: The best algorithm for solving a given problem will *not* be the same in both Pascal and assembly language.

```
FUNCTION Button(StickNumber,ButtonNumber : Integer) :
  Boolean;

VAR
  PortValue : Byte;

BEGIN
  PortValue := Port[$201];    {Read the joystick I/O port}
  IF StickNumber = 1 THEN
    IF ButtonNumber = 1 THEN
      Button := ((PortValue AND $10) = 0)
        ELSE
          IF ButtonNumber = 2 THEN
            Button := ((PortValue AND $20) = 0)
              ELSE Button := False
    ELSE
      IF StickNumber = 2 THEN
        IF ButtonNumber = 1 THEN
          Button := ((PortValue AND $40) = 0)
            ELSE
              IF ButtonNumber = 2 THEN
                Button := ((PortValue AND $80) = 0)
                  ELSE Button := False
      ELSE Button := False
END;
```

The Pascal version of **Button** is simple. The byte at port **$201** is read, and then a convoluted **IF** statement tests only one bit out of the four button bits, depending on the values passed to **Button** in parameters **StickNumber** and **ButtonNumber**. The four literal values **$10, $20, $40,** and **$80** represent a mask for the bit to be tested.

You could translate this procedure literally into assembly language by reading the port into a register, and then testing parameters passed onto the stack to zero in on one test out of four tests actually coded.

This, however, is about twice as much code as you need. It's much better to rethink the procedure in terms of 8086 assembly language. While not the most concise implementation, the following external function is certainly easier than hammering a Pascal function into assembler:

```
1       ;==============================================================================
2       ;
3       ;      B U T T O N  -  Function to return the state of the joystick buttons
4       ;
5       ;==============================================================================
6       ;
7       ;
8       ;
9       ;
10      ;
11      ;
12      ; BUTTON is written to be called from Turbo Pascal V3.0 using the
13      ; EXTERNAL procedure convention.
14      ;
15      ; Declare the procedure itself as external using this declaration:
16      ;
17      ; FUNCTION BUTTON(StickNumber,ButtonNumber : Integer) : Boolean;
18      ;                                  EXTERNAL 'BUTTON.BIN';
19      ;
20      ; StickNumber specifies which joystick to read from, and ButtonNumber
21      ; specifies which of the two buttons on that joystick to read.  If the
22      ; specified button is down, BUTTON returns a Boolean value of TRUE.
23      ;
24      ; Yes, this is the long way 'round; assembly language is in no way required
25      ; to read four bits from an ordinary 8088 I/O port.  BUTTON exists only as
26      ; practice in creating assembly language external functions.
27      ;
28      ; The button information is obtained by reading I/O port $201.  The high
29      ; four bits represent the state of the four buttons (two for each of the
30      ; two possible joysticks) at the instant the port is read.  A LOW bit
31      ; represents a button DOWN.  This is why the byte read from the port is
32      ; inverted via NOT before the selected bit is tested.
33      ;
34      ; Here is a map of the button bits as returned by port $201:
35      ;
36      ;    |7 6 5 4 3 2 1 0|
37      ;     | | | |
38      ;     | | |  - - - - - - -> Button #1, joystick #1
39      ;     | |  - - - - - - - -> Button #2, joystick #1
40      ;     |  - - - - - - - - -> Button #1, joystick #2
41      ;      - - - - - - - - - -> Button #2, joystick #2
42      ;
43      ; Remember that the return value from this function is passed to the runtime
44      ; code in the Zero Flag, which is set by the TEST AL,BL instruction in line
45      ; 103.
46      ;
47      ; To reassemble/relink BUTTON:
48      ;--------------------------------------
49      ; 1. Assemble this file with MASM.  "C>MASM BUTTON;"
```

(continued)

```
50          ; 2. Link it into a .EXE file.        "C>LINK BUTTON;"
51          ; 3. Use EXE2BIN to make a .COM file. "A> EXE2BIN BUTTON.EXE BUTTON.BIN"
52          ; 4. Declare as shown above in your Turbo Pascal program.
53          ; 5. Ignore any minor diagnostic messages that may be generated when
54          ;      this file is assembled and linked.  EXE2BIN is supplied with the
55          ;      supplemental programs for PC-DOS; see the DOS manual.
56          ;
57          ;
58          ; This structure defines the layout of parameters on the stack:
59          ;
60
61          ONSTACK    STRUC
62          OLDBP      DW    ?                      ;TOP OF STACK
63          RETADDR    DW    ?                      ;NEAR RETURN ADDRESS
64          BTN_NO     DW    ?                      ;BUTTON NUMBER
65          STIK_NO    DW    ?                      ;STICK NUMBER
66          RETURN     DB    ?                      ;BOOLEAN RETURN VALUE **A BYTE!**
67          ONSTACK    ENDS
68
69          CODE    SEGMENT PUBLIC
70                  ASSUME  CS:CODE
71                  PUBLIC  BUTTON
72
73          BUTTON  PROC    NEAR
74                  PUSH    BP                      ;SAVE PREVIOUS VALUE OF BP ON STACK
75                  MOV     BP,SP                   ;SP BECOMES NEW VALUE OF BP
76
77          ;-----------------------------------------------------------------
78          ; THE BULK OF THIS ROUTINE SETS UP A TEST MASK BY WHICH ONE SINGLE
79          ; BIT OUT OF THE FOUR BUTTON BITS IS TESTED.
80          ;-----------------------------------------------------------------
81
82                  MOV     BL,010H         ;START WITH HIGH BIT IN BIT 4
83                  CMP     [BP].STIK_NO,2  ;ARE WE TESTING FOR JOYSTICK #2?
84                  JNE     WHICH           ;IF NOT, GO ON TO TEST FOR WHICH BUTTON,
85                  SHL     BL,1            ; OTHERWISE SHIFT TWO POSITIONS LEFTWARD
86                  SHL     BL,1            ; SO THAT THE MASK IS ON BIT 6 FOR STICK 2
87
88          WHICH:  CMP     [BP].BTN_NO,2   ;ARE WE TESTING FOR BUTTON #2?
89                  JNE     READEM          ;IF NOT, MASK IS CORRECT; GO READ PORT
90                  SHL     BL,1            ;OTHERWISE, SHIFT 1 BIT LEFT FOR BUTTON 2
91
92          ;-----------------------------------------------------------------
93          ; THE BIT MASK IS NOW CORRECT.  HERE THE BUTTON BITS ARE READ FROM PORT
94          ; $201 AND TESTED AGAINST THE MASK.  NOTE THAT THE BITS AS READ FROM
95          ; THE PORT MUST BE INVERTED SO THAT THE Z FLAG IS SET RATHER THAN CLEARED
96          ; ON AN ACTIVE BUTTON BIT.  (BITS ARE ACTIVE **LOW**, REMEMBER!)
97          ;-----------------------------------------------------------------
98
```

(continued)

```
 99      READEM: MOV    DX,0201H        ;SET UP 16-BIT ADDRESS FOR PORT READ
100              IN     AL,DX           ;READ BUTTON BITS FROM PORT $201
101              NOT    AL              ;MUST INVERT BITS FOR PROPER SENSE
102                                     ; OF THE Z FLAG AFTER TESTING
103              TEST   AL,BL           ;SEE IF THE DESIRED BIT IS HIGH;
104                                     ;THIS INSTRUCTION SETS THE Z FLAG
105                                     ; FOR THE BOOLEAN FUNCTION RETURN VALUE
106
107      DONE:   MOV    SP,BP           ;RESTORE PRIOR STACK POINTER & BP
108              POP    BP              ; IN CONVENTIONAL RETURN
109              RET    5
110
111      BUTTON  ENDP
112      CODE    ENDS
113              END
```

The algorithm here is different indeed. Rather than read the port value immediately into a register, the function first tests the passed parameters and sets up a bit mask according to those parameters. Instead of picking from four literals, the code begins with a $10 literal (the bit mask for button 1, switch 1) and shifts it one, two, or three bits to the left, depending on the values passed in **ButtonNumber** and **StickNumber**. Note that the Pascal parameter **Button-Number** is named **BTN_NO** in the assembly-language stack structure, and that **StickNumber** becomes **STIK_NO**. Again, there is nothing in the .BIN file loaded at compile time to tell Turbo Pascal what you named the stack fields in your assembly-language source file. The names do not have to relate to one another at all, but, for the sake of sense and readability, they should.

Only when the mask is properly shifted is the port read and the single test actually made. Note the **NOT** instruction at line 101. This inverts the byte read from port $201, so that ones become zeroes and vice versa. Recall that when a button is pressed, its bit goes to *zero*. The **TEST** opcode needs to test for high (one) bits in order to set the zero flag to the value expected by the Turbo Pascal runtime. **TEST** would detect the bit change even without the **NOT** instruction, but in that case the Boolean value returned by **Button** would become **False** when a button was pressed, and remain **True** at all other times. This runs counter to what common sense would indicate in dealing with joystick buttons, so we put the burden of conversion on the assembly-language subprogram and not on the Pascal code that calls it.

Real Numbers

Up to this point, all the simple types which may be returned by a Pascal function have been returned either in machine registers or in the zero flag. Real numbers depart fundamentally from this model in that a function returning a real number actually does return the value on the stack. Real numbers and strings are the only data types for which this is the case.

The *Turbo Pascal Reference Manual* does tell us this much. What it doesn't tell us is that an entirely different return protocol is required to avoid trashing the system. The problem stems from the fact that there is a routine buried in the Turbo Pascal runtime code somewhere that strips the real-number return value off the stack and supplies it in an appropriate fashion to the calling logic. An external function returning a real-number value *cannot* return to the caller via RET n, as is done with every other type of external assembly-language subprogram described so far. The external function must perform an absolute jump to the function-value-stripper routine in the runtime code. The stripper routine does its job, cleans up the stack, and then *it* performs the RET back to the caller.

Worse yet, before this jump can be made, the stack pointer must be adjusted so that it points to the first byte in the function-return value; then the jump is made to the return address. This stack-pointer adjustment is accomplished by adding a value to the stack pointer equal to the sum of the sizes of all the parameters passed on the stack. (Of course, if the function has no parameters, then no adjustment of the stack pointer needs to take place.)

Because the return address is pushed onto the stack after the parameters, it must be saved into a register before the stack pointer is adjusted, or it will be lost. When the jump is finally made, it is to the value stored in the register. There is an 8086 opcode for just that purpose.

To illustrate this extraordinarily tricky business, I have prepared a boiler-plate external assembly-language real-number function, **RealPlate**. It does nothing especially useful. Its only function is to copy its argument into its function-return value. It exists to provide an example so that you can write your own external real-number functions in assembler.

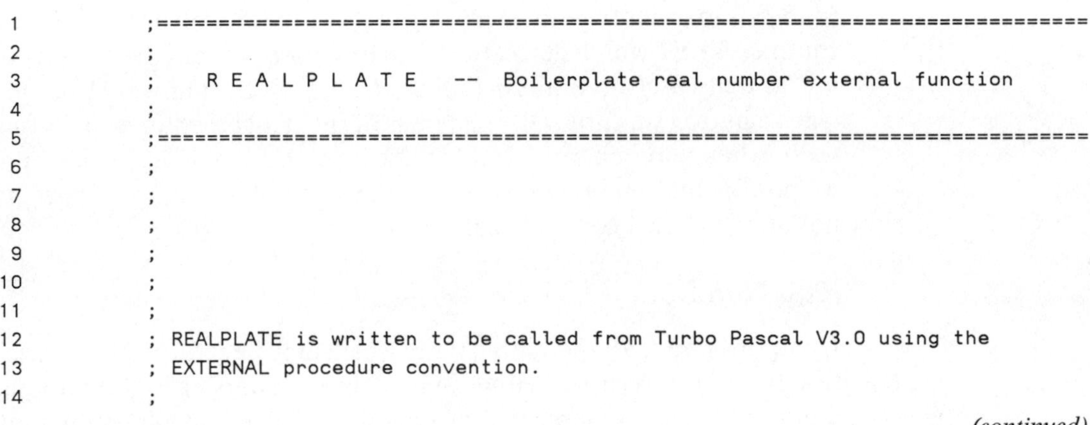

```
 1      ;===============================================================================
 2      ;
 3      ;     R E A L P L A T E    --  Boilerplate real number external function
 4      ;
 5      ;===============================================================================
 6      ;
 7      ;
 8      ;
 9      ;
10      ;
11      ;
12      ; REALPLATE is written to be called from Turbo Pascal V3.0 using the
13      ; EXTERNAL procedure convention.
14      ;
```

(continued)

```
15          ; Declare the procedure itself as external using this declaration:
16          ;
17          ; FUNCTION REALPLATE(Argument : Real) : Real;
18          ;                                     EXTERNAL 'REALPLAT.BIN';
19          ;
20          ; This function doesn't do anything useful; it simply copies the value of
21          ; Argument into the function result.  What it's for is to demonstrate
22          ; the totally peculiar (and utterly undocumented) returning protocol for
23          ; external assembly language real number functions.
24          ;
25          ; Before any external real number function returns to the caller, it must
26          ; make sure that the stack pointer is pointing to the lowest byte of the
27          ; six-byte real number function return value allocated on the stack.  It
28          ; then returns by PERFORMING AN ABSOLUTE JUMP TO THE RETURN ADDRESS!
29          ;
30          ; There is a special routine in the Turbo Pascal runtime library that strips
31          ; the function result off the stack and returns to the calling logic.  This
32          ; routine is the destination of that jump.  That routine will then perform
33          ; the RET necessary to give the caller control in an orderly manner.
34          ;
35          ; Philippe never told us about this one.  Ahh, well.
36          ;
37          ;
38          ; To reassemble/relink REALPLATE:
39          ;----------------------------------------
40          ; 1. Assemble this file with MASM.  "C>MASM REALPLAT;"
41          ; 2. Link it into a .EXE file.      "C>LINK REALPLAT;"
42          ; 3. Use EXE2BIN to make a .COM file. "A> EXE2BIN REALPLAT.EXE REALPLAT.BIN"
43          ; 4. Declare as shown above in your Turbo Pascal program.
44          ; 5. Ignore any minor diagnostic messages that may be generated when
45          ;    this file is assembled and linked.  EXE2BIN is supplied with the
46          ;    supplemental programs for PC-DOS; see the DOS manual.
47          ;
48          ;
49          ; This structure defines the layout of parameters on the stack:
50          ;
51
52          ONSTACK     STRUC
53          OLDBP       DW    ?                 ;CALLER'S BP VALUE
54          RETADDR     DW    ?                 ;RETURN ADDRESS
55
56          PARMANT     DB 5 DUP (?)            ;ALL PARAMETERS MUST BE LISTED HERE;
57          PARMEXP     DB    ?                 ;THE SIZE OF THIS SECTION MAY VARY
58
59          RETMANT     DB 5 DUP (?)            ;REAL NUMBER RETURN VALUE ALWAYS HERE
60          RETEXP      DB    ?                 ;NOTE THAT THERE IS NO "ENDMARK" FIELD!
61          ONSTACK     ENDS
62
63
```

(continued)

```
64          CODE    SEGMENT PUBLIC
65                  ASSUME  CS:CODE
66                  PUBLIC  RLPLATE
67
68          RLPLATE PROC    NEAR
69                  PUSH    BP                      ;SAVE PREVIOUS VALUE OF BP ON STACK
70                  MOV     BP,SP                   ;SP BECOMES NEW VALUE OF BP
71
72
73          ; The real work of your function must be written between the two lines.
74          ; Outside the lines, don't eliminate ANYTHING, and for best results only
75          ; change the portions of the ONSTACK structure that define your parameters.
76          ; Since RETADDR and RETMANT are used by the assembler to calculate the
77          ; stack adjustment constant during exit, changing the names of those two
78          ; fields will prevent MASM from assembling the file correctly.
79
80          ;-----------------------------------------------------------------------------
81
82          ; Strictly brute-force copy of parameter into function return value:
83
84                  MOV     AL,[BP].PARMEXP
85                  MOV     [BP].RETEXP,AL
86                  MOV     AL,[BP].PARMANT
87                  MOV     [BP].RETMANT,AL
88                  MOV     AL,[BP].PARMANT+1
89                  MOV     [BP].RETMANT+1,AL
90                  MOV     AL,[BP].PARMANT+2
91                  MOV     [BP].RETMANT+2,AL
92                  MOV     AL,[BP].PARMANT+3
93                  MOV     [BP].RETMANT+3,AL
94                  MOV     AL,[BP].PARMANT+4
95                  MOV     [BP].RETMANT+4,AL
96
97          ; Somehow I just couldn't let this function do absolutely NOTHING...
98
99          ;-----------------------------------------------------------------------------
100
101         DONE:   MOV     SP,BP                   ;MOVE STACK POINTER UP TO BP POINT
102                 POP     BP                      ;RESTORE CALLER'S BP VALUE
103
104                 POP     BX                      ;POP THE RETURN ADDRESS INTO BX
105                                                 ; SO WE CAN JUMP TO IT LATER
106
107                                                 ;ADJUST STACK POINTER SO THAT IT POINTS
108                 ADD     SP,RETMANT-RETADDR-2
109                                                 ; TO THE FUNCTION RETURN VALUE; THIS
110                                                 ; MEANS MOVING IT UP-MEMORY PAST ALL
111                                                 ; POSSIBLE PARAMETERS.  MASM WILL CALC THIS
112                                                 ; STACK ADJUSTMENT FACTOR UNLESS YOU MESS
```

(continued)

```
113                                          ; UP THE ONSTACK STRUCTURE!
114
115              JMP      BX                 ;NOW JUMP TO THE SAVED RETURN ADDRESS IN BX.
116                                          ; THE TURBO RUNTIME WILL HANDLE THE PASSING
117                                          ; OF THE FUNCTION RETURN VALUE BACK TO THE
118                                          ; CALLING LOGIC.
119
120     RLPLATE  ENDP
121     CODE     ENDS
122              END
```

The tricky part of **RealPlate** lies in the last few instructions. The code between the dashed lines is where the real work of the function is actually done. When you write your own real-number functions, this is where your code should go. Everything else is just housekeeping, and, in general, should not change very much. All that will change will be (perhaps) the necessity to add more parameters to the **ONSTACK** structure. **RealPlate** passes a single real-number parameter, which is perhaps the commonest case in real-number functions. (Things like **SEC(x)** follow this model.) You may have more parameters, or perhaps no parameters. Adjust **ONSTACK** as appropriate. Just remember that you must not change the parts of **ONSTACK** that describe the function-return value, return address, or caller's BP value. These are used by the assembler in calculating the stack-pointer adjustment figure, and if that figure is calculated incorrectly, your function will sink into the murky depths and take your machine with it.

Getting into **RealPlate** is no different than getting into any assembly-language subprogram. Getting *out* again is the trick. The best way to understand what must happen is to follow the diagram in Figure 4.9, showing the stack at four steps along the way. The left portion of the diagram, above bullet 1, is a picture of real-number function's stack (**RealPlate**'s stack, actually) as it exists just before the exit sequence is executed. The dashed lines are borders between bytes on the stack. The solid lines are borders between words. Note that, as with external procedures, BP points to the caller's BP value. Below BP is the function's local work area, including local variables and temporary push/pop storage used during the execution of the function.

The highest item on the stack is the function-return value. The object of the game is to get SP pointing to the first byte in the function-return value without losing anything important. Here's how it works, step by step. (Follow along on the diagram.)

MOV SP,BP (Bullet 2) By copying BP into SP, the function's work area is freed up, and both BP and SP now point to the caller's BP value.

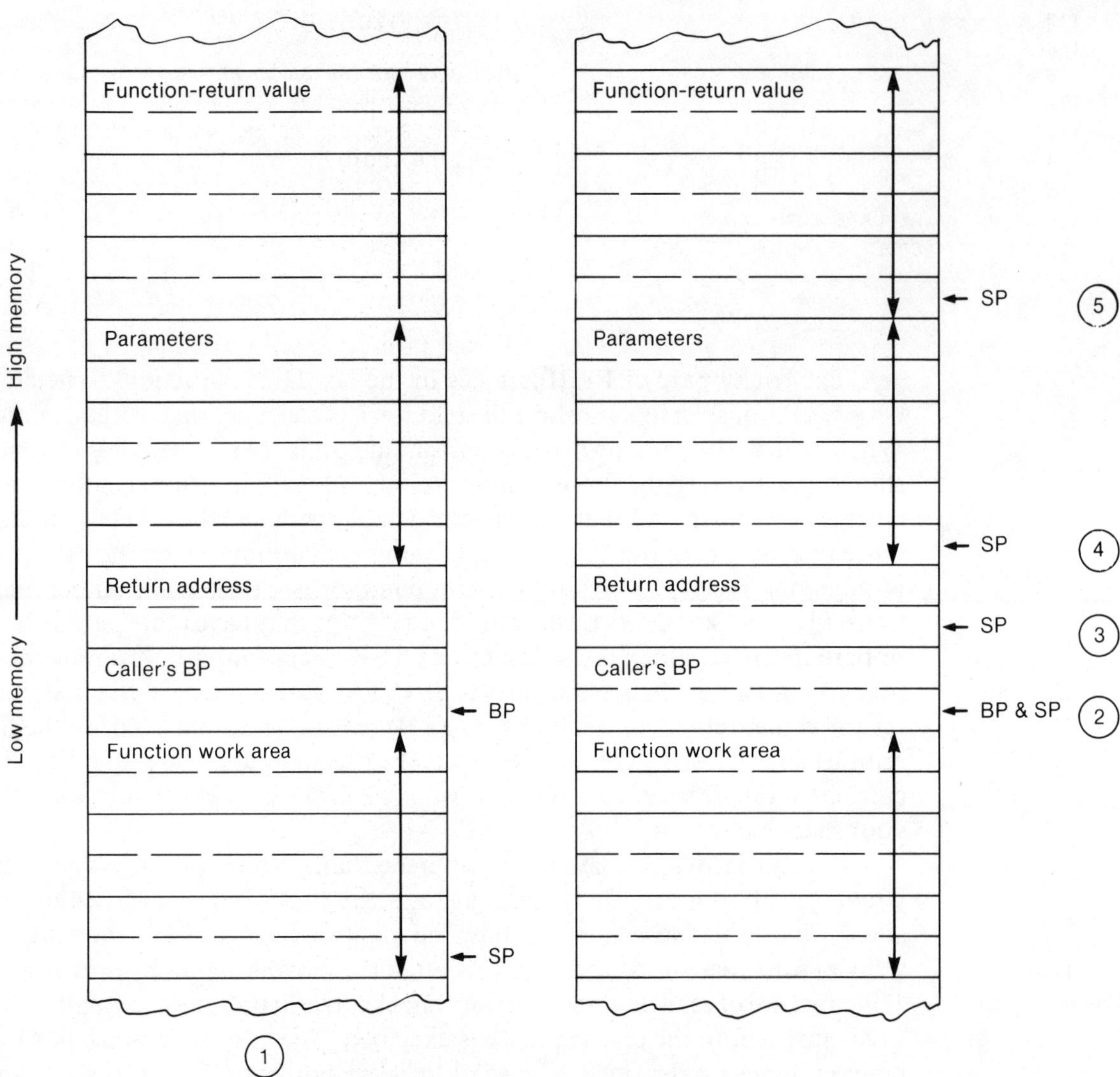

Figure 4.9   **Real-number function-return values**

POP BP (Bullet 3) The caller's saved BP value is popped off the stack back into BP. This gets BP out of the picture as far as the function is concerned, since BP now has a value in it that is of use only to the calling logic. The pop operation leaves SP pointing one word up-stack, to the return address.

POP BX (Bullet 4) The return address gets popped off the stack into register BX, where it will be safe and sound for the time being. (We need it to get back to the caller.) The pop operation leaves SP pointing to the first byte of the function's parameter list.

ADD SP,RETMANT-RETADDR-2 (Bullet 5) Now we have to get rid of the parameter list. This is done by adding a value to the stack pointer SP equal to the total number of bytes in all parameters. In the specific case of **RealPlate**, this is only one parameter, a Turbo Pascal real number that is six bytes long. We could simply add the constant 6 to SP for **RealPlate** and we'd be in business.

But **RealPlate** is, after all, a boilerplate function, and it should be as general as possible. One way to make it more general is to allow the assembler to calculate the total number of bytes represented by the parameter list. It does this by using the **ONSTACK** structure definition.

You must understand what the assembler sees when it sees the structure. **ONSTACK** is just a starting point—an indicator to the assembler that something begins here. Each field identifier within **ONSTACK** represents an offset from that starting point. When the assembler creates its symbol table, it associates an offset from **ONSTACK** for each field within **ONSTACK**. You can see these offset values if you allow MASM to create an .LST file during assembly. Toward the bottom of the .LST file produced during assembly of REALPLAT.ASM, you'll see a table like this:

```
ONSTACK    .............................................  0010 0006
  OLDBP    .............................................  0000
  RETADDR  .............................................  0002
  PARMANT  .............................................  0004
  PARMEXP  .............................................  0009
  RETMANT  .............................................  000A
  RETEXP   .............................................  000F
```

The two numbers beside **ONSTACK** represent the total size of the structure and the number of fields it contains, respectively. (All table figures are in hex.) The numbers beside each of the fields represent their individual offsets from the beginning of the structure.

Any function built around REALPLAT.ASM will have the **OLDBP**, **RETADDR**, **RETMANT**, and **RETEXP** fields. Between **RETADDR** and **RETMANT** may be any number of parameters. **RealPlate** has only one, which has been split into two pieces, a mantissa and an exponent. (The function-return value has also been split into two pieces. In most real-number calculations, these two portions of a real number are dealt with separately, so they were divided in the assembly code for convenience.)

By subtracting the offset represented by **RETADDR** from the offset represented by **RETMANT**, we get a figure representing the number of bytes between **RETADDR** and **RETMANT**, which includes all possible parameters. Unfortunately, it also includes the number of bytes in **RETADDR**, since the **RETADDR** symbol represents the offset from **ONSTACK** at the *beginning* of the **RETADDR** field and not its end. Not to worry—we can subtract the never-changing size of **RETADDR** (2) and get the correct value. Work it out: $0A − $02 − $02 = 6, and 6 is the size of a Turbo Pascal real number and our single parameter (**PARMANT** and **PARMEXP** taken together).

Once this addition has been made, SP points to the first byte in the function-return value stored on the stack, and finally we're where we want to be.

JMP BX (No bullet here) After this instruction is executed, we're off into the depths of the Turbo Pascal runtime code, where the real-number gnomes will strip the result value off the stack and plug it into the caller's expression.

Keep in mind that **RealPlate** will work with standard 6-byte Turbo Pascal real numbers only. It will gag in a big way on the IEEE 8-byte real-number format used in Turbo-87 Pascal. (As attempting to grok the fullness of IEEE reals gives me screaming migraine, I have not attempted the conversion.)

That's all there really is to the mechanics of passing parameters and values between Turbo Pascal code and external assembly-language functions. I took some time and care in explaining the process because that same process is at the heart of the hairier protocol required to get a *string* value out of a function and back to your Pascal code.

Strings

External string functions are a pain, in spades.

As alluded to in the previous section, creating an external assembly-language function that returns a string value is first made difficult by the fact that the *Turbo Pascal Reference Manual* does not completely describe the means by which string function results are returned on the stack. As with real numbers, the Turbo Pascal runtime code allocates a string value on the stack for the function-return value, and as with real-number functions, the code of the external function must do its work and copy the desired data into the string function-return value before it returns.

But, as with real-number functions, going home again is difficult, and the reference manual says nothing about this difficulty; you can't just RET back to the calling logic. You have to make an absolute jump way back into the runtime code, which strips the string function-return value off the stack and *then* returns control to the calling logic.

So far, that's no different from the real-number function described above. But it gets worse: The stripper routine in the runtime code demands that all unused data bytes in the string be removed before it takes control.

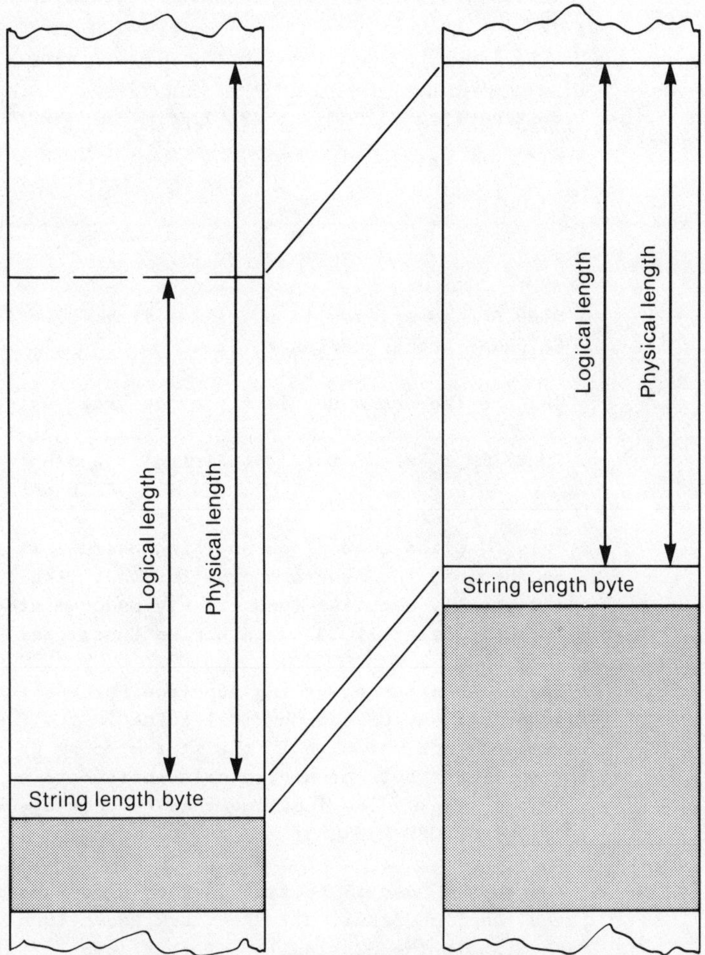

Figure 4.10   **String function-return values**

What has to happen, in effect, is shown in Figure 4.10. A string with a physical length of, say, 80 bytes has been loaded by the code in the external string function with 50 bytes of string data. Before it can go home, the external string function code must move the function-return value up-stack by 30 bytes so that the return value's physical length is the same as its logical length, or 50 bytes.

Why this should be necessary is obscure (I try to avoid crawling around in Turbo Pascal's belly any more than I must) but there's no fighting it. I have prepared a boilerplate external string function called STRPLATE.ASM, shown as follows:

```
 1          ;==============================================================================
 2          ;
 3          ;        S T R P L A T E    --   Boilerplate string external function
 4          ;
 5          ;==============================================================================
 6          ;
 7          ;
 8          ;
 9          ;
10          ;
11          ;
12          ; STRPLATE is written to be called from Turbo Pascal V3.0 using the
13          ; EXTERNAL procedure convention.
14          ;
15          ; Declare the procedure itself as external using this declaration:
16          ;
17          ; FUNCTION STRPLATE(Source : String) : String;
18          ;                                   EXTERNAL 'STRPLATE.BIN';
19          ;
20          ; This function doesn't do anything useful; it simply copies the value of
21          ; Source into the function result.  What it's for is to demonstrate
22          ; the totally peculiar (and utterly undocumented) returning protocol for
23          ; external assembly language string functions.
24          ;
25          ; Before an external string function returns to the caller, it must make
26          ; sure that any unused physical space in the function return string is
27          ; removed, and the data in the string moved up-stack such that the last
28          ; significant byte of string data in the string is the highest byte of data
29          ; on the stack.  The function then returns by PERFORMING AN ABSOLUTE JUMP
30          ; TO THE RETURN ADDRESS!
31          ;
32          ; There is a special routine in the Turbo Pascal runtime library that strips
33          ; the function result off the stack and returns to the calling logic.  This
34          ; routine is the destination of that jump.  That routine will then perform
35          ; the RET necessary to give the caller control in an orderly manner.
36          ;
37          ; Philippe never told us about this one.  Ahh, well.
38          ;
39          ;
40          ; To reassemble/relink STRPLATE:
41          ;-------------------------------------
42          ; 1. Assemble this file with MASM.  "C>MASM STRPLATE;"
43          ; 2. Link it into a .EXE file.      "C>LINK STRPLATE;"
44          ; 3. Use EXE2BIN to make a .COM file. "A> EXE2BIN STRPLATE.EXE STRPLATE.BIN"
45          ; 4. Declare as shown above in your Turbo Pascal program.
46          ; 5. Ignore any minor diagnostic messages that may be generated when
47          ;     this file is assembled and linked.  EXE2BIN is supplied with the
48          ;     supplemental programs for PC-DOS; see the DOS manual.
49          ;
```

(continued)

```
50
51          ; The following value can be set to anything between 1 and 255.  80 and 255
52          ; are the commonest and most useful values.  It represents the physical
53          ; length of the string, and MUST match the length of the return string value
54          ; as declared in the Pascal program for the external function.
55
56      PHYSLEN    EQU    255
57
58          ;
59          ; This structure defines the layout of parameters on the stack:
60          ;
61
62      ONSTACK    STRUC
63      OLDBP      DW     ?                 ;CALLER'S BP VALUE
64      RETADDR    DW     ?                 ;RETURN ADDRESS
65
66      PARMLEN    DB     ?                 ;A STRING PARAMETER; LENGTH BYTE FOLLOWED
67      PARMSTR    DB PHYSLEN DUP (?)       ; BY PHYSLEN DATA BYTES
68
69      RETLEN     DB     ?                 ;LENGTH BYTE OF FUNTION RETURN STRING
70      RETSTR     DB PHYSLEN DUP (?)       ;REAL NUMBER RETURN VALUE ALWAYS HERE
71      ONSTACK    ENDS
72
73
74      CODE       SEGMENT PUBLIC
75                 ASSUME  CS:CODE
76                 PUBLIC  STRPLAT
77
78      STRPLAT PROC    NEAR
79                 PUSH    BP               ;SAVE PREVIOUS VALUE OF BP ON STACK
80                 MOV     BP,SP            ;SP BECOMES NEW VALUE OF BP
81
82
83          ; The real work of your function must be written between the two lines.
84          ; Outside the lines, don't eliminate ANYTHING, and for best results only
85          ; change the portions of the ONSTACK structure that define your parameters.
86          ; Since RETADDR and RETLEN are used by the assembler to calculate the
87          ; stack adjustment constant during exit, changing the names of those two
88          ; fields will prevent MASM from assembling the file correctly.
89          ;------------------------------------------------------------------------
90          ; For an example operation, let's copy the parm into the function result:
91
92                 PUSH    DS               ;SAVE CALLER'S DS
93                 MOV     AX,SS            ;AND SET UP DS AND ES TO BOTH CONTAIN
94                 MOV     ES,AX            ; THE STACK SEGMENT ADDRESS FOR A BLOCK
95                 MOV     DS,AX            ; MOVE FROM ONE POINT ON THE STACK TO
96                                          ; ANOTHER.
97                 XOR     CH,CH            ;ZERO OUT CH
98                 MOV     CL,[BP].PARMLEN  ;MOVE LENGTH BYTE INTO CX FOR BLOCK MOVE
```

(continued)

```
 99                INC     CX                      ;ADD ONE TO CX FOR LENGTH COUNTER
100
101                MOV     SI,BP                   ;THE SOURCE AND DESTINATION INDICES CONTAIN
102                ADD     SI,PARMLEN              ; THE VALUE IN BP PLUS AN OFFSET FROM BP
103                MOV     DI,BP                   ; TO THE STARTS OF THE PARAMETER STRING AND
104                ADD     DI,RETLEN               ; THE FUNCTION RETURN STRING
105
106                CLD                             ;SET DIRECTION FLAG FOR AUTO INCREMENT
107                REPZ MOVSB                       ;PERFORM THE BLOCK MOVE
108
109                POP     DS                      ;RESTORE CALLER'S DS VALUE
110     ;----------------------------------------------------------------------
111     ; By the time you reach label DONE: the string return result must have been
112     ; placed on the stack, and any registers pushed onto the stack for temporary
113     ; safekeeping must have been popped off again.  The following logic should
114     ; not be tampered with or the whole thing won't work.
115
116     DONE:      MOV     CL,PHYSLEN              ;MOVE PHYSICAL LENGTH OF STRING INTO CL
117                MOV     SP,BP                   ;MOVE STACK POINTER UP TO BP POINT
118                POP     BP                      ;RESTORE CALLER'S BP VALUE
119
120                POP     BX                      ;POP THE RETURN ADDRESS INTO BX
121                                                ; SO WE CAN JUMP TO IT LATER
122
123                ADD     SP,RETLEN-RETADDR-2     ;ADJUST THE STACK POINTER UP PAST
124                                                ; ANY PARAMETERS ON THE STACK
125                                                ; SO THAT IT NOW POINTS TO RETLEN,
126                                                ; THE RETURN VALUE'S LENGTH BYTE.
127                MOV     SI,SP                   ;SEE IF THE LOGICAL LENGTH OF THE STRING
128                                                ; IS THE SAME AS THE PHYSICAL LENGTH BY
129                MOV     AL,SS:[SI]               ; COMPARING THE PHYSICAL LENGTH CONSTANT
130                CMP     AL,CL                   ; TO THE LENGTH BYTE.  IF THEY ARE EQUAL,
131                JZ      EXIT                    ; THE BLOCK MOVE IS NOT NECESSARY
132
133     ; The following code performs a block move on strings that are shorter
134     ; logically than physically, moving them up-stack such that any unused
135     ; physical space in the string is eliminated.
136
137                MOV     AH,0                    ;ZERO OUT AH AND CH; RECALL THAT CL CONTAINS
138                MOV     CH,AH                   ; PHYSICAL LENGTH AND AL THE LOGICAL LENGTH
139
140                ADD     SI,AX                   ;ADJUST SI UP-STACK BY LOGICAL LENGTH
141                MOV     DI,SP                   ;COPY STACK POINTER INTO DI
142                ADD     DI,CX                   ;ADJUST DI UP-STACK BY PHYSICAL LENGTH
143                XCHG    CX,AX                   ;EXCHANGE LOGICAL AND PHYSICAL LENGTH
144                INC     CX                      ; AND ADD ONE TO CX FOR THE LENGTH COUNTER
145
146                PUSH    DS                      ;ALL THIS PUSHPOP ACTION DOES IS SAVE THE
```

(continued)

```
147                PUSH    SS         ; CURRENT VALUE OF DS AND COPY SS INTO DS
148                POP     DS         ; AND ES FOR THE TWO ENDS OF THE BLOCK MOVE
149                PUSH    SS
150                POP     ES
151
152                STD                ;SET DIRECTION FLAG FOR AUTO-DECREMENT
153                REPZ MOVSB         ; AND EXECUTE THE BLOCK MOVE
154
155                POP     DS         ;RESTORE THE CALLER'S DS VALUE
156                INC     DI         ;ADJUST DI TO POINT TO THE STRING DATA PROPER
157                MOV     SP,DI      ; AND COPY IT INTO THE STACK POINTER
158
159     EXIT:      JMP     BX         ;NOW JUMP TO THE SAVED RETURN ADDRESS IN BX.
160                                   ; THE TURBO RUNTIME WILL HANDLE THE PASSING
161                                   ; OF THE FUNCTION RETURN VALUE BACK TO THE
162                                   ; CALLING LOGIC.
163
164     STRPLAT ENDP
165     CODE    ENDS
166             END
```

You needn't understand every detail of the workings of the exit code if you don't intend to disturb it, but it merits study as an example of a string block move on the stack. (I've thrown another stack block move in for good measure between the dotted lines that indicate where you should put the meat of your own string functions.)

4.7 Representation of Turbo Pascal Data Items

This section contains a summary of the ways that Turbo Pascal represents its various data types in memory. Sadly, there are some inconsistencies, and these have been noted. In general, be aware that the expression of a data type may be slightly different when pushed onto the stack than when allocated in the data segment.

Something to keep in mind about the representation of data types in memory, especially when perusing hexdumps, is that we tend to write hexadecimal numbers down on paper with the least significant byte on the right and move leftward in order of significance, but hexdumps display bytes increasing in significance from left to right. In other words, on paper we would write the hex equivalent of 17,420 as $440C, but in a hexdump, we would see the two bytes 0C 44.

Bytes, characters, and *Booleans* are represented as single bytes in memory when acting as variables in the data area and function-return values on the stack. When pushed onto the stack as parameters, they are represented as words, with the high-order byte zero-filled. When written to files, they occupy only one byte.

Enumerated types are represented in the same way that bytes, characters, and Booleans are, as no enumerated type may have more than 256 different values. Each constant evaluates to a number, starting with zero. For example, given this enumerated type:

```
TYPE
   Spectrum=(Red,Orange,Yellow,Green,Blue,Indigo,Violet);
```

the constant **Red** evaluates to 0, **Orange** evaluates to 1, and so on. In general terms, a constant from an enumerated type is passed to an external subprogram as the value yielded by Pascal's **Ord** function for that constant.

Integers are always represented as words. Bit 7 of the high-order byte is the sign bit; a high bit in the sign bit indicates a negative quantity.

Pointers are 32-bit quantities (also called "double words"). The lower order word is the segment address, and the higher order word the offset address.

Real numbers come in three distinct and incompatible flavors. Ordinary Turbo Pascal uses a 6-byte real-number format developed by Borland International for Turbo Pascal and used by no one else to my knowledge. Turbo-87 Pascal uses the IEEE standard 8-byte real format, and Turbo BCD Pascal uses a 10-byte format that is also unique to Borland.

Turbo Pascal 6-byte reals keep their exponent in byte 0 and the mantissa in bytes 1–5, with the least significant byte of the mantissa in byte 1, and so on.

Real numbers actually have two signs. Bit 7 of byte 5 is the mantissa's sign bit, which indicates whether the real number as a whole is positive or negative.

The other sign is implied in the representation of the exponent in byte 0. This sign indicates in which direction the decimal point moves when converting the number from scientific to decimal notation. You can see this sign by displaying a real number with a value less than 1; a value such as .00456 will be displayed on the screen as 4.5600000000E−03. The minus sign after the "E" indicates that the decimal point must be moved three places to the left when converting this number to decimal notation.

The value in the exponent is offset by $80. Exponent values greater than $80 indicate that the decimal point must be moved to the right. Exponent values less than $80 indicate that the decimal point must be moved to the left.

Turbo Pascal real numbers are stored internally as base two logarithms. In other words, to represent the number 4,673.45, Turbo Pascal stores the exponent to which the number two must be raised to yield 4,673.45. This makes multiplying and dividing real numbers much easier on the compiler, since numbers may be multiplied by adding their logarithms, and divided by subtracting their logarithms.

The Turbo-87 real-number format is the IEEE 64-bit real, which is well-documented elsewhere, particularly in Richard Startz's book *8087: Applications and Programming for the IBM PC and Other PC's* (Brady Books, 1983. ISBN 0-89303-420-7). Startz's book is surprisingly readable, considering that it must make sense of such numeric arcana as "negative and positive zero" and "wraparound infinity." The book gives many excellent assembly-language examples of IEEE real-number manipulation, much of which can be lifted whole and dropped into a Turbo Pascal external subprogram, with only a little attention paid to Pascal calling conventions. In general, if you intend to do any serious real-number programming and wish to optimize in assembler, the only rational thing to do is to buy an 8087 and use the well-documented IEEE formats.

The Turbo BCD Pascal real-number format occupies 10 bytes. It is not a standard format to my knowledge and is not supported by any other language product.

Arrays

One-dimensional arrays are easy enough to understand: The base type of the array is allocated **n** times, where **n** is the number of elements in the array. The lowest order element of the array is allocated at the lowest memory addresses, and higher order elements are allocated higher in memory.

One example should suffice. Consider an array of 16 integers containing the numbers from 17 to 32:

```
IntArray = ARRAY[0..15] OF Integer;

VAR
  Scores : IntArray;
  I      : Integer;

FOR I := 0 TO 15 DO Scores[I] := I + 17;
```

When **Scores** is displayed in a hexdump, it will look like this:

```
11 00 12 00 13 00 14 00 15 00 16 00 17 00 18 00    ............
19 00 1A 00 1B 00 1C 00 1D 00 1E 00 1F 00 20 00    ............
```

Scores[0] is dumped as the first two bytes, **11 00**; **Scores[1]** as the second two bytes, and so on.

Multidimensional arrays are not as straightforward, and the more dimensions you have, the less obvious it becomes how the compiler allocates array elements in memory. There is a general rule (there has to be; regardless of what you may think amidst a pile of torn hair at three ayem, compilers have no free will), but it still requires some thought to get it straight.

The rule is this: From a given point in memory, the *rightmost* dimension (from the array declaration) increases first, followed by the second rightmost, and so on. This is best shown as a table. Consider a three-dimensional array of integers:

```
TYPE
  Space = ARRAY[0..2,0..2,0..2] OF Integer;
```

```
High Memory    Space[2,2,2]
               Space[2,2,1]
               Space[2,2,0]
               Space[2,1,2]
               Space[2,1,1]
               Space[2,1,0]
               Space[2,0,2]
               Space[2,0,1]
               Space[2,0,0]
               Space[1,2,2]
               Space[1,2,1]
               Space[1,2,0]
               Space[1,1,2]
               Space[1,1,1]
               Space[1,1,0]
               Space[1,0,2]
               Space[1,0,1]
               Space[1,0,0]
               Space[0,2,2]
               Space[0,2,1]
               Space[0,2,0]
               Space[0,1,2]
               Space[0,1,1]
               Space[0,1,0]
               Space[0,0,2]
               Space[0,0,1]
Low Memory     Space[0,0,0]
```

The lowest element in memory is element **[0,0,0]**, followed by **[0,0,1]**, **[0,0,2]**, and so on.

Accessing an individual array element of a one-dimensional array from within an assembly-language subprogram is done by multiplying the size of the individual elements by the index number of the element you want, and adding that offset to the offset of the first element in memory, for which you will already have the address. (The address of the array as a whole will be the address of the first byte of the first element.)

If speed is an overwhelming consideration (and if it isn't, why are you working in assembler?), try to make the size of the individual elements some power of two (2, 4, 8, 16, 32, 64, 128, etc.). If the size of the base type of the array is a power of two, you can multiply the index of the desired element by the size of the base type by using shift opcodes. Shifting a register one bit to the left multiplies that register by 2; shifting it two bits to the left multiplies it by 4, and so on. For example, if your array's base type is 16 bytes in size, you can index to element 29 of the array by placing 29 in a register and shifting the register four bits to the left (2 to the fourth power is 16). The resulting figure is the number of bytes offset into the array where you will find element 29. This is much faster than using the MUL and IMUL hardware multiply opcodes, which are extremely wasteful of machine cycles.

One caution here: Array elements are not always declared as indexing from zero. The array declaration

```
Foo : ARRAY[17..19] OF Integer;
```

is perfectly valid, but it only declares three elements. The Pascal runtime code is smart enough to know that it must subtract **17** from any index value to access an element of array **Foo**, but your assembly-language routines will have to take that into account somehow. As always, when you enter The Assembly Zone, you leave all vestiges of Pascal's range protection behind you.

Records

The allocation of record types in memory is not subtle in any way. The first field of the array is at the lowest memory address, followed by the second field, and so on. The following example will make this clear. Consider this record type, and a record constant defined for the type:

```
TYPE
  FooRec = RECORD
             Alive    : Boolean;
             Points   : Integer;
             Password : String10
           END;
CONST
  Player : FooRec = (Alive    : True;
                     Points   : 42
                     Password : 'CORIOLIS ');
```

If a hexdump of **Player** is displayed, it will look like this:

```
01 2A 00 08 43 4F 52 49 4F 4C 49 53 20 20   | .*..CORIOLIS |
```

As with all hexdumps shown in this book, the lowest memory address dumped is on the left, with addresses increasing toward the right. The first byte in memory is the first field in the record, **Alive**, which is type **Boolean**. The second field, **Points**, is an integer, and thus takes two bytes: **2A 00**, which, in low-byte-first parlance, is hexadecimal for **42**. After **Points** comes **Password**, with the **0A** value representing the logical length of the string (in this case, 10—the same as the physical length).

Records are allocated in much the same way on the stack when passed to subprograms as value parameters. The first field is at the lowest address on the stack, with subsequent fields higher on the stack.

In the case of variant records, space is allocated in memory for the largest variant instance of any variant field. The assembly-language routine must test the tag field to see which variant to use. For free-union variant records, nothing is passed in the record to indicate which variant is currently in force. The assembly-language routine must either be told which variant to use, or to assume one and act accordingly.

4.8   Placing Multiple Subprograms in a Single Module

Turbo Pascal's extended graphics support for the IBM PC family of machines is located in an external machine-code file named GRAPH.BIN. GRAPH .BIN contains many smaller routines, and they are accessed by specifying an offset into GRAPH.BIN when an individual subprogram is declared as EXTERNAL within a Pascal program. A separate file named GRAPH.P contains an external declaration for each subprogram within GRAPH.BIN, along with its offset.

Each individual graphics routine could have been included as a separate machine-code file, but that would involve more than 30 separate machine-code files. Combining multiple subprograms into a single machine-code module saves a lot of clutter, and only slightly complicates the assembly-language source code that produces the module.

An external machine-code file containing more than one subprogram is declared differently than an external file containing only one subprogram. An initial declaration of the module as a whole must be made, naming the module for the Pascal program and giving the module's disk file name:

```
PROCEDURE GameBoard; EXTERNAL 'GAMEBORD.BIN';
```

Note that no parameters are given. Also note that the identifier **GameBoard** is *not* intended to be called as a subroutine. To do so would probably lock up the system.

Each individual subprogram within the module must be declared before it can be used, along with its parameters and an offset figure:

```
PROCEDURE Stick (StickNumber : Integer; VAR X,Y : Integer);
              EXTERNAL GameBoard[0];
```

Note that, unlike a solo external declaration, the qualifier to the reserved word **EXTERNAL** is not a filename in quotes but a Pascal identifier—in this case, the identifier assigned to the external module file GAMEBORD.BIN.

The **[0]** offset figure tells Turbo Pascal where the individual subprogram **Stick** is located within the larger file GAMEBORD.BIN. The integer constant is a byte offset into the machine-code file GAMEBORD.BIN. In this case, the 0 offset indicates that **Stick** is the first subprogram in GAMEBORD.BIN.

Now, our next machine-code subprogram might exist 36 bytes down into GAMEBORD.BIN, so we might declare it as:

```
PROCEDURE Button (StickNumber,ButtonNumber : Integer) : Boolean;
              EXTERNAL GameBoard[36];
```

This will work if **Button** begins precisely 36 bytes into GAMEBORD.BIN. But if you go back and tighten up the code for **Stick**, which precedes **Button** in GAMEBORD.BIN, and manage to eliminate four bytes of code in **Stick**, then **Button** will begin at offset 32 instead of 36. Calling **Button** at offset 36 into GAMEBORD.BIN will skip execution of the first four opcodes of **Button**, and (since the first few opcodes of any external machine-code subprogram generally save critical registers on the stack) will probably crash you hard.

There's a very simple way out: At the top of the combined assembly-code source file that contains both **Stick** and **Button**, create a short "jump table" with one entry for each machine-code subprogram in the file:

```
JMP     STICK
JMP     BUTTON
```

These two mnemonics must be the first executable opcode in the combined machine-code file. The two identifiers **STICK** and **BUTTON** must be the names of the assembly-language "procs" present in the source file. If you remember from our discussion of external machine-code subprograms, within the assembly-language source-code file you must have for each subprogram in the file a line providing this information:

```
STICK     PROC NEAR
```

This declaration names the assembly-language procedure and states that it is a "near" procedure—one that makes no references outside a 64K code segment, and expects to be called from somewhere within the same 64K code segment in which it exists (as will be true in any Turbo Pascal program). The procedure name declared in this line must be the name present in the jump table at the beginning of the assembly-language source file.

With the jump table declared as shown, the assembler will take the responsibility for counting opcode bytes and deciding where within the machine-code file each named subprogram begins. If the jump table is at the beginning of the file, it will remain unaffected by any changes you may make to any of the assembly-language subprograms in the file. They can grow and shrink as you work on them; however, each time you assemble the file as a whole, the assembler will change the addresses in the jump table to reflect the current size and position of each subprogram.

Each jump table entry generates three bytes of machine code. If you were to look at the .LST file generated by MASM for the GAMEBORD.ASM file, the jump table would look something like this:

```
0000  EB 04 90                    JMP     STICK
0003  EB 5A 90                    JMP     BUTTON
```

EB is the **JMP** opcode itself. The **04** and **5A** bytes are displacements for the **JMP** opcode—in other words, the distance forward into the file over which the jump will be made. **04** will jump four bytes forward, past the rest of the jump table and into the first procedure in the file. **5A** must jump past the jump table and the first procedure in the file as well.

0000 and **0003** at the left margin provide additional valuable information. They represent an offset into the machine-code file generated by the assembly. You can lift these numbers as the offset figures to use within the EXTERNAL declaration. In other words, when you declare a procedure in your Pascal program as:

```
PROCEDURE Button (StickNumber,ButtonNumber : Integer) : Boolean;
              EXTERNAL GameBoard[3];
```

the **[3]** offset figure is the offset into the jump table where Turbo Pascal will find the JMP opcode leading into the named subprogram. This offset figure will be the number in the left margin beside the selected JMP opcode.

In short, you don't have to count the sizes of procedures in your combined machine-code subprogram files. Let the assembler do it—it counts better than you can.

One final note: Sharp assembly-language types may wonder why there is a $90 opcode for each entry in the jump table. The $EB opcode requires a one-byte displacement value, and that's all. The 90 seems extraneous . . . but think again. The one-byte displacement value required by the JMP opcode is a "signed" displacement, meaning it can run from −128 to 128. The $EB opcode can jump no further than 128 bytes into the machine-code file. For the time being, that's fine—**STICK** is only about 90 bytes long. But if you should ever decide to make **STICK** more elaborate (perhaps adding code to make the joystick reading independent of CPU speed), you could easily take it over the 128-byte mark. When that happens, the $EB opcode will need to be replaced by the $E9 opcode, which can handle a two-byte displacement. At that point, every entry in the jump table will require three bytes rather than two, since all the later entries will have to jump over **STICK** as well.

The assembler is smart enough to know that a JMP opcode at the start of an assembly-language module is part of a jump table, and it assumes that this jump may eventually become a two-byte jump rather than the (slightly faster) one-byte jump it may need at first. Therefore, in the interest of keeping entries in the jump table at a consistent distance from one another, it always makes a jump table entry three bytes long, and fills in the extra bytes with NOP opcodes—$90.

The following source-code file combines the two joystick interface routines into one assembly-language file, GAMEBORD.ASM. The Pascal program **GameTest** that follows it shows how you declare and use the subprograms within GAMEBORD.BIN.

```
1    ;===============================================================================
2    ;
3    ;    G A M E B O R D  -  Assembly language joystick support for Turbo Pascal
4    ;
5    ;===============================================================================
6    ;
7    ;
8    ;
9    ;
10   ;
11   ;
12   ;
13   ;
14   ; GAMEBORD is a single assembly-language source file that contains both
15   ; STICK.ASM and BUTTON.ASM, which are given separately elsewhere in
16   ; TURBO PASCAL SOLUTIONS.  The purpose of GAMEBORD is to show how multiple
17   ; assembly language source files may be combined into a single machine-code
18   ; mode to lessen program clutter.  This is the same system by which many
19   ; graphics subprograms have been combined into Borland's single module
20   ; GRAPH.P.
21   ;
22   ; Declaring and using the procedures in a combined module like this is a
23   ; little different from using the individual procedures.  The entire
24   ; module as a whole must be declared first so that the file can be loaded
25   ; into memory:
26   ;
27   ; PROCEDURE GameBoard; EXTERNAL 'GAMEBORD.BIN';
```

(continued)

```
28            ;
29            ; That isn't all there is to it, though:  Each individual routine within
30            ; the combined module must also be separately declared, along with an
31            ; offset that specifies the entry point of the routine within the module:
32            ;
33            ; PROCEDURE STICK(StickNumber : Integer VAR X,Y : Integer);
34            ;                                         EXTERNAL GameBoard[0];
35            ;
36            ;
37            ; FUNCTION BUTTON(StickNumber,ButtonNumber : Integer) : Boolean;
38            ;                                         EXTERNAL GameBoard[3];
39            ;
40            ;
41            ; Note the [0] and [3] indices that are not present in ordinary solo
42            ; EXTERNAL declarations, nor in the declaration of the module as a whole.
43            ; The indices refer to offsets into the generated .BIN file, and specify
44            ; where execution is to begin for the named subprogram.  To keep the
45            ; offsets from changing as the routines are altered, a jump table is
46            ; given at the very front of the file.  The first two instructions in
47            ; GAMEBORD.BIN are JMP instructions that take execution to the
48            ; appropriate subprogram.
49            ;
50            ;
51            ; To reassemble/relink GAMEBORD:
52            ;------------------------------------
53            ; 1. Assemble this file with MASM.   "C>MASM GAMEBORD;"
54            ; 2. Link it into a .EXE file.       "C>LINK GAMEBORD;"
55            ; 3. Use EXE2BIN to make a .COM file. "A> EXE2BIN GAMEBORD.EXE GAMEBORD.BIN"
56            ; 4. Declare as shown above in your Turbo Pascal program.
57            ; 5. Ignore any minor diagnostic messages that may be generated when
58            ;    this file is assembled and linked.  EXE2BIN is supplied with the
59            ;    supplemental programs for PC-DOS; see the DOS manual.
60            ;
61            ;
62   GAMEBORD   SEGMENT PUBLIC
63            ASSUME   CS:GAMEBORD
64
65
66            ; This is the jump table;
67
68                 JMP       STICK
69                 JMP       BUTTON
70
71
72            ;===============================================================================
73            ;     S T I C K  -  Procedure to read either joystick
74            ;===============================================================================
75            ;
76            ; Declare the procedure itself as an external using this declaration:
```

(continued)

```
77      ;
78      ;     PROCEDURE STICK(StickNumber : Integer VAR X,Y : Integer);
79      ;                              EXTERNAL GameBoard[0];
80      ;
81      ; StickNumber specifies which joystick to read from, and the X and Y
82      ; parameters return integers proportional to the joystick's position
83      ; at the moment the stick is sampled.  These integers will vary from
84      ; stick to stick depending on the resistance of the potentiometers
85      ; used within the stick, but will typically from from 3 to 150.
86      ;
87      ; The IBM standard game controller board consists of two pairs of
88      ; one-shots, which output a pulse when triggered by an I/O write to
89      ; I/O port $201.  The length of this pulse is determined by an RC
90      ; time constant circuit the resistance portion of which is the
91      ; potentiometer in the joystick.  As the handle is moved around, the
92      ; two potentiometers (one for X, one for Y) run up and back, changing
93      ; resistance as they go.
94      ;
95      ; To read one of the two joysticks, a dummy value (which may be anything
96      ; at all) is written to I/O port $201.  Port $201 must then be polled
97      ; continuously, incrementing a register at each polling event.  When
98      ; the bit corresponding to that stick's X or Y coordinate changes state,
99      ; the count in the register is returned as that coordinate value at the
100     ; time the stick was sampled.
101     ;
102     ; Here is a map of the joystick bits as returned by port $201:
103     ;
104     ;     |7 6 5 4 3 2 1 0|
105     ;            | | | |
106     ;            | | | - - - - - - -> X coordinate, joystick #1
107     ;            | | - - - - - - - -> Y coordinate, joystick #1
108     ;            | - - - - - - - - -> X coordinate, joystick #2
109     ;            - - - - - - - - - -> Y coordinate, joystick #2
110     ;
111     ; One thing to keep in mind is that a bit goes LOW when sampled, and
112     ; you must test for a HIGH on that bit to indicate that the one-shot has
113     ; timed out.
114     ;
115     ;
116     ;
117     ; This structure defines STICK's parameters on the stack.
118     ;
119     ONSTACK1    STRUC
120     OLDBP       DW    ?                ;TOP OF STACK
121     RETADDR     DW    ?                ;NEAR RETURN ADDRESS
122     YADDR       DD    ?                ;FAR ADDRESS OF X VALUE
123     XADDR       DD    ?                ;FAR ADDRESS OF Y VALUE
124     STIK_NO     DW    ?                ;STICK NUMBER
125     ONSTACK1    ENDS
```

(continued)

```
126             ;
127
128             ;   EQUATES FOR ONE-SHOT BITS FOR STICKS 1 & 2
129
130     STICK_X     EQU     1
131     STICK_Y     EQU     2
132
133
134     STICK       PROC    NEAR
135                 PUSH    BP              ;SAVE CALLER'S BP
136                 MOV     BP,SP           ;STACK POINTER BECOMES NEW BP
137                 PUSH    DS
138
139     ;   GET THE X AXIS VALUE FIRST
140
141                 MOV     AH,STICK_X      ; MOVE IN THE X TEST BIT
142                 CMP     [BP].STIK_NO,2  ; SEE IF WE'RE TESTING STICK #1 OR #2
143                 JNE     TEST_X
144                 SHL     AH,1            ; SHIFT BIT NUMBERS 2 LEFT FOR STICK #2
145                 SHL     AH,1
146     TEST_X:     MOV     AL,1            ; INITIALIZE OUTPUT VALUE
147                 MOV     DX,201H         ; SET PORT ADDRESS
148                 MOV     BX,0            ; AND KEEPING THE RUNUP COUNT IN BX
149                 MOV     CX,BX           ; LOOP 64K TIMES MAX
150                 OUT     DX,AL           ; TRIGGER THE ONE-SHOTS
151     AGAIN_X:    IN      AL,DX           ; READ THE ONE-SHOT BITS
152                 TEST    AL,AH           ; TEST FOR A HIGH BIT 0
153                 JE      DELAY           ; WE'RE DONE IF BIT 0 IS HIGH
154                 INC     BX              ; OTHERWISE INCREMENT BX AND LOOP AGAIN
155                 LOOP    AGAIN_X
156                 MOV     BX,-1           ; SET X=-1 IF NO RESPONSE
157
158     ;   DELAY HERE TO LET THE OTHER THREE PULSES MAX OUT
159
160     DELAY:      MOV     CX,256
161     WAIT:       LOOP    WAIT
162
163     ;   NOW WE GET THE Y AXIS VALUE
164
165                 MOV     AH,STICK_Y      ; MOVE IN THE Y TEST BIT
166                 CMP     [BP].STIK_NO,2  ; SEE IF WE'RE TESTING STICK #1 OR #2
167                 JNE     TEST_Y
168                 SHL     AH,1            ; SHIFT BIT NUMBERS 2 LEFT FOR STICK #2
169                 SHL     AH,1
170
171     TEST_Y:     MOV     SI,0            ; KEEP THE RUNUP COUNT FOR Y IN SI
172                 MOV     CX,SI           ; SET LOOP LIMIT TO 64K
173                 OUT     DX,AL           ; FIRE THE ONE-SHOTS AGAIN
174     AGAIN_Y:    IN      AL,DX           ; READ THE ONE-SHOT BITS
```

(continued)

```
175                      TEST    AL,AH          ; TEST FOR A HIGH BIT 1
176                      JE      DONE           ; WE'RE DONE IF BIT 1 IS HIGH
177                      INC     SI             ; OTHERWISE INCREMENT SI AND LOOP AGAIN
178                      LOOP    AGAIN_Y
179                      MOV     SI,-1          ; SET Y=-1 IF NO RESPONSE
180
181              ;   MOVE RETURN VALUES FROM REGISTERS INTO VAR PARAMETERS X & Y
182
183      DONE:           LDS     DI,[BP].XADDR          ;ADDR OF X INTO DS:DI
184                      MOV     [DI],BX                ;X VALUE FROM BX TO DS:DI
185                      LDS     DI,[BP].YADDR          ;DITTO FOR Y VALUE FROM SI
186                      MOV     [DI],SI
187
188              ;   IT'S OVER...NOW CLEAN UP THE STACK AND LEAVE
189
190                      POP     DS
191                      MOV     SP,BP                  ; CLEAN UP STACK AND LEAVE
192                      POP     BP                     ; RESTORE CALLER'S BP
193
194                      RET     10
195
196      STICK   ENDP
197
198
199
200      ;===============================================================================
201      ;     B U T T O N  -  Function to return the state of the joystick buttons
202      ;===============================================================================
203      ;
204      ; Declare the procedure itself as external using this declaration:
205      ;
206      ; FUNCTION BUTTON(StickNumber,ButtonNumber : Integer) : Boolean;
207      ;                                         EXTERNAL GameBoard[3];
208      ;
209      ; StickNumber specifies which joystick to read from, and ButtonNumber
210      ; specifies which of the two buttons on that joystick to read.  If the
211      ; specified button is down, BUTTON returns a Boolean value of TRUE.
212      ;
213      ; Yes, this is the long way 'round; assembly language is in no way required
214      ; to read four bits from an ordinary 8088 I/O port.  BUTTON exists only as
215      ; practice in creating assembly language external functions.
216      ;
217      ; The button information is obtained by reading I/O port $201.  The high
218      ; four bits represent the state of the four buttons (two for each of the
219      ; two possible joysticks) at the instant the port is read.  A LOW bit
220      ; represents a button DOWN.  This is why the byte read from the port is
221      ; inverted via NOT before the selected bit is tested.
222      ;
223      ; Here is a map of the button bits as returned by port $201:
```

(continued)

```
224          ;
225          ;      |7 6 5 4 3 2 1 0|
226          ;        | | | |
227          ;        | | |  - - - - - -> Button #1, joystick #1
228          ;        | |  - - - - - - -> Button #2, joystick #1
229          ;        |  - - - - - - - -> Button #1, joystick #2
230          ;         - - - - - - - - -> Button #2, joystick #2
231          ;
232          ; Remember that the return value from this function is passed to the runtime
233          ; code in the Zero Flag, which is set by the TEST AL,BL instruction in line
234          ; 103.
235          ;
236          ;
237          ; This structure defines the layout of BUTTON's parameters on the stack:
238          ;
239          ONSTACK2    STRUC
240          OLDBP2      DW     ?              ;TOP OF STACK
241          RETADDR2    DW     ?              ;NEAR RETURN ADDRESS
242          BTN_NO      DW     ?              ;BUTTON NUMBER
243          STIK_NO2    DW     ?              ;STICK NUMBER
244          RETURN      DB     ?              ;BOOLEAN RETURN VALUE **A BYTE!**
245          ONSTACK2    ENDS
246
247
248          BUTTON      PROC   NEAR
249                      PUSH   BP             ;SAVE PREVIOUS VALUE OF BP ON STACK
250                      MOV    BP,SP          ;SP BECOMES NEW VALUE OF BP
251
252          ;--------------------------------------------------------------------
253          ; THE BULK OF THIS ROUTINE SETS UP A TEST MASK BY WHICH ONE SINGLE
254          ; BIT OUT OF THE FOUR BUTTON BITS IS TESTED.
255          ;--------------------------------------------------------------------
256
257                      MOV    BL,010H        ;START WITH HIGH BIT IN BIT 4
258                      CMP    [BP].STIK_NO2,2 ;ARE WE TESTING FOR JOYSTICK #2?
259                      JNE    WHICH          ;IF NOT, GO ON TO TEST FOR WHICH BUTTON,
260                      SHL    BL,1           ; OTHERWISE SHIFT TWO POSITIONS LEFTWARD
261                      SHL    BL,1           ; SO THAT THE MASK IS ON BIT 6 FOR STICK 2
262
263          WHICH:      CMP    [BP].BTN_NO,2   ;ARE WE TESTING FOR BUTTON #2?
264                      JNE    READEM         ;IF NOT, MASK IS CORRECT; GO READ PORT
265                      SHL    BL,1           ;OTHERWISE, SHIFT 1 BIT LEFT FOR BUTTON 2
266
267          ;--------------------------------------------------------------------
268          ; THE BIT MASK IS NOW CORRECT.  HERE THE BUTTON BITS ARE READ FROM PORT
269          ; $201 AND TESTED AGAINST THE MASK.  NOTE THAT THE BITS AS READ FROM
270          ; THE PORT MUST BE INVERTED SO THAT THE Z FLAG IS SET RATHER THAN CLEARED
271          ; ON AN ACTIVE BUTTON BIT.  (BITS ARE ACTIVE **LOW**, REMEMBER!)
272          ;--------------------------------------------------------------------
273
```

(continued)

```
274        READEM:    MOV     DX,0201H        ;SET UP 16-BIT ADDRESS FOR PORT READ
275                   IN      AL,DX           ;READ BUTTON BITS FROM PORT $201
276                   NOT     AL              ;MUST INVERT BITS FOR PROPER SENSE
277                                           ; OF THE Z FLAG AFTER TESTING
278                   TEST    AL,BL           ;SEE IF THE DESIRED BIT IS HIGH;
279                                           ;THIS INSTRUCTION SETS THE Z FLAG
280                                           ; FOR THE BOOLEAN FUNCTION RETURN VALUE
281                   MOV     SP,BP           ;RESTORE PRIOR STACK POINTER & BP
282                   POP     BP              ; IN CONVENTIONAL RETURN
283                   RET     5
284
285        BUTTON     ENDP
286
287
288        GAMEBORD   ENDS
289                   END
290
```

```
 1         PROGRAM GameTest;
 2
 3         VAR
 4           X,Y : INTEGER;
 5
 6         PROCEDURE GameBoard; EXTERNAL 'GAMEBORD.BIN';
 7
 8         FUNCTION  Button(StickNumber,ButtonNumber : Integer) : Boolean;
 9                   EXTERNAL GameBoard[3];
10
11         PROCEDURE Stick(StickNumber : Integer;
12                         VAR X       : INTEGER;
13                         VAR Y       : INTEGER);
14                         EXTERNAL GameBoard[0];
15
16
17         BEGIN
18           ClrScr;
19           X := 0; Y := 0;
20           GotoXY(2,9); Writeln('X Axis    Y Axis');
21           WHILE NOT KeyPressed DO
22             BEGIN
23               GotoXY(1,5);
24               IF Button(2,1) THEN Writeln('Button 1 pressed!')
25                 ELSE Writeln('Nothing on 1.....');
26               IF Button(2,2) THEN Writeln('Button 2 pressed!')
27                 ELSE Writeln('Nothing on 2.....');
28               Stick(2,X,Y);
29               GotoXY(1,10);
30               Writeln(X:5,'    ',Y:5);
31             END;
32         END.
```

4.9 Boolean Functions Through INLINE

Part of the difficulty of working with **INLINE** is that the operation of the Turbo Pascal runtime code can get in the way. Runtime is a black box unless you're adept at probing your compiled code step by tortuous step with **DEBUG** (or something stronger like Periscope).

One excellent example of how the runtime can interfere with your plans lies in the creation of a machine-code Boolean function implemented as an **INLINE** statement. If you recall from function **Button** described in Section 4.6, Boolean function results are returned as the state of the 8086 Z flag. This implies that if you wish to create a Boolean function as a single **INLINE** statement, all you have to do is make sure the Z flag is appropriately set or cleared before ending the **INLINE** statement.

A simple working example would be a function that tested two machine words and returned a Boolean value of **True** if the first of two passed integer parameters were greater than the second. The advantage to testing machine words from **INLINE** over simply testing two integers from Pascal is that it allows you to treat the integers as "unsigned machine words"—that is, treat the integer sign bit as numeric data rather than a sign indicator. This allows a machine word to express a value of up to 65,535 rather than only 32,767. (In Chapter 6, Section 6.4, I'll show you a serious use for such a compare machine words function, in determining which of two DOS time stamp words is the greater.)

If all that needed to be done were to compare the two integer parameters and set or clear the Z flag appropriately, the function would look like this:

```
FUNCTION WordComp(Word1,Word2 : Integer) : Boolean;

BEGIN
   INLINE($8B/$86/Word2/     {MOV AX,Word2}
          $3B/$86/Word1)     {CMP AX,Word1}
END;
```

This code does in fact compare the two parameters, and thereby sets the Z flag. (The **CMP** instruction sets the Z flag as part of its operation.) This function, however, does not return the correct Boolean value to follow the state of the Z flag.

What gives?

The heart of the problem lies in the fact that there is more inside this procedure than just the **INLINE** statement. Specifically, there are instructions appended to the end of the function that handle the function-return value. This additional, "invisible" code sets the Z flag before returning to the calling logic.

If you remember from the description of the stack as it is formatted for procedures and functions, there is a single-byte value pushed onto the stack for Boolean functions. This might have seemed odd before, since in the **Button** external machine-code function, this byte value on the stack took no part at all in the computations.

That byte value exists to support the method by which Boolean functions written in Turbo Pascal return their values to the caller. When you assign a Boolean value to the function identifier as a means of assigning a return value to the function, what actually happens is that your Boolean value is stored on the stack as that single-byte return value. It remains there, safe and sound, until all of your code has executed and the function is ready to return control to the caller.

This is when the runtime code kicks in. It reads the Boolean value it previously stored on the stack as the return value into register AL, clears AH to zero, and then ORs AX against itself. The OR operation sets the zero flag if the Boolean value is $00 (Boolean **False**) and clears it if the Boolean value is $01 (Boolean **True**). In this fashion, the runtime sets the zero flag as a means of returning a Boolean value to the caller.

Since there is no way the runtime code can be suppressed during a compile (you would have to NOP it out via **DEBUG** after compilation, which is a lot of extra work), you have to play by the runtime code's rules—even if that means adding more complication to the **INLINE** statement.

It does, although not a great deal. You have to place either a $00 (**False**) or $01 (**True**) on the stack in the function-return value location, so that the runtime code can do its thing as it expects to do after **INLINE** finishes up. The **INLINE** function can be expanded like this:

```
FUNCTION WordComp(Word1,Word2 : Integer) : Boolean;

BEGIN
   INLINE($C6/$46/$08/$00/      {MOV BYTE PTR [BP+8],$00}
          $8B/$86/Word2/        {MOV AX,Word2}
          $3B/$86/Word1/        {CMP AX,Word1}
          $77/$04/              {JA 4  }
          $C6/$46/$08/$01);     {MOV BYTE PTR [BP+8],$01}
END;
```

The new code adds three instructions to the function. The first line now stores a **$00** value into the function-return value on the stack. The **[BP+8]** means that the return value lies eight bytes above **BP** on the stack. You must work this out by counting the bytes in your parameters and, ideally, drawing a picture of the stack as it exists when the function is instantiated.

The last line in the **INLINE** statement stores the opposite Boolean value into that same location on the stack. The line before it performs a conditional jump based on the zero flag: Jump If Above. (This is the unsigned equivalent of

Jump If Greater.) If **Word2** is less than **Word1**, the test will fail, and control will fall through to the instruction that stores a **True** value onto the stack. If **Word2** is greater than **Word1**, the test will succeed, the jump will be made, and the **False** condition stored onto the stack at the beginning of the **INLINE** statement will remain in force.

This time we have a function that works correctly. I disassembled the function with **DEBUG**, along with the runtime code's addendum that reads the function-return value from **BP+8** and sets the zero flag based on the value it finds there. See if you can follow the logic (the comments are mine):

```
;The first five lines are the INLINE statement:
14AC:2DAA C6460800    MOV   BYTE PTR [BP+8],00
14AC:2DAE 8B860400    MOV   AX,[BP+0004]
14AC:2DB2 3B860600    CMP   AX,[BP+0006]
14AC:2DB6 7704        JA    2DBC
14AC;2DB8 C6460801    MOV   BYTE PTR [BP+8],01

14AC:2DBC E90000      JMP   2DBF            ;Ignore this

14AC:2DBF 8A4608      MOV   AL,[BP+08]      ;Move return to AL
14AC:2DC2 32E4        XOR   AH,AH           ;Clear hi byte
14AC:2DC4 0BC0        OR    AX,AX           ;Set zero flag

14AC:2DC6 8BE5        MOV   SP,BP           ;Conventional
14AC:2DC8 5D          POP   BP              ; subprogram return
14AC:2DC9 C20500      RET   0005
```

The disassembly begins with the first line of the **INLINE** statement, and ends up with the **RET** instruction that returns control to the caller. Ignore the **JMP 2DBF** instruction; no one outside of Borland really knows what it's for, and all it does is jump unconditionally to the next instruction in sequence. Undoubtedly, it is used in the generation of code for other kinds of functions, perhaps in "shorting out" the runtime addendum. The **MOV, XOR,** and **OR** instructions perform the zero flag setup based on the value found at **BP+08**.

I included this section in part to show you how to write a Boolean function as an **INLINE** statement. Mostly, I wanted to show you the subtle dangers of writing machine-code routines as **INLINE** code rather than as external machine-code files. If you code something up with **INLINE** and it doesn't work, do this:

1. Add five NOPs to the beginning of the **INLINE** statement.
2. Compile to a .COM file.
3. Load the .COM file into **DEBUG** and search for five NOPS by entering this:

```
-s 90 90 90 90 90
```

You'll get an address (with any luck, only one) where your five NOPs are located. Jot the address down. If you get more than one address, inspect them all, but my experience shows it will usually be the first, or lowest in memory.

4. Unassemble the code starting at that address (or slightly before) by entering **DEBUG's u** command:

```
u <address>
```

Type **u** again to unassemble further into the file. You'll see a listing comparable to the one I included above, which was captured to disk by redirecting **DEBUG's** output to a text file.

5. Get out your 8086 "blue card" and study what you see. It may take some time, and you may have to experiment, but in time you should be able to dope out what's wrong. Make sure you go beyond the end of your own code and try to follow what the runtime is doing. This will be a strange experience indeed, as the Turbo Pascal code generator is, well, brute force, and does not always do what common sense might suggest. It is instead trying to make matters easy on itself and do it quickly.

You will learn a lot—not only about Turbo Pascal, but about the 8086 as well.

CHAPTER 5

Text Video

5.1   Text Mode, the Un-graphics

Graphics gets the glory, but text does the work.

It seems to be an all-or-nothing situation. When people use a graphics metaphor in designing a program, they really go for it: exploding and imploding icons, mice, buttons, control panels, elevators, the works. When they use a text screen, it's either something that could have been scraped right off a 3278 mainframe terminal or (God help us) text scrolling up from line 24 like a 1973 Hazeltine glass teletype.

It doesn't have to be that way. Lots can be done on an ordinary 25×80 text-mode screen, using a set of 255 characters, a handful of character attributes, and a little imagination.

Text mode has two major (and related) advantages over graphics modes:

1. Text mode is *fast*. You can "flash" an entire screen into view in what appears to be an instant—the screen doesn't flow in from top to bottom as graphics screen do. It is simply *there*. Moving graphics information to and from screens takes longer because there's so much more of it. Which leads us to:

2. Text mode is *compact*. A 25×80 text screen with attribute bytes occupies 4000 bytes. The same screen area done in high-resolution monochrome graphics would take 16,000 bytes, and that gives you one color, no attributes. If you want to "sling" screens out onto the heap (as we'll describe later), you will use up heapspace in a tremendous hurry. Graphics objects, in their infinite mutability, occupy much more space than the more mundane IBM character set. If you are programming in an environment where memory is at a premium (the PCjr comes to mind), this can knock a program concept out of the realm of possibility.

I'm not disparaging graphics, which is an important and vast subject that deserves a book to itself. I want to show you in this chapter that you can do a lot of fast and flashy things in text mode.

DMA and Nothing Less!

Part of the reason that text display has gotten a bad rap is that it is usually done in the worst possible way: by sending characters to the screen one at a time through the ultraconservative labyrinth in the IBM PC ROM BIOS. BIOS is *slow* no matter what it does, and nowhere is that slowness more apparent than when you want to display text on the screen. Turbo Pascal's WRITE and WRITELN statements use BIOS, and are therefore not as fast as they could be.

The alternative is called DMA (Direct Memory Access). DMA is a shortcut that cuts BIOS out of the loop; you write characters directly to the RAM buffers of the display adapter card which handles video for you. There's nothing magical or complicated about it. You use MEM or a pointer reference to poke a character into the right location in video memory and *wham*, it appears on the screen.

You probably won't learn about this method in school. DMA screen access is inherently unportable to computers which do not have their screen RAM in the same place and in the same format as the IBM PC standard. On the other hand, these days, only a totally bonkers computer company would offer an MS DOS computer which has an IBM-incompatible text screen. There are only so many ways you can handle an 80×25 text screen, and as far as I'm concerned, IBM's method is as good as anything that could be developed. IBM's Enhanced Graphics Adapter (EGA) has a 43-line text mode using a buffer identical in format to the buffer used in 80×25 text screens and differing only in length. The 80×66 text screen that I use, called the Micro Display Systems Genius VHR Video Display System, is also an extension of the IBM monochrome text screen which (again, aside from the size of its buffer) is completely compatible with the IBM text screen for the first 25 lines. Differences in buffer length can be handled with a little Pascal cleverness.

Standards make life easier for all of us. This is one standard which makes a lot of sense and which I have embraced wholeheartedly.

The Structure of a Video Buffer

IBM currently offers three different display adapters for the IBM PC: the Monochrome Display Adapter (MDA), the Color Graphics Adapter (CGA), and the Enhanced Graphics Adapter (EGA). All three boards operate in text mode. (The MDA does not have a graphics mode.) Each board contains a specific quantity of RAM; this RAM contains each board's video buffer. When you write characters into this RAM, the characters appear on your screen.

The fundamental "atom" of a text-video buffer is a pair of bytes called a *character/attribute pair*. One byte holds a code representing a character; the other holds a code specifying that character's attribute. Think of the character as telling the computer *what* is to be shown on the screen, and the attribute telling the computer *how* it is to be shown.

In a character/attribute pair, the character comes first and the attribute follows. If a video buffer begins at 0, the byte at 0 is the first character byte, and its attribute is byte #1. Throughout the buffer, the even-numbered bytes are characters and the odd-numbered bytes are attributes. This is why there are 160 bytes per 80-column line in a video buffer: Every character byte has an attribute byte right after it.

The CGA and EGA are most different when they are operating in graphics mode. In text mode, they work almost identically to one another and to the MDA. Text-mode buffers are structured the same way regardless of which board contains them; each buffer consists of some number of these character/ attribute pairs. The standard 80×25 text buffer thus holds 160×25 (or 4000) bytes. The EGA's 43-line mode uses a buffer 160×43 (6880) bytes long. The VHR's 66-line screen uses a buffer 160×66 (10560) bytes long.

The attribute byte has radically different meanings in monochrome and color mode. In color mode, the attribute byte specifies the foreground color (the color of the character itself) and the background color (the color of the rest of the "cell" in which the character lies). In monochrome mode, the attribute byte specifies whether or not a character will be displayed in bold, with an underscore, in reverse video, or normally, without any embellishments. (Since manipulating and interpreting attribute bytes is quite complicated, it is discussed in more detail in Section 5.6.)

Figure 5.1 shows the structure of a text buffer on the IBM PC. Note that the diagram reflects the way the characters appear on your screen. Don't forget

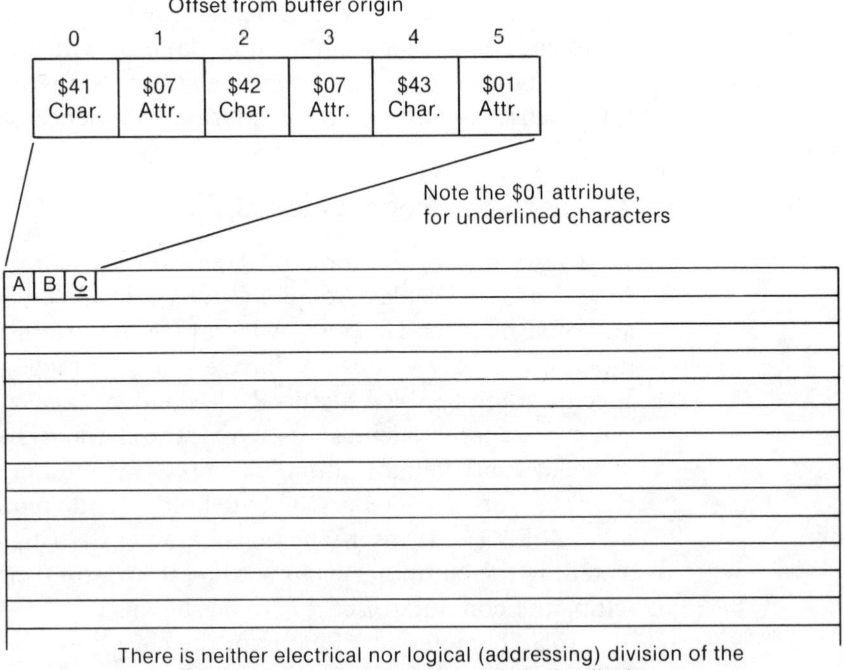

Figure 5.1 **Text buffer structure**

that there is no explicit division of a text buffer into lines. An 80×25 text buffer consists of 2000 character/attribute pairs. It shows up as lines when the video hardware displays a buffer on the screen; however, seen as a block of RAM, a text buffer is just a long row of 4000 bytes. The first 160 bytes of a text buffer appear on the screen as the top line (line 1), the second 160 bytes appear as line 2, and so on.

Because each set of two adjacent bytes in a text buffer functions as a character/attribute pair, it is sometimes more convenient to look at a text buffer as an array of 2000 *integers* rather than 4000 bytes. (An integer in Turbo Pascal contains two bytes.) By writing one integer to the screen, you can write both a character byte and its attribute byte at the same time. This is much faster than separately writing the character byte and its attribute byte. To take advantage of this added speed, text buffers in this chapter will always be treated as arrays of integers. (More properly, arrays of type **Reg**, a free-union variant record of which one variant is type **Integer**.)

5.2 Virtualizing Your Text-Video System

The great headache of software developers is the diversity of hardware in use, even within a "standard" as well-established as the IBM PC. You want your programs to run on as many types of machines as possible; thus, your programs will have to deal with that diversity, and deal with it automatically.

One way to achieve this is to work through the BIOS, using software interrupt 16 ($10), known as VIDEO. If you work through the BIOS, you'll always work correctly with whatever display hardware is installed. However, as I've pointed out, BIOS is too slow.

A more desirable alternative requires spending a little effort to generate a toolkit of text-video functions and procedures that adapt themselves to the currently installed hardware without having to perform every character display through slow BIOS routines. Part of this adaptation relies on BIOS savvy, of course. The trick is knowing which BIOS functions matter critically from a speed standpoint and which do not.

This chapter will present such a toolkit, explaining how it works as we go. The ruling philosophy here is to move away from hardcoded references to specific memory locations and display formats as much as possible. This involves distilling the essence of a display screen and treating it as an object apart from the display adapter. This is called *virtualizing* the screen. The following are my requirements for developing such a virtual screen system:

1. There must be no hardcoded references to the location of a screen buffer in system memory. Screens must be locatable anywhere.

2. There must be allowances for an arbitrary number of screens, with any currently visible screens identified with flags. Screen writes must operate identically on visible and nonvisible screens.
3. There must be no hardcoded references to either the height nor the width of the display screen; i.e., nothing in the program must assume 25×80, 43×80, etc.

Each of these requirements has a host of nonobvious consequences, and each must be discussed in some detail.

The Location of Screen Buffers

A screen buffer is an array of X pairs of bytes acting together, each pair displaying a character on the screen. Every display adapter contains a buffer, consisting of a specific quantity of RAM. When characters are written into this RAM, they appear on the visible screen. The buffer starts at a particular address in the IBM PC memory map.

In the current generation of IBM PC display adapters, there are only two places for a text buffer to reside: $B000 : 0 and $B800 : 0. Until IBM stirs the soup with yet another type of display adapter, a display adapter text buffer will *always* begin at one of these two IBM PC memory addresses.

But which one is which? And why are there two? Doesn't that complicate things?

It certainly does. But the reason for having two separate text-buffer locations is a good one: It allows you to place two video boards in your PC and have two screens active at the same time. If there were only one place for a text buffer to exist, you could only have one screen on display at any given time.

Now, where are they? Follow these rules for locating the three IBM video cards:

```
The CGA buffer ALWAYS begins at $B800 : 0.
The MDA buffer ALWAYS begins at $B000 : 0.
The EGA buffer begins at $B000 : 0 when connected to a Mono-
chrome Display, and $B800 : 0 when connected to a color display.
```

Determining the location of a screen buffer is simple unless you are using the EGA, which is a hat from which you can pull any number of rabbits. The EGA can do almost anything the MDA or CGA can do, *and* it has high-resolution, color text modes. If you have an EGA and can afford a monitor like the Sony Multiscan or NEC Multisync, get one. The high-resolution, color text mode is as comfortable as the Monochrome Display screen, and you get colors, to boot.

Thus, determining the location of a screen buffer first involves knowing which display adapter is installed. (This is only slightly sneaky, and I'll explain how it is done shortly.) If an EGA is found in the machine, the EGA must be queried using another BIOS call to determine what sort of monitor is attached. Given that information, a pointer can be built to indicate the location of the display adapter's buffer. The pointer is built at runtime based on information gathered at that time, and is the sole arbiter of where the screen buffer is located. The code that writes to the buffer can only "get at" the buffer through the pointer. Nothing about the location of the buffer is hardcoded into write routines. The only explicit references to absolute memory locations are isolated in the text-video initialization routines. If IBM ever adds a new video adapter to the fold, these initialization routines should be the only code that needs modification and recompiling to enable use of the new adapter.

I will explain how to perform the equipment determination in Section 5.4.

Multiple Screens

A typical PC has only one screen buffer, which resides inside the display adapter. Some PC's contain two display adapters; those same PC's have two screen buffers, both of them visible at the same time. Although, with current display adapters, no more than two screen buffers can be displayed simultaneously, there's nothing that forbids any number of "invisible" screen buffers to exist elsewhere in memory.

As you may know, Turbo Pascal has a lot of "elsewhere in memory", called the *heap*. Since pointers are used to access data on the heap, and since the only references to screen buffers in toolkit routines work through pointers, the heap is a natural place for multiple screen buffers. The toolkit's screen write routines work identically when writing to both invisible buffers on the heap and to the visible buffer inside the display adapter.

Now, writing invisible text to an invisible buffer on the heap may seem odd, but only until you consider that Turbo Pascal's built-in **Move** procedure can take a screen buffer on the heap and flash it into the display adapter's screen buffer in a fraction of a second. It happens so quickly that the screen simply appears all at once. Given the irrationally impatient nature of humankind (the nature that makes the idiot behind me lean on his horn a nanosecond after the light turns green), a program that flashes its displays all at once will be more satisfying than a program that puts them together while you watch. This will be true even if you must take time to write them into the invisible buffer prior to flashing them into the display adapter. Crosstalk, perhaps the most successful communications program in the PC universe, pulls this trick. While building its invisible screen buffers elsewhere in memory, it gives the user a pithy little aphorism to chuckle over—something like, "On a clear disk you can seek forever. . . ." Sneaky, sneaky.

If you are one of those dour souls who owns the late and unlamented PCjr, the system works even better than that, because the PCjr has a little-known, video-memory remapping feature that can move an invisible buffer into the display adapter in an instant. Jr does a hardware reinterpretation of memory address lines that can take any 16K block of memory and allow the display adapter to display it as though it were located at B800 : 0. Perform a single software-interrupt function call, and *wham*, any 16K block of memory is instantly shown on your screen. Nothing is moved, and no time is lost.

Unfortunately for PCjr owners (but fortunately, I think, for me), I never bought a Jr and can't test a PCjr-specific version of the toolkit. But I'll offer some hints as I go, and if any PCjr owners create a **MoveScreen** routine that works using the PCjr system (using Jr-specific memory remapping rather than the **Move** block-move built-in procedure), I'll include it in a future edition of this book.

Multiple Display Formats

The absurd standard display format of twenty-five 80-column lines was not always as universal as it seems today. My first real computer, the long-extinct Compucolor II, had a very nice 64×32 text screen. My second computer, an S100 machine, contained a long-extinct display board called the Screensplitter, whose display was 40 lines of 86 characters. No, we were condemned to 80×25 by the appearance of cheap serial terminals that used adapted TV video technology. Before the re-emergence of memory-mapped displays with the IBM PC, the cheap serial terminal was the console of choice for most serious desktop computers. The PC display adapters were compatible with this format to allow use of software designed around an 80×25 screen.

So 99 percent of PC users struggle along with 25-line screens. I am not among them. A screen to me is virtual paper, and paper stands the other way, with its long axis vertical. I use a display called the Micro Display Systems Genius VHR, a monochrome screen arranged as 66 lines of 80 characters. Its screen buffer follows the same format and begins at the same place as IBM's Monochrome Display Adapter (B000 : 0); it just continues longer. To know it is to love it.

IBM complicated matters even more by allowing the EGA to display 43 lines of 80 characters through some sleight of hand involving fonts. As with the Genius VHR, the buffer format of character and attribute is the same as for the other IBM adapters, with the buffer simply extending beyond the 4K mark required by 80×25 screens. Unfortunately, 43-line mode is not really a mode in the same sense that 25-line text mode is a mode. (This complicates matters somewhat, as I'll explain shortly.)

There are display adapters, like Tecmar's estimable Graphics Master that have additional, proprietary text modes allowing 90×25 or 90×40, among others. In every case I've seen, the visible buffers begin at the same places in memory as IBM's, and are simply extended and mapped to follow the different number of lines and columns.

Hence my requirement that the toolkit not assume 80×25 or any other screen format. There is enough diversity available to merit a more general approach. Not only is the location of a screen buffer defined at runtime, but also the length of that buffer and its division into rows and columns.

There is a serious hassle involved here, however. I have not yet found a universal and reliable way for software to determine at runtime which screen format is in use. It is possible to query an EGA to discover whether it is operating in 25- or 43-line mode, but what about identifying screen displays such as the Genius VHR, or the Tecmar Graphics Master in one of its own proprietary display formats? There ought to be a BIOS call that returns the display format, but IBM did not see fit to implement one.

What we are left with is a compromise—but a good one. As I explained in Section 2.2, there are two patch points in the first 256 bytes of the Turbo Pascal compiler program that determine the display format assumed by the compiler. These patch points are "inherited" by compiled programs written to disk by Turbo Pascal as .COM files. The toolkit is written to assume that those patch points are the arbiters of the screen size in use. This is done with absolute variables.

```
VAR
   ScreenWidth  : Byte ABSOLUTE CS : $016A;
   ScreenHeight : Byte ABSOLUTE CS : $016B;
```

It would have been easy to return this information to the program through a pair of functions rather than using absolute variables (and using functions would have been somewhat neater), but I wanted to preserve the "patch" nature of the two values, so that if a program somehow discovered it was working with a screen size different from that specified in the patch points, it could repatch the patch points at runtime.

5.3   Mode Setting and Sensing

Setting and sensing modes is messy business. Setting modes, in particular, is hardware-specific, especially when you move to non-IBM modes on non-IBM display adapters such as the Tecmar Graphics Master or the Genius VHR. Turbo Pascal has several built-in procedures for changing modes: **TextMode**, **GraphMode**, **GraphColorMode**, and **HiRes**. These built-in procedures predate the EGA and only support MDA/CGA modes. The better method by far when setting modes is the use of BIOS calls and the IBM-defined mode numbers. The following table summarizes IBM-defined video modes:

Mode #	Valid on	Text/Graphics	Format	Colors	ORG
0	CGA/EGA/Jr	B/W Text	40 × 25	16	B800
1	CGA/EGA/Jr	Color Text	40 × 25	16	B800
2	CGA/EGA/Jr	B/W Text	80 × 25	16	B800
3	CGA/EGA/Jr	Color Text	80 × 25	16	B800
4	CGA/EGA/Jr	Color Graphics	320 × 200	4	B800
5	CGA/EGA/Jr	B/W Graphics	320 × 200	4	B800
6	CGA/EGA/Jr	B/W Graphics	640 × 200	2	B800
7	EGA/MDA	B/W Text	80 × 25	3	B000
8	Jr	Color Graphics	160 × 200	16	B800
9	Jr	Color Graphics	320 × 200	16	B800
A	Jr	Color Graphics	640 × 200	4	B800
B	EGA reserved				
C	EGA reserved				
D	EGA	Color Graphics	320 × 200	16	A000
E	EGA	Color Graphics	640 × 200	16	A000
F	EGA	B/W Graphics	640 × 350	3	A000
10	EGA	Color Graphics	640 × 350	16	A000

This is a lot of modes, most of which aren't worth much. In fact, if we're speaking of text video, we need only examine modes 0–3 and 7, of which only 3 and 7 are important for our purposes. The only difference between modes 0 and 1 is that mode 0 kills the color burst signal sent out with the composite video outputs, creating a black-and-white image on composite color monitors or TV sets. If you're using the RGB outputs of the board, there is no difference between modes 0 and 1. (The same applies to modes 2 and 3, which are identical to 0 and 1, except that they are 80 characters wide.)

Mode 3 is your default text mode when using color monitors, and mode 7 is your default text mode when using a monochrome TTL monitor. In most circumstances, mode 3 displays keep their buffer at B800, while mode 7 displays keep their buffer at B000.

The following general mode-setting procedure is easy to perform and often useful:

```
1        {->>>>SetMode<<<<--------------------------------------------------}
2        {                                                                  }
3        { Filename : SETMODE.SRC -- Last Modified 2/13/87                   }
4        {                                                                  }
5        { This routine will be useful in situations where Turbo's          }
```

(continued)

```
 6        { built-in mode-setting routines (TextMode, HiRes,          }
 7        { GraphColorMode) don't cut it; EGA graphics modes come to   }
 8        { mind.  This is nothing more than a call to VIDEO service 0; }
 9        { there are no safety checks for installed adapter type, etc. }
10        {                                                            }
11        {                                                            }
12        {                                                            }
13        {-----------------------------------------------------------}
14
15        PROCEDURE SetMode(ModeNumber : Integer);
16
17        TYPE
18          Reg      = RECORD
19                       CASE Boolean OF
20                         False : (Word : Integer);
21                         True  : (LoByte,HiByte : Byte)
22                       END;
23
24          Regpack = RECORD
25                      AX,BX,CX,DX,BP,SI,DI,DS,ES,Flags : Reg
26                      END;
27
28        VAR
29          Regs : RegPack;
30
31        BEGIN
32          WITH Regs DO
33            BEGIN
34              AX.HiByte := 0;
35              AX.LoByte := ModeNumber;
36            END;
37          Intr($10,Regs)
38        END;
```

I recommend using **SetMode** over the built-in Turbo Pascal procedures **GraphMode**, **GraphColorMode**, or **TextMode** because **SetMode** allows you complete control over the mode number, both today and in the future, if additional video modes are provided with next-generation display adapters.

Setting 43-line "Mode" on the EGA

The EGA (Enhanced Graphics Adapter) can contain up to 640 pixels on a scan line for either text or graphics, and can display either 200 or 350 lines vertically. The EGA's default text mode scans 350 lines vertically. It has two character fonts in ROM: One is the familiar 8 × 8 character font used on the CGA, and the other is an 8 × 14 font new to the EGA. The 8 × 14 font is the EGA's default text font, used when you set mode 3 on the EGA. By using the 8 × 8 font, 43 lines can be displayed on the EGA text screen. (These are not modes in the usual sense, but are functionally similar to them.)

43-Line mode is less legible than 25-line mode, and the characters are smaller, but it's at least as legible as the (marginal) text we've always endured on the CGA. Still, if an application demands more lines on the screen, it's worth investigating.

Changing from one EGA ROM font to another is accomplished by a single EGA BIOS call, but there is a wrinkle here: If you change from one font to another, the cursor is disrupted by a well-known bug in the EGA BIOS cursor-emulation code. The EGA BIOS attempts to set the cursor to the proper character-cell scan lines when the font is changed, but it gets it all wrong. Consequently, we have to explicitly disable cursor emulation by poking a value into the BIOS data area, and then set the cursor to the correct scan lines ourselves.

I have defined two procedures for changing between the EGA ROM fonts: **Set43Lines**, which sets the screen to 43-line mode, and **Set25Lines**, which sets the screen to the familiar 25-line mode.

```
1        {->>>>Set43Lines<<<<-----------------------------------------------}
2        {                                                                  }
3        { Filename : EGA43LNS.SRC -- Last Modified 2/10/87                  }
4        {                                                                  }
5        { This procedure, which should only be called if an EGA is         }
6        { installed in the host system, will change the EGA font           }
7        { tables to use the 8 X 8 EGA ROM font, thus allowing 43 lines }
8        { on a text screen.  This routine is HIGHLY specific to the        }
9        { EGA!                                                             }
10       {                                                                  }
11       {                                                                  }
12       {                                                                  }
13       {-----------------------------------------------------------------}
14
15       PROCEDURE Set43Lines(VAR Points : Integer);
16
17       TYPE
18         Reg      = RECORD
19                      CASE Boolean OF
20                        False : (Word : Integer);
21                        True  : (LoByte,HiByte : Byte)
22                    END;
23
24         Regpack = RECORD
25                      AX,BX,CX,DX,BP,SI,DI,DS,ES,Flags : Reg
26                    END;
27
28       VAR
```

(continued)

```
29                 Regs : RegPack;
30
31             BEGIN
32               Regs.AX.HiByte := $11;   { Character generator services }
33               Regs.AX.LoByte := $12;   { Load EGA 8X8 font }
34               Regs.BX.Word := 0;
35               Intr($10,regs);
36                                         { Suppress BIOS cursor emulation }
37               MEM[$40 : $87] := mem[$40 : $87] OR $01;
38
39               Regs.AX.Word := $100;    { Set our own cursor to lines 6-7 }
40               Regs.BX.Word := 0;
41               Regs.CX.Word := $0600;
42               Intr($10,regs);
43               Points := 8;             { Tell caller the font is now 8 lines high }
44               { ScreenHeight is the screen height patch point at CS:$016B }
45               ScreenHeight := $2B      { Repatch the patch point for 43 lines! }
46             END;


 1        {->>>>Set25Lines<<<<------------------------------------------------}
 2        {                                                                   }
 3        { Filename : EGA25LNS.SRC -- Last Modified 2/10/87                   }
 4        {                                                                   }
 5        { This procedure, which should ONLY be called if an EGA is          }
 6        { installed in the host system, will change the EGA font            }
 7        { tables to use the 8 X 14 EGA ROM font, thus allowing 25           }
 8        { lines on a text screen.  This routine is HIGHLY specific to       }
 9        { the EGA!                                                          }
10        {                                                                   }
11        {                                                                   }
12        {                                                                   }
13        {-------------------------------------------------------------------}
14
15        PROCEDURE Set25Lines(VAR Points : Integer);
16
17        TYPE
18          Reg      = RECORD
19                       CASE Boolean OF
20                         False : (Word : Integer);
21                         True  : (LoByte,HiByte : Byte)
22                     END;
23
24          Regpack = RECORD
25                       AX,BX,CX,DX,BP,SI,DI,DS,ES,Flags : Reg
26                     END;
27
28        VAR
29          Regs : RegPack;
```

(continued)

```
30
31          BEGIN
32            ClrScr;
33            Regs.AX.HiByte := $11;   { EGA Character generator services }
34            Regs.AX.LoByte := $11;   { Load monochrome ROM font }
35            Regs.BX.Word := 0;
36            Intr($10,regs);
37                                     { Suppress BIOS cursor emulation }
38            MEM[$40 : $87] := MEM[$40 : $87] OR $01;
39            Regs.AX.Word := $100;    { Set our own cursor to lines 12-13 }
40            Regs.BX.Word := 0;
41            Regs.CX.Word := $0C00;
42            Intr($10,Regs);
43            Points := 14;            { Tell caller the font is now 14 lines high }
44            { ScreenHeight is the screen height patch point at CS:$016B }
45            ScreenHeight := $19      { Repatch the patch point for 25 lines! }
46          END;
```

These two routines can be used in a pair of simple utilities that switch the
EGA screen between the two modes from the command line:

```
1
2           {-------------------------------------------------------------}
3           {                          EGA43                             }
4           {                                                            }
5           {              EGA 43-line mode set utility                  }
6           {                                                            }
7           {                             by Jeff Duntemann              }
8           {                             Turbo Pascal V3.01A            }
9           {                             Last update 1/6/87             }
10          {                                                            }
11          { This utility places the EGA in 43-line "mode" by changing  }
12          { the font tables to use the 8 X 8 ROM font via procedure     }
13          { Set43Lines.                                                }
14          {                                                            }
15          {                                                            }
16          {                                                            }
17          {-------------------------------------------------------------}
18
19          PROGRAM EGA43;
20
21          {$I REGPACK.DEF}
22          {$I VSCREEN.DEF}
23
24          VAR
25            Points : Integer;
26
27          {$I ISEGA.SRC}
```

(continued)

```
28    {$I EGA43LNS.SRC}
29
30    BEGIN
31      IF IsEGA THEN
32        BEGIN
33          Set43Lines(Points);
34          ClrScr
35        END
36      ELSE Writeln('>>No EGA detected -- no action taken.')
37    END.
```

```
 1    {---------------------------------------------------------------}
 2    {                            EGA25                              }
 3    {                                                               }
 4    {            EGA 25-line mode set utility                       }
 5    {                                                               }
 6    {                              by Jeff Duntemann                }
 7    {                              Turbo Pascal V3.01A              }
 8    {                              Last update 1/6/87               }
 9    {                                                               }
10    { This utility places the EGA in 25-line "mode" by changing     }
11    { the font tables to use the 8 X 14 ROM font via procedure      }
12    { Set25Lines.                                                   }
13    {                                                               }
14    {                                                               }
15    {                                                               }
16    {---------------------------------------------------------------}
17
18    PROGRAM EGA25;
19
20    {$I REGPACK.DEF}
21    {$I VSCREEN.DEF}
22
23    VAR
24      Points : Integer;
25
26    {$I ISEGA.SRC}
27    {$I EGA25LNS.SRC}
28
29    BEGIN
30      IF IsEGA THEN
31        BEGIN
32          Set25Lines(Points);
33          ClrScr
34        END
35      ELSE Writeln('>>No EGA detected -- no action taken.')
36    END.
37
```

Note that these programs first test for the presence of an EGA with function **IsEGA** before attempting to reset the screen mode. Nothing disastrous occurs when executed on a non-EGA display adapter, but typically the cursor vanishes or becomes some off-the-wall combination of character-cell scan lines.

5.4   Determining Which Display Adapter Is Installed

Without counting the display board from the defunct PCjr, IBM has released only three distinct display adapters: the CGA, MDA, and EGA (as of November 1986). A host of third-party display adapters is available, but, in general, they all try to imitate one of the three IBM boards to software. This mimicry is driven by a need to fall under one of four different DIP switch settings on the PC system board.

Switches 5 and 6 of switch block 1 must be set to reflect the type of display adapter installed in the system. These switch settings are summarized in Figure 5.2. The PC looks at switches 5 and 6 when determining what sort of display it has. It does *not* go out and somehow examine the board to see what is actually present on the bus. This seems to be a risky system on the surface, since there is no guarantee that a third-party board pretending to be an MDA is actually similar enough to an MDA to function properly. In fact, this risk may have driven third-party display board manufacturers to be more concerned with the compatibility of their products with the IBM standard.

It is important to remember that the setting marked "No display adapter installed" means, more properly, a statement from the PC ROM BIOS stating "I don't know what adapter is installed—*yet*." It is a way of allowing ROM BIOS to hedge its bets and defer a decision to a better authority.

What authority? Unlike the older CGA and MDA cards, the EGA contains a ROM BIOS extension in a ROM chip directly on the EGA board. This ROM contains software that is better able to assess the machine environment and decide how to handle video. The EGA BIOS code takes control during the "ROM scan" period after the motherboard-based ROM BIOS completes its power-on self-test (POST) and initializes the BIOS data areas. The EGA BIOS then alters the BIOS data areas as it sees fit.

We know where in memory the BIOS data areas are located, but IBM does not promise not to move them in future releases or future additions to the PC family. Therefore, the safe bet (and speed matters little here since it needs to be done only once) is to access this information through the BIOS. PC ROM BIOS function $11 returns 16 bits of information on what equipment the PC

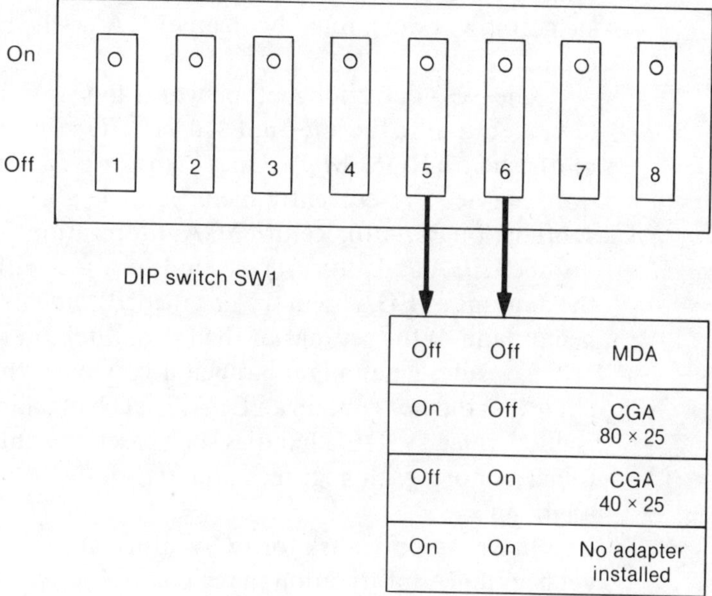

Figure 5.2   **Display adapter DIP switch settings**

thinks it has installed. This information comes from the BIOS data areas, *not* directly from the DIP switches as some people believe. The DIP switches are read *only* at POST time.

This is an important distinction, because the EGA BIOS overwrites the DIP switch information when it performs its test and initialization on the EGA board during ROM scan. Recall that the EGA installation instructions direct the user to set DIP switches 5 and 6 to indicate *no* display adapter installed. The EGA determines, through its own means, whether a color or monochrome monitor is attached to it. If it is a color monitor, the EGA BIOS sets the BIOS data area as though the DIP switches had been set to reflect a CGA. Similarly, if the EGA detects that a monochrome monitor is attached, it sets the BIOS data areas as though the DIP switches had indicated an MDA.

So don't make the mistake of assuming that you will get a 0 code back from BIOS function $11 if the installed video display adapter is an EGA. To re-emphasize, if an EGA is installed, BIOS will tell you that there is a CGA installed if a color monitor is attached to the EGA, or that an MDA is installed if a monochrome display is attached to the EGA.

Obviously, BIOS function $11 alone will *not* tell you whether an EGA is actually installed or not. Remarkably, there is no straightforward way of detecting the presence of an EGA in a system. The method I use has proven reliable for IBM's own EGA, plus a large number of EGA clone boards, and I suspect it will work reliably on any EGA with a responsibly written BIOS on board.

The EGA detection method works this way: The EGA ROM BIOS adds a few extensions to the interrupt $10 VIDEO service included in the PC/XT/AT motherboard ROM BIOS. One extension is service AH=$12, Alternate Function. Service $12 currently includes two subfunctions. We are interested in subfunction BL=$10, Return EGA Information. This subfunction will poll the installed EGA and return:1) the mode in effect, either color or monochrome; 2) the amount of EGA memory installed; 3) the bits from the EGA feature connector; and 4) the settings of the DIP switch on the spine of the EGA.

Consider what might happen if you made this subfunction call on a machine that did *not* contain an EGA. In such machines, VIDEO service AH=$12 is not defined. VIDEO handles such cases in a chivalrous manner and ignores them, restoring all registers and returning to the caller without changing anything.

In a sense, if we ask for EGA information in a machine with an EGA, we get back EGA information in register BX. If we ask for EGA information in a machine *without* an EGA, we get back exactly what we passed to VIDEO in BX, which (thank fate) is not valid EGA information. Thus, the method consists of performing a Return EGA Information call to VIDEO and noting if BX changes in the process. If BX changes, an EGA is present; if BX stays the same, no EGA is installed.

This allows us to write a simple test for the presence of an EGA:

```
1          {->>>>IsEGA<<<<--------------------------------------------------}
2          {                                                                 }
3          { Filename : ISEGA.SRC -- Last Modified 1/27/87                   }
4          {                                                                 }
5          { This function returns a Boolean TRUE value if an EGA is         }
6          { installed in the host system; otherwise FALSE will be           }
7          { returned.  The trick is to perform a VIDEO call that is not     }
8          { defined for the MDA and CGA; a well-behaved BIOS will not       }
9          { alter any registers when an undefined service request          }
10         { is made.                                                        }
11         {                                                                 }
12         {                                                                 }
13         {                                                                 }
14         {-----------------------------------------------------------------}
15
16         FUNCTION IsEGA : Boolean;
17
18         TYPE
19           Reg     = RECORD
```

(continued)

```
20                    CASE Boolean OF
21                      False : (Word : Integer);
22                      True  : (LoByte,HiByte : Byte)
23                  END;
24
25        Regpack = RECORD
26                     AX,BX,CX,DX,BP,SI,DI,DS,ES,Flags : Reg
27                  END;
28
29     VAR
30       Regs : RegPack;
31
32     BEGIN
33       Regs.AX.HiByte := $12;        { Select Alternate Function service }
34       Regs.BX.Word := $10;          { BL=$10 means return EGA information }
35       Intr($10,Regs);               { Call BIOS VIDEO }
36       IF Regs.BX.Word = $10 THEN    { BX unchanged means EGA is NOT there...}
37         IsEGA := False ELSE IsEGA := True   {...anything else means EGA! }
38     END;
```

This function allows us to write another function that tells the entire story
and accurately pins down which of the three display adapter types is installed.
Ideally, a function should return a distinct value for each kind of display card.
While returning 0, 1, or 2 would be adequate, Pascal allows us to define an
enumerated type which will make programs more self-explanatory:

```
TYPE
    AdapterType = (MDA,CGA,EGAMono,EGAColor);
```

The EGA appears in two incarnations, since it can be configured to look
(in text mode, at least) nearly identical to either the CGA or the MDA, including the starting address for the video buffer. The EGA's two incarnations are
sufficiently different (especially since they cannot be switched from one to
another under software control) to consider them, from a software perspective,
as two different kinds of display adapter.

Having predefined this enumerated type, the function itself is simply an
invocation of BIOS equipment determination interrupt $11 for those cases
where an EGA is not detected with **IsEGA**:

```
1       {->>>>QueryAdapterType<<<<------------------------------------------}
2       {                                                                   }
3       { Filename : QUERYDSP.SRC -- Last Modified 2/9/87                    }
4       {                                                                   }
5       { This routine determines the currently installed primary           }
6       { display adapter and returns it in the form of a value from         }
7       { the enumerated type AdapterType.                                   }
```

(continued)

```
8          {                                                              }
9          { AdapterType and IsEGA must be predefined.                    }
10         {                                                              }
11         {                                                              }
12         {                                                              }
13         {--------------------------------------------------------------}
14
15         FUNCTION QueryAdapterType : AdapterType;
16
17         TYPE
18           Reg      = RECORD
19                        CASE Boolean OF
20                           False : (Word : Integer);
21                           True  : (LoByte,HiByte : Byte)
22                      END;
23
24           RegPack = RECORD
25                        AX,BX,CX,DX,BP,SI,DI,DS,ES,Flags : Reg
26                      END;
27
28         VAR
29           Regs : RegPack;
30           Code : Byte;
31
32         BEGIN
33           IF IsEGA THEN
34             BEGIN
35               Regs.AX.HiByte := $12;
36               Regs.BX.LoByte := $10;
37               Intr($10,Regs);
38               IF (Regs.BX.HiByte = 0) THEN QueryAdapterType := EGAColor
39                 ELSE QueryAdapterType := EGAMono
40             END
41           ELSE
42             BEGIN
43               Intr($11,Regs);    { Equipment determination service }
44               Code := (Regs.AX.LoByte AND $30) SHR 4;
45               CASE Code of
46                 1 : QueryAdapterType := CGA;
47                 2 : QueryAdapterType := CGA;
48                 3 : QueryAdapterType := MDA
49               ELSE QueryAdapterType := CGA
50               END { Case }
51             END
52         END;
```

The type **RegPack**, if you recall, was defined and explained in Chapter 3. If the
adapter is found to be an EGA through the use of the **IsEGA** function described earlier, a further query must be made to determine whether the EGA is
configured in a monochrome or color configuration. This is done through the

same BIOS VIDEO Alternate Function service used to determine whether or not the EGA is installed. If the BH register comes back equal to zero, the EGA is attached to a color monitor; if BH comes back equal to one, the EGA is attached to a monochrome monitor.

I deliberately chose *not* to combine the functions of **QueryAdapterType** and **IsEGA** into a single function because I wanted the simplicity of a Boolean yes/no answer to the question of whether the EGA is there at all. And since **QueryAdapterType** must ask that question to accomplish its own mission, it made sense to break out the question as a separate function.

Character-Cell Size and Cursor Manipulation

Before the introduction of the EGA, dealing comprehensively with text video was a much simpler thing. The CGA used an 8×8 character cell; the MDA used an 8×14 character cell. (For the sake of you purists: Yes, it is a 9×14 character cell, but the ninth pixel row doesn't really exist. Nyaa-nyaaah!) The EGA has *both* sizes of fonts in ROM, as we mentioned above, for both monochrome and color modes.

Knowing which font the EGA is using at any given time is important, since turning the cursor on and off correctly depends on it. The reason is this: It's *easy* to turn the cursor off—a simple call to VIDEO service 1 with bit 5 of CX high will do it:

```
1          {->>>>CusorOff<<<<-----------------------------------------------}
2          {                                                                 }
3          { Filename : CURSOFF.SRC -- Last Modified 2/9/87                   }
4          {                                                                 }
5          { A simple BIOS VIDEO call turns off the hardware cursor.          }
6          {                                                                 }
7          { Type RegPack must be predefined.                                 }
8          {                                                                 }
9          {                                                                 }
10         {                                                                 }
11         {-----------------------------------------------------------------}
12
13         PROCEDURE CursorOff;
14
15         VAR
16            Regs : RegPack;
17
18         BEGIN
19           WITH Regs DO
20             BEGIN
21               AX.Word := $0100;
```

(continued)

```
22                CX.Word := $2000;    { Set CH bit 5 hi to suppress cursor }
23            END;
24          INTR($10,Regs);
25        END;
```

Turning the cursor back *on* again is another story. The PC's text cursor is defined as a range of scan lines within the character cell, with the top scan line being line 0, and the bottom scan line either 13 or 7, depending on the font in use at the time. Although any range of scan lines, including the entire character cell, can be set to flash as the cursor, the default text cursor consists of the bottom two scan lines in the character cell. Turning the cursor on again requires passing to VIDEO the starting scan line and ending scan line of the desired cursor. There is no way to "turn the cursor on as it was before we turned it off." VIDEO doesn't remember the old cursor settings; they get thrown away when you turn the cursor off. We need to know how many scan lines are in the current character cell before we can turn the default cursor back on correctly.

I choose to deal with this problem by defining a global variable called **Points**, which specifies the number of scan lines in the font that is currently in use. (Calling it **Points** hearkens back to "point sizes" of printed fonts, although the number of pixels in a font does not map in any way to the standard unit of type-size measure called a "point," which is about 1/72 of an inch.)

The function **DeterminePoints** returns the number of scan lines in the font currently in use. For the CGA, **Points** will always be equal to 8, and, for the MDA, 14. For the EGA it could be either, and an additional query must be made. Again, a call to BIOS VIDEO accomplishes this through the EGA BIOS extension service $11, Character Generator Functions. Subfunction $30, Return Information, provides the number of bytes per character (and hence the number of scan lines, since all characters in IBM text displays are 8 bits or one byte wide) in register CX.

```
1         {->>>>DeterminePoints<<<<-------------------------------------------}
2         {                                                                   }
3         { Filename : FONTSIZE.SRC -- Last Modified 2/9/87                    }
4         {                                                                   }
5         { This routine determines the character cell height for the         }
6         { font currently in use.  For the MDA and EGA this is hard-         }
7         { wired; for the EGA the value must be obtained by querying         }
8         { the EGA ROM BIOS.                                                  }
9         {                                                                   }
10        {                                                                   }
11        {                                                                   }
12        {-------------------------------------------------------------------}
13
```

(continued)

```
14            FUNCTION DeterminePoints : Integer;
15
16            VAR
17              Regs : Regpack;
18
19            BEGIN
20              CASE QueryAdapterType OF
21                CGA       : DeterminePoints := 8;
22                MDA       : DeterminePoints := 14;
23                EGAMono,
24                EGAColor :
25                          BEGIN
26                            WITH Regs DO
27                              BEGIN
28                                AX.HiByte := $11;
29                                AX.LoByte := $30;
30                                BX.LoByte := 0;
31                              END;
32                            Intr($10,Regs);
33                            DeterminePoints := Regs.CX.Word
34                          END
35              END   { CASE }
36            END;
```

The main function of **Points** is to turn the cursor on after it has been
suppressed. The following procedure turns the cursor on, assuming the default
text cursor is the two bottommost scan lines of the character cell. All font sizes
are covered by specifying the cursor's starting scan line as **Points-2** and the
ending scan line as **Points-1**. The bottom scan line is not given by **Points** alone
because **Points** gives the *number* of scan lines in the cell, and VIDEO requires
the ordinal value of a line, counting from zero. For example, for the MDA
font, there are 14 lines in the character cell, and the lines are numbered from 0
to 13.

```
1      {->>>>CursorOn<<<<-------------------------------------------------}
2      {                                                                  }
3      { Filename : CURSON.SRC -- Last Modified 2/9/87                     }
4      {                                                                  }
5      { Assuming a valid value for the height of the character block }
6      { in Points, this routine will turn the hardware cursor back   }
7      { on after it has been turned off.  The standard hardware      }
8      { cursor consisting of the bottom two scan lines in the        }
9      { character block comprise the cursor, regardless of the font  }
10     { height.                                                      }
11     {                                                              }
12     { Type RegPack must be predefined.                             }
```

(continued)

```
13            {                                                              }
14            {                                                              }
15            {                                                              }
16            {--------------------------------------------------------------}
17
18            PROCEDURE CursorOn(Points : Integer);
19
20            VAR
21              Regs : RegPack;
22
23            BEGIN
24              WITH Regs DO
25                BEGIN
26                  AX.Word := $0100;
27                  { 'Points' is the pixel height of the character font }
28                  { currently in use.  'Underscore' cursors always     }
29                  { consist of the bottom two lines in the font cell.  }
30                  { In current display technology, this is either 8 or }
31                  { 14. Here we specify Points-1 and Points-2 because  }
32                  { the character cell lines are counted from 0.       }
33                  CX.HiByte := Points-2;
34                  CX.LoByte := Points-1;
35                END;
36              INTR($10,Regs);
37            END;
```

Note that this procedure **CursorOn** differs significantly from the procedure **CursorOn** that I described in *Complete Turbo Pascal*, which was written before the EGA became popular.

5.5   Screen Descriptors and Screen Buffers

The driving concept behind virtualizing the screen is to remove the application-level concept of a "screen" as much as possible from assumptions based on the physical configuration of the machine. In the ordinary, one-screen-buffer world, the application program can assume that the buffer is always the same—in one place and unchangeable. This makes programming directly to the screen buffer simple.

We are allowing a screen to exist on the heap in a format that may change at runtime—from 25 to 43 lines on the EGA, for example—and that may include more than one visible screen. With all those changeable factors, a screen needs something I call a *descriptor* to describe itself at any given time. This is done well enough by a Pascal record type. As with any complex data structure, this record type is supported by a number of other type definitions, all of which are shown together below:

```
VideoAtom = Reg;                {Same data format as register}
Screen    = Array[0..1] OF VideoAtom;    {Make sure $R is OFF!}
ScreenPtr = ^Screen;
ObjectPtr = ^ScreenRec;

ScreenRec = RECORD
        Handle         : Integer;    {Screen object handle}
        Previous       : ObjectPtr;  {Points to previous screen}
        MyScreen       : ScreenPtr;  {Points to buffer start}
        ScreenLength   : Integer;    {Length of buffer}
        Visible        : Boolean;    {TRUE if screen is visible}
        CursX          : Byte;       {Screen cursor X pos}
        CursY          : Byte;       {Screen cursor Y pos}
        Next           : ObjectPtr;  {Points to next screen}
    END;
```

These definitions are all part of the larger definition file **VSCREEN.DEF**, which is listed in its entirety at the end of this chapter.

The relabeling of **Reg** as **VideoAtom** may seem functionally unnecessary, but it is done for clarity: I don't want to give the impression that a screen buffer is in any way made up of 8086 register types. Because each character/attribute pair in a video buffer needs, at different times, to be treated either as a 16-bit word *or* as two separate 8-bit quantities, the free-union variant record type **Reg** is precisely what we need. The fact that its properties are also useful in dealing with 8086 registers is incidental, and, to preserve sanity, the name should be changed in this independent application of the **Reg** type.

Skirting Pascal Range Errors

Something odd about type **Screen** should leap right off the page at you: According to its type definition, it's only two elements long! That's short for a screen buffer by anyone's definition . . . but there's a reason for it. The routines in this book associated with virtual screens deliberately violate Pascal's insistence that an array have one fixed length set at compile time and un-changeable at runtime. A screen buffer is an array of character/attribute pairs, but because we intend to check the size of the host's video adapters at runtime, we don't know at compile time *how many* character/attribute pairs will be in a screen array. Therefore, we might as well specify the minimum size for any array: two elements.

Simon-pure Pascal would not let us get away with this, but Turbo Pascal will. In a C-like manner, Turbo Pascal allows arrays to be indexed well outside their defined ranges. This can cause trouble when done accidentally, which is the reason Niklaus Wirth built index-checking into his own compiler implementations. On the other hand, if you *know* that indexing beyond the bounds of an array will not damage anything, you should have that option. With Turbo Pascal, you do have that option: Simply don't turn the $R compiler option on. $R is a toggle that specifies whether or not the Turbo Pascal runtime code will check each array reference to ensure that the reference falls into the defined range for that array type. If $R is *on*, an out-of-bounds array reference will generate runtime error 90. If $R is *off*, the runtime code minds its own business, and the programmer is held responsible for the consequences of any out-of-bounds array references.

The default state of the $R toggle is *off*. Thus, unless you explicitly place the {**$R+**} compiler command in your programs, this will not be a problem.

In each **ScreenRec** is an integer field called **Handle**. A *handle* is nothing more than a tag by which something is identified. In PC DOS V2.0 and later, files can be given *file handles* when opened, and can be accessed by specifying the file handle instead of the filename or a descriptor table somewhere in memory. When a screen is created via the **CreateScreen** procedure, a handle value is taken from a typed constant called **LastHandle**, which is then incremented. This handle value is given to field **Handle**.

My use of a handle for screens is not quite the same as DOS's use in regard to files. My screens are accessed through pointers; the handles are used as unique ID tags. In more complex applications, it's sometimes handy to tell which of two otherwise identical screens are which, and since in my scheme no two screens are ever given the same handle (unless your application breaks the rules and resets the handle counter), no two screens are ever precisely alike. (Keep in mind that it's allowable for two screen descriptors to be set to point to the same physical screen on the heap, although the need to do so is unclear and sounds dicey to me. At the very least, their handles will be different.)

Fields **Previous** and **Next** are included to allow the building of singly or doubly linked lists of screen descriptors. When you have a limited number of help screens in an application, you can impress the user with the speed of your help system by placing all the help screens on the heap in a linked list, with some appropriate context-sensitive indexing machinery to access them. When the user presses the help key, the help screen will appear instantly rather than after an annoying grinding of disk heads. (If linked lists are something new to you, refer to their description in Chapter 7.)

The Boolean flag **Visible** indicates whether the descriptor describes a visible screen. A visible screen in my scheme is one in which the screen array (that to which pointer **MyScreen** points) is the physical video display buffer of an actual display adapter. Under IBM's BIOS, two display adapters may be installed at once, one with a buffer at $B000 and the other with a buffer at $B800.

It is possible to create a display adapter with a buffer at any arbitrary memory address (though I don't know of any offhand), and three or four simultaneous displays could exist at once; those beyond two would be without BIOS support but would remain accessible through the virtual-screen software. The virtual-screen code in this chapter can handle such cases easily, by simply tagging a screen descriptor record corresponding to a display adapter's buffer as visible by setting **Visible** to **True**.

Every screen descriptor may record the current cursor position in two **Byte** fields called **CursX** and **CursY**. This becomes useful when several heap-based screens are moved into and out of a visible screen in the course of an application. BIOS makes no provision for multiple text cursors, so if each screen on the heap makes separate use of the hardware text cursor in the visible display adapter, each screen must maintain the location of its text cursor in its screen descriptor. That way, when the screen is saved out and another moved in, the saved-out screen will be able to restore the text cursor to its last-used position once it is moved into the visible screen again. (This action is the responsibility of the application; my virtual screen procedures do not make any use of the hardware cursor. In my own programs, I prefer to just turn the blamed thing off and handle all cursor-positioning myself.)

The pointer **MyScreen** points to the first byte of the screen's buffer. In a visible screen, this is the area of memory used as a video buffer by a display adapter. In a heap-based screen, this is a pointer to a region of the heap reserved for the screen's information.

Creating Screens

Being a Pascal record, a virtual-screen descriptor can exist either in the static data area or on the heap. Creating a screen involves two distinct steps: creating the descriptor, and allocating the screen itself. If a descriptor exists in the static data area, it is defined in the usual fashion in the VAR section of a program or procedure:

```
VAR
    EntryScreen, HelpScreen, ReportScreen : ScreenRec;
```

This statement creates three screen-descriptor records in the static data area. These descriptors are then created at compile time.

If the descriptor is to reside on the heap, it does not exist at compile time and must be created on the heap with Pascal's **New** procedure:

```
VAR
    EntryScreen : ObjectPtr;

        . . . .

New(EntryScreen);
```

Note that the identifier **EntryScreen** is type **ObjectPtr**, which is a pointer to a **ScreenRec** rather than a **ScreenRec** itself.

In both cases, the newly created descriptor cannot be used as is. All of its fields are undefined, and must be initialized. Initializing a descriptor for use is done in two ways, depending on whether the descriptor is for a visible screen or a screen on the heap.

Initializing a visible screen is largely a matter of determining the starting address of the visible display buffer to which it corresponds. There are two ways to go here: Since most systems include only one display adapter, in most cases the system can be queried to determine the type of adapter installed and its starting address. Or, if multiple adapters exist in a system, a starting address can be passed to the initialization routine for the desired display adapter.

The visible screen initialization routine **InitVScreen** works this way. It has a parameter **Segment** that contains the segment address of the start of a video buffer. Since, in the 8086, no display adapter can keep its buffer at segment address 0, a value of 0 passed in **Segment** indicates that the routine is to initialize the descriptor **VScreen** to whatever display adapter is installed in the system. If a non-zero value is passed in **Segment**, that value is used as the address of the video buffer. This address is used to build **MyScreen**, a pointer to the start of the display buffer.

```
 1        {->>>>InitVScreen<<<<-------------------------------------------}
 2        ,{                                                              }
 3        { Filename : INITVSCR.SRC -- Last Modified 2/12/87             }
 4        {                                                              }
 5        { Here we initialize a visible screen.  This involves creating }
 6        { a pointer to the first byte of the video buffer, and filling }
 7        { in the rest of the fields of the ScreenRec.  If a zero is     }
 8        { passed in the Segment parameter, then the code detects the    }
 9        { installed adapter and creates a pointer to the installed      }
10        { adapter's video buffer.  If a segment address is passed in    }
11        { Segment, then that segment is used in the pointer, with an    }
12        { offset of 0.                                                  }
13        {                                                              }
14        { This routine really doesn't stand well alone; it's best to    }
15        { use it within VSCREEN.SRC.  ScreenRec, AdapterType, &         }
16        { RegPack must be predefined, as well as function               }
17        { QueryAdapterType.                                            }
18        {                                                              }
19        {                                                              }
20        {                                                              }
21        {--------------------------------------------------------------}
22
23        PROCEDURE InitVScreen(VAR VScreen : ScreenRec; Segment : Integer);
```

(continued)

```
24
25          VAR
26            Adapter    : AdapterType;
27            VideoSeg   : Integer;
28            Regs       : RegPack;
29
30          BEGIN
31            IF Segment = 0 THEN  { Query hardware for default visible adapter }
32              BEGIN
33                Adapter := QueryAdapterType;
34                CASE Adapter OF
35                  CGA      : VideoSeg := $B800;
36                  MDA      : VideoSeg := $B000;
37                  EGAMono  : VideoSeg := $B000;
38                  EGAColor : VideoSeg := $B800
39                  ELSE VideoSeg := $B800
40                END; {CASE}
41              END
42            ELSE VideoSeg := Segment;
43
44            WITH VScreen DO
45              BEGIN
46                Handle       := Succ(LastHandle);
47                Previous     := NIL;
48                Next         := NIL;
49                MyScreen     := Ptr(VideoSeg,0);
50                ScreenLength := ScreenWidth * ScreenHeight * 2;
51                Visible      := True;
52                LastHandle   := Handle  { LastHandle is a global typed constant! }
53              END;
54          END;
```

The **ScreenLength** field of the descriptor is initialized at this time. **Screen-Length** is the number of bytes in the screen, and it is calculated by reading Turbo Pascal's screen width and screen height parameters at offset $016B into the code segment. These two parameters are defined as absolute variables in the **VSCREEN.DEF** definition file (listed at the end of this chapter), so that they can be accessed by name rather than by address using **MEM**. (These are the screen size "patch points" that are discussed in detail in Chapter 2.)

Initializing a screen on the heap is done with **CreateScreen**. In this case, the hardware does not have to be queried for the starting address of the display buffer. **CreateScreen**, however, must do something that **InitVScreen** does not have to do: allocate memory on the heap for the screen array itself. A visible screen's array is the memory on the display adapter card, and is used for no other purpose. It does not need to be allocated; it is simply there, always ready to be used.

```
1            {->>>>CreateScreen<<<<------------------------------------------}
2            {                                                               }
3            { Filename : CREATSCR.SRC -- Last Modified 2/12/87              }
4            {                                                               }
5            { This routine initializes a screen on the heap.  It fills the }
6            { the ScreenRec passed to it and allocates space for the        }
7            { screen array on the heap.                                     }
8            {                                                               }
9            { ScreenRec and ScreenPtr must be predefined.                  }
10           {                                                               }
11           {                                                               }
12           {                                                               }
13           {-------------------------------------------------------------}
14
15           PROCEDURE CreateScreen(VAR NewScreen : ScreenRec);
16
17           BEGIN
18             WITH NewScreen DO
19               BEGIN
20                 Handle        := Succ(LastHandle);
21                 Previous      := NIL;
22                 Next          := NIL;
23                 ScreenLength := ScreenWidth * ScreenHeight * 2;
24                 GetMem(MyScreen,ScreenLength);
25                 Visible       := False;
26                 LastHandle    := Handle  { LastHandle is a global typed constant! }
27               END;
28           END;
```

Unlike a descriptor record on the heap, the memory for the screen cannot be allocated by the **New** procedure. The reason is that **New** must know at compile time how large a region of memory on the heap it is allocating. We *don't* know, however, how large the screen array is going to be at compile time. **CreateScreen** calculates the size of the screen array from the **ScreenWidth** and **ScreenHeight** absolute variables. It then allocates memory for the screen array on the heap with Turbo Pascal's built-in routine **GetMem**. This procedure works much like **New**, in that it allocates memory on the heap and initializes a pointer to point to the start of that memory. Unlike **New**, however, **GetMem** allows the programmer to pass a parameter to it containing the amount of memory to be allocated. **New** always derives the amount of memory to be allocated from the size of the type that is the target of the pointer passed to **New**.

Both **InitVScreen** and **CreateScreen** assign a unique handle to the screen descriptors they initialize. This handle is the current value of the integer typed constant **LastHandle**. Once the assignment is made, the value of **LastHandle** is incremented, so that the next handle assigned will be one higher. This way, no two handles assigned are ever alike.

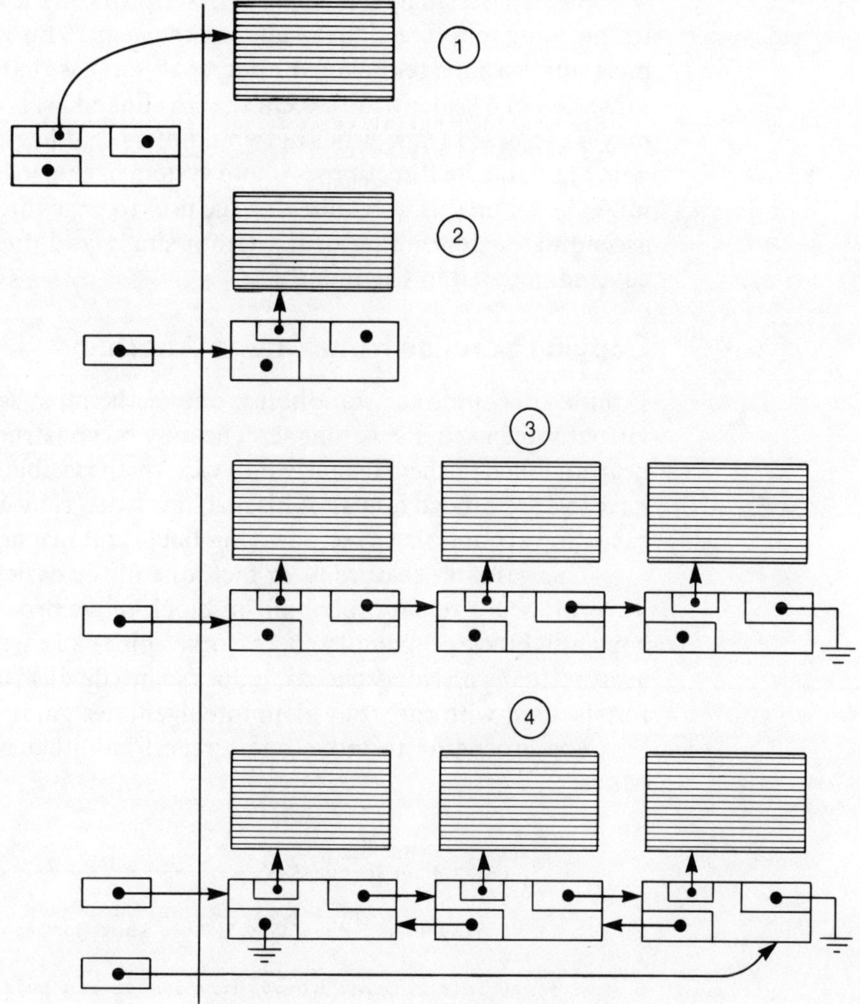

Figure 5.3   **Virtual screens on the heap**

Figure 5.3 summarizes four possible ways of setting up virtual screens. Bullet 1 shows a descriptor in the static data area, pointing to a screen array on the heap. When you know in advance how many screens your application will be using, this method works well; you can declare your descriptor records at compile time and not worry about allocating them on the heap.

Bullet 2 shows a single descriptor record on the heap, accessed through an **ObjectPtr** type in the static data area. This makes little sense; if you need only one screen, you might as well leave the descriptor in the static data area, since it only occupies 19 bytes.

Bullet 3 is a singly linked list of descriptors on the heap, with each descriptor pointing to a screen array also on the heap. This is perfectly adequate for most applications requiring a number of screens that may not always be the same. Bullet 4 is identical, except that the linked list is doubly linked; that is, it may be accessed from either of two pointers that begin paths through the list, going in opposite directions. A help system organized alphabetically by topic might be set up this way, allowing the user to page through the topics in either ascending or descending order. (Both singly and doubly linked lists will be covered in detail in Chapter 7.)

Copying Screens from One to Another

From a user-interface standpoint, one of the most satisfying features of the virtual screen scheme is that screens may be constructed out of sight on the heap and then flashed instantly into view on the visible screen. The user doesn't have to be reminded how slow his machine really is by watching the busy cursor cavorting around the screen, leaving fields and messages in its wake.

This valuable feature is, in fact, one of the easiest to implement, due to Turbo Pascal's remarkable built-in block-move procedure **Move. Move** will copy any block of memory to any other block of memory, and, by throwing away virtually all safety checks, it does so in a devilish hurry. **Move** must therefore be used with care, but in an intelligent design, it works very well.

The procedure to move one screen to another is a single invocation of **Move**:

```
 1          {->>>>MoveScreen<<<<---------------------------------------------}
 2          {                                                                }
 3          { Filename : MOVESCRN.SRC -- Last Modified 2/10/87               }
 4          {                                                                }
 5          { This routine simply moves a screen buffer array from one       }
 6          { place to another.  Screens are ordinarily the same size, but   }
 7          { as unpredictable consequences may come of moving a larger      }
 8          { screen to a smaller, the number of bytes moved is limited to   }
 9          { the size of the smaller of the two screens.                    }
10          {                                                                }
11          {                                                                }
12          {                                                                }
13          {---------------------------------------------------------------}
14
15          PROCEDURE MoveScreen(Source,Target : ScreenRec);
16
17          VAR
18             MoveLength : Integer;
19
```

(continued)

```
20        BEGIN
21          IF Source.ScreenLength > Target.ScreenLength THEN
22            MoveLength := Target.ScreenLength
23          ELSE
24            MoveLength := Source.ScreenLength;
25          Move(Source.MyScreen^,Target.MyScreen^,MoveLength)
26        END;
```

One interesting thing to note about **MoveScreen** is that the number of bytes of memory to be moved in the process is limited by the size of the smaller of the two ends of the line. In theory, all screens are supposed to be the same length, but in the event that a larger screen is copied to a smaller screen, data will be moved only until it fills the smaller screen, and then the move operation will stop. Thus, there is no danger of copying data beyond the end of the destination screen and overwriting other important items on the heap or adjacent to display adapter screen memory.

Disposing of Virtual Screens on the Heap

A virtual screen takes up a fair amount of heap space—4K for a typical 25×80 screen, and almost 11,000 bytes for the 66×80 screen used by the Genius VHR monochrome display. If too many screens are created during the course of an application's execution, it may be necessary to dispose of screens on the heap that have already been created and used. This is especially true if large numbers of screens are created as part of a linked list.

The procedure **DisposeOfScreen** accomplishes this function:

```
1         {->>>>DisposeOfScreen<<<<-------------------------------------}
2         {                                                             }
3         { Filename : DISPSCRN.SRC -- Last Modified 2/12/87            }
4         {                                                             }
5         { This routine disposes of a screen in an orderly fashion, by }
6         { using FreeMem to deallocate the screen array off the heap.  }
7         {                                                             }
8         { ScreenRec must be predefined.                              }
9         {                                                             }
10        {                                                             }
11        {                                                             }
12        {-------------------------------------------------------------}
13
14        PROCEDURE DisposeOfScreen(VAR OldScreen : ScreenRec);
15
16        BEGIN
17          WITH OldScreen DO FreeMem(MyScreen,ScreenLength)
18        END;
19
20
```

Note that visible screens should not be disposed of, and **DisposeOfScreen** checks the **Visible** field of **OldScreen** to be sure that it does not attempt to dispose of a visible screen. In the event that some proprietary third-party display hardware allows the direct mapping of an arbitrary memory block to the screen (the PCjr does something similar to this), the application will have to manually clear the **Visible** flag before attempting to dispose of such a screen. It's impolite to make a screen go poof while the user is still staring at it!

5.6   Writing Information to Virtual Screens

Compared to understanding how virtual screens are created and arranged on the heap, actually writing information to them is almost trivial. The biggest problem lies in emulating a little-appreciated power built into Pascal's **Write** and **Writeln** procedures: binary-to-string data conversion. You take it for granted that you can write an integer to the screen by coding

```
Write(I:5);
```

and have integer **I** right-justified in a five-character field as well. However, writing an integer to a virtual screen on the heap is not so simple. First of all, **Write** and **Writeln** can't do it—they are hardcoded to write to the default display adapter directly, and their output (sadly) cannot be redirected to another destination. Simply writing the two bytes that comprise an integer value into a screen buffer won't work either, because an integer and its displayed representation are *not* the same thing; in fact, they aren't even close.

Screens are meant to be read by human beings, which means that only string information should be written to them, since strings are the only Pascal data types that can be read by a human being *in their native form*. (And that must be modified to mean their native form *minus* the binary value in string element 0 that indicates how long the string is.) In their native form, integers are two bytes of binary-encoded information, with the highest order bit acting as a sign bit. The integer value 748, if "poked" directly into screen memory, would appear as a white smiley face and an infinity sign.

The same applies to Boolean values **True** and **False**, which are not actually strings but binary bytes with values of one and zero, respectively. And everything just said goes in spades for real numbers, which are either 6- or 8-byte binary extravaganzas encoded in formats that nonmathematicians are better off not pondering.

If we weren't working within Turbo Pascal, we'd be in trouble here—performing binary-string conversions from scratch is uglier work than scraping pans that have been sitting in the sink for three weeks. However, Turbo gives us a partial out in the form of its built-in binary-string conversion routine **Str. Str** converts both integer and real-number values to their string equivalents, neatly, quickly and with minimal fuss on the part of the programmer. Basically, you pass a formatted numeric value to **Str** and it passes back the string equivalent in the string variable of your choice:

```
Str(I:5,MyString);
```

This statement converts the integer variable **I** into a string, right-justified in a field five characters wide. Similarly,

```
Str(R:11:3,MyString);
```

converts the real-number variable **R** into a string value right-justified in a field 11 characters wide, with the decimal point three characters from the right.

With that much conversion horsepower at our command, creating string functions that return the string equivalents of integer and real-number values is no tremendous feat. **IntStr** does the job for integers, and **RealStr** does it for reals. If Turbo Pascal had implemented its built-in procedure **Str** as a string *function* instead, these two functions would not be necessary at all.

```
1         {->>>>IntStr<<<<------------------------------------------------------}
2         {                                                                      }
3         { Filename : INTSTR.SRC -- Last Modified 2/12/87                        }
4         {                                                                      }
5         { Because Turbo's Str procedure is a procedure and NOT a               }
6         { function, we need a function to return a string value for            }
7         { given formatted integer value, since WriteAt does not do its }
8         { own binary-string conversion.  This is it.                           }
9         {                                                                      }
10        { Type String10 must be predefined.                                    }
11        {                                                                      }
12        {                                                                      }
13        {                                                                      }
14        {----------------------------------------------------------------------}
15
16        FUNCTION IntStr(IntegerValue,FieldWidth : Integer) : String10;
17
18        VAR
19          Dummy : String10;
20
21        BEGIN
22          Str(IntegerValue : FieldWidth,Dummy);
23          IntStr := Dummy
24        END;
```

```
 1           {->>>>RealStr<<<<---------------------------------------------}
 2           {                                                             }
 3           { Filename : REALSTR.SRC -- Last Modified 2/12/87             }
 4           {                                                             }
 5           { Because Turbo's Str procedure is a procedure and NOT a      }
 6           { function, we need a function to return a string value for   }
 7           { given formatted real number value, since WriteAt does not do }
 8           { its own binary-string conversion.  This is it.              }
 9           {                                                             }
10           { Type String80 must be predefined.                          }
11           {                                                             }
12           {                                                             }
13           {                                                             }
14           {-------------------------------------------------------------}
15
16           FUNCTION RealStr(RealValue : Real; Exponential : Boolean;
17                           FieldWidth,DecimalWidth : Integer) : String80;
18
19           VAR
20             Dummy : String80;
21
22           BEGIN
23             IF Exponential THEN
24               Str(RealValue : FieldWidth,Dummy)
25             ELSE
26               Str(RealValue : FieldWidth : DecimalWidth,Dummy);
27             RealStr := Dummy
28           END;
```

Turbo Pascal has no built-in Boolean-to-string conversion utility, but since there are only two possible string values for any Boolean value (**True** and **False**), creating such a function is essentially trivial.

```
 1           {->>>>BooStr<<<<----------------------------------------------}
 2           {                                                             }
 3           { Filename : BOOSTR.SRC -- Last Modified 2/12/87              }
 4           {                                                             }
 5           { This function provides Boolean-string conversion so that    }
 6           { WriteAt and WriteAtVertical can write Boolean values to     }
 7           { virtual screens.  Values written are TRUE and FALSE, in     }
 8           { upper case.                                                 }
 9           {                                                             }
10           { Type String5 must be predefined.                           }
11           {                                                             }
12           {                                                             }
13           {                                                             }
14           {-------------------------------------------------------------}
```

(continued)

```
15
16      FUNCTION BooStr(BooleanValue : Boolean) : String5;
17
18      BEGIN
19        IF BooleanValue THEN BooStr := 'TRUE'
20          ELSE BooStr := 'FALSE'
21      END;
```

Merging Characters and Attributes on the Way to a Screen

Memory-mapped video is wonderfully simple in concept: Write a character code into a location in memory that is mapped onto a CRT display, and *wham*! It's there for the world to see. For this reason, the essential logic required to write a string into one of our virtual screens comprises only two statements. A few additional statements add some conveniences that even **Write** and **Writeln** don't have, like specifying an X,Y position; centering the text on the screen either horizontally, vertically, or both; and specifying video attributes that are in force *only* for the text written to the screen by a single invocation of the screen-write procedure **WriteAT**.

```
1        {->>>>WriteAt<<<<-------------------------------------------------}
2        {                                                                 }
3        { Filename : WRITEAT.SRC -- Last Modified 2/9/87                   }
4        {                                                                 }
5        { This critter writes information to the virtual screen           }
6        { defined by ScreenRec.  Only strings may be written; for         }
7        { Booleans and numerics you must use IntStr, RealStr, and         }
8        { BooStr to explicitly convert to string form.  Characters        }
9        { must be concatenated to the string, or passed alone if no       }
10       { other information is to be written.                             }
11       {                                                                 }
12       { Type ScreenRec and String255 must be predefined.                }
13       {                                                                 }
14       {                                                                 }
15       {                                                                 }
16       {-----------------------------------------------------------------}
17
18       PROCEDURE WriteAt(Target : ScreenRec; X,Y    : Integer;
19                         How    : Integer; TheText : String255);
20
21       VAR
22         I     : Integer;
23         Inset : Integer;
24
```

(continued)

```
25      BEGIN
26        { Negative X centers string horizontally, negative Y centers }
27        { string vertically. }
28        IF X < 0 THEN X := (ScreenWidth - Length(TheText)) DIV 2;
29        IF Y < 0 THEN Y := ScreenHeight DIV 2;
30        { Inset gives our starting point in the screen buffer: }
31        Inset := (ScreenWidth * (Y-1)) + X - 1;
32        { Now we simply loop and poke char/attribute pairs into the buffer: }
33        WITH Target DO
34          IF MyScreen <> NIL THEN
35            FOR I := 1 TO Length(TheText) DO
36              MyScreen^[Inset + I-1].Word := Ord(TheText[I]) OR How
37      END;
```

To approach the operation of **WriteAt**, think of copying one short string into a much larger string. A screen buffer, after all, is nothing more than a large string of memory locations in a row. The division of a screen into lines is strictly an artifact of the CRT screen; from the perspective of the software, the buffer is one long string of bytes.

To copy a string into the middle of another string you need to know how far into the larger string to begin copying the shorter string. This value could logically be called an *offset*, but this word has more specific meanings in an 8086 context; therefore, I prefer to call it the *inset* (see Figure 5.4). Once this inset is calculated, all that remains to be done is a simple FOR loop that copies the string into the screen array.

The inset into the video buffer is calculated from the X,Y position at which the string is to be written. The Y position indicates the number of full-screen lines that must be skipped from the top of the screen. The X position indicates the number of columns that must be skipped from the left margin. The equation to calculate the inset would thus be

```
Inset := (ScreenWidth * Y) + X;
```

since the length of each line is given by the absolute variable **ScreenWidth**. Unfortunately, the convention in giving screen coordinates is to count them from 1; in other words, the top screen line is line 1, and the leftmost character position on each line is column 1. Computers, however, count everything from zero, so to make the above equation work correctly, we must decrement both X and Y by 1:

```
Inset := (ScreenWidth * (Y-1)) + X-1;
```

This is the statement which **WriteAt** uses to calculate the inset.

WriteAt allows the caller to pass negative values for X and Y. When a negative value is passed in X or Y, **WriteAt** ignores it (its negative nature is used

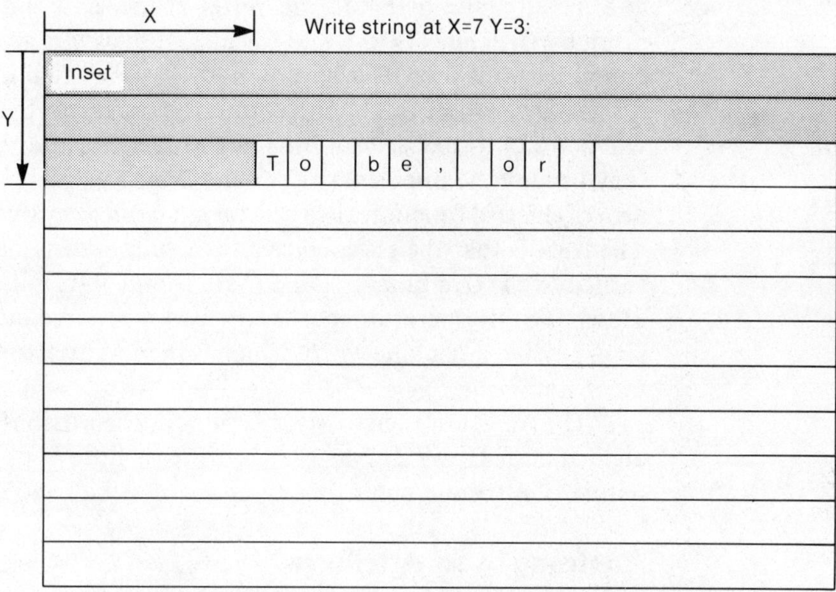

Figure 5.4   **Writing a string onto a virtual screen**

only as a flag) and replaces the negative value with a value that centers the string in either X or Y as appropriate. This works correctly *only* if the length of the string being written to the screen is less than the width of the screen.

There is one aspect to **WriteAt**'s operation that I haven't mentioned yet: the use of attributes. Take a good look at the single statement that writes the string into the screen:

```
WITH Target DO
  IF MyScreen <> NIL THEN
    FOR I := 1 TO Length(TheText) DO
      MyScreen^[Inset + I-1].Word := Ord(TheText[I]) OR How;
```

Understanding that **MyScreen** is a field of the descriptor record **Target**, and that you never write *anything* to a **NIL** pointer's referent, you can see that this is only a **FOR** loop running for the length of the string to be written to the screen. **MyScreen^** is the screen array itself. Its index is the inset plus the current index into the string, decreased by one so that space for the string's length byte will not be copied into the screen.

Notice **.Word** after the array reference. **MyScreen^** is, as you recall, an array of **VideoAtom**, which is nothing more than type **RegPack** wearing a different hat. The **.Word** indicates that we are writing *both* the character byte and the attribute byte into the buffer at the same time. The character byte is given by **Ord(TheText[I])** and the attribute byte is given in **How**. The two are combined with the **OR** operator as they are written into the screen buffer.

Sharp readers might object that the character byte and the attribute byte will conflict if they are simply ORed together, and they would—except that they occupy the opposite ends of the 2-byte value being written to the screen array. The **Ord** function always returns an integer value, and **How** is an integer. The trick is that the character value is in the *lower* eight bits of the value returned by the **Ord** function, and the attribute byte is in the *higher* eight bytes of **How**. The OR operation meshes the two byte-sized quantities smoothly into a single 16-byte machine word, which is then written to the screen by the assignment statement.

The question then arises: How does the attribute byte get into the high eight bits of **How**? The answer requires a little background on the physical nature of attribute bytes.

Anatomy of an Attribute

The character byte indicates which character is to be displayed to the screen. The attribute byte tells *how*, hence the attribute variable **How**. On a color screen, the attribute byte specifies the foreground color (the color of the character figure itself) and the background color (the color of the rest of the character cell not occupied by the character figure). The colors are summarized in Figure 5.5, along with the bit codes necessary to specify those colors from the attribute byte. If the high bit is set in any color pattern, the foreground character figure will blink relative to the background color at the text cursor rate. This is called the *blink bit*.

There are actually only eight distinct colors (including black as a color), but bit 3, when set, modifies the eight colors into "intense" or "bright" colors. Human experience defies comprehension of a color called "bright black," so it is most often called "dark grey." Yellow could more precisely be called "bright brown," since it differs from brown only in the setting of the intensity bit.

On a monochrome screen, the attribute byte is more limited in scope. There is no color in monochrome modes, and rather than speak of "black and white" (since the bulk of monochrome screens operate as either black and green or black and amber), I prefer to say "illuminated and nonilluminated." There are only six possible monochrome attributes in IBM-compatible video, and they occur in two groups that may be combined in various ways. The first group contains four, and involves the relationship of the character to its background: "invisible," which means a nonilluminated character against a nonilluminated background; underlined; reverse video, which means a nonilluminated character against an illuminated background; and "normal," which is an illuminated character against a nonilluminated background. The other group

	1 = Blink	Background Colors			Inten-sity	Foreground Colors		
Black	0	0	0	0	0	0	0	0
Blue	0	0	0	1	0	0	0	1
Green	0	0	1	0	0	0	1	0
Cyan	0	0	1	1	0	0	1	1
Red	0	1	0	0	0	1	0	0
Magenta	0	1	0	1	0	1	0	1
Brown	0	1	1	0	0	1	1	0
Light grey	0	1	1	1	0	1	1	1
Dark grey	0				1	0	0	0
Light blue	0				1	0	0	1
Light green	0				1	0	1	0
Light cyan	0				1	0	1	1
Light red	0				1	1	0	0
Light magenta	0				1	1	0	1
Yellow	0				1	1	1	0
White	0				1	1	1	1

Figure 5.5   **CGA and EGA color mode attributes**

contains two attributes: blink, which causes the character figure to flash on and off at the text cursor rate; and highlight, which sets the video intensity bit and makes whatever illumination falls within the character cell higher in intensity.

In any given character cell, the attribute byte can specify any *one* of the first four conditions and *either or both* of the second two. For example, you can make an underlined character blink, and you can make a high-intensity underlined character blink; but you cannot have an underlined character in reverse video. Of course, some forbidden combinations simply make no sense, like an invisible normal character, or a normal reverse-video character. This would be analogous in the color mode to a character being both red and green at the same time.

The bit patterns for monochrome attributes are shown in Figure 5.6. The blink and highlight attributes are single bits that are available in all attribute bytes, while the other four attributes are specific bit patterns, with only one per attribute byte.

	1 = Blink	Background bits			1 = High- light	Foreground bits		
Invisible	0	0	0	0	0	0	0	0
Underline	0	0	0	0	0	0	0	1
Normal	0	0	0	0	0	1	1	1
Reverse video	0	1	1	1	0	0	0	0

Figure 5.6   **MDA & EGA monochrome attributes**

It is, of course, possible to "hand-assemble" a desired collection of attributes into a single attribute byte, but like hand-assembling code for **INLINE**, that's more work than it has to be. It's always better to let the computer handle such work, and the work falls to a routine called **GenAttribute**:

```
1     {->>>>GenAttribute<<<<-----------------------------------------------}
2     {                                                                     }
3     { Filename : GENATTR.SRC -- Last Modified 2/12/87                      }
4     {                                                                     }
5     { This routine builds an attribute byte, given specifiers for         }
6     { the various attributes passed as parameters.  Note that the         }
7     { actual attribute information is shifted into the high byte          }
8     { of an integer before that integer is assigned to the                }
9     { function return value.                                              }
10    {                                                                     }
11    { Types Color, Adapter, and Attribute must be predefined.             }
12    {                                                                     }
13    {                                                                     }
14    {                                                                     }
15    {---------------------------------------------------------------------}
16
17    FUNCTION GenAttribute(Foreground : Color;
18                          Background : Color;
19                          MonoMethod : Attribute;
20                          Blink      : Boolean;
21                          Bright     : Boolean) : Integer;
22
23    CONST
24      ForegroundColor : ARRAY[Color] OF Byte =
25                                 ($00,$01,$02,$03,$04,$05,$06,$07,
26                                  $08,$09,$0A,$0B,$0C,$0D,$0E,$0F);
27      BackgroundColor : ARRAY[Black..LightGray] OF Byte =
28                                 ($00,$10,$20,$30,$40,$50,$60,$70);
29      MonoAttributes  : ARRAY[Attribute] OF Byte = ($00,$01,$07,$70);
```

(continued)

```
30      BlinkCodes        : ARRAY[Boolean] OF Byte = ($00,$80);
31      BrightCodes       : ARRAY[Boolean] OF Byte = ($00,$08);
32
33   VAR
34     How : Integer;
35
36   BEGIN
37     CASE Adapter OF
38       MDA       : How := MonoAttributes[MonoMethod]
39                          OR BlinkCodes[Blink]
40                          OR BrightCodes[Bright];
41       CGA       : How := BlinkCodes[Blink]
42                          OR BrightCodes[Bright]
43                          OR ForegroundColor[Foreground]
44                          OR BackgroundColor[Background];
45       EGAMono   : How := MonoAttributes[MonoMethod]
46                          OR BlinkCodes[Blink]
47                          OR BrightCodes[Bright];
48       EGAColor : How := BlinkCodes[Blink]
49                          OR BrightCodes[Bright]
50                          OR ForegroundColor[Foreground]
51                          OR BackgroundColor[Background];
52     END; { CASE }
53     How := How SHL 8;  { The attribute proper is in the HIGH byte!!!! }
54     GenAttribute := How
55   END;
```

GenAttribute accepts our selections of attributes and colors and uses
those selections to build an attribute byte, which it returns as its integer function result. Our method of selecting colors and attributes revolves around some
new type definitions. In the **VSCREEN.DEF** file (listed in full at the end of this
chapter) are two enumerated type definitions: **Color** and **Attribute**:

```
Attribute = (Invisible,Underline,Normal,Reverse);
Color     = (Black,Blue,Green,Cyan,Red,Magenta,Brown,
             LightGrey,DarkGrey,LightBlue,LightGreen,
             LightCyan,LightRed,LightMagenta,Yellow,
             White);
```

These enumerated types provide a more human-oriented way of dealing with
the bit patterns comprising a color or attribute.

GenAttribute's translation mechanism uses several local array constants
indexed by the enumerated values of types **Color** and **Attribute**. Indexing into
one of these arrays by the selected enumerated constant for a given attribute
returns a numeric value which represents the bit pattern for that attribute. For
example, the expression **ForegroundColor[Cyan]** evaluates to the byte value
$03, and the expression **MonoAttributes[Reverse]** evaluates to the byte value

$70. **GenAttribute** combines multiple attribute codes into one integer by OR-ing the codes together. Finally, the integer value is shifted eight bits to the left, boosting the attribute information up into the high byte.

This last distinction is critical to remember: **GenAttribute** returns an integer value with the attribute information in the high byte. This way, the attribute information can be combined with character information in the low byte of another integer by using just a single OR operation.

Also note that although the parameter list of **GenAttribute** contains all attribute specifications for both color and monochrome video modes, only the attributes for the current adapter type are actually used to create an attribute byte. Parameters unusued for the current mode are ignored and can be passed dummy variables.

Invoking **WriteAt** always requires an attribute parameter, so you must invoke **GenAttribute** at least once to create a workaday attribute value. If you intend to add emphasis to your screen text by changing attributes, define an integer variable for each different attribute combination you intend to use frequently, and initialize each one with **GenAttribute** before your application gets rolling. You should remember, however, that **GenAttribute** is an integer *function*, and you can pass an attribute value to **WriteAt** by invoking **GenAttribute** as the actual parameter to **WriteAt**'s formal parameter **How**. In other words, while awkward, the following syntax is completely correct:

```
WriteAt(HelpScreen,1,6,
        GenAttribute(White,Black,Normal,Blink,Highlight),
        'The help file JIVEHELP.TXT cannot be read!');
```

Here, the attribute value is generated on the fly as **WriteAt** is being invoked. Certainly it's faster to prepare readymade attribute values in advance, but in practice the difference in speed is undetectable unless you are invoking **WriteAt** hundreds of times in succession.

Changing Attributes for Existing Screen Text

The virtual screen scheme enables a feature not available with **Write** and **Write-ln**: changing the attributes behind text that is already on the screen. This might seem an odd thing to do, but consider this: Suppose you have a data entry application in which a user fills in fields with text and presses Return to indicate a field is ready to be processed. If the data validation logic decides that the entered field is invalid, it can always blank out the field and demand that another string be entered. However, if the fact that this particular piece of data is invalid also invalidates several previously entered fields, you must indicate to the user that he or she must toggle back to several earlier fields and correct them as well.

One way to do that is to change the attributes for each of the displayed fields that needs correcting. This does not involve elaborate redisplay of the data in those fields. As long as the application knows where on the screen the fields are located, it can change the attribute bytes for the fields to be underlined, or highlighted, or blinking *without* disturbing the actual text characters displayed there.

Procedure **SetAttribute** will do that. It's actually very similar to **WriteAt** except that no string data is passed. Instead, an X,Y starting position is passed, along with a string length value.

```
1     {->>>>SetAttribute<<<<-------------------------------------------}
2     {                                                                 }
3     { Filename : SETATTR.SRC -- Last Modified 2/9/87                  }
4     {                                                                 }
5     { This is a way of altering the attributes beneath a line of      }
6     { text on a virtual screen without actually altering the text     }
7     { itself.  How must contain the attribute to be applied to the    }
8     { text, with attribute information in the HIGH eight bits.         }
9     { TextLength is the length of the string at X,Y to be             }
10    { modified.                                                       }
11    {                                                                 }
12    { Type ScreenRec must be predefined.                              }
13    {                                                                 }
14    {                                                                 }
15    {                                                                 }
16    {-----------------------------------------------------------------}
17
18    PROCEDURE SetAttribute(Target          : ScreenRec;
19                           X,Y,TextLength : Integer;
20                           How            : Integer);
21
22    VAR
23      I     : Integer;
24      Inset : Integer;
25
26    BEGIN
27      { Negative X centers string horizontally, negative Y centers }
28      { string vertically. }
29      IF X < 0 THEN X := (ScreenWidth - TextLength) DIV 2;
30      IF Y < 0 THEN Y := ScreenHeight DIV 2;
31      { Inset gives our starting point in the screen buffer: }
32      Inset := (ScreenWidth * (Y-1)) + X - 1;
33      WITH Target DO
34        IF MyScreen <> NIL THEN
35          FOR I := 1 TO TextLength DO
36            MyScreen^[Inset + I-1].HiByte := Hi(How);
37    END;
```

As with **WriteAt**, **SetAttribute** calculates the inset and enters a **FOR** loop to do its work. But take a look at the body of the **FOR** loop:

```
MyScreen^[Inset + I-1].HiByte := Hi(How);
```

Notice that only the **HiByte** field of that particular **VideoAtom** is assigned to, and it is assigned the value stored in the high eight bits of attribute parameter **How**. The actual character value is stored in the **LoByte** field of the **Video-Atom**. No explicit ANDing or ORing complicates the source code here; Pascal "handles" the every-other-byte assignment to the screen buffer behind the scenes. Such is the power of free-union variant records at their best.

Vertically Speaking

There's nothing sacred about the way **WriteAt** writes characters to the screen in a horizontal direction. Writing a string to the screen vertically is no more difficult. In fact, only the **FOR** loop needs to be slightly changed:

```
FOR I := 1 TO Length(TheText) DO
  MyScreen^[Inset + ((I-1) * ScreenWidth)].Word :=
    Ord(TheText[I]) OR How;
```

The only difference is that a screen's width of bytes is added to the inset for each character displayed. As a result, this statement will write characters down the screen, one per screen line, one beneath the other.

```
1      {->>>>WriteAtVertical<<<<---------------------------------------}
2      {                                                                }
3      { Filename : WRITEVRT.SRC -- Last Modified 2/9/87                }
4      {                                                                }
5      { This critter writes information to the virtual screen          }
6      { defined by ScreenRec.  Only strings may be written; for        }
7      { Booleans and numerics you must use IntStr, RealStr, and        }
8      { BooStr to explicitly convert to string form.  Characters       }
9      { must be concatenated to the string, or passed alone if no      }
10     { other information is to be written.  Operation is identical    }
11     { to WriteAt except that information is written downward from    }
12     { X,Y.  Keep in mind that How contains attribute information     }
13     { in the HIGH eight bits!                                        }
14     {                                                                }
15     { Type ScreenRec and String255 must be predefined.              }
16     {                                                                }
17     {                                                                }
18     {                                                                }
19     {--------------------------------------------------------------}
20
21     PROCEDURE WriteAtVertical(Target : ScreenRec; X,Y   : Integer;
```

(continued)

```
22                                      How     : Integer; TheText : String255);
23
24          VAR
25            I     : Integer;
26            Inset : Integer;
27
28          BEGIN
29            { Negative X centers string horizontally, negative Y centers }
30            { string vertically. }
31            IF Y < 0 THEN Y := (ScreenHeight - Length(TheText)) DIV 2;
32            IF X < 0 THEN X := ScreenWidth DIV 2;
33            { Inset gives our starting point in the screen buffer: }
34            Inset := (ScreenWidth * (Y-1)) + X - 1;
35            { Now we simply loop and poke char/attribute pairs into the buffer,   }
36            { remembering that we keep X constant and increment Y with each loop: }
37            WITH Target DO
38              IF MyScreen <> NIL THEN
39                FOR I := 1 TO Length(TheText) DO
40                  MyScreen^[Inset + ((I-1) * ScreenWidth)].Word :=
41                      Ord(TheText[I]) OR How
42            END;
```

Similarly, a variant of **SetAttribute** can be written to alter the attributes behind a vertical line on the screen. I confess to never having used **SetAttributeVertical** in an application, but I include it here to make our discussion complete.

```
1          {->>>>SetAttributeVertical<<<<---------------------------------}
2          {                                                              }
3          { Filename : SETATTRV.SRC -- Last Modified 2/9/87              }
4          {                                                              }
5          { This is a way of altering the attributes beneath a line of   }
6          { text on a virtual screen without actually altering the text  }
7          { itself.  How must contain the attribute to be applied to the }
8          { text, with attribute information in the HIGH eight bits.      }
9          { Operation is just like SetAttribute except that it operates  }
10         { on a vertical line of text from X,Y, to a height of          }
11         { TextLength.                                                  }
12         {                                                              }
13         { Type ScreenRec must be predefined.                          }
14         {                                                              }
15         {                                                              }
16         {                                                              }
17         {--------------------------------------------------------------}
18
19         PROCEDURE SetAttributeVertical(Target          : ScreenRec;
20                                        X,Y,TextLength : Integer;
```

(continued)

```
21                                          How             : Integer);
22
23          VAR
24            I     : Integer;
25            Inset : Integer;
26
27          BEGIN
28            { Negative X centers string horizontally, negative Y centers }
29            { string vertically. }
30            IF Y < 0 THEN Y := (ScreenHeight - TextLength) DIV 2;
31            IF X < 0 THEN X := ScreenWidth DIV 2;
32            { Inset gives our starting point in the screen buffer: }
33            Inset := (ScreenWidth * (Y-1)) + X - 1;
34            WITH Target DO
35              IF MyScreen <> NIL THEN
36                FOR I := 1 TO TextLength DO
37                  MyScreen^[Inset + ((I-1) * ScreenWidth)].HiByte := Hi(How);
38          END;
```

Drawing Boxes in a Hurry

The PC's character set contains a handy suite of special characters that can be used to draw almost any kind of box or form on the screen. However, drawing the four sides of a box is not something that can be done quickly with Turbo Pascal's built-in **GotoXY**, **Write**, and **Writeln** procedures. The top and bottom appear quickly, but writing anything in a vertical direction is slow enough to be followed by the eye (which, by my way of thinking, is always unacceptably slow).

As I have been demonstrating throughout this chapter, working with virtual screens allows much more flexibility in getting character and attribute information to the screen. Drawing characters in a vertical line can be done just as quickly as drawing them horizontally—if the code is set up to work efficiently in a vertical direction.

WriteAt and **WriteAtVertical** together allow the creation of a truly fast box-draw procedure that will place a box on your screen *instantly*—even if the screen is the visible screen.

```
1          {->>>>MakeBox<<<<-------------------------------------------------}
2          {                                                                 }
3          { Filename : MAKEBOX.SRC -- Last Modified 2/12/87                  }
4          {                                                                 }
5          { Here we draw a box at X,Y sized Width by Height, with           }
6          { attribute in How.  (Attribute info in the high 8 bits!)         }
7          { if LineStyle is True, the box will be drawn with the double     }
8          { line drawing characters; False forces use of single line       }
9          { drawing characters.                                            }
```

(continued)

```
10        {                                                                  }
11        { ScreenRec, BarStrings, BoxChars, WriteAt and WriteAtVertical }
12        { must be predefined.                                           }
13        {                                                                  }
14        {                                                                  }
15        {                                                                  }
16        {--------------------------------------------------------------}
17
18        PROCEDURE MakeBox(Target            : ScreenRec;
19                          X,Y,Width,Height : Integer;
20                          LineStyle        : Boolean;
21                          How              : Integer);
22
23        VAR
24          I,J : Integer;
25          HBarLine,
26          VBarLine : BarStrings;
27
28        BEGIN
29          WITH BoxChars DO  { BoxChars is a record constant defined in VSCREEN.DEF }
30            BEGIN
31              { First we create a horizontal bar 80 characters long: }
32              FillChar(HBarLine[LineStyle],Sizeof(HBarLine[LineStyle]),
33                      HBar[LineStyle]);
34              { Next we create a vertical bar 80 characters long: }
35              FillChar(VBarLine[LineStyle],Sizeof(VbarLine[LineStyle]),
36                      VBar[LineStyle]);
37
38              { Negative X centers box horizontally; negative Y vertically: }
39              IF X < 0 THEN X := (ScreenWidth-Width) DIV 2;
40              IF Y < 0 THEN Y := (ScreenHeight-Height) DIV 2;
41
42              { Draw top line: }
43              WriteAt(Target,X,Y,How,ULCorner[LineStyle] +
44                      Copy(HBarLine[LineStyle],1,Width-2) +
45                      URCorner[LineStyle]);
46
47              { Draw bottom line: }
48              WriteAt(Target,X,(Y+Height)-1,How,LLCorner[LineStyle] +
49                      Copy(HBarLine[LineStyle],1,Width-2) +
50                      LRCorner[LineStyle]);
51
52              { Draw left side: }
53              WriteAtVertical
54                (Target,X,Y+1,How,Copy(VBarLine[LineStyle],1,Height-2));
55
56              { Draw right side: }
57              WriteAtVertical
58                (Target,X+Width-1,Y+1,How,Copy(VBarLine[LineStyle],1,Height-2));
59            END
60        END;
```

MakeBox depends upon some new types defined in **VSCREEN.DEF** (listed in full at the end of this chapter). Most important is the notion of a **BoxRec**, which is a PC-specific improvement on the type of the same name I described in *Complete Turbo Pascal*:

```
CONST
  SingleLine = False;
  DoubleLine = True;

TYPE
  LineChars   = ARRAY[SingleLine..DoubleLine] OF Char;
  BoxRec      = RECORD
                  ULCorner,
                  URCorner,
                  LLCorner,
                  LRCorner,
                  HBar,
                  VBar,
                  LineCross,
                  TDown,
                  TUp,
                  TRight,
                  TLeft : LineChars
                END;
```

There are two complete sets of line-drawing characters in the PC character set, one a single-line set and the other a double-line set. Type **LineChars** holds two such characters side by side, and the record **BoxChars**, since it is composed of 11 **LineChars** arrays, holds the entire double set. The notation

```
ARRAY[SingleLine..DoubleLine]
```

is completely equivalent to either

```
ARRAY[False..True]
```

or

```
ARRAY[Boolean]
```

but it conveys the *purpose* of the data type **LineChars** more clearly.

It's much easier to spot the purpose of the **BoxRec** record and what it contains if you see the record constant that actually fills a **BoxRec** with the character values that display the line-drawing characters on the PC screen. This record constant is also defined in **VSCREEN.DEF**:

```
CONST
  BoxChars    = BoxRec =
                  (ULCorner  : (#218,#201);
```

```
URCorner   : (#191,#187);
LLCorner   : (#192,#200);
LRCorner   : (#217,#188);
HBar       : (#196,#205);
VBar       : (#179,#186);
LineCross  : (#197,#206);
TDown      : (#194,#203);
TUp        : (#193,#202);
TRight     : (#195,#185);
TLeft      : (#180,#204));
```

Here, clearly, are the two line-drawing character groups side by side. To work through an example, the expression **HBar[SingleLine]** evaluates to character 196, which is the single-line horizontal line character. **HBar[DoubleLine]** evaluates to character 205, which is the double-line horizontal line character.

MakeBox makes thorough use of **BoxChars**, with the advantage that a single Boolean constant toggles it between drawing boxes in single-line and double-line characters. Some additional Turbo trickery helps **MakeBox** operate more quickly. At the beginning of the procedure, a pair of 80-character strings are filled with horizontal bar and vertical bar characters, respectively, by way of Turbo Pascal's fast **FillChar** character-fill procedure. The four sides of the box being drawn are copied from these two "reference" strings, with the number of characters copied derived from the **Width** and **Height** parameters. The box corner characters are selected from **BoxChars** by the **LineStyle** Boolean parameter.

As with **WriteAt**, the box drawn on the screen by **MakeBox** may be centered either horizontally, vertically, or both, by passing negative values in **X** and/or **Y**.

5.7 Assembly-Language Primitives for Maximum Speed

How fast is fast enough? *Too fast to see.* Period. (Any bets now on why I'm not a Unix fan?) All of the routines described in this chapter until now meet this requirement admirably, even on a 4.77-Mhz 8088. Furthermore, all of them are written completely in Pascal.

In my own explorations of text-video management, I have found three necessary primitive functions implemented in Pascal that run slowly enough to notice: screen clearing, region block moves, and region scrolls. (A *region* is any rectangular subset of a screen.) When Pascal won't hack it, you had better hack it in assembler. The remainder of this chapter describes three assembly-language text primitives implemented as external machine-code files.

Clearing the Screen

In Chapter 4, I described a simple assembly-language routine for clearing a text screen called **ClearScreen**. It amounts to little more than setting up several machine registers and performing one string store opcode. The routine is worth reviewing briefly in the light of what has been discussed in this chapter:

```
 1        ;==============================================================================
 2        ;
 3        ;      C L E A R S C R E E N  -  Screen clear primitive for Turbo Pascal
 4        ;
 5        ;==============================================================================
 6        ;
 7        ;      by Jeff Duntemann      2 February 1987
 8        ;
 9        ;
10        ;
11        ;
12        ; CLEARSCREEN is written to be called from Turbo Pascal V3.0 using the
13        ; EXTERNAL procedure convention.  It has the advantage over ClrScr in that
14        ; it can clear a screen stored on the heap, and also that a screen can be
15        ; cleared with a character other than space, like the IBM PC's halftone
16        ; characters, for the Framework effect.  An attribute can be written to the
17        ; cleared buffer as well as a clear character.
18        ;
19        ; To use CLEARSCREEN, you must have predeclared a screen array and a
20        ; pointer type to that screen array.  For a typical 25 X 80 screen, these
21        ; declarations would like like this:
22        ;
23        ; TYPE
24        ;   Screen    = ARRAY[0..1999] OF Integer;
25        ;   ScreenPtr = ^Screen;
26        ;
27        ; To use CLEARSCREEN on the visible screen, you must "doctor" a declared
28        ; pointer to point to either the monochrome or graphics text buffer:
29        ;
30        ; VAR
31        ;   VisibleScreen : ScreenPtr;
32        ;
33        ; VisibleScreen := Ptr($B000,0);  { For the monochrome adapter }
34        ; VisibleScreen := Ptr($B800,0);  { For the color graphics adapter }
35        ;
36        ; Declare the procedure itself as external using this declaration:
37        ;
38        ; PROCEDURE CLEARSCREEN(Target : ScreenPtr; ScreenSize : Integer;
39        ;                       Attribute : Integer; CharFill : Byte);
40        ;                       EXTERNAL 'CLEARS.BIN'
41        ;
```

(continued)

```
42          ;
43          ; Pass CLEARSCREEN the attribute code you wish to use in Attribute
44          ; (typically $0700 for "normal" text display) and the character to "clear"
45          ; with in CharFill.  Use 32 or Ord(' ') to fill with blanks, or you may use
46          ; the "halftone" characters (176-178) for Framework style screens.  Keep
47          ; in mind that the attribute code must be in the HIGH byte of the actual
48          ; parameter passed to Attribute.
49          ;
50          ; EXAMPLES:
51          ;
52          ; To clear the visible screen to normal blanks:
53          ;     CLEARSCREEN(VisibleScreen,4096,$0700,' ');
54          ;
55          ; To clear a screen on the heap to a halftone screen:
56          ;     CLEARSCREEN(NewScreen,4096,$0700,176);
57          ;
58          ; Obviously, you must have declared VisibleScreen and NewScreen and set
59          ; them up so that they both point to either a screen on the heap or the
60          ; visible screen buffer.  If the pointer Target has a value of NIL,
61          ; CLEARSCREEN will return to the calling logic without taking any action.
62          ; Good thing, too--if it did, it would blank your interrupt vector table!
63          ;
64          ;
65          ; To reassemble/relink CLEARSCREEN:
66          ;--------------------------------------
67          ; 1. Assemble this file with MASM.   "A> MASM CLEARS;"
68          ; 2. Link it into a .EXE file.       "A> LINK CLEARS;"
69          ; 3. Use EXE2BIN to make a .COM file. "A> EXE2BIN CLEARS.EXE CLEARS.COM"
70          ; 4. Declare as shown above in your Turbo Pascal program.
71          ; 5. Ignore any minor diagnostic messages that may be generated when
72          ;    this file is assembled and linked.  EXE2BIN is supplied with the
73          ;    supplemental programs for PC-DOS; see the DOS manual.
74          ;
75
76          CODE    SEGMENT PUBLIC
77                  ASSUME  CS:CODE
78                  PUBLIC  CLEARS
79          ;
80          ; This structure maps the stack at entry to CLEARSCREEN:
81          ;
82          ONSTACK STRUC
83          OLDBP   DW ?       ;CALLER'S BP VALUE SAVED ON STACK
84          RETADDR DW ?       ;RETURN ADDRESS OFFSET
85          FILLER  DW ?       ;CHARACTER THAT FILLS THE CLEARED BUFFER
86          ATTRIB  DW ?       ;ATTRIBUTE FOR THE CLEARED BUFFER
87          BUFSIZE DW ?       ;SIZE OF THE BUFFER TO BE CLEARED, IN BYTES
88          BUFOFS  DW ?       ;OFFSET OF BUFFER ORIGIN
89          BUFSEG  DW ?       ;SEGMENT OF BUFFER ORIGIN
90          ENDMRK  DB ?       ;DUMMY LABEL TO MARK END OF DATA ON STACK
```

(continued)

```
91               ONSTACK ENDS
92               ;
93
94
95      CLEARS   PROC     NEAR
96               PUSH     BP
97               MOV      BP,SP                       ; CALLING CONVENTION
98               ;
99               ;-----------------------------------------------------
100              ; FIRST WE TEST FOR BUFFER = NIL...QUIT IF SO
101              ;-----------------------------------------------------
102              ;
103              CMP      WORD PTR [BP].BUFSEG,0  ; A NIL POINTER IS A SEGMENT AND
104              JNE      START                  ; OFFSET BOTH SET TO 0
105              CMP      WORD PTR [BP].BUFOFS,0
106              JE       BYE
107
108              ;
109              ;-----------------------------------------------------
110              ; PREPARE THE REGISTERS FOR THE STORE WORD OPERATION
111              ;-----------------------------------------------------
112              ;
113      START:  CLD                              ; CLEAR DIRECTION FLAG
114              MOV      AX,[BP].ATTRIB           ; LOAD ATTRIBUTE CODE INTO AX
115              AND      AX,0FF00H                ; MASK OUT LOW BYTE OF ATTRIBUTE CODE
116              MOV      BX,[BP].FILLER           ; LOAD FILLER CODE INTO BX
117              AND      BX,0FFH                  ; MASK OUT HIGH BYTE OF FILLER CODE
118              OR       AX,BX                    ; AND COMBINE ATTRIB & FILLER INTO AX
119              MOV      BX,[BP].BUFOFS           ; SET DI TO TARGET BUFFER OFFSET
120              MOV      DI,BX                    ;   BY WAY OF BX
121              MOV      BX,[BP].BUFSEG           ; SET ES TO TARGET BUFFER SEGMENT
122              MOV      ES,BX                    ;   BY WAY OF BX
123              ;
124              ;------------------------------------------------------------
125              ; LOOP TO STORE CHARACTER AND ATTRIBUTE INTO BUFFER BY WORD MOVE
126              ;------------------------------------------------------------
127              ;
128              MOV      CX,[BP].BUFSIZE          ; SET UP COUNTER WITH BUFFER SIZE
129              REP      STOSW                    ; DO THE STRING STORE
130              ;
131              ;------------------------------------------
132              ; DONE.. CLEAN UP THE STACK AND LEAVE
133              ;------------------------------------------
134              ;
135      BYE:    MOV      SP,BP                    ; RESTORE PRIOR STACK POINTER & BP
136              POP      BP                       ;   IN CONVENTIONAL RETURN
137              RET      ENDMRK-RETADDR-2         ; TRASH 10 BYTES FOR PARMS
138
139      CLEARS   ENDP
140      CODE     ENDS
141               END
```

ClearScreen is passed a pointer to the screen array itself, *not* the screen descriptor, as with most of the text routines written in Pascal. This was done to keep the assembly-language portion of the routine short and simple, and to avoid passing a descriptor's 19 bytes on the stack when the pointer's 4 would do just as well.

The attribute and fill character are passed separately to **ClearScreen**. This contrasts with **Scroller**, in which the attribute and fill character for the inserted lines are passed as a single 16-bit quantity. (Refer to Section 4.5 to review the detailed operation of **ClearScreen**.)

Region Block Moves

One of the most annoying things an application does is "repaint the screen." It amazes me that people think through elaborate user interfaces with pull-down menus, dialog boxes and so on, then "put away" such creatures by clearing the screen and recreating it from scratch. The screen was there, in its entirety, before the dialog box was plopped down on top of it; there is simply no excuse for having to draw the whole screen again once the dialog box has done its job.

There are two solutions—one uses brute force, the other is more elegant. The brute-force method involves simply saving the entire visible screen out to a virtual screen on the heap *before* the dialog box (or whatever) is written to the displayed screen. To erase the dialog box, simply move the saved screen back into the visible screen with **MoveScreen**. This method will consume 4K per 25 × 80 screen, but these days, with 640K PC systems becoming the norm, 4K is not too high a price to pay for instantaneous screen regeneration. You can do it with the tools already described in this chapter.

The elegant method entails saving out only the portion of the screen to be covered by the dialog box, and then moving *only* that saved-out portion back into the visible buffer when the dialog box has done its work. The space required on the heap can usually be kept to 1K or less.

This second method requires an additional, nontrivial tool. This tool must move a rectangular subset of the screen out onto the heap without having to store it in a full-sized screen. And it must be fast (as I said before, it must be too fast to see it work).

For many years, there has existed a necessary tool for graphics work called a BitBLT (Bit Block Transfer), which is a means of moving a rectangular area of pixels on a graphics screen from one location in memory to another. Because virtually all bit-mapped displays store more than one pixel per byte, the BitBLT code must literally split bytes when the edges of the graphics region to be moved do not fall on byte boundaries. The logic for this is painfully arcane.

In the text world, things are made much simpler by the fact that the fundamental atom of a text screen occupies two bytes, or a *machine word*. No splitting of bytes or even words is necessary. Moving a region of a text screen from one place to another is thus a WordBLT (Word Block Transfer). (The routine given below is a WordBLT that meets all my requirements. If you're not at least passingly familiar with 8086 assembly language, you're in for a rough time in attempting to understand it.)

```
 1    ;==============================================================================
 2    ;
 3    ;     W O R D B L T  -   "Word Block Transfer" for text video windowing
 4    ;
 5    ;==============================================================================
 6    ;
 7    ;     by Jeff Duntemann      28 September 1986
 8    ;
 9    ;
10    ;
11    ;
12    ; WORDBLT is written to be called from Turbo Pascal V3.0 using the
13    ; EXTERNAL procedure convention.
14    ;
15    ; Declare the procedure itself as external using this declaration:
16    ;
17    ; PROCEDURE WordBLT(ScreenEnd,StoreEnd : ScrnPtr;
18    ;                     TowardScreen       : Boolean;
19    ;                     ScreenX,ScreenY    : Integer;
20    ;                     ULX,ULY            : Integer;
21    ;                     Width,Height       : Integer);
22    ;             EXTERNAL 'WORDBLT.BIN';
23    ;
24    ; What we have here is a means of moving a rectangular region of a text
25    ; screen (either the visible screen or a screen stored on the heap) from
26    ; the screen array to a storage array.  It is the text analog of a BITBLT
27    ; (BIT BLock Transfer.)  It is an essential component of any windowing or
28    ; menuing system that expects to update the display faster than the eyes
29    ; can follow.
30    ;
31    ; It works like this:  ScreenEnd and StoreEnd are the two pointers pointing
32    ; to the screen array and the storage array, respectively.  If either pointer
33    ; is NIL, WORDBLT returns without taking any action.  TowardScreen specifies
34    ; the direction in which the data is moving.  ScreenX and ScreenY are the
35    ; dimensions of the screen in use.  ULX and ULY are the coordinates of the
36    ; upper left hand corner of the rectangular region to be affected in the
37    ; visible screen.  Width and Height are the dimensions of the region to be
38    ; affected.
39    ;
40    ; There is a critical difference between a screen array and a storage array.
41    ; A screen array has an implied structure of rows and columns, dictated by
```

(continued)

```
42     ; the ScreenX and ScreenY parameters.  A rectangular region within such an
43     ; array is not one contiguous block of elements, but rather a number of
44     ; blocks of elements separated by some quantity of storage not included in
45     ; the block transfer.  Additionally, the rectangular region begins at some
46     ; offset from the beginning of the screen array.  A storage buffer, by
47     ; contrast, is a simple contiguous array of character/attribute pairs without
48     ; any consideration for the row/column structure of a visible screen.  We
49     ; do it this way for the utmost speed and most efficient use of memory.
50     ;
51     ; So while it is true that a single invocation of WORDBLT cannot move a
52     ; text window from one position on a screen to another position on the
53     ; same screen or on a different screen, the operation happens so quickly
54     ; that such moves can be accomplished just as instantaneously to the eyes
55     ; by using two invocations and passing the window through a temporary
56     ; storage array.
57     ;
58     ; Allocation of both screen and storage arrays, of course, is the
59     ; responsibility of the calling logic.  HINT: Use GetMem and FreeMem
60     ; rather than New and Dispose.
61     ;
62     ;
63     ; To reassemble/relink WORDBLT:
64     ;----------------------------------------
65     ; 1. Assemble this file with MASM.   "C>MASM WORDBLT;"
66     ; 2. Link it into a .EXE file.       "C>LINK WORDBLT;"
67     ; 3. Use EXE2BIN to make a .COM file. "A> EXE2BIN WORDBLT.EXE WORDBLT.COM"
68     ; 4. Declare as shown above in your Turbo Pascal program.
69     ; 5. Ignore any minor diagnostic messages that may be generated when
70     ;    this file is assembled and linked.  EXE2BIN is supplied with the
71     ;    supplemental programs for PC-DOS; see the DOS manual.
72     ;
73     ;
74     ;  This creature puts lots of things on the stack.  Study closely:
75     ;
76     ONSTACK STRUC
77     OLDBP   DW ?       ;CALLER'S BP VALUE SAVED ON STACK
78     RETADDR DW ?       ;RETURN ADDRESS OFFSET
79     HEIGHT  DW ?       ;HEIGHT OF WINDOW TO BE MOVED
80     WIDTH   DW ?       ;WIDTH OF WINDOW TO BE MOVED
81     ULY     DW ?       ;Y COORDINATE OF UPPER LEFT CORNER OF WINDOW
82     ULX     DW ?       ;X COORDINATE OF UPPER LEFT CORNER OF WINDOW
83     YSIZE   DW ?       ;GENNED MAX Y DIMENSION OF CURRENT VISIBLE SCREEN
84     XSIZE   DW ?       ;GENNED MAX X DIMENSION OF CURRENT VISIBLE SCREEN
85     TOWARD  DW ?       ;BIT 0 = AWAY FROM SCREEN; BIT 0 = 1 TOWARD SCREEN
86     STORE   DD ?       ;32-BIT POINTER TO STORE BUFFER
87     SCREEN  DD ?       ;32-BIT POINTER TO SCREEN BUFFER
88     ENDMRK  DB ?       ;DUMMY FIELD FOR SIZE CALCULATION PURPOSES
89     ONSTACK ENDS
90
91
```

(continued)

```
92        CODE    SEGMENT PUBLIC
93                ASSUME  CS:CODE
94                PUBLIC  WORDBLT
95
96        WORDBLT PROC    NEAR
97                PUSH    BP                      ;SAVE CALLER'S BP VALUE
98                MOV     BP,SP                   ;SP BECOMES NEW VALUE OF BP
99                PUSH    DS                      ;SAVE CALLER'S DS VALUE
100
101       ;-----------------------------------------------------------------------
102       ;  HERE WE CALCULATE THE INSET FROM THE START OF THE VISIBLE
103       ;     SCREEN BUFFER TO THE FIRST BYTE OF THE WINDOW TO BE BLITTED
104       ;-----------------------------------------------------------------------
105
106               MOV     CX,[BP].XSIZE           ;SCREEN MAX X DIMENSION IN CX
107               MOV     BX,[BP].ULX             ;UL CORNER X DIMENSION IN BX
108               MOV     AX,[BP].ULY             ;UL CORNER Y DIMENSION IN AX
109               SUB     BX,1                    ;CORRECT FOR ORIGIN AT 1 NOT O
110               SUB     AX,1                    ;CORRECT FOR ORIGIN AT 1 NOT O
111               MUL     CX                      ;MULTIPLY SCREEN WIDTH BY UL Y
112               ADD     AX,BX                   ; AND ADD INDENT FROM LEFT MARGIN
113               MOV     CX,AX
114               SHL     CX,1
115
116       ;-----------------------------------------------------------------------
117       ;  CX NOW CONTAINS THE INSET.  THE INCREMENT BETWEEN WINDOW LINES MUST
118       ;     BE CALCULATED NEXT AND STORED IN DX.
119       ;-----------------------------------------------------------------------
120
121               MOV     DX,[BP].XSIZE
122               SUB     DX,[BP].WIDTH           ;INCREMENT IS SCREEN WIDTH MINUS
123                                               ; WINDOW WIDTH
124               SHL     DX,1                    ;INCREMENT IS IN WORDS.  MUST
125                                               ; CONVERT TO BYTES FOR USE; HERE
126                                               ; WE MULTIPLY IT BY TWO BY
127                                               ; SHIFTING LEFT ONE BIT
128
129       ;-----------------------------------------------------------------------
130       ;  NEXT WE HAVE TO FILL THE SOURCE AND DESTINATION SEGMENT AND OFFSET
131       ;     REGISTERS, DEPENDING ON WHICH WAY DATA WILL BE FLOWING.  DS:SI IS
132       ;     ALWAYS THE SOURCE ADDRESS, AND ES:DI IS ALWAYS THE DESTINATION
133       ;     ADDRESS.  TOWARD DETERMINES WHETHER DATA WILL BE FLOWING TOWARD THE
134       ;     SCREEN BUFFER OR TOWARD THE STORAGE BUFFER.  MUCH OF THIS CODE IS
135       ;     CHECKING TO SEE IF EITHER POINTER WAS SET TO NIL, I.E. BOTH WORDS
136       ;     SET TO ZERO.  IF EITHER POINTER WAS PASSED AS NIL, WORDBLT RETURNS
137       ;     WITHOUT TAKING FURTHER ACTION.
138       ;-----------------------------------------------------------------------
139
140               TEST    [BP].TOWARD,1           ;HIGH BIT = 1  MEANS TOWARD SCREEN
141               JZ      STORIT                  ;BIT O MEANS TOWARD STORAGE BUFFER
```

(continued)

```
142
143                 LES      DI,[BP].SCREEN          ;SCREEN IS DESTINATION
144                 LDS      SI,[BP].STORE           ;STORAGE BUFFER IS SOURCE
145
146                 MOV      AX,ES                   ;CAN'T DO A CMP ON A SEGMENT REG.
147                 CMP      AX,0                    ;A NIL POINTER IS A SEGMENT AND
148                 JNE      CHECK2                  ; OFFSET BOTH SET TO 0
149                 CMP      DI,0                    ;RETURN WITHOUT ACTING IF BOTH
150                 JE       GOHOME                  ; ARE SET TO 0
151
152     CHECK2:     MOV      AX,DS                   ;CAN'T DO A CMP ON A SEGMENT REG.
153                 CMP      AX,0                    ;A NIL POINTER IS A SEGMENT AND
154                 JNE      DOMORE                  ; OFFSET BOTH SET TO 0
155                 CMP      SI,0                    ;RETURN WITHOUT ACTING IF BOTH
156                 JE       GOHOME                  ; ARE SET TO 0
157
158     DOMORE:     ADD      DI,CX                   ;SCREEN END MUST ADD INSET VALUE
159                                                  ; TO OFFSET PORTION OF POINTER
160                 XOR      BX,BX                   ;ZERO BX; NO SOURCE INCREMENT
161                                                  ;DESTINATION INCREMENT ALREADY IN DX
162                 JMP      SETUP                   ;HEAD FOR SETUP OF MOVE LOOPS
163
164
165     STORIT:     LES      DI,[BP].STORE           ;HERE, STORAGE BUFFER IS DESTINATION
166                 LDS      SI,[BP].SCREEN          ; AND SCREEN IS SOURCE
167
168                 MOV      AX,ES                   ;CAN'T DO A CMP ON A SEGMENT REG.
169                 CMP      AX,0                    ;A NIL POINTER IS A SEGMENT AND
170                 JNE      CHECK3                  ; OFFSET BOTH SET TO 0
171                 CMP      DI,0                    ;RETURN WITHOUT ACTING IF BOTH
172                 JE       GOHOME                  ; ARE SET TO 0
173
174     CHECK3:     MOV      AX,DS                   ;CAN'T DO A CMP ON A SEGMENT REG.
175                 CMP      AX,0                    ;A NIL POINTER IS A SEGMENT AND
176                 JNE      KEEPON                  ; OFFSET BOTH SET TO 0
177                 CMP      SI,0                    ;RETURN WITHOUT ACTING IF BOTH
178                 JE       GOHOME                  ; ARE SET TO 0
179
180
181     KEEPON:     ADD      SI,CX                   ;SCREEN END MUST ADD INSET VALUE
182                                                  ; TO OFFSET PORTION OF POINTER
183                 MOV      BX,DX                   ;INCREMENT MUST BE IN BX
184                 XOR      DX,DX                   ; AND DX MUST BE ZEROED
185
186
187         ;-------------------------------------------------------------------------
188         ;   THE POINTERS ARE NOW READY FOR WORK.  NOW WE SET UP FOR THE LOOPS.
189         ;     THE DIRECTION FLAG MUST BE SET FOR AUTOINCREMENT DURING LOOPS.
190         ;-------------------------------------------------------------------------
191
```

(continued)

```
192          SETUP:  CLD                         ;SET DIRECTION FLAG FOR AUTOINCREMENT
193                  MOV     AX,[BP].HEIGHT      ;HEIGHT IS COUNT OF LINE MOVES
194
195          ;----------------------------------------------------------------------
196          ;   DOLINE IS THE LABEL FOR THE OUTER LOOP.  THIS LOOP PERFORMS HEIGHT
197          ;     STOSW OPS WHICH EACH MOVE WIDTH WORDS FROM SOURCE TO DESTINATION
198          ;----------------------------------------------------------------------
199
200          DOLINE: MOV     CX,[BP].WIDTH       ;COUNT VALUE FOR INNER LOOP IS WIDTH
201                  REP     MOVSW               ;PERFORM THE INNER LOOP MOVE
202                  ADD     SI,BX               ;ADD SOURCE INCREMENT TO SI
203                  ADD     DI,DX               ;ADD DESTINATION INCREMENT TO DI
204                  DEC     AX                  ;AX IS HEIGHT; I.E. OUTER LOOP COUNTER
205                  JNZ     DOLINE              ;AND LOOP UNTIL AX IS ZERO
206
207          ;----------------------------------------------------------------------
208          ;   WHEN THE OUTER LOOP IS FINISHED, THE WORK IS DONE.  RESTORE REGISTERS
209          ;     AND GO HOME.
210          ;----------------------------------------------------------------------
211
212          GOHOME: POP     DS                  ;RESTORE CALLER'S DS
213                  MOV     SP,BP               ;RESTORE PRIOR STACK POINTER & BP
214                  POP     BP                  ; IN CONVENTIONAL RETURN
215                  RET     ENDMRK-RETADDR-2
216
217          WORDBLT ENDP
218          CODE    ENDS
219                  END
```

Before attempting to understand how it works, it would be best to describe exactly what **WordBLT** does. Like **ClearScreen**, a pointer to a screen array (**ScreenEnd**) is passed to **WordBLT** to avoid having to pass an entire screen descriptor to it on the stack. A rectangular region of the screen is defined by **ULX** and **ULY**, which are the X,Y coordinates of the upper left-hand corner of the region; and **Width** and **Height**, which are, obviously, the width and height of the region, in characters. In one of its two modes, **WordBLT** takes this region of the screen and moves it to a storage area on the heap, pointed to by **StoreEnd**. In the other mode, **WordBLT** takes information stored in a storage area pointed to by **StoreEnd** and moves it back to the defined rectangular region in the screen pointed to by **ScreenEnd**.

WordBLT, then, works both ways. A very important distinction must be made, however, between the two ends of the line. **ScreenEnd** points to a virtual screen's array, in the same manner as the screen arrays we have been working with throughout this chapter. **StoreEnd**, however, does *not* point to a screen array, but simply to a block of heap memory only large enough to contain the video information within the region defined by **ULX**, **ULY**, **Width**, and

Height. Furthermore, this block of memory on the heap is not allocated by **WordBLT**. You must allocate the storage area *before* calling **WordBLT**, typically by using Turbo Pascal's built-in **GetMEM** procedure. The amount of storage required in bytes is equal to the width of the region times its height—which provides the number of characters in the region—times 2, to allocate space for each character's attribute byte as well:

```
GetMEM(StorePointer,(BlockWidth*BlockHeight*2));
```

Once you execute this statement, you can safely pass pointer **StorePointer** to **WordBLT** in parameter **StoreEnd**.

Why the distinction between screen memory and storage memory? It has to do with the real nature of the memory comprising a rectangular region of the screen. Looking at such a nice crisp block on the screen, it's easy to imagine it as a contiguous area of memory in the middle of the screen buffer somewhere. Not so—each text line of the region is a separate area of screen memory, separated by an area of memory that does *not* belong to the region (see Figure 5.7).

On the storage end, **WordBLT** places the separate fragments of memory belonging to the rectangular region together, end to end, without any dead space between them.

This explains why a simple call to Turbo Pascal's **Move** procedure cannot move a rectangular region of a screen—the region doesn't exist all in one place. It also means that **WordBLT** cannot *in one operation* move a rectangular region from one screen to another, or from one part of a screen to another part of the same screen. Such actions require *two* calls to **WordBLT**—one to get a region from one screen into a temporary buffer, and a second call to move the region from the temporary buffer to another screen, or to another location on the same screen. **WordBLT** is fast enough to enable even two consecutive calls to appear instantaneously—which is, after all, the whole idea.

How WordBLT Works

Understanding the operation of **WordBLT**'s assembly code requires understanding two quantities which define the rectangular region on the screen from the larger perspective of the screen array: the inset and the increment. (Both of these quantities will also figure into the working of the **Scroller** region scrolling routine that I'll be describing next.)

The relation of the inset and the increment to the screen array at large is shown in Figure 5.8. The *inset* is simply the distance in bytes from the start of the screen array (that is, the location pointed to by **MyScreen**) to the first byte of the top line of the rectangular region. The inset also figures into the working of many of the Pascal routines described earlier, including **WriteAt** and **Set-Attribute**.

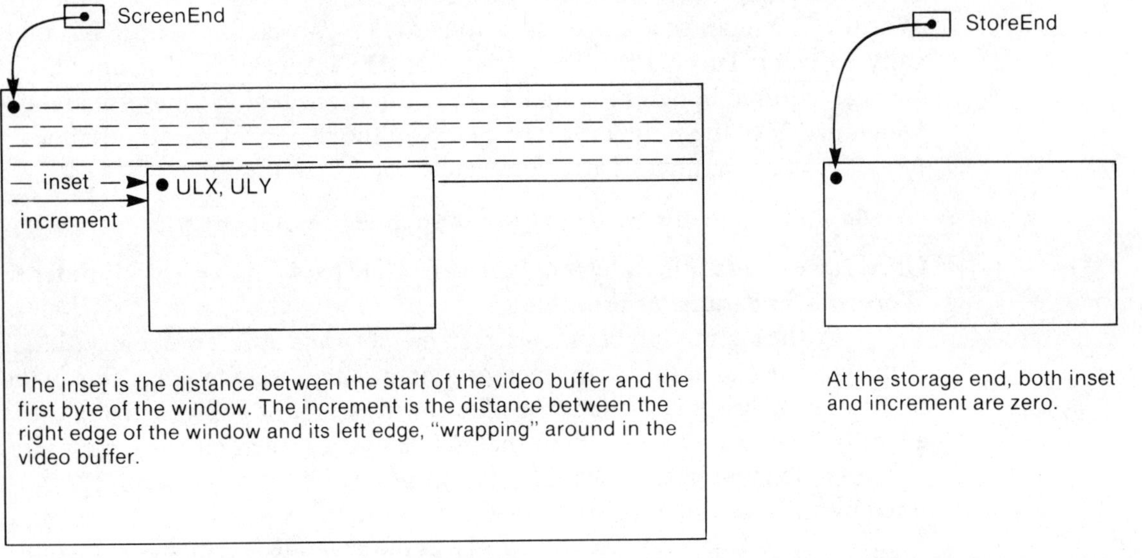

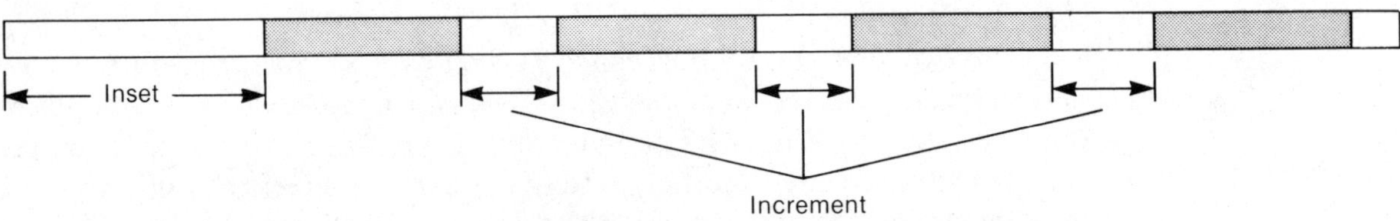

If the video buffer is envisioned as a single long line of memory,
each line of the window may be seen as a separate region of memory,
separated from the others by spaces equal in size to increment.

Figure 5.7   **WordBLT data storage**

The *increment* is the memory gap between successive lines of the rectangular region. (Figure 5.8 should make this clear.) Although this gap exists between any two lines comprising the region, its size is always the same.

The need for these two quantities can best be understood in terms of "getting at" the memory comprising the region. You need the screen pointer **MyScreen** to get at the screen array as a whole. You then need the inset to get at the first line of the region for processing. Finally, after processing each line of the region, you need the increment to get at the next line of the region. This overall scheme will be true for both **WordBLT** and later for **Scroller**. It is a good conceptual base from which to examine both routines' assembly code.

The first two things that **WordBLT** does are calculate the inset and then the increment. The inset *in machine words* is calculated as

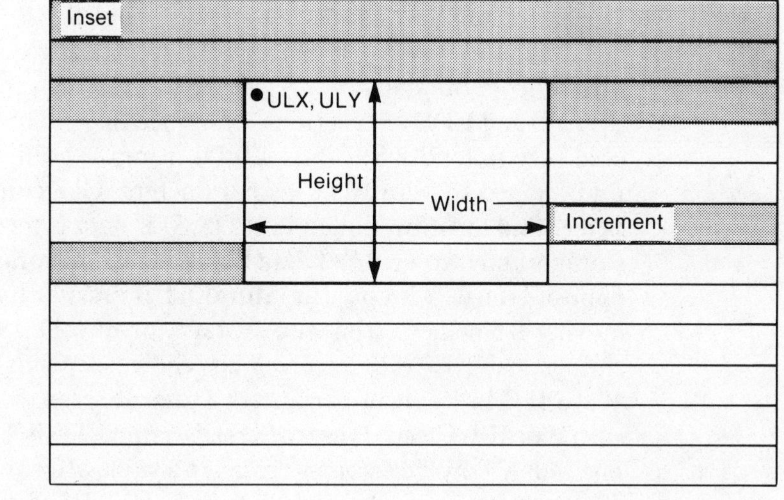

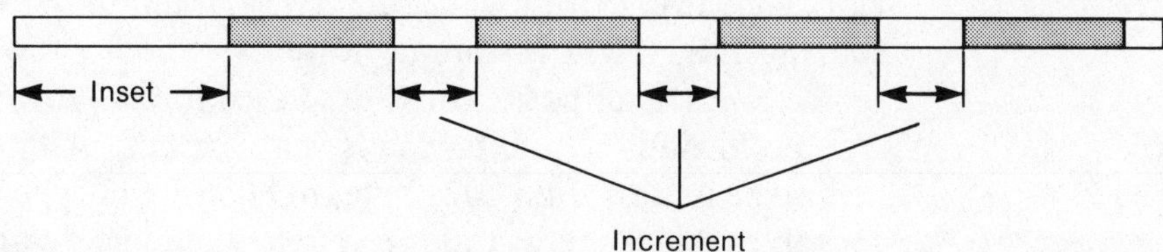

Figure 5.8 **Inset and increment**

```
((ULY * ScreenWidth) + ULX) * 2
```

Note in lines 109–110 that the origins of **ULX** and **ULY** are corrected to zero by subtracting one. We think of the top line of the screen as line 1; your computer is much more comfortable working with it as line 0. Also note that the figure is muliplied by two in line 114 to take character attributes into account. The multiplication by two is accomplished by shifting the value one bit to the left (the same thing if you think about it). This is much faster than using MUL, the 8086's hardware multiply instruction.

The increment is much easier to calculate:

```
(ScreenWidth — RegionWidth) * 2
```

Functionally, **WordBLT** is a series of block moves—one for each line of the region to be moved. Each block move is accomplished with the 8086 REP MOVSW instruction. MOVSW requires that the address of the source data be in the registers DS and SI, with DS containing the segment and SI the offset.

The shorthand form for an address in two registers, as you may recall, is DS:SI. The address of destination data must be in ES:DI.

There are two 8086 instructions specifically designed to load 32-bit addresses from the stack into register pairs such as ES:DI and DS:SI. These are the LES and LDS instructions, described in detail in Chapter 4. They are both used here to load DS:SI and ES:DI from the pointers **ScreenEnd** and **StoreEnd**, passed to **WordBLT** as parameters. One complication is that pointer **ScreenEnd** must be loaded into DS:SI if data is moving from the screen into storage, and into ES:DI if data is moving from storage back to the screen. The opposite is true with pointer **StoreEnd**; it must be loaded into ES:DI if data is moving from the screen into storage, or into DS:SI if data is moving from storage back to the screen. This choice depends on the value passed to **WordBLT** in Boolean parameter **TowardScreen**.

WordBLT tests **TowardScreen** (named **TOWARD** within **WordBLT**) at line 140. If **TowardScreen** were given a value of **True**, the test falls through (the JZ, Jump on Zero, instruction tests **TOWARD** for a value of zero) and executes code in-line for awhile; otherwise, it jumps to label **STORIT**. The code starting at **STORIT** is similar; however, the LES and LDS instructions work on the pointers opposite those described in the previous paragraph.

Following the pointer loads is a series of safety checks. The destination *cannot* be into the first 1024 bytes of 8086 memory, because the interrupt vector table resides there, and the system would go down in flames instantly if a block of screen information were allowed to be written there. Unfortunately, Turbo Pascal implements a NIL pointer as 32 bits of zeroes—essentially 0:0, or the start of the interrupt vector table. The safety check tests the destination pointer to see if it is NIL, and jumps to the end of **WordBLT** (label **GOHOME**) if the destination pointer is NIL.

Note that segment registers cannot be acted upon by the CMP instruction, so they must be copied into AX for the test.

The remainder of **WordBLT** consists of register setup code, and finally the loop of block moves. At labels **DOMORE** and **KEEPON**, the inset value is added to the source offset. (The source offset, remember, is in SI if we're moving data into storage, and DI if we're moving data back to the screen.) This sets up the source pointer to point to the beginning of the data block. The XOR instructions are a sneaky way of zeroing out a register quickly, since, if you XOR a value against itself, the result is always zero.

When the loops begin, the inset is stored in register CX, and the increment in register DX. AX contains the number of block moves that must be executed, which is the height of the region in lines. (Recall that each line is moved with a separate block-move instruction.)

The loop begins at label **DOLINE**. The count value for the block moves always goes into CX; it is the width of the rectangular region being moved, which is also the width of each line. We *don't* multiply it by two here because the block-move instruction is MOVSW, and the "W" on the end means it moves *words* rather than bytes. Each move thus takes both the character *and* its attribute.

What we have here is actually a loop within a loop. The inner loop is in fact a single instruction: REP MOVSW. The REP prefix on the MOVSW word instruction causes the 8086 to repeat the MOVSW instruction, decrementing CX each time, and stopping only when CX becomes zero. It is a *very* tight loop, as you can see, compressing the assembly-language equivalent of a **FOR** loop into a single instruction. It is, hands-down, the fastest way to move information from one area of memory to another in the 8086.

The outer loop executes one inner loop for each line of the rectangular region being moved. It keeps count in register AX, decrementing AX for each line moved and stopping when AX becomes zero. Notice the two ADD instructions within the outer loop (lines 202–203). These add the increment to the source and destination pointers after each line is moved. The storage end, if you recall, has no increment, so either BX or DX here will always be equal to zero, depending on which way information is flowing. The screen end will always have the real increment added to its pointer, whether it is the source or destination.

Following the loop, **WordBLT** cleans house by popping the caller's DS back off the stack, moving the caller's stack pointer from BP into SP, and popping the caller's BP off the stack. Then it returns control to the calling logic.

I haven't attempted to squeeze the very last cycle out of **WordBLT**. There are additional tweaks to be made, but none of them fall within the nested loops, which is where 99% of all of its cycles are spent. In general, if you've optimized your loops, you've made all the difference that a human operator can detect. The rest of the code, which is generally the one-time setting up of registers, can be written for maximum clarity rather than maximum speed.

An additional parameter could perhaps be added to **WordBLT** to allow a region to be moved from one area of a screen to another screen, or to another area on the same screen. This would require an increment and inset for both source and destination, and wold make the code considerably more complex because of the additional test-and-jump code the new parameter would require. Also, if a region were being copied to another region on the same screen, care would have to be taken to ensure that overlapping portions of the source and destination regions are handled correctly, so that data copied to the destination does not overwrite portions of the source before it gets moved.

Scrolling a Region

As with moving a rectangular region of a screen from the screen buffer into storage and back, scrolling a region of a screen without disturbing the surrounding screen data is difficult to do quickly. There is a reasonable routine in the PC's ROM BIOS for scrolling regions, but it is "hardwired" to the currently displayed visible screen buffer. I wanted to be able to scroll a screen whether it was visible or not, so I developed the external assembly-language procedure **Scroller**, shown below:

```
 1    ;===============================================================================
 2    ;
 3    ;     S C R O L L E R  -  Text window scrolling routine
 4    ;
 5    ;===============================================================================
 6    ;
 7    ;     by Jeff Duntemann      23 October 1986
 8    ;
 9    ;
10    ;
11    ;
12    ; SCROLLER is written to be called from Turbo Pascal V3.0 using the
13    ; EXTERNAL procedure convention.
14    ;
15    ; Declare the procedure itself as external using this declaration:
16    ;
17    ; PROCEDURE SCROLLER(Target           : ScrnPtr;
18    ;                    ScrollUp         : Boolean;
19    ;                    ScreenX,ScreenY  : Integer;
20    ;                    ULX,ULY          : Integer;
21    ;                    Width,Height     : Integer;
22    ;                    Attribute        : Integer;
23    ;                    LinesToScroll    : Integer);
24    ;         EXTERNAL 'SCROLLER.BIN';
25    ;
26    ; Scrolling a region within a display buffer is generally hopeless without
27    ; resorting to assembly language.  The region is not a contiguous block of
28    ; memory so Turbo Pascal's MOVE procedure cannot be used.  Hence this
29    ; routine.  It duplicates some of the function of the PC's VIDEO code in
30    ; ROM BIOS, but it's somewhat faster and much more general.  VIDEO can only
31    ; scroll memory in one of the two IBM-style display adapters; SCROLLER can
32    ; scroll a region in any buffer pointed to by a Pascal pointer.  This
33    ; includes screens on the heap or anywhere else, actually--but I don't
34    ; recommend allocating screens anywhere else.
35    ;
36    ; This implies some hazards in using SCROLLER.  To keep speed up, safety
37    ; features were not poured in like hot fudge.  SCROLLER will refuse to
```

(continued)

```
38        ; scroll if the TARGET pointer is NIL.  Still, make sure your pointer is
39        ; initialized to a genuine screen buffer before using it--nothing like
40        ; scrolling a region of your object code, right?
41        ;
42        ; Note that unlike most of the routines in the VSCREEN toolkit, SCROLLER is
43        ; NOT passed a screen descriptor record, but only the pointer to the screen
44        ; array itself.  This was done to keep speed up, by keeping stack grimbling
45        ; to a minimum.  Also, this way the code is simpler and easier to follow.
46        ;
47        ; The SCROLLUP parameter dictates whether the scroll will be up or down; in
48        ; a downward scroll the blank line is inserted at the TOP of the scrolled
49        ; region and the bottom line is lost.
50        ;
51        ; SCREENX and SCREENY are the physical width and height of the current screen.
52        ;
53        ; ULX and ULY are the X,Y coordinates within the screen of the upper left
54        ; corner of the region to be scrolled.
55        ;
56        ; WIIDTH and HEIGHT are the width and height of the region to be scrolled.
57        ; DO NOT confuse with SCREENX and SCREENY.
58        ;
59        ; ATTRIBUTE is the video attribute AND clearing character to be used on
60        ; the top or bottom line(s) of the scrolled region.  You must combine the
61        ; attribute code and character before invoking SCROLLER.  OR them together
62        ; in the parameter line if you like, but the attribute code must be in the
63        ; high eight bits of the parameter while the character must be in the low
64        ; eight bits.
65        ;
66        ; LINESTOSCROLL specifies the number of lines to be scrolled at one shot.
67        ; If this parm receives a zero value, the entire region will be cleared.
68        ; This provides a very fast method of clearing rectangular screen regions.
69        ;
70        ;
71        ; To reassemble/relink SCROLLER:
72        ;--------------------------------------
73        ; 1. Assemble this file with MASM.  "C>MASM SCROLLER;"
74        ; 2. Link it into a .EXE file.     "C>LINK SCROLLER;"
75        ; 3. Use EXE2BIN to make a .COM file. "A> EXE2BIN SCROLLER.EXE SCROLLER.COM"
76        ; 4. Declare as shown above in your Turbo Pascal program.
77        ; 5. Ignore any minor diagnostic messages that may be generated when
78        ;      this file is assembled and linked.  EXE2BIN is supplied with the
79        ;      supplemental programs for PC-DOS; see the DOS manual.
80        ;
81        ;
82        ;   This creature puts lots of things on the stack.  Study closely:
83        ;
84        ONSTACK STRUC
85        OLDBP   DW ?     ;CALLER'S BP VALUE SAVED ON STACK
86        RETADDR DW ?     ;RETURN ADDRESS OFFSET
```

(continued)

```
 87          LINES   DW ?        ;# OF LINES TO SCROLL UP
 88          ATTRIB  DW ?        ;*BOTH* CHARACTER & ATTRIBUTE TO BE USED ON BLANK LINE(S)
 89          HEIGHT  DW ?        ;HEIGHT OF WINDOW TO BE MOVED
 90          WIDTH   DW ?        ;WIDTH OF WINDOW TO BE MOVED
 91          ULY     DW ?        ;Y COORDINATE OF UPPER LEFT CORNER OF WINDOW
 92          ULX     DW ?        ;X COORDINATE OF UPPER LEFT CORNER OF WINDOW
 93          YSIZE   DW ?        ;GENNED MAX Y DIMENSION OF CURRENT VISIBLE SCREEN
 94          XSIZE   DW ?        ;GENNED MAX X DIMENSION OF CURRENT VISIBLE SCREEN
 95          MOVEUP  DW ?        ;BIT 0 = 0 SCROLL DOWN; BIT 0 = 1 SCROLL UP
 96          SCREEN  DD ?        ;32-BIT POINTER TO SCREEN BUFFER
 97          ENDMRK  DB ?        ;DUMMY LABEL TO MARK END OF DATA ON STACK
 98          ONSTACK ENDS
 99
100
101          CODE    SEGMENT PUBLIC
102                  ASSUME  CS:CODE
103                  PUBLIC  SCROLLR
104
105          SCROLLR PROC    NEAR
106
107                  PUSH    BP                      ;SAVE CALLER'S BP VALUE
108                  MOV     BP,SP                   ;SP BECOMES NEW VALUE OF BP
109                  PUSH    DS                      ;SAVE CALLER'S DS VALUE
110
111          ;-------------------------------------------------------------------
112          ;   FIRST ORDER OF BUSINESS IS TO TEST WHETHER THE SCREEN POINTER IS NIL.
113          ;   IF SO, WE EXIT WITHOUT TAKING ANY FURTHER ACTION.
114          ;-------------------------------------------------------------------
115
116                  LES     DI,[BP].SCREEN          ;GET POINTER FROM STACK; BOTH
117                  LDS     SI,[BP].SCREEN          ; SOURCE AND DEST ARE IN SAME SCREEN
118
119                  MOV     AX,ES                   ;CAN'T DO A CMP ON A SEGMENT REG.
120                  CMP     AX,0                    ;A NIL POINTER IS A SEGMENT AND
121                  JNE     INCALC                  ; OFFSET BOTH SET TO 0
122                  CMP     DI,0                    ;RETURN WITHOUT ACTING IF BOTH
123                  JNE     INCALC                  ; ARE SET TO 0
124                  JMP     GOHOME
125
126          ;-------------------------------------------------------------------
127          ;   IT'S SAFE...WE HOPE.  THE INCREMENT BETWEEN WINDOW LINES MUST BE
128          ;   CALCULATED HERE AND STORED IN DX.
129          ;-------------------------------------------------------------------
130
131          INCALC: MOV     DX,[BP].XSIZE
132                  SUB     DX,[BP].WIDTH
133                  SHL     DX,1
134                  PUSH    DX                      ;SAVE INCREMENT ON STACK; WE'LL
135                                                  ; NEED DX FOR MUL OPCODE LATER...
```

(continued)

```
136
137            ;-----------------------------------------------------------------------
138            ;   NEXT WE CALCULATE THE INSET FROM THE START OF THE VISIBLE
139            ;      SCREEN BUFFER TO THE FIRST BYTE OF THE WINDOW TO BE SCROLLED
140            ;-----------------------------------------------------------------------
141
142                   MOV     CX,[BP].XSIZE           ;SCREEN MAX X DIMENSION IN CX
143                   MOV     BX,[BP].ULX             ;UL CORNER X DIMENSION IN BX
144                   MOV     AX,[BP].ULY             ;UL CORNER Y DIMENSION IN AX
145                   SUB     BX,1                    ;CORRECT FOR ORIGIN AT 1 NOT O
146                   SUB     AX,1                    ;CORRECT FOR ORIGIN AT 1 NOT O
147
148                   TEST    [BP].MOVEUP,1           ;IF WE'RE SCROLLING DOWN, WE NEED
149                   JNZ     GOUP                    ; TO PUT LOWER LEFT CORNER Y IN AX
150
151                   ADD     AX,[BP].HEIGHT          ;WE NEED THE LOWER LEFT CORNER Y
152                   SUB     AX,1                    ; MINUS 1 IN AX FOR SCROLL DOWN
153
154            GOUP:   MUL     CX                      ;MULTIPLY SCREEN WIDTH BY UL Y
155                   ADD     AX,BX                   ; AND ADD INDENT FROM LEFT MARGIN
156                   MOV     CX,AX
157                   POP     DX                      ;RESTORE INCREMENT TO DX AFTER MUL
158
159            ;-----------------------------------------------------------------------
160            ;   SI NEEDS TO BE OFFSET FROM DI BY SOME MULTIPLE OF THE SCREEN WIDTH.
161            ;      THIS FIGURE IS CALCULATED HERE AND ADDED IN JUST BEFORE THE ACTUAL
162            ;      SCROLL OPERATION
163            ;-----------------------------------------------------------------------
164
165                   PUSH    DX                      ;SAVE DX BEFORE MUL MUCKS IT UP
166                   MOV     BX,[BP].LINES           ;LOAD LINES TO SCROLL INTO BX
167                   MOV     AX,[BP].XSIZE           ;MOVE SCREEN WIDTH INTO AX
168                   MUL     BX                      ;MULTIPLY SCREEN WIDTH IN AX BY
169                                                   ; NUMBER OF LINES TO ADJUST IN BX
170                                                   ; RESULT IS IN DX:AX
171                   MOV     BX,AX                   ;KEEP ADJUSTMENT IN BX
172                   POP     DX                      ;NOW THAT WE'RE THROUGH WITH MUL,
173                                                   ; RESTORE SAVED INCREMENT TO DX
174
175            ;-----------------------------------------------------------------------
176            ;   NOW WE TEST TO SEE WHETHER WE'RE GOING TO SCROLL UP OR DOWN.  THE
177            ;      SETUP OF REGISTERS AND FLAGS IS SOMEWHAT DIFFERENT AND MORE COMPLEX
178            ;      FOR SCROLLING DOWN.
179            ;-----------------------------------------------------------------------
180
181
182            DTEST:  TEST    [BP].MOVEUP,1           ;HIGH BIT = 1  MEANS SCROLL UP
183                   JZ      GODOWN                  ;BIT = O MEANS SCROLL DOWN
184
```

(continued)

```
185                 MOV     DI,CX                           ;MOVE INSET INTO BOTH SI AND DI
186                 MOV     SI,CX
187
188                 ADD     SI,BX                           ;ADD ADJUSTMENT TO SI
189                 SHL     SI,1
190                 SHL     DI,1
191                 CLD                                     ;SET DIRECTION FLAG FOR
192                 JMP     SCROLL                          ; AUTOINCREMENT OF SI & DI
193
194
195     GODOWN: MOV     AX,[BP].WIDTH
196             SUB     AX,1
197             ADD     CX,AX                               ;ADD WIDTH TO GET SI & DI TO RIGHT EDGE
198             MOV     DI,CX                               ; OF SCROLL WINDOW
199             MOV     SI,CX
200             SUB     SI,BX                               ;SUBTRACT ADJUSTMENT FROM SI
201
202             SHL     SI,1                                ;ADJUST SI AND DI FOR ATTRIBUTE BYTES
203             SHL     DI,1
204             NEG     DX                                  ;INCREMENT MUST BE NEGATIVE FOR
205                                                         ; SCROLLING DOWN
206             STD                                         ;SET DIRECTION FLAG FOR
207                                                         ; AUTODECREMENT
208
209     ;------------------------------------------------------------------------------
210     ;   THE POINTERS ARE READY FOR WORK.  NOW WE SET UP FOR THE LOOPS.
211     ;------------------------------------------------------------------------------
212
213     SCROLL: MOV     BX,[BP].HEIGHT                      ;HEIGHT MINUS LINES TO SCROLL BY
214             SUB     BX,[BP].LINES                       ; IS COUNT OF LINE MOVES REQUIRED
215             CMP     [BP].LINES,1                        ;IF SCROLL BY ZERO, SKIP SCROLL
216             JL      CLRSET
217
218     ;------------------------------------------------------------------------------
219     ;   DOLINE IS THE LABEL FOR THE OUTER LOOP.  THIS LOOP PERFORMS HEIGHT
220     ;     STOSW OPS WHICH EACH MOVE WIDTH WORDS FROM SOURCE TO DESTINATION
221     ;------------------------------------------------------------------------------
222
223     DOLINE: MOV     CX,[BP].WIDTH                       ;COUNT VALUE FOR INNER LOOP IS WIDTH
224             REP     MOVSW                               ;PERFORM THE INNER LOOP MOVE
225             ADD     SI,DX                               ;ADD INCREMENT TO SI
226             ADD     DI,DX                               ;ADD INCREMENT TO DI
227             DEC     BX                                  ;BX IS HEIGHT; I.E. OUTER LOOP COUNTER
228             JNZ     DOLINE                              ;AND LOOP UNTIL AX IS ZERO
229
230     ;------------------------------------------------------------------------------
231     ;   THE SCROLL ITSELF IS NOW DONE.  THE BLANK LINES HAVE TO BE COPIED INTO
232     ;     THE SCROLL WINDOW AT THIS POINT.
233     ;------------------------------------------------------------------------------
```

(continued)

```
234
235         CLRSET: MOV     AX,[BP].ATTRIB          ;MOVE ATTRIBUTE INTO AX
236
237                 MOV     BX,[BP].LINES           ;LINES TO CLEAR = LINES TO SCROLL
238                 CMP     BX,1                    ; EXCEPT WHEN LINES = 0, WHEN LINES
239                 JNL     DOCLR                   ; TO CLEAR = HEIGHT OF WINDOW
240                 MOV     BX,[BP].HEIGHT
241
242         DOCLR:  MOV     CX,[BP].WIDTH
243                 REP     STOSW                   ;BLANK THE LINE WITH STRING STORE
244                 ADD     DI,DX                   ;ADD INCREMENT TO DI
245                 DEC     BX                      ;LINES TO BLANK; OUTER LOOP COUNTER
246                 JNZ     DOCLR                   ;AND LOOP UNTIL AX IS ZERO
247
248                 ;-----------------------------------------------------------------
249                 ;   ONCE THE BLANK LINE IS COPIED, THE WORK IS DONE.   RESTORE REGISTERS
250                 ;       AND GO HOME.
251                 ;-----------------------------------------------------------------
252
253         GOHOME: POP     DS                      ;RESTORE CALLER'S DS
254                 MOV     SP,BP                   ;RESTORE PRIOR STACK POINTER & BP
255                 POP     BP                      ; IN CONVENTIONAL RETURN
256                 RET     ENDMRK-RETADDR-2
257
258         SCROLLR ENDP
259         CODE    ENDS
260                 END
```

Scroller is similar in many ways to **WordBLT**. Because it deals with a region within a screen, it must calculate the inset and increment exactly as **WordBLT** did. It must move the region line by line either up or down (but the top or bottom line is lost), by way of two nested loops. Understanding **WordBLT** is thus a prerequisite to understanding **Scroller**. (If you have not thoroughly read the previous section describing **WordBLT**, do so now, as I will not repeat what the two routines have in common.)

Like the routine in ROM BIOS VIDEO, **Scroller** scrolls a rectangular region of the screen array passed in **Target**. The direction of the scroll may be either up or down; if **ScrollUp** is **True**, the scroll will be upward; if not, it will be downward. Any number of lines (up to the height of the region) may be scrolled at once. Furthermore, if the number of lines to be scrolled (passed in parameter **LinesToScroll**) is set to zero, the entire region will be cleared by scrolling the region by the number of lines it is high.

The **ScreenX**, **ScreenY**, **ULX**, **ULY**, **Width**, and **Height** parameters are exactly the same in **Scroller** as they are in **WordBLT**. **Attribute** is the video attribute *and* fill character for the lines of the region that are blanked in the scroll operation. Unlike **ClearScreen**, which takes the attribute and fill character as separate parameters, I chose to simplify **Scroller** by requiring that they be combined before calling the external routine. It is rare that you need to set the attribute of the fill character for the scrolled lines alone.

A scrolling operation is actually a series of line copies. A lot of information is moved during a scroll, so for the scroll to appear to happen instantaneously, the scrolling routine must be written in assembler. During the following explanation of a simple upward scroll, refer to Figure 5.9.

Bullet 1 shows a rectangular region of a screen before it is scrolled. Its four lines are numbered. Bullet 2 shows the first line copy. Line 2 is copied over line 1. Note that line 1 is simply lost; we say it "scrolls off the top." If your application needs to preserve line 1 after a scroll (perhaps to allow it to reappear after a subsequent downward scroll moves the region's lines in the other direction), your application must save line 1 somewhere before calling **Scroller**.

At Bullet 3, line 3 is copied over line 2. The original line 2 is now gone, since a duplicate of line 3 has been written over it, but because line 2 was previously copied over line 1, a copy of line 2 is still visible. The process continues at Bullet 4, at which line 4 is copied over line 3. There are now two copies of line 4 visible. The final step, shown at Bullet 5, is the blanking of the original line 4. The net effect is that the region has been scrolled upward by one line. The top line has been lost, but all the other lines are visible, even though each is now one line higher in the region than it was originally. A blank line has been inserted at the bottom, ready for your application to write new information on.

Scrolling a region downward is done in the same manner, except that the line copies begin at the bottom of the region rather than at the top, and it is the top line that is blanked as the final step.

How Scroller Works

Scroller's job is to perform those line copies and line blanks, and perform them quickly. **Scroller** is made more complex by having to scroll in either direction *and* having to scroll by more than one line at a time. (Again, if you aren't up on your assembly language, this routine will be a very tough nut to crack.)

After saving the caller's BP,SP, and DS values, **Scroller** begins its work in earnest by checking pointer **Target** to be sure it is not equal to NIL. If **Target** passes muster, **Scroller** then calculates the increment, just as it did with **WordBLT**.

The inset must be calculated next, but it is slightly different in this application. **Scroller**'s inset differs from **WordBLT**'s in that it points to the *first line* to be copied rather than the upper left-hand corner of the region. For an upward scroll, these are the same thing, since the series of line copies (as you can see

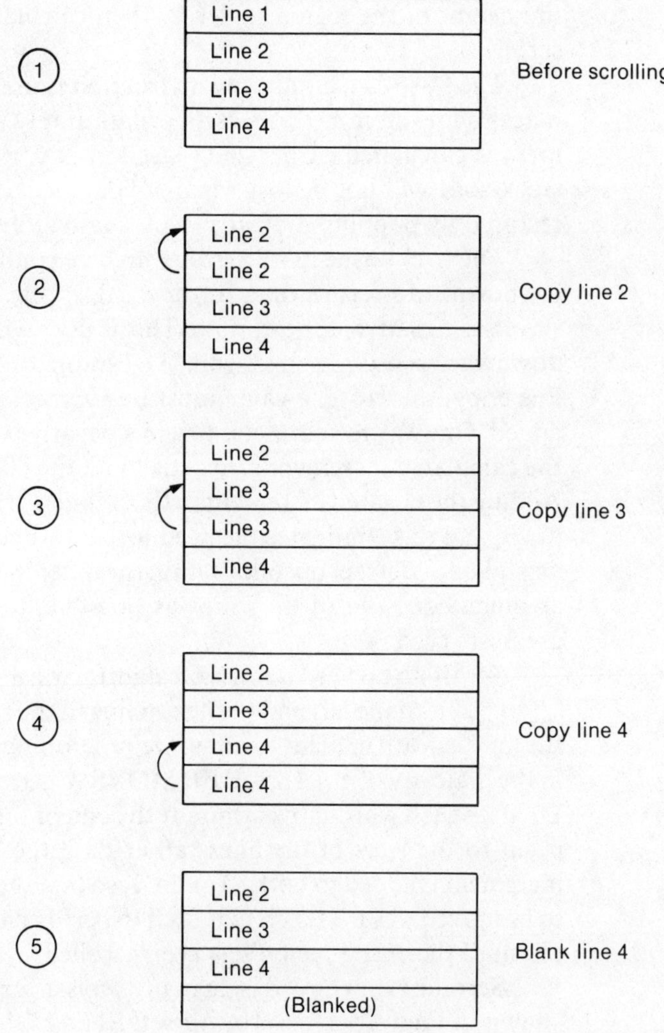

Figure 5.9 **Scrolling a region**

from Figure 5.9) starts at the upper left-hand corner of the region. For a downward scroll, however, the line copies begin at the *lower* left-hand corner. If you remember from **WordBLT**, the algorithm for calculating the inset is this:

```
((ULY * ScreenWidth) + ULX) * 2
```

This will do fine for the inset for an upward scroll. For a downward scroll we must replace **ULY** with the lower left-hand corner Y coordinate for the region.

We don't pass an **LLY** parameter, however, so we have to calculate it by adding the height of the region to **ULY** when calculating the inset for a downward scroll.

The 8086 MUL multiply instruction is used in calculating the inset. This places its result in DX:AX rather than simply AX; therefore, when the increment is calculated earlier and placed in DX, it must also be pushed onto the stack so it will not be lost when MUL calculates the inset. The increment is restored by popping it off the stack again at line 172.

The tricky aspects of **Scroller** involve configuring the registers differently for downward scrolls than for upward scrolls. The increment for downward scrolls is negative, for example. This is due to the fact that the line copies in a downward scroll progress from the bottom of the region upward. After each line copy, therefore, a value must be *subtracted* from SI and DI rather than added. One way to subtract is to add a negative value, so, for downward scrolls, the calculated increment is negated with the 8086 NEG instruction (line 204). Adding the negated increment to the pointers will thus be the same as subtracting it, and this eliminates the need for a test-and-jump code (to select between an add or a subtract opcode) within the outer loop. The idea, as always, is to get as much code *out* of the loops as possible, to allow them to operate at the greatest speed.

Scrolling upward is fairly straightforward. As shown in Figure 5.10, DI is set to point to the left end of the top line in the region, and SI to the left end of the line beneath it. (This assumes we're scrolling by only one line, as will be true in the majority of cases.) A REP MOVSW instruction increments both SI and DI after each word move; thus, at the end of moving an entire line, SI and DI point to the *ends* of the lines rather than the beginnings. At this point, the increment is added to both SI and DI, so that they point to the next pair of lines to be moved. REP MOVSW is used to perform the next line copy down, and so on, until the entire region has been scrolled.

Scrolling downward is, in many ways, the reverse of scrolling upwards, as shown in Figure 5.11. At the outset, SI and DI are set to point to the last two lines in the region rather than the first two. Furthermore, they point to the *right* ends of the last two lines rather than the left ends. The REP MOVSW, when it is executed for each line pair, operates from right to left rather than from left to right, as with an upward scroll. As a result, when they reach the left ends of the line, *subtracting* the increment from both pointers sets them up to begin the next pair of lines. Subtracting the increment from the pointers is done, as mentioned above, by adding a negative increment value.

One thing I haven't mentioned yet is how we set REP MOVSW to work from right to left (decrementing SI and DI as it goes) rather than from left to right. This option is controlled by an 8086 flag bit known as the *direction flag*. In its default state (cleared), the direction flag forces REP MOVSW to auto-

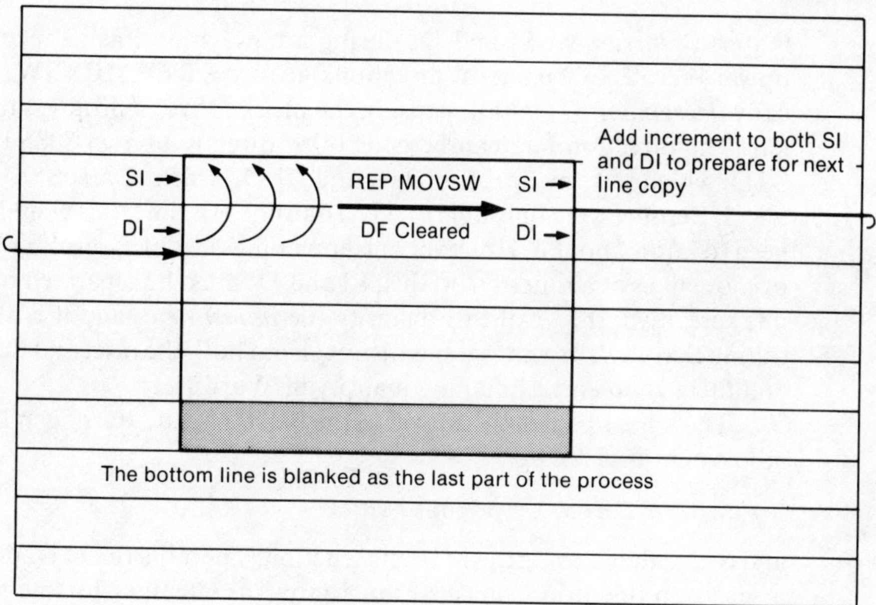

Figure 5.10 **Scrolling upward**

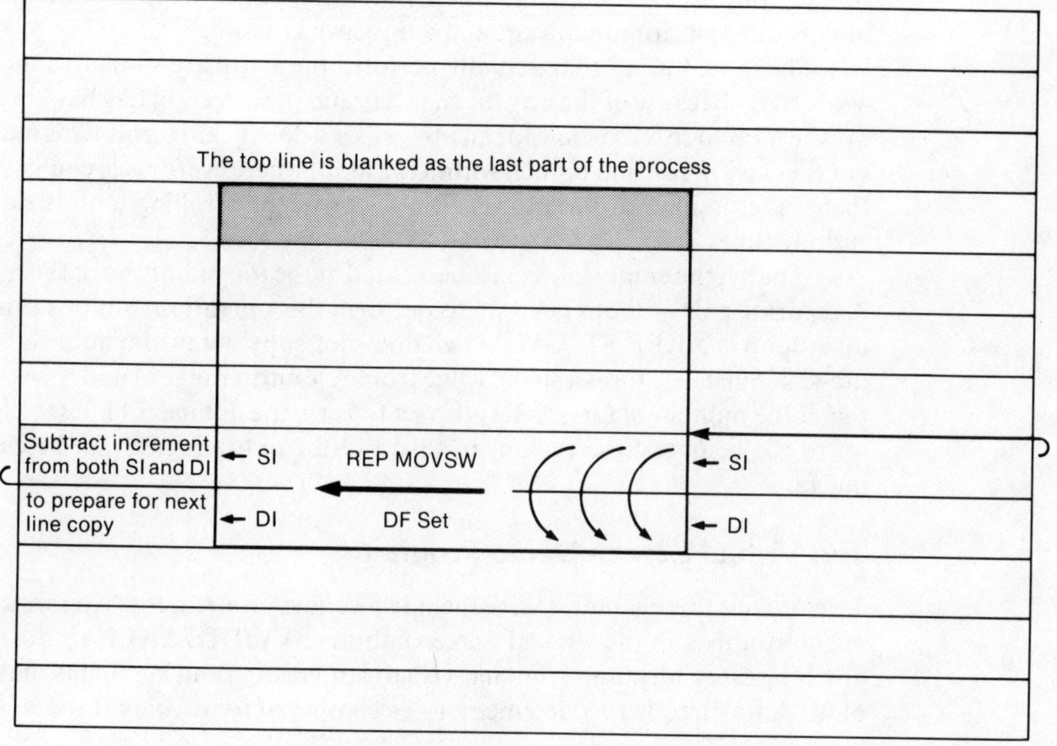

Figure 5.11 **Scrolling downward**

matically *increment* SI and DI during a block move, as happens during an upward scroll. When set, the direction flag forces REP MOVSW to automatically *decrement* SI and DI, causing the block move to progress from right to left. The direction flag can be controlled directly by two 8086 instructions: STD, which sets the direction flag, and CLD, which clears it.

If **Scroller** were only able to scroll one line at a time, this would be all you'd need to know about it. However, it is sometimes useful to scroll a region by two or more lines at a time. To do this, SI and DI must be separated by more than one screen width. I call this quantity the *adjustment*, and it is stored in BX during **Scroller**'s execution. It is distinct from both the inset and the increment, and there is no corresponding quantity in **WordBLT**.

The adjustment is calculated in the block of code starting at line 165. The adjustment is given by

```
LinesToScroll * ScreenWidth
```

and is calculated using the MUL instruction. The adjustment is added to SI for a scroll-up operation, since SI must move up-memory for the scroll. For a downward scroll, SI must be lower in memory than DI, and therefore the adjustment is subtracted from SI for a downward scroll. In both cases, DI is set equal to the inset and is not affected by the adjustment. Keep in mind that the inset is different for an upward and a downward scroll.

The nested loops that actually perform the scroll are similar to those of **WordBLT**. Because of the way the registers and the direction flag have been set up, the loop code is the same for an upward or a downward scroll. This makes it unnecessary to test and branch within the loop, where every cycle counts. Note that if the number of lines to scroll by is zero, the scrolling loop is skipped entirely (lines 215–216).

Finally, the empty lines must be cleared at the top or bottom of the region. A separate pair of loops is set up to perform this operation, but this time the inner loop is a REP STOSW, which does not copy data from address to address, but instead stores a single value from AX into a range of addresses. Note that if the number of lines to scroll is set to zero, the number of lines to clear is set to the height of the region. In this way the entire region can be cleared quickly.

The Virtual Screen Demo Program

To close out this chapter, I have included a short program that exercises most of the routines in the Virtual Screen Library. **VVIDDEMO.PAS** dosn't do anything especially useful, but it is visually interesting and highlights the speed of working directly to video memory as compared to working through BIOS for screen I/O.

The most striking demonstration of speed involves a linked list of 26 virtual screens on the heap. These screens are cleared with a fill character corresponding to their ordinal position in the list. In other words, the first screen is filled with the letter "A", the second screen with "B", and so on. Once the list is built, the screens are flashed into view one by one, with one-third second between each screen's display. Once this is completed, the 26 screens are flashed into view without any delay between them, and it happens so quickly that you probably won't see it happen on a PC/AT or faster machine. (On my 386 machine, the screen only twitches for a fraction of a second, to show that the 26 screens have in fact been displayed.)

The use of **WordBLT** is demonstrated by animating a small region of the screen "bouncing" against the boundaries of the screen. This is done by saving out the background beneath the region to storage, and then alternately erasing and redisplaying the region at a slightly different location each time.

```
1      {--------------------------------------------------------------------}
2      {                              VVIDDEMO                               }
3      {                                                                    }
4      {          Virtual Screen Library Demonstration Program              }
5      {                                                                    }
6      {                                    by Jeff Duntemann                }
7      {                                    Turbo Pascal V3.01A              }
8      {                                    Last update 2/10/87              }
9      {                                                                    }
10     { This program exercises most of the routines in VSCREEN, the        }
11     { Virtual Screen Support Library.  It doesn't do anything            }
12     { utterly spectacular visually and is included as a code             }
13     { example for the use of the various routines.  See Chapter 5        }
14     { for additional details.                                           }
15     {                                                                    }
16     {                                                                    }
17     {                                                                    }
18     {--------------------------------------------------------------------}
19
20     PROGRAM VirtualVideoDemo;
21
22     LABEL
23       100;
24
25     {$I REGPACK.DEF}
26     {$I VSCREEN.DEF}
27
28     VAR
29       VisibleScreen : ScreenRec;
30       Adapter : AdapterType;
```

(continued)

```
31          How     : Integer;
32          Points  : Integer;
33
34          JiveScreen      : ObjectPtr;
35          Root,Current    : ObjectPtr;
36          ZSquare         : ObjectPtr;
37          Blanks          : ScreenPtr;
38          CharVal         : Char;
39          I,ULX,ULY       : Integer;
40          Pause           : Integer;
41
42
43        {$I VSCREEN.SRC}
44
45
46
47        PROCEDURE ShowJivetalkIntroScreen;
48
49        BEGIN
50          New(JiveScreen);                { Create a screen descriptor on the heap... }
51          CreateScreen(JiveScreen^);   { ...and initialize it. }
52          WITH JiveScreen^ DO          { Now fill it with text: }
53            ClearScreen(MyScreen,ScreenLength,How,Ord(' '));
54          MakeBox(JiveScreen^,-1,4,60,11,DoubleLine,How);
55          WriteAt(JiveScreen^,-1,6,
56                  GenAttribute(White,Black,Normal,NoBlink,Highlight),
57                  'J I V E T A L K   L X X I I I');
58          WriteAt(JiveScreen^,-1,8,How,'Release 1.00001Q');
59          WriteAt(JiveScreen^,-1,9,How,
60                  '(c) 1985, 1986, 1987 by Jeff Duntemann');
61          WriteAt(JiveScreen^,-1,10,How,'All rights reserved');
62          WriteAt(JiveScreen^,-1,12,How,'IBM Personal Computer Version');
63
64          MoveScreen(JiveScreen^,VisibleScreen);  { Bring the screen into view }
65          Delay(2000);
66          WriteAt(VisibleScreen,14,20,How,
67                  'No computer is as good as your average hammer.');
68          WriteAt(VisibleScreen,50,21,How,'--Jim Shields');
69          Delay(2000)
70        END;
71
72
73
74        PROCEDURE FlashList(Root : ObjectPtr; DelayCount : Integer);
75
76        VAR
77          Current : ObjectPtr;
78
79        BEGIN
```

(continued)

```
80          Current := Root;
81          WHILE Current <> NIL DO
82            BEGIN
83              MoveScreen(Current^,VisibleScreen);
84              Current := Current^.Next;
85              IF DelayCount > 0 THEN Delay(DelayCount)
86            END
87        END;
88
89
90        PROCEDURE ZSquareIn(X,Y : Integer);
91
92        BEGIN
93          WordBLT(VisibleScreen.MyScreen,    { The "screen end," here visible }
94                  ZSquare^.MyScreen,         { The "storage end," on the heap }
95                  TowardScreen,              { Here we move from storage to screen }
96                  ScreenWidth,ScreenHeight,  { Physical size of screen in use }
97                  X,Y,                       { Upper left corner X,Y of screen window }
98                  17,8);                     { Width and height of screen window }
99        END;
100
101
102       PROCEDURE BlanksIn(X,Y : Integer; Pause : Integer);
103
104       BEGIN
105         WordBLT(VisibleScreen.MyScreen,    { The "screen end," here visible }
106                 Blanks,                    { The "storage end," on the heap }
107                 TowardScreen,              { Here we move from storage to screen }
108                 ScreenWidth,ScreenHeight,  { Physical size of screen in use }
109                 X,Y,                       { Upper left corner X,Y of screen window }
110                 17,8);                     { Width and height of screen window }
111         Delay(Pause)
112       END;
113
114
115
116       BEGIN
117         Adapter := QueryAdapterType;
118         Points  := DeterminePoints;
119         InitVScreen(VisibleScreen,0);
120         How := GenAttribute(White,Black,Normal,NoBlink,NoHighlight);
121
122         ShowJivetalkIntroScreen;
123
124         { Here we create a linked list of 26 screens on the heap, each filled }
125         { with a letter of the alphabet: }
126         Root := NIL;
127         How := GenAttribute(White,Black,Reverse,NoBlink,NoHighlight);
128         FOR CharVal := 'Z' DOWNTO 'A' DO
```

(continued)

```
129          BEGIN
130            New(Current);
131            CreateScreen(Current^);
132            WITH Current^ DO
133              ClearScreen(MyScreen,ScreenLength,How,Ord(CharVal));
134            Current^.Next := Root;
135            Root := Current;
136          END;
137
138      100:
139      How := GenAttribute(White,Black,Normal,NoBlink,NoHighlight);
140      FlashList(Root,300);     { Move in the heap-stored screens slowly... }
141      FlashList(Root,0);       { ...and now at top speed }
142
143
144      ZSquare := Root^.Next^.Next^.Next; { Pick a screen for Z square storage }
145
146      { Allocate heapspace for blank region storage: }
147      GetMEM(Blanks,(17 * 8 * 2));
148
149      { Blit out a square section of the visible screen to temporary storage: }
150      WordBLT(VisibleScreen.MyScreen,    { The "screen end," here on the heap }
151              ZSquare^.MyScreen,         { The "storage end" also on the heap }
152              AwayFromScreen,            { Move screen data into storage }
153              ScreenWidth,ScreenHeight,  { Physical size of screen in use }
154              40,9,                      { Upper left corner X,Y of screen window }
155              17,8);                     { Width and height of screen window }
156
157      { Blit out a section of the B screen to temporary storage: }
158      WordBLT(Root^.Next^.MyScreen,      { The "screen end," here on the heap }
159              Root^.MyScreen,            { The "storage end" also on the heap }
160              AwayFromScreen,            { Move screen data into storage }
161              ScreenWidth,ScreenHeight,  { Physical size of screen in use }
162              12,4,                      { Upper left corner X,Y of screen window }
163              17,8);                     { Width and height of screen window }
164
165      { Blit the B's back into the visible screen full of Z's: }
166      WordBLT(VisibleScreen.MyScreen,    { The "screen end," here visible }
167              Root^.MyScreen,            { The "storage end," on the heap }
168              TowardScreen,              { Here we move from storage to screen }
169              ScreenWidth,ScreenHeight,  { Physical size of screen in use }
170              40,9,                      { Upper left corner X,Y of screen window }
171              17,8);                     { Width and height of screen window }
172
173      Delay(2000);  { Look at the B's, mommy! }
174
175      { Now we scroll the window full of B's up and out of sight: }
176      FOR I := 1 TO 8 DO
177        BEGIN
```

(continued)

```
178            Scroller(VisibleScreen.MyScreen,ScrollUp,
179                    ScreenWidth,ScreenHeight,
180                    40,9,               { X,Y of upper left corner of scroll window }
181                    17,8,               { Width and height of scroll window }
182                    How OR Ord(' '),    { Attribute & char for cleared line(s) }
183                    1);                 { # of lines to scroll at a crack }
184         Delay(350)
185       END;
186
187    Delay(3000);
188
189    { Blit the square of blanks out to temporary storage: }
190    WordBLT(VisibleScreen.MyScreen,    { The "screen end," here on the heap }
191            Blanks,                    { The "storage end" also on the heap }
192            AwayFromScreen,            { Move screen data into storage }
193            ScreenWidth,ScreenHeight,  { Physical size of screen in use }
194            40,9,                      { Upper left corner X,Y of screen window }
195            17,8);                     { Width and height of screen window }
196
197    { Here we animate the blank square around the screen: }
198
199    ULX := 40; ULY := 9; Pause := 30;
200    FOR I := 1 TO 4 DO
201      BEGIN
202        WHILE (ULY > 0) AND (ULX > 0) DO
203          BEGIN
204            ZSquareIn(ULX,ULY);
205            ULX := ULX-2; ULY := ULY-1;
206            BlanksIn(ULX,ULY,Pause);
207          END;
208        WHILE (ULX > 0) AND (ULY < (ScreenHeight - 8)) DO
209          BEGIN
210            ZSquareIn(ULX,ULY);
211            ULX := ULX-2; ULY := ULY + 1;
212            BlanksIn(ULX,ULY,Pause);
213          END;
214        WHILE (ULX < (ScreenWidth - 17)) AND (ULY < (ScreenHeight - 8)) DO
215          BEGIN
216            ZSquareIn(ULX,ULY);
217            ULX := ULX+2; ULY := ULY+1;
218            BlanksIn(ULX,ULY,Pause);
219          END;
220        WHILE (ULX < (ScreenWidth - 17)) AND (ULY > 0) DO
221          BEGIN
222            ZSquareIn(ULX,ULY);
223            ULX := ULX+2; ULY := ULY-1;
224            BlanksIn(ULX,ULY,Pause);
225          END;
226      END;
```

(continued)

```
227
228            WITH VisibleScreen DO        { Clear screen to halftones: }
229              ClearScreen(MyScreen,ScreenLength,
230                           GenAttribute(White,Black,Reverse,NoBlink,NoHighlight),
231                           177);
232
233            WriteAt(VisibleScreen,-1,3,How,'Now you, too, can clone Framework!');
234            Delay(2000);
235
236                                          { Display blinking 'good bye' message in box: }
237            MakeBox(VisibleScreen,-1,-1,42,5,DoubleLine,How);
238            WriteAt(VisibleScreen,-1,-1,
239                    GenAttribute(White,Black,Normal,Blink,Highlight),
240                    'Th..th..th..that''s all, f..f..folks!');
241
242            Delay(5000);
243            ClrScr;
244          END.
```

Finally, although each of the individual routines has been listed at the point of its discussion in this chapter, I find it more convenient to treat them as a group and place them in a single include file. Because some of the routines call one another, declaration order is also important. VSCREEN, which begins on page 258, includes all the Pascal routines described in this chapter, plus additional comments not included in the individual subprogram listings elsewhere in this chapter. It must be included *after* VSCREEN.DEF.

```
1        {----------------------------------------------------------------}
2        {                   VSCREEN DEFINITION FILE                      }
3        {                                                                }
4        {        FOR: VScreen, the Virtual screen support library        }
5        {                                                                }
6        {                        by Jeff Duntemann                       }
7        {                        Turbo Pascal V3.01A                     }
8        {                        Last update 1/30/87                     }
9        {                                                                }
10       {     NOTE: The file REGPACK.DEF must be INCLUDEd before this    }
11       {     file so that Reg and RegPack will be defined.              }
12       {                                                                }
13       {                                                                }
14       {                                                                }
15       {----------------------------------------------------------------}
16
17       { Simple constants in the old Pascal tradition are declared first: }
18
```

(continued)

```
19      CONST
20         SingleLine    = False;      { These two constants are used in generating }
21         DoubleLine    = True;       { figures incorporating the box-draw characters }
22
23         Blink         = True;       { These four constants are used for passing }
24         NoBlink       = False;      { attribute selections to GenAttribute }
25         Highlight     = True;
26         NoHighlight   = False;
27
28         ScrollUp      = True;       { These two constants are used to indicate }
29         ScrollDown    = False;      { scrolling direction in Scroller }
30
31         TowardScreen    = True;     { These two constants indicate the direction }
32         AwayFromScreen  = False;    { text is moved in WordBLT }
33
34
35      TYPE
36         String5     = String[5];
37         String10    = String[10];
38         String80    = String[80];
39         String255   = String[255];
40
41         AdapterType = (CGA,MDA,EGAMono,EGAColor); { Enumerated type! }
42
43         VideoAtom   = Reg;                        { Same data format as register }
44         Screen      = Array[0..1] OF VideoAtom;
45         ScreenPtr   = ^Screen;
46         ObjectPtr   = ^ScreenRec;
47         ScreenRec   = RECORD
48                          Handle        : Integer;   { Screen object handle }
49                          Previous      : ObjectPtr; { Pointer to previous screen }
50                          MyScreen      : ScreenPtr; { Pointer to start of buffer }
51                          ScreenLength  : Integer;   { Length of buffer in bytes }
52                          Visible       : Boolean;   { TRUE if screen is visible }
53                          CursX         : Byte;      { Screen cursor X position }
54                          CursY         : Byte;      { Screen cursor Y position }
55                          Next          : ObjectPtr; { Pointer to next screen }
56                       END;
57
58         Attribute   = (Invisible,Underline,Normal,Reverse);
59         Color       = (Black,Blue,Green,Cyan,Red,Magenta,Brown,LightGray,
60                        DarkGray,LightBlue,LightGreen,LightCyan,LightRed,
61                        LightMagenta,Yellow,White);
62
63
64         LineChars   = ARRAY[SingleLine..DoubleLine] OF Char;
65         BarStrings  = ARRAY[SingleLine..DoubleLine] OF String80;
66         BoxRec      = RECORD
67                          ULCorner,
```

(continued)

```
68                                  URCorner,
69                                  LLCorner,
70                                  LRCorner,
71                                  HBar,
72                                  VBar,
73                                  LineCross,
74                                  TDown,
75                                  TUp,
76                                  TRight,
77                                  TLeft : LineChars
78                               END;
79
80
81        { After all VScreen's types have been defined, we declare structured }
82        { constants: }
83
84        CONST
85          LastHandle  : Integer = 0;    { Last assigned screen handle }
86          BoxChars    : BoxRec =
87                          (ULCorner  : (#218,#201);
88                           URCorner  : (#191,#187);
89                           LLCorner  : (#192,#200);
90                           LRcorner  : (#217,#188);
91                           HBar      : (#196,#205);
92                           VBar      : (#179,#186);
93                           LineCross : (#197,#206);
94                           TDown     : (#194,#203);
95                           TUp       : (#193,#202);
96                           TRight    : (#195,#185);
97                           TLeft     : (#180,#204));
98
99
100
101       VAR
102         ScreenWidth  : Byte ABSOLUTE CSeg : $016A;
103         ScreenHeight : Byte ABSOLUTE CSeg : $016B;


1         {------------------------------------------------------------------}
2         {                          VSCREEN                                  }
3         {                                                                  }
4         {              Virtual screen support library                      }
5         {                                                                  }
6         {                               by Jeff Duntemann                  }
7         {                               Turbo Pascal V3.01A                }
8         {                               Last update 2/10/87                }
9         {                                                                  }
10        {  NOTE:  The file VSCREEN.DEF must be included into the           }
11        {  main program file before this file is included.                 }
```

(continued)

```
12            {  VSCREEN.DEF contains essential constant and type        }
13            {  definitions for the use of the procedures and functions  }
14            {  in this library.                                         }
15            {                                                           }
16            {                                                           }
17            {                                                           }
18            {-----------------------------------------------------------}
19
20
21            { First we define and load assembly-language text primitives:  }
22
23
24            PROCEDURE ClearScreen(Target : ScreenPtr; ScreenSize : Integer;
25                             How    : Integer; CharFill : Byte);
26                             EXTERNAL 'CLEARS.BIN';
27
28
29            PROCEDURE Scroller(Target         : ScreenPtr;
30                             ScrollUp         : Boolean;
31                             ScreenX,ScreenY  : Integer;
32                             ULX,ULY          : Integer;
33                             Width,Height     : Integer;
34                             Clearit          : Integer;
35                             Lines            : Integer);
36                             EXTERNAL 'SCROLLER.BIN';
37
38
39            PROCEDURE WordBLT(ScreenEnd,StoreEnd : ScreenPtr;
40                             TowardScreen     : Boolean;
41                             ScreenX,ScreenY  : Integer;
42                             ULX,ULY          : Integer;
43                             Width,Height     : Integer);
44                             EXTERNAL 'WORDBLT.BIN';
45
46
47            {-----------------------------------------------------------}
48            { The first several routines in this library are very hardware-}
49            { specific, moreso than the later ones.  These handle mode    }
50            { setting and sensing, adapter and font identification.       }
51            {-----------------------------------------------------------}
52
53
54            PROCEDURE Set43Lines(VAR Points : Integer);
55
56            TYPE
57              Reg        = RECORD
58                             CASE Boolean OF
59                               False : (Word : Integer);
60                               True  : (LoByte,HiByte : Byte)
```

(continued)

```
61                          END;
62
63                 Regpack = RECORD
64                             AX,BX,CX,DX,BP,SI,DI,DS,ES,Flags : Reg
65                          END;
66
67             VAR
68               Regs : RegPack;
69
70             BEGIN
71               Regs.AX.HiByte := $11;   { Character generator services }
72               Regs.AX.LoByte := $12;   { Load EGA 8X8 font }
73               Regs.BX.Word := 0;
74               Intr($10,regs);
75                                        { Suppress BIOS cursor emulation }
76               MEM[$40 : $87] := mem[$40 : $87] OR $01;
77
78               Regs.AX.Word := $100;    { Set our own cursor to lines 6-7 }
79               Regs.BX.Word := 0;
80               Regs.CX.Word := $0600;
81               Intr($10,regs);
82               Points := 8;             { Tell caller the font is now 8 lines high }
83               ScreenHeight := $2B      { Repatch the patch point for 43 lines! }
84             END;
85
86
87             PROCEDURE Set25Lines(VAR Points : Integer);
88
89             TYPE
90               Reg      = RECORD
91                             CASE Boolean OF
92                                False : (Word : Integer);
93                                True  : (LoByte,HiByte : Byte)
94                          END;
95
96                 Regpack = RECORD
97                             AX,BX,CX,DX,BP,SI,DI,DS,ES,Flags : Reg
98                          END;
99
100            VAR
101              Regs : RegPack;
102
103            BEGIN
104              ClrScr;
105              Regs.AX.HiByte := $11;   { EGA Character generator services }
106              Regs.AX.LoByte := $11;   { Load monochrome ROM font }
107              Regs.BX.Word := 0;
108              Intr($10,regs);
109                                       { Suppress BIOS cursor emulation }
```

(continued)

```pascal
110        MEM[$40 : $87] := MEM[$40 : $87] OR $01;
111        Regs.AX.Word := $100;    { Set our own cursor to lines 12-13 }
112        Regs.BX.Word := 0;
113        Regs.CX.Word := $0C00;
114        Intr($10,Regs);
115        Points := 14;            { Tell caller the font is now 14 lines high }
116        ScreenHeight := $19      { Repatch the patch point for 25 lines! }
117     END;
118
119
120
121
122     FUNCTION IsEGA : Boolean;
123
124     TYPE
125       Reg     = RECORD
126                     CASE Boolean OF
127                         False : (Word : Integer);
128                         True  : (LoByte,HiByte : Byte)
129                     END;
130
131       Regpack = RECORD
132                     AX,BX,CX,DX,BP,SI,DI,DS,ES,Flags : Reg
133                     END;
134
135     VAR
136       Regs : RegPack;
137
138     BEGIN
139       Regs.AX.HiByte := $12;       { Select Alternate Function service }
140       Regs.BX.Word := $10;         { BL=$10 means return EGA information }
141       Intr($10,Regs);              { Call BIOS VIDEO }
142       IF Regs.BX.Word = $10 THEN   { BX unchanged means EGA is NOT there...}
143         IsEGA := False ELSE IsEGA := True   {...anything else means EGA! }
144     END;
145
146
147
148
149     FUNCTION QueryAdapterType : AdapterType;
150
151     TYPE
152       Reg     = RECORD
153                     CASE Boolean OF
154                         False : (Word : Integer);
155                         True  : (LoByte,HiByte : Byte)
156                     END;
157
158       RegPack = RECORD
```

(continued)

```
159                          AX,BX,CX,DX,BP,SI,DI,DS,ES,Flags : Reg
160                    END;
161
162        VAR
163          Regs : RegPack;
164          Code : Byte;
165
166        BEGIN
167          IF IsEGA THEN
168            BEGIN
169              Regs.AX.HiByte := $12;
170              Regs.BX.LoByte := $10;
171              Intr($10,Regs);
172              IF (Regs.BX.HiByte = 0) THEN QueryAdapterType := EGAColor
173                  ELSE QueryAdapterType := EGAMono
174            END
175          ELSE
176            BEGIN
177              Intr($11,Regs);    { Equipment determination service }
178              Code := (Regs.AX.LoByte AND $30) SHR 4;
179              CASE Code of
180                 1 : QueryAdapterType := CGA;
181                 2 : QueryAdapterType := CGA;
182                 3 : QueryAdapterType := MDA
183              ELSE QueryAdapterType := CGA
184              END { Case }
185            END
186        END;
187
188
189        FUNCTION DeterminePoints : Integer;
190
191        VAR
192          Regs : Regpack;
193
194        BEGIN
195          CASE QueryAdapterType OF
196            CGA       : DeterminePoints := 8;
197            MDA       : DeterminePoints := 14;
198            EGAMono,
199            EGAColor :
200                        BEGIN
201                          WITH Regs DO
202                            BEGIN
203                                AX.HiByte := $11;
204                                AX.LoByte := $30;
205                                BX.LoByte := 0;
206                            END;
207                          Intr($10,Regs);
```

(continued)

```
208                        DeterminePoints := Regs.CX.Word
209                     END
210            END   { CASE }
211         END;
212
213
214         {------------------------------------------------------------------}
215         { The following two routines deal with the hardware cursor.    }
216         {------------------------------------------------------------------}
217
218         PROCEDURE CursorOn(Points : Integer);
219
220         VAR
221           Regs : RegPack;
222
223         BEGIN
224           WITH Regs DO
225             BEGIN
226               AX.Word := $0100;
227               { 'Points' is the pixel height of the character font }
228               { currently in use.  'Underscore' cursors always      }
229               { consist of the bottom two lines in the font cell.  }
230               { In current display technology, this is either 8 or }
231               { 14. Here we specify Points-1 and Points-2 because  }
232               { the character cell lines are counted from 0.        }
233               CX.HiByte := Points-2;
234               CX.LoByte := Points-1;
235             END;
236           INTR($10,Regs);
237         END;
238
239
240         PROCEDURE CursorOff;
241
242         VAR
243           Regs : RegPack;
244
245         BEGIN
246           WITH Regs DO
247             BEGIN
248               AX.Word := $0100;
249               CX.Word := $2000;   { Set CH bit 5 hi to suppress cursor }
250             END;
251           INTR($10,Regs);
252         END;
253
254
255         {------------------------------------------------------------------}
256         { This routine builds an attribute byte, given specifiers for   }
```

(continued)

```
257          { the various attributes passed as parameters.  Note that the  }
258          { actual attribute information is shifted into the high byte   }
259          { of an integer before that integer is assigned to the         }
260          { function return value.                                       }
261          {--------------------------------------------------------------}
262
263          FUNCTION GenAttribute(Foreground : Color;
264                                Background : Color;
265                                MonoMethod : Attribute;
266                                Blink      : Boolean;
267                                Bright     : Boolean) : Integer;
268
269          CONST
270            ForegroundColor : ARRAY[Color] OF Byte =
271                                         ($00,$01,$02,$03,$04,$05,$06,$07,
272                                          $08,$09,$0A,$0B,$0C,$0D,$0E,$0F);
273            BackgroundColor : ARRAY[Black..LightGray] OF Byte =
274                                         ($00,$10,$20,$30,$40,$50,$60,$70);
275            MonoAttributes  : ARRAY[Attribute] OF Byte = ($00,$01,$07,$70);
276            BlinkCodes      : ARRAY[Boolean] OF Byte = ($00,$80);
277            BrightCodes     : ARRAY[Boolean] OF Byte = ($00,$08);
278
279          VAR
280            How : Integer;
281
282          BEGIN
283            CASE Adapter OF
284              MDA      : How := MonoAttributes[MonoMethod]
285                               OR BlinkCodes[Blink]
286                               OR BrightCodes[Bright];
287              CGA      : How := BlinkCodes[Blink]
288                               OR BrightCodes[Bright]
289                               OR ForegroundColor[Foreground]
290                               OR BackgroundColor[Background];
291              EGAMono  : How := MonoAttributes[MonoMethod]
292                               OR BlinkCodes[Blink]
293                               OR BrightCodes[Bright];
294              EGAColor : How := BlinkCodes[Blink]
295                               OR BrightCodes[Bright]
296                               OR ForegroundColor[Foreground]
297                               OR BackgroundColor[Background];
298            END; { CASE }
299            How := How SHL 8;  { The attribute proper is in the HIGH byte!!!! }
300            GenAttribute := How
301          END;
302
303
304          {--------------------------------------------------------------}
305          { The following four procedures manipulate virtual screens as  }
```

(continued)

```
306          { units; initializing them, creating them, moving them, or      }
307          { disposing of them:                                            }
308          {----------------------------------------------------------------}
309
310
311          PROCEDURE InitVScreen(VAR VScreen : ScreenRec; Segment : Integer);
312
313          VAR
314            Adapter   : AdapterType;
315            VideoSeg  : Integer;
316            Regs      : RegPack;
317
318          BEGIN
319            IF Segment = 0 THEN  { Query hardware for default visible adapter }
320              BEGIN
321                Adapter := QueryAdapterType;
322                CASE Adapter OF
323                  CGA      : VideoSeg := $B800;
324                  MDA      : VideoSeg := $B000;
325                  EGAMono  : VideoSeg := $B000;
326                  EGAColor : VideoSeg := $B800
327                  ELSE VideoSeg := $B800
328                END; {CASE}
329              END
330            ELSE VideoSeg := Segment;
331
332            WITH VScreen DO
333              BEGIN
334                Handle       := Succ(LastHandle);
335                Previous     := NIL;
336                Next         := NIL;
337                MyScreen     := Ptr(VideoSeg,0);
338                ScreenLength := ScreenWidth * ScreenHeight * 2;
339                Visible      := True;
340                LastHandle   := Handle  { LastHandle is a global typed constant! }
341              END;
342          END;
343
344
345
346          PROCEDURE CreateScreen(VAR NewScreen : ScreenRec);
347
348          BEGIN
349            WITH NewScreen DO
350              BEGIN
351                Handle       := Succ(LastHandle);
352                Previous     := NIL;
353                Next         := NIL;
354                ScreenLength := ScreenWidth * ScreenHeight * 2;
```

(continued)

```
355                  GetMem(MyScreen,ScreenLength);
356                  Visible        := False;
357                  LastHandle     := Handle   { LastHandle is a global typed constant! }
358               END;
359           END;
360
361
362
363       PROCEDURE DisposeOfScreen(VAR OldScreen : ScreenRec);
364
365       BEGIN
366         WITH OldScreen DO FreeMem(MyScreen,ScreenLength)
367       END;
368
369
370       PROCEDURE MoveScreen(Source,Target : ScreenRec);
371
372       VAR
373         MoveLength : Integer;
374
375       BEGIN
376         IF Source.ScreenLength > Target.ScreenLength THEN
377           MoveLength := Target.ScreenLength
378         ELSE
379           MoveLength := Source.ScreenLength;
380         Move(Source.MyScreen^,Target.MyScreen^,MoveLength)
381       END;
382
383
384       {--------------------------------------------------------------}
385       { The following functions convert non-text data types to       }
386       { string form, so that we can emulate Write and Writeln, which }
387       { contain their own binary/string conversion machinery:        }
388       {--------------------------------------------------------------}
389
390       FUNCTION BooStr(BooleanValue : Boolean) : String5;
391
392       BEGIN
393         IF BooleanValue THEN BooStr := 'TRUE'
394           ELSE BooStr := 'FALSE'
395       END;
396
397
398       FUNCTION IntStr(IntegerValue,FieldWidth : Integer) : String10;
399
400       VAR
401         Dummy : String10;
402
403       BEGIN
```

(continued)

```
404          Str(IntegerValue : FieldWidth,Dummy);
405           IntStr := Dummy
406         END;
407
408
409         FUNCTION RealStr(RealValue : Real; Exponential : Boolean;
410                         FieldWidth,DecimalWidth : Integer) : String80;
411
412         VAR
413           Dummy : String80;
414
415         BEGIN
416           IF Exponential THEN
417             Str(RealValue : FieldWidth,Dummy)
418           ELSE
419             Str(RealValue : FieldWidth : DecimalWidth,Dummy);
420           RealStr := Dummy
421         END;
422
423
424         {------------------------------------------------------------------}
425         { These two functions set the attributes "behind" a given          }
426         { set of screen locations without disturbing the text in those }
427         { same screen locations:                                           }
428         {------------------------------------------------------------------}
429
430         PROCEDURE SetAttribute(Target           : ScreenRec;
431                                X,Y,TextLength : Integer;
432                                How              : Integer);
433
434         VAR
435           I     : Integer;
436           Inset : Integer;
437
438         BEGIN
439           { Negative X centers string horizontally, negative Y centers }
440           { string vertically. }
441           IF X < 0 THEN X := (ScreenWidth - TextLength) DIV 2;
442           IF Y < 0 THEN Y := ScreenHeight DIV 2;
443           { Inset gives our starting point in the screen buffer: }
444           Inset := (ScreenWidth * (Y-1)) + X - 1;
445           WITH Target DO
446             IF MyScreen <> NIL THEN
447               FOR I := 1 TO TextLength DO
448                 MyScreen^[Inset + I-1].HiByte := Hi(How);
449         END;
450
451
452         PROCEDURE SetAttributeVertical(Target           : ScreenRec;
```

(continued)

```
453                                            X,Y,TextLength : Integer;
454                                            How           : Integer);
455
456             VAR
457               I     : Integer;
458               Inset : Integer;
459
460             BEGIN
461               { Negative X centers string horizontally, negative Y centers }
462               { string vertically. }
463               IF Y < 0 THEN Y := (ScreenHeight - TextLength) DIV 2;
464               IF X < 0 THEN X := ScreenWidth DIV 2;
465               { Inset gives our starting point in the screen buffer: }
466               Inset := (ScreenWidth * (Y-1)) + X - 1;
467               WITH Target DO
468                 IF MyScreen <> NIL THEN
469                   FOR I := 1 TO TextLength DO
470                     MyScreen^[Inset + ((I-1) * ScreenWidth)].HiByte := Hi(How);
471             END;
472
473
474             {------------------------------------------------------------}
475             { These last routines actually write text information to a    }
476             { virtual screen.                                             }
477             {------------------------------------------------------------}
478
479             PROCEDURE WriteAt(Target : ScreenRec; X,Y   : Integer;
480                               How     : Integer; TheText : String255);
481
482             VAR
483               I     : Integer;
484               Inset : Integer;
485
486             BEGIN
487               { Negative X centers string horizontally, negative Y centers }
488               { string vertically. }
489               IF X < 0 THEN X := (ScreenWidth - Length(TheText)) DIV 2;
490               IF Y < 0 THEN Y := ScreenHeight DIV 2;
491               { Inset gives our starting point in the screen buffer: }
492               Inset := (ScreenWidth * (Y-1)) + X - 1;
493               { Now we simply loop and poke char/attribute pairs into the buffer: }
494               WITH Target DO
495                 IF MyScreen <> NIL THEN
496                   FOR I := 1 TO Length(TheText) DO
497                     MyScreen^[Inset + I-1].Word := Ord(TheText[I]) OR How
498             END;
499
500
501             PROCEDURE WriteAtVertical(Target : ScreenRec; X,Y   : Integer;
```

(continued)

```
502                                   How     : Integer; TheText : String255);
503
504            VAR
505              I     : Integer;
506              Inset : Integer;
507
508            BEGIN
509              { Negative X centers string horizontally, negative Y centers }
510              { string vertically. }
511              IF Y < 0 THEN Y := (ScreenHeight - Length(TheText)) DIV 2;
512              IF X < 0 THEN X := ScreenWidth DIV 2;
513              { Inset gives our starting point in the screen buffer: }
514              Inset := (ScreenWidth * (Y-1)) + X - 1;
515              { Now we simply loop and poke char/attribute pairs into the buffer,   }
516              { remembering that we keep X constant and increment Y with each loop: }
517              WITH Target DO
518                IF MyScreen <> NIL THEN
519                  FOR I := 1 TO Length(TheText) DO
520                    MyScreen^[Inset + ((I-1) * ScreenWidth)].Word :=
521                      Ord(TheText[I]) OR How
522            END;
523
524
525
526
527            PROCEDURE MakeBox(Target             : ScreenRec;
528                              X,Y,Width,Height : Integer;
529                              LineStyle          : Boolean;
530                              How                : Integer);
531
532            VAR
533              I,J : Integer;
534              HBarLine,
535              VBarLine : BarStrings;
536
537            BEGIN
538              WITH BoxChars DO  { BoxChars is a record constant defined in VSCREEN.DEF }
539                BEGIN
540                  { First we create a horizontal bar 80 characters long: }
541                  FillChar(HBarLine[LineStyle],Sizeof(HBarLine[LineStyle]),
542                        HBar[LineStyle]);
543                  { Next we create a vertical bar 80 characters long: }
544                  FillChar(VBarLine[LineStyle],Sizeof(VbarLine[LineStyle]),
545                        VBar[LineStyle]);
546
547                  { Negative X centers box horizontally; negative Y vertically: }
548                  IF X < 0 THEN X := (ScreenWidth-Width) DIV 2;
549                  IF Y < 0 THEN Y := (ScreenHeight-Height) DIV 2;
550
```

(continued)

```
551                        { Draw top line: }
552                        WriteAt(Target,X,Y,How,ULCorner[LineStyle] +
553                                 Copy(HBarLine[LineStyle],1,Width-2) +
554                                 URCorner[LineStyle]);
555
556                        { Draw bottom line: }
557                        WriteAt(Target,X,(Y+Height)-1,How,LLCorner[LineStyle] +
558                                 Copy(HBarLine[LineStyle],1,Width-2) +
559                                 LRCorner[LineStyle]);
560
561                        { Draw left side: }
562                        WriteAtVertical
563                          (Target,X,Y+1,How,Copy(VBarLine[LineStyle],1,Height-2));
564
565                        { Draw right side: }
566                        WriteAtVertical
567                          (Target,X+Width-1,Y+1,How,Copy(VBarLine[LineStyle],1,Height-2));
568               END
569          END;
```

Time, Date, and Duration

"I can give you anything but Time," said Napoleon Bonaparte. Your PC won't provide you with an empire, but time . . . well, time is easy. (The day of the week is another matter, but we'll get to that . . .) Setting and reading the time and date from the PC's real-time clock are simple matters that many people don't know how to do. Using the clock's time values to measure duration (the distance in time from one point to another) is simple and can be quite useful. This section will cover the details of dealing with time on the PC, with a little help from Turbo Pascal.

1   How the PC Keeps Time

Understanding *how* the PC keeps time is best begun by knowing *where* it "keeps" time. At $0040 : $006C is a 4-byte storage area that keeps a count of clock "ticks." These ticks occur roughly 18.2 times per second. Four bytes of zeroes at this location indicates midnight, and the count increases by 18.2 for every second past midnight. When DOS sets the clock to a particular time of day, it works backwards from the requested time to the number of ticks that should have occurred by that time each day, and forces that number into the count storage location. When DOS needs to read the current time of day, it reads the four bytes from that storage location and converts the number of ticks to hours, minutes, and seconds. (The date is kept elsewhere, as I'll describe shortly.)

Now 18.2 ticks per second is a peculiar number, but it can be understood in the context of the PC's hardware. As Figure 6.1 indicates, the PC's timing mechanism provides several different frequencies for several different purposes, all from the same master reference frequency. On the PC motherboard is an 8284 clock controller chip with a crystal-controlled reference oscillator that produces a 14.31818-Mhz square wave signal. This frequency was chosen as a convenience to the Color Graphics Adapter, which requires a 3.579545-Mhz input to correctly create what is called the *color burst* signal. The color burst signal helps format color information onto the composite video output produced in the CGA. As some quick work with your Sidekick calculator will show, 3.579545 is 14.31818 divided by 4. (Those unfamiliar with computer hardware should understand that dividing a frequency by a factor of 2 or 3 or some power of 2 or 3 is easily done with a couple of standard flip-flop circuits.)

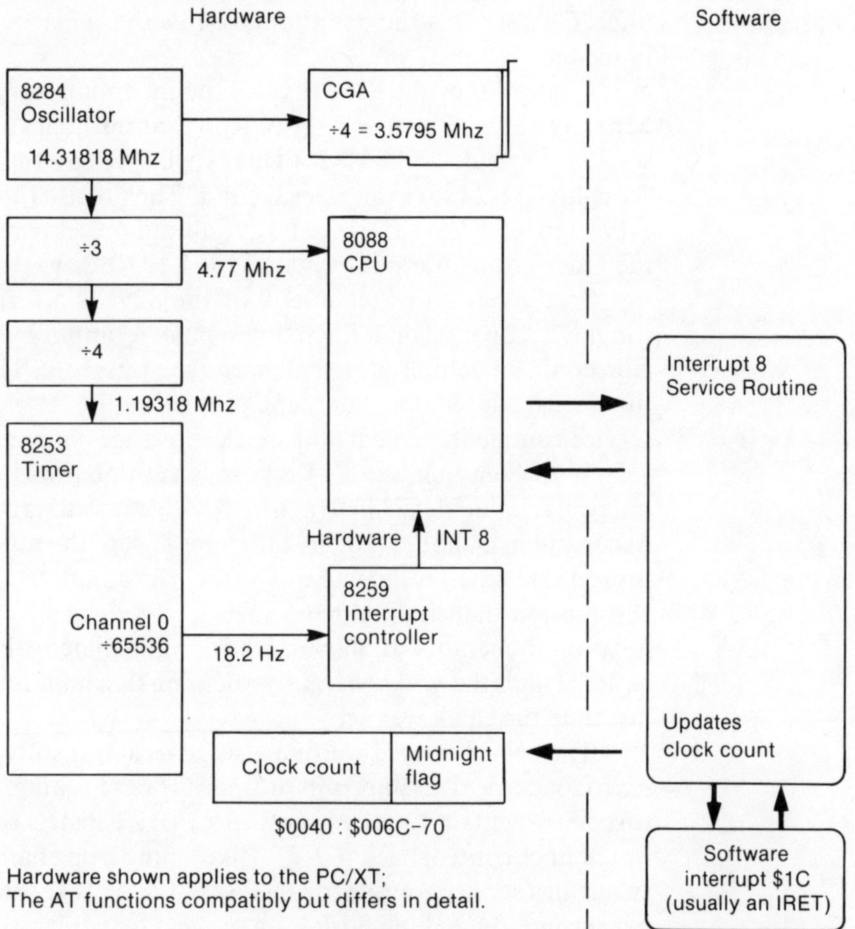

Figure 6.1   **The PC/XT clock/timer mechanism**

Another familiar number will appear if you divide 14.31818 by 3: 4.7727, which, in Mhz, is the CPU clock speed of the IBM PC. So if you have ever wondered why the PC is so slow, allow yourself to get even angrier by answering yourself that it is due to a courtesy to a video format (composite color) that virtually no one uses anymore.

Well, one can accuse IBM of many things, but rarely are they guilty of foresight. It's done—let's explore further. Dividing 14.31818 Mhz by 12 yields 1.19318 Mhz. This frequency is used as an input to a 3-channel counter/timer chip called the 8253 (8254 on the PC/AT). The 8253 is a busy creature, controlling the timer tick interrupt, dynamic RAM refresh, and speaker output, all at once. Channel 0 is the one that controls the timer tick, which is of the most immediate interest.

Channel 0 of the 8253 divides the incoming signal (in this case, 1.19318 Mhz) by up to 16 bits, or 65,536. Run that through your calculator and you'll see that it yields 18.206482. (This is why we say that the PC clock ticks at "roughly" 18.2 timer ticks per second. The precise figure is given by the ratio 1,193,180/65,536.) 18.2 is the fewest output pulses per second obtainable from the 8253, given an input frequency of 1.19318 Mhz.

So the output of channel 0 of the 8253 is a series of pulses coming at roughly 18.2 per second. Each time a pulse is output by the 8253, the 8259 interrupt controller chip generates a hardware interrupt. The interrupt service routine for this interrupt (interrupt 8) is in the PC ROM BIOS. This interrupt service routine increments the clock reference count at $0040 : $006C.

With each tick, the INT 8 service routine tests the reference count for a particular value: 1,573,040 (in hex, $1800B0). This is the number of timer ticks occurring in 24 hours (18.206482 times 86400, the number of seconds in a 24-hour day). When it detects this value, the count "rolls over" to zero, on the assumption that midnight has just occurred. It also writes a 1 into another location in memory at $0040 : $0070, immediately above the clock reference count. This is the *midnight flag*, indicating that midnight has occurred since the last time the clock was set.

The INT 8 service routine also generates a software interrupt $1C with each clock tick. This interrupt ordinarily does nothing, and the interrupt vector associated with it initially points to an IRET instruction, which does nothing but bounce control back to INT 8 like a ping-pong ball. However, it is possible to install a service routine for INT $1C that will execute a given task 18.2 times per second. By making this task a process scheduler, some minimal multitasking support is possible. Of course, as anyone who has ever tried to run Unix on a 4.77-Mhz IBM PC should be aware, you can't expect much in terms of performance. The interrupt can be very useful in certain limited applications, like print spoolers. "Background" tunes can also be played by using interrupt $1C to feed new timer values to 8253 channel 2, which controls the speaker. (Consider that application a *tone spooler* if you will.)

Another note: Some people have jumped to the conclusion that 65,536 clock ticks occur in an hour, which is close but not true, since the true figure is 65,543 clocks and change.

Obviously, the clock count is only maintained while the PC is powered up and working properly. During periods when the power is off, the correct time must be maintained elsewhere—usually on a multifunction board, although some PC clone motherboards include a battery-operated clock chip. A small lithium battery keeps an oscillator and a clock chip alive, and when the PC is powered up, a transient utility or a DOS device driver reads the battery-powered clock and loads its value into the clock reference count at $0040 : $006C.

In the PC/XT world, there are no standards at all in terms of how a battery-operated clock chip is to be read, so it's pointless going into that here. It's usually nothing more than a series of I/O port reads, which may easily be done using Turbo Pascal's **PORT** array. The PC/AT has a battery-operated clock chip as standard equipment, and a series of AT-specific ROM BIOS calls can set and read the time and date on the battery-operated clock.

6.2   Reading and Setting the Time Through DOS

PC DOS provides several functions connected with time and date. As are most simple DOS functions, they are called by loading control values in pertinent registers and executing INT 21. Turbo Pascal's built-in **MSDOS** procedure hides the explicit interrupt call, but the register manipulations remain the same. (If you are unfamiliar with DOS function calls and how Turbo Pascal handles them, you might look ahead to the beginning of Chapter 7, where the process is explained in detail.)

Function 44 ($2C) returns the time as currently maintained in the PC. Its information ultimately comes from the clock reference count at $0040 : $006C, but DOS converts the raw count of ticks since midnight into the familiar hours, minutes, seconds, and a slightly ersatz hundredths of seconds figure. The hours figure (expressed as a 24-hour clock) is returned in CH, the minutes in CL, seconds in DH, and hundredths of seconds in DL.

The hundredths figure is questionable because the PC's clock doesn't really resolve to a single hundredth of a second. Since there are only 18.2 clock ticks per second, the duration of a single tick is about 0.055 seconds (the reciprocal of 18.2). What DOS does is interpolate a given tick to its closest decimal equivalent within a second. This figure can be useful as long as you understand that there is that inescapable roundoff to the closest near-twentieth of a second.

Retrieving the time through DOS is trivial, then—as long as all we need is time in the form of four integers. In everyday programming, time values are useful in a number of forms. A time-fetch routine can start with DOS's basic integer time values and calculate these additional forms.

One common use of time is simply to display it, in a convenient format, for a human reader. The format I like is the one most familiar to IBM PC users: the DOS DIR time format, which is a colon-separated 12-hour format with a single-letter AM/PM indicator (**12:17p**). Creating a string containing such a time format can be done with the use of Turbo's built-in **Str** procedure and some concatenation.

A more intriguing use of time is in the comparison of two time values to see which is the older of the two. Using the four different integer values in a comparison would involve a lot of IF/THEN testing, since if the hours are equal, then the minutes have to be tested, and if the minutes are also equal, then the seconds have to be tested, and so on. It would be handy if there were a way to combine the elements of a time value into a single number that could be used in a compare operation to tell if one value is older than another. A number like this is often called a *time stamp*.

The obvious way is simply to express a time as the number of hundredths of a second in all the hours, minutes, and seconds of a day. In a 24-hour day, this works out to 8,640,000. This would fit nicely in a 32-bit "long" integer— but we don't have long integers in Turbo Pascal. (After years of pestering Philippe Kahn for long integers in Turbo, he has told me that Turbo 4.0, which with some luck we will see in 1987, will include long integers. Turbo Pascal for the Macintosh, which is a syntactic preview of Turbo 4.0, already contains type **LongInt**.)

We can drop the hundredths—they're a little too ersatz for my tastes anyway. This cuts the figure to 86,400—agonizingly close to 65,536, but still too high to express in 16 bits.

Compromises must then be made. By dividing the maximum number of seconds in the time stamp by two—to 30 instead of 60—the number of bits required to express the seconds in a minute drops from five to four. Granting this slight reduction in the time stamp's precision, we can now express the number of hours in day in five bits (0-23); the number of minutes in an hour in six bits (0-59); and the number of "seconds" in five bits (0-29). 5 + 6 + 5 = 16 (see Figure 6.2).

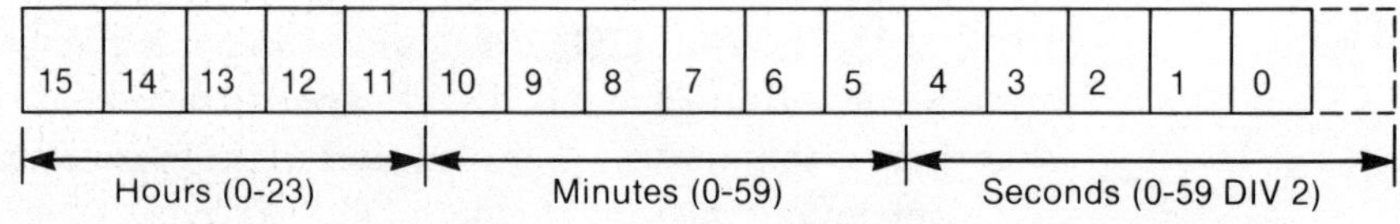

TimeStamp := (Hours SHL 11) OR (Minutes SHL 5) OR (Seconds SHR 1);

Figure 6.2 **DOS time stamp format**

Losing hundredths and every other second means that if two time stamps are within a second of one another, they will be identical. This might not be the time stamp method of choice in a system making rapid laboratory measurements in real-time, but for expressing the creation time of a file (which usually takes more than one second to create, write, and close anyway), it works out quite well.

I won't take credit for the 16-bit time stamp outlined here. It's used by DOS to time stamp its own files, and the time stamp figure can be obtained for any DOS file by reading that file's directory entry. (I'll show you how to do this in Section 7.5.)

In my own programming, I have combined these three different expressions of time into a single Pascal record:

```
TimeRec = RECORD
             TimeComp    : Integer; {DOS time stamp format}
             TimeString : String80;
             Hours,Minutes,Seconds,Hundredths : Integer
          END;
```

Filling such a record with the current time can be done easily with a routine that makes DOS function call $2C:

```
1        {->>>>GetTime<<<<-------------------------------------------------}
2        {                                                                  }
3        { Filename: GETTIME.SRC -- Last Modified 12/31/86                  }
4        {                                                                  }
5        { This routine returns the current system time  through  DOS      }
6        { call $2C.  It requires a prior definition of type TimeRec:       }
7        {                                                                  }
8        {      TimeRec = RECORD                                            }
9        {                      TimeComp    : Integer;    (DTA time stamp)  }
10       {                      TimeString : String80;                     }
11       {                      Hours,Minutes,Seconds,Hundredths : Integer }
12       {                  END;                                           }
13       {                                                                  }
14       { which, of course, also requires definition of type String80. }
15       { GetTime also calls CalcTime, which fills in the other fields }
16       { in the TimeRec that GetTime returns to the caller.              }
17       {                                                                  }
18       {                                                                  }
19       {                                                                  }
20       {----------------------------------------------------------------}
21
22       PROCEDURE GetTime(VAR TimeNow : TimeRec);
23
24       TYPE
25         Reg      = RECORD
26                      CASE Boolean OF
27                        False : (Word : Integer);
28                        True  : (LoByte,HiByte : Byte)
29                    END;
30
```

(continued)

```
31                 Regpack = RECORD
32                             AX,BX,CX,DX,BP,SI,DI,DS,ES,Flags : Reg
33                           END;
34
35           VAR
36             Regs          : RegPack;
37
38           BEGIN
39             Regs.AX.HiByte := $2C; MSDOS(Regs);
40             WITH TimeNow DO
41               BEGIN
42                 Hours := Regs.CX.HiByte; Minutes := Regs.CX.LoByte;
43                 Seconds := Regs.DX.HiByte; Hundredths := Regs.DX.LoByte;
44               END;
45             CalcTime(TimeNow);
46           END;
47
```

GetTime itself only makes the DOS call and loads the **TimeRec** integer fields. A separate routine, **CalcTime** is used to calculate the string version of the time value and the time stamp value. I broke this out as a separate procedure so that time values originating elsewhere than the system clock can be put into the same format as system time values.

```
1         {->>>>CalcTime<<<<--------------------------------------------------}
2         {                                                                   }
3         { Filename: CALCTIME.SRC -- Last Modified 1/7/87                     }
4         {                                                                   }
5         { This routine "fills out" a TimeRec passed to it with only         }
6         { the DOS time values (hours, minutes, seconds, hundredths)         }
7         { valid.  It generates the TimeComp and TimeString fields.          }
8         {                                                                   }
9         {     TimeRec = RECORD                                              }
10        {                   TimeComp   : Integer;    (DTA time stamp)       }
11        {                   TimeString : String80;                         }
12        {                   Hours,Minutes,Seconds,Hundredths : Integer      }
13        {                END;                                              }
14        {                                                                   }
15        { which, of course, also requires definition of type String80. }
16        {                                                                   }
17        {                                                                   }
18        {                                                                   }
19        {-------------------------------------------------------------------}
20
21        PROCEDURE CalcTime(VAR ThisTime : TimeRec);
22
23        TYPE
```

(continued)

```
24                     String5 = String[5];
25
26             VAR
27               Temp1,Temp2 : String5;
28               AMPM        : Char;
29               I           : Integer;
30
31             BEGIN
32               WITH ThisTime DO
33                 BEGIN
34                   I := Hours;
35                   IF Hours = 0 THEN I := 12;    { "0" hours = 12am }
36                   IF Hours > 12 THEN I := Hours - 12;
37                   IF Hours > 11 THEN AMPM := 'p' ELSE AMPM := 'a';
38                   Str(I:2,Temp1); Str(Minutes,Temp2);
39                   IF Length(Temp2) < 2 THEN Temp2 := '0' + Temp2;
40                   TimeString := Temp1 + ':' + Temp2 + AMPM;
41                   TimeComp :=
42                     (Hours SHL 11) OR (Minutes SHL 5) OR (Seconds SHR 1)
43                 END
44             END;
45
```

Note that while the integer value **Hours** is left in 24-hour format, the string representation of the time converts its hours figure to a 12-hour format with the "a" and "p" to indicate AM or PM. Also note how the time stamp is created by shifting the hours, minutes, and seconds numbers into their proper orientation and then ORing them into what amounts to a bitmap. Since the high bit of the integer is a portion of the time stamp's value rather than a sign indicator, the time stamp cannot be calculated by multiplying the hours figure by 2048—even though this is identical to and clearer than shifting the hours value left by 11 bits.

Setting the time is even easier, since no time format conversion is involved. It's nothing more than a simple DOS function call:

```
1          {->>>>>SetTime<<<<---------------------------------------------}
2          {                                                              }
3          { Filename: SETTIME.SRC -- Last Modified 12/31/86              }
4          {                                                              }
5          { This routine sets the PC clock to a given time through DOS   }
6          { call $2D.  It requires a prior definition of type TimeRec:   }
7          {                                                              }
8          {     TimeRec = RECORD                                         }
9          {                 TimeComp   : Integer;   (DTA time stamp)     }
10         {                 TimeString : String80;                      }
11         {                 Hours,Minutes,Seconds,Hundredths : Integer   }
```

(continued)

```
12    {                    END;                                              }
13    {                                                                      }
14    { which, of course, also requires definition of type String80  }
15    { as String[80].                                                       }
16    {                                                                      }
17    {                                                                      }
18    {                                                                      }
19    {----------------------------------------------------------------}
20
21    PROCEDURE SetTime(TimeNow : TimeRec);
22
23    TYPE
24      Reg      = RECORD
25                    CASE Boolean OF
26                        False : (Word : Integer);
27                        True  : (LoByte,HiByte : Byte)
28                    END;
29
30      Regpack = RECORD
31                    AX,BX,CX,DX,BP,SI,DI,DS,ES,Flags : Reg
32                    END;
33
34    VAR
35      Regs        : RegPack;
36
37    BEGIN
38      WITH TimeNow DO
39        BEGIN
40          Regs.CX.HiByte := Hours; Regs.CX.LoByte := Minutes;
41          Regs.DX.HiByte := Seconds; Regs.DX.LoByte := Hundredths;
42        END;
43      Regs.AX.HiByte := $2D; MSDOS(Regs);
44    END;
45
```

If you use these routines in your own applications, you will have to prede-fine **TimeRec** somewhere. On the listings diskette for *Turbo Pascal Solutions*, I have provided a file called **TIMEREC.DEF**, containing the required defini-tions:

```
1      {->>>>Time Record Definition<<<<-------------------------------}
2      {                                                              }
3      { Filename : TIMEREC.DEF -- Last Modified 12/31/86             }
4      {                                                              }
5      { This type should be declared (via this include file)        }
6      { anywhere you intend to use Solutions Toolkit routines that   }
7      { make use of time values.  TimeComp is organized as a DOS    }
8      { time stamp, exactly as used in DOS directory entries.        }
```

(continued)

```
 9             { Remember to declare String80 = String[80] before including  }
10             { this file.                                                   }
11             {                                                              }
12             { And don't forget...you CAN'T include this file inside        }
13             { another include file!                                        }
14             {                                                              }
15             {                                                              }
16             {                                                              }
17             {-------------------------------------------------------------}
18
19             TYPE
20               TimeRec = RECORD
21                     TimeComp    : Integer;    { DOS time stamp format }
22                     TimeString  : String80;
23                     PM          : Boolean;
24                     Hours,Minutes,Seconds,Hundredths : Integer
25                   END;
```

6.3 Reading and Setting the Date Through DOS

There's a little understood but critical difference between the way the PC handles the time and the date. Actually, the difference is that the PC *doesn't* handle the date at all in the same sense that it keeps time. Time on the PC is almost a hardware function. The hardware timer generates time-of-day interrupts (INT 8), which are serviced by a routine in ROM, which updates the clock reference count at $0040 : $006C. The only information relevant to date-keeping is a single flag at $0040 : $0070. This is the midnight flag, and it is set by the time-of-day interrupt service routine to a value of 1 when the clock reference count rolls over to zero at midnight.

That's it. The date, if it is to be kept at all, must be kept either by the operating system or by the application software. PC DOS maintains the current date, but it keeps the date value in a peculiar place—inside COMMAND .COM, the DOS command processor program. This location can be found by some DEBUG snooping, but it's different for each version of DOS and, like any "undocumented" DOS location, could disappear entirely or reappear in a completely incompatible form without any warning. So while you can muck around with the clock reference count and derive your own time values from it by going directly to memory at $0040 : $006C, the *only* way to set or read the date is to do it DOS's way, through DOS function calls 42 ($2A) and 43 ($2B).

DOS uses the midnight flag to determine when to increment its date value. If DOS goes out to read the clock reference count through ROM BIOS service

$1A and discovers that the midnight flag has been set, it increments its date value within COMMAND.COM. It always does this at boot time, but for a PC that is left on continuously, it is unclear when DOS actually goes out and looks at the clock reference count.

There is an excellent reason not to use ROM BIOS service $1A to read the clock reference count in your own programs: *Any* reading of the count through this service (by you or by DOS) clears the midnight flag to zero. If your program uses BIOS service $1A before DOS updates its date value (again, on a PC that stays on all the time), your date will fall one day behind. For this reason, consider BIOS service $1A DOS's private creature; if you must read the clock reference count, go directly to memory with **MEMW** at $0040 : $006C.

When you read the date from DOS through DOS service $2A, it provides the year, month, day, and day of the week, all as integer quantities. As with the time, I created a record type to hold DOS's date values, two string representations of the date, and a *date stamp* integer that follows the DOS date stamp format used in its directory entries:

```
TYPE
  DateRec = RECORD
              DateComp       : Integer;
              LongDateString : String80;
              DateString     : String80;
              Year,Month,Day : Integer;
              DayOfWeek      : Integer
            END;
```

In setting up procedures to read the date through DOS, I followed the same strategy as with reading the time. A simple routine makes the DOS function $2A call and returns a **DateRec** with the **Year**, **Month**, **Day**, and **DayOf-Week** fields filled. A separate routine, **CalcDate**, calculates the date stamp and the two string representations of the date.

```
1          {->>>>GetDate<<<<-------------------------------------------------}
2          {                                                                 }
3          { Filename: GETDATE.SRC -- Last Modified 1/1/87                    }
4          {                                                                 }
5          { This routine returns the current system date through DOS        }
6          { call $2A.  It requires a prior definition of types DateRec      }
7          { and String80.  DateString is formatted this way:                }
8          {                                                                 }
9          {      Wednesday, July 17, 1986                                   }
```

(continued)

```
10          {                                                                      }
11          {       DateRec = RECORD                                               }
12          {                       DateComp        : Integer;                     }
13          {                       LongDateString : String80;                     }
14          {                       DateString     : String80;                     }
15          {                       Year,Month,Day : Integer;                      }
16          {                       DayOfWeek       : Integer                      }
17          {                  END;                                                }
18          {                                                                      }
19          { DayOfWeek is a code from 0-6, with 0 = Sunday.                       }
20          { DateComp is an integer generated by the formula:                     }
21          {      DateComp = (Year-1980)*512 + (Month*64) + Day                   }
22          { It is used for comparing two dates to determine which is             }
23          { earlier, and is the same format as the date stamp used in            }
24          { DOS directory entries.                                               }
25          { GetDate calls CalcDate, which fills in the other fields in           }
26          { the DateRec not filled by DOS call $2A.                              }
27          {                                                                      }
28          {                                                                      }
29          {                                                                      }
30          {----------------------------------------------------------------------}
31
32          PROCEDURE GetDate(VAR Today : DateRec);
33
34          TYPE
35            Reg      = RECORD
36                         CASE Boolean OF
37                             False : (Word : Integer);
38                             True  : (LoByte,HiByte : Byte)
39                       END;
40
41            Regpack = RECORD
42                         AX,BX,CX,DX,BP,SI,DI,DS,ES,Flags : Reg
43                       END;
44
45          VAR
46            Regs   : RegPack;
47
48          BEGIN
49            Regs.AX.HiByte := $2A; MSDOS(Regs);
50            WITH Today DO
51              BEGIN
52                Year := Regs.CX.Word;
53                Month := Regs.DX.HiByte;
54                Day := Regs.DX.LoByte;
55                DayOfWeek := Regs.AX.LoByte;
56              END;
57            CalcDate(Today)
58          END;
```

```
 1          {->>>>CalcDate<<<<-------------------------------------------------}
 2          {                                                                  }
 3          { Filename: CALCDATE.SRC -- Last Modified 4/26/87                   }
 4          {                                                                  }
 5          { This routine fills in the DateString, LongDateString, and        }
 6          { DateComp fields of the DateRec record passed to it.  It          }
 7          { requires that the Year, Month, and Day fields be valid on        }
 8          { entry.  It also requires prior definition of types DateRec       }
 9          { and String80.  DateString is formatted this way:                 }
10          {                                                                  }
11          {     Wednesday, July 17, 1986                                     }
12          {                                                                  }
13          { DateRec is declared this way:                                    }
14          {                                                                  }
15          {     DateRec = RECORD                                             }
16          {                 DateComp       : Integer;                        }
17          {                 LongDateString : String80;                       }
18          {                 DateString     : String80;                       }
19          {                 Year,Month,Day : Integer;                        }
20          {                 DayOfWeek      : Integer                         }
21          {               END;                                              }
22          {                                                                  }
23          { DayOfWeek is a code from 0-6, with 0 = Sunday.                   }
24          { DateComp is an integer generated by the formula:                 }
25          {                                                                  }
26          {     DateComp = (Year-1980)*512 + (Month*32) + Day                }
27          {                                                                  }
28          { It is used for comparing two dates to determine which is         }
29          { earlier, and is the same format used in the date stamp in        }
30          { DOS directory entries.                                           }
31          {                                                                  }
32          {                                                                  }
33          {                                                                  }
34          {------------------------------------------------------------------}
35
36          PROCEDURE CalcDate(VAR ThisDate : DateRec);
37
38          TYPE
39            String9 = String[9];
40
41          CONST
42            MonthTags : ARRAY [1..12] of String9 =
43              ('January','February','March','April','May','June','July',
44               'August','September','October','November','December');
45            DayTags   : ARRAY [0..6] OF String9 =
46              ('Sunday','Monday','Tuesday','Wednesday',
47               'Thursday','Friday','Saturday');
48
49          VAR
```

(continued)

```
50              Temp1 : String80;
51
52            BEGIN
53              WITH ThisDate DO
54                BEGIN
55                  DayOfWeek := DateToDayOfWeek(Year,Month,Day);
56                  Str(Month,DateString);
57                  Str(Day,Temp1);
58                  DateString := DateString + '/' + Temp1;
59                  LongDateString := DayTags[DayOfWeek] + ', ';
60                  LongDateString := LongDateString +
61                    MonthTags[Month] + ' ' + Temp1 + ', ';
62                  Str(Year,Temp1);
63                  LongDateString := LongDateString + Temp1;
64                  DateString := DateString + '/' + Copy(Temp1,3,2);
65                  DateComp := (Year - 1980) * 512 + (Month * 32) + Day
66                END
67            END;
```

The two string representations cover the two most common expressions of
a date in human-readable form: a short form with slashes, **6/29/87**; and a long
form spelling it all out, **Friday, January 2, 1987**. Subsets of the long form can
easily be extracted (for example, without the day of the week or simply the
month and day) by using the Turbo Pascal built-in string function **Copy**.

The date stamp is constructed by shifting the years figure nine bits to the
left (actually by multiplying it by 512, which is the same thing); adding that to
the months figure shifted left by seven bits (i.e., multiplying the months figure
by 64), and then adding in the days value unchanged. Because the "19" portion
of the year value is not incorporated into the date stamp, there are plenty of bits
to go around. In fact, only 14 bits are required, so ordinary multiplication can
be used to generate the date stamp without worrying about getting snared by
the integer's sign bit.

As with **TimeRec**, I have added a small include file to the listings diskette
for this book, containing the **DateRec** declaration:

```
1      {->>>>Date Record Definition<<<<--------------------------------}
2      {                                                               }
3      { Filename : DATEREC.DEF -- Last Modified 12/31/86              }
4      {                                                               }
5      { This type should be declared (via this include file)         }
6      { anywhere you intend to use Solutions Toolkit routines that    }
7      { make use of date values.  DateComp is organized as a DOS      }
8      { date stamp, exactly as used in DOS directory entries.         }
9      { Remember to declare String80 = String[80] before including    }
10     { this file.                                                    }
```

(continued)

```
11              {                                                            }
12              { And don't forget...you CAN'T include this file inside      }
13              { another include file!                                      }
14              {                                                            }
15              {                                                            }
16              {                                                            }
17              {----------------------------------------------------------}
18
19              TYPE
20                DateRec = RECORD
21                            DateComp         : Integer;
22                            LongDateString  : String80;
23                            DateString       : String80;
24                            Year,Month,Day  : Integer;
25                            DayOfWeek        : Integer
26                          END;
```

Calculating the Day of the Week

DOS contains a (slightly flawed) algorithm for calculating the day of the week given the date, so that when you read the date through DOS function $2A, you get a day-of-the-week indicator free of charge. Sunday is represented as a 0, and Saturday as a 6. Under the assumption that I would, at some point, need to fill a **DateRec** that did not come from DOS function $2A, I needed a means to calculate the day of the week from the date.

There are a number of published methods for doing this, all of them messy and involved. Peter Norton was kind enough to point out that DOS already knows how to figure the day of the week. All you have to do is save the current date, set the DOS date to the date in question, read it back with DOS's calculated day-of-the-week code, and then reset the DOS date to the true date.

This is quick and convenient, but there are two catches: 1) DOS does not "understand" dates prior to 1/1/80, which is "Year Zero" as far as the PC is concerned; and 2) the DOS date algorithm does not return the correct day of the week for leap-year day (February 29 in leap year).

The first problem could be important, if you need to deal with dates prior to 1980, say in connection with birth dates, old contract dates, etc.

The second problem is minor, since DOS is entirely consistent about its errant ways: The day of the week returned for leap-year day is always exactly one day code higher than it should be. In other words, if DOS returns a 0, the real code is 6; if DOS returns a 1, the real code is 0, etc. This correction is simplified by the fact that the year 2000 is special. Ordinarily, "century years" are *not* leap years, even though they are divisible by 4, since a day has to be dropped every 100 years to make things come out even. But every 400 years, a century year *is* a leap year. (Again, to compensate for a very *very* minor cumulative error in the calendar.) The year 1600 was the last time this happened, and 2000 will be the next. For this reason, 2000 may be treated as an ordinary leap year.

I trust you will not be programming in Turbo Pascal in the year 2100.

```
{->>>>DateToDayOfWeek<<<<--------------------------------------}
{                                                              }
{ Filename : DAYOWEEK.SRC -- Last Modified 1/1/87              }
{                                                              }
{ This function "calculates" the day of week from the month,   }
{ day, and year values passed to it.  The actual calculation   }
{ is done by DOS, by setting the current date in the PC to the }
{ date passed, and then reading back the current date          }
{ to get the day of week in AL.  (The real current date was    }
{ read and saved and is restored before control returns to the }
{ caller.)  The bulk of the routine deals with the fact that   }
{ DOS cannot correctly calculate the day of the week for any   }
{ leap year day.  Fortunately, it's consistant in its error,   }
{ and the error can be easily corrected for.                   }
{                                                              }
{                                                              }
{                                                              }
{--------------------------------------------------------------}

FUNCTION DateToDayOfWeek(Year,Month,Day : Integer) : Integer;

TYPE
  Reg      = RECORD
                CASE Boolean OF
                   False : (Word : Integer);
                   True  : (LoByte,HiByte : Byte)
              END;

  Regpack = RECORD
                AX,BX,CX,DX,BP,SI,DI,DS,ES,Flags : Reg
              END;


VAR
   SaveDate,WorkDate : RegPack;
   DayNumber         : Integer;
   LeapYearDay       : Boolean;

CONST
   DayArray : ARRAY[1..12] OF Integer =
       (31,28,31,30,31,30,31,31,30,31,30,31);

BEGIN
```

(continued)

```
44            LeapYearDay := False;
45            IF (Month = 2) AND ((Year MOD 4)=0) AND (Day = 29) THEN
46              LeapYearDay := True;
47            IF (NOT LeapYearDay) AND (Day > DayArray[Month]) THEN
48              DateToDayOfWeek := -1
49            ELSE
50              BEGIN
51                WorkDate.AX.HiByte := $2B;
52                SaveDate.AX.HiByte := $2A;    { Saves date encoded in registers }
53                MSDOS(SaveDate);              { Fetch & save today's date }
54                WITH WorkDate DO
55                  BEGIN
56                    CX.Word   := Year;        { Set the clock to the input date }
57                    DX.HiByte := Month;
58                    DX.LoByte := Day;
59                    MSDOS(WorkDate);
60                    AX.HiByte := $2A;         { Turn around and read it back }
61                    MSDOS(WorkDate);          {  to find the day-of-week indicator }
62                    DayNumber := AX.LoByte;   {  in AL. }
63                    IF LeapYearDay THEN       { Correct for DOS's leap year bug }
64                      IF DayNumber = 0 THEN DayNumber := 6
65                         ELSE DayNumber := Pred(DayNumber);
66                    DateToDayOfWeek := DayNumber
67                  END;
68                SaveDate.AX.HiByte := $2B;  { Restore clock to today's date }
69                MSDOS(SaveDate);
70              END
71        END;
```

Setting the date is, like setting the time, a trivial matter. DOS requires the year (in full 4-digit form) in register CX, the month in DH, and the day in DL. The day of the week does not need to be set; DOS calculates that for itself. Function call $2B does the work.

```
1          {->>>>SetDate<<<<----------------------------------------------}
2          {                                                              }
3          { Filename: SETDATE.SRC -- Last Modified 1/1/87                }
4          {                                                              }
5          { This routine sets the current system date through DOS call   }
6          { $2B.  It requires a prior definition of types DateRec and    }
7          { String80.  DateRec is declared this way:                     }
8          {                                                              }
9          {     DateRec = RECORD                                         }
10         {                 DateComp       : Integer;                    }
11         {                 LongDateString : String80;                   }
12         {                 DateString     : String80;                   }
13         {                 Year,Month,Day : Integer;                    }
```

(continued)

```
14         {                    DayOfWeek       : Integer                    }
15         {                 END;                                            }
16         {                                                                 }
17         { Only Year, Month, and Day are necessary to set the date.        }
18         { The other fields are ignored.                                   }
19         {                                                                 }
20         {                                                                 }
21         {                                                                 }
22         {----------------------------------------------------------------}
23
24         PROCEDURE SetDate(DateToday : DateRec);
25
26         TYPE
27           Reg      = RECORD
28                        CASE Boolean OF
29                          False : (Word : Integer);
30                          True  : (LoByte,HiByte : Byte)
31                      END;
32
33           Regpack = RECORD
34                       AX,BX,CX,DX,BP,SI,DI,DS,ES,Flags : Reg
35                     END;
36
37         VAR
38           Regs : RegPack;
39
40         BEGIN
41           WITH DateToday DO
42             BEGIN
43               Regs.CX.Word := Year;
44               Regs.DX.HiByte := Month; Regs.DX.LoByte := Day;
45             END;
46           Regs.AX.HiByte := $2B; MSDOS(Regs);
47         END;
```

6.4 Measuring Duration

Yet another task that doesn't seem especially tricky until you attempt to dash it off in five lines of code is the measuring of the duration of a given event. Overall, it involves taking a snapshot of the "before" time with **GetTime**, taking a second, "after" time sampling, and then subtracting to get the difference between the two.

Rather than trying to get the hours difference first, and then the minutes difference, and so on, it makes more sense to convert everything to seconds and then subtract the earlier seconds figure from the later. This works well unless your measured time interval falls across a midnight boundary between days, in which case your "before" time is apparently later than your "after" time. The solution in this case is to use the **TimeComp** field to determine if "before" is larger than "after," indicating a midnight crossover sometime in between. Compensating for the midnight rollover is done by adding the number of seconds in a day (86400) to "after."

Note that the two time stamps have to be compared by using the **Word-Comp** word-oriented compare function described at the end of Chapter 4. The DOS time stamp must be treated as an unsigned quantity because *all* bits, including integer sign bit 15, are used to represent numeric data.

The obvious thing to do here would be to subtract the earlier time stamp from the later; this might work if we had full precision in the time stamp. The time stamp, however, rounds off hundredths and every other second to make the stamp fit into 16 bits. The overhead involved in converting the two time figures to seconds is minor, and it occurs *after* the second time sample is taken, so it does not affect the accuracy of the measured interval.

The procedure **MarkTime** provides a convenient means of measuring duration. Take the "before" time sample with **GetTime** and keep the sample in a **TimeRec** while duration is being measured. When it's time to take the "after" sample and calculate the duration, invoke **MarkTime** with the "before" **Time-Rec** and an empty **TimeRec** that will be returned with the duration between the two samples.

For example, in a benchmarking situation, you might wish to determine how long it takes to execute 100 iterations of that ol' devil Sieve of Eratosthenes. It could be coded this way:

```
VAR
  Mark,Duration : TimeRec;

GetTime(Mark);
PerformSieve(100);
MarkTime(Mark,Duration);
```

The example assumes a procedure called **PerformSieve** that executes the Sieve benchmark the number of times specified in its single parameters. On completion of the benchmark, **MarkTime** takes the "after" time sample and returns the calculated duration in **Duration**.

```
1          {->>>>MarkTime<<<<-------------------------------------------------}
2          {                                                                  }
3          { Filename: MARKTIME.SRC -- Last Modified 1/2/87                    }
4          {                                                                  }
5          { This routine returns in TimeRec Delta the time difference        }
6          { between the time passed to it in Mark and the current time.      }
```

(continued)

```pascal
 7          { It requires a prior definition of types String80 & TimeRec:  }
 8          {                                                               }
 9          {       TimeRec = Record                                        }
10          {                    TimeComp    : Integer;                     }
11          {                    TimeString : String80;                     }
12          {                    Hours,Minutes,Seconds,Hundredths : Integer  }
13          {                  END;                                         }
14          {                                                               }
15          { Additionally, Solutions Toolkit routines GetTime and          }
16          { CalcTime must be included in the work file BEFORE this file   }
17          { is included!                                                  }
18          {                                                               }
19          { NOTE:   Although this routine will operate correctly across   }
20          {         a midnight boundary, it will NOT operate correctly    }
21          {         for intervals longer than 24 hours!                   }
22          {                                                               }
23          {                                                               }
24          {                                                               }
25          {---------------------------------------------------------------}
26
27          PROCEDURE MarkTime(Var Mark,Delta : TimeRec);
28
29          TYPE
30            Reg      = RECORD
31                         CASE Boolean OF
32                           False : (Word : Integer);
33                           True  : (LoByte,HiByte : Byte)
34                       END;
35
36            Regpack = RECORD
37                        AX,BX,CX,DX,BP,SI,DI,DS,ES,Flags : Reg
38                      END;
39
40          VAR
41            TempTime : TimeRec;
42            TempSeconds,DeltaSeconds : Real;
43
44          FUNCTION TimeToSeconds(T : TimeRec) : Real;
45
46          BEGIN
47            WITH T DO TimeToSeconds := (Hours * 3600.0) + (Minutes * 60.0) +
48              Seconds + (Hundredths * 0.01);
49          END;
50
51          BEGIN
52            GetTime(TempTime);
53            { Test if midnight fell between the two time points: }
54            IF WordComp(Mark.TimeComp,TempTime.TimeComp) THEN
55              BEGIN  { "Add" a day to the later time point: }
56                TempSeconds := TimeToSeconds(TempTime) + 86400.0;
```

(continued)

```
57              DeltaSeconds := TempSeconds - TimeToSeconds(Mark)
58          END
59        ELSE  { Otherwise it's a simple difference }
60          DeltaSeconds := TimeToSeconds(TempTime)-TimeToSeconds(Mark);
61      WITH Delta DO { Convert the delta from seconds to hh:mm:ss:hh }
62        BEGIN
63          Hundredths := Trunc(Frac(DeltaSeconds) * 100);
64          DeltaSeconds := Int(DeltaSeconds);
65          TempSeconds :=  Int(DeltaSeconds / 3600.0);
66          Hours := Trunc(TempSeconds);
67          DeltaSeconds := DeltaSeconds - (Hours * 3600.0);
68          Minutes := Trunc(DeltaSeconds / 60);
69          Seconds := Trunc(DeltaSeconds - (Minutes * 60.0))
70        END;
71      CalcTime(Delta)  { Fill in the rest of the TimeRec }
72    END;
```

DOS, Directories, and Linked Lists

The best 8086 software toolkit bargain going is PC DOS. For $90.00, you get a host of machine-code subprograms of remarkable power, that together do most of the dullest and most difficult routine work of a PC program: telling the time and date, spinning the disks, and managing memory. All of this power is available through one Turbo Pascal built-in procedure. Although I won't be covering all DOS functions in this book (that would take a book several times this size), I hope to give you enough general information and examples so that you can work out the means to use any DOS function from Turbo Pascal.

Linked lists made it into the title because they are a natural for manipulating DOS disk directories, and, in that context, I will also be explaining how to manipulate doubly linked lists. The treatment should be general enough for you to build your own linked-list managers for lists of any purpose and data type.

7.1   The Evolution of a Toolkit

Those of us who shrug at the thought of an application program that *requires* 640K (like Xerox's superb Ventura Publisher) might find the notion of an operating system that resided in less than 12K almost miraculous—until we ponder how little such an operating system actually accomplished. The operating system, of course, was CP/M-80, the overwhelming favorite personal computer OS before the appearance of the IBM PC. Today, in 1987, CP/M-80 is almost forgotten, but to forget it is to lose sight of why PC DOS has evolved the way it has.

DOS 1.X was simply a clone of CP/M-80 written in 8086 assembler rather than 8080/Z80 assembler. The first 36 function calls (up to function $24, Set Random Record) are virtually identical to CP/M-80's function calls. Though tightly written, CP/M-80 cannot be accused of having been beautifully designed, and its function calls have a haphazard way of dealing with input values, return values, and error codes. Fortunately, the more fundamental DOS calls are hidden by the Turbo Pascal runtime code, and you'll have little need to call them directly through the **MSDOS** procedure. When you do, pay attention to the documentation and make no assumptions.

When it accessed files, CP/M-80 set up control blocks in memory called FCB's (File Control Blocks). In general terms, an application wrote necessary information into an FCB and then made the CP/M function call. PC DOS 1.X inherited this system for file I/O function calls, and all of the file I/O function calls in the first 36 DOS functions require the use of FCB's.

The break between PC DOS 1.X and DOS 2.0 was a fundamental one—far more fundamental than the break between 2.X and 3.X. For Version 2, Microsoft rewrote DOS from scratch, modeling it on the Unix minicomputer operating system developed by AT&T. DOS 2 and 3 may be seen as stripped-down single-user, single-tasking Unix clones, containing most of the genuine Unix innovations without Unix's wretchedly slow performance.

Unix's most important contributions to DOS are subdirectories and their associated pathnames, allowing structure to be imposed on massive linear directories containing hundreds of separate files. The file I/O code within DOS 1.X was too set in its ways to be expanded to support pathnames and subdirectories, so Microsoft created a whole "second set" of file I/O function calls for DOS 2.X. These new calls provide all the functions of the original set and then some, and do it in a much cleaner fashion. DOS 2.X hid the FCB's within itself, making interface to files much simpler and more consistent. Rather than being associated with an FCB, a file, when opened, became associated with a *file handle*—a 16-bit code number associated with a file control table somewhere inside DOS.

Most of the fooling around connected with file I/O is, again, handled transparently by the Turbo Pascal runtime code, and, therefore, you needn't study the arcane details of working with file handles. What you need to understand is the reason why there are two DOS function calls for most file operations: The old ones do not understand pathnames or subdirectories; the new ones do. There are subtler reasons for using the newer set of file function calls, but, for brevity's sake, I'll ask you to take my word for it. Since Turbo Pascal 3.0 does not run under DOS 1.X, you have absolutely no reason *not* to use the newer function calls.

A handful of new function calls were added to DOS 3.X. They are arcane to the nines (seeming to point the way to yet more future enhancements rather than being immediately useful), and I will not be covering them here.

7.2 How DOS Calls Are Made from Turbo Pascal

Like most everything else in an 8088 environment, PC DOS is called through a software interrupt. We could, in fact, call PC DOS using Turbo Pascal's INTR software interrupt routine, by setting up values in a register structure and calling interrupt $21.

Turbo Pascal provides a somewhat more readable DOS call facility:

```
MSDOS(Registers);
```

where **Registers** is a structure containing exactly 20 bytes, representing the following 8088 16-bit registers: AX, BX, CX, DX, BP, SI, DI, DS, ES, and Flags. Interrupt 21 does not have to be specified, as it is always the same for DOS calls and the interrupt calling code is built into Turbo Pascal's runtime library.

The best way to handle the register structure under Turbo Pascal is to define a free-union variant record type allowing us to access the registers as either whole 16-bit registers (type Integer) or as 8-bit register halves (type Byte). (This was described in detail in Section 3.2.) The structure itself looks like this:

```
TYPE
  Reg      = RECORD
                CASE Boolean OF
                  False : (Word : Integer);
                  True  : (LoByte,HiByte : Byte)
             END;

  RegPack = RECORD
                AX,BX,CX,DX,BP,SI,DI,DS,ES,Flags : Reg
             END;
```

Each register in the record **RegPack** is itself a record of type **Reg**. Values are stored in the registers by specifying both the register name field of **RegPack** and the word/byte field specifier of each register record. Assuming a variable named **Registers** of type **RegPack**, loading a $30 into register AH (the high half of register AX) is done with this notation:

```
Registers.AX.HiByte := $30;
```

Each of the various functions performed by DOS has a number. To invoke a function, this number must be loaded into register AH. Most individual DOS services require that additional parameters be loaded into various other registers before making the actual DOS call.

DOS Error Messages

Things go wrong. When a DOS function cannot complete successfully, DOS takes its best guess at what the problem is and returns an appropriate code in register AX. I say "best guess" because unusual situations have been known to knock DOS for a loop and return completely inappropriate error codes. You must therefore interpret DOS error codes carefully, and make provision for situations when the returned error codes don't bear any relation to the problem at hand.

Beginning with DOS 2.0, a set of 19 error-code values was defined and used in a standard fashion across all the new DOS function calls first included in DOS 2.0. This set begins with function call $2F, Set DTA Address. Function calls with numbers lower than $2F probably *don't* return error codes from this set. I have tried, whenever possible, to use the newer DOS function calls in this book, especially those connected with disk file I/O, since those are the calls most likely to return error messages. If you use function calls with numbers prior to $2F, double-check the DOS documentation to be sure you understand the errors such a call may return.

The following table summarizes the standard DOS error codes.

DOS Standard Error Codes

$00	No error; function call completed correctly
$01	Invalid function number
$02	File not found
$03	Path not found
$04	No handle available; all are in use
$05	Access denied
$06	Invalid handle
$07	Memory control blocks destroyed
$08	Insufficient memory
$09	Invalid memory block address
$0A	Invalid DOS environment
$0B	Invalid format
$0C	Invalid access code
$0D	Invalid data
$0E	<not used by DOS>
$0F	Invalid drive specification
$10	Attempt to remove current directory
$11	Not same device
$12	No more files to be found

In summary: To make a DOS call, define a register variable of type **Reg-Pack** as described previously, load the DOS service number into AH, load any other required parameters into the proper registers, and pass the structure to Turbo Pascal's **MSDOS** procedure:

```
Registers.AX.HiByte := $36;      {Get free disk space service}
Registers.DX.LoByte := $01;      {Request A; (drive 1)}

MSDOS(Registers);                {Make the DOS call}
```

If an error occurs, the error code will be returned in AX.

A warning about DOS function call $4B, Execute Program (EXEC): This function call *cannot* be made safely from Turbo Pascal's **MSDOS** procedure because of certain hassles involving the destruction of registers. I have not satisfied myself that a truly reliable method of calling EXEC from within a Turbo Pascal program has been developed; I have always managed to crash the system by doing seemingly innocuous things before returning. (If this book sells well enough to merit a second edition, I will try to incorporate a truly reliable EXEC function.)

IBM's documentation of DOS services is not always the best, especially if you're just learning your way around the PC at the system level. I don't have room to go over every DOS service (there are about 85 in all) in this book. Experiment, but keep in mind that this is strong stuff—if you misunderstand the purpose of a parameter or put it in the wrong register, you could easily blow your DOS session away and force a warm or cold reboot. Be careful—read it twice—and keep your cool!

7.3   The DOS Version Number

DOS call 48 ($30) returns the version number of the copy of DOS installed on the computer. This allows your programs to determine what version of DOS is running beneath them.

Why is this important? Well, DOS evolves. Version 1.0 can't deal with double-sided disk drives. Version 1.1 can't deal with pathnames. Version 3.0 lacks the "hooks" into the PC Network that version 3.1 includes. And that's just a sampler. Each version of DOS has numerous abilities not shared by prior versions.

If you had written a program which creates a subdirectory in which it stores temporary files, and then someone tries to run it under DOS 1.1—which doesn't understand the concept of subdirectories—what would happen? Your program would attempt to make a DOS call with an undefined (as far as DOS 1.1 was concerned) function-call number. Certainly, this would cause an error. In some cases, it might lock up your machine.

To be safe, your program ought to know what DOS facilities are available to it. This is the reason for DOS call 48. When it begins running, a program should perform DOS call 48 and then make a decision based on the returned value. If DOS 1.1 is running, the safest thing to do would be to print a helpful message such as this:

```
[Error 42] JIVETALK LXXIII requires DOS 2.0 or later!
```

and return to DOS without attempting anything else.

An even more intelligent program might rearrange its menus to hide certain features which are not supported by older versions of DOS. If the program discovered that it were running under DOS 1.1, it could eschew the use of subdirectories and file handles, but continue operating using FCB file I/O and "flat" disk directories. A program which supports local area networking as an option could suppress LAN-oriented commands and menus if it found that it was running under DOS 3.0 or earlier.

There's an important wrinkle in using DOS function 48 with Turbo Pascal. You probably know that Turbo Pascal V3.0 requires at least DOS 2.0 to run at all. What is less well-known is that programs compiled to disk as .COM files also check for DOS V1, whether you, the programmer, do or not. Although function 48 will allow you to determine if DOS V1.0 or DOS V1.1 is running on a machine, the Turbo Pascal V3.0 runtime code will not necessarily let it get that far. Before your program actually begins executing, the Turbo Pascal V3.0 runtime code will check the DOS version itself, and it will terminate your program with an error message if it discovers any DOS version prior to 2.0.

Turbo Pascal V2.0 will, however, allow you to run on DOS V1.X.

Using DOS call 48 is simplicity itself. No input parameters (other than the DOS call number in AH) are required. Turbo Pascal's MSDOS procedure does the work:

```
1              {->>>>DOSVersion<<<<-------------------------------------------------}
2              {                                                                     }
3              { Filename: DOSVERSN.SRC -- Last modified 12/14/85                     }
4              {                                                                     }
5              { This routine returns the current DOS version as a real              }
6              { number.  It uses DOS call 48.  If you are using DOS 2.1 it           }
7              { will return the value 2.1.  If you need to test only the             }
8              { major or minor portions of the DOS version number, use the          }
9              { VAR parameters Major, which contains the major release              }
10             { number ("2" for DOS 2.1) and Minor, which contains the minor }
11             { release number ("10" for DOS 2.1).                                  }
12             {                                                                     }
13             {                                                                     }
14             {                                                                     }
15             {---------------------------------------------------------------------}
16
17             FUNCTION DOSVersion(VAR Major,Minor : Integer) : Real;
18
19             TYPE
20               Reg      = RECORD
21                             CASE Boolean OF
22                                 False : (Word : Integer);
```

(continued)

```
23                              True  : (LoByte,HiByte : Byte)
24                    END;
25
26           Regpack = RECORD
27                        AX,BX,CX,DX,BP,SI,DI,DS,ES,Flags : Reg
28                    END;
29
30           String15 = String[15];
31
32        VAR
33           I              : Integer;
34           R              : Real;
35           Dummy1,Dummy2 : String15;
36           Registers     : Regpack;
37
38        BEGIN
39           Registers.AX.HiByte := 48;
40           MSDOS(Registers);
41           WITH Registers DO
42             BEGIN
43               Major := AX.LoByte;
44               Minor := AX.HiByte;
45               Str(Major,Dummy1);
46               Str(Minor,Dummy2);
47             END;
48           Dummy1 := Dummy1 + '.' + Dummy2;
49           Val(Dummy1,R,I);
50           DOSVersion := R
51        END;
```

The first two lines in the body of the procedure do all the important work of making the DOS call. This rest of the procedure is nothing more than code to reformat the returned value. DOS returns the major portion of the version number (that is, the "3" of DOS 3.1) in AL, and the minor portion of the version number (the "1" in DOS 3.1) in AH. Note that any non-zero minor version is always returned as a 2-digit number. In other words, for DOS 2.1 and 3.1, the minor version number will be 10 rather than 1. For DOS 2.0, 3.0, or 4.0, of course, the minor version number will be 0.

A short program, VERTEST, demonstrates how **DOSVersion** is used:

```
1          PROGRAM VersionTest;
2
3          VAR
4            Major,Minor : Integer;
5
6          {$I DOSVERSN.SRC}
```

(continued)

```
7
8            BEGIN
9              Writeln
10             ('The currently running version of DOS is ',
11               DOSVersion(Major,Minor):3:2);
12           END.
```

DOSVersion combines major and minor portions into a real-number value, which DOS version numbers resemble. It does this by converting major and minor portions into strings, concatenating the strings with a decimal point in the middle, and then using the built-in **Val** procedure to turn this string representation of the version number into a real number. You can still use the major and minor release numbers separately as returned in **Major** and **Minor**.

There are advantages to combining the major and minor release numbers into a single real value: 1) The real-number equivalent can be printed to the screen and it will look like a DOS version number, and 2) a single value can be compared with another single value to determine which of the two represents a "later" DOS version.

Point 1 is cosmetic. Point 2 is important. It allows you to test for a particular version of DOS with a simple numeric comparison:

```
RunningVersion := DOSVersion(Major,Minor);
IF RunningVersion < 3.1 THEN AllowNetworking := FALSE;
```

There's a small "gotcha" involved with **DOSVersion**: DOS function call 48 did not exist in DOS 1.0 or 1.1. Technically, if you execute **DOSVersion** under DOS 1.0 or 1.1, you risk an error—or worse. However, Peter Norton claims (and my experimentation confirms) that DOS 1.0 and 1.1 will reliably—and without disruption—return a 0 in AL when DOS call 48 is made under these two versions. What you must do, then, is test *first* if **DOSVersion** returns a value *less than one*. If the return value is less than one, the DOS version running is DOS 1.0 or 1.1:

```
RunningVersion := DOSVersion(Major,Minor)
IF RunningVersion < 1.0 THEN
  Writeln('[Error 17] DOS version 2.0 or later required!');
```

7.4 Reading the DOS Environment

One of the peculiarities of PC DOS V2 and later is an item called the *DOS environment block* (usually referred to as *the environment*). What was at the outset a good idea was implemented so peculiarly that it leads me to wonder if the lights are on with nobody home up in Washington State.

The underlying idea is this: DOS reserves a region of memory somewhere, in a location that doesn't change, as a "bulletin board" reserved for the posting of notices. These notices are for applications programs that load, run for awhile under DOS, and then terminate. They have the ability to peek at the bulletin board and see what notices have been posted.

The notices can be anything at all, but are typically useful items about the DOS configuration of the system: where COMMAND.COM is stored, what the current DOS search path is for program execution, and so on. Additionally, the user has the ability to place notices in the DOS environment by using DOS's SET command. By entering a command such as this:

```
SET SYMLIB=D:\M2LIB\SYM
```

it's possible to post the string **SYMLIB=D:\M2LIB\SYM** on the DOS environment's bulletin board. Then, when a utility program needs to know where the Modula 2 symbol files are kept, it can peek at the environment and get the path attached to the identifier **SYMLIB**.

So far, so good. This solves the knotty problem of sharing critical information among sequentially transient but related programs. Now, however, for the catch: DOS only reserves 160 bytes of space for its environment block. The latest in DOS versions (3.2) allows this size to be increased to a maximum of 32K, but, to my mind, the additional features of DOS 3.2 don't warrant another $90 out of my pocket.

For the vast majority of DOS users, 160 bytes is all you get. That's room for a typical 80-byte search path, COMSPEC, and one (or *maybe* two) other things. It does *not* provide room for a search path, COMSPEC, and the five or ten environment variables requested by many language systems, such as Logitech's excellent Modula 2/86. Every time I need to use Logitech Modula 2, I must reboot my machine with a special batch file that eliminates my search path to make room for the five Modula 2 environment variables.

In short, the DOS environment is close to useless. If you wish to use it, however, the following Pascal function will allow you to read the DOS environment:

```
1      {->>>>SearchEnvironment<<<<------------------------------------}
2      {                                                              }
3      { Filename: SRCHENV.SRC -- Last modified 10/20/85              }
4      {                                                              }
5      { This routine searches the DOS environment for a parameter,   }
6      { and if it finds the parameter, returns the value of that     }
7      { parameter as read from the environment.  The function return }
8      { value is set to True if the parameter is found.  The value   }
```

(continued)

```
 9     { of the found parameter is placed in Value.  If the parameter }
10     { is not found, Value will be set to the null string. ('')      }
11     { The requested parameter is forced to upper-case before the    }
12     { search is begun, since COMMAND.COM capslocks the parameter     }
13     { when it is entered via the SET DOS command.                    }
14     {                                                                }
15     { Type String80 must be predefined.                             }
16     {                                                                }
17     {                                                                }
18     {                                                                }
19     {--------------------------------------------------------------}
20
21     FUNCTION SearchEnvironment(Parm        : String80;
22                                   VAR Value : String80) : Boolean;
23
24     TYPE
25         String255 = String[255];
26
27     VAR
28         I,J,K       : Integer;
29         EnvSegment : Integer;
30         EnvOffset  : Integer;
31         TempString : String255;
32
33     BEGIN
34       SearchEnvironment := False;         { Defaults to "not found" }
35       Value := '';                        { Set Value to null string }
36       FOR I := 1 TO Length(Parm) DO       { Caps lock the parm }
37         Parm[I] := UpCase(Parm[I]);
38       EnvSegment := MEMW[CSEG:$2C];        { Locate the DOS environment }
39       EnvOffset  := 0;  J := 0;
40       { Until we run out of environment, search: }
41       WHILE MEM[EnvSegment : EnvOffset] <> 0 DO
42         BEGIN
43           TempString := '';
44           I := 1;
45           { Here we copy an environment string into TempString: }
46           REPEAT
47             TempString[I] := CHR(MEM[EnvSegment : EnvOffset]);
48             I := SUCC(I);
49             EnvOffset := SUCC(EnvOffset)
50           UNTIL MEM[EnvSegment : EnvOffset]=0;
51           TempString[0] := CHR(EnvOffset-J); { Set length of TempString }
52           K := Pos('=',TempString);          { Locate "=" in TempString }
53           IF K > 0 THEN           { If there is an "=" in this string... }
54             IF Copy(TempString,1,K-1) = Parm THEN   { If Parm is found }
55               BEGIN
56                   SearchEnvironment := True;  { We found it! }
```

(continued)

```
57                          { Copy procedure's value into Value... }
58                          Value := Copy(TempString,K+1,Length(TempString)-K);
59                          Exit                        { ...and duck out of proc    }
60                        END;
61                    J := EnvOffset+1;
62                    EnvOffset := SUCC(EnvOffset)
63                  END
64              END;
```

SearchEnvironment is a Boolean function that checks to see if a value has been posted in the DOS environment for a given identifier. If a value has been posted for this identifier, the value is returned. In other words, to check to see if a value has been posted for SYMLIB, you would load the string SYMLIB into parameter **Parm** and call **SearchEnvironment**. If the return value of **Search-Environment** comes back **TRUE**, a value has been posted for SYMLIB, and that value will be returned in VAR parameter **Value**. If no value has been posted for SYMLIB, the function returns **FALSE**, and **Value** comes back holding a null string.

The strings stored in the environment are ASCIIZ strings, meaning that they are arrays of characters terminated with a binary 0 [in Pascal, Chr(0)]. The end of significant information in the environment is signaled by the presence of another binary 0 *after* the binary 0 signaling the end of the last string in the environment. If the environment *begins* with a binary 0, nothing has been stored into it.

The location of the DOS environment is stored at the beginning of the code segment of your Pascal program, in a 256-byte area called the Program Segment Prefix (PSP). At offset $2C into the PSP is a 2-byte segment address, which is the segment of the first byte of the DOS environment. (The offset of the first byte of the environment is always assumed to be 0.) So finding the environment is only as difficult as saying:

```
EnvSegment := MEMW[CSEG : $2C];
```

where **EnvSegment** is an integer.

The remainder of **SearchEnvironment** is nothing more than looping through character arrays searching for binary 0's and copying the identified ASCIIZ strings into more tractable Pascal strings.

SearchEnvironment is interesting in another sense. I feel that it is a good example of an occasion where using Turbo Pascal's **Exit** procedure to jump out of a procedure in the middle somewhere does *not* harm readability, compared to the fooling around necessary to terminate the procedure on a string match using traditional control structures.

7.5   Understanding and Using Disk Directories

There are two ways to look at disk files: the physical and the logical. The physical file is a collection of magnetic disturbances arranged on a floppy disk. The logical file is a sequence of sectors stored on a disk, where a sector is a "slice" of a disk file comprising some number of bytes of data. The physical location of all individual sector on the disk itself is of no concern in the logical view of the file. The physical file has no name; it is only a collection of sectors scattered buckshot-style across the face of the disk.

DOS intermediates between the two views of a file. It is possible to go around DOS and take charge of the physical reality of the file's naked sectors, but there's plenty of danger in that and very little profit, unless you intend to play copy-protection games, and I think I'd rather run a school for child molesters than teach people how to copy-protect their diskettes.

Therefore, I won't go into the physical view of a file here, nor explain the FAT (File Allocation Table)—which is the ultimate arbiter between physical and logical—nor most of the other DOS internals that could fill a book on their own. At the logical level, the most important entities aside from the disk files themselves are disk directories. By and large, this section concerns disk directories, how DOS formats them, and how the information contained there can be used.

Root Directories and Subdirectories

A directory is like a phone book; there is one entry in a directory on a disk for every file on that disk, and this entry contains information essential for opening and using that file. There are two types of directories available under DOS. Every disk volume (which is a mass storage entity responding to a drive specifier like A:, B:, C:, etc.) has one and only one root directory. The root directory is of a fixed size, although the size of root directories varies, depending on the type of disk you're dealing with.

Subdirectories may exist within the root directories, or within other subdirectories. They are tools for organizing groups of disk files into logical structures, revealing those of interest in their entirety, while hiding those that are not needed for the time being. They also serve to keep unused directory space from hogging precious disk space; like dynamic variables in Pascal, subdirectories can be created as needed in unlimited numbers (since they can be nested) and erased when no longer required.

A subdirectory is in fact a special type of file. Until DOS 3.0, in fact, subdirectories could be read and processed by the same function calls used to process ordinary data files. As part of DOS's ongoing evolution toward a protected-mode multitasking operating system, this, as well as other shortcuts, have been removed. DOS provides adequate tools for dealing with subdirectories at a Turbo Pascal program level. For disk diagnostic routines and other low-level utilities, stronger measures (such as tracing through the labyrinth of the FAT) are required.

Directory Entries vs. DTA

Echoing the logical/physical dichotomy of the disk file, there are two faces to a directory entry. One is the entry as it is actually stored on the disk, and the other is the way DOS shows us that entry when we search for it and find it. There are two reasons for this split personality: 1) The "real" directory entry contains information—specifically, the starting FAT cluster—that DOS would prefer to keep to itself, and 2) there is information that is useful for repeated directory searches that is created and deleted after the searches are completed, and does not need to be stored away on disk.

The directory entry as it is stored on disk is not of any serious concern except for writing low-level disk utilities such as the Norton Utilities. For everyday work with files, the second manifestation of the directory entry—the entry as it is shown to us in a place called the Disk Transfer Area (DTA)—is the one I will be describing and using here.

As you might expect, there are DOS function calls that go out to the directory and search for entries that match a particular file spec. These calls can help repair a crucial failing in Turbo Pascal—the compiler gives the programmer no facilities to read and inspect disk directories. If a program needs to know whether or not a file exists on a given disk drive, it can attempt to open the file, and the **IOResult** function will return an error code if the file does not exist. There is no method provided by Turbo Pascal, however, which enables a program to go out and see what is actually on the disk before it tries to open something. To do this, we have to resort to DOS function calls and the built-in **MSDOS** procedure.

The most useful DOS calls we'll be discussing shortly place information about files in a table called the Disk Transfer Area, or DTA. The DTA table is the closest DOS will let us get to a directory entry without goosing it beneath the belt. The DTA's organization is best explained and used by setting it up as a Pascal record:

```
DWord   = RECORD
             LoInteger,HiInteger : Integer
          END;

DTARec  = RECORD
```

```
Reserved  : ARRAY[0..20] OF Byte;
Attrib    : Byte;
TimeComp  : Integer;
DateComp  : Integer;
DTASize   : DWord;
FileName  : ARRAY[1..13] OF Char
END;
```

The **DWord** type is an unsigned 32-bit integer—a type Turbo Pascal should have, but doesn't. Even a signed 32-bit integer would do nicely here, but we won't see that until Turbo Pascal 4.0 appears. The DTA keeps the DOS file size figure as a 32-bit integer, hence the need for type **DWord**.

The first 21 bytes are reserved, and DOS *means* that—don't think that in this case "reserved" means "unused." DOS uses those 21 bytes to hold information over from one type of DOS call to the next, and if you try tucking something away in there, your file searches won't work.

TimeComp and **DateComp** should be familiar from the previous section. They are the time and date stamps DOS keeps for every file in its directory entry, and have the same format as described in connection with the **TimeRec** and **DateRec** definitions.

DTASize is the size of the file as it exists on disk, in bytes.

FileName is the name of the file. This includes the dot *if* there are more than eight characters in the name. The file name is an ASCIIZ string. This means that it is a string of characters without a length byte, plus a "null" character (character 0) appended to the end to indicate that it does, in fact, end somewhere. ASCIIZ is the lazy language's way to handle strings and I hate it a bunch. Resist the pull of C, my friends. For all the supposed "freedom" it offers you, it makes you work 50 percent harder by making you keep track of your own string lengths, and a multitude of other things that Pascal already does for you. Still, it generally doesn't offer you anything close to 100 percent improvement in performance over Pascal, which is the minimum considered significant by most experts in the field. C is a ripoff. End of sermon.

Attrib is the DOS file-attribute byte. File attributes are "colors" that a file may take on under certain conditions so that it may be treated in special ways. Six of the eight bits in the attribute byte are significant, and they are outlined in Figure 7.1. Bits are considered "active" if set to 1.

Bit 0, if set to 1, marks a file as *read-only*, meaning it cannot be deleted or modified via normal DOS operations. To delete or change the file you must first use a particular DOS call (CHMOD) to zero out the read-only bit, or use a DOS utility called ATTRIB from the command line to lower the read-only flag. NOTE: One of the bugs in DOS 1.X's bug collection ignores this flag; if you're working under DOS 1.X with Turbo V1 or V2, keep this in mind.

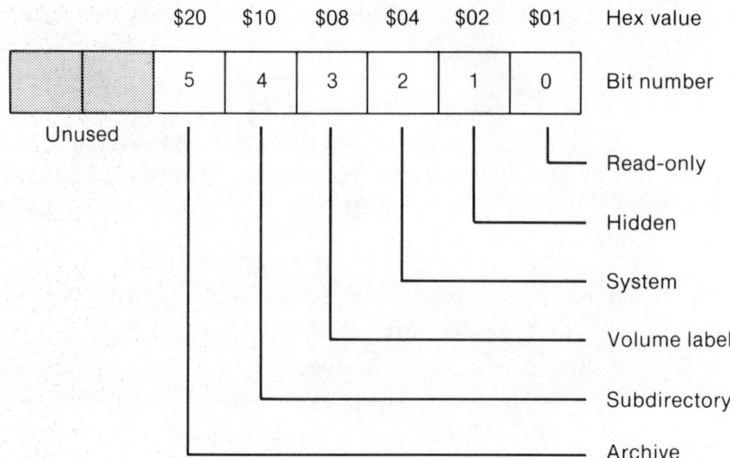

Figure 7.1   **DOS file attribute bits**

Bit 1 marks a file as *hidden*, which means the file exists but cannot be seen or modified by most DOS operations. Some DOS calls will detect hidden files (FIND FIRST and FIND NEXT, notably), but, in most cases, you need to use CHMOD to "unhide" them before you can do much with them. Out of sight, out of mind, I guess—and that old devil ERASE *.* won't touch hidden files.

Bit 2 marks a file as a *system* file, but has no real significance that I can identify. Peter Norton says it is a holdover from CP/M-80, but that's unclear to me. Ignore it.

Bit 3, if set, marks the file as the current *volume label*, an 11-character name that can be given to any disk volume. Volume labels are seldom used, in part because of a DOS bug that prevents you from altering a volume label once it is created (more on this later).

Bit 4 marks a file as a *subdirectory*. Subdirectories are, in fact, files—and, in DOS 2.X, they could even be read as files using ordinary DOS calls. DOS 3.X will not allow subdirectories to be opened and read as files, but this attribute bit still allows you to identify such files as subdirectories, as we'll see in designing the **Locate** program shortly.

Bit 5 is the *archive* bit, and is set to 1 every time a file is changed somehow. The idea is that a backup utility can inspect a directory and only back up files with the archive bit set. Then, once a file is archived, the utility can set its archive bit back to 0, so that it will be ignored by the next archiving operation. When the file is again modified, its archive bit will be set back to 1, making it fair game for the backup utility. Unless you use a backup utility, this bit will be set to 1 on nearly all files all the time.

Telling DOS about the DTA

When a program begins running, DOS sets up a default DTA at offset $80 into
the file. This is the same address at which the "command line tail" is placed,
which is why you must pick up and save the command parameters *before* you
begin opening and reading any files. While it is certainly possible to use the
DTA at offset $80, I feel it is a better idea to declare a **DTARec** as a variable,
and then instruct DOS to use that variable as its DTA.

A DOS call, $1A, exists for this purpose. You can use it to set up a
DTARec as the current DTA:

```
VAR
  CurrentDTA  : DTARec;
  Regs        : RegPack;

  . . . . .

WITH Regs DO
  BEGIN
    AX.HiByte  := $1A;
    DS.Word    := Seg(CurrentDTA);
    DX.Word    := Ofs(CurrentDTA);
  END;
MSDOS(Regs);
```

The idea here is to place the address of the first byte of the new **DTA** in **DS** (the
segment portion) and **DX** (the offset portion). As with all DOS calls, the
number of the function goes in register AH.

You might get a little nervous about placing a new value in DS, when DS
holds the segment address for Turbo Pascal's data segment, but, in fact, the
current value of DS is saved and restored by the code generated for the
MSDOS procedure by Turbo Pascal.

After this code is executed, any time DOS requires the use of a DTA, it
will use the one mapped out at the address passed in DS : DX—in this case,
record variable **CurrentDTA**. This particular **DTARec** was declared as a variable, but you can also pass DOS the addresses of **DTARec**s passed as parameters or declared as record constants.

A Better Record Format for Directory Information

The DTA format is what DOS gives us, but it's not necessarily the best that can
be done. On many counts, the DTA doesn't mesh well with Pascal's data types.
The 4-byte integer file size maps onto nothing Turbo Pascal offers, and AS-
CIIZ strings are simply nuisances. The time stamp and date stamp are compact, but not very useful, except for determining the older of two files. The time

stamp in particular does not map well onto a Pascal integer because the high-order bit is needed to carry numeric precision rather than sign information.

To make directory information from the DTA more accessible to Turbo Pascal programs, I have defined a different record type providing better Pascal representation of DTA information, and pointers for use in linked lists:

```
DIRRec = RECORD
            FileName   : String15;
            Attrib     : Byte;
            FileSize   : Real;
            TimeStamp  : TimeRec;
            DateStamp  : DateRec;
            Prior      : DIRPtr;
            Next       : DIRPtr;
         END;
```

(This record definition is included in the listings diskette for this book under the name **DIRREC.DEF**.) The reserved DOS work area in the DTA has been omitted. The filename field is now a Pascal string with a length byte. The file size is now expressed as a real number. This isn't ideal, because rounding errors and comparison problems can intrude when you're trying to perform "integer" arithmetic on real numbers, but with some care it can be done; besides, there isn't any better alternative.

The time and date stamps have been replaced with the time and date records described in Chapter 6. The original time and date stamp values are present in these records, but have been expanded to individual values for hours, minutes, and seconds; month, day, and year, and English-reading string representations of time and date.

The two pointer fields allow doubly linked lists of these records to be constructed on the heap. (I'll be describing this process in considerable detail in Section 7.8.)

Converting between the DTA format and the **DIRRec** format is accomplished by a single routine, **DTAToDIR**. The routine is not especially subtle.

```
1
2          {->>>>DTAtoDIR<<<<-------------------------------------------------}
3          {                                                                  }
4          { FILENAME DTATODIR.SRC -- Last modified 1/7/87                    }
5          {                                                                  }
6          { This procedure converts data as returned by DOS FIND            }
7          { calls $4E & $4F in the Disk Transfer Area (DTA) to a more        }
8          { tractable form as defined by my own record type DIRRec.          }
9          { This involves converting the time from a two byte integer to }
10         { a TimeRec, and the date from an integer to a DateRec.            }
```

(continued)

```
11        {                                                            }
12        { DTAToDIR requires the prior definition of types DWord,      }
13        { DIRRec, DTARec, DIRPtr, and DTAPtr; and procedures CalcTime }
14        { and CalcDate.                                               }
15        {                                                            }
16        {                                                            }
17        {                                                            }
18        {------------------------------------------------------------}
19
20        PROCEDURE DTAtoDIR(VAR OutRec : DIRRec);
21
22        TYPE
23          DTAPtr  = ^DTARec;
24
25        VAR
26          I           : Integer;
27          TempReal    : Real;
28          InRec       : DTARec;
29          Registers   : RegPack;
30          CurrentDTA  : DTAPtr;
31
32        BEGIN
33          Registers.AX.Word := $2F00; { Find current location of DTA }
34          MSDOS(Registers);
35          WITH Registers DO CurrentDTA := Ptr(ES.Word,BX.Word);
36          InRec := CurrentDTA^;
37          WITH OutRec DO                { Now extract and reformat data }
38            BEGIN
39              I := 1;                   { Extract the file name field }
40              WHILE InRec.FileName[I] <> Chr(0) DO
41                BEGIN
42                  FileName[I] := InRec.FileName[I];
43                  I := Succ(I)
44                END;
45              FileName[0] := CHR(I-1);
46              Attrib := InRec.Attrib; { Extract the attribute field }
47              WITH TimeStamp DO      { Expand integer time stamp }
48                BEGIN
49                  TimeComp := InRec.TimeComp;
50                  Hours := TimeComp SHR 11;
51                  Minutes := (TimeComp AND $07E0) SHR 5;
52                  Seconds := (TimeComp AND $1F) SHL 1;
53                  Hundredths := 0;
54                END;
55              CalcTime(TimeStamp);    { Fill in the other time fields }
56              WITH DateStamp DO       { Expand integer date stamp }
57                BEGIN
58                  DateComp := InRec.DateComp;
59                  Day := DateComp AND $1F;
```

(continued)

```
60                      Month := (DateComp AND $01FF) SHR 5;
61                      Year  := (DateComp SHR 9) + 1980;
62                    END;
63                  CalcDate(DateStamp);    { Fill in the other date fields }
64                  WITH InRec.DTASize DO   { Convert 4-byte filesize to real }
65                    BEGIN
66                      TempReal := LoInteger;
67                      If TempReal < O THEN TempReal := TempReal + 65536.0;
68                      FileSize := (HiInteger * 65536.0) + TempReal;
69                    END;
70                  Next := NIL;                  { Initialize the "next" pointer }
71                  Prior := NIL;                 { Ditto the "prior" pointer }
72                END
73            END;  { DTAtoDIR }
```

One point of interest is that you don't explicitly pass **DTAToDIR** a **DTARec** to act as input. **DTAToDIR** gets its input in a somewhat unusual fashion, by querying DOS (by way of DOS function call $2F) to find out where the current DTA is, and assigning the address returned from DOS in ES : BX to a pointer. The DTA information is then accessed through that pointer.

It didn't have to be done that way, but I looked upon it as some guarantee that only the most current DTA would get converted (as encouragement to get information out of it and be done with the DTA format), and also as a demonstration of a DOS function call I might not otherwise be able to demonstrate. If you intend to keep **DTARec**s around and need to convert them regardless of whether or not they are set as the current DOS DTA, it's trivial to pass a **DTARec** as a value parameter.

DTAToDIR uses the **CalcDate** and **CalcTime** procedures from Chapter 6 to fill in the time and data stamp records in the **DIRRec** returned to the calling logic.

From Directory to String

Because directory information needs to be displayed to the user in many applications, it would be handy to have a further conversion between information as stored in a **DIRRec** record and a string easily displayable via **Write** or **Writeln**. Such a conversion function is provided by the string function **DIRToString**.

```
1          {->>>>DIRToString<<<<-------------------------------------------------}
2          {                                                                     }
3          { Filename : DIRSTRIN.SRC -- Last Modified 1/13/87                     }
4          {                                                                     }
5          { This routine returns a String80 value containing all the           }
6          { significant information from a directory record, formatted         }
```

(continued)

```
  7       { in a fashion similar to that used by the DOS DIR command      }
  8       { when it displays a file and its information.  A typical        }
  9       { string returned by DIRToString would look like this:          }
 10       {                                                               }
 11       {         DIRSTRIN.BAK 1697  01/07/87    3:04p                  }
 12       {                                                               }
 13       { Types DIRRec and String80 must be predefined.                 }
 14       {                                                               }
 15       {                                                               }
 16       {                                                               }
 17       {-------------------------------------------------------------}
 18
 19       FUNCTION DIRToString(InputDIR : DIRRec) : String80;
 20
 21       CONST
 22         Blanker = '
 23
 24       VAR
 25         Temp,WorkString : String80;
 26         DotPos : Integer;
 27
 28       BEGIN
 29         WITH InputDIR DO
 30           BEGIN
 31             Temp := '
 32             {If the entry has the directory attribute, format differently: }
 33             IF (Attrib AND $10) <> 0 THEN    { Bit 4 is the directory attribute }
 34               BEGIN
 35                 Insert(FileName,Temp,1);   { No extensions on subdirectory names }
 36                 Insert('<DIR>',Temp,14)    { Tell the world it's a subdirectory  }
 37               END
 38             ELSE
 39               {This compound statement separates the file from its extension  }
 40               { and converts the file size to a string.  Note that we did not }
 41               { insert a file size figure into Temp for subdirectory entries. }
 42               BEGIN
 43                 DotPos := Pos('.',FileName);
 44                 WorkString := Copy(FileName,1,DotPos-1) +
 45                   Copy(Blanker,1,9-DotPos) + '.' +
 46                   Copy(FileName,DotPos+1,Length(FileName)-DotPos);
 47                 Insert(WorkString,Temp,1);
 48                 Str(FileSize:7:0,WorkString);
 49                 Insert(WorkString,Temp,15)
 50               END;
 51             WITH DateStamp DO
 52               BEGIN
 53                 { This is what it takes to assemble three separate integer  }
 54                 { figures for month, day, and year into a string equivalent.}
 55                 IF Month < 10 THEN Insert('0',DateString,1);
```

(continued)

```
56                   IF Day < 10 THEN Insert('0',DateString,4);
57                   Insert(DateString,Temp,24);
58                END;
59             Insert(TimeStamp.TimeString,Temp,34); { Finally, insert the time }
60          END;
61       Delete(Temp,42,Length(Temp)-42);
62       DIRToString := Temp
63    END;
```

There's nothing especially subtle about **DIRToString**; it fills a string with information plucked from the **DIRRec** passed in parameter **InputDIR**. For a typical directory entry of a DOS file, the string returned by **DIRToString** looks like this:

```
DIRSTRIN.BAK    2623  01/13/87    7:53p
```

This string value returned by **DIRToString** is exactly 39 characters long, meaning that two such strings can be displayed side by side on an 80-column screen, with two spaces between them in the middle.

DIRToString will play a key role in two utility programs described later in this chapter, **Locate** and **Spacer**.

Search and Search Again

On the surface of it, you'd think that the simplest method possible for searching for a given file would simply be to attempt to open it. However, that ignores the possibility of using ambiguous filenames—that is, filenames containing "wild card" characters that can match one file or many files. These filenames are valid at the keyboard, and from within a program as well. For example, making use of ambiguous filenames would allow your program to identify every file on a disk with an extension of .PAS—by using the ambiguous filename *.PAS—and work only with those files.

There are two kinds of wild card characters: ? and *. The question mark character replaces one character in a filename, and no more; in other words, MODE?ERR.MSG would apply equally to MODE1ERR.MSG, MODE-2ERR.MSG, MODE3ERR.MSG, and so on. The asterisk means, "I match anything from here to the end." The "end" is either the dot character for the main portion of the filename, or the end of the filename proper for the filename extension. In other words, MODE*.MSG would match all of the three filenames mentioned earlier in this paragraph, while the familiar *.* matches anything at all.

DOS's mechanism for dealing with one file specification matching many files involves two separate DOS calls: FIND FIRST and FIND NEXT. It works like this: Assemble a *file spec* for the file or files you wish to locate. A file spec is the string containing a full file specifier, including the drive unit and pathname. For example, while LOCATE.PAS is a filename, its full file spec might be something like D:\TURBO\HACKS\LOCATE.PAS. Pass this file spec to FIND FIRST, and it will locate the first file matching that file spec if one exists, or return an error message if there is no match at all. If at least one is found, you then can call FIND NEXT repeatedly, and FIND NEXT will keep returning matching directory entries in the DTA until no more files match the file spec. Then an appropriate error code is returned in AX.

At first glance, it seems odd that two DOS calls would be required to do this. A single FIND call could both begin the search and keep searching until it found all directory entries matching the file spec passed to it. DOS's 2-call system is actually very efficient, since FIND FIRST does all the setting up of the file spec, and arranges some special information in the DTA to make the search possible. Once that setup has been done, it need not be done again, and if the DTA is not disturbed, FIND NEXT need only continue the search, and not bother setting up all the search machinery for each additional search on the same file spec.

7.6   Creating and Reading Volume Labels

Reading volume labels provides an interesting initial exercise in the use of the DOS FIND FIRST function call. Before we get into that, some discussion of volume labels and their role in PC DOS must come first.

Volume labels are a tip of the DOS hat to mainframe operating systems, which have long provided for the application of a unique machine-readable label to a storage volume, be it removable disk pack, fixed disk pack, or magnetic tape. Anyone can stick an adhesive label on a diskette, of course, but volume labels allow both the user and the application program to "read" the label on the diskette. That way, if the program directs the user to "Insert the ACCOUNTS diskette in drive A:," the program can immediately determine if the right diskette made it into the drive without having to poll the names of the files on the disk to make sure.

PC DOS first supported volume labels with V2.0, but the support in DOS 2.X is limited and crude. My recommendation is that you do *not* try to build volume label support into your applications unless they can be guaranteed to run only under DOS 3.X or higher.

For that reason, this particular section makes the same assumption—that the **CreateLabel** and **GetLabel** routines will only be run under DOS 3.X. I have not tested them under DOS 2.X and cannot guarantee that they will work under all circumstances for DOS 2.X.

A volume label is physically nothing more than an empty file (that is, a file with zero bytes in it) with the volume label attribute bit set to 1 (see Figure 7.1). All directory entry fields—aside from creation time and date, filename, and attribute byte—are zeroed out. DOS will only set attribute bit 3 (the volume label bit) on a file created in the root directory. By going beneath the level of DOS, it is possible to set the volume label bit on a file in a subdirectory, of course—but how DOS would deal with such a file, I couldn't say.

It's also possible to set the volume label bit on multiple files in the root directory, but only the one having the physically first directory entry will be treated as the real DOS volume label.

Reading and creating volume labels is easy. Changing or deleting them is *not*. Once a directory entry has had its volume label bit raised to 1, none of the familiar DOS function calls will touch it, and only FIND FIRST will be able to detect its presence, and then only if it's the *first* directory entry with the bit set. Whether this is a bug due to Microsoft's forgetfulness or a feature supporting media security is unclear; that depends on how much you love Microsoft *or* how paranoid you are. I lean toward the former view; it seems silly to restrict the modification of volume labels so severely when *creating* them is so simple.

So once again, care must be counseled. Before you create a volume label for a disk volume, make triple sure the label you're creating is the label you want. The only safe recourse to an undesired label is to reformat the disk and recreate the label in the process.

There have been, of course, published methods of deleting and changing volume labels by locating the directory sectors on the disk and physically altering the sectors to change the directory entry tagged as the volume label. This operates beneath the level at which DOS wants you to work, and there's more than just "sticking to the rules" at stake here. The number of disk storage devices has grown explosively in the last few years, and some of them (the Bernoulli Box comes to mind) are significantly different from either floppy disks or traditional hard disks. I have not yet seen any truly reliable way of determining where the directory physically begins on the disk for any arbitrary disk type, and, when you're talking about writing to sectors involving the disk directory or FAT, *you do not want to get it wrong*. If your application tries to alter the volume label on a customer's 200MB odd-format Winchester disk drive and scrambles it in the process, you will, at the very least, lose the customer and possibly hear from his lawyers as well, since the likelihood of a disk device being fully backed up at all times varies inversely with its capacity.

For this reason, the two volume label routines presented here either read or create a volume label, but do not alter or delete volume labels that already exist. My hunch is that future releases of DOS will correct this oversight, since history has shown that volume label support has grown better as DOS has evolved. Furthermore, when DOS begins to support multitasking and multiple users, it must get very hard-nosed about keeping applications from snooping critical DOS resources (such as the FAT and disk directories) from under the table. The ability to alter volume labels is not there now, but I don't think you'll have to wait very long for it.

Reading a Volume Label

Since a DOS volume label is the first file in the root directory of a volume with bit 3 of the attribute byte set, the FIND FIRST function call is an intuitive means of reading a volume label. It is, in fact, the only means short of directly reading the directory sectors on the disk. The function **GetLabel** uses FIND FIRST to return the DOS volume label in the DTA.

```
1       {->>>>GetLabel<<<<-------------------------------------------------}
2       {                                                                  }
3       { Filename : GETLABEL.SRC -- Last Modified 1/9/87                   }
4       {                                                                  }
5       { This function returns a String80 value that is the volume        }
6       { label of the drive passed in DriveSpec.  No check is made        }
7       { as to the validity of the character in DriveSpec; if there       }
8       { is no corresponding drive the system may hang or return an       }
9       { error depending on the specifics.  If no volume label exists }
10      { for the specified volume, a null string (zero length) will       }
11      { be returned and parameter LabelFound will be set to FALSE.       }
12      {                                                                  }
13      { Types DTARec and String80 must be predefined.                    }
14      {                                                                  }
15      {                                                                  }
16      {                                                                  }
17      {------------------------------------------------------------------}
18
19
20      FUNCTION GetLabel(DriveSpec : Char; VAR LabelFound : Boolean) : String80;
21
22      TYPE
23        Reg      = RECORD
24                     CASE Boolean OF
25                       False : (Word : Integer);
26                       True  : (LoByte,HiByte : Byte)
27                     END;
28
```

(continued)

```pascal
29              Regpack = RECORD
30                          AX,BX,CX,DX,BP,SI,DI,DS,ES,Flags : Reg
31                        END;
32
33         VAR
34           I          : Integer;
35           SearchSpec : String80;
36           Temp       : String80;
37           Regs       : RegPack;
38           ASCIIZ     : ARRAY[1..81] OF Char;
39           CurrentDTA : DTARec;
40
41         BEGIN
42           { Start by setting the DOS DTA to CurrentDTA: }
43           WITH Regs DO
44             BEGIN
45               DS.Word := Seg(CurrentDTA);
46               DX.Word := Ofs(CurrentDTA);
47               AX.Word := $1A00
48             END;
49           MSDOS(Regs);
50
51           SearchSpec :=  DriveSpec + ':\*.*' + Chr(0);
52           Move(SearchSpec[1],ASCIIZ,Sizeof(SearchSpec));
53           WITH Regs DO
54             BEGIN
55               AX.Word := $4E00;           { $4E = Find First }
56               DS.Word := Seg(ASCIIZ);     { Put address of ASCIIZ }
57               DX.Word := Ofs(ASCIIZ);     { in DS : DX }
58               CX.LoByte := $08;           { Set Volume Label attribute }
59             END;
60           MSDOS(Regs);                    { Make FIND FIRST DOS call... }
61
62           Temp := '';                     { Default to null string }
63           IF (Regs.AX.Word = 2) OR (Regs.AX.Word = 18) THEN  { Label not found }
64             LabelFound := False
65           ELSE
66             BEGIN
67               LabelFound := True;
68               I := 1;                      { Move label from ASCIIZ to Pascal string }
69               WHILE CurrentDTA.FileName[I] <> Chr(0) DO
70                 BEGIN
71                   Temp[I] := CurrentDTA.FileName[I];
72                   I := Succ(I)
73                 END;
74               Temp[0] := Chr(I-1);        { Set volume label length byte }
75               { If a dot exists in the DTA file name, get rid of it: }
76               IF Pos('.',Temp) > 0 THEN Delete(Temp,Pos('.',Temp),1);
77             END;
78           GetLabel := Temp;               { Assign function return value }
79         END;
```

The first step in using FIND FIRST is to establish a DTA for DOS. In the previous section, we used DOS function call $2F to query DOS as to the location of the current DTA, creating a pointer from the segment and offset values DOS passed back to us in machine registers. The reverse process is used here: DOS function call $1A sets the DTA to an address passed in two registers, the segment portion in DS and the offset portion in DX. Once call $1A is executed, DOS will place directory information at the address we gave it. In the case of **GetLabel**, this address is the address of **CurrentDTA**, a record of type **DTARec** declared as a local variable within **GetLabel**. What we have done, in a sense, is pass **CurrentDTA** to DOS as a VAR parameter, since, with a VAR parameter, all that is actually passed to a subprogram is the address of the parameter, not the parameter itself.

With the DTA established, the next step is to make the FIND FIRST call itself. FIND FIRST requires a *search spec*, which is the full pathname of the file to be searched for, including the drive specifier. In this case, the filename we want to locate is the familiar *.*, meaning any filename at all. Since we don't know what the volume label is, we need to use a completely ambiguous filename. In other applications, we might want to find a file with a particular name, perhaps to see if it exists on the specified volume. In that case, the filename would be part of the search spec, rather than *.*.

The search spec is constructed in a string variable by concatenating the drive specifier and the pathname *.*, meaning any filename in the root directory. In other applications, the search spec could include a path down through several levels of subdirectories to a specific file or *.* within a specific subdirectory. An ASCII NUL character (character 0) is appended to the end of the search spec. This is for the sake of DOS, which is too stupid to understand real Pascal strings, and must scan a string until it finds a NUL character to determine where the string ends. The **Move** statement physically moves the string information from the string **SearchSpec** into an array of characters called **AS-CIIZ**. Strictly speaking, this move is unnecessary. You could as well have passed DOS the address of **SearchSpec[1]** and skipped the move, since all we really need to do is avoid passing DOS the length byte (element 0) of **Search-Spec**. I included the move to make apparent the need of DOS for an ASCIIZ string rather than a Pascal string.

The address of **ASCIIZ** is passed to DOS in registers DS and DX, with the segment in DS. Our program's DS value, by which all global variables are accessed, is not destroyed in the process; the Turbo Pascal runtime pushes the current value of DS on the stack before making the DOS call, and restores it when the DOS call has been accomplished.

The statement that sets this particular FIND FIRST call apart from a search for an ordinary file is:

```
CX.LoByte := $08;
```

FIND FIRST expects an attribute byte passed to it in register CL. The $08 value is a byte with only the volume label attribute bit (bit 3) set. This is how we direct FIND FIRST to locate a volume label directory entry and nothing else.

This exclusive treatment of the volume label attribute bit is a special case. The other attribute bits are treated very differently by FIND FIRST, as I will explain in the next section when we start looking for ordinary files.

With the search spec and attribute bit set into the appropriate registers, DOS function call $4E is made. When DOS returns, two situations are possible: Either an error message comes back in register AX, or the DTA has been filled with a directory entry containing the DOS volume label on the specified volume.

DOS documentation states that the error message will be either 2 (File not found) or 18 (No more files to be found), but in practice I have never seen anything but error 18 returned under DOS 3.1. **GetLabel** does not return an error code to the calling logic; if the volume label was not found, VAR parameter **LabelFound** will return a value of **FALSE**.

One peculiarity about volume labels is that, although they are actually filenames, DOS displays them without splitting them into the traditional filename/file extension duo, divided by a period character. So when you retrieve a volume label from a DTA, you need to remove the period character *if* the volume label is longer than eight characters. In other words, the volume label CALIBAN will be found in the DTA as CALIBAN, but the longer volume label WIDDERSHINS will be found as WIDDERSH.INS. One **Delete** statement does the job.

Creating a Volume Label

If a disk volume does not already have a label, you can create one with a single DOS function call. DOS function call $3C (CREATE) is used to create a file anywhere on a disk, given its full file spec including path. Function $3C does not actually write any information into the file. It simply creates a directory entry and fills out the time and date stamps, name, and attribute byte. The resulting file has zero length, and occupies no space on the disk other than the space taken by the directory entry. Furthermore, if the attribute byte passed to function $3C contains bit 3 set to 1, the created file will become the volume's label (that is, of course, assuming that the volume in question doesn't already have a label).

```
1          {->>>>CreateLabel<<<<----------------------------------------}
2          {                                                            }
3          { Filename : CREATLBL.SRC -- Last Modified 1/12/87           }
4          {                                                            }
5          { This procedure creates a new volume label on the unlabeled }
```

(continued)

```
 6         { DOS volume passed in DriveSpec.  No check is made          }
 7         { as to the validity of the character in DriveSpec; if there  }
 8         { is no corresponding drive the system may hang or return an  }
 9         { error depending on the specifics.  If a volume label already }
10         { exists on the specified volume, CreatedLabel will return     }
11         { FALSE with an ErrorReturn value of 0.  This is not really an }
12         { error condition, but DOS makes no provision for altering a   }
13         { volume label that already exists, so at best we go home with }
14         { our tail between our legs.  If some sort of true error        }
15         { occurs, the DOS error code will be returned in ErrorReturn,  }
16         { and CreatedLabel will be set to FALSE.  If CreatedLabel       }
17         { comes back TRUE, the label was in fact created.              }
18         {                                                             }
19         { Function GetLabel must be predefined.                       }
20         { Types DTARec and String80 must be predefined.               }
21         {                                                             }
22         {                                                             }
23         {                                                             }
24         {-------------------------------------------------------------}
25
26         PROCEDURE CreateLabel(DriveSpec         : Char;
27                               NewLabel          : String80;
28                               VAR CreatedLabel  : Boolean;
29                               VAR ErrorReturn   : Integer;
30                               ShowError         : Boolean);
31
32         TYPE
33           Reg      = RECORD
34                        CASE Boolean OF
35                          False : (Word : Integer);
36                          True  : (LoByte,HiByte : Byte)
37                      END;
38
39           Regpack = RECORD
40                       AX,BX,CX,DX,BP,SI,DI,DS,ES,Flags : Reg
41                     END;
42
43           ErrorCode = 0..18;    { DOS function call error codes }
44
45         VAR
46           I             : Integer;
47           SearchSpec    : String80;
48           FileSpec      : String80;
49           CurrentLabel  : String80;
50           Regs          : RegPack;
51           ASCIIZ        : ARRAY[1..81] OF Char;
52           CurrentDTA    : DTARec;
53           Error         : ErrorCode;
54           FoundLabel    : Boolean;
55
```

(continued)

```
56        BEGIN
57          CurrentLabel := GetLabel(DriveSpec,FoundLabel);
58          IF NOT FoundLabel THEN { No label exists yet }
59            BEGIN
60              FileSpec := DriveSpec + ':\' + NewLabel + Chr(0);
61              Move(FileSpec[1],ASCIIZ,Sizeof(FileSpec));
62
63              WITH Regs DO
64                BEGIN
65                  AX.HiByte := $3C;            { $3C = Create File }
66                  DS.Word := Seg(ASCIIZ);      { Put address of ASCIIZ }
67                  DX.Word := Ofs(ASCIIZ);      { in DS : DX }
68                  CX.LoByte := $08;            { Set Volume Label attribute }
69                END;
70              MSDOS(Regs);                     { Make CHMOD DOS call }
71
72              { If the Carry Flag is found to be set, it's an error: }
73              IF (Regs.Flags.Word AND $01) = $01 THEN
74                BEGIN
75                  CreatedLabel := False;       { No luck }
76                  ErrorReturn := Regs.AX.Word; { Return error code as parameter }
77                  Error := ErrorReturn;        { Make an ordinal of the error code }
78                  IF ShowError THEN
79                    CASE Error OF
80                      2 : Writeln('Label file not found.');
81                      3 : Writeln('Bad path error -- possible disk failure.');
82                      5 : Writeln('Access to label denied -- Disk write protected?');
83                      ELSE Writeln('Unexpected DOS error ',Error,' on label write.')
84                    END; { CASE }
85                END
86              ELSE CreatedLabel := True   { No error - created the label }
87            END
88          ELSE    { Label already exists; can't re-create it... }
89            BEGIN
90              CreatedLabel := False;
91              ErrorReturn := 0;
92            END
93        END;
```

DOS function call $3C is used to create a volume label in the procedure
CreateLabel. To determine if a label already exists on the requested volume,
CreateLabel calls **GetLabel**. If a label already exists, the Boolean variable
CreatedLabel is returned to the calling logic set to **FALSE**. If no label is found,
CreateLabel sets up function call $3C with $08 in CL—again, $08 is the nu-
meric value of the attribute byte with bit 3, the volume label bit, set to 1.

    CreateLabel gives you the option of returning an error code without any
visible display of an error message, or actually displaying an error message on
the console for the user.

Ordinarily, you wouldn't need to use DOS function $3C to create a file, since you can create a zero-length file simply by using **Assign** to assign a file variable to a pathname, and **Rewrite** to write the directory entry to the disk. **Assign** and **Rewrite** do not, however, give you access to the attribute byte, which is why function $3C must be used to create a volume label.

7.7   Searching for Groups of Files

FIND FIRST will locate the first file matching a given file spec. DOS has a streamlined method to take it from there: Once FIND FIRST has set up the necessary criteria, the FIND NEXT function call will repeatedly search the specified path until no more files are found that match the file spec specified to FIND FIRST.

Calling FIND NEXT is simplicity itself: Set the function number in register AH and call **MSDOS**. When control returns to your Turbo Pascal program, either a found directory entry will be in the current DTA, or an error code will be in AX, indicating that no more files are to be found on that path.

The example program I've written to illustrate the use of FIND FIRST and FIND NEXT is a very useful one, now that 20- and 30-megabyte hard disks are common and 80-megabyte hard disks are not out of reach. If it hasn't already, a situation like this will soon arise: Somewhere on your hard disk you suspect there is a public domain utility program called FASTVID.COM—or was it FASTV.COM? Or FASTVID.EXE? Or were you imagining it all along? With 500 files scattered across 40 nested subdirectories, it could take quite a bit of searching to locate the mystery utility.

Or you could let the computer do what it does best and find it for you. This is the purpose of the program **Locate** which I will be describing shortly. **Locate** searches any directory and all its child subdirectories for files that match a given file specification, including wild cards. (If no directory is given, **Locate** will search the entire disk.)

Locate is a more difficult program than most to understand because it operates *recursively*. Some people just have a hard time dealing with recursion, and if you're one of those, **Locate** will have that uncomfortable feeling of black magic about it. (I recommend picking up my book *Complete Turbo Pascal* and boning up on it if recursion isn't cleanly in your grasp.)

Recursive Tree Search

You may have heard the term "tree-structured directories" in reference to PC DOS V2.X subdirectory structures, particularly when there are several layers of nested subdirectories involved. The "tree" metaphor stems from the fact that one "root" directory can have any number of "branch" directories, each of which can have more "branch" directories, and so on. The directory structure spreads out from one single root directory into a structure reminiscent of a tree.

Figure 7.2 is a simplified diagram of a system of nested subdirectories. The top directory is the root, with each vertical partition representing one directory entry. Directory entries are either files or subdirectories. Each subdirectory entry in a directory points to its own subdirectory proper, and subdirectories may be nested in this fashion as deeply as desired.

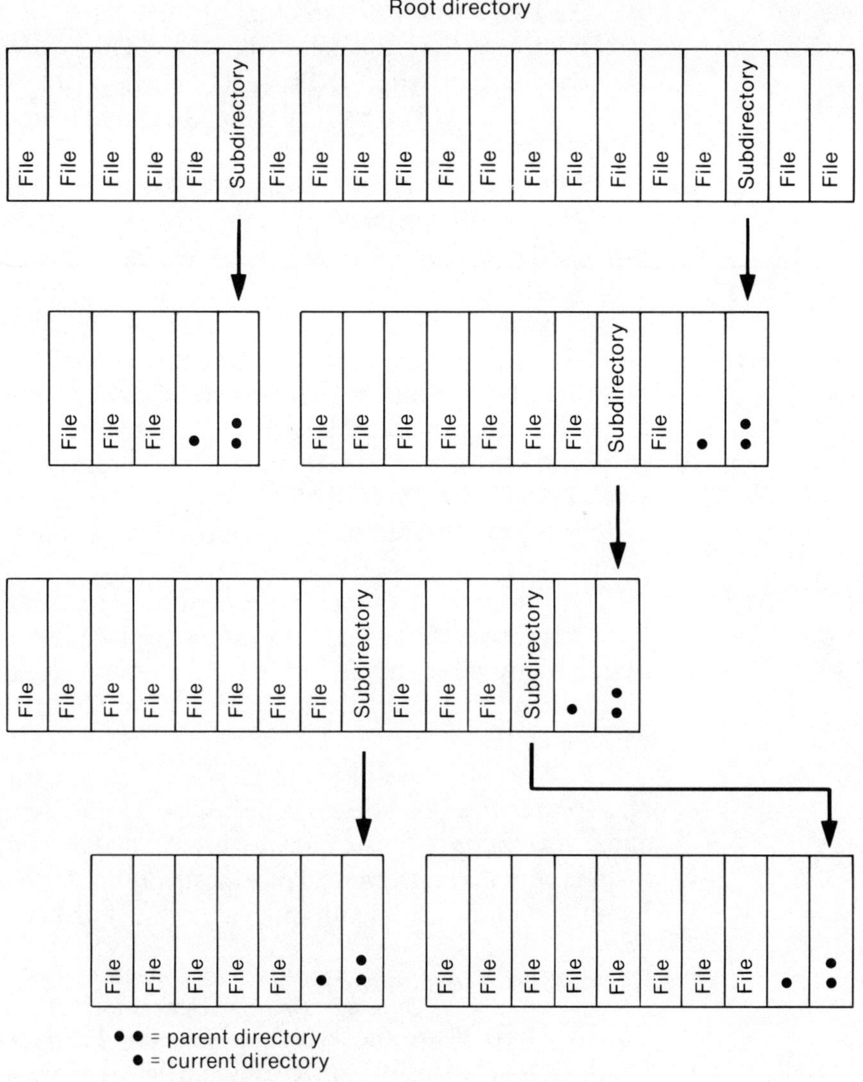

Figure 7.2 **Tree-structured directories**

The single-dot and double-dot symbols should be familiar from DIR listings of subdirectories. The single dot represents the current directory, and the double dot the parent directory. Why directory entries are required for the current and parent directories is complex and has to do with the way DOS keeps track of disk storage. In a sense, a tree-structured directory is a doubly linked list of directories, but if that makes no sense to you, forget it; it is not germane to the current discussion. Note that the root directory has entries for neither parent directory (obviously) nor for itself; this is one way in which the root directory is unique and distinct from subdirectories.

Searching a tree structure like this *recursively* can best be explained by following the search path on a diagram (refer to Figure 7.3). For the sake of discussion, imagine a Pascal procedure named **SearchDirectory**. If you pass it a directory specifier and a filename, it will search that directory and any of its child directories for anything matching that filename, and print out the name and full path of any file it finds.

The search begins at the root directory. **SearchDirectory** is called, given the root directory specifier (the solo backslash "\") as the directory to search. Directory entries are examined one by one, to see if the filenames match the search spec. This prosaic process continues until **SearchDirectory** encounters a subdirectory entry; let's call it subdirectory **TURBO**. **TURBO** needs to be searched, too. This is where recursion happens.

SearchDirectory calls itself. What happens here is that the current "state" of **SearchDirectory** is pushed onto the stack, and an entirely new copy of **SearchDirectory**'s local variables and parameters is created. This is called an "instantiation" of **SearchDirectory**. The new "copy" of **SearchDirectory** is passed the root directory specifier "\" *plus* the name of the new subdirectory, **TURBO**. It then begins searching directory **TURBO** for file matches.

As it did with the root directory, **SearchDirectory** examines the directory entries in **TURBO** one by one for matches and displays any that it finds. Along the way it discovers another subdirectory, a child directory to **TURBO** called **HACKS**. **HACKS** needs to be searched, just as any other directory does. So **SearchDirectory** calls itself once again.

This time, the parent directory specifier **TURBO** is prefixed to **HACKS** (with a backslash separator) making the new directory specifier **TURBO** **HACKS**. A third instantiation of **SearchDirectory** is created after the second has been safely pushed onto the stack. Yet again, directory entries are examined one by one for file matches, keeping an eye out for more subdirectories.

HACKS, however, has no subdirectories. When the scan of **HACKS** is completed, the third instantiation of **SearchDirectory** terminates. As with any Pascal subprogram that finishes execution, it returns control to the calling logic. In this case, the calling logic was the second instantiation of **SearchDirectory**. The second instantiation is popped from the stack and begins run-

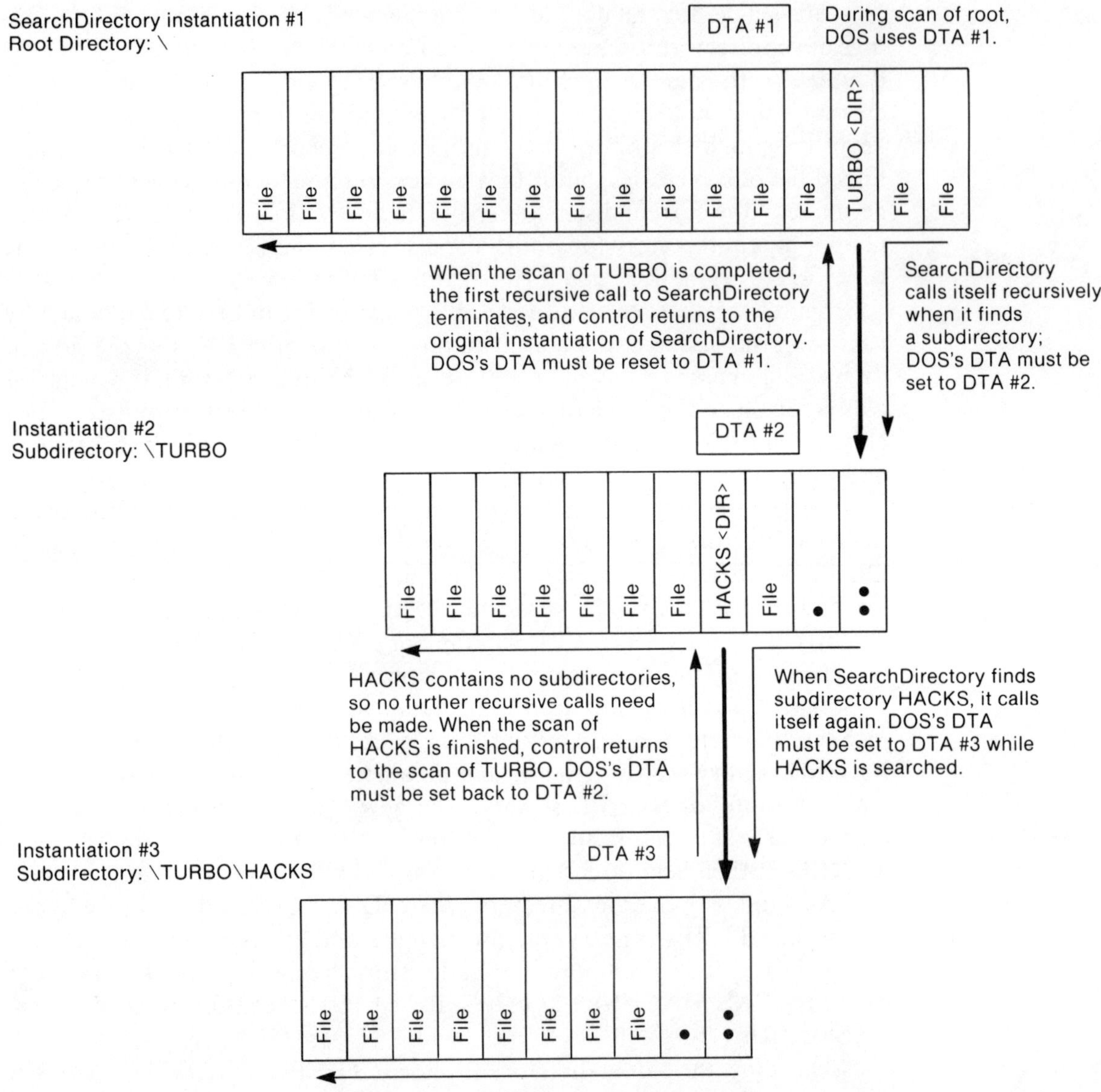

Figure 7.3 Recursive directory search

ning again, checking directory entries in **\TURBO** for file matches as though nothing had interrupted it.

Subdirectory **\TURBO**, as it happens, has no more subdirectories. If it had, they would have been searched in the same way **HACKS** was searched, via another recursive call to **SearchDirectory**. Thus, the rest of **\TURBO** is searched for matching files. Eventually the search is completed. The second instantiation of **SearchDirectory** terminates, and returns control to the first instantiation—the one searching the root directory. The first instantiation of **SearchDirectory** is popped off the stack, and the search of the root directory continues. Once the scan of the root is completed, the original instantiation of **SearchDirectory** terminates, having searched the entire disk for files matching the given file spec.

From ten steps back, this is all that happens. There is one somewhat jarring detail that has to be tended to, however: the current DTA.

The actual search mechanism used by **SearchDirectory** is DOS's FIND FIRST and FIND NEXT, which require the use of the DOS DTA. FIND NEXT only works over a single directory, and each directory being searched needs its own exclusive use of a DTA. From a Pascal perspective, this is no problem; Pascal creates a new **DTARec** variable for each new instantiation of **SearchDirectory**. However, *DOS doesn't "know" that it must switch to the new instantiation's* **DTARec**. DOS, in a sense, isn't in on the recursion process, which is handled entirely by the Turbo Pascal runtime code.

Therefore, each time a call to **SearchDirectory** is made, DOS must be told which DTA to use. Furthermore, each time control returns to **SearchDirectory** from a recursive call to itself, DOS must be told *again* which DTA to use, since the recursive call to **SearchDirectory** had its *own* DTA and told DOS to use it. DOS must be informed both coming and going, as it were.

It's enough to make your head spin. The process is best followed along on a diagram; again, trace through the three instantiations of **SearchDirectory** in Figure 7.3. Each directory needs its own DTA for the search process, and the three DTA's are numbered from one to three. DTA #1 is used during the search of the root directory. When the first recursive call to **SearchDirectory** is made, an explicit call to DOS function $1A is made, changing the current DTA (that is, the one DOS will use) to DTA #2. DTA #2 remains the current DTA as long as the second instantiation of **SearchDirectory** has control. But when the third instantiation is created to search the third directory **TURBO\\HACKS**, the current DTA must be changed yet again, to DTA #3. DTA #3 remains the current DTA as long as subdirectory **TURBO\\HACKS** is being searched.

TURBO\\HACKS is the bottom of the tree; from that point we start going home, and the whole process of changing DTA's as we wove our way downward through the directory tree must be undone as we move back upward again. The first change happens as we leave the third instantiation behind. DTA #3 was in force during the search of **TURBO\\HACKS**; now we are returning to the search of **TURBO**, and we need to go back to DTA #2. (DTA #2 was waiting on the stack, safe and sound, still containing setup information from the FIND FIRST call that began the search of **TURBO**.) When the search of **TURBO** is finished, DTA #2's job is done. Control returns to the first instantiation of **SearchDirectory** to finish out the search of the root directory, and the current DTA must be changed again from DTA #2 to DTA #1, again on the stack, waiting to go back to work and finish the FIND NEXT sequence that inspects directory entries one by one.

Each time we need to change from one DTA to another, a call must be made to DOS function $1A. In program **Locate**, this is done in a small local procedure called **SetDTA**.

Program Locate

With all of that convolution safely beneath your belt, take a long, close look at the actual code for the program **Locate**. The entirety of **Locate** is only a frame for procedure **SearchDirectory**, which does the only real work in **Locate**. The search process was built into a procedure so that it could call itself; programs in Pascal cannot call themselves recursively.

```
 1        {--------------------------------------------------------------------}
 2        {                              LOCATE                                 }
 3        {                                                                    }
 4        {            Disk file tree-search search utility                    }
 5        {                                                                    }
 6        {                                    by Jeff Duntemann                }
 7        {                                    Turbo Pascal V3.01A              }
 8        {                                    Last update 1/14/87              }
 9        {                                                                    }
10        { This utility searches a tree of directories (from the root   }
11        { or from any child directory of the root) for a given file    }
12        { spec, either unique or ambiguous.  It provides a good        }
13        { example of the use of the DOS 2.X/3.X FIND FIRST/NEXT        }
14        { function calls.  See the main program block for instructions }
15        { on its use.                                                  }
16        {                                                                    }
17        {                                                                    }
18        {                                                                    }
19        {--------------------------------------------------------------------}
20
21        {$P512}   { This allows the output to be redirected by DOS;    }
22                  { very handy for keeping "snapshots" of a big search. }
23
24        PROGRAM Locate;
25
26        TYPE
27          String80 = String[80];
28          String15 = String[15];
29
30
31        {$I REGPACK.DEF}
32        {$I TIMEREC.DEF}
```

(continued)

```
33          {$I DATEREC.DEF}
34          {$I DIRREC.DEF}
35          {$I DTAREC.DEF}
36
37
38          VAR
39            I,J               : Integer;
40            SearchSpec        : String80;
41            InitialDirectory  : String80;
42
43
44          {$I DAYOWEEK.SRC}    { FUNCTION DateToDayOfWeek }
45          {$I CALCDATE.SRC}    { PROCEDURE CalcDate }
46          {$I CALCTIME.SRC}    { PROCEDURE CalcTime }
47          {$I DIRSTRIN.SRC}    { FUNCTION DIRToString }
48          {$I DTATODIR.SRC}    { PROCEDURE DTAToDIR }
49
50
51          {->>>>SearchDirectory<<<<--------------------------------------}
52          {                                                              }
53          { This is the real meat of program LOCATE.  The machinery      }
54          { for using FIND FIRST and FIND NEXT are placed in a procedure }
55          { so that it may be recursively called.  Recursion is used     }
56          { because it is the most elegant way to search a tree, which   }
57          { is really all we're doing here.  All the messiness (and it   }
58          { IS messy!) exists to cater to DOS's peculiarities.           }
59          {                                                              }
60          { For example, note that each recursive instantiation of       }
61          { SearchDirectory needs its own DTA.  No problem--one is       }
62          { created on the stack each time SearchDirectory is called.    }
63          { BUT--DOS is not a party to the recursion, so the DTA address }
64          { must be set both before AND after the recursive call, so     }
65          { that once control comes BACK to an instance of              }
66          { SearchDirectory that has been left via recursion, DOS can    }
67          { "come back" to the temporarily dormant DTA, which may still  }
68          { contain information necessary to execute a FIND NEXT call.    }
69          {                                                              }
70          { Much of the rest of the fooling around involves formatting   }
71          { the search strings correctly for passing to the next        }
72          { instantiation of SearchDirectory.                           }
73          {                                                              }
74          { It's not documented, but I have found that DOS returns error }
75          { code 3 (Bad Path) on a file FIND when the path includes a    }
76          { nonexistant directory name.  Error code 2, on the other     }
77          { hand, while documented, never seems to come up at all.       }
78          {--------------------------------------------------------------}
79
80
81          PROCEDURE SearchDirectory(Directory,SearchSpec : String80);
```

(continued)

```
 82

 83        VAR
 84          ASCIIZ          : ARRAY[1..81] OF Char;
 85          NextDirectory   : String80;
 86          TempDirectory   : String80;
 87          CurrentDTA      : DTARec;
 88          CurrentDIR      : DIRRec;
 89          Regs            : RegPack;

 90

 91

 92        {>>>>DisplayData<<<<}
 93        { Displays file data and full path for the passed file }

 94

 95        PROCEDURE DisplayData(Directory : String80; CurrentDIR : DIRRec);

 96

 97        VAR
 98          Temp : String80;

 99

100        BEGIN
101          Temp := DIRToString(CurrentDIR);
102          Delete(Temp,1,13);
103          Write(Temp,Directory);
104          IF Directory <> '\' THEN Write('\');
105          Writeln(CurrentDIR.FileName);
106        END;

107

108

109        {>>>>SetDTA<<<<}
110        { Sets the DTA address to the DTARec CurrentDTA }

111

112        PROCEDURE SetDTA;
113

114        BEGIN
115          WITH Regs DO
116            BEGIN
117              DS.Word := Seg(CurrentDTA);   { DTA address is passed in }
118              DX.Word := Ofs(CurrentDTA);   { DS : DX }
119              AX.Word := $1A00
120            END;
121          MSDOS(Regs);
122        END;

123

124

125

126        BEGIN
127          SetDTA;     { Set the Disk Transfer Area for this invocation }

128

129          { First we look for any subdirectories.  If any are found, }
130          { we make a recursive call and search 'em too: }
```

(continued)

```
131
132       { Suppress unnecessary backslashes if we're searching the root: }
133       IF Directory = '\' THEN
134         TempDirectory := Directory + '*.*' + Chr(0)
135       ELSE
136         TempDirectory := Directory + '\*.*' + Chr(0);
137
138       { Turn the search string into ASCIIZ format: }
139       Move(TempDirectory[1],ASCIIZ,Sizeof(TempDirectory));
140
141       { Now make the FIND FIRST call for directories: }
142       WITH Regs DO
143         BEGIN
144           AX.Word := $4E00;            { $4E = Find First }
145           DS.Word := Seg(ASCIIZ);      { Put address of ASCIIZ }
146           DX.Word := Ofs(ASCIIZ);      { in DS:DX   (DOS saves our DS...) }
147           CX.LoByte := $10;            { Set file attribute for directory }
148         END;
149       MSDOS(Regs);                     { Make FIND FIRST DOS call... }
150
151       { Here's the tricky stuff.  If we get an indication that there is }
152       { at least one more subdirectory within the current directory,    }
153       { (indicated by lack of error codes 2 or 18) we must search it     }
154       { by making a recursive call to SearchDirectory.  We continue      }
155       { recursing and returning from the searched subdirectories until  }
156       { we get a code indicating none are left.   Much of this involves }
157       { formatting the string containing the directory path from Pascal }
158       { strings into that misbegotten C-freaks' beloved ASCIIZ format.  }
159       WHILE (Regs.AX.Word <> 2) AND (Regs.AX.Word <> 18) DO
160         BEGIN
161           IF  ((CurrentDTA.Attrib AND $10) = $10)    { If it's a directory }
162           AND (CurrentDTA.FileName[1] <> '.') THEN { and not '.' or '..' }
163             BEGIN
164               { Add a slash separating sections of the path if we're not }
165               { currently searching the root: }
166               IF Directory <> '\' THEN NextDirectory := Directory + '\'
167                 ELSE NextDirectory := Directory;
168
169               { This begins with the current directory name, and copies }
170               { the name of the found directory from the current DTA to }
171               { the end of the current directory string.  Then the new  }
172               { path is passed to the next recursive instantiation of   }
173               { SearchDirectory.  ASCIIZ conversion is done "there."     }
174               J := Length(NextDirectory);
175               I := 1;
176               WHILE CurrentDTA.FileName[I] <> Chr(0) DO
177                 BEGIN
178                   NextDirectory[J + I] := CurrentDTA.FileName[I];
179                   I := I + 1;
```

(continued)

```
180                    END;
181                    NextDirectory[0] := Chr(J + I-1);
182
183                    { Here's where we call "ourselves." }
184                    SearchDirectory(NextDirectory,SearchSpec);
185
186                    { Look back up to the beginning of this procedure and note }
187                    { that the first thing it does is set DOS to a new DTA      }
188                    { address.  DOS goes quietly, but remember that we have to }
189                    { explicitly reset DOS back to the "old" DTA we were using }
190                    { before the recursive call. }
191                    SetDTA;
192                  END;
193                Regs.AX.Word := $4F00;        { $4F = Find Next }
194                MSDOS(Regs);                   { Make FIND NEXT DOS call... }
195              END;
196
197        { Now we can search for files, once we've run out of directories.   }
198        { This is conceptually simpler, as recursion is not involved.       }
199        { We combine the path and the file spec into one string, convert    }
200        { it to ASCIIZ, and make the FIND FIRST call: }
201
202        { Suppress unnecessary slashes for root search: }
203        IF Directory <> '\' THEN
204           TempDirectory := Directory + '\' + SearchSpec + Chr(0)
205        ELSE TempDirectory := Directory + SearchSpec + Chr(0);
206
207        Move(TempDirectory[1],ASCIIZ,Sizeof(TempDirectory));
208        WITH Regs DO
209          BEGIN
210            AX.Word := $4E00;          { $4E = Find First }
211            DS.Word := Seg(ASCIIZ);    { Put address of ASCIIZ }
212            DX.Word := Ofs(ASCIIZ);    { in DS : DX }
213            CX.LoByte := $00;          { Set no file attributes }
214          END;
215        MSDOS(Regs);                   { Make FIND FIRST DOS call... }
216
217        IF Regs.AX.Word = 3 THEN       { Bad path error }
218           Writeln('Path not found; check spelling.')
219
220        { If we found something in the current directory matching the filespec, }
221        { format it nicely into a single string and display it: }
222        ELSE IF (Regs.AX.Word = 2) OR (Regs.AX.Word = 18) THEN
223           { Null; Directory is empty }
224        ELSE
225          BEGIN
226            DTAtoDIR(CurrentDIR);       { Convert first find to DIR format.. }
227            DisplayData(Directory,CurrentDIR);       { Show it pretty-like }
228
```

(continued)

```
229           IF Regs.AX.Word <> 18 THEN { More files are out there... }
230             REPEAT
231               Regs.AX.Word := $4F00; { Set up for FIND NEXT DOS call }
232               MSDOS(Regs);           { Make FIND NEXT DOS call }
233               IF Regs.AX.Word <> 18 THEN  { More entries exist }
234                 BEGIN
235                   DTAtoDIR(CurrentDIR); { Convert further finds to DIR format }
236                   DisplayData(Directory,CurrentDIR)        { and display 'em }
237                 END
238             UNTIL (Regs.AX.Word = 18) OR (Regs.AX.Word = 2)  { Ain't no more! }
239         END
240     END;
241
242
243     BEGIN
244       IF ParamCount = 0 THEN
245         BEGIN
246           Writeln('>>LOCATE<<  V1.01  By Jeff Duntemann');
247           Writeln('             From the book, TURBO PASCAL SOLUTIONS');
248           Writeln('             Scott, Foresman & Co. 1986');
249           Writeln('             ISBN ');
250           Writeln;
251           Writeln('This program searches for all files matching a given ');
252           Writeln('filespec on the current disk device, in any subdirectory.');
253           Writeln('Now that 32MB disks are getting cheap, we can pile up');
254           Writeln('great heaps of files and easily forget where we put things.');
255           Writeln('Given only the filespec, LOCATE prints out the FULL PATH');
256           Writeln('of any file matching that filespec.');
257           Writeln;
258           Writeln('CALLING SYNTAX:');
259           Writeln;
260           Writeln('LOCATE <filespec>');
261           Writeln;
262           Writeln('For example, to find out where your screen capture files');
263           Writeln('(ending in .CAP) are, you would enter:');
264           Writeln;
265           Writeln('LOCATE *.CAP');
266           Writeln;
267           Writeln('and LOCATE will show the pathname of any file ending in .CAP.');
268         END
269       ELSE
270         BEGIN
271           Writeln;
272           SearchSpec := ParamStr(1);
273           { A "naked" filespec searches the entire volume: }
274           IF Pos('\',SearchSpec) = 0 THEN
275             SearchDirectory('\',SearchSpec)
276           ELSE
277             BEGIN
```

(continued)

```
278                          { This rigamarole separates the filespec from the path: }
279                          I := Length(SearchSpec);
280                          WHILE SearchSpec[I] <> '\' DO I := Pred(I);
281                          InitialDirectory := Copy(SearchSpec,1,I-1);
282                          Delete(SearchSpec,1,I);
283                          SearchDirectory(InitialDirectory,SearchSpec);
284                      END;
285                  END
286              END.
```

The operation of **Locate** differs in small ways from the recursive search process described in connection with Figure 7.3. A single FIND FIRST/FIND NEXT operation cannot, in fact, inspect directories for both subdirectory and file entries. To find all subdirectories, we have to use a search spec of *.*, due to the way DOS handles attribute bits during file searches (more on this below); to find a specific file or group of files, we need a search spec naming that file or group. Obviously, this means we must search first for directories and then, once all of a directory's child directories have been searched, inspect the files.

So **SearchDirectory** searches for subdirectories first. Notice that the first thing done by **SearchDirectory** is to call **SetDTA**, which informs DOS that the variable **CurrentDTA** is to be used as its DTA for all file operations. **CurrentDTA** is local to **SearchDirectory**. This will become important when we get to the recursive call.

To make the FIND FIRST call in its search for directories, **SearchDirectory** must assemble a search spec. For directories, this is nothing more than the current path passed to **SearchDirectory** in parameter **Directory** plus the totally ambiguous file specifier, *.*. The search spec is moved into an ASCIIZ variable, and the full address of the ASCIIZ variable is loaded into registers DS and DX. Note the $10 value loaded into CL. This is an attribute byte with the subdirectory flag set to 1. The idea is that we are searching for any directory entry that has this bit set to 1.

We did something like this in searching for volume labels, by using FIND FIRST with CL set to $08, which is the volume label flag set to 1. Unfortunately, DOS is inconsistent here. Executing FIND FIRST with CL set to $08 finds *only* the first directory entry with bit 3 of the attribute byte set to 1. Executing FIND FIRST with bit 4 (subdirectory) set to 1 will find a subdirectory entry, but it will also find any ordinary file as well. A search for directory entries with the volume label bit set is *exclusive*, in that it finds *only* volume label entries. A search for subdirectory entries is *inclusive* because it finds ordinary file entries *and* subdirectory entries.

This means we have to test any directory entry returned from a FIND FIRST or FIND NEXT in our search for subdirectories to make sure the returned entry is not just an ordinary file. This is done by masking out the subdirectory bit in the attribute byte and testing it:

```
IF (CurrentDTA.Attrib AND $10) = $10
```

The Boolean expression here will return true only if the directory entry in **CurrentDTA** is a subdirectory entry.

Yet (as life is wont), there is another catch. All subdirectories (but *not* the root directory) contain two additional directory entries that are not really subdirectories. You've seen these on DOS DIR displays: "." (current directory) and ".." (parent directory). Both these directory entries have bit 4 set to 1, so our search will find them. They are not part of **SearchDirectory**'s search strategy, however. We are already searching the current directory, so making a recursive call to search "." is meaningless. And due to the way **SearchDirectory** operates, we have already searched the parent directory by the time we are searching any child directory, so searching ".." is redundant.

This is why we must also discriminate against "." and ".." in testing for subdirectory entries. Therefore, if the following Boolean expression turns up a value of **TRUE**, we know we have a subdirectory in hand:

```
IF ((CurrentDTA.Attrib AND $10) = $10
AND (CurrentDTA.FileName[1] <> '.') THEN
```

This test is made within a **WHILE** loop that inherits the initialized **DTA** from FIND FIRST and makes FIND NEXT calls continuously until an error message indicates no more files are to be found.

Once we know we have a subdirectory entry in the DTA, we have to search it. The only tricky part to making the recursive call is passing the correct directory path to the next instantiation of **SearchDirectory**. A string variable, **NextDirectory**, is provided to hold the string carrying the directory path to be searched by the recursive call. **NextDirectory** is loaded with the path of the directory currently being searched. Then, after a backslash acting as a separator, the name of the "found" directory (in **CurrentDTA**) needs to be appended to **NextDirectory**. This needs to be done character by character, rather than by Turbo Pascal's string functions, because the **FileName** field of the DTA is not a Pascal string but an array of characters.

Generating the new path involves copying the name of the subdirectory out of the DTA and appending it to the end of the directory path we are currently searching. A backslash needs to be added as a separator—unless we're still searching the root directory, whose path *is* a backslash.

Once the new path has been created in string variable **NextDirectory**, we're ready to make the recursive call. The search spec in **SearchSpec** (that is, the filename or ambiguous filename we're searching for) is unchanged, and the directory path in **NextDirectory** reflects the name of the subdirectory we found in executing FIND FIRST and FIND NEXT.

The only unusual thing about this recursive call is the need to drag DOS along, by setting the DTA both at the beginning of each instantiation of **SearchDirectory** and also immediately upon return *from* any recursive call to **SearchDirectory**. If **SearchDirectory** did not have to be called recursively (in other words, if all we had were "flat" directories as in DOS 1.X), *neither* of **SearchDirectory**'s calls to DOS function $1A (Set DTA Address) would be necessary; we could simply set the DTA address when the program began running and forget about it.

But we can't. While being searched, each directory demands exclusive use of a DTA. Each time **SearchDirectory** is instantiated, a local variable called **CurrentDTA** is allocated on the stack. **CurrentDTA** is meant to function as the DOS DTA for as long as its instantiation of **SearchDirectory** has control. When an instantiation of **SearchDirectory** takes control, it must set the address of the DOS DTA to its own copy of **CurrentDTA**. When it terminates and returns control to the prior instantiation of **SearchDirectory**, *that* instantiation must *again* set the address of the DOS DTA to its own copy of **CurrentDTA**. Hence the need for two calls to procedure **SetDTA**—once when an instantiation of **SearchDirectory** is entered for the first time, and again when it is *re-entered* after passing control recursively to another instantiation of **SearchDirectory**.

The first scan of a directory takes action only on subdirectories; files are ignored. Once a given scan determines that no further subdirectories exist within the current directory, a second scan is begun, this time a search for the file or files specified in string variable **SearchSpec**.

As with the search for directories, the current directory string must be combined with the search spec to produce the full pathname of the file or files to be searched for. In setting up FIND FIRST to look for subdirectories, we used a search spec of *.*. This won't do here—**SearchSpec** contains the very filename we're trying to match. This string is loaded into an ASCIIZ string as a courtesy to the operating system, and the address of the ASCIIZ string is loaded into DS and DX.

The attribute byte is set to $00 for this search; in other words, no attribute bits are set. An attribute of $00 causes FIND FIRST to return *only* ordinary files. It will not locate directories, hidden files, system files, or volume labels. This means that any file turned up as a match is indeed a match, and no further testing (as was necessary in looking for subdirectories) of the found files needs to be done.

If FIND FIRST returns DOS error message 2 or 18, then the directory is empty, and that particular instantiation of **SearchDirectory** has done its job. It terminates, either ending the **Locate** program completely or passing control upward to the prior instantiation of **SearchDirectory** to continue the search.

More likely, a file will be turned up. Its information is translated and moved from **CurrentDTA** to a more compliant form, embodied by the **DIR-Rec** record variable **CurrentDIR**. This translation is accomplished by the **DTAToDIR** procedure described earlier in this chapter. The information in **CurrentDIR** is then displayed along with the full pathname of the found file by rearranging the information generated by the **DIRToSTRING** procedure (also described earlier).

Once any information turned up by FIND FIRST is displayed, control enters a **REPEAT** loop that calls FIND NEXT repeatedly, displaying any matching files it finds, until DOS error 2 or 18 turns up. Either error indicates that no more matching files remain in the current directory. At this point, **SearchDirectory** terminates, and either ends **Locate** or passes control back to the prior instantiation of **SearchDirectory**.

That is about all there is to **Locate**. A typical session looks like this:

```
D:\>LOCATE *.BAK
     1101    11/06/86     7:26p     \TEXT\HEADER.BAK
    11503    01/14/87    11:15a     \TURBO\LOCATE.BAK
     2623    01/13/87     7:53p     \TURBO\DIRSTRIN.BAK
     6055    01/14/87     9:33a     \TURBO\SPACER.BAK
     8595    01/14/87     9:31a     \TURBO\GETDIR.BAK
     2701    01/13/87    11:18a     \TURBO\DTATODIR.BAK
      215    12/12/86     1:12p     \CONFIG.BAK
```

It's interesting to note that the only file found in the root directory, **CONFIG .BAK**, turns up *last* in the display, even though DOS DIR lists it *before* both subdirectories **TURBO** and **TEXT**. Given your understanding of the workings of **Locate**, can you explain why this happens?

If you can, you are more than capable of writing and using recursive procedures such as **SearchDirectory** and utilities that turn on their particular brand of black magic.

7.8   Linked Lists of Directory Entries

When multiple files match a given file spec in a given directory, FIND NEXT will keep popping up appropriate directory entries, one after the other. There could be three, a dozen, a hundred, or five hundred; with today's inexpensive 32MB hard disks and tomorrow's gigabyte WORM and CD ROM drives, you have to be ready to deal with a lot of files. Unless you were prepared to process the files you found on the spot (as **Locate** does, by simply displaying their pathnames and other information to the screen), you wouldn't keep calling FIND NEXT without somehow planning to keep the directory entries it returns somewhere for later use.

Where to put them? You could define an array of **DIRRec**, but in Pascal the size of the array must be set at compile time. Therefore, if you plan for a worst-case scenario of holding an array of 500 directory entries, that array will occupy close to 48K of RAM—and 64K is as large as any single Pascal data item can be. Worse, even if you only want to store three directory entries, the entire array must exist, taking up room with 497 records full of dead space.

A better solution is to string them together in a linked list on the heap, by creating a dynamically allocated **DIRRec** record on the heap for each directory entry, and connecting them with pointers. Heapspace under Turbo Pascal is very large, occupying *all* available memory beyond the end of compiler, code, and data—all the way up to 640K. (This is called a *long heap*, and only a few Pascal compilers support it.)

The remainder of Chapter 7 will explore the uses of heap storage in managing large numbers of directory entries returned by repeated calls to FIND NEXT. I'll be including a number of diagrams to help make this somewhat abstract concept a little more visual. Figure 7.4 summarizes the different symbols I'll be using to represent pointers and the records that make up singly and doubly linked lists.

Singly Linked Lists

Doubly linked lists are perhaps the most useful dynamic data structures in the Pascal pantheon. (I'll be using doubly linked lists later in this chapter to solve the problem of managing hundreds of directory entries.) The best way to approach doubly linked lists—if you are new to linked lists in general—is to begin with singly linked lists. What follows is a brief review of singly linked lists.

In a *singly linked list*, a pointer in the static data area of the program (called the "root") points to a record on the heap. A pointer in that record points to another record on the heap, which points to yet another record on the heap, and so on to the end of the list, with each record pointing to the next record. The pointer in the last record is set to **Nil**, a special Pascal pointer value that must be interpreted as "pointing to nothing" rather than simply being undefined. A **Nil** pointer value indicates the end of the list.

Consider a very simple record:

```
TYPE
  NamePtr = ^NameRec;
```

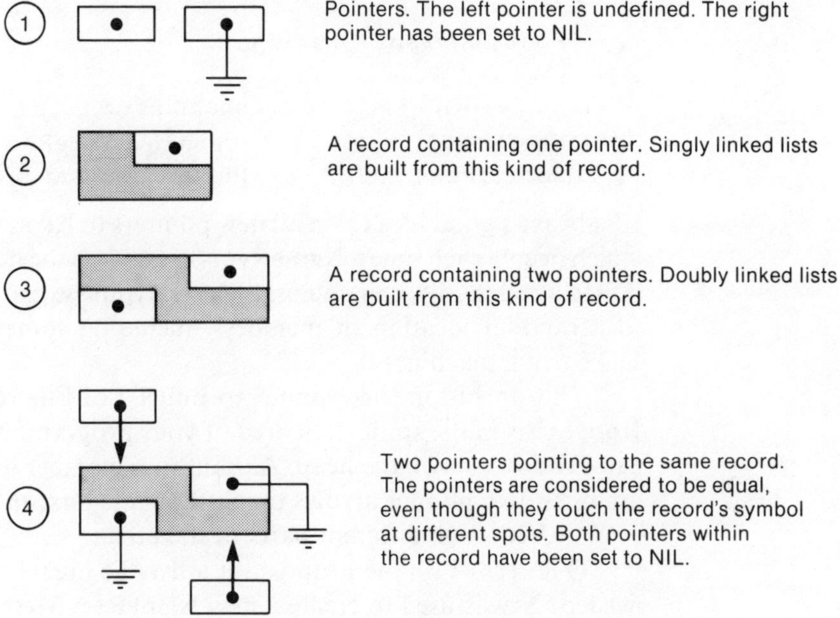

Figure 7.4   **Typographical conventions for linked lists**

```
NameRec = RECORD
            Name : String80;
            Next : NamePtr
          END;
```

The record contains nothing but a string for name data and a pointer to the next record. On the linked-list diagrams in this section, a shaded rectangular box represents a **NameRec**. Each **NameRec** box contains a smaller, unshaded box with a dot in the middle. This is the **Next** field of the **NameRec** record. When the **NameRec** is created, the **Next** pointer is undefined, and an undefined pointer is shown as a dot without any arrow or line leading away from it. Once defined, a pointer has either an arrow proceeding from the dot or an inverted line pyramid resembling the "ground" symbol from radio schematics; this symbol indicates a **Nil** pointer.

Note the exception to Pascal's requirement that all data types be defined before they are used; it is legal to define a pointer to a record type before the record itself is defined. (Because both types refer to one another, a chicken/egg paradox would exist if *one* were not allowed to be used "on the honor system" before the other is defined.)

A pointer variable of type **NamePtr** must be defined before a **NameRec** can be created out on the heap. A **NameRec** can be created by using **New**:

```
VAR
  Root, Current : NamePtr;

        .   .   .

  New(Root);           {Create a NameRec on the heap}
  Root^.Next := Nil;   {Never leave an undefined pointer!}
```

It's always a good idea to set all new pointers to **Nil** as soon as they are created, which occurs each time a **NameRec** is created on the heap. Undefined pointers, if used accidentally, can potentially crash your system by allowing you to write to a random location in memory—including somewhere in the middle of DOS's vital machinery!

This operation corresponds to Bullet 1 of Figure 7.5. Keep in mind that **Root** exists in the static data area of your program, while the **NameRec** we'll call **Frodo** exists on the heap. A point to remember in reading linked-list diagrams: If two pointer arrows touch the same box, *they are considered equal*, even if they touch different parts of the box.

One record on the heap is not a list. To create a list, another pointer is needed. **New** is used to create a new **NameRec**, **Merry**, pointed to by pointer **Current**:

```
  New(Current);
  Current^.Next := Nil;
```

("Merry" and "Frodo" are only names I've given to the records for the purposes of this discussion to tell them apart—perhaps the names are data in the **Name** field. From the compiler's perspective, objects on the heap have no names.) Now there are two **NameRec**s and two pointers, as in Bullet 2 of Figure 7.5. Connecting the two records into a list is done by pointing the **Next** field of record **Merry** to record **Frodo**. This is done by assigning the value of **Root** to **Current^.Next**. (This notation is hard to pronounce, aside from saying, "The **Next** field of the **NameRec** record pointed to by **Current**." You might decide to do what I do when I see such notation, and think, "**Current**'s target dot **Next**.")

```
  Current^.Next := Root;
```

Assigning **Root**'s value to **Current^.Next** has the effect of pointing **Current^.Next** to the same record that **Root** points to. This is the way pointers work. Equal pointers point to the same object. This is the situation in Bullet 3 of Figure 7.5. The last step is to get **Root** pointed to the beginning of the list again:

```
  Root := Current;
```

This time we assign **Current**'s value to **Root**, making **Current** and **Root** equal by virtue of their pointing to the same object, **Merry**. This corresponds to

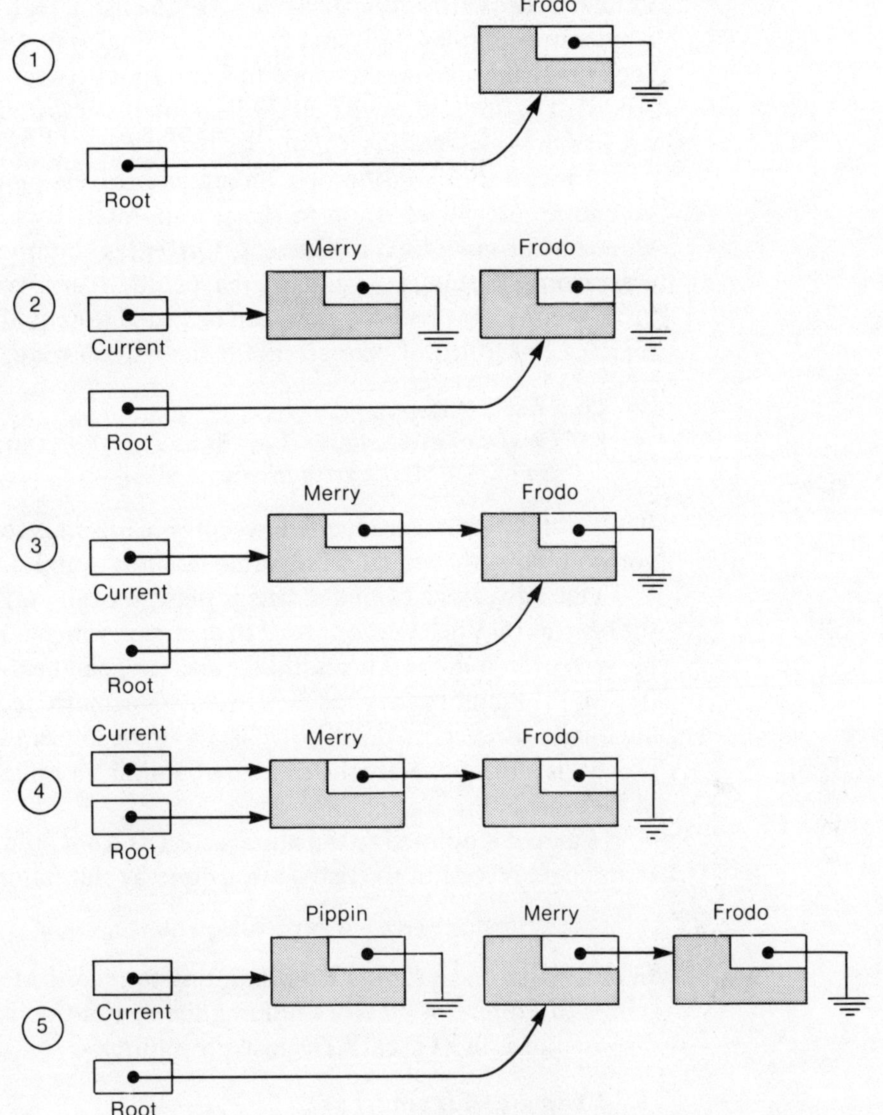

Figure 7.5 **Building a singly linked list**

Bullet 4 of Figure 7.5. **Current** can now be used for other things, because **Root** once again is acting as the "root" of the linked list.

In continuing the process, the list would be built by creating new records pointed to by **Current** and inserting them at the head of the list by using the process just described (Bullet 5 of Figure 7.5). This creates an unsorted linked list, as the first record becomes the end of the list, moving farther from the root as new records are added at the head of the list. Creating a sorted list is somewhat more complex, as it involves "traversing" (i.e., stepping through) the list each time a new record is created to find a spot between two records for the new record to be inserted, such that the list remains in sorted order. (I described this process in some detail in *Complete Turbo Pascal*.)

As with the building of a linked list, traversing a linked list requires a second pointer in addition to the root pointer. By repeatedly assigning the value of **Current^.Next** to **Current**, **Current** is "bumped" along the linked list one record at a time, pointing to each record in turn. When **Current** points to a given record, that record's data can be tested for equality to a given value. To search a linked list of **NameRec**s for the name **Frodo**, this code will do:

```
Current := Root;
WHILE (Current^.Name <> 'Frodo') AND (Current <> Nil) DO
  Current := Current^.Next;
```

If, after this **WHILE** statement executes, **Current** is found to be equal to **Nil**, you will know that the desired name was not found in the list.

One advantage of linked lists is that they only take up as much room on the heap as they need (as opposed to an array, which is always its largest possible size, even if it contains nothing) and they can be disposed of as desired to free up the memory they take. In order to properly reclaim their memory for later use, however, disposing of a list has to be done in an orderly fashion. The process is almost exactly the reverse of building a linked list, and is illustrated in Figure 7.6.

Current is pointed to the same record as **Root**, and then **Root** is "stepped" to the next record in the list. This is done by the statement:

```
Root := Current^.Next;
```

In our diagram, that puts **Root** pointing to record Merry, while **Current** still points to Pippin. With **Root** holding the rest of the list, Pippin can be safely disposed of using Pascal's **Dispose** procedure:

```
Dispose(Current);
```

This statement makes Pippin go poof, and leaves **Current** undefined. The list is now one record shorter, and all of the memory previously allocated to Pippin is now available for other uses. To dispose of the entire list, a **REPEAT/UNTIL** loop ratchets **Root** and **Current** along the list, disposing of records until they're all gone:

```
REPEAT
  Current := Root;
  Root := Current^.Next;
```

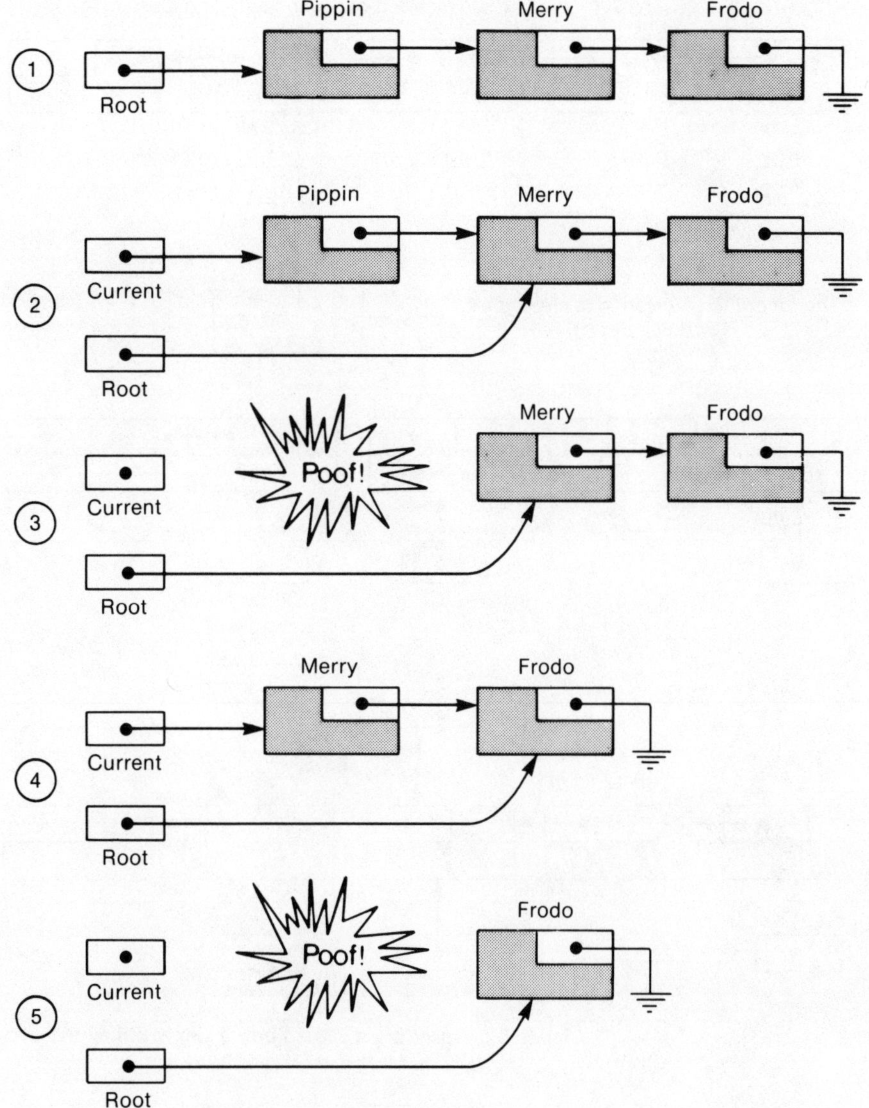

Figure 7.6   Disposing of a singly linked list

```
Dispose(Current);
UNTIL Root = Nil;
```

The last important operation is list insertion. Figure 7.7 outlines the insertion process for a singly linked list. A third pointer is required here, in addition to **Root** and **Current**. This pointer must point to the record in the list immediately prior to **Current**. Let's call it **Last**, since, if we are traversing the list in

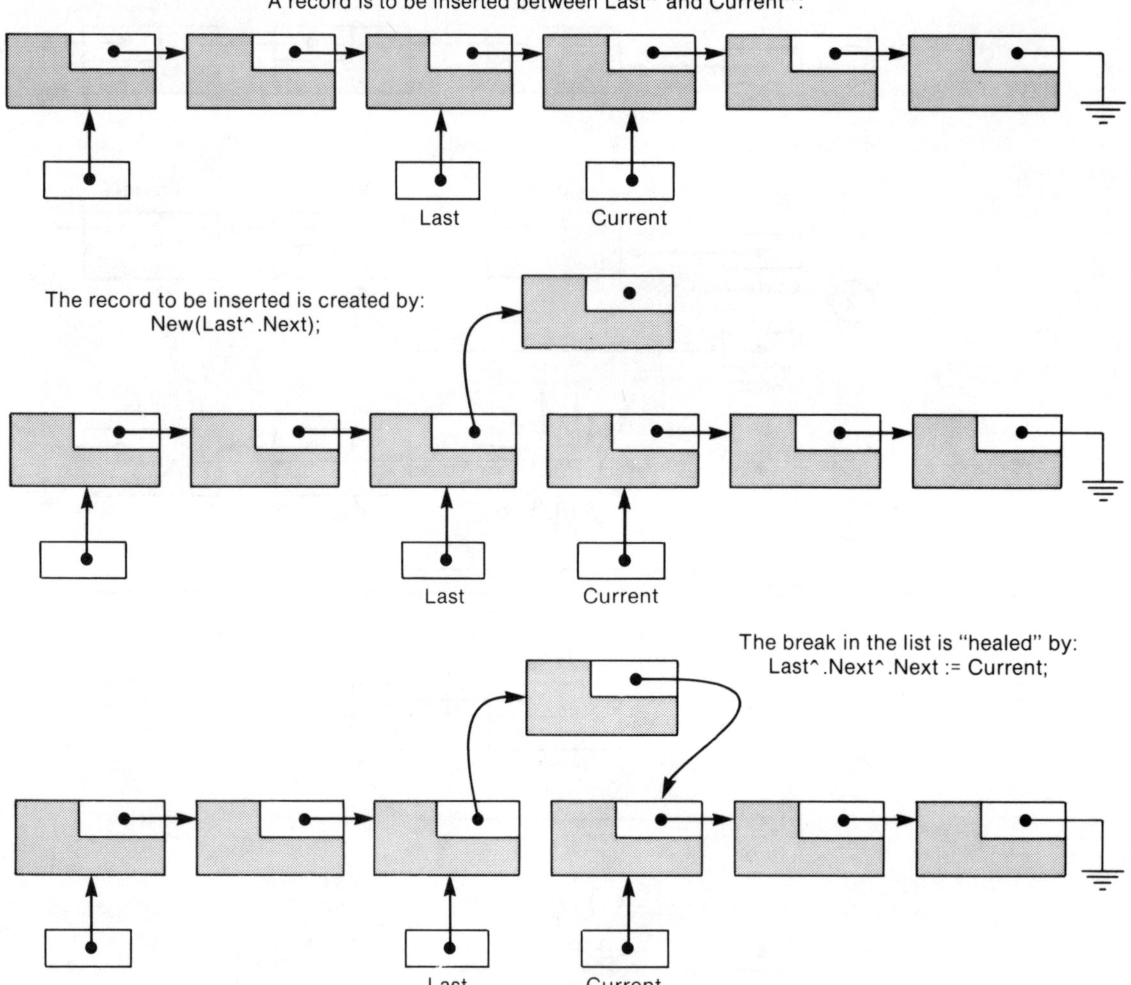

Figure 7.7 **Inserting a record into a singly linked list**

order to find the proper point at which to insert a new record, **Last** points to the last record we examined before the current record.

Assume for the diagram that we have decided to insert a record between **Last**^ and **Current**^. Don't forget that all three pointers (**Root, Last,** and **Current**) reside in the static data area of the program and can be accessed independently of one another. With **Current** maintaining contact with the rest of the list, the list is broken at **Last** by creating a new record for **Last**^.**Next** to point to:

```
New(Last^.Next);
```

(This corresponds to Bullet 2 of Figure 7.7.) Of course, when a record is created on the heap by the **New** procedure, all its fields are undefined. We need to "fill" the new record with its information by using assignment statements and working through **Last**:

```
Last^.Next^.Name := CustomerName;
```

Once the new record has been filled with whatever data it needs, the list can be "healed" again by pointing the **Next** field of the newly created record to **Current^**:

```
Last^.Next^.Next := Current;
```

At this point, the list is whole again, starting at **Root** and running uninterrupted right to the **Nil** pointer marking the list's end. **Current** and **Last** can be stepped further down the list for more insertions, or they can be used for other things. The insertion is complete.

All other manipulations of linked lists are some combination or variation of these basic operations: building, traversing, disposing, and inserting.

Doubly Linked Lists

Singly linked lists have a serious limitation: You can only traverse them in one direction, starting from the root. To simply search a list in order to tell if a particular data item is present, traversing a list in one direction is sufficient. You might, however, wish to display the items in a linked list in ascending or descending order. You might wish to display the items in a list in a screen menu, and select one item from the list by moving a "bounce bar" of inverse video up and down the list, finally choosing one item by pressing a particular key, as in Word Perfect Corporation's P-Edit and Word Perfect editors. For applications like these, a *doubly linked list* is needed.

Figure 7.8 represents a doubly linked list of four items. Note that each record in the list contains two pointers instead of one, and that there is a pointer variable in the static data area pointing to each end of the list. **Root** is still there, by convention on the left, but the pointer at the opposite end of the list I call **Descending**, because to traverse a sorted list in descending order, you must begin at the end of the list *opposite* **Root**.

The two pointers within each record are called **Next** and **Prior**. The **Next** fields in the list point "away" from **Root** toward **Descending**, and the **Prior** fields point away from **Descending** toward **Root**. Assuming a sorted list with the first item pointed to by **Root** and the last by **Descending**, we now have a second way to traverse the list:

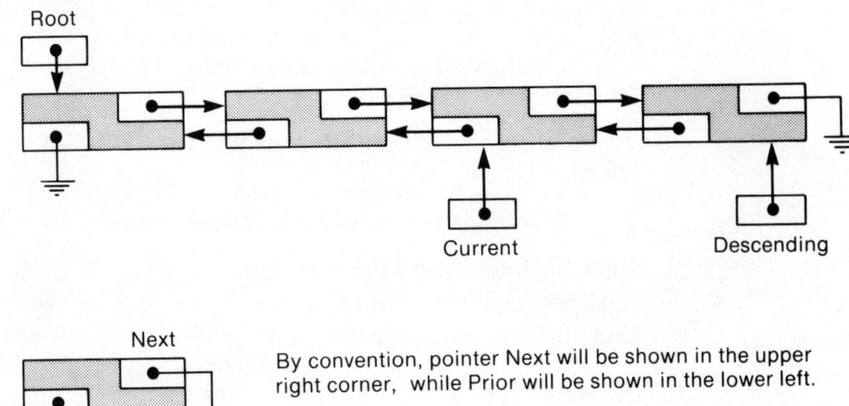

Figure 7.8 A doubly linked list

```
Current := Descending;
WHILE (Current^.Name <> 'Frodo') AND (Current <> Nil) DO
  Current := Current^.Prior;
```

This **WHILE** loop begins at **Descending**'s end of the list and searches the list rootward until it either finds a record containing the name **Frodo** or until it reaches the record **Root^**, whose **Prior** field is set to **Nil**.

Structurally, a doubly linked list is completely symmetrical. Anything you can do in one direction you can also do in the other direction.

In the previous discussion of singly linked lists, the process of building a list was very simple because the list was not an "ordered" list. Its records were placed in the list as created without any regard for how the data in one related to the data in any of the others. Essentially, building a nonordered list is no more complex than inserting each record at the head of the list (rather like letting out the string of a kite).

Building an ordered list involves more overhead. For each insertion, the list must be traversed in order to find the correct place in the list for the inserted record. When the proper point is found, the new record is inserted at that point. Three possible scenarios can arise in locating the proper spot for a new record: The new record can fall 1) at the root end of the list, 2) at the descending end of the list, or 3) somewhere in the middle. The code for handling each situation is different.

The code for list insertion follows. Assume that the list is to be ordered on a record field called **KeyField**. Also assume that the record to be inserted has

been created through a pointer called **Holder**, and that it has already been filled
with data.

```
Current := Root;
REPEAT
  IF Current^.KeyField > Holder^.KeyField THEN
    PositionFound := True ELSE PositionFound := False;
  IF NOT PositionFound THEN Current := Current^.Next
UNTIL PositionFound OR (Current = Nil);
IF PositionFound THEN {Record falls at beginning or middle}
  BEGIN
    IF Current = Root THEN            {Insert at the beginning}
      BEGIN
        Holder^.Next := Root;
        Current^.Prior := Holder;
        Root := Holder;
        Root^.Prior := Nil
      END
    ELSE        {Insert in the middle, right before Current^}
      BEGIN
        Holder^.Next := Current;
        Holder^.Prior := Current^.Prior;
        Current^.Prior^.Next := Holder;
        Current^.Prior := Holder
      END
  END
ELSE                      {Record falls at the end}
  BEGIN
    Descending^.Next := Holder;
    Descending^.Next^.Prior := Descending;
    Descending := Descending^.Next;
    Descending^.Next := Nil
  END;
```

The **REPEAT** statement accomplishes the traversal of the linked list. At each
record in the list, the data in **Holder**^ is compared to the data in **Current**^. If
Current^ is not found to be greater than **Holder**^, then the pointer **Current** is
bumped to point to the next record in the list. Boolean flag **PositionFound**
simply marks when the code decides that it knows where the record should go.

This traversal could apply to a singly linked list as well as a doubly linked
list, since it is only testing in one direction. The **Prior** field of the records in the
list has no function during traversal.

Inserting records into the list at any point must be done with some care.
The order in which the pointers are modified is important. Changing the order

could "break" the list, and, while doubly linked lists are easier to mend than singly linked lists (since there are two independent threads holding the list together), there's no sense in doing more than you have to in managing the list.

Inserting a record at the beginning of the list first involves pointing **Holder^** at **Root^**. This places the inserted record at the head of the list. The **Prior** pointer in the record that used to be the first record in the list must be pointed "back" at the new head of the list. (Its previous value was **Nil**.) **Root** must now be moved so that it points to the new head of the list. This is done by assigning it **Holder**'s value. Finally, the **Prior** field of the new head record is set to **Nil**, as it now points to nothing (there is no prior record).

Appending a record to the opposite end of the list is the mirror image of that process. The tail end record's **Next** pointer is pointed to the new record. The **Prior** pointer of the new end record is pointed back at the old end record. **Descending** is moved to point to the new end of the list. Finally, the **Next** field of the new end record is set to **Nil**, since there is no next record.

Inserting a record into the middle of a doubly linked list is summarized by Figure 7.9. Bullet 1 shows the situation before the insertion: A new record pointed to by **Holder** is ready for insertion. The next step, shown by Bullet 2, involves pointing the **Prior** and **Next** pointers in the new record to their appropriate new target records in the list. At this point it might seem that the new record has somehow become attached to the list, but not so. If something happened to **Holder**, the new record would be completely inaccessible, because although it points to two records in the list, nothing points to *it*. Pointers are strictly a one-way street. The target of a pointer cannot look "back along the pointer" to identify who is pointing to it.

Bullet 3 completes the process by repointing the two records between which the new record falls back to the new record. All in all, four records must be altered to insert the new record.

The process of deleting a record in the middle of a list is considerably simpler, as shown in Figure 7.10. Two pointers are required, because deleting an entire record breaks *both* threads running through the list. The record is deleted by way of the **Dispose** procedure, and it can be disposed of from either the **Current** side or the **Holder** side:

```
Dispose(Current^.Prior);
Dispose(Holder^.Next);
```

After that, "healing" the break simply involves pointing the two records along-side the break to one another:

```
Holder^.Next := Current;
Current^.Prior := Holder;
```

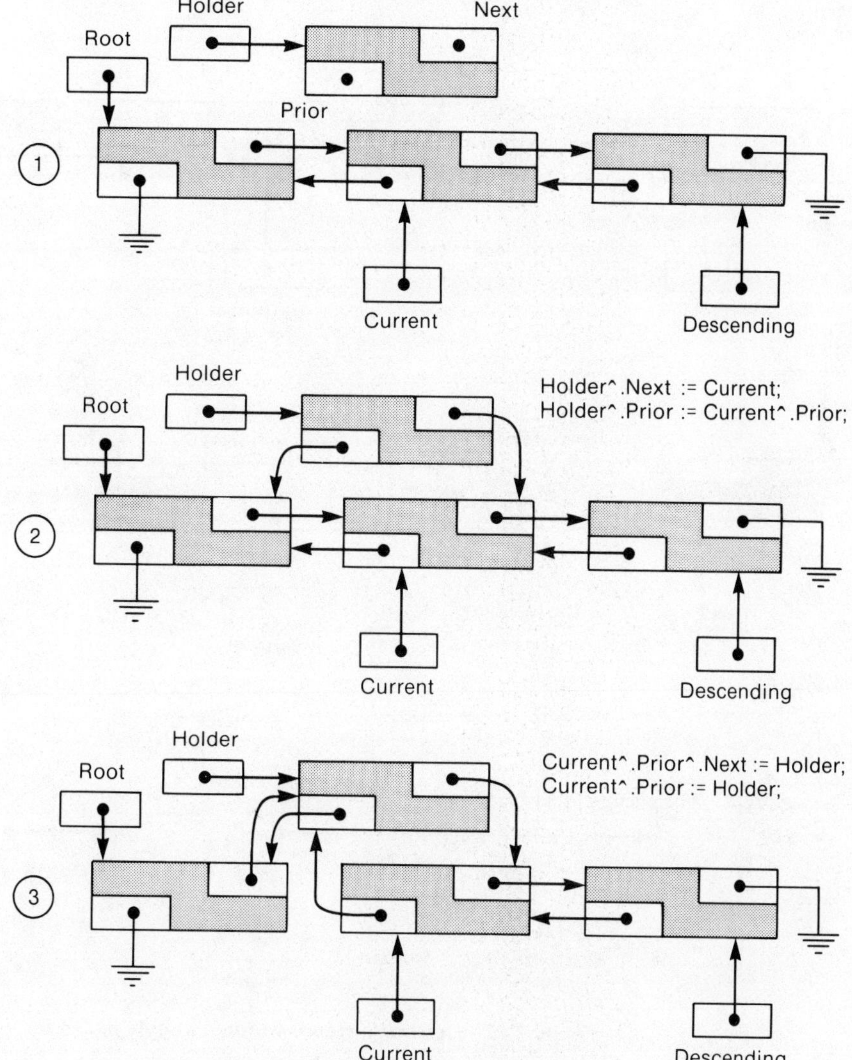

Figure 7.9   **Inserting a record into a doubly linked list**

Creating a List of Directory Entries

Because of Pascal's strong typing restrictions, it is impossible to create a "black box" linked-list handler that creates and manages linked lists of arbitrarily typed records. This being the case, you will have to build linked-list management into any application that requires it. Understanding the concept thor-

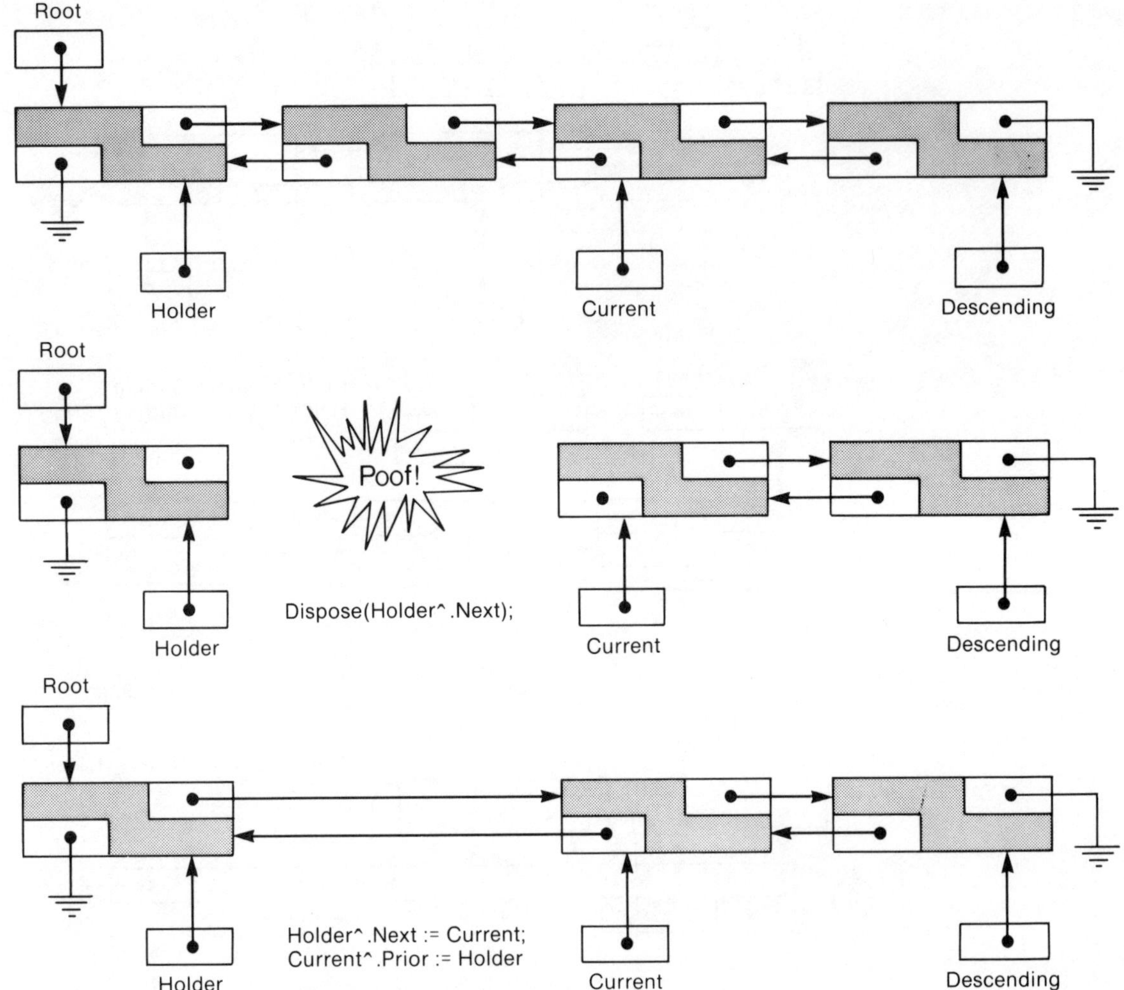

Figure 7.10 **Deleting a record within a doubly linked list**

oughly is crucial to implementing it. And the best way to understand it is to develop a useful toolkit routine that uses it.

Procedure **GetDirectory** returns two pointers to a doubly linked list of directory entries matching a given file spec. The two pointers are called **Ascending** and **Descending**, but in fact **Ascending** is our old friend **Root** with a new name. Figure 7.9 in particular will be helpful in understanding the operating of **GetDirectory**.

```
 1          {->>>>GetDirectory<<<<-------------------------------------------}
 2          {                                                                }
 3          { Filename: GETDIR.SRC -- Last modified 4/26/87                   }
 4          {                                                                }
 5          { This routine returns a pointer to a linked list of type         }
 6          { DIRRec, which must have been previously defined this way,        }
 7          { along with pointer type DIRPtr to point to it:                   }
 8          {                                                                }
 9          { DIRPtr = ^DIRRec;                                               }
10          { DIRRec = RECORD                                                 }
11          {               FileName  : String15;                            }
12          {               Attrib    : Byte;                                }
13          {               FileSize  : Real;                                }
14          {               TimeStamp : TimeRec;                             }
15          {               DateStamp : DateRec;                             }
16          {               Prior     : DIRPtr;                              }
17          {               Next      : DIRPtr;                              }
18          {            END;                                                }
19          {                                                                }
20          { The linked list will contain a record for every file in the     }
21          { current directory.  Since the linked list is out in heap,        }
22          { your directory data takes up NO space in your data segment.      }
23          { If there are no files in the current directory, the pointer      }
24          { returned is equal to NIL.                                       }
25          {                                                                }
26          { The types TimeRec and DateRec must be defined prior to using }
27          { GetDirectory.  String80 & DTAToDIR must be defined as well.  }
28          {                                                                }
29          {                                                                }
30          {                                                                }
31          {----------------------------------------------------------------}
32
33
34          PROCEDURE GetDirectory(Filespec   : String80;
35                                 Sorted     : Boolean;
36                                 SortOnName : Boolean;
37                                 VAR Ascending  : DIRPtr;
38                                 VAR Descending : DIRPtr);
39
40          TYPE
41            String9 = String[9];
42            Reg     = RECORD
43                        CASE Boolean OF
44                          False : (Word : Integer);
45                          True  : (LoByte,HiByte : Byte)
46                        END;
47
48            Regpack = RECORD
```

(continued)

```
49                           AX,BX,CX,DX,BP,SI,DI,DS,ES,Flags : Reg
50                       END;
51
52         DWord     = RECORD
53                         LoInteger,HiInteger : Integer
54                       END;
55
56
57       VAR
58          I          : Integer;
59          Registers : RegPack;
60          Root       : DIRPtr;
61          Current    : DIRPtr;
62          Last       : DIRPtr;
63          Holder     : DIRPtr;
64          ASCIIZ     : ARRAY[1..81] OF Char;
65          PositionFound : Boolean;
66
67
68       FUNCTION LaterThan(LeftEntry,RightEntry : DirPtr) : Boolean;
69
70       BEGIN
71         IF LeftEntry^.DateStamp.DateComp > RightEntry^.DateStamp.DateComp THEN
72           LaterThan := True
73         ELSE
74           IF (LeftEntry^.DateStamp.DateComp = RightEntry^.DateStamp.DateComp)
75              AND  { Remember that time stamps must be treated as WORDs... }
76              WordComp(LeftEntry^.TimeStamp.TimeComp,RightEntry^.TimeStamp.TimeComp)
77           THEN LaterThan := True
78           ELSE LaterThan := False
79       END;
80
81
82       PROCEDURE AppendToEnd(VAR Holder,Descending : DIRPtr);
83
84       BEGIN
85         Descending^.Next := Holder;      { Add record to end of list }
86         Descending^.Next^.Prior := Descending;  { Set reverse pointer }
87         Descending := Descending^.Next;    { Bump Current to next record }
88       END;
89
90
91
92       BEGIN
93         {First step is to convert Filespec string to ASCIIZ:}
94         Filespec := Filespec + CHR(0);  { Append binary zero to Filespec }
95         Move(Filespec[1],ASCIIZ,Sizeof(Filespec));
96         WITH Registers DO
97           BEGIN
```

(continued)

```
 98              AX.Word := $4E00;        { $4E = Find First }
 99              DS.Word := Seg(ASCIIZ); { Put address of ASCIIZ }
100              DX.Word := Ofs(ASCIIZ); { in DS : DX }
101              CX.LoByte := $16;        { Set file attributes for search: }
102                                       {   normal, directory, hidden, system }
103           END;
104         MSDOS(Registers);             { Make FIND FIRST DOS call... }
105         IF Registers.AX.Word = 2 THEN
106           BEGIN
107             Ascending := NIL;
108             Descending := NIL
109           END
110         ELSE
111           BEGIN
112             New(Root);              { Create a record for the first find }
113             DTAtoDIR(Root^);        { Convert first find to DIR format }
114             Current := Root;        { The current record is now the root record }
115             Descending := Root;     { And also the last record in the list! }
116             IF Registers.AX.Word <> 18 THEN
117               REPEAT
118                 Registers.AX.Word := $4F00; { Set up for FIND NEXT DOS call }
119                 MSDOS(Registers);              { Make FIND NEXT DOS call }
120                 IF Registers.AX.Word <> 18 THEN  { More entries exist }
121                   BEGIN
122                     New(Holder);          { Create a record with temporary pointer }
123                     DTAtoDIR(Holder^);  { Convert additional finds to DIR format }
124                     { Sorted and unsorted lists are constructed differently. }
125                     { If we're building a sorted list we have to scan it for }
126                     { each entry to find the proper place in the list.  For  }
127                     { unsorted lists we just hang the latest found entry on   }
128                     { the end of the list and bump Current to the Next. }
129                     IF Sorted THEN
130                       BEGIN
131                         Current := Root;    { Traverse list to find insert spot: }
132                         REPEAT
133                           IF SortOnName THEN     { To sort list on file name }
134                             IF Current^.FileName > Holder^.FileName THEN
135                               PositionFound := True ELSE PositionFound := False
136                           ELSE                   { To sort list by time/date }
137                             IF LaterThan(Current,Holder) THEN
138                               PositionFound := True ELSE PositionFound := False;
139                           IF NOT PositionFound THEN
140                             Current := Current^.Next; { Bump to next item }
141                         UNTIL (Current = NIL) OR PositionFound;
142                         { When PositionFound becomes True, the record needs }
143                         { to be inserted in the list BEFORE Current^-- }
144                         { This needs to be done differently if Current^ is }
145                         { at the head of the list. (i.e., Current = Root)}
146                         IF PositionFound THEN  { Insert at beginning... }
```

(continued)

```
147            BEGIN                    { ...or in the middle somewhere }
148              { NOTE:   DO NOT change the order of the }
149              { pointer assignments in the following }
150              { IF/THEN/ELSE statement!! }
151              IF Current = Root THEN  { Insert at beginning }
152                BEGIN
153                  Holder^.Next := Root;
154                  Current^.Prior := Holder;
155                  Root := Holder;
156                END
157              ELSE    { Insert in the middle: }
158                BEGIN
159                  Holder^.Next  := Current;
160                  Holder^.Prior := Current^.Prior;
161                  Current^.Prior^.Next := Holder;
162                  Current^.Prior := Holder
163                END
164            END
165          ELSE  { The new record belongs at the end of the list }
166              AppendToEnd(Holder,Descending)
167        END
168      ELSE    { If no sort, we add the record to the end of the list: }
169          AppendToEnd(Holder,Descending)
170    END
171    UNTIL Registers.AX.Word = 18;
172    Ascending := Root
173  END
174  END;  {GetDirectory}
```

The full search spec, including the path and disk specifier, is passed to
GetDirectory in parameter **FileSpec**. As with any use of DOS's FIND FIRST/
FIND NEXT sequence, the search spec must be assembled into an ASCIIZ
string, and the string's address loaded into registers DS and DX. The attribute
byte is also set, but we've chosen to read every kind of file except for the volume
label: hidden files, system files, subdirectories, and, of course, ordinary DOS
data files. Taken together, the hidden file bit, the system file bit, and the subdirectory bit represent a binary value of $16, which is passed to DOS in register
CL.

If DOS error messages 2 or 18 are returned by FIND FIRST, the directory
is empty, and both **Ascending** and **Descending** are returned with a value of **Nil**.
Otherwise, a new **DIRRec** record is created as the root of the new list, and filled
with information returned by DOS in the DTA. Repeated calls by FIND
NEXT will read the remainder of the directory, until an error message indicates
no further entries to be read. As each directory entry is read, **GetDirectory**
adds the entry to the doubly linked list it is building.

GetDirectory offers two different ways to build the list: in the order the directory entries physically appear on the disk, or in sorted order. The caller's preference is passed to **GetDirectory** in Boolean parameter **Sorted**. If sorted order is selected (**Sorted** set to **True**), there is the further choice of sorting the list on either the name of the file or subdirectory (**SortOnName** = **True**), or on the time and date of last modification (**SortOnName** = **False**).

Determining which of two string records is greater than another in alphanumeric sort order is simple: They can be compared via Pascal's Boolean operators. Determining which of two time/date combinations is the earlier is trickier, even with the time and date present as single integer quantities in variables **TimeComp** and **DateComp** (see Sections 6.2 and 6.3). If the "left" date is greater than the "right" date, then the time does not have to be taken into account, but, if the dates are equal, the time stamps must also be compared. To aid the readability of the procedure, this process was set off in a short function called **LaterThan**, which accepts pointers to **DIRRec**s and returns a Boolean value of **True** if the left entry is greater than the right entry as passed in the parameter line.

The logic of adding a record to the list is very similar to the code example given on page 347, with some additional conditional logic to allow ordering the list on either the name or the time/date fields. Read the code example, and compare it to the actual code for **GetDirectory**.

A File Size Tally Utility

As a practical example of **GetDirectory** in use, let me present **Spacer,** a utility that does something I have always wished DOS DIR would do: It presents a tally of the sizes of the displayed files. Many times I've had to clear out a couple of megabytes from a 20-megabyte hard disk (which always seems to stay stuck at 18.5 megabytes full, no matter what I do!), and I have had to become a good eyeball estimator of the space I'll save if I just do an ERASE *.BAK or something along those lines. **Spacer** eliminates the guesswork. To find out the space taken up in the current directory by backup files (or any other kind of files you specify), type:

```
LOCATE   .BAK    11503    01/14/87    11:15a
DIRSTRIN.BAK     2623     01/13/87     7:53p
SPACER   .BAK     6055    01/14/87     9:33a
GETDIR   .BAK     8595    01/14/87     9:31a
DTEST    .BAK     5328    01/15/87     5:54p
DISPDIR  .BAK      443    01/15/87     5:59p
DTATODIR.BAK      2701    01/13/87    11:18a

Total space occupied by these files is    37248 bytes.
```

Spacer works by generating a doubly linked list of the requested files, using **GetDirectory**. It then displays the list, keeping a running total of the sizes of the files as it displays them. When the display has been completed, **Spacer** adds an additional line giving the total number of bytes of disk space occupied by the files whose names have just been displayed.

At first glance, you might wonder why a linked list needs to be built at all. After all, the **Locate** program from the previous section displays files from directories—why couldn't you just add a little code to keep a running tally of files displayed from **Locate**? Well, of course, you could, and it's probably a worthwhile improvement on **Locate**. But when you display 'em as you find 'em, you lose the ability to display them sorted by name or by last-modified time and date; you can only display them in the order that the directory entries physically appear on the disk. For that you need a linked list, and to offer the choice of displaying them either in ascending or descending order by your chosen sort field, you need a *doubly* linked list.

Also notice the compiler directive immediately beneath the comment header:

```
{$P512}
```

This directs the program's **Write** and **Writeln** output to the DOS standard output device, which (unlike Turbo Pascal's default sneaky direct access to the screen) can be redirected to a DOS file. In other words, if you wanted to capture **Spacer**'s output to a file for further reference, you would only need to type:

```
C:\>SPACER *.BAK > BAKSPACE.TXT
```

and, rather than see the output on the screen, you will notice the disk-drive indicator working, as DOS instead writes the text output from **Spacer** to disk file **BAKSPACE.TXT**.

The "512" in the compiler directive specifies the buffer size of the file buffer for the standard output device. The larger the buffer, the fewer writes to disk need to be made on a long listing, and the faster the process will be.

```
 1       {-----------------------------------------------------------------}
 2       {                            SPACER                                }
 3       {                                                                 }
 4       {            Directory lister with file size tally                }
 5       {                                                                 }
 6       {                              by Jeff Duntemann                  }
 7       {                              Turbo Pascal V3.01A                }
 8       {                              Last update 4/26/87                }
 9       {                                                                 }
10       {  This utility functions similarly to DOS DIR in that it         }
```

(continued)

```
11        {  displays a directory of files in a subdirectory, but unlike }
12        {  DIR it keeps a running total of the size of the files        }
13        {  displayed.  It exists mostly to demonstrate the generation   }
14        {  of a linked list of directory entries through the procedure  }
15        {  GetDirectory.  Ideally, it should be expanded into a         }
16        {  utility similar to SWEEP.                                     }
17        {                                                               }
18        {                                                               }
19        {                                                               }
20        {---------------------------------------------------------------}
21
22        {$P512}   { This allows the output to be redirected by DOS;     }
23                  { very handy for keeping "snapshots" of DIR listing. }
24
25        PROGRAM Spacer;
26
27        CONST
28          SortByName = True;
29          SortByDate = False;
30
31
32        TYPE
33         String80 = String[80];
34         String15 = String[15];
35
36        {$I REGPACK.DEF}
37        {$I TIMEREC.DEF}
38        {$I DATEREC.DEF}
39        {$I DTAREC.DEF}
40        {$I DIRREC.DEF}
41
42
43        VAR
44           Parms      : Byte;
45           SpaceTaken : Real;
46           RunUp      : DIRPtr;
47           RunDown    : DIRPtr;
48           Current    : DIRPtr;
49           FileSpec   : String80;
50           WorkString : String80;
51           Sorted     : Boolean;
52           SortSpec   : Boolean;
53           Ascending  : Boolean;
54           I          : Integer;
55
56
57        {$I DAYOWEEK.SRC}
58        {$I CALCDATE.SRC}
59        {$I CALCTIME.SRC}
```

(continued)

```
60      {$I DTATODIR.SRC}
61      {$I WORDCOMP.SRC}
62      {$I GETDIR.SRC}
63      {$I DIRSTRIN.SRC}
64
65
66      BEGIN
67        Sorted := False;               { Set default values }
68        SortSpec := SortByName;
69        Ascending := True;
70        Parms := ORD(ParamCount);  { Convert parm count to ordinal value }
71        CASE Parms OF
72          0 :
73          BEGIN
74            Writeln('>>SPACER<<  V1.05  By Jeff Duntemann');
75            Writeln('              From the book, TURBO PASCAL SOLUTIONS');
76            Writeln('              Scott, Foresman & Co. 1987');
77            Writeln('              ISBN 0-673-18584-2 ');
78            Writeln;
79            Writeln('This program displays ALL files matching a given filespec.');
80            Writeln('Hidden and system files are not immune.');
81            Writeln('Additionally, it will add up the cumulative file sizes of');
82            Writeln('the files matching the filespec, so you can tell how much');
83            Writeln('space files in a given subdirectory subtend, or how much');
84            Writeln('space you have invested in .PAS files, and so on.');
85            Writeln;
86            Writeln('CALLING SYNTAX:');
87            Writeln;
88            Writeln('SPACER <filespec> N|D A|D');
89            Writeln;
90            Writeln('where <filespec> is a legal DOS filespec, including wildcards.');
91            Writeln('The second parameter is either N or D:');
92            Writeln('N indicates sort by file name;');
93            Writeln('D indicates sort by time and date stamp.');
94            Writeln('If not given, entries are displayed in physical order.');
95            Writeln;
96            Writeln('The third parameter is either A or D:');
97            Writeln('A indicates ascending order of display;');
98            Writeln('D indicates descending order of display.');
99            Writeln('If not given, sort is ascending.');
100           Writeln;
101           Writeln('For example:');
102           Writeln;
103           Writeln('SPACER *.PAS N');
104           Writeln('  will display all files with the .PAS extension,');
105           Writeln('  in ascending sorted order by file name.  Or,');
106           Writeln;
107           Writeln('SPACER *.PAS D D');
108           Writeln('  will display all files with the .PAS extension,');
```

(continued)

```
109            Writeln('  in descending order by last-modification date.');
110            Halt;
111          END;
112        1 : FileSpec := ParamStr(1);
113        2 : BEGIN
114              Sorted := True;
115              FileSpec := ParamStr(1);
116              WorkString := ParamStr(2);
117              CASE UpCase(WorkString[1]) OF
118                'D' : SortSpec := SortByDate;
119                'N' : SortSpec := SortByName;
120                ELSE Sorted := False
121              END
122            END;
123        3 : BEGIN
124              Sorted := True;
125              FileSpec := ParamStr(1);
126              WorkString := ParamStr(2);
127              CASE UpCase(WorkString[1]) OF
128                'D' : SortSpec := SortByDate;
129                'N' : SortSpec := SortByName;
130                ELSE Sorted := False
131              END;
132              IF Sorted THEN
133                BEGIN
134                  WorkString := ParamStr(3);
135                  CASE UpCase(WorkString[1]) OF
136                    'A' : Ascending := True;
137                    'D' : Ascending := False;
138                    ELSE Ascending := True
139                  END
140                END
141            END;
142    END; { CASE }
143    { Now we actually go out and build a linked list of directory entries, }
144    { based on the parms we have parsed out of the command line: }
145    GetDirectory(FileSpec,Sorted,SortSpec,RunUp,RunDown);
146    IF Ascending THEN Current := RunUp
147      ELSE Current := RunDown;
148    IF Current = Nil THEN Writeln('No files found.')
149      ELSE
150        BEGIN
151          SpaceTaken := 0.0;
152          IF Ascending THEN
153            WHILE Current <> NIL DO
154              BEGIN
155                Writeln(DirToString(Current^));
156                SpaceTaken := SpaceTaken + Current^.FileSize;
157                Current := Current^.Next
```

(continued)

```
158                        END
159                    ELSE
160                      WHILE Current <> NIL DO
161                        BEGIN
162                          Writeln(DirToString(Current^));
163                          SpaceTaken := SpaceTaken + Current^.FileSize;
164                          Current := Current^.Prior
165                        END;
166                    Writeln;
167                    Writeln
168                    ('Total space occupied by these files is ',SpaceTaken:9:0,' bytes.');
169                  END
170            END.
```

Disposing of a List of Directory Entries

The lists of directory entries created by **GetDirectory** exist on the heap, and take up heapspace. For utilities such as **Spacer**, this is not especially important, since the utility creates the linked list, displays it, and then returns to DOS. For more complicated applications that need to re-use heapspace, some method of disposing of the directory lists is required.

Such a routine, by this time, should seem almost trivial. Singly and doubly linked lists can be disposed of in nearly identical fashion, since only one thread is required to tether the list while the rootmost entry is disposed of. Procedure **DisposeOfDirectory** will do the job quickly and safely.

```
1    {->>>>DisposeOfDirectory<<<<-------------------------------------}
2    {                                                               }
3    { Filename : DISPDIR.SRC -- Last Modified 1/15/87               }
4    {                                                               }
5    { This routine disposes of lists of DIRRec records as built by  }
6    { GetDirectory.  Type DIRRec and DIRPtr must be defined prior   }
7    { to its inclusion.                                             }
8    {                                                               }
9    {                                                               }
10   {                                                               }
11   {---------------------------------------------------------------}
12
13   PROCEDURE DisposeOfDirectory(RootPointer : DIRPtr);
14
15   VAR
16     Holder : DIRPtr;
17
18   BEGIN
19     IF RootPointer <> NIL THEN        { Can't dispose if no list! }
```

(continued)

```
20        REPEAT
21           Holder := RootPointer^.Next;    { Grab the next record. }
22           Dispose(RootPointer);           { Dispose of the first... }
23           RootPointer := Holder           { ...and make the next the first... }
24        UNTIL RootPointer = NIL            { ...until the list is all gone. }
25     END;
```

```
1    {->>>>DIRRec definition<<<<-------------------------------------}
2    {                                                               }
3    { Filename : DIRREC.DEF -- Last Modified 1/6/87                 }
4    {                                                               }
5    { This is the definition for the DIRRec record and its pointer }
6    { type.  Many of the directory routines from Chapter 7 use it. }
7    {                                                               }
8    { Types TimeRec, DateRec, and String15 must be predefined.     }
9    {                                                               }
10   {                                                               }
11   {                                                               }
12   {---------------------------------------------------------------}
13
14   TYPE
15     DIRPtr = ^DIRRec;
16     DIRRec = RECORD
17              FileName  : String15;
18              Attrib    : Byte;
19              FileSize  : Real;
20              TimeStamp : TimeRec;
21              DateStamp : DateRec;
22              Prior     : DIRPtr;
23              Next      : DIRPtr;
24           END;
```

```
1    {->>>>DTARec definition<<<<-------------------------------------}
2    {                                                               }
3    { Filename : DTAREC.DEF -- Last Modified 1/6/87                 }
4    {                                                               }
5    { This is the definition for the DTARec record and its pointer }
6    { type.  Many of the directory routines from Chapter 7 use it. }
7    { The DWord type used in the DOS time and date stamps is also  }
8    { defined here.                                                 }
9    {                                                               }
10   {                                                               }
11   {                                                               }
12   {---------------------------------------------------------------}
13
```

(continued)

```
14

15          DWord    = RECORD
16                      LoInteger,HiInteger : Integer
17                    END;
18          DTAPtr   = ^DTARec;
19          DTARec   = RECORD
20                      Reserved : ARRAY[0..20] OF Byte;
21                      Attrib   : Byte;
22                      TimeComp : Integer;
23                      DateComp : Integer;
24                      DTASize  : DWord;
25                      FileName : ARRAY[1..13] OF Char
26                    END;
```

The Eyeball INLINE Assembler

Many years ago, in my first job as dishwasher in a Walgreen's Drug Store Dinette, I had the responsibility of opening up the creaky old dishwashing machine and removing trays full of slimy, pale-green slop that had accumulated over the day's work. These had to be cleaned and scrubbed and returned to their slots, ready to receive the next day's slop. Lousy work, but somebody had to do it—and for $1.45 an hour, at that.

Emptying slop trays at the Walgreen's Dinette may be one of the few things I like less than hand-assembling 8086 machine code. The 8086 instruction set was never intended to be *orthogonal*; that is, symmetric in treating all machine registers identically and lacking in "special cases." Intel, in fact, never really intended that the 8086 would be programmed in assembler by human beings. Its "native" language was supposed to have been Intel's PL/M-86— and might have been, had Intel not insisted on selling PL/M-86 for many thousands of dollars.

One of the reasons I shunned Turbo Pascal's INLINE facility early on was an unwillingness to build individual 8086 instructions with mental tweezers, bit by nonorthagonal bit. The other reason was Borland's poor documentation of the Turbo Pascal runtime environment, which made it hard to understand why INLINE statements would sometimes work correctly and sometimes not. Experience has made the second problem less fierce than it once was, since dogged **DEBUG** work has shown us where most of the bodies are buried.

And, in answer to Reason #1, I have constructed the Eyeball INLINE Assembler, which occupies the next 70-odd pages of this book. The idea is simple: In the left column is a near-exhaustive list of 8086 assembly-language mnemonics, and in the right column is a list of INLINE-formatted machine-code equivalents to those mnemonics.

All register/register operations are included, as far as I know. The list is only near-exhaustive because I have not included all of the many exotic 8086 addressing modes for the memory/register opcodes. There are 8086 opcodes allowing you to address memory through combinations such as:

```
ES:[BX+SI+<16-bit displacement>]
CS:[BX+DI]
SS:[BP+DI+<8-bit displacement>]
```

and if you wish to use creatures like this, you will have to go back to your mental tweezers. What I have done is included memory/register opcodes for the three important classes of Turbo Pascal data accessible from within IN-

LINE statements: global variables, subprogram local variables and parameters, and subprogram VAR parameters and pointer references. (These last two are essentially the same thing, since VAR parameters are actually pointers to their parameters.)

The addressing mode given for global variables is:

```
DS:[<16-bit displacement>]
```

since Turbo Pascal replaces global variable identifiers with the 16-bit displacement of that identifier from the beginning of the data segment. This mode is indicated in the Eyeball Assembler by the use of the word **Global** in a mnemonic. Replace the word **Global** with a global variable identifier and you're in business.

To keep the size of the list down, I have not included a separate line for typed constants. Typed constants are essentially global variables that live in the code segment, and you can modify a global variable opcode to address a typed constant simply by placing the CS segment override prefix $2E in front of it.

For example, taking a line from the Eyeball Assembler:

```
ADD AL,Global          $02/$06/Global
```

This opcode can be modified to address a typed constant by changing it to:

```
$2E/$02/$06/TypedConstant
```

The addressing mode given for subprogram value parameters and local variables is:

```
SS:[BP+<16-bit displacement>]
```

since Turbo Pascal replaces value parameter and local variable identifiers with their 16-bit displacements from the **BP** register, assuming the use of the stack segment, **SS**. Again, replace the word **LocalOrParm** with your own value parameter or local variable identifier and you've got it.

Finally, I've included opcodes for use in addressing subprogram VAR parameters and pointer references. The addressing mode here is

```
ES:[DI]
```

meaning that the register **DI** contains an offset from the segment address in **ES**, and that the two taken together contain the full 32-bit address of a memory location upon which the opcode does its work.

VAR parameters, if you recall, are passed to subprograms as 32-bit addresses. Pointers are themselves nothing more than 32-bit addresses of the things they point to. The only problem in using the ES:[DI] opcodes is that the addresses must somehow be gotten into ES and DI.

Loading an address into ES and DI is done with the LES instruction. For loading an address passed on the stack (a VAR parameter, in other words), LES is used this way:

```
LES DI,VarParm          $C4/$BE/VarParm
```

Examples of **LES** used in this fashion are given in Section 4.3. For using **LES** to load an address stored as a global variable pointer, the following form of **LES** is used:

```
LES DI,MyPtr            $C4/$3E/MyPtr
```

It is important to remember that, in this case, the identifier **MyPtr** is replaced with its 16-bit offset from DS, as with any global variable. Examples of accessing data pointed to by a global variable pointer are also given in Section 4.3.

Once an address has been loaded into ES:DI in this fashion, any of the opcodes that address memory via ES:[DI] can be used.

As you might have guessed from the presence of semicolons in column 1, the Eyeball Assembler was originally generated by processing an assembler source file through Microsoft's MASM V4.0. The resulting .LST file (which contains binary opcode information in the left margin) was massaged by a Turbo Pascal utility and a number of Word Perfect macros to get it into its current form. No hand-assembled opcodes are included, and, for this reason, I feel that the Eyeball Assembler is quite reliable, assuming you understand what each of the opcodes is actually supposed to do.

If not, again, I recommend studying up on the 8086 instruction set. Learning by tearing your hair out can be effective, as long as you remember (as I failed to do) that eventually you run out of hair.

```
 1              ;   THE EYEBALL INLINE ASSEMBLER
 2              ;
 3              ;   by Jeff Duntemann
 4              ;
 5              ;   Last Modified 12/28/86
 6              ;
 7              ;
 8              ;
 9              ;   Arithmetic adjust instructions:
10              ;
11              AAA                         $37
12              AAD                         $D5/$0A
13              AAM                         $D4/$0A
14              AAS                         $3F
15              ;
16              ;
```

(continued)

```
17              ;   Add with carry.  8-bit operations first:
18              ;
19              ADC AL,AH                    $12/$C4
20              ADC AL,BL                    $12/$C3
21              ADC AL,BH                    $12/$C7
22              ADC AL,CL                    $12/$C1
23              ADC AL,CH                    $12/$C5
24              ADC AL,DL                    $12/$C2
25              ADC AL,DH                    $12/$C6
26              ADC AL,01H                   $14/$01
27              ADC AL,LocalOrParm           $12/$86/LocalOrParm
28              ADC LocalOrParm,AL           $10/$86/LocalOrParm
29              ADC AL,Global                $12/$06/Global
30              ADC Global,AL                $10/$06/Global
31              ADC AL,ES:[DI]               $26/$12/$05
32              ADC ES:[DI],AL               $26/$10/$05
33              ;
34              ADC AH,AL                    $12/$E0
35              ADC AH,BL                    $12/$E3
36              ADC AH,BH                    $12/$E7
37              ADC AH,CL                    $12/$E1
38              ADC AH,CH                    $12/$E5
39              ADC AH,DL                    $12/$E2
40              ADC AH,DH                    $12/$E6
41              ADC AH,01H                   $80/$D4/$01
42              ADC AH,LocalOrParm           $12/$A6/LocalOrParm
43              ADC LocalOrParm,AH           $10/$A6/LocalOrParm
44              ADC AH,Global                $12/$26/Global
45              ADC Global,AH                $10/$26/Global
46              ADC AH,ES:[DI]               $26/$12/$25
47              ADC ES:[DI],AH               $26/$10/$25
48              ;
49              ADC BL,BH                    $12/$DF
50              ADC BL,AL                    $12/$D8
51              ADC BL,AH                    $12/$DC
52              ADC BL,CL                    $12/$D9
53              ADC BL,CH                    $12/$DD
54              ADC BL,DL                    $12/$DA
55              ADC BL,DH                    $12/$DE
56              ADC BL,01H                   $80/$D3/$01
57              ADC BL,LocalOrParm           $12/$9E/LocalOrParm
58              ADC LocalOrParm,BL           $10/$9E/LocalOrParm
59              ADC BL,Global                $12/$1E/Global
60              ADC Global,BL                $10/$1E/Global
61              ADC BL,ES:[DI]               $26/$12/$1D
62              ADC ES:[DI],BL               $26/$10/$1D
63              ;
64              ADC BH,BL                    $12/$FB
65              ADC BH,AL                    $12/$F8
```

(continued)

66	ADC BH,AH	$12/$FC
67	ADC BH,CL	$12/$F9
68	ADC BH,CH	$12/$FD
69	ADC BH,DL	$12/$FA
70	ADC BH,DH	$12/$FE
71	ADC BH,01H	$80/$D7/$01
72	ADC BH,LocalOrParm	$12/$BE/LocalOrParm
73	ADC LocalOrParm,BH	$10/$BE/LocalOrParm
74	ADC BH,Global	$12/$3E/Global
75	ADC Global,BH	$10/$3E/Global
76	ADC BH,ES:[DI]	$26/$12/$3D
77	ADC ES:[DI],BH	$26/$10/$3D
78	;	
79	ADC CL,CH	$12/$CD
80	ADC CL,AL	$12/$C8
81	ADC CL,AH	$12/$CC
82	ADC CL,BL	$12/$CB
83	ADC CL,BH	$12/$CF
84	ADC CL,DL	$12/$CA
85	ADC CL,DH	$12/$CE
86	ADC CL,01H	$80/$D1/$01
87	ADC CL,LocalOrParm	$12/$8E/LocalOrParm
88	ADC LocalOrParm,CL	$10/$8E/LocalOrParm
89	ADC CL,Global	$12/$0E/Global
90	ADC Global,CL	$10/$0E/Global
91	ADC CL,ES:[DI]	$26/$12/$0D
92	ADC ES:[DI],CL	$26/$10/$0D
93	;	
94	ADC CH,CL	$12/$E9
95	ADC CH,AL	$12/$E8
96	ADC CH,AH	$12/$EC
97	ADC CH,BL	$12/$EB
98	ADC CH,BH	$12/$EF
99	ADC CH,DL	$12/$EA
100	ADC CH,DH	$12/$EE
101	ADC CH,01H	$80/$D5/$01
102	ADC CH,LocalOrParm	$12/$AE/LocalOrParm
103	ADC LocalOrParm,CH	$10/$AE/LocalOrParm
104	ADC CH,Global	$12/$2E/Global
105	ADC Global,CH	$10/$2E/Global
106	ADC CH,ES:[DI]	$26/$12/$2D
107	ADC ES:[DI],CH	$26/$10/$2D
108	;	
109	ADC DL,DH	$12/$D6
110	ADC DL,AL	$12/$D0
111	ADC DL,AH	$12/$D4
112	ADC DL,BL	$12/$D3
113	ADC DL,BH	$12/$D7
114	ADC DL,CL	$12/$D1

(continued)

```
115               ADC DL,CH                    $12/$D5
116               ADC DL,01H                   $80/$D2/$01
117               ADC DL,LocalOrParm           $12/$96/LocalOrParm
118               ADC LocalOrParm,DL           $10/$96/LocalOrParm
119               ADC DL,Global                $12/$16/Global
120               ADC Global,DL                $10/$16/Global
121               ADC DL,ES:[DI]               $26/$12/$15
122               ADC ES:[DI],DL               $26/$10/$15
123               ;
124               ADC DH,DL                    $12/$F2
125               ADC DH,AL                    $12/$F0
126               ADC DH,AH                    $12/$F4
127               ADC DH,BL                    $12/$F3
128               ADC DH,BH                    $12/$F7
129               ADC DH,CL                    $12/$F1
130               ADC DH,CH                    $12/$F5
131               ADC DH,01H                   $80/$D6/$01
132               ADC DH,LocalOrParm           $12/$B6/LocalOrParm
133               ADC LocalOrParm,DH           $10/$B6/LocalOrParm
134               ADC DH,Global                $12/$36/Global
135               ADC Global,DH                $10/$36/Global
136               ADC DH,ES:[DI]               $26/$12/$35
137               ADC ES:[DI],DH               $26/$10/$35
138               ;
139               ;    Now the 16-bit ADCs:
140               ;
141               ADC AX,BX                    $13/$C3
142               ADC AX,CX                    $13/$C1
143               ADC AX,DX                    $13/$C2
144               ADC AX,BP                    $13/$C5
145               ADC AX,SI                    $13/$C6
146               ADC AX,DI                    $13/$C7
147               ADC AX,SP                    $13/$C4
148               ADC AX,01H                   $15/$01/$00
149               ADC AX,07733H                $15/$33/$77
150               ADC AX,LocalOrParm           $13/$86/LocalOrParm
151               ADC LocalOrParm,AX           $11/$86/LocalOrParm
152               ADC AX,Global                $13/$06/Global
153               ADC Global,AX                $11/$06/Global
154               ADC AX,ES:[DI]               $26/$13/$05
155               ADC ES:[DI],AX               $26/$11/$05
156               ;
157               ADC BX,AX                    $13/$D8
158               ADC BX,CX                    $13/$D9
159               ADC BX,DX                    $13/$DA
160               ADC BX,BP                    $13/$DD
161               ADC BX,SI                    $13/$DE
162               ADC BX,DI                    $13/$DF
163               ADC BX,SP                    $13/$DC
```

(continued)

164	ADC BX,01H	$83/$D3/$01
165	ADC BX,07733H	$81/$D3/$33/$77
166	ADC BX,LocalOrParm	$13/$9E/LocalOrParm
167	ADC LocalOrParm,BX	$11/$9E/LocalOrParm
168	ADC BX,Global	$13/$1E/Global
169	ADC Global,BX	$11/$1E/Global
170	ADC BX,ES:[DI]	$26/$13/$1D
171	ADC ES:[DI],BX	$26/$11/$1D
172	;	
173	ADC CX,AX	$13/$C8
174	ADC CX,BX	$13/$CB
175	ADC CX,DX	$13/$CA
176	ADC CX,BP	$13/$CD
177	ADC CX,SI	$13/$CE
178	ADC CX,DI	$13/$CF
179	ADC CX,SP	$13/$CC
180	ADC CX,01H	$83/$D1/$01
181	ADC CX,07733H	$81/$D1/$33/$77
182	ADC CX,LocalOrParm	$13/$8E/LocalOrParm
183	ADC LocalOrParm,CX	$11/$8E/LocalOrParm
184	ADC CX,Global	$13/$0E/Global
185	ADC Global,CX	$11/$0E/Global
186	ADC CX,ES:[DI]	$26/$13/$0D
187	ADC ES:[DI],CX	$26/$11/$0D
188	;	
189	ADC DX,AX	$13/$D0
190	ADC DX,BX	$13/$D3
191	ADC DX,CX	$13/$D1
192	ADC DX,BP	$13/$D5
193	ADC DX,SI	$13/$D6
194	ADC DX,DI	$13/$D7
195	ADC DX,SP	$13/$D4
196	ADC DX,01H	$83/$D2/$01
197	ADC DX,07733H	$81/$D2/$33/$77
198	ADC DX,LocalOrParm	$13/$96/LocalOrParm
199	ADC LocalOrParm,DX	$11/$96/LocalOrParm
200	ADC DX,Global	$13/$16/Global
201	ADC Global,DX	$11/$16/Global
202	ADC DX,ES:[DI]	$26/$13/$15
203	ADC ES:[DI],DX	$26/$11/$15
204	;	
205	ADC BP,AX	$13/$E8
206	ADC BP,BX	$13/$EB
207	ADC BP,CX	$13/$E9
208	ADC BP,DX	$13/$EA
209	ADC BP,SI	$13/$EE
210	ADC BP,DI	$13/$EF
211	ADC BP,SP	$13/$EC
212	ADC BP,01H	$83/$D5/$01

(continued)

```
213             ADC BP,07733H           $81/$D5/$33/$77
214             ADC BP,Global           $13/$2E/Global
215             ADC Global,BP           $11/$2E/Global
216             ADC BP,ES:[DI]          $26/$13/$2D
217             ADC ES:[DI],BP          $26/$11/$2D
218             ;
219             ADC SI,AX               $13/$F0
220             ADC SI,BX               $13/$F3
221             ADC SI,CX               $13/$F1
222             ADC SI,DX               $13/$F2
223             ADC SI,BP               $13/$F5
224             ADC SI,DI               $13/$F7
225             ADC SI,SP               $13/$F4
226             ADC SI,01H              $83/$D6/$01
227             ADC SI,07733H           $81/$D6/$33/$77
228             ADC SI,LocalOrParm      $13/$B6/LocalOrParm
229             ADC LocalOrParm,SI      $11/$B6/LocalOrParm
230             ADC SI,Global           $13/$36/Global
231             ADC Global;SI           $11/$36/Global
232             ADC SI,ES:[DI]          $26/$13/$35
233             ADC ES:[DI],SI          $26/$11/$35
234             ;
235             ADC DI,AX               $13/$F8
236             ADC DI,BX               $13/$FB
237             ADC DI,CX               $13/$F9
238             ADC DI,DX               $13/$FA
239             ADC DI,BP               $13/$FD
240             ADC DI,SI               $13/$FE
241             ADC DI,SP               $13/$FC
242             ADC DI,01H              $83/$D7/$01
243             ADC DI,07733H           $81/$D7/$33/$77
244             ADC DI,LocalOrParm      $13/$BE/LocalOrParm
245             ADC LocalOrParm,DI      $11/$BE/LocalOrParm
246             ADC DI,Global           $13/$3E/Global
247             ADC Global,DI           $11/$3E/Global
248             ;
249             ADC SP,AX               $13/$E0
250             ADC SP,BX               $13/$E3
251             ADC SP,CX               $13/$E1
252             ADC SP,DX               $13/$E2
253             ADC SP,BP               $13/$E5
254             ADC SP,SI               $13/$E6
255             ADC SP,DI               $13/$E7
256             ADC SP,01H              $83/$D4/$01
257             ADC SP,07733H           $81/$D4/$33/$77
258             ADC SP,LocalOrParm      $13/$A6/LocalOrParm
259             ADC LocalOrParm,SP      $11/$A6/LocalOrParm
260             ADC SP,Global           $13/$26/Global
261             ADC Global,SP           $11/$26/Global
```

(continued)

```
262                ADC SP,ES:[DI]                      $26/$13/$25
263                ADC ES:[DI],SP                      $26/$11/$25
264                ;
265                ADC BYTE PTR LocalOrParm,01H        $80/$96/LocalOrParm/$01
266                ADC WORD PTR LocalOrParm,01H        $83/$96/LocalOrParm/$01
267                ADC BYTE PTR Global,01H             $80/$16/Global/$01
268                ADC WORD PTR Global,01H             $83/$16/Global/$01
269                ADC BYTE PTR ES:[DI],01H            $26/$80/$15/$01
270                ADC WORD PTR ES:[DI],01H            $26/$83/$15/$01
271                ;
272                ;
273                ;    ADDs.   8-bit operations first:
274                ;
275                ADD AL,AH                           $02/$C4
276                ADD AL,BL                           $02/$C3
277                ADD AL,BH                           $02/$C7
278                ADD AL,CL                           $02/$C1
279                ADD AL,CH                           $02/$C5
280                ADD AL,DL                           $02/$C2
281                ADD AL,DH                           $02/$C6
282                ADD AL,01H                          $04/$01
283                ADD AL,LocalOrParm                  $02/$86/LocalOrParm
284                ADD LocalOrParm,AL                  $00/$86/LocalOrParm
285                ADD AL,Global                       $02/$06/Global
286                ADD Global,AL                       $00/$06/Global
287                ADD AL,ES:[DI]                      $26/$02/$05
288                ADD ES:[DI],AL                      $26/$00/$05
289                ;
290                ADD AH,AL                           $02/$E0
291                ADD AH,BL                           $02/$E3
292                ADD AH,BH                           $02/$E7
293                ADD AH,CL                           $02/$E1
294                ADD AH,CH                           $02/$E5
295                ADD AH,DL                           $02/$E2
296                ADD AH,DH                           $02/$E6
297                ADD AH,01H                          $80/$C4/$01
298                ADD AH,LocalOrParm                  $02/$A6/LocalOrParm
299                ADD LocalOrParm,AH                  $00/$A6/LocalOrParm
300                ADD AH,Global                       $02/$26/Global
301                ADD Global,AH                       $00/$26/Global
302                ADD AH,ES:[DI]                      $26/$02/$25
303                ADD ES:[DI],AH                      $26/$00/$25
304                ;
305                ADD BL,BH                           $02/$DF
306                ADD BL,AL                           $02/$D8
307                ADD BL,AH                           $02/$DC
308                ADD BL,CL                           $02/$D9
309                ADD BL,CH                           $02/$DD
310                ADD BL,DL                           $02/$DA
```

(continued)

```
311             ADD BL,DH                    $02/$DE
312             ADD BL,01H                    $80/$C3/$01
313             ADD BL,LocalOrParm            $02/$9E/LocalOrParm
314             ADD LocalOrParm,BL            $00/$9E/LocalOrParm
315             ADD BL,Global                 $02/$1E/Global
316             ADD Global,BL                 $00/$1E/Global
317             ADD BL,ES:[DI]                $26/$02/$1D
318             ADD ES:[DI],BL                $26/$00/$1D
319             ;
320             ADD BH,BL                     $02/$FB
321             ADD BH,AL                     $02/$F8
322             ADD BH,AH                     $02/$FC
323             ADD BH,CL                     $02/$F9
324             ADD BH,CH                     $02/$FD
325             ADD BH,DL                     $02/$FA
326             ADD BH,DH                     $02/$FE
327             ADD BH,01H                    $80/$C7/$01
328             ADD BH,LocalOrParm            $02/$BE/LocalOrParm
329             ADD LocalOrParm,BH            $00/$BE/LocalOrParm
330             ADD BH,Global                 $02/$3E/Global
331             ADD Global,BH                 $00/$3E/Global
332             ADD BH,ES:[DI]                $26/$02/$3D
333             ADD ES:[DI],BH                $26/$00/$3D
334             ;
335             ADD CL,CH                     $02/$CD
336             ADD CL,AL                     $02/$C8
337             ADD CL,AH                     $02/$CC
338             ADD CL,BL                     $02/$CB
339             ADD CL,BH                     $02/$CF
340             ADD CL,DL                     $02/$CA
341             ADD CL,DH                     $02/$CE
342             ADD CL,01H                    $80/$C1/$01
343             ADD CL,LocalOrParm            $02/$8E/LocalOrParm
344             ADD LocalOrParm,CL            $00/$8E/LocalOrParm
345             ADD CL,Global                 $02/$0E/Global
346             ADD Global,CL                 $00/$0E/Global
347             ADD CL,ES:[DI]                $26/$02/$0D
348             ADD ES:[DI],CL                $26/$00/$0D
349             ;
350             ADD CH,CL                     $02/$E9
351             ADD CH,AL                     $02/$E8
352             ADD CH,AH                     $02/$EC
353             ADD CH,BL                     $02/$EB
354             ADD CH,BH                     $02/$EF
355             ADD CH,DL                     $02/$EA
356             ADD CH,DH                     $02/$EE
357             ADD CH,01H                    $80/$C5/$01
358             ADD CH,LocalOrParm            $02/$AE/LocalOrParm
359             ADD LocalOrParm,CH            $00/$AE/LocalOrParm
```

(continued)

```
360                 ADD CH,Global              $02/$2E/Global
361                 ADD Global,CH              $00/$2E/Global
362                 ADD CH,ES:[DI]             $26/$02/$2D
363                 ADD ES:[DI],CH             $26/$00/$2D
364                 ;
365                 ADD DL,DH                  $02/$D6
366                 ADD DL,AL                  $02/$D0
367                 ADD DL,AH                  $02/$D4
368                 ADD DL,BL                  $02/$D3
369                 ADD DL,BH                  $02/$D7
370                 ADD DL,CL                  $02/$D1
371                 ADD DL,CH                  $02/$D5
372                 ADD DL,01H                 $80/$C2/$01
373                 ADD DL,LocalOrParm         $02/$96/LocalOrParm
374                 ADD LocalOrParm,DL         $00/$96/LocalOrParm
375                 ADD DL,Global              $02/$16/Global
376                 ADD Global,DL              $00/$16/Global
377                 ADD DL,ES:[DI]             $26/$02/$15
378                 ADD ES:[DI],DL             $26/$00/$15
379                 ;
380                 ADD DH,DL                  $02/$F2
381                 ADD DH,AL                  $02/$F0
382                 ADD DH,AH                  $02/$F4
383                 ADD DH,BL                  $02/$F3
384                 ADD DH,BH                  $02/$F7
385                 ADD DH,CL                  $02/$F1
386                 ADD DH,CH                  $02/$F5
387                 ADD DH,01H                 $80/$C6/$01
388                 ADD DH,LocalOrParm         $02/$B6/LocalOrParm
389                 ADD LocalOrParm,DH         $00/$B6/LocalOrParm
390                 ADD DH,Global              $02/$36/Global
391                 ADD Global,DH              $00/$36/Global
392                 ADD DH,ES:[DI]             $26/$02/$35
393                 ADD ES:[DI],DH             $26/$00/$35
394                 ;
395                 ;    Now the 16-bit ADCs:
396                 ;
397                 ADD AX,BX                  $03/$C3
398                 ADD AX,CX                  $03/$C1
399                 ADD AX,DX                  $03/$C2
400                 ADD AX,BP                  $03/$C5
401                 ADD AX,SI                  $03/$C6
402                 ADD AX,DI                  $03/$C7
403                 ADD AX,SP                  $03/$C4
404                 ADD AX,01H                 $05/$01/$00
405                 ADD AX,07733H              $05/$33/$77
406                 ADD AX,LocalOrParm         $03/$86/LocalOrParm
407                 ADD LocalOrParm,AX         $01/$86/LocalOrParm
408                 ADD AX,Global              $03/$06/Global
```

(continued)

```
409          ADD  Global,AX              $01/$06/Global
410          ADD  AX,ES:[DI]             $26/$03/$05
411          ADD  ES:[DI],AX             $26/$01/$05
412          ;
413          ADD  BX,AX                  $03/$D8
414          ADD  BX,CX                  $03/$D9
415          ADD  BX,DX                  $03/$DA
416          ADD  BX,BP                  $03/$DD
417          ADD  BX,SI                  $03/$DE
418          ADD  BX,DI                  $03/$DF
419          ADD  BX,SP                  $03/$DC
420          ADD  BX,01H                 $83/$C3/$01
421          ADD  BX,07733H              $81/$C3/$33/$77
422          ADD  BX,LocalOrParm         $03/$9E/LocalOrParm
423          ADD  LocalOrParm,BX         $01/$9E/LocalOrParm
424          ADD  BX,Global              $03/$1E/Global
425          ADD  Global,BX              $01/$1E/Global
426          ADD  BX,ES:[DI]             $26/$03/$1D
427          ADD  ES:[DI],BX             $26/$01/$1D
428          ;
429          ADD  CX,AX                  $03/$C8
430          ADD  CX,BX                  $03/$CB
431          ADD  CX,DX                  $03/$CA
432          ADD  CX,BP                  $03/$CD
433          ADD  CX,SI                  $03/$CE
434          ADD  CX,DI                  $03/$CF
435          ADD  CX,SP                  $03/$CC
436          ADD  CX,01H                 $83/$C1/$01
437          ADD  CX,07733H              $81/$C1/$33/$77
438          ADD  CX,LocalOrParm         $03/$8E/LocalOrParm
439          ADD  LocalOrParm,CX         $01/$8E/LocalOrParm
440          ADD  CX,Global              $03/$0E/Global
441          ADD  Global,CX              $01/$0E/Global
442          ADD  CX,ES:[DI]             $26/$03/$0D
443          ADD  ES:[DI],CX             $26/$01/$0D
444          ;
445          ADD  DX,AX                  $03/$D0
446          ADD  DX,BX                  $03/$D3
447          ADD  DX,CX                  $03/$D1
448          ADD  DX,BP                  $03/$D5
449          ADD  DX,SI                  $03/$D6
450          ADD  DX,DI                  $03/$D7
451          ADD  DX,SP                  $03/$D4
452          ADD  DX,01H                 $83/$C2/$01
453          ADD  DX,07733H              $81/$C2/$33/$77
454          ADD  DX,LocalOrParm         $03/$96/LocalOrParm
455          ADD  LocalOrParm,DX         $01/$96/LocalOrParm
456          ADD  DX,Global              $03/$16/Global
457          ADD  Global,DX              $01/$16/Global
```

(continued)

458	ADD DX,ES:[DI]	$26/$03/$15
459	ADD ES:[DI],DX	$26/$01/$15
460	;	
461	ADD BP,AX	$03/$E8
462	ADD BP,BX	$03/$EB
463	ADD BP,CX	$03/$E9
464	ADD BP,DX	$03/$EA
465	ADD BP,SI	$03/$EE
466	ADD BP,DI	$03/$EF
467	ADD BP,SP	$03/$EC
468	ADD BP,01H	$83/$C5/$01
469	ADD BP,07733H	$81/$C5/$33/$77
470	ADD BP,Global	$03/$2E/Global
471	ADD Global,BP	$01/$2E/Global
472	ADD BP,ES:[DI]	$26/$03/$2D
473	ADD ES:[DI],BP	$26/$01/$2D
474	;	
475	ADD SI,AX	$03/$F0
476	ADD SI,BX	$03/$F3
477	ADD SI,CX	$03/$F1
478	ADD SI,DX	$03/$F2
479	ADD SI,BP	$03/$F5
480	ADD SI,DI	$03/$F7
481	ADD SI,SP	$03/$F4
482	ADD SI,01H	$83/$C6/$01
483	ADD SI,07733H	$81/$C6/$33/$77
484	ADD SI,LocalOrParm	$03/$B6/LocalOrParm
485	ADD LocalOrParm,SI	$01/$B6/LocalOrParm
486	ADD SI,Global	$03/$36/Global
487	ADD Global,SI	$01/$36/Global
488	ADD SI,ES:[DI]	$26/$03/$35
489	ADD ES:[DI],SI	$26/$01/$35
490	;	
491	ADD DI,AX	$03/$F8
492	ADD DI,BX	$03/$FB
493	ADD DI,CX	$03/$F9
494	ADD DI,DX	$03/$FA
495	ADD DI,BP	$03/$FD
496	ADD DI,SI	$03/$FE
497	ADD DI,SP	$03/$FC
498	ADD DI,01H	$83/$C7/$01
499	ADD DI,07733H	$81/$C7/$33/$77
500	ADD DI,LocalOrParm	$03/$BE/LocalOrParm
501	ADD LocalOrParm,DI	$01/$BE/LocalOrParm
502	ADD DI,Global	$03/$3E/Global
503	ADD Global,DI	$01/$3E/Global
504	;	
505	ADD SP,AX	$03/$E0
506	ADD SP,BX	$03/$E3

(continued)

```
507              ADD  SP,CX                        $03/$E1
508              ADD  SP,DX                        $03/$E2
509              ADD  SP,BP                        $03/$E5
510              ADD  SP,SI                        $03/$E6
511              ADD  SP,DI                        $03/$E7
512              ADD  SP,01H                       $83/$C4/$01
513              ADD  SP,07733H                    $81/$C4/$33/$77
514              ADD  SP,LocalOrParm               $03/$A6/LocalOrParm
515              ADD  LocalOrParm,SP               $01/$A6/LocalOrParm
516              ADD  SP,Global                    $03/$26/Global
517              ADD  Global,SP                    $01/$26/Global
518              ADD  SP,ES:[DI]                   $26/$03/$25
519              ADD  ES:[DI],SP                   $26/$01/$25
520              ;
521              ADD  BYTE PTR LocalOrParm,01H     $80/$86/LocalOrParm/$01
522              ADD  WORD PTR LocalOrParm,01H     $83/$86/LocalOrParm/$01
523              ADD  BYTE PTR Global,01H          $80/$06/Global/$01
524              ADD  WORD PTR Global,01H          $83/$06/Global/$01
525              ADD  BYTE PTR ES:[DI],01H         $26/$80/$05/$01
526              ADD  WORD PTR ES:[DI],01H         $26/$83/$05/$01
527              ;
528              ;
529              ;    ANDs. 8-bit operations first:
530              ;
531              AND  AL,AH                        $22/$C4
532              AND  AL,BL                        $22/$C3
533              AND  AL,BH                        $22/$C7
534              AND  AL,CL                        $22/$C1
535              AND  AL,CH                        $22/$C5
536              AND  AL,DL                        $22/$C2
537              AND  AL,DH                        $22/$C6
538              AND  AL,01H                       $24/$01
539              AND  AL,LocalOrParm               $22/$86/LocalOrParm
540              AND  LocalOrParm,AL               $20/$86/LocalOrParm
541              AND  AL,Global                    $22/$06/Global
542              AND  Global,AL                    $20/$06/Global
543              AND  AL,ES:[DI]                   $26/$22/$05
544              AND  ES:[DI],AL                   $26/$20/$05
545              ;
546              AND  AH,AL                        $22/$E0
547              AND  AH,BL                        $22/$E3
548              AND  AH,BH                        $22/$E7
549              AND  AH,CL                        $22/$E1
550              AND  AH,CH                        $22/$E5
551              AND  AH,DL                        $22/$E2
552              AND  AH,DH                        $22/$E6
553              AND  AH,01H                       $80/$E4/$01
554              AND  AH,LocalOrParm               $22/$A6/LocalOrParm
555              AND  LocalOrParm,AH               $20/$A6/LocalOrParm
```

(continued)

556	AND AH,Global	$22/$26/Global
557	AND Global,AH	$20/$26/Global
558	AND AH,ES:[DI]	$26/$22/$25
559	AND ES:[DI],AH	$26/$20/$25
560	;	
561	AND BL,BH	$22/$DF
562	AND BL,AL	$22/$D8
563	AND BL,AH	$22/$DC
564	AND BL,CL	$22/$D9
565	AND BL,CH	$22/$DD
566	AND BL,DL	$22/$DA
567	AND BL,DH	$22/$DE
568	AND BL,01H	$80/$E3/$01
569	AND BL,LocalOrParm	$22/$9E/LocalOrParm
570	AND LocalOrParm,BL	$20/$9E/LocalOrParm
571	AND BL,Global	$22/$1E/Global
572	AND Global,BL	$20/$1E/Global
573	AND BL,ES:[DI]	$26/$22/$1D
574	AND ES:[DI],BL	$26/$20/$1D
575	;	
576	AND BH,BL	$22/$FB
577	AND BH,AL	$22/$F8
578	AND BH,AH	$22/$FC
579	AND BH,CL	$22/$F9
580	AND BH,CH	$22/$FD
581	AND BH,DL	$22/$FA
582	AND BH,DH	$22/$FE
583	AND BH,01H	$80/$E7/$01
584	AND BH,LocalOrParm	$22/$BE/LocalOrParm
585	AND LocalOrParm,BH	$20/$BE/LocalOrParm
586	AND BH,Global	$22/$3E/Global
587	AND Global,BH	$20/$3E/Global
588	AND BH,ES:[DI]	$26/$22/$3D
589	AND ES:[DI],BH	$26/$20/$3D
590	;	
591	AND CL,CH	$22/$CD
592	AND CL,AL	$22/$C8
593	AND CL,AH	$22/$CC
594	AND CL,BL	$22/$CB
595	AND CL,BH	$22/$CF
596	AND CL,DL	$22/$CA
597	AND CL,DH	$22/$CE
598	AND CL,01H	$80/$E1/$01
599	AND CL,LocalOrParm	$22/$8E/LocalOrParm
600	AND LocalOrParm,CL	$20/$8E/LocalOrParm
601	AND CL,Global	$22/$0E/Global
602	AND Global,CL	$20/$0E/Global
603	AND CL,ES:[DI]	$26/$22/$0D
604	AND ES:[DI],CL	$26/$20/$0D

(continued)

```
605                     ;
606                     AND  CH,CL                    $22/$E9
607                     AND  CH,AL                    $22/$E8
608                     AND  CH,AH                    $22/$EC
609                     AND  CH,BL                    $22/$EB
610                     AND  CH,BH                    $22/$EF
611                     AND  CH,DL                    $22/$EA
612                     AND  CH,DH                    $22/$EE
613                     AND  CH,01H                   $80/$E5/$01
614                     AND  CH,LocalOrParm           $22/$AE/LocalOrParm
615                     AND  LocalOrParm,CH           $20/$AE/LocalOrParm
616                     AND  CH,Global               $22/$2E/Global
617                     AND  Global,CH               $20/$2E/Global
618                     AND  CH,ES:[DI]               $26/$22/$2D
619                     AND  ES:[DI],CH               $26/$20/$2D
620                     ;
621                     AND  DL,DH                    $22/$D6
622                     AND  DL,AL                    $22/$D0
623                     AND  DL,AH                    $22/$D4
624                     AND  DL,BL                    $22/$D3
625                     AND  DL,BH                    $22/$D7
626                     AND  DL,CL                    $22/$D1
627                     AND  DL,CH                    $22/$D5
628                     AND  DL,01H                   $80/$E2/$01
629                     AND  DL,LocalOrParm           $22/$96/LocalOrParm
630                     AND  LocalOrParm,DL           $20/$96/LocalOrParm
631                     AND  DL,Global               $22/$16/Global
632                     AND  Global,DL               $20/$16/Global
633                     AND  DL,ES:[DI]               $26/$22/$15
634                     AND  ES:[DI],DL               $26/$20/$15
635                     ;
636                     AND  DH,DL                    $22/$F2
637                     AND  DH,AL                    $22/$F0
638                     AND  DH,AH                    $22/$F4
639                     AND  DH,BL                    $22/$F3
640                     AND  DH,BH                    $22/$F7
641                     AND  DH,CL                    $22/$F1
642                     AND  DH,CH                    $22/$F5
643                     AND  DH,01H                   $80/$E6/$01
644                     AND  DH,LocalOrParm           $22/$B6/LocalOrParm
645                     AND  LocalOrParm,DH           $20/$B6/LocalOrParm
646                     AND  DH,Global               $22/$36/Global
647                     AND  Global,DH               $20/$36/Global
648                     AND  DH,ES:[DI]               $26/$22/$35
649                     AND  ES:[DI],DH               $26/$20/$35
650                     ;
651                     ;    Now the 16-bit ANDs:
652                     ;
653                     AND  AX,BX                    $23/$C3
```

(continued)

654	AND AX,CX	$23/$C1
655	AND AX,DX	$23/$C2
656	AND AX,BP	$23/$C5
657	AND AX,SI	$23/$C6
658	AND AX,DI	$23/$C7
659	AND AX,SP	$23/$C4
660	AND AX,01H	$25/$01/$00
661	AND AX,07733H	$25/$33/$77
662	AND AX,LocalOrParm	$23/$86/LocalOrParm
663	AND LocalOrParm,AX	$21/$86/LocalOrParm
664	AND AX,Global	$23/$06/Global
665	AND Global,AX	$21/$06/Global
666	AND AX,ES:[DI]	$26/$23/$05
667	AND ES:[DI],AX	$26/$21/$05
668	;	
669	AND BX,AX	$23/$D8
670	AND BX,CX	$23/$D9
671	AND BX,DX	$23/$DA
672	AND BX,BP	$23/$DD
673	AND BX,SI	$23/$DE
674	AND BX,DI	$23/$DF
675	AND BX,SP	$23/$DC
676	AND BX,01H	$81/$E3/$01/$00
677	AND BX,07733H	$81/$E3/$33/$77
678	AND BX,LocalOrParm	$23/$9E/LocalOrParm
679	AND LocalOrParm,BX	$21/$9E/LocalOrParm
680	AND BX,Global	$23/$1E/Global
681	AND Global,BX	$21/$1E/Global
682	AND BX,ES:[DI]	$26/$23/$1D
683	AND ES:[DI],BX	$26/$21/$1D
684	;	
685	AND CX,AX	$23/$C8
686	AND CX,BX	$23/$CB
687	AND CX,DX	$23/$CA
688	AND CX,BP	$23/$CD
689	AND CX,SI	$23/$CE
690	AND CX,DI	$23/$CF
691	AND CX,SP	$23/$CC
692	AND CX,01H	$81/$E1/$01/$00
693	AND CX,07733H	$81/$E1/$33/$77
694	AND CX,LocalOrParm	$23/$8E/LocalOrParm
695	AND LocalOrParm,CX	$21/$8E/LocalOrParm
696	AND CX,Global	$23/$0E/Global
697	AND Global,CX	$21/$0E/Global
698	AND CX,ES:[DI]	$26/$23/$0D
699	AND ES:[DI],CX	$26/$21/$0D
700	;	
701	AND DX,AX	$23/$D0
702	AND DX,BX	$23/$D3

(continued)

```
703              AND DX,CX                     $23/$D1
704              AND DX,BP                     $23/$D5
705              AND DX,SI                     $23/$D6
706              AND DX,DI                     $23/$D7
707              AND DX,SP                     $23/$D4
708              AND DX,01H                    $81/$E2/$01/$00
709              AND DX,07733H                 $81/$E2/$33/$77
710              AND DX,LocalOrParm            $23/$96/LocalOrParm
711              AND LocalOrParm,DX            $21/$96/LocalOrParm
712              AND DX,Global                 $23/$16/Global
713              AND Global,DX                 $21/$16/Global
714              AND DX,ES:[DI]                $26/$23/$15
715              AND ES:[DI],DX                $26/$21/$15
716              ;
717              AND BP,AX                     $23/$E8
718              AND BP,BX                     $23/$EB
719              AND BP,CX                     $23/$E9
720              AND BP,DX                     $23/$EA
721              AND BP,SI                     $23/$EE
722              AND BP,DI                     $23/$EF
723              AND BP,SP                     $23/$EC
724              AND BP,01H                    $81/$E5/$01/$00
725              AND BP,07733H                 $81/$E5/$33/$77
726              AND BP,Global                 $23/$2E/Global
727              AND Global,BP                 $21/$2E/Global
728              AND BP,ES:[DI]                $26/$23/$2D
729              AND ES:[DI],BP                $26/$21/$2D
730              ;
731              AND SI,AX                     $23/$F0
732              AND SI,BX                     $23/$F3
733              AND SI,CX                     $23/$F1
734              AND SI,DX                     $23/$F2
735              AND SI,BP                     $23/$F5
736              AND SI,DI                     $23/$F7
737              AND SI,SP                     $23/$F4
738              AND SI,01H                    $81/$E6/$01/$00
739              AND SI,07733H                 $81/$E6/$33/$77
740              AND SI,LocalOrParm            $23/$B6/LocalOrParm
741              AND LocalOrParm,SI            $21/$B6/LocalOrParm
742              AND SI,Global                 $23/$36/Global
743              AND Global,SI                 $21/$36/Global
744              AND SI,ES:[DI]                $26/$23/$35
745              AND ES:[DI],SI                $26/$21/$35
746              ;
747              AND DI,AX                     $23/$F8
748              AND DI,BX                     $23/$FB
749              AND DI,CX                     $23/$F9
750              AND DI,DX                     $23/$FA
751              AND DI,BP                     $23/$FD
```

(continued)

```
752              AND  DI,SI                         $23/$FE
753              AND  DI,SP                         $23/$FC
754              AND  DI,01H                        $81/$E7/$01/$00
755              AND  DI,07733H                     $81/$E7/$33/$77
756              AND  DI,LocalOrParm                $23/$BE/LocalOrParm
757              AND  LocalOrParm,DI                $21/$BE/LocalOrParm
758              AND  DI,Global                     $23/$3E/Global
759              AND  Global,DI                     $21/$3E/Global
760              ;
761              AND  SP,AX                         $23/$E0
762              AND  SP,BX                         $23/$E3
763              AND  SP,CX                         $23/$E1
764              AND  SP,DX                         $23/$E2
765              AND  SP,BP                         $23/$E5
766              AND  SP,SI                         $23/$E6
767              AND  SP,DI                         $23/$E7
768              AND  SP,01H                        $81/$E4/$01/$00
769              AND  SP,07733H                     $81/$E4/$33/$77
770              AND  SP,LocalOrParm                $23/$A6/LocalOrParm
771              AND  LocalOrParm,SP                $21/$A6/LocalOrParm
772              AND  SP,Global                     $23/$26/Global
773              AND  Global,SP                     $21/$26/Global
774              AND  SP,ES:[DI]                    $26/$23/$25
775              AND  ES:[DI],SP                    $26/$21/$25
776              ;
777              AND  BYTE PTR LocalOrParm,01H      $80/$A6/LocalOrParm/$01
778              AND  WORD PTR LocalOrParm,01H      $81/$A6/LocalOrParm/$01/$00
779              AND  BYTE PTR Global,01H           $80/$26/Global/$01
780              AND  WORD PTR Global,01H           $81/$26/Global/$01/$00
781              AND  BYTE PTR ES:[DI],01H          $26/$80/$25/$01
782              AND  WORD PTR ES:[DI],01H          $26/$81/$25/$01/$00
783              ;
784              ;
785              ;    CALLs
786              ;
787              CALL AX                            $FF/$D0
788              CALL BX                            $FF/$D3
789              CALL CX                            $FF/$D1
790              CALL DX                            $FF/$D2
791              CALL BP                            $FF/$D5
792              CALL SI                            $FF/$D6
793              CALL DI                            $FF/$D7
794              CALL SP                            $FF/$D4
795              ;
796              ;
797              ;    Convert Byte to Word
798              ;
799              CBW                                $98
800              ;
```

(continued)

```
801                     ;
802                     ;    Clear/complement Flags
803                     ;
804                     CLC                         $F8
805                     CLD                         $FC
806                     CLI                         $FA
807                     CMC                         $F5
808                     ;
809                     ;
810                     ;    Compares:
811                     ;
812                     CMP AL,AH                    $3A/$C4
813                     CMP AL,BL                    $3A/$C3
814                     CMP AL,BH                    $3A/$C7
815                     CMP AL,CL                    $3A/$C1
816                     CMP AL,CH                    $3A/$C5
817                     CMP AL,DL                    $3A/$C2
818                     CMP AL,DH                    $3A/$C6
819                     CMP AL,01H                   $3C/$01
820                     CMP AL,LocalOrParm           $3A/$86/LocalOrParm
821                     CMP LocalOrParm,AL           $38/$86/LocalOrParm
822                     CMP AL,Global               $3A/$06/Global
823                     CMP Global,AL               $38/$06/Global
824                     CMP AL,ES:[DI]              $26/$3A/$05
825                     CMP ES:[DI],AL              $26/$38/$05
826                     ;
827                     CMP AH,AL                    $3A/$E0
828                     CMP AH,BL                    $3A/$E3
829                     CMP AH,BH                    $3A/$E7
830                     CMP AH,CL                    $3A/$E1
831                     CMP AH,CH                    $3A/$E5
832                     CMP AH,DL                    $3A/$E2
833                     CMP AH,DH                    $3A/$E6
834                     CMP AH,01H                   $80/$FC/$01
835                     CMP AH,LocalOrParm           $3A/$A6/LocalOrParm
836                     CMP LocalOrParm,AH           $38/$A6/LocalOrParm
837                     CMP AH,Global               $3A/$26/Global
838                     CMP Global,AH               $38/$26/Global
839                     CMP AH,ES:[DI]              $26/$3A/$25
840                     CMP ES:[DI],AH              $26/$38/$25
841                     ;
842                     CMP BL,BH                    $3A/$DF
843                     CMP BL,AL                    $3A/$D8
844                     CMP BL,AH                    $3A/$DC
845                     CMP BL,CL                    $3A/$D9
846                     CMP BL,CH                    $3A/$DD
847                     CMP BL,DL                    $3A/$DA
848                     CMP BL,DH                    $3A/$DE
849                     CMP BL,01H                   $80/$FB/$01
```

(continued)

850	CMP BL,LocalOrParm	$3A/$9E/LocalOrParm
851	CMP LocalOrParm,BL	$38/$9E/LocalOrParm
852	CMP BL,Global	$3A/$1E/Global
853	CMP Global,BL	$38/$1E/Global
854	CMP BL,ES:[DI]	$26/$3A/$1D
855	CMP ES:[DI],BL	$26/$38/$1D
856	;	
857	CMP BH,BL	$3A/$FB
858	CMP BH,AL	$3A/$F8
859	CMP BH,AH	$3A/$FC
860	CMP BH,CL	$3A/$F9
861	CMP BH,CH	$3A/$FD
862	CMP BH,DL	$3A/$FA
863	CMP BH,DH	$3A/$FE
864	CMP BH,01H	$80/$FF/$01
865	CMP BH,LocalOrParm	$3A/$BE/LocalOrParm
866	CMP LocalOrParm,BH	$38/$BE/LocalOrParm
867	CMP BH,Global	$3A/$3E/Global
868	CMP Global,BH	$38/$3E/Global
869	CMP BH,ES:[DI]	$26/$3A/$3D
870	CMP ES:[DI],BH	$26/$38/$3D
871	;	
872	CMP CL,CH	$3A/$CD
873	CMP CL,AL	$3A/$C8
874	CMP CL,AH	$3A/$CC
875	CMP CL,BL	$3A/$CB
876	CMP CL,BH	$3A/$CF
877	CMP CL,DL	$3A/$CA
878	CMP CL,DH	$3A/$CE
879	CMP CL,01H	$80/$F9/$01
880	CMP CL,LocalOrParm	$3A/$8E/LocalOrParm
881	CMP LocalOrParm,CL	$38/$8E/LocalOrParm
882	CMP CL,Global	$3A/$0E/Global
883	CMP Global,CL	$38/$0E/Global
884	CMP CL,ES:[DI]	$26/$3A/$0D
885	CMP ES:[DI],CL	$26/$38/$0D
886	;	
887	CMP CH,CL	$3A/$E9
888	CMP CH,AL	$3A/$E8
889	CMP CH,AH	$3A/$EC
890	CMP CH,BL	$3A/$EB
891	CMP CH,BH	$3A/$EF
892	CMP CH,DL	$3A/$EA
893	CMP CH,DH	$3A/$EE
894	CMP CH,01H	$80/$FD/$01
895	CMP CH,LocalOrParm	$3A/$AE/LocalOrParm
896	CMP LocalOrParm,CH	$38/$AE/LocalOrParm
897	**CMP CH,Global**	**$3A/$2E/Global**
898	**CMP Global,CH**	**$38/$2E/Global**

(continued)

```
899                 CMP CH,ES:[DI]              $26/$3A/$2D
900                 CMP ES:[DI],CH              $26/$38/$2D
901                 ;
902                 CMP DL,DH                   $3A/$D6
903                 CMP DL,AL                   $3A/$D0
904                 CMP DL,AH                   $3A/$D4
905                 CMP DL,BL                   $3A/$D3
906                 CMP DL,BH                   $3A/$D7
907                 CMP DL,CL                   $3A/$D1
908                 CMP DL,CH                   $3A/$D5
909                 CMP DL,01H                  $80/$FA/$01
910                 CMP DL,LocalOrParm          $3A/$96/LocalOrParm
911                 CMP LocalOrParm,DL          $38/$96/LocalOrParm
912                 CMP DL,Global               $3A/$16/Global
913                 CMP Global,DL               $38/$16/Global
914                 CMP DL,ES:[DI]              $26/$3A/$15
915                 CMP ES:[DI],DL              $26/$38/$15
916                 ;
917                 CMP DH,DL                   $3A/$F2
918                 CMP DH,AL                   $3A/$F0
919                 CMP DH,AH                   $3A/$F4
920                 CMP DH,BL                   $3A/$F3
921                 CMP DH,BH                   $3A/$F7
922                 CMP DH,CL                   $3A/$F1
923                 CMP DH,CH                   $3A/$F5
924                 CMP DH,01H                  $80/$FE/$01
925                 CMP DH,LocalOrParm          $3A/$B6/LocalOrParm
926                 CMP LocalOrParm,DH          $38/$B6/LocalOrParm
927                 CMP DH,Global               $3A/$36/Global
928                 CMP Global,DH               $38/$36/Global
929                 CMP DH,ES:[DI]              $26/$3A/$35
930                 CMP ES:[DI],DH              $26/$38/$35
931                 ;
932                 ;   Now the 16-bit CMPs:
933                 ;
934                 CMP AX,BX                   $3B/$C3
935                 CMP AX,CX                   $3B/$C1
936                 CMP AX,DX                   $3B/$C2
937                 CMP AX,BP                   $3B/$C5
938                 CMP AX,SI                   $3B/$C6
939                 CMP AX,DI                   $3B/$C7
940                 CMP AX,SP                   $3B/$C4
941                 CMP AX,01H                  $3D/$01/$00
942                 CMP AX,07733H               $3D/$33/$77
943                 CMP AX,LocalOrParm          $3B/$86/LocalOrParm
944                 CMP LocalOrParm,AX          $39/$86/LocalOrParm
945                 CMP AX,Global               $3B/$06/Global
946                 CMP Global,AX               $39/$06/Global
947                 CMP AX,ES:[DI]              $26/$3B/$05
```

(continued)

948	CMP ES:[DI],AX	$26/$39/$05
949	;	
950	CMP BX,AX	$3B/$D8
951	CMP BX,CX	$3B/$D9
952	CMP BX,DX	$3B/$DA
953	CMP BX,BP	$3B/$DD
954	CMP BX,SI	$3B/$DE
955	CMP BX,DI	$3B/$DF
956	CMP BX,SP	$3B/$DC
957	CMP BX,01H	$83/$FB/$01
958	CMP BX,07733H	$81/$FB/$33/$77
959	CMP BX,LocalOrParm	$3B/$9E/LocalOrParm
960	CMP LocalOrParm,BX	$39/$9E/LocalOrParm
961	CMP BX,Global	$3B/$1E/Global
962	CMP Global,BX	$39/$1E/Global
963	CMP BX,ES:[DI]	$26/$3B/$1D
964	CMP ES:[DI],BX	$26/$39/$1D
965	;	
966	CMP CX,AX	$3B/$C8
967	CMP CX,BX	$3B/$CB
968	CMP CX,DX	$3B/$CA
969	CMP CX,BP	$3B/$CD
970	CMP CX,SI	$3B/$CE
971	CMP CX,DI	$3B/$CF
972	CMP CX,SP	$3B/$CC
973	CMP CX,01H	$83/$F9/$01
974	CMP CX,07733H	$81/$F9/$33/$77
975	CMP CX,LocalOrParm	$3B/$8E/LocalOrParm
976	CMP LocalOrParm,CX	$39/$8E/LocalOrParm
977	CMP CX,Global	$3B/$0E/Global
978	CMP Global,CX	$39/$0E/Global
979	CMP CX,ES:[DI]	$26/$3B/$0D
980	CMP ES:[DI],CX	$26/$39/$0D
981	;	
982	CMP DX,AX	$3B/$D0
983	CMP DX,BX	$3B/$D3
984	CMP DX,CX	$3B/$D1
985	CMP DX,BP	$3B/$D5
986	CMP DX,SI	$3B/$D6
987	CMP DX,DI	$3B/$D7
988	CMP DX,SP	$3B/$D4
989	CMP DX,01H	$83/$FA/$01
990	CMP DX,07733H	$81/$FA/$33/$77
991	CMP DX,LocalOrParm	$3B/$96/LocalOrParm
992	CMP LocalOrParm,DX	$39/$96/LocalOrParm
993	CMP DX,Global	$3B/$16/Global
994	CMP Global,DX	$39/$16/Global
995	CMP DX,ES:[DI]	$26/$3B/$15
996	CMP ES:[DI],DX	$26/$39/$15

(continued)

```
997                     ;
998                     CMP BP,AX                    $3B/$E8
999                     CMP BP,BX                    $3B/$EB
1000                    CMP BP,CX                    $3B/$E9
1001                    CMP BP,DX                    $3B/$EA
1002                    CMP BP,SI                    $3B/$EE
1003                    CMP BP,DI                    $3B/$EF
1004                    CMP BP,SP                    $3B/$EC
1005                    CMP BP,01H                   $83/$FD/$01
1006                    CMP BP,07733H                $81/$FD/$33/$77
1007                    CMP BP,Global                $3B/$2E/Global
1008                    CMP Global,BP                $39/$2E/Global
1009                    CMP BP,ES:[DI]               $26/$3B/$2D
1010                    CMP ES:[DI],BP               $26/$39/$2D
1011                    ;
1012                    CMP SI,AX                    $3B/$F0
1013                    CMP SI,BX                    $3B/$F3
1014                    CMP SI,CX                    $3B/$F1
1015                    CMP SI,DX                    $3B/$F2
1016                    CMP SI,BP                    $3B/$F5
1017                    CMP SI,DI                    $3B/$F7
1018                    CMP SI,SP                    $3B/$F4
1019                    CMP SI,01H                   $83/$FE/$01
1020                    CMP SI,07733H                $81/$FE/$33/$77
1021                    CMP SI,LocalOrParm           $3B/$B6/LocalOrParm
1022                    CMP LocalOrParm,SI           $39/$B6/LocalOrParm
1023                    CMP SI,Global                $3B/$36/Global
1024                    CMP Global,SI                $39/$36/Global
1025                    CMP SI,ES:[DI]               $26/$3B/$35
1026                    CMP ES:[DI],SI               $26/$39/$35
1027                    ;
1028                    CMP DI,AX                    $3B/$F8
1029                    CMP DI,BX                    $3B/$FB
1030                    CMP DI,CX                    $3B/$F9
1031                    CMP DI,DX                    $3B/$FA
1032                    CMP DI,BP                    $3B/$FD
1033                    CMP DI,SI                    $3B/$FE
1034                    CMP DI,SP                    $3B/$FC
1035                    CMP DI,01H                   $83/$FF/$01
1036                    CMP DI,07733H                $81/$FF/$33/$77
1037                    CMP DI,LocalOrParm           $3B/$BE/LocalOrParm
1038                    CMP LocalOrParm,DI           $39/$BE/LocalOrParm
1039                    CMP DI,Global                $3B/$3E/Global
1040                    CMP Global,DI                $39/$3E/Global
1041                    ;
1042                    CMP SP,AX                    $3B/$E0
1043                    CMP SP,BX                    $3B/$E3
1044                    CMP SP,CX                    $3B/$E1
1045                    CMP SP,DX                    $3B/$E2
```

(continued)

```
1046                CMP SP,BP                     $3B/$E5
1047                CMP SP,SI                     $3B/$E6
1048                CMP SP,DI                     $3B/$E7
1049                CMP SP,01H                    $83/$FC/$01
1050                CMP SP,07733H                 $81/$FC/$33/$77
1051                CMP SP,LocalOrParm            $3B/$A6/LocalOrParm
1052                CMP LocalOrParm,SP            $39/$A6/LocalOrParm
1053                CMP SP,Global                 $3B/$26/Global
1054                CMP Global,SP                 $39/$26/Global
1055                CMP SP,ES:[DI]                $26/$3B/$25
1056                CMP ES:[DI],SP                $26/$39/$25
1057                ;
1058                CMP BYTE PTR LocalOrParm,01H  $80/$BE/LocalOrParm/$01
1059                CMP WORD PTR LocalOrParm,01H  $83/$BE/LocalOrParm/$01
1060                CMP BYTE PTR Global,01H       $80/$3E/Global/$01
1061                CMP WORD PTR Global,01H       $83/$3E/Global/$01
1062                CMP BYTE PTR ES:[DI],01H      $26/$80/$3D/$01
1063                CMP WORD PTR ES:[DI],01H      $26/$83/$3D/$01
1064                ;
1065                ;
1066                ;   Compare String:
1067                ;
1068                CMPSB                         $A6
1069                CMPSW                         $A7
1070                ;
1071                ;
1072                ;   Convert Word to Double Word:
1073                ;
1074                CWD                           $99
1075                ;
1076                ;
1077                ;   Decimal Adjust instructions:
1078                ;
1079                DAA                           $27
1080                DAS                           $2F
1081                ;
1082                ;
1083                ;   Decrements:
1084                ;
1085                DEC AL                        $FE/$C8
1086                DEC BL                        $FE/$CB
1087                DEC CL                        $FE/$C9
1088                DEC DL                        $FE/$CA
1089                DEC AH                        $FE/$CC
1090                DEC BH                        $FE/$CF
1091                DEC CH                        $FE/$CD
1092                DEC DH                        $FE/$CE
1093                DEC AX                        $48
1094                DEC BX                        $4B
```

(continued)

```
1095          DEC CX                          $49
1096          DEC DX                          $4A
1097          DEC BP                          $4D
1098          DEC SI                          $4E
1099          DEC DI                          $4F
1100          DEC SP                          $4C
1101          DEC BYTE PTR LocalOrParm        $FE/$8E/LocalOrParm
1102          DEC WORD PTR LocalOrParm        $FF/$8E/LocalOrParm
1103          DEC BYTE PTR Global             $FE/$0E/Global
1104          DEC WORD PTR Global             $FF/$0E/Global
1105          DEC BYTE PTR ES:[DI]            $26/$FE/$0D
1106          DEC WORD PTR DS:[DI]            $FF/$0D
1107          ;
1108          ;
1109          ;    Unsigned Divide instructions:
1110          ;
1111          DIV AL                          $F6/$F0
1112          DIV BL                          $F6/$F3
1113          DIV CL                          $F6/$F1
1114          DIV DL                          $F6/$F2
1115          DIV AH                          $F6/$F4
1116          DIV BH                          $F6/$F7
1117          DIV CH                          $F6/$F5
1118          DIV DH                          $F6/$F6
1119          DIV AX                          $F7/$F0
1120          DIV BX                          $F7/$F3
1121          DIV CX                          $F7/$F1
1122          DIV DX                          $F7/$F2
1123          DIV BP                          $F7/$F5
1124          DIV SI                          $F7/$F6
1125          DIV DI                          $F7/$F7
1126          DIV SP                          $F7/$F4
1127          DIV BYTE PTR LocalOrParm        $F6/$B6/LocalOrParm
1128          DIV WORD PTR LocalOrParm        $F7/$B6/LocalOrParm
1129          DIV BYTE PTR Global             $F6/$36/Global
1130          DIV WORD PTR Global             $F7/$36/Global
1131          DIV BYTE PTR ES:[DI]            $26/$F6/$35
1132          DIV WORD PTR DS:[DI]            $F7/$35
1133          ;
1134          ;
1135          ;    ESCape instructions to the coprocessor:
1136          ;
1137          ESC 0,AX                         $D8/$C0
1138          ESC 0,BX                         $D8/$C3
1139          ESC 0,CX                         $D8/$C1
1140          ESC 0,DX                         $D8/$C2
1141          ESC 0,BP                         $D8/$C5
1142          ESC 0,SI                         $D8/$C6
1143          ESC 0,DI                         $D8/$C7
```

(continued)

1144	ESC 0,SP	$D8/$C4
1145	;	
1146	ESC 1,AX	$D8/$C8
1147	ESC 1,BX	$D8/$CB
1148	ESC 1,CX	$D8/$C9
1149	ESC 1,DX	$D8/$CA
1150	ESC 1,BP	$D8/$CD
1151	ESC 1,SI	$D8/$CE
1152	ESC 1,DI	$D8/$CF
1153	ESC 1,SP	$D8/$CC
1154	;	
1155	ESC 2,AX	$D8/$D0
1156	ESC 2,BX	$D8/$D3
1157	ESC 2,CX	$D8/$D1
1158	ESC 2,DX	$D8/$D2
1159	ESC 2,BP	$D8/$D5
1160	ESC 2,SI	$D8/$D6
1161	ESC 2,DI	$D8/$D7
1162	ESC 2,SP	$D8/$D4
1163	;	
1164	ESC 3,AX	$D8/$D8
1165	ESC 3,BX	$D8/$DB
1166	ESC 3,CX	$D8/$D9
1167	ESC 3,DX	$D8/$DA
1168	ESC 3,BP	$D8/$DD
1169	ESC 3,SI	$D8/$DE
1170	ESC 3,DI	$D8/$DF
1171	ESC 3,SP	$D8/$DC
1172	;	
1173	ESC 4,AX	$D8/$E0
1174	ESC 4,BX	$D8/$E3
1175	ESC 4,CX	$D8/$E1
1176	ESC 4,DX	$D8/$E2
1177	ESC 4,BP	$D8/$E5
1178	ESC 4,SI	$D8/$E6
1179	ESC 4,DI	$D8/$E7
1180	ESC 4,SP	$D8/$E4
1181	;	
1182	ESC 5,AX	$D8/$E8
1183	ESC 5,BX	$D8/$EB
1184	ESC 5,CX	$D8/$E9
1185	ESC 5,DX	$D8/$EA
1186	ESC 5,BP	$D8/$ED
1187	ESC 5,SI	$D8/$EE
1188	ESC 5,DI	$D8/$EF
1189	ESC 5,SP	$D8/$EC
1190	;	
1191	ESC 6,AX	$D8/$F0
1192	ESC 6,BX	$D8/$F3

(continued)

```
1193            ESC  6,CX                        $D8/$F1
1194            ESC  6,DX                        $D8/$F2
1195            ESC  6,BP                        $D8/$F5
1196            ESC  6,SI                        $D8/$F6
1197            ESC  6,DI                        $D8/$F7
1198            ESC  6,SP                        $D8/$F4
1199            ;
1200            ESC  7,AX                        $D8/$F8
1201            ESC  7,BX                        $D8/$FB
1202            ESC  7,CX                        $D8/$F9
1203            ESC  7,DX                        $D8/$FA
1204            ESC  7,BP                        $D8/$FD
1205            ESC  7,SI                        $D8/$FE
1206            ESC  7,DI                        $D8/$FF
1207            ESC  7,SP                        $D8/$FC
1208            ;
1209            ;
1210            ;    HALT instruction:
1211            ;
1212            HLT                              $F4
1213            ;
1214            ;
1215            ;    Signed Divide instructions:
1216            ;
1217            IDIV AL                          $F6/$F8
1218            IDIV BL                          $F6/$FB
1219            IDIV CL                          $F6/$F9
1220            IDIV DL                          $F6/$FA
1221            IDIV AH                          $F6/$FC
1222            IDIV BH                          $F6/$FF
1223            IDIV CH                          $F6/$FD
1224            IDIV DH                          $F6/$FE
1225            IDIV AX                          $F7/$F8
1226            IDIV BX                          $F7/$FB
1227            IDIV CX                          $F7/$F9
1228            IDIV DX                          $F7/$FA
1229            IDIV BP                          $F7/$FD
1230            IDIV SI                          $F7/$FE
1231            IDIV DI                          $F7/$FF
1232            IDIV SP                          $F7/$FC
1233            IDIV BYTE PTR LocalOrParm        $F6/$BE/LocalOrParm
1234            IDIV WORD PTR LocalOrParm        $F7/$BE/LocalOrParm
1235            IDIV BYTE PTR Global             $F6/$3E/Global
1236            IDIV WORD PTR Global             $F7/$3E/Global
1237            IDIV BYTE PTR ES:[DI]            $26/$F6/$3D
1238            IDIV WORD PTR DS:[DI]            $F7/$3D
1239            ;
1240            ;    Signed Multiply instructions:
1241            ;
```

(continued)

```
1242            IMUL AL                         $F6/$E8
1243            IMUL BL                         $F6/$EB
1244            IMUL CL                         $F6/$E9
1245            IMUL DL                         $F6/$EA
1246            IMUL AH                         $F6/$EC
1247            IMUL BH                         $F6/$EF
1248            IMUL CH                         $F6/$ED
1249            IMUL DH                         $F6/$EE
1250            IMUL AX                         $F7/$E8
1251            IMUL BX                         $F7/$EB
1252            IMUL CX                         $F7/$E9
1253            IMUL DX                         $F7/$EA
1254            IMUL BP                         $F7/$ED
1255            IMUL SI                         $F7/$EE
1256            IMUL DI                         $F7/$EF
1257            IMUL SP                         $F7/$EC
1258            IMUL BYTE PTR LocalOrParm       $F6/$AE/LocalOrParm
1259            IMUL WORD PTR LocalOrParm       $F7/$AE/LocalOrParm
1260            IMUL BYTE PTR Global            $F6/$2E/Global
1261            IMUL WORD PTR Global            $F7/$2E/Global
1262            IMUL BYTE PTR ES:[DI]           $26/$F6/$2D
1263            IMUL WORD PTR DS:[DI]           $F7/$2D
1264            ;
1265            ;
1266            ;    Port input:
1267            ;
1268            IN   AL,74H                      $E4/$74
1269            IN   AX,8BH                      $E5/$8B
1270            IN   AL,DX                       $EC
1271            IN   AX,DX                       $ED
1272            ;
1273            ;
1274            ;    Increments:
1275            ;
1276            INC AL                           $FE/$C0
1277            INC BL                           $FE/$C3
1278            INC CL                           $FE/$C1
1279            INC DL                           $FE/$C2
1280            INC AH                           $FE/$C4
1281            INC BH                           $FE/$C7
1282            INC CH                           $FE/$C5
1283            INC DH                           $FE/$C6
1284            INC AX                           $40
1285            INC BX                           $43
1286            INC CX                           $41
1287            INC DX                           $42
1288            INC BP                           $45
1289            INC SI                           $46
1290            INC DI                           $47
```

(continued)

```
1291              INC SP                          $44
1292              INC BYTE PTR LocalOrParm        $FE/$86/LocalOrParm
1293              INC WORD PTR LocalOrParm        $FF/$86/LocalOrParm
1294              INC BYTE PTR Global             $FE/$06/Global
1295              INC WORD PTR Global             $FF/$06/Global
1296              INC BYTE PTR ES:[DI]            $26/$FE/$05
1297              INC WORD PTR DS:[DI]            $FF/$05
1298              ;
1299              ;
1300              ;   Software interrupts:
1301              ;
1302              INT  33H                         $CD/$33
1303              INT  3                           $CC
1304              INTO                             $CE
1305              IRET                             $CF
1306              ;
1307              ;
1308              ;   JUMP instructions:
1309              ;
1310              ;   NOTE: The '8' value is an example only; any 8-bit
1311              ;   signed displacement can be used here.
1312              ;
1313              JMP 256                          $E9/$00/$01
1314              JMP AX                           $FF/$E0
1315              JMP BX                           $FF/$E3
1316              JMP CX                           $FF/$E1
1317              JMP DX                           $FF/$E2
1318              JMP BP                           $FF/$E5
1319              JMP SI                           $FF/$E6
1320              JMP DI                           $FF/$E7
1321              JMP SP                           $FF/$E4
1322              JMP  8                           $EB/$08
1323              JCXZ 8      $E3/$08
1324              JA   8      $77/$08
1325              JNA  8      $76/$08
1326              JAE  8      $73/$08
1327              JNAE 8      $72/$08
1328              JB   8      $72/$08
1329              JNB  8      $73/$08
1330              JBE  8      $76/$08
1331              JNBE 8      $77/$08
1332              JC   8      $72/$08
1333              JNC  8      $73/$08
1334              JE   8      $74/$08
1335              JNE  8      $75/$08
1336              JG   8      $7F/$08
1337              JNG  8      $7E/$08
1338              JGE  8      $7D/$08
1339              JNGE 8      $7C/$08
```

(continued)

```
1340            JL    8    $7C/$08
1341            JLE   8    $7E/$08
1342            JNL   8    $7D/$08
1343            JNLE  8    $7F/$08
1344            JO    8    $70/$08
1345            JNO   8                        $71/$08
1346            JP    8                        $7A/$08
1347            JNP   8                        $7B/$08
1348            JPE   8                        $7A/$08
1349            JPO   8    $7B/$08
1350            JS    8    $78/$08
1351            JNS   8    $79/$08
1352            JZ    8    $74/$08
1353            JNZ   8    $75/$08
1354            ;
1355            ;
1356            ;    Load AH from low byte of Flags:
1357            ;
1358            LAHF                            $9F
1359            ;
1360            ;
1361            ;    Pointer load instructions
1362            ;
1363            ;    NOTE:  There are many more variations on LDS and LES
1364            ;    than are included here, to support different addresssing
1365            ;    modes like BX+SI, CX+DI, etc.  For working in INLINE,
1366            ;    you will generally need only access VAR parameters or
1367            ;    the referents of pointers declared as global variables.
1368            ;    Opcodes referencing VARParm use SS:[BP+<16-bit offset>].
1369            ;    Opcodes referencing GlobalPtr use DS:[<16-bit offset>].
1370            ;
1371            ;    Load pointer through DS:
1372            ;
1373            LDS AX,VARParm                  $C5/$86/VARParm
1374            LDS AX,GlobalPtr                $C5/$06/GlobalPtr
1375            LDS BX,VARParm                  $C5/$9E/VARParm
1376            LDS BX,GlobalPtr                $C5/$1E/GlobalPtr
1377            LDS CX,VARParm                  $C5/$8E/VARParm
1378            LDS CX,GlobalPtr                $C5/$0E/GlobalPtr
1379            LDS DX,VARParm                  $C5/$96/VARParm
1380            LDS DX,GlobalPtr                $C5/$16/GlobalPtr
1381            LDS DI,VARParm                  $C5/$BE/VARParm
1382            LDS DI,GlobalPtr                $C5/$3E/GlobalPtr
1383            LDS SI,VARParm                  $C5/$B6/VARParm
1384            LDS SI,GlobalPtr                $C5/$36/GlobalPtr
1385            ;
1386            ;    Load pointer through ES:
1387            ;
1388            LES AX,VARParm                  $C4/$86/VARParm
```

(continued)

```
1389                   LES AX,GlobalPtr               $C4/$06/GlobalPtr
1390                   LES BX,VARParm                 $C4/$9E/VARParm
1391                   LES BX,GlobalPtr               $C4/$1E/GlobalPtr
1392                   LES CX,VARParm                 $C4/$8E/VARParm
1393                   LES CX,GlobalPtr               $C4/$0E/GlobalPtr
1394                   LES DX,VARParm                 $C4/$96/VARParm
1395                   LES DX,GlobalPtr               $C4/$16/GlobalPtr
1396                   LES DI,VARParm                 $C4/$BE/VARParm
1397                   LES DI,GlobalPtr               $C4/$3E/GlobalPtr
1398                   LES SI,VARParm                 $C4/$B6/VARParm
1399                   LES SI,GlobalPtr               $C4/$36/GlobalPtr
1400                   ;
1401                   ;
1402                   ;   LOCK prefix:
1403                   ;
1404                   LOCK                           $F0
1405                   ;
1406                   ;
1407                   ;   Load String instructions:
1408                   ;
1409                   LODSB                          $AC
1410                   LODSW                          $AD
1411                   ;
1412                   ;
1413                   ;   LOOP instructions:
1414                   ;
1415                   ;   NOTE:  The $FA value is the 2's complement equivalent of
1416                   ;   -6.  It is given here as an example; any 8-bit value is
1417                   ;   legal, and represents the number of bytes to move away
1418                   ;   from the byte AFTER the LOOP opcode, in the course of
1419                   ;   re-executing the instructions making up the LOOP.
1420                   ;
1421                   LOOP -6                        $E2/$FA
1422                   LOOPE -6                       $E1/$FA
1423                   LOOPNE -6                      $E0/$FA
1424                   ;
1425                   ;
1426                   ;   MOV opcodes.  Begin with the 8-bit moves:
1427                   ;
1428                   MOV AL,AH                      $8A/$C4
1429                   MOV AL,BL                      $8A/$C3
1430                   MOV AL,BH                      $8A/$C7
1431                   MOV AL,CL                      $8A/$C1
1432                   MOV AL,CH                      $8A/$C5
1433                   MOV AL,DL                      $8A/$C2
1434                   MOV AL,DH                      $8A/$C6
1435                   MOV AL,01H                     $B0/$01
1436                   MOV AL,LocalOrParm             $8A/$86/LocalOrParm
1437                   MOV LocalOrParm,AL             $88/$86/LocalOrParm
```

(continued)

1438	MOV AL,Global	$A0/Global
1439	MOV Global,AL	$A2/Global
1440	MOV AL,ES:[DI]	$26/$8A/$05
1441	MOV ES:[DI],AL	$26/$88/$05
1442	;	
1443	MOV AH,AL	$8A/$E0
1444	MOV AH,BL	$8A/$E3
1445	MOV AH,BH	$8A/$E7
1446	MOV AH,CL	$8A/$E1
1447	MOV AH,CH	$8A/$E5
1448	MOV AH,DL	$8A/$E2
1449	MOV AH,DH	$8A/$E6
1450	MOV AH,01H	$B4/$01
1451	MOV AH,LocalOrParm	$8A/$A6/LocalOrParm
1452	MOV LocalOrParm,AH	$88/$A6/LocalOrParm
1453	MOV AH,Global	$8A/$26/Global
1454	MOV Global,AH	$88/$26/Global
1455	MOV AH,ES:[DI]	$26/$8A/$25
1456	MOV ES:[DI],AH	$26/$88/$25
1457	;	
1458	MOV BL,BH	$8A/$DF
1459	MOV BL,AL	$8A/$D8
1460	MOV BL,AH	$8A/$DC
1461	MOV BL,CL	$8A/$D9
1462	MOV BL,CH	$8A/$DD
1463	MOV BL,DL	$8A/$DA
1464	MOV BL,DH	$8A/$DE
1465	MOV BL,01H	$B3/$01
1466	MOV BL,LocalOrParm	$8A/$9E/LocalOrParm
1467	MOV LocalOrParm,BL	$88/$9E/LocalOrParm
1468	MOV BL,Global	$8A/$1E/Global
1469	MOV Global,BL	$88/$1E/Global
1470	MOV BL,ES:[DI]	$26/$8A/$1D
1471	MOV ES:[DI],BL	$26/$88/$1D
1472	;	
1473	MOV BH,BL	$8A/$FB
1474	MOV BH,AL	$8A/$F8
1475	MOV BH,AH	$8A/$FC
1476	MOV BH,CL	$8A/$F9
1477	MOV BH,CH	$8A/$FD
1478	MOV BH,DL	$8A/$FA
1479	MOV BH,DH	$8A/$FE
1480	MOV BH,01H	$B7/$01
1481	MOV BH,LocalOrParm	$8A/$BE/LocalOrParm
1482	MOV LocalOrParm,BH	$88/$BE/LocalOrParm
1483	MOV BH,Global	$8A/$3E/Global
1484	MOV Global,BH	$88/$3E/Global
1485	MOV BH,ES:[DI]	$26/$8A/$3D
1486	MOV ES:[DI],BH	$26/$88/$3D

(continued)

```
1487                  ;
1488                  MOV CL,CH                    $8A/$CD
1489                  MOV CL,AL                    $8A/$C8
1490                  MOV CL,AH                    $8A/$CC
1491                  MOV CL,BL                    $8A/$CB
1492                  MOV CL,BH                    $8A/$CF
1493                  MOV CL,DL                    $8A/$CA
1494                  MOV CL,DH                    $8A/$CE
1495                  MOV CL,01H                   $B1/$01
1496                  MOV CL,LocalOrParm           $8A/$8E/LocalOrParm
1497                  MOV LocalOrParm,CL           $88/$8E/LocalOrParm
1498                  MOV CL,Global               $8A/$0E/Global
1499                  MOV Global,CL               $88/$0E/Global
1500                  MOV CL,ES:[DI]               $26/$8A/$0D
1501                  MOV ES:[DI],CL               $26/$88/$0D
1502                  ;
1503                  MOV CH,CL                    $8A/$E9
1504                  MOV CH,AL                    $8A/$E8
1505                  MOV CH,AH                    $8A/$EC
1506                  MOV CH,BL                    $8A/$EB
1507                  MOV CH,BH                    $8A/$EF
1508                  MOV CH,DL                    $8A/$EA
1509                  MOV CH,DH                    $8A/$EE
1510                  MOV CH,01H                   $B5/$01
1511                  MOV CH,LocalOrParm           $8A/$AE/LocalOrParm
1512                  MOV LocalOrParm,CH           $88/$AE/LocalOrParm
1513                  MOV CH,Global               $8A/$2E/Global
1514                  MOV Global,CH               $88/$2E/Global
1515                  MOV CH,ES:[DI]               $26/$8A/$2D
1516                  MOV ES:[DI],CH               $26/$88/$2D
1517                  ;
1518                  MOV DL,DH                    $8A/$D6
1519                  MOV DL,AL                    $8A/$D0
1520                  MOV DL,AH                    $8A/$D4
1521                  MOV DL,BL                    $8A/$D3
1522                  MOV DL,BH                    $8A/$D7
1523                  MOV DL,CL                    $8A/$D1
1524                  MOV DL,CH                    $8A/$D5
1525                  MOV DL,01H                   $B2/$01
1526                  MOV DL,LocalOrParm           $8A/$96/LocalOrParm
1527                  MOV LocalOrParm,DL           $88/$96/LocalOrParm
1528                  MOV DL,Global               $8A/$16/Global
1529                  MOV Global,DL               $88/$16/Global
1530                  MOV DL,ES:[DI]               $26/$8A/$15
1531                  MOV ES:[DI],DL               $26/$88/$15
1532                  ;
1533                  MOV DH,DL                    $8A/$F2
1534                  MOV DH,AL                    $8A/$F0
1535                  MOV DH,AH                    $8A/$F4
```

(continued)

```
1536              MOV DH,BL                 $8A/$F3
1537              MOV DH,BH                 $8A/$F7
1538              MOV DH,CL                 $8A/$F1
1539              MOV DH,CH                 $8A/$F5
1540              MOV DH,01H                $B6/$01
1541              MOV DH,LocalOrParm        $8A/$B6/LocalOrParm
1542              MOV LocalOrParm,DH        $88/$B6/LocalOrParm
1543              MOV DH,Global             $8A/$36/Global
1544              MOV Global,DH             $88/$36/Global
1545              MOV DH,ES:[DI]            $26/$8A/$35
1546              MOV ES:[DI],DH            $26/$88/$35
1547              ;
1548              ;    Next come the 16-bit moves:
1549              ;
1550              MOV AX,BX                 $8B/$C3
1551              MOV AX,CX                 $8B/$C1
1552              MOV AX,DX                 $8B/$C2
1553              MOV AX,BP                 $8B/$C5
1554              MOV AX,SI                 $8B/$C6
1555              MOV AX,DI                 $8B/$C7
1556              MOV AX,SP                 $8B/$C4
1557              MOV AX,CS                 $8C/$C8
1558              MOV AX,DS                 $8C/$D8
1559              MOV AX,SS                 $8C/$D0
1560              MOV AX,ES                 $8C/$C0
1561              MOV AX,01H                $B8/$01/$00
1562              MOV AX,07733H             $B8/$33/$77
1563              MOV AX,LocalOrParm        $8B/$86/LocalOrParm
1564              MOV LocalOrParm,AX        $89/$86/LocalOrParm
1565              MOV AX,Global             $A1/Global
1566              MOV Global,AX             $A3/Global
1567              MOV AX,ES:[DI]            $26/$8B/$05
1568              MOV ES:[DI],AX            $26/$89/$05
1569              ;
1570              MOV BX,AX                 $8B/$D8
1571              MOV BX,CX                 $8B/$D9
1572              MOV BX,DX                 $8B/$DA
1573              MOV BX,BP                 $8B/$DD
1574              MOV BX,SI                 $8B/$DE
1575              MOV BX,DI                 $8B/$DF
1576              MOV BX,SP                 $8B/$DC
1577              MOV BX,CS                 $8C/$CB
1578              MOV BX,DS                 $8C/$DB
1579              MOV BX,SS                 $8C/$D3
1580              MOV BX,ES                 $8C/$C3
1581              MOV BX,01H                $BB/$01/$00
1582              MOV BX,07733H             $BB/$33/$77
1583              MOV BX,LocalOrParm        $8B/$9E/LocalOrParm
1584              MOV LocalOrParm,BX        $89/$9E/LocalOrParm
```

(continued)

1585	MOV BX,Global	$8B/$1E/Global
1586	MOV Global,BX	$89/$1E/Global
1587	MOV BX,ES:[DI]	$26/$8B/$1D
1588	MOV ES:[DI],BX	$26/$89/$1D
1589	;	
1590	MOV CX,AX	$8B/$C8
1591	MOV CX,BX	$8B/$CB
1592	MOV CX,DX	$8B/$CA
1593	MOV CX,BP	$8B/$CD
1594	MOV CX,SI	$8B/$CE
1595	MOV CX,DI	$8B/$CF
1596	MOV CX,SP	$8B/$CC
1597	MOV CX,CS	$8C/$C9
1598	MOV CX,DS	$8C/$D9
1599	MOV CX,SS	$8C/$D1
1600	MOV CX,ES	$8C/$C1
1601	MOV CX,01H	$B9/$01/$00
1602	MOV CX,07733H	$B9/$33/$77
1603	MOV CX,LocalOrParm	$8B/$8E/LocalOrParm
1604	MOV LocalOrParm,CX	$89/$8E/LocalOrParm
1605	MOV CX,Global	$8B/$0E/Global
1606	MOV Global,CX	$89/$0E/Global
1607	MOV CX,ES:[DI]	$26/$8B/$0D
1608	MOV ES:[DI],CX	$26/$89/$0D
1609	;	
1610	MOV DX,AX	$8B/$D0
1611	MOV DX,BX	$8B/$D3
1612	MOV DX,CX	$8B/$D1
1613	MOV DX,BP	$8B/$D5
1614	MOV DX,SI	$8B/$D6
1615	MOV DX,DI	$8B/$D7
1616	MOV DX,SP	$8B/$D4
1617	MOV DX,CS	$8C/$CA
1618	MOV DX,DS	$8C/$DA
1619	MOV DX,SS	$8C/$D2
1620	MOV DX,ES	$8C/$C2
1621	MOV DX,01H	$BA/$01/$00
1622	MOV DX,07733H	$BA/$33/$77
1623	MOV DX,LocalOrParm	$8B/$96/LocalOrParm
1624	MOV LocalOrParm,DX	$89/$96/LocalOrParm
1625	MOV DX,Global	$8B/$16/Global
1626	MOV Global,DX	$89/$16/Global
1627	MOV DX,ES:[DI]	$26/$8B/$15
1628	MOV ES:[DI],DX	$26/$89/$15
1629	;	
1630	MOV DS,AX	$8E/$D8
1631	MOV DS,BX	$8E/$DB
1632	MOV DS,CX	$8E/$D9
1633	MOV DS,DX	$8E/$DA

(continued)

```
1634             MOV DS,BP                            $8E/$DD
1635             MOV DS,SI                            $8E/$DE
1636             MOV DS,DI                            $8E/$DF
1637             MOV DS,SP                            $8E/$DC
1638             MOV DS,LocalOrParm                   $8E/$9E/LocalOrParm
1639             MOV LocalOrParm,DS                   $8C/$9E/LocalOrParm
1640             MOV DS,ES:[DI]                       $26/$8E/$1D
1641             MOV ES:[DI],DS                       $26/$8C/$1D
1642             ;
1643             MOV SS,AX                            $8E/$D0
1644             MOV SS,BX                            $8E/$D3
1645             MOV SS,CX                            $8E/$D1
1646             MOV SS,DX                            $8E/$D2
1647             MOV SS,BP                            $8E/$D5
1648             MOV SS,SI                            $8E/$D6
1649             MOV SS,DI                            $8E/$D7
1650             MOV SS,SP                            $8E/$D4
1651             MOV SS,LocalOrParm                   $8E/$96/LocalOrParm
1652             MOV LocalOrParm,SS                   $8C/$96/LocalOrParm
1653             MOV SS,Global                        $8E/$16/Global
1654             MOV Global,SS                        $8C/$16/Global
1655             MOV SS,ES:[DI]                       $26/$8E/$15
1656             MOV ES:[DI],SS                       $26/$8C/$15
1657             ;
1658             MOV ES,AX                            $8E/$C0
1659             MOV ES,BX                            $8E/$C3
1660             MOV ES,CX                            $8E/$C1
1661             MOV ES,DX                            $8E/$C2
1662             MOV ES,BP                            $8E/$C5
1663             MOV ES,SI                            $8E/$C6
1664             MOV ES,DI                            $8E/$C7
1665             MOV ES,SP                            $8E/$C4
1666             MOV ES,LocalOrParm                   $8E/$86/LocalOrParm
1667             MOV LocalOrParm,ES                   $8C/$86/LocalOrParm
1668             MOV ES,Global                        $8E/$06/Global
1669             MOV Global,ES                        $8C/$06/Global
1670             ;
1671             MOV BYTE PTR LocalOrParm,01H         $C6/$86/LocalOrParm/$01
1672             MOV WORD PTR LocalOrParm,01H         $C7/$86/LocalOrParm/$01/$00
1673             MOV BYTE PTR Global,01H              $C6/$06/Global/$01
1674             MOV WORD PTR Global,01H              $C7/$06/Global/$01/$00
1675             MOV BYTE PTR ES:[DI],01H             $26/$C6/$05/$01
1676             MOV WORD PTR DS:[DI],01H             $C7/$05/$01/$00
1677             ;
1678             ;
1679             ;    Segment Override Prefixes, using MOV as examples:
1680             ;
1681             MOV AX,DS:0441H                      $A1/$41/$04
1682             MOV DS:0441H,AX                      $A3/$41/$04
```

(continued)

```
1683            MOV AX,CS:0441H                  $2E/$A1/$41/$04
1684            MOV CS:0441H,AX                  $2E/$A3/$41/$04
1685            MOV AX,SS:0441H                  $36/$A1/$41/$04
1686            MOV SS:0441H,AX                  $36/$A3/$41/$04
1687            MOV AX,ES:0441H                  $26/$A1/$41/$04
1688            MOV ES:0441H,AX                  $26/$A3/$41/$04
1689            ;
1690            ;
1691            ;   Move String instructions:
1692            ;
1693            MOVSB                            $A4
1694            MOVSW                            $A5
1695            ;
1696            ;
1697            ;   Unsigned Multiply instructions:
1698            ;
1699            MUL AL                           $F6/$E0
1700            MUL BL                           $F6/$E3
1701            MUL CL                           $F6/$E1
1702            MUL DL                           $F6/$E2
1703            MUL AH                           $F6/$E4
1704            MUL BH                           $F6/$E7
1705            MUL CH                           $F6/$E5
1706            MUL DH                           $F6/$E6
1707            MUL AX                           $F7/$E0
1708            MUL BX                           $F7/$E3
1709            MUL CX                           $F7/$E1
1710            MUL DX                           $F7/$E2
1711            MUL BP                           $F7/$E5
1712            MUL SI                           $F7/$E6
1713            MUL DI                           $F7/$E7
1714            MUL SP                           $F7/$E4
1715            MUL BYTE PTR LocalOrParm         $F6/$A6/LocalOrParm
1716            MUL WORD PTR LocalOrParm         $F7/$A6/LocalOrParm
1717            MUL BYTE PTR Global              $F6/$26/Global
1718            MUL WORD PTR Global              $F7/$26/Global
1719            MUL BYTE PTR ES:[DI]             $26/$F6/$25
1720            MUL WORD PTR DS:[DI]             $F7/$25
1721            ;
1722            ;
1723            ;   Twos complements and ones complements:
1724            ;
1725            NEG AL                           $F6/$D8
1726            NEG BL                           $F6/$DB
1727            NEG CL                           $F6/$D9
1728            NEG DL                           $F6/$DA
1729            NEG AH                           $F6/$DC
1730            NEG BH                           $F6/$DF
1731            NEG CH                           $F6/$DD
```

(continued)

```
1732            NEG DH                              $F6/$DE
1733            NEG AX                              $F7/$D8
1734            NEG BX                              $F7/$DB
1735            NEG CX                              $F7/$D9
1736            NEG DX                              $F7/$DA
1737            NEG BP                              $F7/$DD
1738            NEG SI                              $F7/$DE
1739            NEG DI                              $F7/$DF
1740            NEG SP                              $F7/$DC
1741            NEG BYTE PTR LocalOrParm            $F6/$9E/LocalOrParm
1742            NEG WORD PTR LocalOrParm            $F7/$9E/LocalOrParm
1743            NEG BYTE PTR Global                 $F6/$1E/Global
1744            NEG WORD PTR Global                 $F7/$1E/Global
1745            NEG BYTE PTR ES:[DI]                $26/$F6/$1D
1746            NEG WORD PTR DS:[DI]                $F7/$1D
1747            ;
1748            NOT AL                              $F6/$D0
1749            NOT BL                              $F6/$D3
1750            NOT CL                              $F6/$D1
1751            NOT DL                              $F6/$D2
1752            NOT AH                              $F6/$D4
1753            NOT BH                              $F6/$D7
1754            NOT CH                              $F6/$D5
1755            NOT DH                              $F6/$D6
1756            NOT AX                              $F7/$D0
1757            NOT BX                              $F7/$D3
1758            NOT CX                              $F7/$D1
1759            NOT DX                              $F7/$D2
1760            NOT BP                              $F7/$D5
1761            NOT SI                              $F7/$D6
1762            NOT DI                              $F7/$D7
1763            NOT SP                              $F7/$D4
1764            NOT BYTE PTR LocalOrParm            $F6/$96/LocalOrParm
1765            NOT WORD PTR LocalOrParm            $F7/$96/LocalOrParm
1766            NOT BYTE PTR Global                 $F6/$16/Global
1767            NOT WORD PTR Global                 $F7/$16/Global
1768            NOT BYTE PTR ES:[DI]                $26/$F6/$15
1769            NOT WORD PTR DS:[DI]                $F7/$15
1770            ;
1771            ;
1772            ;   Our old friend No Op:
1773            ;
1774            NOP                                 $90
1775            ;
1776            ;
1777            ;   ORs. 8-bit operations first:
1778            ;
1779            OR AL,AH                            $0A/$C4
1780            OR AL,BL                            $0A/$C3
```

(continued)

```
1781          OR AL,BH              $0A/$C7
1782          OR AL,CL              $0A/$C1
1783          OR AL,CH              $0A/$C5
1784          OR AL,DL              $0A/$C2
1785          OR AL,DH              $0A/$C6
1786          OR AL,01H             $0C/$01
1787          OR AL,LocalOrParm     $0A/$86/LocalOrParm
1788          OR LocalOrParm,AL     $08/$86/LocalOrParm
1789          OR AL,Global          $0A/$06/Global
1790          OR Global,AL          $08/$06/Global
1791          OR AL,ES:[DI]         $26/$0A/$05
1792          OR ES:[DI],AL         $26/$08/$05
1793          ;
1794          OR AH,AL              $0A/$E0
1795          OR AH,BL              $0A/$E3
1796          OR AH,BH              $0A/$E7
1797          OR AH,CL              $0A/$E1
1798          OR AH,CH              $0A/$E5
1799          OR AH,DL              $0A/$E2
1800          OR AH,DH              $0A/$E6
1801          OR AH,01H             $80/$CC/$01
1802          OR AH,LocalOrParm     $0A/$A6/LocalOrParm
1803          OR LocalOrParm,AH     $08/$A6/LocalOrParm
1804          OR AH,Global          $0A/$26/Global
1805          OR Global,AH          $08/$26/Global
1806          OR AH,ES:[DI]         $26/$0A/$25
1807          OR ES:[DI],AH         $26/$08/$25
1808          ;
1809          OR BL,BH              $0A/$DF
1810          OR BL,AL              $0A/$D8
1811          OR BL,AH              $0A/$DC
1812          OR BL,CL              $0A/$D9
1813          OR BL,CH              $0A/$DD
1814          OR BL,DL              $0A/$DA
1815          OR BL,DH              $0A/$DE
1816          OR BL,01H             $80/$CB/$01
1817          OR BL,LocalOrParm     $0A/$9E/LocalOrParm
1818          OR LocalOrParm,BL     $08/$9E/LocalOrParm
1819          OR BL,Global          $0A/$1E/Global
1820          OR Global,BL          $08/$1E/Global
1821          OR BL,ES:[DI]         $26/$0A/$1D
1822          OR ES:[DI],BL         $26/$08/$1D
1823          ;
1824          OR BH,BL              $0A/$FB
1825          OR BH,AL              $0A/$F8
1826          OR BH,AH              $0A/$FC
1827          OR BH,CL              $0A/$F9
1828          OR BH,CH              $0A/$FD
1829          OR BH,DL              $0A/$FA
```

(continued)

1830	OR BH,DH	$0A/$FE
1831	OR BH,01H	$80/$CF/$01
1832	OR BH,LocalOrParm	$0A/$BE/LocalOrParm
1833	OR LocalOrParm,BH	$08/$BE/LocalOrParm
1834	OR BH,Global	$0A/$3E/Global
1835	OR Global,BH	$08/$3E/Global
1836	OR BH,ES:[DI]	$26/$0A/$3D
1837	OR ES:[DI],BH	$26/$08/$3D
1838	;	
1839	OR CL,CH	$0A/$CD
1840	OR CL,AL	$0A/$C8
1841	OR CL,AH	$0A/$CC
1842	OR CL,BL	$0A/$CB
1843	OR CL,BH	$0A/$CF
1844	OR CL,DL	$0A/$CA
1845	OR CL,DH	$0A/$CE
1846	OR CL,01H	$80/$C9/$01
1847	OR CL,LocalOrParm	$0A/$8E/LocalOrParm
1848	OR LocalOrParm,CL	$08/$8E/LocalOrParm
1849	OR CL,Global	$0A/$0E/Global
1850	OR Global,CL	$08/$0E/Global
1851	OR CL,ES:[DI]	$26/$0A/$0D
1852	OR ES:[DI],CL	$26/$08/$0D
1853	;	
1854	OR CH,CL	$0A/$E9
1855	OR CH,AL	$0A/$E8
1856	OR CH,AH	$0A/$EC
1857	OR CH,BL	$0A/$EB
1858	OR CH,BH	$0A/$EF
1859	OR CH,DL	$0A/$EA
1860	OR CH,DH	$0A/$EE
1861	OR CH,01H	$80/$CD/$01
1862	OR CH,LocalOrParm	$0A/$AE/LocalOrParm
1863	OR LocalOrParm,CH	$08/$AE/LocalOrParm
1864	OR CH,Global	$0A/$2E/Global
1865	OR Global,CH	$08/$2E/Global
1866	OR CH,ES:[DI]	$26/$0A/$2D
1867	OR ES:[DI],CH	$26/$08/$2D
1868	;	
1869	OR DL,DH	$0A/$D6
1870	OR DL,AL	$0A/$D0
1871	OR DL,AH	$0A/$D4
1872	OR DL,BL	$0A/$D3
1873	OR DL,BH	$0A/$D7
1874	OR DL,CL	$0A/$D1
1875	OR DL,CH	$0A/$D5
1876	OR DL,01H	$80/$CA/$01
1877	OR DL,LocalOrParm	$0A/$96/LocalOrParm
1878	OR LocalOrParm,DL	$08/$96/LocalOrParm

(continued)

```
1879          OR DL,Global              $0A/$16/Global
1880          OR Global,DL              $08/$16/Global
1881          OR DL,ES:[DI]             $26/$0A/$15
1882          OR ES:[DI],DL             $26/$08/$15
1883          ;
1884          OR DH,DL                  $0A/$F2
1885          OR DH,AL                  $0A/$F0
1886          OR DH,AH                  $0A/$F4
1887          OR DH,BL                  $0A/$F3
1888          OR DH,BH                  $0A/$F7
1889          OR DH,CL                  $0A/$F1
1890          OR DH,CH                  $0A/$F5
1891          OR DH,01H                 $80/$CE/$01
1892          OR DH,LocalOrParm         $0A/$B6/LocalOrParm
1893          OR LocalOrParm,DH         $08/$B6/LocalOrParm
1894          OR DH,Global              $0A/$36/Global
1895          OR Global,DH              $08/$36/Global
1896          OR DH,ES:[DI]             $26/$0A/$35
1897          OR ES:[DI],DH             $26/$08/$35
1898          ;
1899          ;   Now the 16-bit ORs:
1900          ;
1901          OR AX,BX                  $0B/$C3
1902          OR AX,CX                  $0B/$C1
1903          OR AX,DX                  $0B/$C2
1904          OR AX,BP                  $0B/$C5
1905          OR AX,SI                  $0B/$C6
1906          OR AX,DI                  $0B/$C7
1907          OR AX,SP                  $0B/$C4
1908          OR AX,01H                 $0D/$01/$00
1909          OR AX,07733H              $0D/$33/$77
1910          OR AX,LocalOrParm         $0B/$86/LocalOrParm
1911          OR LocalOrParm,AX         $09/$86/LocalOrParm
1912          OR AX,Global              $0B/$06/Global
1913          OR Global,AX              $09/$06/Global
1914          OR AX,ES:[DI]             $26/$0B/$05
1915          OR ES:[DI],AX             $26/$09/$05
1916          ;
1917          OR BX,AX                  $0B/$D8
1918          OR BX,CX                  $0B/$D9
1919          OR BX,DX                  $0B/$DA
1920          OR BX,BP                  $0B/$DD
1921          OR BX,SI                  $0B/$DE
1922          OR BX,DI                  $0B/$DF
1923          OR BX,SP                  $0B/$DC
1924          OR BX,01H                 $81/$CB/$01/$00
1925          OR BX,07733H              $81/$CB/$33/$77
1926          OR BX,LocalOrParm         $0B/$9E/LocalOrParm
1927          OR LocalOrParm,BX         $09/$9E/LocalOrParm
```

(continued)

1928	OR BX,Global	$0B/$1E/Global
1929	OR Global,BX	$09/$1E/Global
1930	OR BX,ES:[DI]	$26/$0B/$1D
1931	OR ES:[DI],BX	$26/$09/$1D
1932	;	
1933	OR CX,AX	$0B/$C8
1934	OR CX,BX	$0B/$CB
1935	OR CX,DX	$0B/$CA
1936	OR CX,BP	$0B/$CD
1937	OR CX,SI	$0B/$CE
1938	OR CX,DI	$0B/$CF
1939	OR CX,SP	$0B/$CC
1940	OR CX,01H	$81/$C9/$01/$00
1941	OR CX,07733H	$81/$C9/$33/$77
1942	OR CX,LocalOrParm	$0B/$8E/LocalOrParm
1943	OR LocalOrParm,CX	$09/$8E/LocalOrParm
1944	OR CX,Global	$0B/$0E/Global
1945	OR Global,CX	$09/$0E/Global
1946	OR CX,ES:[DI]	$26/$0B/$0D
1947	OR ES:[DI],CX	$26/$09/$0D
1948	;	
1949	OR DX,AX	$0B/$D0
1950	OR DX,BX	$0B/$D3
1951	OR DX,CX	$0B/$D1
1952	OR DX,BP	$0B/$D5
1953	OR DX,SI	$0B/$D6
1954	OR DX,DI	$0B/$D7
1955	OR DX,SP	$0B/$D4
1956	OR DX,01H	$81/$CA/$01/$00
1957	OR DX,07733H	$81/$CA/$33/$77
1958	OR DX,LocalOrParm	$0B/$96/LocalOrParm
1959	OR LocalOrParm,DX	$09/$96/LocalOrParm
1960	OR DX,Global	$0B/$16/Global
1961	OR Global,DX	$09/$16/Global
1962	OR DX,ES:[DI]	$26/$0B/$15
1963	OR ES:[DI],DX	$26/$09/$15
1964	;	
1965	OR BP,AX	$0B/$E8
1966	OR BP,BX	$0B/$EB
1967	OR BP,CX	$0B/$E9
1968	OR BP,DX	$0B/$EA
1969	OR BP,SI	$0B/$EE
1970	OR BP,DI	$0B/$EF
1971	OR BP,SP	$0B/$EC
1972	OR BP,01H	$81/$CD/$01/$00
1973	OR BP,07733H	$81/$CD/$33/$77
1974	OR BP,Global	$0B/$2E/Global
1975	OR Global,BP	$09/$2E/Global
1976	OR BP,ES:[DI]	$26/$0B/$2D

(continued)

1977	OR ES:[DI],BP	$26/$09/$2D
1978	;	
1979	OR SI,AX	$0B/$F0
1980	OR SI,BX	$0B/$F3
1981	OR SI,CX	$0B/$F1
1982	OR SI,DX	$0B/$F2
1983	OR SI,BP	$0B/$F5
1984	OR SI,DI	$0B/$F7
1985	OR SI,SP	$0B/$F4
1986	OR SI,01H	$81/$CE/$01/$00
1987	OR SI,07733H	$81/$CE/$33/$77
1988	OR SI,LocalOrParm	$0B/$B6/LocalOrParm
1989	OR LocalOrParm,SI	$09/$B6/LocalOrParm
1990	OR SI,Global	$0B/$36/Global
1991	OR Global,SI	$09/$36/Global
1992	OR SI,ES:[DI]	$26/$0B/$35
1993	OR ES:[DI],SI	$26/$09/$35
1994	;	
1995	OR DI,AX	$0B/$F8
1996	OR DI,BX	$0B/$FB
1997	OR DI,CX	$0B/$F9
1998	OR DI,DX	$0B/$FA
1999	OR DI,BP	$0B/$FD
2000	OR DI,SI	$0B/$FE
2001	OR DI,SP	$0B/$FC
2002	OR DI,01H	$81/$CF/$01/$00
2003	OR DI,07733H	$81/$CF/$33/$77
2004	OR DI,LocalOrParm	$0B/$BE/LocalOrParm
2005	OR LocalOrParm,DI	$09/$BE/LocalOrParm
2006	OR DI,Global	$0B/$3E/Global
2007	OR Global,DI	$09/$3E/Global
2008	;	
2009	OR SP,AX	$0B/$E0
2010	OR SP,BX	$0B/$E3
2011	OR SP,CX	$0B/$E1
2012	OR SP,DX	$0B/$E2
2013	OR SP,BP	$0B/$E5
2014	OR SP,SI	$0B/$E6
2015	OR SP,DI	$0B/$E7
2016	OR SP,01H	$81/$CC/$01/$00
2017	OR SP,07733H	$81/$CC/$33/$77
2018	OR SP,LocalOrParm	$0B/$A6/LocalOrParm
2019	OR LocalOrParm,SP	$09/$A6/LocalOrParm
2020	OR SP,Global	$0B/$26/Global
2021	OR Global,SP	$09/$26/Global
2022	OR SP,ES:[DI]	$26/$0B/$25
2023	OR ES:[DI],SP	$26/$09/$25
2024	;	
2025	OR BYTE PTR LocalOrParm,01H	$80/$8E/LocalOrParm/$01

(continued)

```
2026          OR WORD PTR LocalOrParm,01H        $81/$8E/LocalOrParm/$01/$00
2027          OR BYTE PTR Global,01H             $80/$0E/Global/$01
2028          OR WORD PTR Global,01H             $81/$0E/Global/$01/$00
2029          OR BYTE PTR ES:[DI],01H            $26/$80/$0D/$01
2030          OR WORD PTR ES:[DI],01H            $26/$81/$0D/$01/$00
2031          ;
2032          ;
2033          ;    Port output instructions:
2034          ;
2035          OUT 03H,AL                         $E6/$03
2036          OUT 03H,AX                         $E7/$03
2037          OUT DX,AL                          $EE
2038          OUT DX,AX                          $EF
2039          ;
2040          ;
2041          ;    POPs and PUSHes:
2042          ;
2043          POP AX                             $58
2044          POP BX                             $5B
2045          POP CX                             $59
2046          POP DX                             $5A
2047          POP BP                             $5D
2048          POP SI                             $5E
2049          POP DI                             $5F
2050          POP SP                             $5C
2051          POP DS                             $1F
2052          POP SS                             $17
2053          POP ES                             $07
2054          POPF                               $9D
2055          POP LocalOrParm                    $8F/$86/LocalOrParm
2056          POP Global                         $8F/$06/Global
2057          POP ES:[DI]                        $26/$8F/$05
2058          ;
2059          ;
2060          PUSH AX                            $50
2061          PUSH BX                            $53
2062          PUSH CX                            $51
2063          PUSH DX                            $52
2064          PUSH BP                            $55
2065          PUSH SI                            $56
2066          PUSH DI                            $57
2067          PUSH SP                            $54
2068          PUSH CS                            $0E
2069          PUSH DS                            $1E
2070          PUSH SS                            $16
2071          PUSH ES                            $06
2072          PUSHF                              $9C
2073          PUSH LocalOrParm                   $FF/$B6/LocalOrParm
2074          PUSH Global                        $FF/$36/Global
```

(continued)

```
2075          PUSH ES:[DI]                      $26/$FF/$35
2076          ;
2077          ;
2078          ;   Rotate Left Through Carry instructions:
2079          ;
2080          RCL AL,1                          $D0/$D0
2081          RCL BL,1                          $D0/$D3
2082          RCL CL,1                          $D0/$D1
2083          RCL DL,1                          $D0/$D2
2084          RCL AH,1                          $D0/$D4
2085          RCL BH,1                          $D0/$D7
2086          RCL CH,1                          $D0/$D5
2087          RCL DH,1                          $D0/$D6
2088          RCL AX,1                          $D1/$D0
2089          RCL BX,1                          $D1/$D3
2090          RCL CX,1                          $D1/$D1
2091          RCL DX,1                          $D1/$D2
2092          RCL BP,1                          $D1/$D5
2093          RCL SI,1                          $D1/$D6
2094          RCL DI,1                          $D1/$D7
2095          RCL SP,1                          $D1/$D4
2096          RCL BYTE PTR LocalOrParm,1        $D0/$96/LocalOrParm
2097          RCL WORD PTR LocalOrParm,1        $D1/$96/LocalOrParm
2098          RCL BYTE PTR Global,1             $D0/$16/Global
2099          RCL WORD PTR Global,1             $D1/$16/Global
2100          RCL BYTE PTR ES:[DI],1            $26/$D0/$15
2101          RCL WORD PTR ES:[DI],1            $26/$D1/$15
2102          ;
2103          RCL AL,CL                         $D2/$D0
2104          RCL BL,CL                         $D2/$D3
2105          RCL CL,CL                         $D2/$D1
2106          RCL DL,CL                         $D2/$D2
2107          RCL AH,CL                         $D2/$D4
2108          RCL BH,CL                         $D2/$D7
2109          RCL CH,CL                         $D2/$D5
2110          RCL DH,CL                         $D2/$D6
2111          RCL AX,CL                         $D3/$D0
2112          RCL BX,CL                         $D3/$D3
2113          RCL CX,CL                         $D3/$D1
2114          RCL DX,CL                         $D3/$D2
2115          RCL BP,CL                         $D3/$D5
2116          RCL SI,CL                         $D3/$D6
2117          RCL DI,CL                         $D3/$D7
2118          RCL SP,CL                         $D3/$D4
2119          RCL BYTE PTR LocalOrParm,CL       $D2/$96/LocalOrParm
2120          RCL WORD PTR LocalOrParm,CL       $D3/$96/LocalOrParm
2121          RCL BYTE PTR Global,CL            $D2/$16/Global
2122          RCL WORD PTR Global,CL            $D3/$16/Global
2123          RCL BYTE PTR ES:[DI],CL           $26/$D2/$15
```

(continued)

```
2124                RCL WORD PTR ES:[DI],CL          $26/$D3/$15
2125                ;
2126                ;
2127                ;   Rotate Right Through Carry instructions:
2128
2129                ;
2130                ;
2131                RCR AL,1                         $D0/$D8
2132                RCR BL,1                         $D0/$DB
2133                RCR CL,1                         $D0/$D9
2134                RCR DL,1                         $D0/$DA
2135                RCR AH,1                         $D0/$DC
2136                RCR BH,1                         $D0/$DF
2137                RCR CH,1                         $D0/$DD
2138                RCR DH,1                         $D0/$DE
2139                RCR AX,1                         $D1/$D8
2140                RCR BX,1                         $D1/$DB
2141                RCR CX,1                         $D1/$D9
2142                RCR DX,1                         $D1/$DA
2143                RCR BP,1                         $D1/$DD
2144                RCR SI,1                         $D1/$DE
2145                RCR DI,1                         $D1/$DF
2146                RCR SP,1                         $D1/$DC
2147                RCR BYTE PTR LocalOrParm,1       $D0/$9E/LocalOrParm
2148                RCR WORD PTR LocalOrParm,1       $D1/$9E/LocalOrParm
2149                RCR BYTE PTR Global,1            $D0/$1E/Global
2150                RCR WORD PTR Global,1            $D1/$1E/Global
2151                RCR BYTE PTR ES:[DI],1           $26/$D0/$1D
2152                RCR WORD PTR ES:[DI],1           $26/$D1/$1D
2153                ;
2154                RCR AL,CL                        $D2/$D8
2155                RCR BL,CL                        $D2/$DB
2156                RCR CL,CL                        $D2/$D9
2157                RCR DL,CL                        $D2/$DA
2158                RCR AH,CL                        $D2/$DC
2159                RCR BH,CL                        $D2/$DF
2160                RCR CH,CL                        $D2/$DD
2161                RCR DH,CL                        $D2/$DE
2162                RCR AX,CL                        $D3/$D8
2163                RCR BX,CL                        $D3/$DB
2164                RCR CX,CL                        $D3/$D9
2165                RCR DX,CL                        $D3/$DA
2166                RCR BP,CL                        $D3/$DD
2167                RCR SI,CL                        $D3/$DE
2168                RCR DI,CL                        $D3/$DF
2169                RCR SP,CL                        $D3/$DC
2170                RCR BYTE PTR LocalOrParm,CL      $D2/$9E/LocalOrParm
2171                RCR WORD PTR LocalOrParm,CL      $D3/$9E/LocalOrParm
2172                RCR BYTE PTR Global,CL           $D2/$1E/Global
```

(continued)

```
2173              RCR WORD PTR Global,CL           $D3/$1E/Global
2174              RCR BYTE PTR ES:[DI],CL          $26/$D2/$1D
2175              RCR WORD PTR ES:[DI],CL          $26/$D3/$1D
2176              ;
2177              ;
2178              ;   Repeat Prefixes:
2179              ;
2180              REP                              $F3
2181              REPNE                            $F2
2182              ;
2183              ;
2184              ;   Intrasegment RETURN:
2185              ;
2186              ;   NOTE: Intersegment opcodes are not included
2187              ;   because Turbo Pascal supports only a single
2188              ;   code segment.  Also, '6' is only an example
2189              ;   figure; it indicates the number of bytes to
2190              ;   POP from the stack on return.
2191              ;
2192              RET                              $C3
2193              RET 6                            $C2/$06/$00
2194              ;
2195              ;
2196              ;   Rotate Left Instructions:
2197              ;
2198              ROL AL,1                         $D0/$C0
2199              ROL BL,1                         $D0/$C3
2200              ROL CL,1                         $D0/$C1
2201              ROL DL,1                         $D0/$C2
2202              ROL AH,1                         $D0/$C4
2203              ROL BH,1                         $D0/$C7
2204              ROL CH,1                         $D0/$C5
2205              ROL DH,1                         $D0/$C6
2206              ROL AX,1                         $D1/$C0
2207              ROL BX,1                         $D1/$C3
2208              ROL CX,1                         $D1/$C1
2209              ROL DX,1                         $D1/$C2
2210              ROL BP,1                         $D1/$C5
2211              ROL SI,1                         $D1/$C6
2212              ROL DI,1                         $D1/$C7
2213              ROL SP,1                         $D1/$C4
2214              ROL BYTE PTR LocalOrParm,1       $D0/$86/LocalOrParm
2215              ROL WORD PTR LocalOrParm,1       $D1/$86/LocalOrParm
2216              ROL BYTE PTR Global,1            $D0/$06/Global
2217              ROL WORD PTR Global,1            $D1/$06/Global
2218              ROL BYTE PTR ES:[DI],1           $26/$D0/$05
2219              ROL WORD PTR ES:[DI],1           $26/$D1/$05
2220              ;
2221              ROL AL,CL                        $D2/$C0
```

(continued)

```
2222          ROL BL,CL                         $D2/$C3
2223          ROL CL,CL                         $D2/$C1
2224          ROL DL,CL                         $D2/$C2
2225          ROL AH,CL                         $D2/$C4
2226          ROL BH,CL                         $D2/$C7
2227          ROL CH,CL                         $D2/$C5
2228          ROL DH,CL                         $D2/$C6
2229          ROL AX,CL                         $D3/$C0
2230          ROL BX,CL                         $D3/$C3
2231          ROL CX,CL                         $D3/$C1
2232          ROL DX,CL                         $D3/$C2
2233          ROL BP,CL                         $D3/$C5
2234          ROL SI,CL                         $D3/$C6
2235          ROL DI,CL                         $D3/$C7
2236          ROL SP,CL                         $D3/$C4
2237          ROL BYTE PTR LocalOrParm,CL       $D2/$86/LocalOrParm
2238          ROL WORD PTR LocalOrParm,CL       $D3/$86/LocalOrParm
2239          ROL BYTE PTR Global,CL            $D2/$06/Global
2240          ROL WORD PTR Global,CL            $D3/$06/Global
2241          ROL BYTE PTR ES:[DI],CL           $26/$D2/$05
2242          ROL WORD PTR ES:[DI],CL           $26/$D3/$05
2243          ;
2244          ;
2245          ;    Rotate Right Instructions:
2246          ;
2247          ROR AL,1                          $D0/$C8
2248          ROR BL,1                          $D0/$CB
2249          ROR CL,1                          $D0/$C9
2250          ROR DL,1                          $D0/$CA
2251          ROR AH,1                          $D0/$CC
2252          ROR BH,1                          $D0/$CF
2253          ROR CH,1                          $D0/$CD
2254          ROR DH,1                          $D0/$CE
2255          ROR AX,1                          $D1/$C8
2256          ROR BX,1                          $D1/$CB
2257          ROR CX,1                          $D1/$C9
2258          ROR DX,1                          $D1/$CA
2259          ROR BP,1                          $D1/$CD
2260          ROR SI,1                          $D1/$CE
2261          ROR DI,1                          $D1/$CF
2262          ROR SP,1                          $D1/$CC
2263          ROR BYTE PTR LocalOrParm,1        $D0/$8E/LocalOrParm
2264          ROR WORD PTR LocalOrParm,1        $D1/$8E/LocalOrParm
2265          ROR BYTE PTR Global,1             $D0/$0E/Global
2266          ROR WORD PTR Global,1             $D1/$0E/Global
2267          ROR BYTE PTR ES:[DI],1            $26/$D0/$0D
2268          ROR WORD PTR ES:[DI],1            $26/$D1/$0D
2269          ;
2270          ROR AL,CL                         $D2/$C8
```

(continued)

```
2271          ROR BL,CL                        $D2/$CB
2272          ROR CL,CL                        $D2/$C9
2273          ROR DL,CL                        $D2/$CA
2274          ROR AH,CL                        $D2/$CC
2275          ROR BH,CL                        $D2/$CF
2276          ROR CH,CL                        $D2/$CD
2277          ROR DH,CL                        $D2/$CE
2278          ROR AX,CL                        $D3/$C8
2279          ROR BX,CL                        $D3/$CB
2280          ROR CX,CL                        $D3/$C9
2281          ROR DX,CL                        $D3/$CA
2282          ROR BP,CL                        $D3/$CD
2283          ROR SI,CL                        $D3/$CE
2284          ROR DI,CL                        $D3/$CF
2285          ROR SP,CL                        $D3/$CC
2286          ROR BYTE PTR LocalOrParm,CL      $D2/$8E/LocalOrParm
2287          ROR WORD PTR LocalOrParm,CL      $D3/$8E/LocalOrParm
2288          ROR BYTE PTR Global,CL           $D2/$0E/Global
2289          ROR WORD PTR Global,CL           $D3/$0E/Global
2290          ROR BYTE PTR ES:[DI],CL          $26/$D2/$0D
2291          ROR WORD PTR ES:[DI],CL          $26/$D3/$0D
2292          ;
2293          ;
2294          ;    Store AH into low byte of flags:
2295          ;
2296          SAHF                             $9E
2297          ;
2298          ;
2299          ;    Shift Arithmetic Left instructions:
2300          ;
2301          SAL AL,1                         $D0/$E0
2302          SAL BL,1                         $D0/$E3
2303          SAL CL,1                         $D0/$E1
2304          SAL DL,1                         $D0/$E2
2305          SAL AH,1                         $D0/$E4
2306          SAL BH,1                         $D0/$E7
2307          SAL CH,1                         $D0/$E5
2308          SAL DH,1                         $D0/$E6
2309          SAL AX,1                         $D1/$E0
2310          SAL BX,1                         $D1/$E3
2311          SAL CX,1                         $D1/$E1
2312          SAL DX,1                         $D1/$E2
2313          SAL BP,1                         $D1/$E5
2314          SAL SI,1                         $D1/$E6
2315          SAL DI,1                         $D1/$E7
2316          SAL SP,1                         $D1/$E4
2317          SAL BYTE PTR LocalOrParm,1       $D0/$A6/LocalOrParm
2318          SAL WORD PTR LocalOrParm,1       $D1/$A6/LocalOrParm
2319          SAL BYTE PTR Global,1            $D0/$26/Global
```

(continued)

2320	SAL WORD PTR Global,1	$D1/$26/Global
2321	SAL BYTE PTR ES:[DI],1	$26/$D0/$25
2322	SAL WORD PTR ES:[DI],1	$26/$D1/$25
2323	;	
2324	SAL AL,CL	$D2/$E0
2325	SAL BL,CL	$D2/$E3
2326	SAL CL,CL	$D2/$E1
2327	SAL DL,CL	$D2/$E2
2328	SAL AH,CL	$D2/$E4
2329	SAL BH,CL	$D2/$E7
2330	SAL CH,CL	$D2/$E5
2331	SAL DH,CL	$D2/$E6
2332	SAL AX,CL	$D3/$E0
2333	SAL BX,CL	$D3/$E3
2334	SAL CX,CL	$D3/$E1
2335	SAL DX,CL	$D3/$E2
2336	SAL BP,CL	$D3/$E5
2337	SAL SI,CL	$D3/$E6
2338	SAL DI,CL	$D3/$E7
2339	SAL SP,CL	$D3/$E4
2340	SAL BYTE PTR LocalOrParm,CL	$D2/$A6/LocalOrParm
2341	SAL WORD PTR LocalOrParm,CL	$D3/$A6/LocalOrParm
2342	SAL BYTE PTR Global,CL	$D2/$26/Global
2343	SAL WORD PTR Global,CL	$D3/$26/Global
2344	SAL BYTE PTR ES:[DI],CL	$26/$D2/$25
2345	SAL WORD PTR ES:[DI],CL	$26/$D3/$25
2346	;	
2347	;	
2348	; Shift Arithmetic Right instructions:	
2349	;	
2350	SAR AL,1	$D0/$F8
2351	SAR BL,1	$D0/$FB
2352	SAR CL,1	$D0/$F9
2353	SAR DL,1	$D0/$FA
2354	SAR AH,1	$D0/$FC
2355	SAR BH,1	$D0/$FF
2356	SAR CH,1	$D0/$FD
2357	SAR DH,1	$D0/$FE
2358	SAR AX,1	$D1/$F8
2359	SAR BX,1	$D1/$FB
2360	SAR CX,1	$D1/$F9
2361	SAR DX,1	$D1/$FA
2362	SAR BP,1	$D1/$FD
2363	SAR SI,1	$D1/$FE
2364	SAR DI,1	$D1/$FF
2365	SAR SP,1	$D1/$FC
2366	SAR BYTE PTR LocalOrParm,1	$D0/$BE/LocalOrParm
2367	SAR WORD PTR LocalOrParm,1	$D1/$BE/LocalOrParm
2368	SAR BYTE PTR Global,1	$D0/$3E/Global

(continued)

```
2369          SAR WORD PTR Global,1             $D1/$3E/Global
2370          SAR BYTE PTR ES:[DI],1            $26/$D0/$3D
2371          SAR WORD PTR ES:[DI],1            $26/$D1/$3D
2372          ;
2373          SAR AL,CL                         $D2/$F8
2374          SAR BL,CL                         $D2/$FB
2375          SAR CL,CL                         $D2/$F9
2376          SAR DL,CL                         $D2/$FA
2377          SAR AH,CL                         $D2/$FC
2378          SAR BH,CL                         $D2/$FF
2379          SAR CH,CL                         $D2/$FD
2380          SAR DH,CL                         $D2/$FE
2381          SAR AX,CL                         $D3/$F8
2382          SAR BX,CL                         $D3/$FB
2383          SAR CX,CL                         $D3/$F9
2384          SAR DX,CL                         $D3/$FA
2385          SAR BP,CL                         $D3/$FD
2386          SAR SI,CL                         $D3/$FE
2387          SAR DI,CL                         $D3/$FF
2388          SAR SP,CL                         $D3/$FC
2389          SAR BYTE PTR LocalOrParm,CL       $D2/$BE/LocalOrParm
2390          SAR WORD PTR LocalOrParm,CL       $D3/$BE/LocalOrParm
2391          SAR BYTE PTR Global,CL            $D2/$3E/Global
2392          SAR WORD PTR Global,CL            $D3/$3E/Global
2393          SAR BYTE PTR ES:[DI],CL           $26/$D2/$3D
2394          SAR WORD PTR ES:[DI],CL           $26/$D3/$3D
2395          ;
2396          ;
2397          ;   Subtract with Borrow.  8-bit operations first:
2398          ;
2399          SBB AL,AH                         $1A/$C4
2400          SBB AL,BL                         $1A/$C3
2401          SBB AL,BH                         $1A/$C7
2402          SBB AL,CL                         $1A/$C1
2403          SBB AL,CH                         $1A/$C5
2404          SBB AL,DL                         $1A/$C2
2405          SBB AL,DH                         $1A/$C6
2406          SBB AL,01H                        $1C/$01
2407          SBB AL,LocalOrParm                $1A/$86/LocalOrParm
2408          SBB LocalOrParm,AL                $18/$86/LocalOrParm
2409          SBB AL,Global                     $1A/$06/Global
2410          SBB Global,AL                     $18/$06/Global
2411          SBB AL,ES:[DI]                    $26/$1A/$05
2412          SBB ES:[DI],AL                    $26/$18/$05
2413          ;
2414          SBB AH,AL                         $1A/$E0
2415          SBB AH,BL                         $1A/$E3
2416          SBB AH,BH                         $1A/$E7
2417          SBB AH,CL                         $1A/$E1
```

(continued)

2418	SBB AH,CH	$1A/$E5
2419	SBB AH,DL	$1A/$E2
2420	SBB AH,DH	$1A/$E6
2421	SBB AH,01H	$80/$DC/$01
2422	SBB AH,LocalOrParm	$1A/$A6/LocalOrParm
2423	SBB LocalOrParm,AH	$18/$A6/LocalOrParm
2424	SBB AH,Global	$1A/$26/Global
2425	SBB Global,AH	$18/$26/Global
2426	SBB AH,ES:[DI]	$26/$1A/$25
2427	SBB ES:[DI],AH	$26/$18/$25
2428	;	
2429	SBB BL,BH	$1A/$DF
2430	SBB BL,AL	$1A/$D8
2431	SBB BL,AH	$1A/$DC
2432	SBB BL,CL	$1A/$D9
2433	SBB BL,CH	$1A/$DD
2434	SBB BL,DL	$1A/$DA
2435	SBB BL,DH	$1A/$DE
2436	SBB BL,01H	$80/$DB/$01
2437	SBB BL,LocalOrParm	$1A/$9E/LocalOrParm
2438	SBB LocalOrParm,BL	$18/$9E/LocalOrParm
2439	SBB BL,Global	$1A/$1E/Global
2440	SBB Global,BL	$18/$1E/Global
2441	SBB BL,ES:[DI]	$26/$1A/$1D
2442	SBB ES:[DI],BL	$26/$18/$1D
2443	;	
2444	SBB BH,BL	$1A/$FB
2445	SBB BH,AL	$1A/$F8
2446	SBB BH,AH	$1A/$FC
2447	SBB BH,CL	$1A/$F9
2448	SBB BH,CH	$1A/$FD
2449	SBB BH,DL	$1A/$FA
2450	SBB BH,DH	$1A/$FE
2451	SBB BH,01H	$80/$DF/$01
2452	SBB BH,LocalOrParm	$1A/$BE/LocalOrParm
2453	SBB LocalOrParm,BH	$18/$BE/LocalOrParm
2454	SBB BH,Global	$1A/$3E/Global
2455	SBB Global,BH	$18/$3E/Global
2456	SBB BH,ES:[DI]	$26/$1A/$3D
2457	SBB ES:[DI],BH	$26/$18/$3D
2458	;	
2459	SBB CL,CH	$1A/$CD
2460	SBB CL,AL	$1A/$C8
2461	SBB CL,AH	$1A/$CC
2462	SBB CL,BL	$1A/$CB
2463	SBB CL,BH	$1A/$CF
2464	SBB CL,DL	$1A/$CA
2465	SBB CL,DH	$1A/$CE
2466	SBB CL,01H	$80/$D9/$01

(continued)

```
2467        SBB CL,LocalOrParm          $1A/$8E/LocalOrParm
2468        SBB LocalOrParm,CL          $18/$8E/LocalOrParm
2469        SBB CL,Global               $1A/$0E/Global
2470        SBB Global,CL               $18/$0E/Global
2471        SBB CL,ES:[DI]              $26/$1A/$0D
2472        SBB ES:[DI],CL              $26/$18/$0D
2473        ;
2474        SBB CH,CL                   $1A/$E9
2475        SBB CH,AL                   $1A/$E8
2476        SBB CH,AH                   $1A/$EC
2477        SBB CH,BL                   $1A/$EB
2478        SBB CH,BH                   $1A/$EF
2479        SBB CH,DL                   $1A/$EA
2480        SBB CH,DH                   $1A/$EE
2481        SBB CH,01H                  $80/$DD/$01
2482        SBB CH,LocalOrParm          $1A/$AE/LocalOrParm
2483        SBB LocalOrParm,CH          $18/$AE/LocalOrParm
2484        SBB CH,Global               $1A/$2E/Global
2485        SBB Global,CH               $18/$2E/Global
2486        SBB CH,ES:[DI]              $26/$1A/$2D
2487        SBB ES:[DI],CH              $26/$18/$2D
2488        ;
2489        SBB DL,DH                   $1A/$D6
2490        SBB DL,AL                   $1A/$D0
2491        SBB DL,AH                   $1A/$D4
2492        SBB DL,BL                   $1A/$D3
2493        SBB DL,BH                   $1A/$D7
2494        SBB DL,CL                   $1A/$D1
2495        SBB DL,CH                   $1A/$D5
2496        SBB DL,01H                  $80/$DA/$01
2497        SBB DL,LocalOrParm          $1A/$96/LocalOrParm
2498        SBB LocalOrParm,DL          $18/$96/LocalOrParm
2499        SBB DL,Global               $1A/$16/Global
2500        SBB Global,DL               $18/$16/Global
2501        SBB DL,ES:[DI]              $26/$1A/$15
2502        SBB ES:[DI],DL              $26/$18/$15
2503        ;
2504        SBB DH,DL                   $1A/$F2
2505        SBB DH,AL                   $1A/$F0
2506        SBB DH,AH                   $1A/$F4
2507        SBB DH,BL                   $1A/$F3
2508        SBB DH,BH                   $1A/$F7
2509        SBB DH,CL                   $1A/$F1
2510        SBB DH,CH                   $1A/$F5
2511        SBB DH,01H                  $80/$DE/$01
2512        SBB DH,LocalOrParm          $1A/$B6/LocalOrParm
2513        SBB LocalOrParm,DH          $18/$B6/LocalOrParm
2514        SBB DH,Global               $1A/$36/Global
2515        SBB Global,DH               $18/$36/Global
```

(continued)

```
2516            SBB DH,ES:[DI]              $26/$1A/$35
2517            SBB ES:[DI],DH             .$26/$18/$35
2518            ;
2519            ;    Now the 16-bit SBBs:
2520            ;
2521            SBB AX,BX                   $1B/$C3
2522            SBB AX,CX                   $1B/$C1
2523            SBB AX,DX                   $1B/$C2
2524            SBB AX,BP                   $1B/$C5
2525            SBB AX,SI                   $1B/$C6
2526            SBB AX,DI                   $1B/$C7
2527            SBB AX,SP                   $1B/$C4
2528            SBB AX,01H                  $1D/$01/$00
2529            SBB AX,07733H               $1D/$33/$77
2530            SBB AX,LocalOrParm          $1B/$86/LocalOrParm
2531            SBB LocalOrParm,AX          $19/$86/LocalOrParm
2532            SBB AX,Global               $1B/$06/Global
2533            SBB Global,AX               $19/$06/Global
2534            SBB AX,ES:[DI]              $26/$1B/$05
2535            SBB ES:[DI],AX             $26/$19/$05
2536            ;
2537            SBB BX,AX                   $1B/$D8
2538            SBB BX,CX                   $1B/$D9
2539            SBB BX,DX                   $1B/$DA
2540            SBB BX,BP                   $1B/$DD
2541            SBB BX,SI                   $1B/$DE
2542            SBB BX,DI                   $1B/$DF
2543            SBB BX,SP                   $1B/$DC
2544            SBB BX,01H                  $83/$DB/$01
2545            SBB BX,07733H               $81/$DB/$33/$77
2546            SBB BX,LocalOrParm          $1B/$9E/LocalOrParm
2547            SBB LocalOrParm,BX          $19/$9E/LocalOrParm
2548            SBB BX,Global               $1B/$1E/Global
2549            SBB Global,BX               $19/$1E/Global
2550            SBB BX,ES:[DI]              $26/$1B/$1D
2551            SBB ES:[DI],BX             $26/$19/$1D
2552            ;
2553            SBB CX,AX                   $1B/$C8
2554            SBB CX,BX                   $1B/$CB
2555            SBB CX,DX                   $1B/$CA
2556            SBB CX,BP                   $1B/$CD
2557            SBB CX,SI                   $1B/$CE
2558            SBB CX,DI                   $1B/$CF
2559            SBB CX,SP                   $1B/$CC
2560            SBB CX,01H                  $83/$D9/$01
2561            SBB CX,07733H               $81/$D9/$33/$77
2562            SBB CX,LocalOrParm          $1B/$8E/LocalOrParm
2563            SBB LocalOrParm,CX          $19/$8E/LocalOrParm
2564            SBB CX,Global               $1B/$0E/Global
```

(continued)

2565	SBB Global,CX	$19/$0E/Global
2566	SBB CX,ES:[DI]	$26/$1B/$0D
2567	SBB ES:[DI],CX	$26/$19/$0D
2568	;	
2569	SBB DX,AX	$1B/$D0
2570	SBB DX,BX	$1B/$D3
2571	SBB DX,CX	$1B/$D1
2572	SBB DX,BP	$1B/$D5
2573	SBB DX,SI	$1B/$D6
2574	SBB DX,DI	$1B/$D7
2575	SBB DX,SP	$1B/$D4
2576	SBB DX,01H	$83/$DA/$01
2577	SBB DX,07733H	$81/$DA/$33/$77
2578	SBB DX,LocalOrParm	$1B/$96/LocalOrParm
2579	SBB LocalOrParm,DX	$19/$96/LocalOrParm
2580	SBB DX,Global	$1B/$16/Global
2581	SBB Global,DX	$19/$16/Global
2582	SBB DX,ES:[DI]	$26/$1B/$15
2583	SBB ES:[DI],DX	$26/$19/$15
2584	;	
2585	SBB BP,AX	$1B/$E8
2586	SBB BP,BX	$1B/$EB
2587	SBB BP,CX	$1B/$E9
2588	SBB BP,DX	$1B/$EA
2589	SBB BP,SI	$1B/$EE
2590	SBB BP,DI	$1B/$EF
2591	SBB BP,SP	$1B/$EC
2592	SBB BP,01H	$83/$DD/$01
2593	SBB BP,07733H	$81/$DD/$33/$77
2594	SBB BP,Global	$1B/$2E/Global
2595	SBB Global,BP	$19/$2E/Global
2596	SBB BP,ES:[DI]	$26/$1B/$2D
2597	SBB ES:[DI],BP	$26/$19/$2D
2598	;	
2599	SBB SI,AX	$1B/$F0
2600	SBB SI,BX	$1B/$F3
2601	SBB SI,CX	$1B/$F1
2602	SBB SI,DX	$1B/$F2
2603	SBB SI,BP	$1B/$F5
2604	SBB SI,DI	$1B/$F7
2605	SBB SI,SP	$1B/$F4
2606	SBB SI,01H	$83/$DE/$01
2607	SBB SI,07733H	$81/$DE/$33/$77
2608	SBB SI,LocalOrParm	$1B/$B6/LocalOrParm
2609	SBB LocalOrParm,SI	$19/$B6/LocalOrParm
2610	SBB SI,Global	$1B/$36/Global
2611	SBB Global,SI	$19/$36/Global
2612	SBB SI,ES:[DI]	$26/$1B/$35
2613	SBB ES:[DI],SI	$26/$19/$35

(continued)

```
2614                    ;
2615                    SBB DI,AX                          $1B/$F8
2616                    SBB DI,BX                          $1B/$FB
2617                    SBB DI,CX                          $1B/$F9
2618                    SBB DI,DX                          $1B/$FA
2619                    SBB DI,BP                          $1B/$FD
2620                    SBB DI,SI                          $1B/$FE
2621                    SBB DI,SP                          $1B/$FC
2622                    SBB DI,01H                         $83/$DF/$01
2623                    SBB DI,07733H                      $81/$DF/$33/$77
2624                    SBB DI,LocalOrParm                 $1B/$BE/LocalOrParm
2625                    SBB LocalOrParm,DI                 $19/$BE/LocalOrParm
2626                    SBB DI,Global                      $1B/$3E/Global
2627                    SBB Global,DI                      $19/$3E/Global
2628                    ;
2629                    SBB SP,AX                          $1B/$E0
2630                    SBB SP,BX                          $1B/$E3
2631                    SBB SP,CX                          $1B/$E1
2632                    SBB SP,DX                          $1B/$E2
2633                    SBB SP,BP                          $1B/$E5
2634                    SBB SP,SI                          $1B/$E6
2635                    SBB SP,DI                          $1B/$E7
2636                    SBB SP,01H                         $83/$DC/$01
2637                    SBB SP,07733H                      $81/$DC/$33/$77
2638                    SBB SP,LocalOrParm                 $1B/$A6/LocalOrParm
2639                    SBB LocalOrParm,SP                 $19/$A6/LocalOrParm
2640                    SBB SP,Global                      $1B/$26/Global
2641                    SBB Global,SP                      $19/$26/Global
2642                    SBB SP,ES:[DI]                     $26/$1B/$25
2643                    SBB ES:[DI],SP                     $26/$19/$25
2644                    ;
2645                    SBB BYTE PTR LocalOrParm,01H       $80/$9E/LocalOrParm/$01
2646                    SBB WORD PTR LocalOrParm,01H       $83/$9E/LocalOrParm/$01
2647                    SBB BYTE PTR Global,01H            $80/$1E/Global/$01
2648                    SBB WORD PTR Global,01H            $83/$1E/Global/$01
2649                    SBB BYTE PTR ES:[DI],01H           $26/$80/$1D/$01
2650                    SBB WORD PTR ES:[DI],01H           $26/$83/$1D/$01
2651                    ;
2652                    ;
2653                    ;    Scan String instructions:
2654                    ;
2655                    SCASB                              $AE
2656                    SCASW                              $AF
2657                    ;
2658                    ;
2659                    ;    Segment Override Prefixes, using MOV as examples:
2660                    ;
2661                    MOV AX,DS:0441H                    $A1/$41/$04
2662                    MOV DS:0441H,AX                    $A3/$41/$04
```

(continued)

```
2663              MOV AX,CS:0441H              $2E/$A1/$41/$04
2664              MOV CS:0441H,AX              $2E/$A3/$41/$04
2665              MOV AX,SS:0441H              $36/$A1/$41/$04
2666              MOV SS:0441H,AX              $36/$A3/$41/$04
2667              MOV AX,ES:0441H              $26/$A1/$41/$04
2668              MOV ES:0441H,AX              $26/$A3/$41/$04
2669              ;
2670              ;
2671              ;    Shift Logical Left instructions:
2672              ;
2673              SHL AL,1                      $D0/$E0
2674              SHL BL,1                      $D0/$E3
2675              SHL CL,1                      $D0/$E1
2676              SHL DL,1                      $D0/$E2
2677              SHL AH,1                      $D0/$E4
2678              SHL BH,1                      $D0/$E7
2679              SHL CH,1                      $D0/$E5
2680              SHL DH,1                      $D0/$E6
2681              SHL AX,1                      $D1/$E0
2682              SHL BX,1                      $D1/$E3
2683              SHL CX,1                      $D1/$E1
2684              SHL DX,1                      $D1/$E2
2685              SHL BP,1                      $D1/$E5
2686              SHL SI,1                      $D1/$E6
2687              SHL DI,1                      $D1/$E7
2688              SHL SP,1                      $D1/$E4
2689              SHL BYTE PTR LocalOrParm,1    $D0/$A6/LocalOrParm
2690              SHL WORD PTR LocalOrParm,1    $D1/$A6/LocalOrParm
2691              SHL BYTE PTR Global,1         $D0/$26/Global
2692              SHL WORD PTR Global,1         $D1/$26/Global
2693              SHL BYTE PTR ES:[DI],1        $26/$D0/$25
2694              SHL WORD PTR ES:[DI],1        $26/$D1/$25
2695              ;
2696              SHL AL,CL                     $D2/$E0
2697              SHL BL,CL                     $D2/$E3
2698              SHL CL,CL                     $D2/$E1
2699              SHL DL,CL                     $D2/$E2
2700              SHL AH,CL                     $D2/$E4
2701              SHL BH,CL                     $D2/$E7
2702              SHL CH,CL                     $D2/$E5
2703              SHL DH,CL                     $D2/$E6
2704              SHL AX,CL                     $D3/$E0
2705              SHL BX,CL                     $D3/$E3
2706              SHL CX,CL                     $D3/$E1
2707              SHL DX,CL                     $D3/$E2
2708              SHL BP,CL                     $D3/$E5
2709              SHL SI,CL                     $D3/$E6
2710              SHL DI,CL                     $D3/$E7
2711              SHL SP,CL                     $D3/$E4
```

(continued)

```
2712            SHL BYTE PTR LocalOrParm,CL        $D2/$A6/LocalOrParm
2713            SHL WORD PTR LocalOrParm,CL        $D3/$A6/LocalOrParm
2714            SHL BYTE PTR Global,CL             $D2/$26/Global
2715            SHL WORD PTR Global,CL             $D3/$26/Global
2716            SHL BYTE PTR ES:[DI],CL            $26/$D2/$25
2717            SHL WORD PTR ES:[DI],CL            $26/$D3/$25
2718            ;
2719            ;
2720            ;    Shift Logical Right instructions:
2721            ;
2722            SHR AL,1                           $D0/$E8
2723            SHR BL,1                           $D0/$EB
2724            SHR CL,1                           $D0/$E9
2725            SHR DL,1                           $D0/$EA
2726            SHR AH,1                           $D0/$EC
2727            SHR BH,1                           $D0/$EF
2728            SHR CH,1                           $D0/$ED
2729            SHR DH,1                           $D0/$EE
2730            SHR AX,1                           $D1/$E8
2731            SHR BX,1                           $D1/$EB
2732            SHR CX,1                           $D1/$E9
2733            SHR DX,1                           $D1/$EA
2734            SHR BP,1                           $D1/$ED
2735            SHR SI,1                           $D1/$EE
2736            SHR DI,1                           $D1/$EF
2737            SHR SP,1                           $D1/$EC
2738            SHR BYTE PTR LocalOrParm,1         $D0/$AE/LocalOrParm
2739            SHR WORD PTR LocalOrParm,1         $D1/$AE/LocalOrParm
2740            SHR BYTE PTR Global,1              $D0/$2E/Global
2741            SHR WORD PTR Global,1              $D1/$2E/Global
2742            SHR BYTE PTR ES:[DI],1             $26/$D0/$2D
2743            SHR WORD PTR ES:[DI],1             $26/$D1/$2D
2744            ;
2745            SHR AL,CL                          $D2/$E8
2746            SHR BL,CL                          $D2/$EB
2747            SHR CL,CL                          $D2/$E9
2748            SHR DL,CL                          $D2/$EA
2749            SHR AH,CL                          $D2/$EC
2750            SHR BH,CL                          $D2/$EF
2751            SHR CH,CL                          $D2/$ED
2752            SHR DH,CL                          $D2/$EE
2753            SHR AX,CL                          $D3/$E8
2754            SHR BX,CL                          $D3/$EB
2755            SHR CX,CL                          $D3/$E9
2756            SHR DX,CL                          $D3/$EA
2757            SHR BP,CL                          $D3/$ED
2758            SHR SI,CL                          $D3/$EE
2759            SHR DI,CL                          $D3/$EF
2760            SHR SP,CL                          $D3/$EC
```

(continued)

```
2761          SHR BYTE PTR LocalOrParm,CL      $D2/$AE/LocalOrParm
2762          SHR WORD PTR LocalOrParm,CL      $D3/$AE/LocalOrParm
2763          SHR BYTE PTR Global,CL           $D2/$2E/Global
2764          SHR WORD PTR Global,CL           $D3/$2E/Global
2765          SHR BYTE PTR ES:[DI],CL          $26/$D2/$2D
2766          SHR WORD PTR ES:[DI],CL          $26/$D3/$2D
2767          ;
2768          ;
2769          ;    Set Flag instructions:
2770          ;
2771          STC                              $F9
2772          STD                              $FD
2773          STI                              $FB
2774          ;
2775          ;
2776          ;    Store String instruction:
2777          ;
2778          STOSB                            $AA
2779          STOSW                            $AB
2780          ;
2781          ;
2782          ;    Subtract.   8-bit operations first:
2783          ;
2784          SUB AL,AH                        $2A/$C4
2785          SUB AL,BL                        $2A/$C3
2786          SUB AL,BH                        $2A/$C7
2787          SUB AL,CL                        $2A/$C1
2788          SUB AL,CH                        $2A/$C5
2789          SUB AL,DL                        $2A/$C2
2790          SUB AL,DH                        $2A/$C6
2791          SUB AL,01H                       $2C/$01
2792          SUB AL,LocalOrParm               $2A/$86/LocalOrParm
2793          SUB LocalOrParm,AL               $28/$86/LocalOrParm
2794          SUB AL,Global                    $2A/$06/Global
2795          SUB Global,AL                    $28/$06/Global
2796          SUB AL,ES:[DI]                   $26/$2A/$05
2797          SUB ES:[DI],AL                   $26/$28/$05
2798          ;
2799          SUB AH,AL                        $2A/$E0
2800          SUB AH,BL                        $2A/$E3
2801          SUB AH,BH                        $2A/$E7
2802          SUB AH,CL                        $2A/$E1
2803          SUB AH,CH                        $2A/$E5
2804          SUB AH,DL                        $2A/$E2
2805          SUB AH,DH                        $2A/$E6
2806          SUB AH,01H                       $80/$EC/$01
2807          SUB AH,LocalOrParm               $2A/$A6/LocalOrParm
2808          SUB LocalOrParm,AH               $28/$A6/LocalOrParm
2809          SUB AH,Global                    $2A/$26/Global
```

(continued)

2810	SUB Global,AH	$28/$26/Global
2811	SUB AH,ES:[DI]	$26/$2A/$25
2812	SUB ES:[DI],AH	$26/$28/$25
2813	;	
2814	SUB BL,BH	$2A/$DF
2815	SUB BL,AL	$2A/$D8
2816	SUB BL,AH	$2A/$DC
2817	SUB BL,CL	$2A/$D9
2818	SUB BL,CH	$2A/$DD
2819	SUB BL,DL	$2A/$DA
2820	SUB BL,DH	$2A/$DE
2821	SUB BL,01H	$80/$EB/$01
2822	SUB BL,LocalOrParm	$2A/$9E/LocalOrParm
2823	SUB LocalOrParm,BL	$28/$9E/LocalOrParm
2824	SUB BL,Global	$2A/$1E/Global
2825	SUB Global,BL	$28/$1E/Global
2826	SUB BL,ES:[DI]	$26/$2A/$1D
2827	SUB ES:[DI],BL	$26/$28/$1D
2828	;	
2829	SUB BH,BL	$2A/$FB
2830	SUB BH,AL	$2A/$F8
2831	SUB BH,AH	$2A/$FC
2832	SUB BH,CL	$2A/$F9
2833	SUB BH,CH	$2A/$FD
2834	SUB BH,DL	$2A/$FA
2835	SUB BH,DH	$2A/$FE
2836	SUB BH,01H	$80/$EF/$01
2837	SUB BH,LocalOrParm	$2A/$BE/LocalOrParm
2838	SUB LocalOrParm,BH	$28/$BE/LocalOrParm
2839	SUB BH,Global	$2A/$3E/Global
2840	SUB Global,BH	$28/$3E/Global
2841	SUB BH,ES:[DI]	$26/$2A/$3D
2842	SUB ES:[DI],BH	$26/$28/$3D
2843	;	
2844	SUB CL,CH	$2A/$CD
2845	SUB CL,AL	$2A/$C8
2846	SUB CL,AH	$2A/$CC
2847	SUB CL,BL	$2A/$CB
2848	SUB CL,BH	$2A/$CF
2849	SUB CL,DL	$2A/$CA
2850	SUB CL,DH	$2A/$CE
2851	SUB CL,01H	$80/$E9/$01
2852	SUB CL,LocalOrParm	$2A/$8E/LocalOrParm
2853	SUB LocalOrParm,CL	$28/$8E/LocalOrParm
2854	SUB CL,Global	$2A/$0E/Global
2855	SUB Global,CL	$28/$0E/Global
2856	SUB CL,ES:[DI]	$26/$2A/$0D
2857	SUB ES:[DI],CL	$26/$28/$0D
2858	;	

(continued)

```
2859            SUB CH,CL              $2A/$E9
2860            SUB CH,AL              $2A/$E8
2861            SUB CH,AH              $2A/$EC
2862            SUB CH,BL              $2A/$EB
2863            SUB CH,BH              $2A/$EF
2864            SUB CH,DL              $2A/$EA
2865            SUB CH,DH              $2A/$EE
2866            SUB CH,01H             $80/$ED/$01
2867            SUB CH,LocalOrParm     $2A/$AE/LocalOrParm
2868            SUB LocalOrParm,CH     $28/$AE/LocalOrParm
2869            SUB CH,Global          $2A/$2E/Global
2870            SUB Global,CH          $28/$2E/Global
2871            SUB CH,ES:[DI]         $26/$2A/$2D
2872            SUB ES:[DI],CH         $26/$28/$2D
2873            ;
2874            SUB DL,DH              $2A/$D6
2875            SUB DL,AL              $2A/$D0
2876            SUB DL,AH              $2A/$D4
2877            SUB DL,BL              $2A/$D3
2878            SUB DL,BH              $2A/$D7
2879            SUB DL,CL              $2A/$D1
2880            SUB DL,CH              $2A/$D5
2881            SUB DL,01H             $80/$EA/$01
2882            SUB DL,LocalOrParm     $2A/$96/LocalOrParm
2883            SUB LocalOrParm,DL     $28/$96/LocalOrParm
2884            SUB DL,Global          $2A/$16/Global
2885            SUB Global,DL          $28/$16/Global
2886            SUB DL,ES:[DI]         $26/$2A/$15
2887            SUB ES:[DI],DL         $26/$28/$15
2888            ;
2889            SUB DH,DL              $2A/$F2
2890            SUB DH,AL              $2A/$F0
2891            SUB DH,AH              $2A/$F4
2892            SUB DH,BL              $2A/$F3
2893            SUB DH,BH              $2A/$F7
2894            SUB DH,CL              $2A/$F1
2895            SUB DH,CH              $2A/$F5
2896            SUB DH,01H             $80/$EE/$01
2897            SUB DH,LocalOrParm     $2A/$B6/LocalOrParm
2898            SUB LocalOrParm,DH     $28/$B6/LocalOrParm
2899            SUB DH,Global          $2A/$36/Global
2900            SUB Global,DH          $28/$36/Global
2901            SUB DH,ES:[DI]         $26/$2A/$35
2902            SUB ES:[DI],DH         $26/$28/$35
2903            ;
2904            ;   Now the 16-bit SUBs:
2905            ;
2906            SUB AX,BX              $2B/$C3
2907            SUB AX,CX              $2B/$C1
```

(continued)

2908	SUB AX,DX	$2B/$C2
2909	SUB AX,BP	$2B/$C5
2910	SUB AX,SI	$2B/$C6
2911	SUB AX,DI	$2B/$C7
2912	SUB AX,SP	$2B/$C4
2913	SUB AX,01H	$2D/$01/$00
2914	SUB AX,07733H	$2D/$33/$77
2915	SUB AX,LocalOrParm	$2B/$86/LocalOrParm
2916	SUB LocalOrParm,AX	$29/$86/LocalOrParm
2917	SUB AX,Global	$2B/$06/Global
2918	SUB Global,AX	$29/$06/Global
2919	SUB AX,ES:[DI]	$26/$2B/$05
2920	SUB ES:[DI],AX	$26/$29/$05
2921	;	
2922	SUB BX,AX	$2B/$D8
2923	SUB BX,CX	$2B/$D9
2924	SUB BX,DX	$2B/$DA
2925	SUB BX,BP	$2B/$DD
2926	SUB BX,SI	$2B/$DE
2927	SUB BX,DI	$2B/$DF
2928	SUB BX,SP	$2B/$DC
2929	SUB BX,01H	$83/$EB/$01
2930	SUB BX,07733H	$81/$EB/$33/$77
2931	SUB BX,LocalOrParm	$2B/$9E/LocalOrParm
2932	SUB LocalOrParm,BX	$29/$9E/LocalOrParm
2933	SUB BX,Global	$2B/$1E/Global
2934	SUB Global,BX	$29/$1E/Global
2935	SUB BX,ES:[DI]	$26/$2B/$1D
2936	SUB ES:[DI],BX	$26/$29/$1D
2937	;	
2938	SUB CX,AX	$2B/$C8
2939	SUB CX,BX	$2B/$CB
2940	SUB CX,DX	$2B/$CA
2941	SUB CX,BP	$2B/$CD
2942	SUB CX,SI	$2B/$CE
2943	SUB CX,DI	$2B/$CF
2944	SUB CX,SP	$2B/$CC
2945	SUB CX,01H	$83/$E9/$01
2946	SUB CX,07733H	$81/$E9/$33/$77
2947	SUB CX,LocalOrParm	$2B/$8E/LocalOrParm
2948	SUB LocalOrParm,CX	$29/$8E/LocalOrParm
2949	SUB CX,Global	$2B/$0E/Global
2950	SUB Global,CX	$29/$0E/Global
2951	SUB CX,ES:[DI]	$26/$2B/$0D
2952	SUB ES:[DI],CX	$26/$29/$0D
2953	;	
2954	SUB DX,AX	$2B/$D0
2955	SUB DX,BX	$2B/$D3
2956	SUB DX,CX	$2B/$D1

(continued)

2957	SUB DX,BP	$2B/$D5
2958	SUB DX,SI	$2B/$D6
2959	SUB DX,DI	$2B/$D7
2960	SUB DX,SP	$2B/$D4
2961	SUB DX,01H	$83/$EA/$01
2962	SUB DX,07733H	$81/$EA/$33/$77
2963	SUB DX,LocalOrParm	$2B/$96/LocalOrParm
2964	SUB LocalOrParm,DX	$29/$96/LocalOrParm
2965	SUB DX,Global	$2B/$16/Global
2966	SUB Global,DX	$29/$16/Global
2967	SUB DX,ES:[DI]	$26/$2B/$15
2968	SUB ES:[DI],DX	$26/$29/$15
2969	;	
2970	SUB BP,AX	$2B/$E8
2971	SUB BP,BX	$2B/$EB
2972	SUB BP,CX	$2B/$E9
2973	SUB BP,DX	$2B/$EA
2974	SUB BP,SI	$2B/$EE
2975	SUB BP,DI	$2B/$EF
2976	SUB BP,SP	$2B/$EC
2977	SUB BP,01H	$83/$ED/$01
2978	SUB BP,07733H	$81/$ED/$33/$77
2979	SUB BP,Global	$2B/$2E/Global
2980	SUB Global,BP	$29/$2E/Global
2981	SUB BP,ES:[DI]	$26/$2B/$2D
2982	SUB ES:[DI],BP	$26/$29/$2D
2983	;	
2984	SUB SI,AX	$2B/$F0
2985	SUB SI,BX	$2B/$F3
2986	SUB SI,CX	$2B/$F1
2987	SUB SI,DX	$2B/$F2
2988	SUB SI,BP	$2B/$F5
2989	SUB SI,DI	$2B/$F7
2990	SUB SI,SP	$2B/$F4
2991	SUB SI,01H	$83/$EE/$01
2992	SUB SI,07733H	$81/$EE/$33/$77
2993	SUB SI,LocalOrParm	$2B/$B6/LocalOrParm
2994	SUB LocalOrParm,SI	$29/$B6/LocalOrParm
2995	SUB SI,Global	$2B/$36/Global
2996	SUB Global,SI	$29/$36/Global
2997	SUB SI,ES:[DI]	$26/$2B/$35
2998	SUB ES:[DI],SI	$26/$29/$35
2999	;	
3000	SUB DI,AX	$2B/$F8
3001	SUB DI,BX	$2B/$FB
3002	SUB DI,CX	$2B/$F9
3003	SUB DI,DX	$2B/$FA
3004	SUB DI,BP	$2B/$FD
3005	SUB DI,SI	$2B/$FE

(continued)

```
3006              SUB DI,SP                       $2B/$FC
3007              SUB DI,01H                      $83/$EF/$01
3008              SUB DI,07733H                   $81/$EF/$33/$77
3009              SUB DI,LocalOrParm              $2B/$BE/LocalOrParm
3010              SUB LocalOrParm,DI              $29/$BE/LocalOrParm
3011              SUB DI,Global                   $2B/$3E/Global
3012              SUB Global,DI                   $29/$3E/Global
3013              ;
3014              SUB SP,AX                       $2B/$E0
3015              SUB SP,BX                       $2B/$E3
3016              SUB SP,CX                       $2B/$E1
3017              SUB SP,DX                       $2B/$E2
3018              SUB SP,BP                       $2B/$E5
3019              SUB SP,SI                       $2B/$E6
3020              SUB SP,DI                       $2B/$E7
3021              SUB SP,01H                      $83/$EC/$01
3022              SUB SP,07733H                   $81/$EC/$33/$77
3023              SUB SP,LocalOrParm              $2B/$A6/LocalOrParm
3024              SUB LocalOrParm,SP              $29/$A6/LocalOrParm
3025              SUB SP,Global                   $2B/$26/Global
3026              SUB Global,SP                   $29/$26/Global
3027              SUB SP,ES:[DI]                  $26/$2B/$25
3028              SUB ES:[DI],SP                  $26/$29/$25
3029              ;
3030              SUB BYTE PTR LocalOrParm,01H    $80/$AE/LocalOrParm/$01
3031              SUB WORD PTR LocalOrParm,01H    $83/$AE/LocalOrParm/$01
3032              SUB BYTE PTR Global,01H         $80/$2E/Global/$01
3033              SUB WORD PTR Global,01H         $83/$2E/Global/$01
3034              SUB BYTE PTR ES:[DI],01H        $26/$80/$2D/$01
3035              SUB WORD PTR ES:[DI],01H        $26/$83/$2D/$01
3036              ;
3037              ;
3038              ;   Test instructions.  8-bit operations first:
3039              ;
3040              TEST AL,AH                      $84/$C4
3041              TEST AL,BL                      $84/$C3
3042              TEST AL,BH                      $84/$C7
3043              TEST AL,CL                      $84/$C1
3044              TEST AL,CH                      $84/$C5
3045              TEST AL,DL                      $84/$C2
3046              TEST AL,DH                      $84/$C6
3047              TEST AL,01H                     $A8/$01
3048              TEST AL,LocalOrParm             $84/$86/LocalOrParm
3049              TEST LocalOrParm,AL             $84/$86/LocalOrParm
3050              TEST AL,Global                  $84/$06/Global
3051              TEST Global,AL                  $84/$06/Global
3052              TEST AL,ES:[DI]                 $26/$84/$05
3053              TEST ES:[DI],AL                 $26/$84/$05
3054              ;
```

(continued)

3055	TEST AH,AL	$84/$E0
3056	TEST AH,BL	$84/$E3
3057	TEST AH,BH	$84/$E7
3058	TEST AH,CL	$84/$E1
3059	TEST AH,CH	$84/$E5
3060	TEST AH,DL	$84/$E2
3061	TEST AH,DH	$84/$E6
3062	TEST AH,01H	$F6/$C4/$01
3063	TEST AH,LocalOrParm	$84/$A6/LocalOrParm
3064	TEST LocalOrParm,AH	$84/$A6/LocalOrParm
3065	TEST AH,Global	$84/$26/Global
3066	TEST Global,AH	$84/$26/Global
3067	TEST AH,ES:[DI]	$26/$84/$25
3068	TEST ES:[DI],AH	$26/$84/$25
3069	;	
3070	TEST BL,BH	$84/$DF
3071	TEST BL,AL	$84/$D8
3072	TEST BL,AH	$84/$DC
3073	TEST BL,CL	$84/$D9
3074	TEST BL,CH	$84/$DD
3075	TEST BL,DL	$84/$DA
3076	TEST BL,DH	$84/$DE
3077	TEST BL,01H	$F6/$C3/$01
3078	TEST BL,LocalOrParm	$84/$9E/LocalOrParm
3079	TEST LocalOrParm,BL	$84/$9E/LocalOrParm
3080	TEST BL,Global	$84/$1E/Global
3081	TEST Global,BL	$84/$1E/Global
3082	TEST BL,ES:[DI]	$26/$84/$1D
3083	TEST ES:[DI],BL	$26/$84/$1D
3084	;	
3085	TEST BH,BL	$84/$FB
3086	TEST BH,AL	$84/$F8
3087	TEST BH,AH	$84/$FC
3088	TEST BH,CL	$84/$F9
3089	TEST BH,CH	$84/$FD
3090	TEST BH,DL	$84/$FA
3091	TEST BH,DH	$84/$FE
3092	TEST BH,01H	$F6/$C7/$01
3093	TEST BH,LocalOrParm	$84/$BE/LocalOrParm
3094	TEST LocalOrParm,BH	$84/$BE/LocalOrParm
3095	TEST BH,Global	$84/$3E/Global
3096	TEST Global,BH	$84/$3E/Global
3097	TEST BH,ES:[DI]	$26/$84/$3D
3098	TEST ES:[DI],BH	$26/$84/$3D
3099	;	
3100	TEST CL,CH	$84/$CD
3101	TEST CL,AL	$84/$C8
3102	TEST CL,AH	$84/$CC
3103	TEST CL,BL	$84/$CB

(continued)

3104	TEST CL,BH	$84/$CF
3105	TEST CL,DL	$84/$CA
3106	TEST CL,DH	$84/$CE
3107	TEST CL,01H	$F6/$C1/$01
3108	TEST CL,LocalOrParm	$84/$8E/LocalOrParm
3109	TEST LocalOrParm,CL	$84/$8E/LocalOrParm
3110	TEST CL,Global	$84/$0E/Global
3111	TEST Global,CL	$84/$0E/Global
3112	TEST CL,ES:[DI]	$26/$84/$0D
3113	TEST ES:[DI],CL	$26/$84/$0D
3114	;	
3115	TEST CH,CL	$84/$E9
3116	TEST CH,AL	$84/$E8
3117	TEST CH,AH	$84/$EC
3118	TEST CH,BL	$84/$EB
3119	TEST CH,BH	$84/$EF
3120	TEST CH,DL	$84/$EA
3121	TEST CH,DH	$84/$EE
3122	TEST CH,01H	$F6/$C5/$01
3123	TEST CH,LocalOrParm	$84/$AE/LocalOrParm
3124	TEST LocalOrParm,CH	$84/$AE/LocalOrParm
3125	TEST CH,Global	$84/$2E/Global
3126	TEST Global,CH	$84/$2E/Global
3127	TEST CH,ES:[DI]	$26/$84/$2D
3128	TEST ES:[DI],CH	$26/$84/$2D
3129	;	
3130	TEST DL,DH	$84/$D6
3131	TEST DL,AL	$84/$D0
3132	TEST DL,AH	$84/$D4
3133	TEST DL,BL	$84/$D3
3134	TEST DL,BH	$84/$D7
3135	TEST DL,CL	$84/$D1
3136	TEST DL,CH	$84/$D5
3137	TEST DL,01H	$F6/$C2/$01
3138	TEST DL,LocalOrParm	$84/$96/LocalOrParm
3139	TEST LocalOrParm,DL	$84/$96/LocalOrParm
3140	TEST DL,Global	$84/$16/Global
3141	TEST Global,DL	$84/$16/Global
3142	TEST DL,ES:[DI]	$26/$84/$15
3143	TEST ES:[DI],DL	$26/$84/$15
3144	;	
3145	TEST DH,DL	$84/$F2
3146	TEST DH,AL	$84/$F0
3147	TEST DH,AH	$84/$F4
3148	TEST DH,BL	$84/$F3
3149	TEST DH,BH	$84/$F7
3150	TEST DH,CL	$84/$F1
3151	TEST DH,CH	$84/$F5
3152	TEST DH,01H	$F6/$C6/$01

(continued)

```
3153            TEST  DH,LocalOrParm          $84/$B6/LocalOrParm
3154            TEST  LocalOrParm,DH          $84/$B6/LocalOrParm
3155            TEST  DH,Global              $84/$36/Global
3156            TEST  Global,DH              $84/$36/Global
3157            TEST  DH,ES:[DI]             $26/$84/$35
3158            TEST  ES:[DI],DH             $26/$84/$35
3159            ;
3160            ;    Now the 16-bit TESTs:
3161            ;
3162            TEST  AX,BX                   $85/$C3
3163            TEST  AX,CX                   $85/$C1
3164            TEST  AX,DX                   $85/$C2
3165            TEST  AX,BP                   $85/$C5
3166            TEST  AX,SI                   $85/$C6
3167            TEST  AX,DI                   $85/$C7
3168            TEST  AX,SP                   $85/$C4
3169            TEST  AX,01H                  $A9/$01/$00
3170            TEST  AX,07733H               $A9/$33/$77
3171            TEST  AX,LocalOrParm          $85/$86/LocalOrParm
3172            TEST  LocalOrParm,AX          $85/$86/LocalOrParm
3173            TEST  AX,Global              $85/$06/Global
3174            TEST  Global,AX              $85/$06/Global
3175            TEST  AX,ES:[DI]             $26/$85/$05
3176            TEST  ES:[DI],AX             $26/$85/$05
3177            ;
3178            TEST  BX,AX                   $85/$D8
3179            TEST  BX,CX                   $85/$D9
3180            TEST  BX,DX                   $85/$DA
3181            TEST  BX,BP                   $85/$DD
3182            TEST  BX,SI                   $85/$DE
3183            TEST  BX,DI                   $85/$DF
3184            TEST  BX,SP                   $85/$DC
3185            TEST  BX,01H                  $F7/$C3/$01/$00
3186            TEST  BX,07733H               $F7/$C3/$33/$77
3187            TEST  BX,LocalOrParm          $85/$9E/LocalOrParm
3188            TEST  LocalOrParm,BX          $85/$9E/LocalOrParm
3189            TEST  BX,Global              $85/$1E/Global
3190            TEST  Global,BX              $85/$1E/Global
3191            TEST  BX,ES:[DI]             $26/$85/$1D
3192            TEST  ES:[DI],BX             $26/$85/$1D
3193            ;
3194            TEST  CX,AX                   $85/$C8
3195            TEST  CX,BX                   $85/$CB
3196            TEST  CX,DX                   $85/$CA
3197            TEST  CX,BP                   $85/$CD
3198            TEST  CX,SI                   $85/$CE
3199            TEST  CX,DI                   $85/$CF
3200            TEST  CX,SP                   $85/$CC
3201            TEST  CX,01H                  $F7/$C1/$01/$00
```

(continued)

```
3202          TEST CX,07733H            $F7/$C1/$33/$77
3203          TEST CX,LocalOrParm       $85/$8E/LocalOrParm
3204          TEST LocalOrParm,CX       $85/$8E/LocalOrParm
3205          TEST CX,Global            $85/$0E/Global
3206          TEST Global,CX            $85/$0E/Global
3207          TEST CX,ES:[DI]           $26/$85/$0D
3208          TEST ES:[DI],CX           $26/$85/$0D
3209          ;
3210          TEST DX,AX                $85/$D0
3211          TEST DX,BX                $85/$D3
3212          TEST DX,CX                $85/$D1
3213          TEST DX,BP                $85/$D5
3214          TEST DX,SI                $85/$D6
3215          TEST DX,DI                $85/$D7
3216          TEST DX,SP                $85/$D4
3217          TEST DX,01H               $F7/$C2/$01/$00
3218          TEST DX,07733H            $F7/$C2/$33/$77
3219          TEST DX,LocalOrParm       $85/$96/LocalOrParm
3220          TEST LocalOrParm,DX       $85/$96/LocalOrParm
3221          TEST DX,Global            $85/$16/Global
3222          TEST Global,DX            $85/$16/Global
3223          TEST DX,ES:[DI]           $26/$85/$15
3224          TEST ES:[DI],DX           $26/$85/$15
3225          ;
3226          TEST BP,AX                $85/$E8
3227          TEST BP,BX                $85/$EB
3228          TEST BP,CX                $85/$E9
3229          TEST BP,DX                $85/$EA
3230          TEST BP,SI                $85/$EE
3231          TEST BP,DI                $85/$EF
3232          TEST BP,SP                $85/$EC
3233          TEST BP,01H               $F7/$C5/$01/$00
3234          TEST BP,07733H            $F7/$C5/$33/$77
3235          TEST BP,Global            $85/$2E/Global
3236          TEST Global,BP            $85/$2E/Global
3237          TEST BP,ES:[DI]           $26/$85/$2D
3238          TEST ES:[DI],BP           $26/$85/$2D
3239          ;
3240          TEST SI,AX                $85/$F0
3241          TEST SI,BX                $85/$F3
3242          TEST SI,CX                $85/$F1
3243          TEST SI,DX                $85/$F2
3244          TEST SI,BP                $85/$F5
3245          TEST SI,DI                $85/$F7
3246          TEST SI,SP                $85/$F4
3247          TEST SI,01H               $F7/$C6/$01/$00
3248          TEST SI,07733H            $F7/$C6/$33/$77
3249          TEST SI,LocalOrParm       $85/$B6/LocalOrParm
3250          TEST LocalOrParm,SI       $85/$B6/LocalOrParm
```

(continued)

```
3251            TEST SI,Global              $85/$36/Global
3252            TEST Global,SI              $85/$36/Global
3253            TEST SI,ES:[DI]             $26/$85/$35
3254            TEST ES:[DI],SI             $26/$85/$35
3255            ;
3256            TEST DI,AX                  $85/$F8
3257            TEST DI,BX                  $85/$FB
3258            TEST DI,CX                  $85/$F9
3259            TEST DI,DX                  $85/$FA
3260            TEST DI,BP                  $85/$FD
3261            TEST DI,SI                  $85/$FE
3262            TEST DI,SP                  $85/$FC
3263            TEST DI,01H                 $F7/$C7/$01/$00
3264            TEST DI,07733H              $F7/$C7/$33/$77
3265            TEST DI,LocalOrParm         $85/$BE/LocalOrParm
3266            TEST LocalOrParm,DI         $85/$BE/LocalOrParm
3267            TEST DI,Global              $85/$3E/Global
3268            TEST Global,DI              $85/$3E/Global
3269            ;
3270            TEST SP,AX                  $85/$E0
3271            TEST SP,BX                  $85/$E3
3272            TEST SP,CX                  $85/$E1
3273            TEST SP,DX                  $85/$E2
3274            TEST SP,BP                  $85/$E5
3275            TEST SP,SI                  $85/$E6
3276            TEST SP,DI                  $85/$E7
3277            TEST SP,01H                 $F7/$C4/$01/$00
3278            TEST SP,07733H              $F7/$C4/$33/$77
3279            TEST SP,LocalOrParm         $85/$A6/LocalOrParm
3280            TEST LocalOrParm,SP         $85/$A6/LocalOrParm
3281            TEST SP,Global              $85/$26/Global
3282            TEST Global,SP              $85/$26/Global
3283            TEST SP,ES:[DI]             $26/$85/$25
3284            TEST ES:[DI],SP             $26/$85/$25
3285            ;
3286            TEST BYTE PTR LocalOrParm,01H    $F6/$86/LocalOrParm/$01
3287            TEST WORD PTR LocalOrParm,01H    $F7/$86/LocalOrParm/$01/$00
3288            TEST BYTE PTR Global,01H         $F6/$06/Global/$01
3289            TEST WORD PTR Global,01H         $F7/$06/Global/$01/$00
3290            TEST BYTE PTR ES:[DI],01H        $26/$F6/$05/$01
3291            TEST WORD PTR ES:[DI],01H        $26/$F7/$05/$01/$00
3292            ;
3293            ;
3294            ;    The WAIT instruction:
3295            ;
3296            WAIT                        $9B
3297            ;
3298            ;
3299            ; Register exchanges.  8-bit first:
```

(continued)

```
3300                     ;
3301                     XCHG AL,AH                    $86/$C4
3302                     XCHG AL,BL                    $86/$C3
3303                     XCHG AL,BH                    $86/$C7
3304                     XCHG AL,CL                    $86/$C1
3305                     XCHG AL,CH                    $86/$C5
3306                     XCHG AL,DL                    $86/$C2
3307                     XCHG AL,DH                    $86/$C6
3308                     XCHG AL,LocalOrParm           $86/$86/LocalOrParm
3309                     XCHG AL,Global                $86/$06/Global
3310                     XCHG AL,ES:[DI]               $26/$86/$05
3311                     XCHG AH,BL                    $86/$E3
3312                     XCHG AH,BH                    $86/$E7
3313                     XCHG AH,CL                    $86/$E1
3314                     XCHG AH,CH                    $86/$E5
3315                     XCHG AH,DL                    $86/$E2
3316                     XCHG AH,DH                    $86/$E6
3317                     XCHG AH,LocalOrParm           $86/$A6/LocalOrParm
3318                     XCHG AH,Global                $86/$26/Global
3319                     XCHG AH,ES:[DI]               $26/$86/$25
3320                     XCHG BL,BH                    $86/$DF
3321                     XCHG BL,CL                    $86/$D9
3322                     XCHG BL,CH                    $86/$DD
3323                     XCHG BL,DL                    $86/$DA
3324                     XCHG BL,DH                    $86/$DE
3325                     XCHG BL,LocalOrParm           $86/$9E/LocalOrParm
3326                     XCHG BL,Global                $86/$1E/Global
3327                     XCHG BL,ES:[DI]               $26/$86/$1D
3328                     XCHG BH,CL                    $86/$F9
3329                     XCHG BH,CH                    $86/$FD
3330                     XCHG BH,DL                    $86/$FA
3331                     XCHG BH,DH                    $86/$FE
3332                     XCHG BH,LocalOrParm           $86/$BE/LocalOrParm
3333                     XCHG BH,Global                $86/$3E/Global
3334                     XCHG BH,ES:[DI]               $26/$86/$3D
3335                     XCHG CL,CH                    $86/$CD
3336                     XCHG CL,DL                    $86/$CA
3337                     XCHG CL,DH                    $86/$CE
3338                     XCHG CL,LocalOrParm           $86/$8E/LocalOrParm
3339                     XCHG CL,Global                $86/$0E/Global
3340                     XCHG CL,ES:[DI]               $26/$86/$0D
3341                     XCHG CH,DL                    $86/$EA
3342                     XCHG CH,DH                    $86/$EE
3343                     XCHG CH,LocalOrParm           $86/$AE/LocalOrParm
3344                     XCHG CH,Global                $86/$2E/Global
3345                     XCHG CH,ES:[DI]               $26/$86/$2D
3346                     ;
3347                     ;    Exchanges involving AX generate single-byte opcodes:
3348                     ;
```

(continued)

```
3349                   XCHG AX,BX                    $93
3350                   XCHG AX,CX                    $91
3351                   XCHG AX,DX                    $92
3352                   XCHG AX,BP                    $95
3353                   XCHG AX,SI                    $96
3354                   XCHG AX,DI                    $97
3355                   XCHG AX,SP                    $94
3356                   ;
3357                   ;     Now the generalized 16-bit register exchanges:
3358                   ;
3359                   XCHG AX,LocalOrParm           $87/$86/LocalOrParm
3360                   XCHG AX,Global               $87/$06/Global
3361                   XCHG AX,ES:[DI]              $26/$87/$05
3362                   XCHG BX,CX                    $87/$D9
3363                   XCHG BX,DX                    $87/$DA
3364                   XCHG BX,BP                    $87/$DD
3365                   XCHG BX,SI                    $87/$DE
3366                   XCHG BX,DI                    $87/$DF
3367                   XCHG BX,SP                    $87/$DC
3368                   XCHG BX,LocalOrParm           $87/$9E/LocalOrParm
3369                   XCHG BX,Global               $87/$1E/Global
3370                   XCHG BX,ES:[DI]              $26/$87/$1D
3371                   XCHG CX,DX                    $87/$CA
3372                   XCHG CX,BP                    $87/$CD
3373                   XCHG CX,SI                    $87/$CE
3374                   XCHG CX,DI                    $87/$CF
3375                   XCHG CX,SP                    $87/$CC
3376                   XCHG CX,LocalOrParm           $87/$8E/LocalOrParm
3377                   XCHG CX,Global               $87/$0E/Global
3378                   XCHG CX,ES:[DI]              $26/$87/$0D
3379                   XCHG DX,BP                    $87/$D5
3380                   XCHG DX,SI                    $87/$D6
3381                   XCHG DX,DI                    $87/$D7
3382                   XCHG DX,SP                    $87/$D4
3383                   XCHG DX,LocalOrParm           $87/$96/LocalOrParm
3384                   XCHG DX,Global               $87/$16/Global
3385                   XCHG DX,ES:[DI]              $26/$87/$15
3386                   XCHG BP,SI                    $87/$EE
3387                   XCHG BP,DI                    $87/$EF
3388                   XCHG BP,SP                    $87/$EC
3389                   XCHG BP,Global               $87/$2E/Global
3390                   XCHG BP,ES:[DI]              $26/$87/$2D
3391                   XCHG SI,DI                    $87/$F7
3392                   XCHG SI,SP                    $87/$F4
3393                   XCHG SI,LocalOrParm           $87/$B6/LocalOrParm
3394                   XCHG SI,Global               $87/$36/Global
3395                   XCHG SI,ES:[DI]              $26/$87/$35
3396                   XCHG DI,SP                    $87/$FC
3397                   XCHG DI,LocalOrParm           $87/$BE/LocalOrParm
```

(continued)

```
3398            XCHG SI,Global               $87/$36/Global
3399            ;
3400            ;
3401            ;   The translate instruction:
3402            ;
3403            XLAT O3H                      $D7
3404            ;
3405            ;
3406            ;   XORs. 8-bit operations first:
3407            ;
3408            XOR AL,AH                     $32/$C4
3409            XOR AL,BL                     $32/$C3
3410            XOR AL,BH                     $32/$C7
3411            XOR AL,CL                     $32/$C1
3412            XOR AL,CH                     $32/$C5
3413            XOR AL,DL                     $32/$C2
3414            XOR AL,DH                     $32/$C6
3415            XOR AL,O1H                    $34/$01
3416            XOR AL,LocalOrParm            $32/$86/LocalOrParm
3417            XOR LocalOrParm,AL            $30/$86/LocalOrParm
3418            XOR AL,Global                $32/$06/Global
3419            XOR Global,AL                $30/$06/Global
3420            XOR AL,ES:[DI]               $26/$32/$05
3421            XOR ES:[DI],AL               $26/$30/$05
3422            ;
3423            XOR AH,AL                     $32/$E0
3424            XOR AH,BL                     $32/$E3
3425            XOR AH,BH                     $32/$E7
3426            XOR AH,CL                     $32/$E1
3427            XOR AH,CH                     $32/$E5
3428            XOR AH,DL                     $32/$E2
3429            XOR AH,DH                     $32/$E6
3430            XOR AH,O1H                    $80/$F4/$01
3431            XOR AH,LocalOrParm            $32/$A6/LocalOrParm
3432            XOR LocalOrParm,AH            $30/$A6/LocalOrParm
3433            XOR AH,Global                $32/$26/Global
3434            XOR Global,AH                $30/$26/Global
3435            XOR AH,ES:[DI]               $26/$32/$25
3436            XOR ES:[DI],AH               $26/$30/$25
3437            ;
3438            XOR BL,BH                     $32/$DF
3439            XOR BL,AL                     $32/$D8
3440            XOR BL,AH                     $32/$DC
3441            XOR BL,CL                     $32/$D9
3442            XOR BL,CH                     $32/$DD
3443            XOR BL,DL                     $32/$DA
3444            XOR BL,DH                     $32/$DE
3445            XOR BL,O1H                    $80/$F3/$01
3446            XOR BL,LocalOrParm            $32/$9E/LocalOrParm
```

(continued)

```
3447          XOR LocalOrParm,BL          $30/$9E/LocalOrParm
3448          XOR BL,Global               $32/$1E/Global
3449          XOR Global,BL               $30/$1E/Global
3450          XOR BL,ES:[DI]              $26/$32/$1D
3451          XOR ES:[DI],BL              $26/$30/$1D
3452          ;
3453          XOR BH,BL                   $32/$FB
3454          XOR BH,AL                   $32/$F8
3455          XOR BH,AH                   $32/$FC
3456          XOR BH,CL                   $32/$F9
3457          XOR BH,CH                   $32/$FD
3458          XOR BH,DL                   $32/$FA
3459          XOR BH,DH                   $32/$FE
3460          XOR BH,01H                  $80/$F7/$01
3461          XOR BH,LocalOrParm          $32/$BE/LocalOrParm
3462          XOR LocalOrParm,BH          $30/$BE/LocalOrParm
3463          XOR BH,Global               $32/$3E/Global
3464          XOR Global,BH               $30/$3E/Global
3465          XOR BH,ES:[DI]              $26/$32/$3D
3466          XOR ES:[DI],BH              $26/$30/$3D
3467          ;
3468          XOR CL,CH                   $32/$CD
3469          XOR CL,AL                   $32/$C8
3470          XOR CL,AH                   $32/$CC
3471          XOR CL,BL                   $32/$CB
3472          XOR CL,BH                   $32/$CF
3473          XOR CL,DL                   $32/$CA
3474          XOR CL,DH                   $32/$CE
3475          XOR CL,01H                  $80/$F1/$01
3476          XOR CL,LocalOrParm          $32/$8E/LocalOrParm
3477          XOR LocalOrParm,CL          $30/$8E/LocalOrParm
3478          XOR CL,Global               $32/$0E/Global
3479          XOR Global,CL               $30/$0E/Global
3480          XOR CL,ES:[DI]              $26/$32/$0D
3481          XOR ES:[DI],CL              $26/$30/$0D
3482          ;
3483          XOR CH,CL                   $32/$E9
3484          XOR CH,AL                   $32/$E8
3485          XOR CH,AH                   $32/$EC
3486          XOR CH,BL                   $32/$EB
3487          XOR CH,BH                   $32/$EF
3488          XOR CH,DL                   $32/$EA
3489          XOR CH,DH                   $32/$EE
3490          XOR CH,01H                  $80/$F5/$01
3491          XOR CH,LocalOrParm          $32/$AE/LocalOrParm
3492          XOR LocalOrParm,CH          $30/$AE/LocalOrParm
3493          XOR CH,Global               $32/$2E/Global
3494          XOR Global,CH               $30/$2E/Global
3495          XOR CH,ES:[DI]              $26/$32/$2D
```

(continued)

```
3496              XOR ES:[DI],CH               $26/$30/$2D
3497              ;
3498              XOR DL,DH                    $32/$D6
3499              XOR DL,AL                    $32/$D0
3500              XOR DL,AH                    $32/$D4
3501              XOR DL,BL                    $32/$D3
3502              XOR DL,BH                    $32/$D7
3503              XOR DL,CL                    $32/$D1
3504              XOR DL,CH                    $32/$D5
3505              XOR DL,01H                   $80/$F2/$01
3506              XOR DL,LocalOrParm           $32/$96/LocalOrParm
3507              XOR LocalOrParm,DL           $30/$96/LocalOrParm
3508              XOR DL,Global                $32/$16/Global
3509              XOR Global,DL                $30/$16/Global
3510              XOR DL,ES:[DI]               $26/$32/$15
3511              XOR ES:[DI],DL               $26/$30/$15
3512              ;
3513              XOR DH,DL                    $32/$F2
3514              XOR DH,AL                    $32/$F0
3515              XOR DH,AH                    $32/$F4
3516              XOR DH,BL                    $32/$F3
3517              XOR DH,BH                    $32/$F7
3518              XOR DH,CL                    $32/$F1
3519              XOR DH,CH                    $32/$F5
3520              XOR DH,01H                   $80/$F6/$01
3521              XOR DH,LocalOrParm           $32/$B6/LocalOrParm
3522              XOR LocalOrParm,DH           $30/$B6/LocalOrParm
3523              XOR DH,Global                $32/$36/Global
3524              XOR Global,DH                $30/$36/Global
3525              XOR DH,ES:[DI]               $26/$32/$35
3526              XOR ES:[DI],DH               $26/$30/$35
3527              ;
3528              ;    Now the 16-bit XORs:
3529              ;
3530              XOR AX,BX                    $33/$C3
3531              XOR AX,CX                    $33/$C1
3532              XOR AX,DX                    $33/$C2
3533              XOR AX,BP                    $33/$C5
3534              XOR AX,SI                    $33/$C6
3535              XOR AX,DI                    $33/$C7
3536              XOR AX,SP                    $33/$C4
3537              XOR AX,01H                   $35/$01/$00
3538              XOR AX,07733H                $35/$33/$77
3539              XOR AX,LocalOrParm           $33/$86/LocalOrParm
3540              XOR LocalOrParm,AX           $31/$86/LocalOrParm
3541              XOR AX,Global                $33/$06/Global
3542              XOR Global,AX                $31/$06/Global
3543              XOR AX,ES:[DI]               $26/$33/$05
3544              XOR ES:[DI],AX               $26/$31/$05
```

(continued)

```
3545                     ;
3546                     XOR BX,AX                  $33/$D8
3547                     XOR BX,CX                  $33/$D9
3548                     XOR BX,DX                  $33/$DA
3549                     XOR BX,BP                  $33/$DD
3550                     XOR BX,SI                  $33/$DE
3551                     XOR BX,DI                  $33/$DF
3552                     XOR BX,SP                  $33/$DC
3553                     XOR BX,01H                 $81/$F3/$01/$00
3554                     XOR BX,07733H              $81/$F3/$33/$77
3555                     XOR BX,LocalOrParm         $33/$9E/LocalOrParm
3556                     XOR LocalOrParm,BX         $31/$9E/LocalOrParm
3557                     XOR BX,Global              $33/$1E/Global
3558                     XOR Global,BX              $31/$1E/Global
3559                     XOR BX,ES:[DI]             $26/$33/$1D
3560                     XOR ES:[DI],BX             $26/$31/$1D
3561                     ;
3562                     XOR CX,AX                  $33/$C8
3563                     XOR CX,BX                  $33/$CB
3564                     XOR CX,DX                  $33/$CA
3565                     XOR CX,BP                  $33/$CD
3566                     XOR CX,SI                  $33/$CE
3567                     XOR CX,DI                  $33/$CF
3568                     XOR CX,SP                  $33/$CC
3569                     XOR CX,01H                 $81/$F1/$01/$00
3570                     XOR CX,07733H              $81/$F1/$33/$77
3571                     XOR CX,LocalOrParm         $33/$8E/LocalOrParm
3572                     XOR LocalOrParm,CX         $31/$8E/LocalOrParm
3573                     XOR CX,Global              $33/$0E/Global
3574                     XOR Global,CX              $31/$0E/Global
3575                     XOR CX,ES:[DI]             $26/$33/$0D
3576                     XOR ES:[DI],CX             $26/$31/$0D
3577                     ;
3578                     XOR DX,AX                  $33/$D0
3579                     XOR DX,BX                  $33/$D3
3580                     XOR DX,CX                  $33/$D1
3581                     XOR DX,BP                  $33/$D5
3582                     XOR DX,SI                  $33/$D6
3583                     XOR DX,DI                  $33/$D7
3584                     XOR DX,SP                  $33/$D4
3585                     XOR DX,01H                 $81/$F2/$01/$00
3586                     XOR DX,07733H              $81/$F2/$33/$77
3587                     XOR DX,LocalOrParm         $33/$96/LocalOrParm
3588                     XOR LocalOrParm,DX         $31/$96/LocalOrParm
3589                     XOR DX,Global              $33/$16/Global
3590                     XOR Global,DX              $31/$16/Global
3591                     XOR DX,ES:[DI]             $26/$33/$15
3592                     XOR ES:[DI],DX             $26/$31/$15
3593                     ;
```

(continued)

3594	XOR BP,AX	$33/$E8
3595	XOR BP,BX	$33/$EB
3596	XOR BP,CX	$33/$E9
3597	XOR BP,DX	$33/$EA
3598	XOR BP,SI	$33/$EE
3599	XOR BP,DI	$33/$EF
3600	XOR BP,SP	$33/$EC
3601	XOR BP,01H	$81/$F5/$01/$00
3602	XOR BP,07733H	$81/$F5/$33/$77
3603	XOR BP,Global	$33/$2E/Global
3604	XOR Global,BP	$31/$2E/Global
3605	XOR BP,ES:[DI]	$26/$33/$2D
3606	XOR ES:[DI],BP	$26/$31/$2D
3607	;	
3608	XOR SI,AX	$33/$F0
3609	XOR SI,BX	$33/$F3
3610	XOR SI,CX	$33/$F1
3611	XOR SI,DX	$33/$F2
3612	XOR SI,BP	$33/$F5
3613	XOR SI,DI	$33/$F7
3614	XOR SI,SP	$33/$F4
3615	XOR SI,01H	$81/$F6/$01/$00
3616	XOR SI,07733H	$81/$F6/$33/$77
3617	XOR SI,LocalOrParm	$33/$B6/LocalOrParm
3618	XOR LocalOrParm,SI	$31/$B6/LocalOrParm
3619	XOR SI,Global	$33/$36/Global
3620	XOR Global,SI	$31/$36/Global
3621	XOR SI,ES:[DI]	$26/$33/$35
3622	XOR ES:[DI],SI	$26/$31/$35
3623	;	
3624	XOR DI,AX	$33/$F8
3625	XOR DI,BX	$33/$FB
3626	XOR DI,CX	$33/$F9
3627	XOR DI,DX	$33/$FA
3628	XOR DI,BP	$33/$FD
3629	XOR DI,SI	$33/$FE
3630	XOR DI,SP	$33/$FC
3631	XOR DI,01H	$81/$F7/$01/$00
3632	XOR DI,07733H	$81/$F7/$33/$77
3633	XOR DI,LocalOrParm	$33/$BE/LocalOrParm
3634	XOR LocalOrParm,DI	$31/$BE/LocalOrParm
3635	XOR DI,Global	$33/$3E/Global
3636	XOR Global,DI	$31/$3E/Global
3637	;	
3638	XOR SP,AX	$33/$E0
3639	XOR SP,BX	$33/$E3
3640	XOR SP,CX	$33/$E1
3641	XOR SP,DX	$33/$E2
3642	XOR SP,BP	$33/$E5

(continued)

```
3643              XOR  SP,SI                       $33/$E6
3644              XOR  SP,DI                       $33/$E7
3645              XOR  SP,01H                      $81/$F4/$01/$00
3646              XOR  SP,07733H                   $81/$F4/$33/$77
3647              XOR  SP,LocalOrParm              $33/$A6/LocalOrParm
3648              XOR  LocalOrParm,SP              $31/$A6/LocalOrParm
3649              XOR  SP,Global                   $33/$26/Global
3650              XOR  Global,SP                   $31/$26/Global
3651              XOR  SP,ES:[DI]                  $26/$33/$25
3652              XOR  ES:[DI],SP                  $26/$31/$25
3653              ;
3654              XOR  BYTE PTR LocalOrParm,01H    $80/$B6/LocalOrParm/$01
3655              XOR  WORD PTR LocalOrParm,01H    $81/$B6/LocalOrParm/$01/$00
3656              XOR  BYTE PTR Global,01H         $80/$36/Global/$01
3657              XOR  WORD PTR Global,01H         $81/$36/Global/$01/$00
3658              XOR  BYTE PTR ES:[DI],01H        $26/$80/$35/$01
3659              XOR  WORD PTR ES:[DI],01H        $26/$81/$35/$01/$00
3660              ;
3661              ;  Keep hacking!  --JD--
3662              ;
```

APPENDIX B

How This Book Was Produced

*T*urbo Pascal Solutions came together over a 14-month period beginning in November 1985, and was interrupted in late winter and early spring of 1986 while I updated *Complete Turbo Pascal* to its second edition. In the process, I used a fair number of tools—some successfully, some disastrously. Perhaps you can learn something from my experiences.

The word processor that I used, as always, was Word Perfect, a workhorse of a program that beats everything else I have ever tried all hollow. Some accuse it of being slow, but it's much faster than WordStar, and, while slower than XyWrite, it allows me to use Sidekick beneath it, and I would not be without Sidekick. You lose, XyWrite. Actually, Word Perfect is slow in just a few areas, including macro processing, spell-checking, and moving from one end of a large document to the other. I avoided the spelling problem by not using the spelling checker on the entire document. I can get away with this because I am an intuitive speller and only stumble over an occasional schwa. For a time I tried Turbo Lightning, but combined with Sidekick it just took too much memory. If you have trouble spelling, however, Lightning is jack-fine and might be more valuable than Sidekick's hex calculator.

Word Perfect is certainly slow in moving between ends of a document. I solved that problem late in the game by assembling a 16-Mhz 386 machine. Problem gone.

For awhile I tried running under Microsoft Windows, so that I could flash between Word Perfect and Turbo Pascal without having to leave one and enter the other. It worked (hogging memory I'd rather devote to other purposes), but it was slow indeed. I was going to try DesqView as a text-based environment when I realized that Word Perfect allows you to EXEC to DOS, where Turbo Pascal can be easily and quickly loaded and run. Not quite as slick as being able to hot-key between the two programs, but with a stopwatch I found it was no slower than listening to Windows grind the hard disk while it switched contexts. I retained that system for the remainder of the project.

The host machine changed many times. I still have an original IBM PC purchased in January 1984, and it works as well as ever. The PC took me up until April 1986. A slot shortage prompted me to assemble a minimal Taiwan clone box in mid-1986, using a 640K motherboard purchased at the Dayton Hamvention from an anonymous Chinese chap for $85. It has never dropped a bit since then, even though most of its add-in boards are the most wretchedly despised no-name knockoffs I could find. At this point, *I'd* fire you for buying IBM—Big Blue offers nothing to individuals and small business customers that can't be had for one-fifth the price from a reputable mail-order vendor.

The PC and the Taiwan box changed roles periodically as my hardware configuration changed. Finally, in December 1986, I received my 386 motherboard and dutifully installed it in an $89 Taiwan AT cabinet with a Fortron power supply and a 43MB 29ms fixed disk from PC Source. The speed improvement is truly frightening after five years on a stock IBM PC. CPU speed, like money, isn't everything—but it sure makes most things more pleasant.

Mass storage was your typical PC's Limited 20MB hard disk backed up by FastBack until mid-1986, when I broke down and bought a Bernoulli Box. This became necessary when *Turbo Pascal Solutions* began to soak up 40 percent of my fixed disk space, crowding out other projects in space the way it had long since crowded out other projects in time. The Bernoulli Box is a godsend—but the devil *ticks*! If you ever think about buying one of these creatures, try to spend some time sitting in front of one. That persistent, soft-edged, slightly metallic, 2-per-second percussion is the sort of thing that you can either ignore outright or be driven totally mad by. Too often I found myself whistling Copland's "Appalachian Spring" in cadence with it—the men with the butterfly nets were right around the corner at that point.

Nonetheless, the ability to keep an entire major project on a single 10MB cartridge is wonderful. They are bulky but fast, about as fast as your typical Winchester hard disk. An image backup from one cartridge to another happens in 2 minutes 14 seconds every time. So far (seven months later) it has been utterly reliable. If you write for money, it may be worth the space and the racket. Just turn up "Appalachian Spring" loud enough to drown it out.

For the rest of you, it's still tough to beat FastBack, especially now that they've removed the copy protection.

I've mentioned the MDS Genius VHR here and there throughout the text, particularly in Chapter 5, and I'll say it again: This screen beats anything else I have ever used for text processing. It's an 80×66 line portrait-oriented monochrome-compatible subsystem that has a 728×1003 graphics option supported by GEM and Microsoft Windows. At $1595, it's hardly cheap, but I live by my writing and I'm very particular about screens, keyboards, and printers. The graphics option came in handy in creating the figures, which was done with Media Cybernetics' Halo DPE (Desktop Publishing Editor). I'm not sure how effective it is in the desktop publishing field, but DPE is a mighty potent paint program. The mouse I use is Logitech's, which is the best nonoptical mouse you can buy.

Hardcopy output has been a problem. The 500 pages of manuscript for this book were printed on a Canon LBP-8 A1 laser printer, which started to smear the copy midway across the sheet about halfway through the print job, and is still doing it. The listings in this book are camera-ready output from the Canon, courtesy of their Line Printer Gothic font cartridge and a short Turbo Pascal lister utility of my own design. I chose the Canon A1 laser because it's cheap and well-supported by Word Perfect. It was a mistake. The Canon documentation is written in something that seems calculated to take the most amount of page space saying absolutely nothing, and the Canon "authorized" dealers I have spoken with know virtually nothing about the product. Canon's central office seemed to care nothing about helping me; they were primarily concerned with protecting the turf of their dealership network. I finally managed to obtain the Line Printer Gothic font cartridge from an unauthorized mail-order dealer who treated me with much courtesy and apologized for otherwise unbelievable foulups on Canon's part that, by that time, I found all too believable. Avoid the A1 like the plague. It has been unreliable, font cartridges are virtually impossible to find, and the arrogance of Canon, Inc. defies quantification.

That cannot be said for Tall Tree Systems, whose JLaser Plus board actually fed images to the Canon printer. The board worked the first time and has never failed; each time I suspected there was a problem with it, further investigation showed the problem to belong to the Canon printer. JLaser Plus is an EMS board in which graphics images are constructed, with a daughterboard that converts the graphics image into video information fed directly to the Canon's laser controller. It's fast and wonderful. Their support people are brilliant and always willing to help. If you need good 300 DPI APA graphics, get one—just don't plug it into a Canon printer.

NEC falls right in beside Canon in their ability to get on my bad side. I ordered an APC IV keyboard as a separate item, since it's an excellent AT-style keyboard without IBM's excessively clicky feel, and after four months there's still no sign of it. There's no authorized NEC dealer within 50 miles of Baltimore, and the authorized dealers I was forced to deal with repeatedly lost my order, forgot my phone number, and generally acted like Keystone Kops hung over on antifreeze. After a fortune in phone calls and much lost time, I still have no keyboard to show for it. Again and again, I pleaded with NEC to put me in touch with a mail-order dealer with half a brain, only to be told that "Mail-order dealers cannot adequately support you."

Are you worried about the Japanese taking over the American computer market? I'm not.

Index to Programs, Functions, and Procedures

Index

Notes

Notes

Notes

Notes

Notes

Notes

Here's how to receive your free catalog and save money on your next book order from Scott, Foresman and Company

Simply mail in the response card below to receive your free copy of our latest catalog featuring computer and business books. After you've looked through the catalog and you're ready to place your order, attach the coupon below to receive $1.00 off of catalog price on your next order of Scott, Foresman and Company Professional Publishing Group business or computer books.

■ ■ ■ ■ ■ ■ ■ ■ ■ ■ ■ ■ ■ ■ ■ ■ ■ ■

[ ] **YES**, please send me my *free* catalog of your latest computer and business books! I am especially interested in

[ ] IBM	[ ] Programming	
[ ] MACINTOSH	[ ] Business Applications	
[ ] AMIGA	[ ] Networking/Telecommunications	
[ ] APPLE IIc, IIe, IIGS	[ ] Other _______________	
[ ] COMMODORE	_______________	

Name (please print) _______________________________________

Company _______________________________________

Address _______________________________________

City _______________________ State _______ Zip _________

Mail response card to: **Scott, Foresman and Company
Professional Publishing Group
1900 East Lake Avenue
Glenview, IL 60025**

■ ■ ■ ■ ■ ■ ■ ■ ■ ■ ■ ■ ■ ■ ■ ■ ■

Publisher's Coupon   No Expiration Date

SAVE
$1.00

Limit one per order. Good only on Scott, Foresman and Company Professional Publishing Group publications. Consumer pays any sales tax. Coupon may not be assigned, transferred, or reproduced. Coupon will be redeemed by Scott, Foresman and Company, Professional Publishing Group, 1900 E. Lake Ave., Glenview, IL 60025.

Customer's Signature _______________________________________